BECOME AMERICA

BECOME AMERICA

Civic Sermons on Love, Responsibility,
and Democracy

ERIC LIU

SASQUATCH BOOKS

SEATTLE

Copyright © 2019 by Eric Liu

Printed in the United States of America

SASQUATCH BOOKS with colophon is a registered trademark of Penguin Random House LLC

23 22 21 20 19   9 8 7 6 5 4 3 2 1

"Refugee in America" © Langston Hughes | "Summer Sparks" © Claudia Castro Luna | "38" © Layli Long Soldier | Full text credits on page 301

Editor: Gary Luke
Production editors: Rachelle Longé McGhee | Jill Saginario
Cover illustration: © Doomko | Dreamstime.com
Design: Tony Ong

Library of Congress Cataloging-in-Publication Data

Names: Liu, Eric, author.
Title: Become America : civic sermons on love, responsibility, and democracy / Eric Liu.
Description: Seattle : Sasquatch Books, [2019]
Identifiers: LCCN 2018049487 | ISBN 9781632172570 (hard cover)
Subjects: LCSH: Political culture--United States. | Citizenship--United States. | Political participation--United States.
Classification: LCC JK1726 .L577 2019 | DDC 323.6/50973--dc23
LC record available at https://lccn.loc.gov/2018049487

ISBN: 978-1-63217-257-0

Sasquatch Books
1904 Third Avenue, Suite 710
Seattle, WA 98101

SasquatchBooks.com

SUSTAINABLE FORESTRY INITIATIVE

Certified Chain of Custody
Promoting Sustainable Forestry
www.sfiprogram.org
SFI-01268

SFI label applies to the text stock

To the team at Citizen University

CONTENTS

PREFACE

This is a book of reckoning and repair.

Throughout 2016, Jená Cane and I kicked around ideas for a new civic ritual that would have the moral pull and communal feel of a faith gathering. We're the cofounders of a nonprofit called Citizen University, whose mission is to foster a culture of powerful citizenship in the United States. (We're also spouses!) Jená and I were drawn viscerally to this idea of a civic analogue to church but never had time to develop it. Then came the presidential election. The morning after, we and our team decided to act.

Four days later, we put together the first ever Civic Saturday. It was held in the basement reading room of Elliott Bay Book Company in Seattle. Given the short notice and scramble, we expected maybe forty people. More than 220 showed up, packing every corner of that low-ceilinged underground space. Together, we began to make sense of our tumultuous moment—and its origins in decades of degradation and predation in public life under the rule of both parties.

Civic Saturday has the arc of a faith gathering: we sing together, we turn to the strangers next to us and talk about a common question, we hear poetry and readings, there is a sermon that ties those texts to the issues and ethical choices of the times, and then we sing together again and reflect on what actions we commit to taking. But this gathering is not about church or temple or mosque religion. It is about American *civic religion*: the creed of ideals stated at our nation's founding and restated at junctures of crisis (like today), and the deeds by which we and those before us live up to the creed.

Why the analogy to faith gatherings? In part because over the millennia the major faiths have figured out something about how to help people find meaning and belonging, how to interpret texts and to reckon with the gap between our ideals and our reality, how to sustain hope and heart in a sea of cynicism and hate. And in part because we truly believe that democracy in America is an act of faith. Not faith in the divine but in the people with whom we hold the fate of this fragile experiment.

That's always been true: we Americans have little to hold us together, really, but some words on parchment and a collective uncoordinated habit of investing those words with meaning. But the habit is waning. Our belief in self-government is eroding. This is a time of unchecked concentration of wealth, tectonic demographic shifts, resurgent white nationalism, creeping authoritarianism, hyperpolarization, decaying institutions. A time when so many feel so wronged and yearn for strongmen and saviors to right things.

In short, it is a time to rekindle our faith in each other.

Since that first morning in November 2016, there have been dozens of Civic Saturday gatherings across the United States. In theaters and coworking spaces and churches, on street corners, in public parks, and on college campuses. Our team has held them continuously in Seattle. As word spread, people started asking us to come to *their* towns. So we've brought Civic Saturdays to Des Moines and Detroit, Nashville and New York, Atlanta, Omaha, Los Angeles, and Portland, Maine. More importantly, we've launched a Civic Seminary to train people to understand American civic religion, to hold their own Civic Saturdays, and to build their own civic congregations.

Our seminarians, like those who attend Civic Saturdays, come from red states and blue, small towns and big. Not all are citizens in the sense of documentation status but all are citizens in the more capacious ethical sense of being contributors to community. They are young and old, of "every hue and caste," as Whitman put it, "every rank and religion." Some are indeed religious and others are not. Most are kin to someone with diametrically opposed political views. Whether they are from the left, right, or center, they are willing to challenge each other and themselves to test their beliefs, to do more than indulge in the righteousness of their own side. They are educators and artists and organizers and active neighbors who want to be more than mere bystanders.

They are just like you.

This volume consists of the sermons I've written and delivered at our first nineteen Civic Saturday gatherings, from November 2016 to August 2018. It is organized by the date of the gathering. Before each sermon, you'll find several readings—pieces of American "civic scripture"—selected by me to give shape to the sermon and to be read aloud by community members. Some of these readings are foundational, like Lincoln's Second Inaugural; others, like Susan B. Anthony's speech at her trial for attempted voting, are less well known but still at the core of the creed we are meant to steward. The sermons are all about what it means to live like a citizen in this age of brokenness. What it means to take risks like a citizen, to make art like a citizen, to remember like a citizen, and to forgive like one. What it means, from head, heart, and gut, to heal the body politic.

You can read this book from start to finish, following the chronological progression of sermons and the unfolding of our new political reality over the last two years. Or you can take the sermons in a random sequence and sense for yourself the motifs that recur. The sermons aren't chapters of a novel or an argument, so you won't have missed "backstory" or "setup" if you start in the middle. But they do compound. I've woven chords of connection across and within these sermons that echo the chords of connection across and within our country. Listen for them.

They are chords of love, responsibility, and democracy. Chords of pain, fear, hope, and moral courage.

To open this book is to do something countercultural. As I often say to our Civic Saturday community: we are the counterculture now. In a culture of celebrity worship and consumerism, we stand for service and citizenship. In an age of hyperindividualism, we practice collective action and common cause. In a time of fundamentalism and showy sanctimony, we stand for discernment and humility. In the smog of hypocrisy and situational ethics, we still live and breathe the universal timeless values and ideals of the Golden Rule, the Tao, the Declaration, and the Preamble of the Constitution.

That is radical. If we do our jobs right, we will spark a great civic awakening across the land and make today's crisis of democracy an age of civic rebirth. A renewal of people power and a replenishment of civic character. That's why we invite you to join us. Share this book. Find a Civic Saturday near you. Apply for our Civic Seminary. Learn more broadly about our work and other programs at Citizen University. (Visit our website at CitizenUniversity.us.)

Most of all, practice civic spirit. Know your own mind. Plumb the depths of your own heart. Nurture the conscience of a citizen, in yourself first and then in those you encounter. Build the muscle of acting with others for the good of all. Always open with questions rather than answers. If you must argue, argue to understand and not to win.

Can we deliver the country we've been promising ourselves all our lives? Can we face our history and truly animate words like "equal justice under law" and *E Pluribus Unum*? Can we, at long last, become America?

I believe we can. I believe we are doing it at this very moment. Turn the page and join us.

1.

A DIVIDED HEART

Elliott Bay Book Company · Seattle, WA
November 12, 2016

SUSAN B. ANTHONY
*From the statement at her trial for
the crime of attempting to vote*
June 1873

The preamble of the Federal Constitution says:

> We, the people of the United States, in order to
> form a more perfect union, establish justice, insure
> domestic tranquility, provide for the common
> defense, promote the general welfare and secure
> the blessings of liberty to ourselves and our
> posterity, do ordain and establish this Constitution
> for the United States of America.

It was we, the people, not we, the white male citizens, nor we,
the male citizens, but we, the whole people, who formed this
Union. We formed it not to give the blessings of liberty but to

secure them, not to the half of ourselves and the half of our posterity, but to the whole people—women as well as men.

JUDGE LEARNED HAND
From his speech on "I Am an American Day"
Central Park, New York
May 21, 1944

I often wonder whether we do not rest our hopes too much upon constitutions, upon laws and upon courts. These are false hopes; believe me, these are false hopes. Liberty lies in the hearts of men and women; when it dies there, no constitution, no law, no court can even do much to help it. While it lies there it needs no constitution, no law, no court to save it. . . . What then is the spirit of liberty? I cannot define it; I can only tell you my own faith. The spirit of liberty is the spirit which is not too sure that it is right; the spirit of liberty is the spirit which seeks to understand the mind of other men and women; the spirit of liberty is the spirit which weighs their interests alongside its own without bias; the spirit of liberty remembers that not even a sparrow falls to earth unheeded; . . . that there may be a kingdom where the least shall be heard and considered side by side with the greatest.

LANGSTON HUGHES
"Refugee in America"
Saturday Evening Post
Published 1943

There are words like "Freedom,"
Sweet and wonderful to say.
On my heartstrings freedom sings
All day everyday.

There are words like "Democracy"
That almost make me cry.
If you had known what I knew
You would know why.

We have come together this morning not to affirm a faith but to question it—and, if we are lucky, to renew it.

This week's election result can be understood as an earthquake. It certainly was seismic. But an actual earthquake brings people together, wiping away differences and distinctions and forcing them to help one another. As Rebecca Solnit writes in her book *A Paradise Built in Hell*, natural disasters create spontaneous utopias of fellow-feeling and joyful, even euphoric, mutual aid. A political earthquake is different, though. This one in particular leaves us more divided and isolated and disoriented than ever. Many of you feel not just shocked but betrayed. Not just sad but grief-stricken.

So we gather today in search of a spirit of fellowship and common purpose.

We've called Civic Saturday an analogue to church, but I wish to be clear: this is about *civic* religion, not church or synagogue or mosque religion.

What do I mean by *civic* religion? I mean that the United States has a creed, contained in foundational documents and given life in fateful collective acts. Devotion to that creed—and the mystic memory of such devotion—is what makes us American. The *creed* defines American. Not whiteness or Christianity or birth on these shores or certain documents. That creed is found in the Preamble to the Constitution and the Fourteenth Amendment, in the Gettysburg Address and the "I Have a Dream" speech, in the Declaration of Independence and in the Seneca

Falls Declaration of Sentiments. And it is only made real by what we *do*. Words are just words until they become *works*.

My spirit is an American hybrid. I'm the son of immigrants from China and I wasn't raised in any faith tradition. I've found inspiration from the Puritans, the preachers of the Second Great Awakening, the Jews, the Jesuits, Zen Buddhists. But mainly my civic faith has been shaped by a pantheon of great Americans, some known to us like Lincoln and King, some not so widely known but in this very room.

Lincoln and King fought to make the Union more than words. They had moral clarity and an abiding sense of moral responsibility. They took the Founders and Framers at their word and held them unrelentingly, unflinchingly to account, whatever the cost.

Most of all, they *felt*; they felt the pain of a nation divided against itself. They understood the convoluted knots of denial that form like a thicket around fragile, unearned privilege. They knew the way that despised people create stories to endure their status and then stay within those stories. They knew that true liberation liberates the oppressor as much as the oppressed. They recognized that you can fight and love the same people at the same time.

I've looked to them both as I've tried to feel my way through this week. And I've asked three questions that I'd like to explore with you today.

What do I do with my divided heart? What is the threat we now face? And how do we know what to do next?

WHAT DO I DO WITH MY DIVIDED HEART?

Let me confess: My heart has been divided, not just since November 8 but throughout this election season. Sometimes I've wanted to understand the people who supported Donald Trump, other times I've wanted to vanquish and isolate them. Sometimes I empathize with their yearnings; other times I want to shame and judge them harshly.

Do we owe Trump, as Hillary Clinton said this week, an open mind? Do we owe him a closed fist?

When Trump won, one of the many emotions I felt, besides fear and shock and disgust and sadness, was awe. This was one of the most stunning demonstrations of bottom-up citizen power in American history. It was also, alas, the greatest and most candid national legitimization of bigotry since Redemption, which is what people in the South like to call the end of Reconstruction.

The morning after the election, while my progressive friends were still in a daze, one of the first phone calls I got came from my friend Mark. Mark was a founder of the Tea Party. And though he did not support Trump—in fact, he's very wary of Trump—he was calling to say, if I may paraphrase, *This is what I've been trying to tell you. Millions of Americans have felt left out and put down, told that they're deplorable racists and bigots and sexists if they challenge the elites and insiders who are tolerant of everyone but them. They're tired of it, and with Trump they found a way to say so.*

What struck me about Mark's call was first of all that he called. He felt the need to say this to me. Why? It wasn't a gloating *I told you so.* It was partly a plea for understanding, but it was an angry plea. He still feels beleaguered. He is still feeling persecuted—in his case, specifically, because he was one of the people the IRS targeted in the Tea Party case that became a scandal. He chided me and people on the left I've introduced him to for not coming to his aid then. He felt let down.

He then went on to say of most progressives everything I've heard progressives say of most people on the right: They don't want to understand the other side; they just want to hate. They are insanely ideological and can't see the humanity of their opponents. They don't just disagree with you; they say you're a bad person—that *all* people on your side are bad if one person is.

I listened. I told him I appreciated his call, which I did. I agreed with much of his analysis of what Trump voters were saying. But I pointed out that a significant part of the Trump base is in fact deplorably bigoted and sexist and anti-Semitic and Islamophobic. And I asked him to consider that the feeling of persecution he's had is something that millions of people who are immigrants or gay or Muslim or people of color are contending with in a newly poisonous way.

Mark said—and I believe him—that he would be the first to call out someone on the right who's being hateful or intolerant. But then he turned back to the idea that he shouldn't be lumped in with them. And he got amped up again about all the terrible ways the left has behaved in this era.

If this were someone I did not already know, I would have suited up for a talking-points war and my temperature would have risen until perhaps I did indeed come to despise him. But I know this man. I think he's right in part and very wrong in part. And he's complicated all around. As we all are. Jená has siblings and in-laws and nephews and nieces in south Louisiana who are Trump supporters. They love their kin and they have deep endurance for the hard parts of life. She cannot excise them or deny what she shares with them, which is more than blood. And she doesn't want to.

After my call with Mark I had a meeting with my team and other colleagues. The feeling in these progressive rooms was what many of you have felt, which is grief, even betrayal. And the real fear of becoming the objects of hate. But because I'd so recently heard Mark, I realized something about *all* of us. We live in the bubbles of our dreams, unaware that we share so many fears.

And we all have to wake up.

This moment feels to many progressives like sudden death, but what has died is only ignorance about people who have been our countrymen all this time. Not just poor whites in Appalachia. Educated whites in exurban office parks or suburban soccer fields. What has died is an illusion of security—economic or physical or psychic—and a delusion about how inclusive America was becoming and how ready the new American electorate was to claim its potential power. So this moment now demands awakening: a readiness to fight hate and a willingness to *see* who we really are.

To many others, this moment feels like vindication and victory, or at least satisfying comeuppance for an arrogant, insular cosmopolitan establishment elite. But what really has been won here? "Make America White Again" cannot win in the long term: among babies being born today that cause is already lost. And a vision of walls will not in the long term prevail either because, as King said in his "Letter from a Birmingham Jail," the very goal of America is freedom. This moment is not a permanent triumph for nativism or closedness; it is a rebalancing, and it won't cure the status anxiety that brought us here—anxiety shared by Sanders supporters as much as by Trump supporters.

There's been a lot of talk about reconciliation now. But we should think about the process in South Africa after the end of apartheid called Truth and Reconciliation Commissions. The key thing there is that truth must precede reconciliation. There must be reckoning before there is reconciling.

If I am honest, my enthusiasm for the work of reconciliation followed the needle on the *New York Times* website that tracked Hillary Clinton's chances of winning. As that needle sank over the course of hours, so did my appetite for such work. Once it became clear she was going to lose, my mind went not to reconciliation but to resistance. If Trump follows through on half of his campaign threats, there is danger in the land of deeply un-American action. So I had a real-time look at how my own heart is split between ideals of Union and facing facts.

What I've come to think about my divided heart is this: let it be divided. But remember that blood flows between the chambers. Fight when you must, love when you can. Find in yourself all that you hate in others. Know that *everyone* is operating out of fear. Remember that everyone wants to be the hero of their own story, to justify their place in the world, and that revolutions are made of such yearnings. Use that knowledge as skillfully as, well, Donald Trump has.

To say that is not to engage in moral equivalence or relativism. The white man's fear created by the diminishing returns to being white and male is not the moral equivalent of the woman of color's fear created by the rise of Trump and the alt-right. Your liberty to discriminate against me is not the same as my liberty to be secure from discrimination.

What I'm saying is simply this: we must rehumanize our politics. That means not seeing our adversaries or ourselves as either-or beings. We are all subject to the same pressures to oversimplify each other. We must listen and see anew. I must see Mark or my sister-in-law Sally in my mind's eye before I indulge the impulse to demonize the right. At the same time, I must name and *judge* and combat injustice with all my soul when I encounter it, even if Mark or Sally are the agents of that injustice.

The most famous part of Lincoln's Second Inaugural, delivered in the final year of the Civil War, comes at the end: "With malice toward none, with charity for all," he seeks to "bind up the nation's wounds." There is the echo of Jesus here. But we forget the part that precedes it, which has more of the Old Testament: "Fondly do we hope, fervently do we pray, that this mighty scourge of war may speedily pass away. Yet, if God wills that it continue, until all the wealth piled by the bondsman's two hundred and fifty years of unrequited toil shall be sunk, and until every drop of blood drawn with the lash shall be repaid by another drawn with the sword, as was said three thousand years ago, so still it must be said 'the judgments of the Lord are true and righteous altogether.'"

Lincoln was both Old and New Testament. So are we all. The goal of rehumanization isn't false reconciliation or fake consensus. We have deep divides, within us as well as between us. The goal is to be able to take responsibility for where we are, how we got here, and how to preserve this Union. Which brings me to the second question:

HOW GREAT IS THE THREAT NOW?

Let me offer another confession: I've always wished I could have been alive (and allowed to participate in politics) in the 1850s or the 1930s—periods of peril and disunion. I've always been drawn in my history readings to books like *The Impending Crisis*, by David Potter, about the slow-motion unfolding of secession in the decades before the Civil War. I've always been drawn to novels like Philip Roth's *The Plot Against America*, a counterfactual work that imagines what this country would've been like if Lindbergh had run and beaten FDR, then made peace with the Nazis, then dispersed American Jews across the corn-fed Midwest and de-Judified them.

Well, be careful what you wish for. To any student of history or of such fiction, these times are frighteningly familiar. Times of peril and potential disunion.

Last month, Jená and I took a trip to Germany. The occasion was a ceremony in a little town in the former East Germany called Aschersleben. This is where Jená's great-grandaunt lived until she was 76 years old, in the year 1942, when she was deported to a concentration camp called Theresienstadt and killed by the Nazis. Jená's father and uncle and grandparents had lived there too but had fled to the U.S. in 1936.

Here a group of citizens, amateur local historians from 18 to 80 years old, had researched the lives of Jews who had once lived in this town. They'd worked with an artist to create these brass cobble-stones—*stolpersteine*, or stumble-stones—placed in front of the last place that someone had lived before fleeing Germany or being murdered. And that's what it says: "murdered." This artist has created 60,000 of these stones, all across the country and continent. They have reckoned with their past.

On that same trip we also went to Berlin. There's a place there called the Topography of Terror. It is a museum set on the several square blocks where the SS, Gestapo, and Reich Main Security headquarters once stood. The nerve center of the Nazi leviathan. Those buildings were reduced to rubble at the end of WWII. But the museum documents, with unflinching honesty and detail, how the people of Germany made Hitler and how he then remade the people of Germany.

What struck me when I was there was not the later Nazi history, which popular culture has made all too familiar: the *Schindler's List* scenes of deportation and the camps. What struck me was the early history, the way the German parliament, following the mechanisms of democracy, voted to ban parties. Voted to allow Hitler to suspend the Constitution as needed. All under the color of law, with every "i" dotted and "t" crossed.

What the people of Germany in the 1930s wanted was freedom *from* freedom. As Eric Hoffer writes in *The True Believer*, his classic study of how people fall into mass movements, freedom had become unbearable for the average German who could not make sense of how to navigate a crushingly unequal economy, a marketplace of choices that made him feel like he wasn't keeping up, a sense of national drift. The average German wanted someone to come and take care of things. To make order.

This was all too familiar. I posted on Facebook at the time about the parallels between Hitler's rise and Trump's, and one of Jená's sisters commented, "Come on—isn't that a stretch?" I said, yes, a bit, but the echoes are real. John Adams once noted that there was not a democracy yet that had not committed suicide. And that's what I thought when I was in the Topography of Terror.

Of course, Trump lacks the discipline or the conviction of Hitler, and that's one thing we have going for us. But Americans today lack the coherence and moral clarity and civic self-possession to resist a *real* Hitler, and that's one thing we'd better work on.

With so much unknown as the transition unfolds, it's tempting to say "we'll see." We will now see just how much of a stretch it is. But it's not enough to say that. We are not just spectators or an audience, awaiting the action in the next scene, held in suspense. We are the authors too of what happens next. *We* will decide.

If you want proof of that remember that we are the authors of Donald Trump. We made him. He did not take power. We gave it to him. Even those of us who opposed and detested him. We gave it to him with our attention, which craven media companies knew could be converted into revenue, and so they gave us more and so we gave him more and he gave us more excuses to give him more. The half of the electorate that didn't vote gave it to him by not voting, because there truly is no such thing as not voting.

Power is a gift. Remember that. Power is a gift that resides within us, and every day we give it away. Those who opposed Trump but did not vote are a case in point. There is no such thing as not voting.

But there's another scenario besides the mini-Hitler strongman who forces a sudden and violent break with the norms of American civic religion. The other scenario is creeping, seeping, and ultimately fatal corruption. The early days of this transition are full of what I find to be still unbelievable and revolting reports that people like Steve Bannon of Breitbart, tribune of the alt-right, might become White House chief of staff.

The analogue here is the period after Reconstruction. After the Civil War, the North undertook a great effort to remake the polity of the South. Black citizens were encouraged to vote and to run for office. Freedmen's Bureaus were created to help the once enslaved make the transition to civic life. But ten years in, white society was tired. The South was tired of being led around by Northern Republicans. And the North, preoccupied with the emerging opportunities of what would become the Gilded Age, the chance to make money, were tired of policing the South. So they agreed to stop, in a corrupt bargain that allowed the robber barons to take over Washington and Jim Crow to reign in the South. White supremacy was enshrined in a vulgar, racist democracy.

In counterfactual spirit, I sometimes wonder how things would've gone had Lincoln not been assassinated. Had he been succeeded not by Andrew Johnson, who sympathized with the South and lost appetite for

Reconstruction, but by someone else. Then I stop daydreaming. And wake up. Remember, in the world we did have, the cycle turned. The People's Party, the populists of that age who would have more in common with Sanders than with Trump, came along. Then the Progressives came on the scene. The social reformers from Jane Addams to Jacob Riis to Teddy Roosevelt to Bob La Follette came and laid the groundwork for reform and helped heal this very sick body politic. It took a generation, but this country did rejuvenate itself. We did not commit suicide then, and there's no reason to assume we will now.

So now let's consider the final question:

HOW CAN WE KNOW WHAT TO DO NEXT?

In the depths of the Great Depression, President Franklin Roosevelt had a simple strategy: try everything. He cooked up recovery and relief programs and initiatives at a dizzying rate. Many of them flopped or failed to make an appreciable difference. But it was the totality of the effort—the message of the energy—that pulled citizens out of their passivity and created an upward spiral of confidence.

We are a long way from the New Deal now and, God knows, a long way from President Roosevelt. We have to flip the roles now. Citizens today have to be the ones who try everything. We have to cook up recovery and relief and defense and justice and compassion initiatives at a dizzying rate. It's already starting to happen, as we get woke.

We have to find ways to create together, serve together, sing together, make together. And the one thing all these efforts must have in common, whether they come from cities or rural areas, red or blue states, is this: they have to give citizens a sense of being the boss of their own lives. A sense of agency and not just spectatordom.

It's no accident that in the Brexit, in the nationalism that's spreading across Europe and Asia, and in the Trump victory, one throughline is a deep-seated fear of the loss of *sovereignty*. People fear loss of control of borders. That's not just the U.S.-Mexico border. That's the realization that in this age the borders between genders, between men's rooms and women's rooms, have been blurred. The borders between the Chinese and the Scotch-Irish-Jewish parts of my daughter. You hear this refrain that our nation will soon cease to exist. That we cannot govern ourselves. This fear is not about public policy only, or even primarily. It is primal. Vast global economic forces, distant bureaucrats, unseen political game-riggers: all of these we can feel have eroded our integrity—our wholeness—and feed a sense that we've lost control of our own lives. That's what the loss-of-sovereignty fear is about on a deeper level.

I think all of us can relate to this. All of us. It won't do to mock or look down on people who feel so strongly this way that they vote for someone like Trump. And we have to keep this in mind and in our hearts. In a way, the question of what we do next is simple. You know already:

First: Push back against the bigotry and hatred that's been normalized. Not just on major national issues but in every moment of everyday life. What you see someone saying at work. Or on the Number 2 bus. Or in your kid's lunch line at school.

Second: Organize. Organize at every level. Organize like there is no point to life except organizing. We've come together today in that spirit, not even sure what will come of it but sure that showing up will matter. That can be protests or it can be plans for legislative action or it can be meetings like this. Exercise that citizen muscle with others.

Third: Learn to read and write power, to understand its dynamics and flow. To be literate in power isn't just about understanding the workings of Washington, DC. I bet half of this room wouldn't know how to move a piece of legislation through the Seattle City Council. And that's just formal government. Then you've got to learn the informal dimension, the power structure of who really runs this town. You voted on ballot measures, and that's good. But do you know how those measures got on the ballot? Do you know how you could put something on the ballot yourself? Get literate in power. Get literate by practicing.

Fourth: Claim the American creed and language. My friend Nick Hanauer and I wrote a book called *The True Patriot* nine years ago in which we noted that progressives often have an ambivalent, arm's-length relationship to patriotism. Our message, in short, was *get over it*. Claim this language. Frame your fights in the context of American antecedents and American values and our creed. That's how you win.

Fifth: Make it local. I would be saying this even if Trump had not won. In our time, Washington, DC is not the locus of action and reform. Renewal starts where we live and radiates outward. Our city and state have been innovating on the minimum wage, marijuana, gun responsibility, marriage equality, democracy vouchers. We show the way by achieving reform and justice here.

And then, most of all, learn to see in your fellow citizens this yearning for a sense of being in charge of something again. Channel it to constructive and inclusive ends even as Trump and his followers may channel it to division and scapegoating. And tell a new story of us that is about *us*—not isolated rugged individuals scavenging the landscape but groups coming together to build and unite.

This is why we are all here. This is Black Lives Matter. It is Standing Rock. It is $15 Now. It was Feel the Bern. But it was also the Tea Party. And now it's the Trump Train. This is the age of citizen power, and even if we don't like all the directions that power is flowing, there's no question that the general direction is from the bottom up and the middle out. Not the top down. That's the moment we are in and this moment demands that we be ready and *woke*.

So listen to your complex and divided heart. Understand where we sit in history. Act as if you could change the course of American democracy just by showing up. You can. It may take a generation still. But we've got to have faith in things unseen, in just the way that religions teach, and in just the way every generation of Americans has done.

You are the authors of what comes next. You're more powerful than you think.

2.

PRESENT AT THE CREATION

Madrona Commons · Seattle, WA
November 26, 2016

THOMAS PAINE
From his pamphlet "Common Sense"
December 1776

These are the times that try men's souls. The summer soldier
and the sunshine patriot will, in this crisis, shrink from the
service of his country; but he that stands by it NOW, deserves
the love and thanks of man and woman. Tyranny, like hell, is
not easily conquered; yet we have this consolation with us,
that the harder the conflict, the more glorious the triumph.

U.S. SENATOR MARGARET CHASE SMITH (R-Maine)
From her Declaration of Conscience speech
June 1950

Those of us who shout the loudest about Americanism
in making character assassinations are all too frequently
those who, by our own words and acts, ignore some of the
principles of Americanism—
The right to criticize.
The right to hold unpopular beliefs.
The right to protest.
The right of independent thought.
The exercise of these rights should not cost one single
American citizen his reputation or his right to a livelihood nor
should he be in danger of losing his reputation or livelihood
merely because he happens to know someone who holds
unpopular beliefs. Who of us does not? Otherwise none of us
could call our own souls our own.

EMMA LAZARUS
"The New Colossus"
Published 1883

Not like the brazen giant of Greek fame,
With conquering limbs astride from land to land;
Here at our sea-washed, sunset gates shall stand
A mighty woman with a torch, whose flame
Is the imprisoned lightning, and her name
Mother of Exiles. From her beacon-hand
Glows world-wide welcome; her mild eyes command
The air-bridged harbor that twin cities frame.

"Keep, ancient lands, your storied pomp!" cries she
With silent lips. "Give me your tired, your poor,
Your huddled masses yearning to breathe free,
The wretched refuse of your teeming shore.
Send these, the homeless, tempest-tost to me,
I lift my lamp beside the golden door!"

We find ourselves this morning still digesting.
Yes, we're still working on leftover Thanksgiving turkey and stuffing and pie, and various stupefying combinations thereof. But of course we are also digesting our new political reality, which, though not three weeks old, is also stupefying and already exhausting.

There's an unreality to this new reality, just as there is to reality television. And actually, reality TV is one of the main models for what the coming years in America might look like: a self-enclosed and self-referential dome of manufactured drama and competition.

Another template, of course, is the Twitter feed, an endless current of trumped-up controversies that disappear as quickly as they flare up. Another still is the fake news—or, to speak more plainly, the welter of lies and propaganda from Russia and the extreme American right—that's been spreading like a rash across your Face(book).

These three templates, these metaphors for how we take in politics today, all have one thing in common. They disrespect truth and they enshrine subjectivity. Sometimes the subjectivity poses as truth. Sometimes it mocks and dismisses truth. Either way, the message today is that facts are old-fashioned and truth is simply what *I* feel—and when that *I* is very powerful, truth becomes simply what power says it is.

Today I'd like to help us make sense of this new era of narrative, this post-truth, fact-optional era of fragmented shards of story all refracting the light in crazy ways.

I'd like to share three thoughts in particular: first, that there is some good in all this fragmentation; second, that we are called now to be citizens in new ways; and third, that as shattered as the public square may seem, there is one thing—and it's counterintuitive—that can bring us back together. Let me begin with the first topic:

WHAT'S GOOD ABOUT THIS AGE OF STORY FRAGMENTATION

I want to tell you about a delightful fellow I met last week. He was born in England and schooled in Scotland, and his slightly high voice has a Highland accent. When I first laid eyes on him, at a buttoned-down DC conference, he was wearing a Scottish kilt with a fur-lined silver sporran, or man-purse. He moved to the United States several years ago. Specifically, he came to Jonesborough, Tennessee, to run something called the International Storytelling Center, which every year gathers tens of thousands of people for a conference on the art of story. In his years in Appalachia, he's become friends with his neighbors, many of whom supported Trump and some of whom didn't.

Got a picture of him? His name is Kiran Singh Sirah. He is of Indian descent. The pattern of his kilt was the Sikh tartan, which was invented only about twenty years ago. And though he admitted he was a bit nervous about stepping outside his home the morning after the election, he has in the weeks since remembered that he doesn't care what story you tell about him: he's going to make it more complex.

Complexity is the watchword of our time. It is why so many people crave simplicity. Donald Trump—and I do not mean this as criticism, or only as criticism—is a genius of simplicity. But only a certain kind of simplicity.

The great Supreme Court Justice Oliver Wendell Holmes was shaped by his experience as a Union officer in the Civil War. He never forgot the carnage that could spill forth from simple ideas. And he once said, "I would not give a fig for the simplicity on this side of complexity, but I would give my life for the simplicity on the other side of complexity."

Sit with that a moment. This sentence lays out the arc we are in now. We used to think we had simplicity. Now we are confronting complexity. Trump wants to take us back to the old imagined simplicity. Someone else will have to lead us forward, to push through to the other side to the kind of enlightened simplicity for which Holmes would've given his life.

I remember an essay by the novelist Saul Bellow about his Depression-era childhood in Chicago. He described walking along Lake Michigan one summer evening and seeing cars parked by the water, all with their doors open and windows down. The passengers were listening to the same thing at the same time: President Roosevelt, giving a fireside chat. And Bellow could pick up the entire radio address as he strolled by one parked car after another, FDR's reassuring voice ebbing and flowing from vehicle to vehicle. That image, that memory of sound, has always stayed with me.

Of course, it's Bellow's memory, not mine. But when I first read it, in my twenties, it stirred within *me* a strange sense of nostalgia. My reaction was, *Wow, I wish I still lived in a time when we all listened to the same thing, all knew the same things, all were part of the same story like that.* I lamented, even in the 1990s, the fragmentation of narrative and common things in America.

But as I've grown older, I've come to realize something. I was kidding myself. The notion that there was ever a time when all Americans were on the same page and of the same mind and agreeing upon the same reality is, well, an illusion. A dream.

It was a dream made possible in part by a lack of democracy, by a set of walls around the public square that made it accessible to whites only, more to men than to women, and more to people of means than without. Another book I read when I was young, by Walter Isaacson and Evan Thomas, was called *The Wise Men*. It told the story of a handful of WASP American men who made the postwar world. They'd gone to Groton and Andover, then to Yale and Princeton; they were named Harriman and Lovett and Kennan and Acheson; they came from wealth and made more of it before serving in government. And even before World War II had ended, they were the wise men who designed and built the multilateral institutions that were meant to keep nationalism and short-sightedness in check: NATO, the UN, the IMF, the World Bank.

Dean Acheson, the most famous and patrician of these Wise Men, who served as Truman's secretary of state, titled his memoir *Present at the Creation*. But at the very moment that the Wise Men were designing the postwar world, the seeds of the destruction of that world were already proliferating.

And at the very moment Saul Bellow was taking in President Roosevelt's voice, an unbroadcast cacophony of other American voices was in fact at full pitch: labor radicals who found FDR too tame; conservative capitalists who found him alarmingly socialistic; isolationists who resented the way he was nudging the U.S. into war;

African Americans fighting a culture of unchecked lynching; women who wanted not just a vote but a *say*.

All those voices were always there. They just didn't have the microphone of the one or two radio corporations that created much of public life in the 1930s. Even the 1960s, for all their upheaval, look today like a time of storytelling simplicity. There were just three TV networks, all of which beamed Bull Connor and Andy Griffith into tens of millions of living rooms at once. People still read newspapers every day, local and national. As late as the 1990s, before Fox News and of course before the Web became the Web, it was still possible to sustain the pretense of a common narrative.

So does this mean we're screwed now? Does it mean society is trending ever more rapidly toward entropy and chaos? I don't think so. I think society is trending toward *growing up*. Toward seeing the true complexity of social reality.

The Nigerian novelist Chimamanda Ngozi Adichie warns us of the "danger of a single story." That danger is great indeed. A single story is usually told by a few to rationalize their domination of the many— to give the few a sense of coherence they wouldn't otherwise have. Adichie was talking about the story the West invented about Africa—a narrative that helped *make* the West and became both cause and effect of a global machinery of racism. But her insight is universal.

Think about how the most elemental stories begin. "In the beginning." "Once upon a time." We are hardwired as humans to tell stories, and part of that hardwiring makes us imagine big bang moments when the story begins, when what preceded the story is voided out, darkened into oblivion. *Present at the creation.*

But the American Revolution itself, that biggest of our country's big bangs, was not really a thing that sprung out of insensate silence and darkness. It was only the inflection point, the coming to boil, of a turbulence that had been brewing for decades.

Rewind further. In celebrating Thanksgiving two days ago, we perpetuated, if tacitly, a storyline that says America began with the Pilgrims' arrival. We did so even as Native Americans today, at Standing Rock, are reminding us, as they face fire hoses fed by the very waters they wish to protect, that what preceded the Pilgrims here was *people* and the *land* and the *relationship* between people and the land.

In eleven days we will mark the seventy-fifth anniversary of Pearl Harbor. For the Japanese Americans who were rounded up and put into internment camps in the weeks following, the first part of their story—the part where they'd grown up here, farmed here, run grocery stores here, gone to church here, played Little League here—that part was obliterated. A new single story descended upon them, which began on December 7, and it deemed them alien to the core and presumed them hostile to the United States.

It took decades for the Congress and the country to acknowledge the sin of that story and its consequences. And here's the thing: it's only taken a few more decades for us to begin to *forget* that acknowledgment. We are beginning to not know what we once knew. A new world is emerging from that forgetting.

We are *always* present at the creation, for better or worse. And the creation is always a "bloomin' buzzin' confusion," in the words of William James, the American pragmatist philosopher. We make sense of that confusion with our story filters. But we should never mistake the filters for what's actually out there, the shadow for the act.

I think it's good that we are facing this fact. For one thing, today's is a world where my voice and that of my new friend Kiran Singh Sirah from Jonesborough by way of Glasgow, who just got his green card, can be part of the cosmology of American stories. Yes, it's also a time for unsavory, hateful voices who no longer have to wait for wise men and elite gatekeepers to let them speak. They are definitely speaking now. They have megaphones, and soon they'll have access to the White House.

And yet net-net, I still think this centrifugal storm, this fracking of the single story and this explosion of perspectives and truths, is *progress*. Because it's forcing us to see the world as it has always been.

To listen for voices that were always there. To stop saying that when people of color demand to be heard it's "identity politics" and to stop pretending there was some prelapsarian paradise when America was unsullied by identity politics. Identity politics here started when the first Puritan stepped ashore.

Somewhere on the other side of this complexity is a better kind of simplicity—if we know how to find it. Which brings me to the second topic I want to address today:

WHY WE AS CITIZENS MUST CHANGE OUR HABITS OF MIND

Last week, when I was in the other Washington, I spent a day meeting with a range of leaders in science, both from big institutions and community-based organizations, about how to make citizens more science-literate and scientists more civics-literate. As you can imagine, we talked a lot about the truth-challenged, fact-denying ways of not just the president-elect but also the private interests that are eager to take advantage of his ascendancy. Climate change deniers, public health deniers, gun violence deniers.

I was reminded of the line by Upton Sinclair, the muckraking journalist from a century ago, who said, "It's difficult to get a man to understand something when his salary depends on his not understanding it!"

But also, I would add, if his *self-image* depends on not understanding it. We are all ardent, often unconscious defenders of the images we've constructed of ourselves. That defense is a primary human reflex. This is why I've always been dissatisfied with Thomas Frank's thesis in *What's the Matter with Kansas?*—that poor conservatives who vote for billionaire-coddling Republicans are "voting against their interests."

Self-image, more than salary, determines what most people think of as "their interests." And self-image is bound up with status—*relative* status—in ways that salary can't fully express and indeed often obscures. Self-image is more often about fears of decline than hopes for advancement, but in all cases it's more about emotion than rationality.

This actually makes me optimistic. Because it hints at a set of things we can do. The first is to be humble: to realize we hardly know ourselves. We think we have a self and we think it consists of experiences and memories and predispositions that we can label and name, and yet at the very same time we are nearly blind to how much we are formed by people around us; one, two, three network links away. Heck, we are *totally* blind to how much we are formed by our own microbiome—the blooms of bacteria in our gut—that not only gives us our "gut feelings" but whose genetic volume and diversity exceed that of our human DNA. As it is with the body so it is with the body politic.

Starting with humility enables us to begin to see our own patterns of truth-making and truth-evading. And foremost among those patterns is self-justification.

In his deeply wise book *Bonds That Make Us Free*, C. Terry Warner describes a universal human dynamic of self-justification. It goes like this: I *accuse* you in order to *excuse* me. You, in turn, return the favor. And then we are off on a cycle of blame and evasion that defines interpersonal, interracial, international dynamics. It starts with

– *Why didn't you take out the trash?*
– *Well, why didn't you do the dishes?*

And it goes to

– *Why don't you fund failing schools?*
– *Well, why don't you fire failing teachers?*

Or to

– *Why don't black lives matter?*
– *Well, why don't blue lives matter?*

We accuse to excuse, incessantly, in private and public life. But Warner teaches that we can reset this loop. We can convert it from a vicious circle of *denying* responsibility into a virtuous cycle of *accepting* it. We can start that in our smallest conversations, over the seemingly smallest things. Because all things are made of small things.

When we admit our piece of the problem we free ourselves from the burdens of constant self-serving justification. We influence others by letting them influence us, which awakens *their* sense of responsibility:

– *You're right, I should've taken out the trash.*
– *Well, you know, I still haven't done the dishes.*

This is not preemptively surrendering high ground. It is leading people who are stuck in self-justification by sharing your example of getting *unstuck*. That example is contagious. In fact, contagion, not persuasion, is what really ever changes minds and self-images. Warner has helped people at every scale apply these insights, from families in crisis to nations at war. Every scale holds the same truth: We make one another. We can remake one another. No one is blameless. Yield to advance.

Does this sound like woo-woo left-wing hippie talk? That's OK. Some of my best friends are woo-woo left-wing hippies. I note, though, that C. Terry Warner is a professor at Brigham Young University, where, decades ago, he was a mentor to an earnest man in search of himself named Mitt Romney. Warner's work is informed by his Mormon faith, as he says up front, though he takes great pains not to proselytize or even to name that faith. What I, a non-Mormon, non-Christian believer in American *civic* religion, took away from Warner is simply this: how to live like a citizen.

Once you see through the lens that Warner crafted, you begin to question yourself in other constructive ways. During my meeting last week with the citizen-scientists in DC, what became clear is that Americans can find scientific information easily if they want it. What they can't get so easily is the desire to want it. What they—we—need is to remember that we can deal with a changing world more effectively when we learn how to think like the best scientists. How to ask great questions. How to ruthlessly prune away bad assumptions. How to stay aware of ignorance while gaining expertise.

And also this: how to build communities of practice to keep you honest. This is what we've got to do now as citizens. Make circles of friends and newcomers alike to talk about the news, to expand the number of sources you're getting information from.

The best scientists have the soul of an artist and the decisiveness of a warrior. They can face themselves, their accumulated patterns, their own body of work and ask: What here is obsolete? What must I release to move forward? They can then say, to use the title of an anthology by John Brockman, *This Idea Must Die.*

Ask of yourself each day: Which idea of mine must die? Which way of thinking about other people—whether my allies or those I've decided are my enemies—is holding me back? Here's one idea that I think must die in American civic life: the idea that *we all have to get along.* Which brings me to the third and final topic I'd like to speak to today:

WHAT IT REALLY MEANS TO COME TOGETHER

How in this age when everyone has their own truth and facts can we ever manage to reestablish the commons? Here's a hint: it's not about empathy and reconciliation.

In fact, I'd say today that what America needs is not forced reconciliation that papers over our actual and deep philosophical divides. What we need now is to argue more. *More?* Most people, it is true, would say we have such dysfunction today because we already argue too much about too many things. But that's a misdiagnosis of what ails

American politics. We don't need fewer arguments today; we need less stupid ones.

The arguments in American politics today are stupid in many ways: they're stuck in a decaying two-party institutional framework; they fail to challenge foundational assumptions about capitalism or government; they center on symbolic proxy skirmishes instead of naming the underlying change; they focus excessively on style and surface.

Americans can do better. Remember: America doesn't just have arguments; America *is* an argument—between Federalist and Anti-Federalist worldviews, strong national government and local control, liberty and equality, individual rights and collective responsibility, color-blindness and color-consciousness, *Pluribus* and *Unum*.

The point of civic life in this country is not to avoid such tensions. Nor is it for one side to achieve "final" victory. The point is for us all to wrestle perpetually with these polarities, to fashion hybrid solutions that work for the times until they don't, then to start again.

Imagine if in public libraries, civic clubs, neighborhood groups, and spaces like this we taught ourselves how to argue better, how to identify and name our foundational fights over principle, how to argue all sides and not just one's own, how to change one's own mind as well as another's, and how to put together solutions that draw from each pole of principle—as if we had responsibility for solutions, not just posturing. Because we do.

This is reconciliation for grown-ups. It doesn't pretend that all will be peaceful—or that it should be. It acknowledges the never-endingness of our fights. But it acknowledges too that to be a citizen means fighting to make our fights more useful: more honest, more open to change, more human.

Knowing how to have better arguments is the job of every American now. And perhaps paradoxically, it is the way we can come together. Let's come together to fight. To fight better. Let's invite each other out of our virtual bubbles and engage each other for real.

It's also our job to point out to each other, in the spirit of *Bonds That Make Us Free*, the blind spots we don't know we have. To be, in the most loving sense possible, the blind leading the blind.

I want to close with the words of a great citizen. Grace Lee Boggs was a Chinese American who defied conventions of race and gender to become a leading activist in the Civil Rights Movement and a revolutionary activist in Detroit to the end of her 100 years of life. "History is not the past," she said. "It is the stories we tell about the past. How we tell these stories—triumphantly or self-critically, metaphysically or dialectally—has a lot to do with whether we cut short or advance our evolution as human beings."

There are a lot more stories in the mix now. Let's find the good in that, and search out the simplicity of universal human yearnings in all those complex stories. Let's learn how to lead by an example of humility and responsibility-taking that will, in the end, be the greatest antidote to the pathological braggadocio and responsibility-shirking of the next president. And let's learn to argue not in the manner of social media impression-managers but in the manner of humans who must face one another.

And let's always remember just how blessed we are to be present at the creation.

3.

IF WE CAN KEEP IT

Madrona Commons · Seattle, WA
December 17, 2016

JANE JACOBS
From a reply to a McCarthyite committee
investigating her beliefs
1952

I was brought up to believe there is no virtue in conforming meekly to the dominant opinion of the moment. I was encouraged to believe that simple conformity results in stagnation for a society, and that American progress has been largely owing to the opportunity for experimentation, the leeway given initiative, and to a gusto and a freedom for chewing over odd ideas.

I was taught that the American's right to be a free individual, not at the mercy of the state, was hard-won and that its price was eternal vigilance, that I too would have to be vigilant.

> I was not tired physically, or no more tired than I usually was
> at the end of a working day. I was not old, although some
> people have an image of me as being old then. I was forty-
> two. No, the only tired I was, was tired of giving in.

H ow many of you have ever been to a United States naturalization ceremony?

If you've never been, I urge you to find one in town and go. There are few experiences more moving, especially the "roll call of nations," in which the applicants, who've already taken and passed their citizenship exam, are asked to stand up as their native country is called. *Azerbaijan, China, France, Kenya, Mexico, New Zealand.* When the roll call is complete the immigrants are told, "The next time you sit down, you will be Americans." They then raise their right hands, swear an oath, and become United States citizens.

It gives me goosebumps just telling you about it.

A few years ago, after we'd been to a naturalization ceremony, my wife, Jená, had an idea. What if we created a ceremony like that—with ritual and emotion and an oath—not just for immigrants who were becoming citizens but for citizens of long standing as well? A ceremony where everyone, whether they were brand-new Americans or people who'd had the dumb luck to be born here, could renew their vows?

We were in a meeting and Jená got up to the whiteboard and sketched an image of a revival tent and described this not as a swearing-in but as a chance to be "sworn-again." And so was born a little project of Citizen University called "Sworn-Again America."

We created a simple template for a ceremony—readings, remarks, and an oath—then primed it with a few great partner organizations and put it out into the world. There have been countless Sworn-Again America ceremonies ever since, at public libraries and college campuses and military bases. At the National Constitution Center and Monticello and the White House. At Starbucks headquarters here in Seattle and at house parties across the country. With a few people or a few thousand, all of them reflecting—some for the first time—on the content of their citizenship.

As folks create their own ceremonies, adapting them to local circumstances, the one constant is the "Sworn-Again" oath we created. Let me share it with you:

I pledge to be an active American.
To show up for others,
To govern myself,
To help govern my community.
I recommit myself to my country's creed:
To cherish liberty as a responsibility.
I pledge to serve and to push my country:
When right, to be kept right; when wrong, to be set right.
Wherever my ancestors and I were born,
I claim America
And I pledge to live like a citizen.

You'll notice a few things about this oath. It's nonpartisan, of course. But it is *not* morally neutral. It contains a judgment about what it is to be a useful contributor to the body. And it's written in a way that applies regardless of your documentation status: for there are plenty of people in this country who lack the papers but live like great citizens, and plenty of people who have the papers but don't.

Today I want to talk about three commitments from this Sworn-Again American oath. First: *To cherish liberty as a responsibility.* Second: *To govern myself.* And third: *To help govern my community.* In unpacking these three phrases, I am truly asking what civic responsibility really means when the body politic is as unhealthy and corrupted as it is today. Let's start with the first phrase:

LIBERTY AS A RESPONSIBILITY

This sounds nice. But I wonder how many people in this country truly practice it.

To many Americans, liberty means, roughly, *It's a free country, man. Don't tell me what to do.* Or, to use more historically resonant language: *Don't Tread On Me.* This notion of negative liberty is deep in our nation's DNA. And that makes sense, given that the big bang of our nation was founded to throw off monarchical tyranny. The idea that liberty is the removal of encumbrance has a long and distinguished history. My fellow civic nerds who celebrated Bill of Rights Day on Thursday can appreciate this.

But a funny thing happened on the way to Trump Tower. We Americans forgot that real liberty requires more than just the removal of encumbrance. We forgot that a society cannot stand on rights alone. We forgot that only toddlers and sociopaths believe in rights without responsibilities. And we forgot that the colonists in the 1770s who made flags that said "Don't Tread On Me" didn't need to make other flags that said liberty is a responsibility because it was profoundly obvious to them. It was second nature. It was the very definition of adulthood back then.

Rights don't just come with duties. Rights *are* duties. Freedoms *are* responsibilities. Liberties *are* obligations. You figure that out pretty quickly when you have to sustain your own outpost in the woods with little outside help. Historians like Garry Wills and Bernard Bailyn have written about the deep culture of self-government that existed in the colonies before 1776 and that formed what Bailyn calls "the ideological origins of the American Revolution." Over a century and a half, subjects of the British Crown evolved gradually and subtly into citizens of a new nation. They made assemblies. They made town meetings. They made common law. They also made, thanks to people like Benjamin Franklin, fire departments and libraries and public health organizations. That evolution was a byproduct of the unforgiving environment: of having to figure out how not to die, and realizing that mutual aid and strong reciprocity and a code of responsibility are as necessary to liberty as oxygen is to flame.

It's the same lesson the Americans of 1787 had to relearn when they faced the collapse of the Articles of Confederation and decided they had to ratify a Constitution to form a more perfect Union. Without that Constitution, each state was like a toddler, asserting rights and evading responsibilities and paying no heed to a continental tragedy of the commons. The states had to grow up if they wanted liberty to mean anything in the United States. The alternative, they knew from a decade of experience, was not utopia but bedlam.

The story goes that when Ben Franklin walked out of Independence Hall in Philadelphia after the Constitutional Convention was over, a woman passing on the street asked him what the convention had created. He replied, "A republic, if you can keep it." In other words: "We didn't create anything. It's on you."

And so here we are today. Hardly anyone talks like this now. The closest you get, in our militarized post-9/11 age, is the slogan "Freedom isn't free." I remember one recent summer during Seafair, when my family went down to Lake Washington to watch the Blue Angels—and I do appreciate the Blue Angels—as those fearsome F/A-18s buzzed past, a beer-drinking man with skulls and tanks on his T-shirt screamed out to no one in particular, "YEAH, BABY!! FREEDOM AIN'T FREE!! WOO-HOOOO!"

But *this* articulation of the idea has more in common with the late Roman empire than it does with the early Roman republic—or the American republic that we were supposed to keep. *This* articulation of the idea is simply a reminder that our professional warriors—the 1 percent of our population to whom a morally avoidant nation has subcontracted a decade and a half of war, when we all should have been drafted and all should have served—that these warriors now have semi-sacred status as guardians of our liberties.

The natural conclusion of *this* articulation of the idea—freedom ain't free, so show respect to your military—is a presidential cabinet overstocked with generals.

No, I'm talking about the *Founders'* articulation of the idea. *Liberty as responsibility.* And I'm talking about their knowledge, as Bernard Bailyn wrote, that "free states are fragile and degenerate easily into tyrannies unless vigilantly protected by a free, knowledgeable, and uncorrupted electorate working through institutions that balance and distribute rather than concentrate power."

A free, knowledgeable, and uncorrupted electorate. Well, we have catastrophically failed in our responsibility to be *that*. The American electorate today is half-absent and the other half is half-ignorant.

Each passing day confirms that Donald Trump is a menace to our form of self-government. But in a sense, he is also a blessing. For in this odious, cynical, incurious, pathological person is now *personified* all the sicknesses in our political culture: rampant materialism and celebrity worship, profound ignorance of history and the world, disregard for fact or fairness, addiction to instant gratification. He is not the cause of our democratic sickness. He is the result of it. (Although he may yet cause a collapse.)

And what Donald Trump does for *all* of us is force us to ask whether we, too, are the personification of all the sicknesses in our political culture. How should we, civic physicians, heal *ourselves*? Which brings me to the second commitment of our oath:

TO GOVERN MYSELF

What does this mean?

Well, it means first to remember that society becomes how *you* behave. Every social change, welcome or unwelcome, begins with the individual. Your choice to be compassionate or not, civil or not, courageous or not, becomes rapidly, immediately, imperceptibly contagious. To realize that society becomes how you behave is to leave behind the myth of what economists call "externalities"—the idea that you don't have to bear the costs of your bad or selfish behavior. But to realize that society becomes how you behave is also to leave behind the myth that you are just one in a billion, one helpless inconsequential individual. You are at *all* times a node of contagion.

That is especially true in *these* times—times when prosocial moral norms are teetering and when the people threatening those norms most vividly have titles like "president-elect" and "senior counselor to the president-elect." Those men have chosen to govern themselves a certain way, which is to indulge the darker demons of their nature, and they've given permission to many millions to act just as deplorably.

You—we—must generate the counter-contagion. We must create a countervailing kind of permission. Permission to speak truth to power. Permission to disrupt the disrupter-in-chief and to answer his cynicism and self-dealing with integrity and moral clarity. Permission to show some guts and to spend some capital and clout, if you have any, on behalf of those who have less.

For instance: How on earth did all those tech sector titans like Jeff Bezos and Sheryl Sandberg and Brad Smith go to the meeting that Trump called this week without one of them saying one word to decry the odious things Trump has said and done against women, immigrants, labor leaders, and everyday citizens? Those tech titans, each with their vast hoards of capital of every kind, were profiles in cowardice this week.

Imagine if all of them—if one of them—had held a press conference after that meeting and said, with all civility, that while their meeting was pleasant and interesting, they'd told the president-elect and they were telling the public now that they would never be party to the construction of an online registry to round up Muslim Americans and that the president-elect's rhetoric this fall against immigrants was especially harmful to a sector of American innovation that depends on making immigrants feel valued.

We should not wait on our leaders. We should lead them. *We* have to be the ones who signal that we will disable any such registry by flooding it with all our names. *We* have to be the ones who make that choice in our heart, and then vocalize it. To carry ourselves in a way that is conscious of the power of example and the example of power.

To govern oneself means figuring out exactly what you believe and why. Doing this is hard. It will illuminate how challenging it is to apply your beliefs evenhandedly. It'll also reveal what principles you won't ever sacrifice for personal gain.

Let me confess, on the point about applying beliefs evenhandedly, that these last few years I was not that troubled by President Obama's use of executive orders and administrative rulemaking powers to bypass an obstructionist Congress and Article I of the Constitution. Why? Because his *ends* were appealing to me: ends like protecting our undocumented friends from deportation, like protecting the environment from coal-fired despoliation. But now that it's going to be President Trump using those same powers, I have a belated respect for checks and balances and for Article I and for the reasons why Congress and not the president was the focus of Article I.

If I'm to govern myself honestly, I must admit my hypocrisy about ends and means. And I've got to try to hold myself and my side to account with integrity. Because otherwise I remain too vulnerable to the temptation to sacrifice principle when the ends demand it.

I was reading recently about Elliot Richardson, an old upright Establishment figure who was United States Attorney General when

Richard Nixon ordered him on October 20, 1973, to fire Archibald Cox, the special prosecutor investigating the Watergate scandal. In what became known as the "Saturday Night Massacre," Richardson refused the order and he resigned. His deputy, Seattle's own Bill Ruckelshaus, also refused and resigned. Finally, Solicitor General Robert Bork, third in command but least in command of himself morally, carried out the president's order and fired Cox. And Watergate approached its disgraceful endgame.

There are likely going to be moments like this in the coming administration. But not just for Trump's equivalents of Richardson and Ruckelshaus and Bork. For you. And me. You want to be ready when that moment comes. It may not be in the White House and it may not be national news. It may be on your block, when someone emboldened by the times mistreats a neighbor. It might be at your kid's school. It might be at work, when good old boys feel like it's OK again to be politically incorrect and tell their female colleague how much they like the way she walks. To govern yourself is to know yourself morally. To know what will come out under the crucible of a crisis or in a random revealing moment. To know that you'll know right from wrong when the pressure's on.

To govern oneself also means regulating your behavior and your reactions to things. You can't control what Donald Trump does. But you can control how you react to what Donald Trump does. For starters, let's stop jumping at everything that little man tweets, or at everything someone posts about what that little man tweets. In fact, let's take a social media Sabbath. Let's *decelerate*. Trump thrives on relentless acceleration, on creating a whirlwind of controversy that obliterates memory and disorients us from fact and truth and gets the body politic so stressed out and hopped-up that it's in a state of constant agitation that's like an autoimmune disorder. To govern oneself means saying no to all that. Taking control of your own metabolism and mind.

To govern oneself also means to experiment relentlessly in search of a better way to be of use to others. Mohandas Gandhi titled his autobiography *The Story of My Experiments with Truth*. I love that title. I love the idea that to live like a citizen is to be running experiments all the time, personal experiments that may be invisible to all, in pursuit of a truer and better way to live out your ideals and to enact justice.

When Gandhi was a young lawyer still in his native South Africa, he wrote a letter to the great Russian novelist Leo Tolstoy seeking advice on how to liberate India. Tolstoy's answer cut right to the chase. Describing how the British East India Company had come to take over India, Tolstoy wrote: "What does it mean that thirty thousand men, not athletes, but rather weak and ordinary people, have enslaved two hundred million vigorous, clever, capable, and freedom-loving people? Do not the figures make it clear that . . . the Indians . . . have enslaved themselves?"

And after that wake-up call, Gandhi began tinkering with his own imagination, his own way of living, his own notions of convention and normality and what he would accept as conventional and normal. He began to see, as he later wrote, that "The moment the slave resolves that he will no longer be a slave, his fetters fall. He frees himself and he shows the way to others. Freedom and slavery are mental states." The rest, as we know, is history. But you don't go from zero to Gandhi after one sermon. (Even if it is crazy-inspiring to learn that Tolstoy lit the flame for Gandhi.) And you don't leap from being a couch potato and Twitter addict to strong citizenship in one move.

So, finally, to govern oneself means to get in shape civically. That means setting goals and finding places to work out: *I will, in the next year, be able to give a five-minute extemporaneous speech on a civic topic.* Or: *I will organize (and meet) my neighbors to do something together for the good of the neighborhood.* Or: *I will, starting now, read national and local news every day, as well as trusted opinions from left and right.* Or: *I will, by midyear, learn what the core arguments are in American civic life.*

When you're civically fit, you can organize people through word and deed. You can recognize the patterns and the echoes from history when modern politicians argue, the way we now sense Hamilton and Jefferson reverberating in contemporary politics thanks to Lin-Manuel Miranda.

Of course, 'tis the season to be thinking about how out of shape we are *physically* and to make resolutions to remedy that. Well, it's the same civically. We commit. We pace ourselves. We make a routine. And the routine will go better and last longer if we show up with others and make progress together.

This gathering, at an hour when there is *so much else to do*, is proof of that. We are a community, and part of a larger one. So the final commitment we must make is this:

TO HELP GOVERN MY COMMUNITY

There's so much going around social media these days in the "What Should I Do?" category. The latest thing I saw is a document written by an anonymous group of congressional staffers—an insiders' guide for everyday citizens about how to lobby and apply pressure on members of Congress to resist Trump's agenda.

I think this is exactly the right idea—and exactly the wrong arena. It's the right idea because every one of us now must become far more fluent in how power operates in civic life. Every one of us now must be able to understand in civic life who decides, who drives decision, and what gets left off the agenda for decision and why. Every one of us needs to learn how to read and rearrange the array of sources and conduits of power that comprise what we call the power structure.

To govern your community means to become literate in power— and to know how to read *and* write power. Too many of us know too little about how to make stuff happen.

But the congressional insiders' guide focuses on the wrong arena, I think, because the place for you, the citizen, to exercise your power and to achieve civic fitness most effectively today is *here*. Your community. That's partly because a gerrymandered and challenger-proof

Congress is deaf to people outside each member's base electorate. But it's also because it is at the level of the city and the small town that we can learn anew how to run things like we are responsible for them. Because we are.

Let me tell you, as someone who worked in the United States Senate and then the Clinton White House twice and who now serves on a federal board as an Obama appointee, that my true and best education in democratic self-government came during my ten years as a trustee of the Seattle Public Library, from 2002 to 2012.

In Washington, DC, the game was mainly talking points and positioning and the appearance of doing something. When you are one of five trustees overseeing an institution that's beloved by the city, there's no hiding behind talking points. You either build and program these neighborhood libraries in accordance with the hopes and dreams of the neighbors—or you fail to. You either learn who can make stuff happen in Seattle neighborhoods like Lake City or Ballard or the International District—or you proceed at your own peril.

So take that insiders' guide to Congress and apply it to city hall or the school board. Organize other people, your neighbors and friends, for simple teach-ins about how those institutions work and how they could work better. And then, crowdsource a supplement to that insiders' guide that's not about the formal institutions like the city council and the state legislature and people with public titles and salaries but is about the informal web of *who really runs this town*.

To govern your community is to know the answer to that question. The mayor is surely part of the answer. But so is Paul Allen, who holds no office but owns South Lake Union and the Seattle Seahawks and is defining the shape of this city's landscape and demographic profile. And so is Estela Ortega, who also holds no office but who runs El Centro de la Raza and is a power broker for immigrants and communities of color in the Beacon Hill neighborhood. And so on and so on. You can do a roll call of power brokers that is longer than the list of elected officials; it may leave many of them off.

To govern your community is not only to understand who *really* runs this town, but then to insert yourself into the answer. To participate. To volunteer. To serve. To take leadership roles in established committees. Or to establish your own. The three greatest words in American civic life, words that Ben Franklin lived by, are *start a club*. On anything useful. To govern your community is to start a club or join one so that in the company of others you can practice power. And practice some more. And some more.

Now how, you might ask, will this stop Congress from repealing Obamacare or enacting Trump's tax cuts for the rich or doing worse? It may not, immediately. But starting and joining clubs, and signing up to make change happen where you live, rebuilds citizen muscle and it redistributes citizen power. Address homelessness. Fix mental health systems. Feed schoolchildren real food. Fund our schools right. And all that muscle and power can then be deployed in any arena, whether national or local. Sending emails to Senator X or Congressperson Y or sharing outraged posts on Facebook does not build power in the same way or at the same rate.

It's not an either-or, of course, and many of us are simultaneously practicing power locally and applying what we have nationally too. As a people, we must all be in that spirit of tinkering and experimenting with truth and hammering out new practical ways to make change happen. Let an ecosystem flower from our diverse efforts. But wherever we choose to focus our energies, the thing to remember is what James Madison said in 1792. "In Europe," he observed, "charters of liberty have been granted by power. America has set the example . . . of charters of power granted by liberty."

If we in our liberty grant power to others to rule for a time, then we must also renew the covenant behind the grant—a covenant that says that they rule not *over* us but *with* us. *By* us. *For* us. The idea of a covenant has Puritan overtones, and covenant theology is what propelled the Pilgrims to Plymouth. But the American covenant belongs to us all. It's not just a Mayflower thing. And it is not a commitment to consensus; it is a promise to argue perpetually over the meaning of our creed. It is a hammering out of disputes and of often irreconcilable visions of the good life. It is a reckoning with dangers. It is a binding of fates that can be unpleasant and hard.

We agree to form and to reform this Union, to try to keep this republic, challenging and contradictory as it is, because we imagine that we are better off with it than without.

A nation, Benedict Anderson wrote, is an "imagined community." That is particularly true of a nation like ours that has no mythic common bond of blood or soil. We are a nation bound together by the flimsiest thing in the world: a creed. But that creed, that cloud of intangible words like *liberty* and *equality* and *justice*, can also, when spoken together, bind our best selves together.

I commit to using all my powers to resist authoritarianism in this country.

I commit to teaching everything I know about civic power to as many people as I can.

I commit to helping remedy economic and political inequality in Seattle.

I commit to defending disfavored people whom Donald Trump tries to bully.

I commit to building the kind of beloved community I want to be part of.

Join me in these covenants. Let's recommit ourselves to our country's creed.

4.

_____

ALTERNATE REALITIES

Washington Hall · Seattle, WA
January 14, 2017

WALT WHITMAN

From Leaves of Grass: *"Song of Myself," Section 16*
1891–92 edition

I am of old and young, of the foolish as much as the wise,
Regardless of others, ever regardful of others,
Maternal as well as paternal, a child as well as a man,
Stuff'd with the stuff that is coarse and stuff'd with the stuff that
    is fine,
One of the Nation of many nations, the smallest the same and
    the largest the same,
A Southerner soon as a Northerner, a planter nonchalant and
    hospitable down by the Oconee I live,
A Yankee bound by my own way ready for trade, my joints the
    limberest joints on earth and the sternest joints on earth,

A Kentuckian walking the vale of the Elkhorn in my deerskin
    leggings, a Louisianian or Georgian,
A boatman over lakes or bays or along coasts, a Hoosier, Badger,
    Buckeye;
At home on Kanadian snow-shoes or up in the bush, or with
    fishermen off Newfoundland,
At home in the fleet of ice-boats, sailing with the rest and tacking,
At home on the hills of Vermont or in the woods of Maine, or the
    Texan ranch,
Comrade of Californians, comrade of free North-Westerners,
    (loving their big proportions,)
Comrade of raftsmen and coalmen, comrade of all who shake
    hands and welcome to drink and meat,
A learner with the simplest, a teacher of the thoughtfullest,
A novice beginning yet experient of myriads of seasons,
Of every hue and caste am I, of every rank and religion,
A farmer, mechanic, artist, gentleman, sailor, quaker,
Prisoner, fancy-man, rowdy, lawyer, physician, priest.

I resist any thing better than my own diversity,
Breathe the air but leave plenty after me,
And am not stuck up, and am in my place.

(The moth and the fish-eggs are in their place,
The bright suns I see and the dark suns I cannot see are in
    their place,
The palpable is in its place and the impalpable is in its place.)

ABRAHAM LINCOLN
From the first debate with Stephen Douglas
August 21, 1858

Judge Douglas is going back to the era of our Revolution, and to the extent of his ability, muzzling the cannon which thunders its annual joyous return. When he invites any people willing to have slavery, to establish it, he is blowing out the moral lights around us. When he says he "cares not whether slavery is voted down or voted up,"—that it is a sacred right of self-government—he is, in my judgment, penetrating the human soul and eradicating the light of reason and the love of liberty in this American people.

RALPH WALDO EMERSON
From the essay "Experience"
Published 1844

We must be very suspicious of the deceptions of the element of time. It takes a good deal of time to eat or to sleep, or to earn a hundred dollars, and a very little time to entertain a hope and an insight which becomes the light of our life. We dress our garden, eat our dinners, discuss the household with our wives, and these things make no impression, are forgotten next week; but in the solitude to which every man is always returning, he has a sanity and revelations, which in his passage into new worlds he will carry with him. Never mind the ridicule, never mind the defeat: up again, old heart!—it seems to say,—there is victory yet for all justice; and the true romance which the world exists to realize, will be the transformation of genius into practical power.

Our first reading today, from Walt Whitman, is perhaps best known for a single line: "Of every hue and caste am I, of every rank and religion." This is not just a line celebrating American diversity and pluralism. It is a line about metaphysics, about how each part contains the whole. It is a line about how the infinite spectrum of human possibility—possible lives, possible selves, possible futures—resides here and now in *each* of us.

"The palpable is in its place and the impalpable is in its place."

I love that. And I want to talk with you today about this idea, this suggestion of alternate simultaneous realities.

As a quantum physicist might joke, alternate realities are *everywhere* these days. (Sorry; it's a little early in the morning for a quantum physics joke.) But really, they do seem to be all around us now, in our culture and our politics alike.

Over the holidays, Jená and I fell into the alternate reality of a show called *The Man in the High Castle*. It's on Amazon Prime in its second season, and is itself about alternate realities. It's based on a Philip K. Dick sci-fi novel in which the Nazis and the Japanese Empire won the Second World War and divvied up the territory of what used to be the United States, leaving a no-man's-land in the Rocky Mountains.

That premise alone is very chilling. It's jarring to watch an all-American family in a suburban 1959 home with their dad, John Smith . . . who comes down to breakfast wearing a spit-shined, squared-away black-and-silver SS uniform and is addressed by his driver as *Obergruppenfuhrer* Smith. But it's especially jarring now, when we have a president-elect who won't hesitate to lash out at John Lewis or the pope or Meryl Streep but just cannot bring himself to disavow white nationalists, and whose election was aided by Russia and cheered by neo-Nazis and authoritarians. As I say, chilling.

Nevertheless, the show is great. And what makes it great is not just the imaginative leap of its historical premise. What makes it great is that many of the characters, starting with a frail and paranoid Adolf

Hitler, are freaking out because strange, subversive films are appearing out of nowhere that show a different world: a world in which the Americans, not the Germans, developed the A-bomb first; in which it was Hiroshima and not Washington, DC, that was leveled by that bomb; in which FDR was never assassinated and in which Hitler committed suicide; in which San Francisco is not the capital of the Japanese Pacific States but is a hub of baseball, jazz, and beat poets.

Both the regime and the resistance are trying to get their hands on these films but no one knows where they're coming from. They're too detailed to be fakes. As a viewer, as someone primed for science fiction, you begin to wonder: Did they drop in from some other quantum reality? Has the veil between this universe and another been pierced? Who has broken through?

Well, I hope I've sold you on the show. It's an imagination-bender, because it gives you the exhilarating sense that *you* could be the one to break through. And so was another work of fiction that I consumed hungrily over the holidays: Colson Whitehead's new novel *The Underground Railroad*.

On the surface, it's a straight narrative about an enslaved woman in 1830s Georgia who flees from her plantation and is aided by many people along the way in her escape from slavery. But its genius is that it takes the metaphor of the Underground Railroad literally. So Cora, the main character, finds herself literally going underground and entering vast tunnels built by *who knows who*, and taking powerful locomotives in an unknown, unseen network from North Carolina to Tennessee to Indiana to freedom. And what this simple, subtle device does is make you wonder what our world would look like if we actually did make the subterranean yearnings, the metaphors and symbols cherished by all those who labor under oppression, into *reality*.

So that's what I did over Christmas break. I left this world for a while. But break is over, isn't it? We are, as they say, "back to reality." And yet even *this* reality is about alternate realities. Consider the twenty-four-hour period this week when we saw the jagged, stomach-churning contrast between President Obama's inspiring and earnest farewell address, in which he tried to awaken us to our responsibilities as citizens, and Donald Trump's cynical first press conference postelection, in which he tried to discredit reports that Russia had blackmail-worthy videos of him and, more troublingly, that his campaign had colluded with the Putin regime to undermine American policy.

Both halves of that day were enough to make you cry.

That same day, as we found ourselves fluctuating between a president and a president-elect, I *personally* experienced a similarly disorienting immersion into two very different worlds. First I had coffee that morning with my friend Sarah Jaynes, who runs the Progress Alliance, a Washington-statewide network of progressive donors who invest in organizations that promote social and economic justice.

Sarah has been doing activism and civic engagement since she was six, when she was writing letters to President Jimmy Carter. All her remembered life, she has been fighting for inclusion and fairness. Which is maybe why, as we were sitting at the Hi-Spot coffee shop, and she was talking about the recommitment she and the Progress Alliance were making to their work, her eyes welled with tears. They were not, by my reckoning, tears either of hopelessness *or* resolve. They were tears simply of love: love for the ideals of this country, love for her work, love for this life, which cannot be taken for granted.

An hour later I was en route to Dallas. And there I went to meet a son of Mount Vernon, Washington. A man who endured a childhood of great trial and trauma, including the death under mysterious circumstances of his mother. A man who never managed to get a college degree but who hustled his way into a medium where he could find his voice, and along the way found a stabilizing faith through the Mormon Church. A man who now works in a giant studio building, like a Hollywood set, and has become one of the modern era's most powerful and effective political communicators. And a man who now, a multimillionaire and a few years into grandparenthood, is asking anew what it's all about. That man is named Glenn Beck.

Most everyone knows who he is, and how much damage he has done to civic and political life by being for so many years an inflammatory right-wing radio and television host, most notoriously on Fox News. And most everyone in this predominantly progressive room today is thinking, *What the F? Glenn Beck?*

Well, let me share with you why I went and what I learned, and then return to this idea of alternate realities.

WHY I WENT

If you've been following the media in the last couple of years and especially in the last few months, you know Glenn Beck is in the midst of an interesting metamorphosis. He has very publicly, in mainstream media outlets, disavowed some of his most egregious past statements. He has apologized for being a prime creator of our polarized, scorched-earth political culture. He has said he now understands and appreciates Black Lives Matter. He rejected Trump during the primaries and has consistently warned about the authoritarian dangers of a Trump presidency. He has joined with the liberal comic talk-show host Samantha Bee in a televised segment about searching for a way to undo the damage he's done and to rehumanize politics and combat Trumpism.

As I watched this shift, I thought, here I've stood at this very lectern talking about the need to rehumanize those with whom we disagree. Why not put my money where my mouth is? Why not engage Glenn Beck? So I asked my friend Matt Kibbe, who was an early Tea Party leader and now runs a libertarian organization called Free the People, if he would introduce me to Beck's team. He did. I talked on the phone with Beck's trusted lieutenant, Jon Schreiber, who runs his media business. We talked about how much we disagreed about the role of government. We also talked about how much we agreed that the role of the citizen, especially today, is to take more responsibility for problems and to learn how to make change with skill and with principle. And at the end of that call Jon invited me to come down to Dallas to spend some time with him and Glenn.

That's how I found myself on Wednesday morning sitting on one of the soft, comfy couches on Glenn Beck's set, the kind of couch where you can do a TV show viewed by millions while wearing jeans and an old cowboy shirt, and I sat across from Glenn Beck, who was wearing jeans and an old cowboy shirt. The cameras and microphones were off. And Glenn and Jon and I began a conversation that went well past the hour we'd allotted. He was warm, down-to-earth, funny, and inquisitive. He started by asking me, in all sincerity, how I could square my progressive philosophy with a belief in the individual. By instinct, I began with Whitman. I had a thought ready to unspool about how Whitman's life and poetry remind us so vividly that there is no such thing as an individual disconnected from a society, and that governments help create the social context within which the individual can thrive and become his or her fullest self.

But before I could get going, Beck smiled and pointed at the coffee table between us. I hadn't even noticed but right there in front of me was a photo of Whitman in old age, sitting on top of a copy of *Leaves of Grass*. Glenn and I nodded at each other. Then I finished unspooling my answer, and from there we were off on a discussion that was sometimes political, sometimes personal, and throughout, very candid.

We quickly got to definitions. In his mind, "progressive" means someone who wants to use the government to make everyone else do what *he* wants to do. Which means Donald Trump is as dangerous a progressive as Barack Obama. In my mind, "progressive" means someone who believes that American life is about closing the gap between our stated ideals and our actual condition, rather than being resigned to the status quo. Government exists to help us close that gap.

But just as Jon Schreiber and I had over the phone, Glenn Beck and I found ourselves agreeing that this is the age of citizen power, whether you're looking at the Tea Party or Black Lives Matter, and that the more ordinary citizens are equipped to make decisions and make change, the better. He and I sit at such distant points along the spectrum from libertarian to communitarian, from belief in minimalist to maximalist government, but we agree that civic life cannot be just one or the other. Democracies are gardens, I said. Citizens are gardeners. And gardening is about *degrees* of letting nature run its course. As a native Northwesterner, he understood just what I was saying.

We talked about the difference between liberty and freedom, and I told him about one of my favorite books, called *Liberty and Freedom*, by the Brandeis historian David Hackett Fischer. The book lays out the history of these two ideas, and makes the argument that these are two *different* ideas, even though Americans have always conflated them. *Liberty* has roots in Latin and signifies a status of nondependence and an absence of obligations in a hierarchical society. *Freedom* has roots in Old Norse and Icelandic and arises from the bands of self-governing tribesmen for whom being free meant being bonded to others in a community that kept danger at bay. Both Glenn and Jon were deeply interested in this, and when I told them that the book is mainly about icons, symbols, and images, from liberty trees and liberty poles and liberty bells to Freedom Rides and Freedom Summer, they got fired up and made a note to get the book.

And before long we got to a deeper level, the spirit level. I told Glenn about a book I've described at past Civic Saturdays called *Bonds That Make Us Free*. It's by C. Terry Warner, a BYU organizational behavior professor who described a simple universal human cycle of "I *accuse* you to *excuse* me." Which then got us to the shift Beck is now making so publicly, and the way he is trying to break his own circuit of "accuse to excuse"—the very circuit that spun him into power and fueled his success.

We agreed that most people most of the time don't know *what they believe or why*. And they don't have opportunity to figure it out. Then I told him about all of you—about this Civic Saturday experiment we are creating together. I told him about this simple structure of a gathering, this civic analogue to church, where people find fellowship in song, sermon, and civic scripture. He was intrigued. We talked about how he chose to become a Mormon and how I chose to become a believer in the American creed, and how neither of us believes that belief of any kind should ever be too sure of itself.

And here at last we got to the power of example. Beck is now trying to *model* a different way of being, in real time, even as he is *inventing* it. He's trying to show his audience and his base of followers that it's possible to be a different kind of person forming a different kind of reality. He wants to learn from me—from you—and others on the left. He wants to disagree with me in a way that everyone else can learn from: with respect and genuine openness. It's challenging. He can't get too far ahead of his base. He is a businessman and entertainer with many millions of dollars at stake. And I can't forget that for all his changes, he still supported Ted Cruz for president and we still disagree sharply about issues like the minimum wage. He still runs a media empire called TheBlaze that still is home to flamethrowers and hyperbolic fearmongering.

But I do believe he is sincere in his desire to shift, to trip the circuit, as he put it. I believe he is interesting and thoughtful. And I intend to continue this conversation and see where it takes us, whether it's collaboration or simply having better arguments.

But all that I've told you here does not sum up what I truly learned from my time with Glenn Beck. That is what I'd like to turn to next.

WHAT I LEARNED

As I flew home from Dallas, digesting this unexpectedly enjoyable encounter, I realized three things. They aren't about Glenn Beck per se but are about the reality we find ourselves in six days before the inauguration of a nakedly dishonest, dishonorable man as our president.

First, I realized that empathy is not enough—you have to own responsibility for both the wrong you've done and for your role in the right that must be done.

Second, democracy is not enough—you have to cultivate virtue and moral clarity.

Third, resistance is not enough—you have to build something folks want to be part of.

Let me say a word about each of these learnings.

Empathy is not enough. In *New York* magazine a couple of weeks ago there was a fascinating feature on an experiment they conducted on radical empathy. Working with a nonprofit called Narrative 4, they paired off gun-rights champions, including the guy who shamelessly auctioned off the handgun George Zimmerman used to murder Trayvon Martin, with victims of gun violence, including the still-shattered mom of a boy killed at Sandy Hook Elementary School. They asked the people in each pair to listen to the story of their counterpart. Then they asked them to inhabit the other person's story. To retell it to the rest of the group, not in the third person but in the first.

So the gun auctioneer had to say to the room, "*I* love being a mother and *I* took my son to school that morning and *I* saw his little body shot through four times." And the young black man from the South Side of Chicago had to become the black woman cop from Baltimore and say, "*I* was scared to be shot at by criminals, and scared to fire my own weapon because *I* didn't want to hurt the wrong person."

Initially, this process was cathartic and transformative. Tears streamed and the participants were moved by the simple act of occupying another person's *I*—to enter an alternate reality. People on both sides said they could truly begin to understand the other on a deeper level. But before long, things broke down. Some folks were too deeply threatened by the exercise, and snapped back, doubling down on their original worldview and attitudes. Others were changed for a moment but as the magic wore off found themselves reverting to old talking points. The cohesion began to disintegrate.

In the wake of the presidential election there has been so much talk, some of it from me, about empathy. About liberal Seattleites stepping into the shoes of the Michigan Trump voter. About that Trump voter stepping into the shoes of the young Muslim immigrant. And so on. Empathy is better than no empathy, to be sure. I'm glad I'd read about Glenn Beck's childhood before I met the man. It helped me hear him and see him. But as the *New York* magazine story and experiment reminds us, empathy has its limits. You can't swap out identities. You shouldn't want to. What you *can* do is practice enough empathy to become aware of your own failings and blind spots so that you can handle and even appreciate challenges to your worldview—and so that you can understand other people's reactions when you challenge theirs.

But the key here is being willing to *challenge* each other. Now that I've spent time thinking about how that Trump supporter from the Rust Belt came to feel disenfranchised and forgotten and left behind, it's time to for me to stop patronizing him and for him to stop pitying himself. It's time to say that he is welcome to nurture his wounded ego but he is not welcome to do so at the expense of the rights and dignity of other Americans. It's time to say that I have a part in how polarized and unequal our society has become, and so does he. And it's time for me to challenge him to do better, and vice versa. It's nice to enter another man's reality. But it's more important to take responsibility for the reality we now inhabit together.

This is what Glenn Beck is trying to do, and it's what I want to join him on. Not a maudlin empathy tour, but a grown-up demonstration of how to push each other to be better, how to find the places where we can do things together and serve and love and work together, and how to fight with more wisdom and self-knowledge when we must fight.

This brings me to my second learning from my time with Beck, which is that *democracy is not enough*. Here's what I mean. Donald Trump is the essential product of democracy: not technically, since he lost the popular vote and was elected via the Electoral College, an intermediary institution designed out of *mistrust* of democracy.

But he's the product of democracy in the sense that his tastes are low, his style is broad, his method is visceral. The fact that he is the stylistic and ethical opposite of Obama is in fact a big part of his appeal. Obama was almost too good. Admirable, self-controlled, nearly perfect. But not exactly *representative*. Trump is representative of something deeper and truer in our coarse and narcissistic popular culture and rapacious market economy. He is, more than Obama, a man of the people. And that is so not enough.

Here's another sense of my meaning: democracy can yield terrible things. Democracy, when considered the opposite of autocracy, honors the value of freedom, and that's to be cherished. But democracy as a method of decision-making is utterly value-neutral. It can be used to destroy freedom. It can be used to enshrine slavery.

This was the point at the heart of the Lincoln-Douglas Debates of 1858. Senator Stephen Douglas had a slippery way of cloaking pro-slavery sympathies in democratic principle. He preached "popular sovereignty." What Douglas meant is that if the white settlers of the Nebraska territory voted to enter the Union as a slave state, then American democratic principle must honor that choice. The people (the white squatters, that is) were sovereign. Lincoln saw the danger of this argument and throughout those seven debates up and down the state of Illinois, he attacked it. No, he said. It's not sufficient that the people democratically choose slavery and that we then ritualistically say their decision is final. Somewhere, he said, there must be a moral reckoning. Somewhere it must be said that voting for an evil is evil.

Yes, democracy is better than not-democracy. But democracy alone guarantees nothing except that we can choose to imprison or degrade ourselves. We need to summon the moral clarity to distinguish between the will of the people and actual justice. We need instruction in that kind of moral discernment, and practice in speaking out against modern-day Stephen Douglases. We need to be the next Abraham Lincolns. We need mediating institutions to help us do that, whether they are small circles of friends or formal classes or the kinds of clubs I talked about last sermon.

That's what this is, what we are trying to be here today. That's what I think Glenn Beck is trying to find his way toward. Donald Trump is the fusion of the lowest form of democracy and the lowest form of capitalism. The lowest form of "free choice" and popular sovereignty. Our job is to do better. To show that democracy, when coupled with ethics, with character, can yield something better.

Thus the third and final thing I learned after my time with Beck: *resistance is not enough.* The closer we get to Inauguration Day, the more the left and some on the right are becoming fixated on resistance. There is a romantic and purposeful vibe to the word. You think of Paris under swastika flags. You think of the Underground Railroad.

A show like *The Man in the High Castle* can give us the strange thrill of feeling like we're living out a grand and horrible prophecy. But let's not forget: we don't in fact live in *The Man in the High Castle.* America is sick but it is not a dystopia yet. We aren't forced to go underground. We are not part of a resistance under oppression. We who did not vote for Donald Trump are the great majority of Americans. We are citizens, and we are the rightful and necessary stewards of the liberties and freedoms of the Constitution.

We should start acting like it. That means that for every cause that will be dedicated to resisting Trump's most harmful plans, we need another one that will embody an *alternative affirmative* agenda. We need offense. We have to believe *in* something. We have to give others something to believe in. Glenn Beck, for all his stylistic and tonal shifts, believes in an affirmative philosophy of liberty and rights. I believe in an affirmative philosophy of community and responsibility. Between us and the likes of us there is an American fusion to be fashioned that people will want to be part of.

We have to show it's possible. And we have to start locally, where we can make our ideas tangible most immediately. It can be on wages or homelessness or funding our schools or reducing carbon emissions or closing prisons or welcoming refugees. We've got to create a beacon here so that across this land people will remember that the people are not powerless before this tainted, possibly treasonous king of the Big Lie. We are not the audience for a reality show. We are makers of our own reality.

ALTERNATE REALITIES

So let me close today by returning to this idea of alternate realities.

I read something recently about how traumatic brain injuries can sometimes unleash what scientists call "hidden savants." A guy who gets a concussion in a biking accident suddenly becomes a prolific composer, even though he'd shown neither interest nor skill prior to the accident. A woman injured in a car crash finds months later that she can draw by hand the most elaborate, detailed fractal images that usually a computer would create. A once shy and taciturn man becomes an eloquent public speaker. And so on.

What captured my imagination about this was both the speed and the depth of the transformation. In an instant, a human can discover that there was this whole other human inside: this hidden artist, scientist, preacher, healer, builder. And the elasticity of time makes the savant feel that the new self has always been there. As Emerson said in our final reading, it can take just "a very little time to entertain a hope and an insight which becomes the light of our life." By the way, he wrote that line, that essay called "Experience," in the immediate aftermath of the death of his child.

I've said it before: as it is with the body, so it is with the body politic. Our system of self-government has just suffered a traumatic brain injury, and this on top of decades of being unfit and congested in every artery.

How terrible.

How potentially beautiful.

Who is the hidden civic savant we shall now discover? What is the untapped infinity of public selves and identities and realities that we will now unleash? It's time for you to discover that you're a master organizer. A powerful orator. A magical listener. A brilliant strategist. A dogged advocate. A relentless squeaky wheel. You've been bonked hard on the head. It's time for your civic imagination to spill forth.

The tagline for the new season of *The Man in the High Castle* is "The future belongs to those who change it." It's meant to sound ominous or sci-fi mystical. But I take it as a statement of self-evident fact. We can change the future. That's why I want to propose an alternative way to think about alternate realities. See the word as a *verb*: alter*nate* realities. Change them. Toggle back and forth between and among them.

It is simultaneously true right now that American democracy is at its most fragile state in generations *and* that American democracy is more primed than ever for renewal.

It is simultaneously true that millions of our fellow citizens are becoming drones, programmed by people like Glenn Beck *used* to be to attack their enemies without thinking, *and* that millions of our fellow citizens are reprogramming themselves to understand our times better, to build bridges, to serve together and to fix things.

It is simultaneously true that you have an encrusted story of self that says you're not powerful, you're not a changemaker or a catalyst, *and* that within you right now, waiting to be tapped, are an unlimited number of other possible selves and stories of self.

See with Whitman's eyes, Emerson's heart, and Lincoln's soul just how thin a margin separates one you from another, or me from Glenn Beck, or today's civic life from a better one. Pass through that thin margin. You don't need time travel or quantum mechanics to change the future. You just need commitment.

5.

WHERE IS AMERICA?

Jones Playhouse, University of Washington · Seattle, WA
February 4, 2017

FREDERICK DOUGLASS
From his speech "What to the Slave is the Fourth of July?"
July 5, 1852

Fellow-citizens! I will not enlarge further on your national inconsistencies. The existence of slavery in this country brands your republicanism as a sham, your humanity as a base pretense, and your Christianity as a lie. It destroys your moral power abroad; it corrupts your politicians at home. It saps the foundation of religion; it makes your name a hissing, and a bye-word to a mocking earth. It is the antagonistic force in your government, the only thing that seriously disturbs and endangers your *Union*. It fetters your progress; it is the enemy of improvement, the deadly foe of education; it fosters pride; it breeds insolence; it promotes vice; it shelters crime; it is a curse to the earth that supports it; and yet, you cling to it, as if it were the sheet anchor of all your hopes. Oh! be warned! be warned! a horrible reptile is coiled up in your nation's bosom; the venomous creature is nursing at the tender breast of your youthful republic; *for the love of God*, tear away, and fling from you the hideous monster, and *let the weight of twenty millions, crush and destroy it forever!*

CLAUDIA CASTRO LUNA
"Summer Sparks"
From the All of Us Belong project
February 2017

In New York a colossal woman raises
a burning torch, a promise to harbor
the tired, the poor, the homeless, the tempest-tossed.
In Seattle another *woman* fades,
homeless in a park, with the racing butterfly
of her child's heart her only compass.
A pendulum swings, all over the land,
from the luscious forests of generous imaginations
to the ruinous bigotry that clipped
Emmett Till's wings. Echoes of yesteryear's
Ghost Dance over Wounded Knee,
that sideway shuffle call for ancestors' aid,
beats time before us again and again.
Fruit plump on summer's light
in a New England vale ripens
alongside Southwestern's border
bruised and battered fruit.
4th of July fireworks bravado,
the feeling of losing yourself in the jubilee
of the crowd after winning, collapses
under the crushing evidence
of the country that we've never been.

The sparks lighting up the sky then falling,
folding back into night,
are they a celebration, *the best part of summer,*
or more of a weeping?
Love and pain don't strike
some over others with different strength.
We are equally susceptible to kindness
and to cold, and board together
the destiny of our shared country.
On an occasion like this,
from sea to shining sea,
it is a good place to begin not end.

CARLOS BULOSAN

From his novel America Is in the Heart
Published 1946

America is also the nameless foreigner, the homeless
refugee, the hungry boy begging for a job and the black
body dangling from a tree. America is the illiterate immigrant
who is ashamed that the world of books and intellectual
opportunities is closed to him. We are that nameless
foreigner, that homeless refugee, that hungry boy, that illiterate
immigrant and that lynched black body. All of us, from the first
Adams to the last Filipino, native born or alien, educated or
illiterate—We are America!

GERDA WEISSMANN KLEIN

From her memoir All But My Life

Published 1957

"Wasn't it traumatic to make the transition to normality?" How often I have been asked that question, and I have come to the conclusion that, yes, perhaps it was. But I didn't know what the word "trauma" implied, and I would have been ashamed to admit any dissatisfaction, believing it to be selfish and ungrateful to complain about anything here.

In retrospect, I think that coming to America was like stepping out of a dark, oppressive room in which I had been locked up for a long, long time. Once I was free and exposed to light again, the most ordinary objects, the simplest things acquired an aura of extraordinary beauty, desirability, and value. I reveled in the joy of discovery, and my gratitude was boundless.

A long time ago, in a city far, far away, it was unclear how the people of this vast land would respond to the words and deeds of an unstable president in unholy alliance with autocrats abroad and white nationalists at home.

That was last week. And now we know.

We know just how we the people have responded—and how we are capable of responding. With passion. With presence. With purpose. With power. And with a fair amount of joy. (I'll have more to say later about joy.)

We—and I mean not just social-justice progressives but liberty-loving conservatives and skeptical independents too; not just in the cities of the coasts but in the towns of the heartland; not just at airport terminals but in Facebook groups and coffee shops; not just those most at risk of persecution but all those determined to prevent it—we have reminded ourselves and the current executive that while he for a time may control the machinery of state, we forever control its *legitimacy*.

Political legitimacy is the acceptance by the people of a leader's claim to authority. It is a fragile unspoken hybrid of laws and norms. It is one of the most fascinating aspects of civic power because you can't put your finger on it, yet you can't lift a finger without it. You can be legally elected and have no legitimacy, like Nixon in 1974, or you can be powerless under the law yet have plenty of legitimacy, like Mandela in 1989.

At 5:12 this morning Donald Trump tweeted about the "so-called judge" who blocked his anti-refugee and anti-immigrant executive order. This is tantamount to calling the Constitution the "so-called Constitution." To Trump the Constitution is just another contract to break, another terrible deal he inherited and refuses to honor.

And you know what? There is in fact nothing magical about the Constitution that forces us to abide by it. Just like there's nothing magical about the office of the presidency that forces us to respect him. As a minority president aided by an adversary of the United States, Trump craves legitimacy. But he forgets what that great philosopher Tony Soprano once said: "Those who want respect, give respect."

If Trump wants legitimacy, let him earn it. He can start by showing the people and the Constitution some more respect. Because legitimacy is in the eye of the collective beholder. It is always contested, not just on Election Day. It is what *we* say it is.

There will be countless more challenges to our Constitution and the norms that give it life. For the moment, however, we have reminded each other that the president does not *wield* power except as we *yield* it. And we are not in a yielding mood.

At the same time, of course, folks can be excused for feeling a bit out of breath. The last week or two have been testament to Trump's impressive ability to speed up time while slowing it down. His barrage of executive orders, real or notional, vetted or not, sparks an accelerating cycle of action and reaction. But out of all that action and reaction accumulates a residue of spent emotion and stress, clogging our neurons, making a day feel like a month, a week like a year.

For many folks, including me, it's been hard sometimes to make sense of things. Paranoia creeps in. We lose our moral bearings. So I thought one simple approach would be to share some moments from the last week of my life—and ours. And what I've been wondering during these days of peril is this: Where is America?

I mean that in a specific way. Not really "Where is public opinion?" (Answer: not with Trump.) Nor do I mean "Where is our attention?" (Answer: it's the day before Lady Gaga plays the Super Bowl.) And though I acknowledge, angrily, that a president of the United States who owes his election in part to Vladimir Putin cannot rightly be called the Leader of the Free World—and that his alienation of allies and his disregard for freedom is creating a vacuum of moral leadership in the world—that also is not the sense in which I mean "Where is America?" No, I mean something even deeper. I mean: Where can we find the true spirit of this country, especially in such extraordinary times?

There are days when it appears that the United States is devolving into a society like modern Russia, where there is a thin crust of cosmopolitan capitalist comfort atop a rotting core of mistrust and conspiracy thinking. Then there are days when it appears that we are evolving into a truly participatory democracy and experiencing, from the inside out and the bottom up, a new birth of freedom.

The truth is not somewhere in between. The truth is both at the same time. We are in a thoroughly rigged system of radical inequality. We are in an exhilarating age of bottom-up power. And the challenge is to ask the question "Where is America?" in a way that can nudge the answer toward hope and not despair.

So this morning I want to explore three propositions with you:

America is in the laws. America is in the acts. America is in the heart.

Let me be clear: I'm not sure any of these is right. But I hope that examining them will reveal something useful about our times and ourselves.

AMERICA IS IN THE LAWS

On the citizenship exam that naturalizing immigrants take—a test, by the way, that I bet most native-born Americans would fail—there are many simple, fact-based questions about how many states there are or who the first president was. But there is one ringer of a question that I am *certain* would stump most native-born Americans:

What is the rule of law?

One conception of America is that it is a nation of laws. It is a place built not on blood or soil or religion but on a set of neutral rules that are universally applied and that derive from our creed and our foundational documents like the Constitution and Declaration. This is the notion we heard last night when my friend Bob Ferguson, our attorney general here in Washington State, sought and secured in federal court a nationwide stay on Trump's refugee and immigration ban. "Nobody is above the law," the AG said.

But another, more complicated conception is implied in the title of today's first reading: "What to the slave is the Fourth of July?" What, to someone tormented or oppressed by the law, is the value of celebrating the law?

Donald Trump, from minute one in the Oval Office, has tested the premise that rule of law trumps all else. Deliberately, with the persistence of a toddler and the menace of a sociopath, he has broken rules of every kind. Rules governing how rules should get made. Rules about courtesy to other heads of state. Rules for how to staff one's own agencies. Rules about self-dealing and venality and nepotism and conflicts of interest.

Some of these rules are written in the form of law. Some are unwritten and take the form of convention and tradition. Trump delights in breaking them all. And what many of his critics don't seem to get is that when you say he is an amateurish wrecker of institutions, he and his base hear that as praise. They take it as a badge of honor and as a marker of success. Because he promised, and his base took him to mean, that he would in fact blow up an establishment power structure—rules, norms, conventions, and institutions—that they felt had screwed them all their lives.

Are they wrong to think that, to wish for that? Were the poor, indebted farmers who brought Andrew Jackson to the White House wrong to wish for the destruction of the Hamiltonian power structure in Washington, with its national bank and Wall Street bias? Was Frederick Douglass—may he rest in peace—wrong to wish for the obliteration of a power structure that had extracted wealth and dignity from his body and the bodies of countless millions of other African Americans?

Now, hold on a minute, you must be thinking. How can you equate the self-pity of status-anxious white Trump voters who in fact still have loads of privilege with the existential suffering of enslaved black Americans who were defiled by American life?

I can't. I don't. But I do point out that at various points in history, very different kinds of people have had cause to disrespect and reject the rule of law.

We will see just how regularly this president brings the country to the brink of constitutional crisis. Will the people who work in his agencies abide by court orders and temporary injunctions? Will they respect the judicial branch? Will enough of us know enough to know what's at stake?

Two days before Trump issued his executive order against refugees and Muslim immigrants, I had coffee with a friend who served in the administration of President George W. Bush. Though she now works at a nonpartisan organization, she has her beliefs and she knows they're different from mine. But I was struck in this conversation by two things: first, her strong sense of the threat that Trump's behavior poses—not to specific groups but to the rule of law itself; and second, her fear that if other Republicans knew just how she felt, she might be called a RINO (Republican in Name Only) and this would kill her ability to advance reform. That's why I am not even naming her. She is a Republican. She is a patriot. And she has limited room for maneuver.

So what is the rule of law? It is still too often what men—and it's mainly men—say it is.

The new nominee to the United States Supreme Court, Neil Gorsuch, is a member of the Federalist Society. So were all the men on Trump's short list. The Federalist Society is a conservative legal organization that has been remarkably effective over recent decades at building out a network of law school chapters that feeds a network of educators, litigators, and jurists that then generates candidates for the high court.

To many progressives, the Federalist Society is a bogeyman, a key node in what Hillary Clinton once called the "vast right-wing conspiracy." But I think this organization has a lot to teach people across the political spectrum. One of their initiatives is called the Article I Initiative. As in: the first Article of the Constitution is about the legislative power—*not* the executive power, which is in Article II. They began this project in 2015 out of frustration with what they regarded as President Obama's overuse of executive orders and administrative rules. Their goal was to reassert Congress's primacy.

But in truth, the growth of what scholars call "the imperial presidency" has been a multigenerational and bipartisan affair. And shortly after the election, U.S. Senator Ben Sasse, Republican of Nebraska, gave an interesting and thoughtful speech at the Federalist Society conference. You can watch it on YouTube. Sasse is a rising star: a principled conservative, a Gen X leader who was a college president before he became a politician, and a Republican who never got on the Trump Train.

Sasse praised the Federalist Society for the Article I Initiative. He buttered them up. And then he challenged them. He said that if the conservatives in the room believed Congress should rein in presidential powers when the president was named Obama, they should also believe it when the president is named Trump. This, he said, was the very meaning of conservatism: consistent humility in the exercise of state power.

Well, in the first two weeks of the Trump presidency, GOP leaders have said little about Article I or taming an out-of-control executive branch. Trump has issued one after another executive order as if Congress didn't even exist. Congressional Republicans have acted as if Congress didn't exist. A few have dared to suggest that perhaps the executive orders weren't perfectly well drafted. Not quite profiles in courage.

And yet before I get too righteous about presidential overreach and congressional diffidence, I am obligated to ask myself: Where was I when President Obama interpreted *his* power expansively? I didn't complain when he used executive orders or rulemaking authority to shut down polluters or to welcome undocumented Dreamers or to advance the radical idea that financial advisors shouldn't stack the deck against their own clients. Why? Because I *liked* those outcomes.

Perhaps I should have spoken up then on principle. Let me amend that: I should have. I should have said that although I support the outcome I have qualms about the process. I know that's easy for me to say now, when President Obama already seems a distant memory, but I am saying it so that someone will remind me when it's *not* easy for me to say. I should have been as vocally concerned then as I am now about a creeping imbalance of constitutional power.

Why? Because the alternative plays right into Trump's hands. The alternative is to say, as senators on both sides of the aisle now say through their actions on Supreme Court nominations, that rules are just window dressing for who has the muscle to get what they want. And each side blames the other, placing the origin of the problem at 2009 or 2000 or 1994 or some other year where it all broke down.

The question of "who started it" is not unanswerable—I can say the Republicans started it in the mid-1990s when they blew up the norms of Congress and impeached a president for having an affair. Someone else might say it started when Court nominee Judge Robert Bork, the good soldier of the Saturday Night Massacre, was "Borked" by Senator Joe Biden and the Democrats on the Judiciary Committee in 1988. But it is irrelevant now. What matters now even to people who care not about process but only about outcome is that *President Trump is the outcome*. He and his institution-destroying ways are the product of years of this kind of corrosive gamesmanship.

Rules matter. Attorney General Ferguson was right, and so was U.S. District Court Judge James Robart, the Bush 43 appointee based here in Seattle, who granted Ferguson the stay of Trump's immigration order. Rules have to be something more than a cloak of convenience for the powerful. Not because rules are always right or fair but because they are the agreement we make to keep each other aloft, above the stinking pit of cynicism that other societies have long fallen into. Rules force us to take actions and make choices that are inconvenient. Which brings me to my second proposition:

AMERICA IS IN THE ACTS

One of the ways that Jená and I count ourselves lucky is that we have neighbors we love, who are good friends and something like family. Some of them are here today. Our little block—not even quite fully a block, but more like a rectangle of homes—has something that is hard to describe, much less to replicate. It's trust, to be sure. It's also a spirit of mutual aid. We're always helping each other, cooking for each other, taking each other to the light rail. It's a sense of ease, making the street and sidewalks that separate our dwellings into a common area—an outdoor room—and not just a thoroughfare. But most of all, it's a sense that we're in this thing together.

I've been cherishing this good fortune lately because I know how little neighborly love there is in so much of this broad land. We are a people who've become isolated and atomized and insensate to the human hearts aching and striving and singing right alongside our own. And in that isolation Americans have become susceptible to people selling untruth as truth, scapegoating as solution, and crisis as purpose.

I've also been thinking about what it means to be a neighbor because a week ago my Citizen University colleagues and I were in the other Washington. We were at the United States Holocaust Memorial Museum for two gatherings we had helped to organize. The first was a meeting of the Civic Collaboratory, a mutual-aid society of catalytic civic leaders from the left and right who meet every quarter. The second was a leadership summit of campus leaders from ten colleges across the country.

Downstairs at the museum, there is an exhibition that our groups toured and that I wish every American could experience—and indeed, you can see much of it on the museum's website. It's a departure from Holocaust histories that focus on the Nazi machinery of state. Instead it focuses on everyday acts of complicity by ordinary people.

Friends betrayed friends, joining the mobs that ransacked the homes and businesses of Jews. Classmates informed on classmates, coworkers sent coworkers to the camps and took their possessions, out of jealousy or greed or a desire to please authority or the inability to resist the tide. The exhibition is called "Some Were Neighbors."

Some are always neighbors. Indeed, whenever authoritarianism takes hold, its most effective agents are neighbors. There are only so many uniformed officers of the government. Only when the people become collaborators can the leviathan truly work. Their capacity for mutual aid must be redirected to mutual suspicion and containment.

All of that collaboration and complicity boils down to acts. To simple choices that then compound and become contagious.

Do you choose to rush to the airport to stand in solidarity with a refugee you never met who's being detained without cause? Or do you choose to tell Homeland Security that you have suspicions about your Arab neighbor when in fact all you have is a beef with him about the property line or his noisy parties or something else so mundane?

Small acts. Small compromises. Small stands. Small choices that turn large tides. That's what every nation's culture is made of. Where do we find America today? In the infinite catalog of unseen and unrecorded acts that we the people commit. You—not just the president of the United States—have the power the rewrite that catalog.

I recently read a powerful article in *New York* magazine about life in Putin's Russia. It was by a reporter named Michael Idov who'd been born in the Soviet Union but emigrated here as a child and returned for five years to write about Moscow. It began with an anecdote about being in traffic on a Moscow highway when an ambulance siren started blaring. Instinctively, as an American, Idov expected cars to yield and make way. No one moved. The ambulance crawled along with everyone else. Why? The driver explained that "Everyone knows ambulance drivers make money on the side selling VIP airport rides. Who knows who's in that van right now?"

Who knows? The safe bet, the smart bet, was not to trust. And so it went. Idov chronicles the deep kleptocracy, the expectation of corruption that implicates you in the corruption, the absolutely self-fulfilling way that "everyone knows" life is just a series of bribes and betrayals. Add a few laws pushed through by Putin to criminalize protest. A few mysterious deaths of dissident activists. The rest takes care of itself. The title of his piece is "Life After Trust." It is a story of cynicism as a way of life. It is chilling.

What inoculates us from that kind of cynicism is acts, repeated acts of principle. We have to build our principle reflex into a principle muscle. We can't just have a twinge of conscience. We have to have bursts of it, sustained bursts that enable us to move great obstacles and surmount high walls. We learn to trust by being trustworthy. We become trustworthy by trusting. I do not want to find out what Life After Trust is like in America.

This is a time to sharpen our moral faculties, to contemplate what we will do when principle is tested. This is what I told those student leaders we organized at the Holocaust Museum. We were gathered on the day after the refugee ban was issued. The day after the president failed to mention Jews in his statement marking Holocaust Remembrance Day. The warning of history was self-evident but also sobering. In 1938 over 70 percent of Americans recognized that Germany was oppressing Jews—and over 70 percent opposed letting in any Jewish refugees. Which is why no American politician, from Franklin Roosevelt down, felt the need to act with moral courage on behalf of the Jews. Their inaction *became* action. Our borders closed first in their hearts.

Which brings me to the final proposition to explore today.

AMERICA IS IN THE HEART

In 1942 a teenager named Gerda Weissmann was delivered from her hometown in Poland, via the trains of the Third Reich, to a Nazi labor camp in Czechoslovakia. Her parents had been sent in a different direction—to Auschwitz. She survived the extremity, the unspeakable horrors of the Holocaust, by holding on to a dream of a new life, by honing her will to live into something vivid. She dreamed of the small details of freedom, picturing the ball she would one day attend, and deciding whether to wear the red dress or the blue dress. She imagined her way to freedom.

When Gerda Weissmann was liberated at war's end she was twenty-one years old and weighed sixty-eight pounds. She had not had a bath in three years. Her hair had turned white. She was liberated by an

American GI named Kurt Klein. He had been born in Germany, a Jew, and had fled to America to escape the Nazis. His parents too had been sent to Auschwitz, never to be heard from again.

When Kurt met Gerda, he did a simple thing that restored her to humanity: he held a door open for her. Gerda would eventually marry that GI Kurt Klein, move to America, and raise a family to live a life both extraordinary and beautifully ordinary. She wrote a bestselling memoir called *All But My Life*, which became an Oscar-winning film, and created a nonprofit called Citizenship Counts. She was given the Presidential Medal of Freedom. But as she says, she didn't cure cancer. She wasn't Mother Teresa. All she did was enjoy the simple freedom to be a wife and a mother and a grandmother, and to make friends who would become like family to her. A subsequent book she titled *A Boring Evening at Home*. That was her wish, her ambition: the humble, grateful experience of everyday freedom.

Gerda and I have become like family. She has a magical spirit in her heart and eyes. And I suppose she is drawn to my earnest idealism. She demands that I call her Grandma instead of Mrs. Klein. And though we speak in the idioms of different generations, we are asking the same question. What does it mean to be American?

The other night I had dinner in Los Angeles with my friend Melvin Mar. Melvin is what they call a "showrunner." He's the creator of the pioneering and acclaimed ABC sitcom *Fresh Off the Boat*, about a Taiwanese American family, and another new sitcom called *Speechless*, centering on a boy with a disability that prevents him from speaking. And Melvin's got other ideas for shows that will include the faces and voices of once-marginalized Americans into this most American format of myth-making.

Melvin told me something that his dad, an immigrant from the Toishan region of China, once said to him. It's something I think many children of immigrants have heard at one time or another. It's basically this: *You're not of them, and they are not of you. Don't kid yourself. Keep your head down and don't speak your mind.*

Thank God Melvin didn't internalize that message. Thank God he believed he belonged and decided to make the change he wanted to see. His body of work embodies and literally broadcasts a message: I *am* of them, because they are of me. He is claiming America. He is redefining America by rewriting the storyline of who *us* is.

The next morning, I had breakfast with another such claimer and rewriter. My friend Jose Antonio Vargas, who I've spoken of before, is a Pulitzer Prize–winning journalist. He is a creator of an organization called Define American, which is using popular culture and campus activism to spark more inclusive conversations about immigration reform. And he is perhaps America's most famous undocumented immigrant.

Born in the Philippines, brought to the U.S. as a two-year-old, raised by his grandparents in California, growing up an average American suburban kid, Jose didn't learn he was undocumented until he was in high school. He kept it a secret for many years, with the complicity and collaboration of teachers and neighbors and mentors and bosses. Then finally, a few years ago, he came out as undocumented in the *New York Times*. Since then he's been a representative and a heat shield for other undocumented people. He is courage incarnate. And now, every day, he gets tweets from gleefully malicious Trump trolls telling him, "Tick tock—you're getting deported any minute now."

It's true that Jose and eleven million other undocumented people in this country now live in great peril. His stress is palpable. And what made my heart hurt was hearing him say how much he loves this country—the only country he has ever known, the country to which he has contributed so much. Jose quoted the Filipino American novelist Carlos Bulosan yesterday, not in a flight of rhetorical fancy but to console himself. Wherever he may live, America *is* his heart. And all he wants is simply to enjoy freedom. To not have to look over his shoulder. To enjoy a boring evening at home.

So now I must ask: Does my love of Jose outweigh my belief in the rule of law? How do I reconcile what I just said about rules mattering with the fact that his residence here breaks the rules? Here's how. I remember that *ruleness* is not what makes a rule legitimate. Justice is. And a rule that would deport Jose to the Philippines, where he has no memories or life and where the Trumpish strongman Rodrigo Duterte has set loose murderous vigilante gangs against journalists and dissidents, is unjust.

That was the day before yesterday. After a day of meetings and events, I flew home from LAX—a place Jose is now afraid to enter—to Sea-Tac, where seven days earlier a spontaneous throng of people arrived to defend not just the suddenly disfavored but the rule of law itself. I drove straight to Benaroya Hall to meet Jená and our friends and neighbors Tom and Barb. We heard a Seattle Symphony concert that opened with an ambitious project called "All of Us Belong."

This project takes four pieces by the early-twentieth-century composer Charles Ives that he combined into a symphony for New England holidays. Quiet dissonance and roiling storms of sound, all interleaved with snippets and faint echoes of old American folk tunes. Ives, if you don't know the music, can be described as *cacophony plus memory*. America, if you don't know it, can be described the same way.

The performance Thursday night combined the music of Ives with images of and by many homeless Seattleites, projected onto a great screen. And it combined all that, in turn, with four gorgeous poems composed and read by Seattle's first Civic Poet, Claudia Castro Luna. We read today her poem for the Fourth of July movement of the symphony. It moved me so much to hear the music of her words, the spirit of her Americanness: "We are equally susceptible to kindness and to cold."

In the program for the performance it says "Home is Where the Art Is." And with Jose in my heart, I scribbled on the program: *What are we made of?* Are we a cruel, indifferent people? Or a people with basic decency? Do we stand and speak when others won't? Or do we too bend like serfs to power?

We Americans are made of more than fear. We are made of more than shame. We are made of more than loss and pain.

ODE TO JOY

I want to close with some words about joy.

Joy? Really? In these times? Yes, really. Not a Pollyanna joy that can't or won't see what's dark and terrible out there. But a defiant joy. Last night in front of the new Trump hotel in DC there was a protest. It was a dance party. That's what I'm talking about. At Citizen University we've launched a project called The Joy of Voting that's bringing raucous creativity and art and fun communal rituals to voting in cities around the U.S.

Joy is not frivolity. Joy is the generative spirit that emerges when there is underlying trust, respect, imagination, openness. Joy is a symptom that we haven't given in.

And we haven't. Certainly the citizen surge of the last two weeks shows that. People are willing to fight. But it's not just about fighting Trump. It's about fighting the thing that feeds Trump, which is self-fulfilling cynicism.

Don't fall into doom loops of conspiracy theory and powerlessness. I can't tell you how many people have asked me what I make of the article on Medium depicting the actions of Bannon and Trump as a dry run for a coup. De-staff agencies like State and Justice of their professionals. Stack decision-making councils like the NSC with loyal insiders and remove independent generals who could check them. Attack the courts. Lie incessantly. Enrich self. Punish minorities. Claim to represent the majority.

To be sure, these are all things the Trump circle is doing. And I know the weird thrill that smart people get when they read a piece that suggests sophisticated hidden motives and plans. But having worked in American government, I'm here to tell you: any inner-circle master plan cannot move very far or fast. Our institutions, though weak, are not so weak that they could be that easily captured. At the same time, they are just weak enough that they would be inefficient and unresponsive tools for would-be autocrats. The bureaucracy is a quagmire for the good and evil alike.

And in any case, the answer to world-class levels of cynicism is not more cynicism. We who believe in inclusion and integrity can't out-cynicism the likes of Bannon and Trump. We can out-believe them. We can out-love them, out-trust them, out-mobilize them, out-imagine them. Out-*joy* them. Have you ever seen Donald J. Trump smile with joy? He cannot. We must. We must do that at home. With our neighbors. With strangers we encounter face to face. And with strangers we can't see or touch but can imagine.

Trump is weak, not strong. That's why he has to use a strategy of chaos creation. The people are strong, not weak. That's why we mustn't panic. Persist, believe, organize. Do so with love, and with joy. In our laws, our acts, and our hearts, this land is *our* land.

6.

A GREAT AWAKENING

Town Hall · Seattle, WA
April 8, 2017

REBECCA SOLNIT
From A Paradise Built in Hell: The Extraordinary
Communities That Arise in Disaster
Published 2009

You can read recent history as a history of privatization not just of the economy but also of society, as marketing and media shove imagination more and more toward private life and private satisfaction, as citizens are redefined as consumers, as public participation falters and with it any sense of collective or individual political power, as even the language for public emotions and satisfactions withers. There is no money in what is aptly called free association: we are instead encouraged by media and advertising to fear each other and regard public life as a danger and a nuisance, to live in secured spaces, communicate by electronic means, and acquire our information from media rather than each other.

But in disaster people come together, and though some fear this gathering as a mob, many cherish it as an experience of a civil society that is close enough to paradise.

CAROL TAVRIS AND ELLIOT ARONSON
From Mistakes Were Made (But Not by Me)
Published 2007

Depression is not "anger turned inward"; if anything, anger is depression turned outward. Follow the trail of anger inward, and there you will find the small, still voice of pain. . . .

In the horrifying calculus of self-deception, the greater the pain we inflict on others, the greater the need to justify it to maintain our feelings of decency and self-worth. . . .

Rebels and dissidents challenge the complacent belief in a just world, and, as the theory would predict, they are usually denigrated for their efforts. While they are alive, they may be called "cantankerous," "crazy," "hysterical," "uppity," or "duped." Dead, some of them become saints and heroes, the sterling characters of history. It's a matter of proportion. One angry rebel is crazy, three is a conspiracy, fifty is a movement.

Welcome. It's great and very fitting that we are gathering today in a space that was once a Christian Science church and is now a civic temple at the heart of our city's life.

I've just spent a week with Jená in the other Washington and in New York, speaking to all kinds of audiences and organizations about my new book, *You're More Powerful Than You Think*, which is a citizen's guide to exercising power.

The trip was fantastic, and I'll tell you today about some of the things I learned. But I was running hard every hour of every day and I didn't sleep much. So now my body clock is a bit off. I've been hovering in that space where wakefulness and sleep are commingled, where the line between a dream and a memory becomes blurred.

From that interstitial state of mind emerges the question I'd like to ponder today: *What's the difference between a promise you've never kept and a lie?* At what point does a failure to deliver become not just an omission or a condition of regrettable tardiness but an act, an act of malicious deceit?

That, my friends, is the American question.

The American promise, is what Thomas Jefferson wrote and others extended, clause by clause. It is our creedal pledge of equality under law, of liberty and justice for all, of government by, of, and for the people. It's a creed we haven't yet lived up to.

More than that, it is a dream. It is a dream in the sense of an aspiration, for economic security and material comfort. It is a dream too in the sense of Martin Luther King's vision of racial integration and equal opportunity for all.

A dream exists both above and below "real" life—above, in that experiences of time and space are intensified and heightened by our unleashed imaginations; below, in that every dream trawls through the murky waters of animal instinct and sense memory.

The American Dream is just like that. It's a great feat of imagination—and a stirring of our basest nature. We're not sure if it's real, yet we can't seem to shake it. Today I want to talk about three states of being in the American body politic and spirit politic: the states of sleeping, dreaming, and awakening.

SLEEPING

On our last night in New York, Jená and I went to Studio 54 in Manhattan. It's no longer the disco of hedonistic '70s lore—which is too bad, because you should see us on the dance floor (especially her)—but it's now a gorgeous, intimate Broadway theater. There we saw a celebrated and new play by Lynn Nottage called *Sweat*.

Sweat is set in Reading, Pennsylvania, between 2000 and 2008. It chronicles a group of friends who've worked all their lives at the town's steel tubing plant, as they reckon with the slow-motion decimation of their factory and their community. Things get complicated when one of the friends, who's black, gets promoted off the line and into management. Things get even more complicated when upper management starts squeezing the workers and locking them out until they agree to a 60 percent pay cut. Jobs and machines go to Mexico. A Colombian American bartender crosses the picket line.

Disaster ensues—not the acts of God that generate surges of fellow feeling and collective action, as Rebecca Solnit described in our first reading; but rather the acts of capitalists that yield only tragic isolation.

Nottage, who wrote *Sweat* before the election, has said her subject was the human cost of "America's de-industrial revolution." Donald Trump, more bluntly, has called it "American carnage," and he vacuumed up votes from the real Reading in November.

But Lynn Nottage is no Donald Trump. She is an African American woman, she is a genius not of the self-proclaimed kind but of the MacArthur Fellowship kind, and she listens to other humans. She spent two years living in Reading, listening to the women and men, black and white and Hispanic, of every generation, who grew up believing in the certainty of their work and their sweat and their pride and their dignity—even as evidence mounted all around them that all would be outsourced and shipped away.

Out of that listening came this play. From the first moments, it gave me the kind of lump in the throat that precedes a deep and long-deferred cry. At various moments, often unexpected ones, I did cry. And in the final scene, many tears were flowing.

I'm not going to give away the plot points that pressed those tears out. But the particulars aren't important. What made me cry was the grinding, inexorable tragedy of these characters who had believed in a promise that became a lie.

At each scene break, images from national news are projected onto the sets, without commentary or explicit connection to the plot—images of President Clinton and President George W. Bush, images of the stock market booming and then collapsing, Wall Street bailouts being announced. Barack Obama is never mentioned, and what made me cry was the unsaid truth that we learned between 2009 and today: that it wouldn't matter. "Hope and Change" didn't happen in the Rust Belt. W's promise was "compassionate conservatism." Bill Clinton's slogan in '92 was "Putting People First."

The truth was that no matter who was president, these people were getting screwed. Global capital was gutting local labor. There was no compassion to it. What made me cry that night was feeling the sheer distance—the awful silent chasm—between the elites who've rigged the game during my lifetime and the people who've paid the price.

And what haunted me was how long I'd been *asleep* while this was happening in America—the complicity in my slumber.

Let me back up a step. Two weeks ago, we at Citizen University held our annual national conference. The theme was "Reckoning and Repair" in a polarized and severely unequal America, and we had speakers and teachers from many domains there to share ideas and lessons from history and politics.

But I was struck by how much the learning and teaching at the conference was either above or below politics. Above, in that it was on a spiritual plane, about values and moral aspiration; below, in that it was about the forgotten fundamentals of respect and human presence—how to see each other and feel each other and recognize each other, deeply—fundamentals that we've neglected in American civic life. Speaker after speaker returned to this theme of re-presenting ourselves face-to-face.

I recently learned about a theater company called 600 Highwaymen that stages beautifully immersive performances in which lines between audience and performer are smudged by invitations to touch, to sense, to feel the faces and see the eyes and bear the weight and the spirit of the people all around you. That's what we all need now.

So when I was watching Sweat, I was highly attuned to those moments onstage—heartbreaking, endowed moments—when characters would hold or touch or see one another. To provide small mercies and fleeting comforts that would still not be enough to compensate for the stripping away of dignity, of place and purpose. There's a refrain throughout the play, many variations of "They don't even see you."

And later, "I'm gonna make 'em see me."

This is why people have been flocking to see Sweat the same way they're flocking to read J. D. Vance's Appalachian memoir Hillbilly Elegy: to figure out how it happened. To empathize with the folks whose suffering and bottled-up rage and shame begat Trump.

Empathizing with the pain of another is good, of course. But empathy can be dangerous if it masks the underlying imbalances of power that create the pain in the first place. The prime task in the United States today is not for the privileged to witness the suffering of others. The prime task is to ask how this suffering came to be—to understand how power was monopolized by a few to betray and diminish so many people into invisibility. And then for all of us, together, to change the story. Even if it costs us something.

The whole time I was watching Sweat, because I am a teacher of civic power, I was asking myself what else these Reading steelworkers could have done. How else could they have organized against the financiers and the company owners? Could they have mobilized allies from other states, to expand the arena? Could they have pressed the media to publicize NAFTA's effects earlier? Why didn't they band together in the face of economic disaster to revive civic clubs and associations and generate power? Could they have put out a call for people who seemingly had nothing to do with their sector and their lives, to come to Reading and stand with them? People, for instance, like me?

Then I had to ask: What else could *I* have done while the American Dream was evaporating for so many Americans? Why did it take me so long to wake up and *see* my fellow citizens?

DREAMING

Maybe it's because I was dreaming too hard.

Often people look at my life and early career—son of Chinese immigrants, product of public schools in tiny Wappingers Falls, New York, goes off to Yale and becomes a White House speechwriter— as an embodiment of the American Dream. I tell the story that way myself sometimes.

But today I think that when I was a young man, lost in my dreams, I was rather blind.

Let me tell you about the first set of speeches I wrote for President Clinton. It was 1993, and we were planning a trip to Moscow. This was going to be the first time an American president had visited Russia since the fall of the Berlin Wall, the implosion of the Soviet Union, and the end of the Cold War.

A few weeks before the trip, a fellow speechwriter and I sat down in the Oval Office with the president, to take notes as he riffed on the kinds of themes and topics he would want to address on this historic trip. I figured he would go to policy issues. I was wrong. He spent the whole time musing aloud about psychology and national character.

Russia, he said, was a great nation. More, it was a great civilization. And though we in the U.S. might celebrate the end of communism and the beginning of democracy there, and though we might frame this as a narrative of progress, we had to be careful. We had to be careful, he said, to attend to the wounded pride of the Russian people, who, after all, were now in a shaky economic situation and at the mercy of their former enemies. Though the average Russian might be relieved to be rid of a militaristic totalitarian government, much of that relief was canceled out by the anxiety and even shame of having lost superpower status.

So the key, the president told us, was to help the Russian people channel their yearning for greatness and pride in a healthy and constructive direction. To tell them that meeting the challenges of creating a free-market liberal democracy would be a new chance to prove in a new way the enduring greatness and resilience of this nation.

I thought this was so astute at the time. It was certainly vintage Clinton, applying X-ray insight into the human psyche, and at the international scale rather than only the interpersonal. I followed the president's direction closely, layering his speeches with soulful references to the poetry and literature and music and spirit of Mother Russia. He made people feel good on that trip. He felt their pain.

Of course, we know how things turned out. Clinton's counterpart, Boris Yeltsin, had been courageous in the days of liberation but turned out to be an undisciplined leader whose cronies strip-mined the state for personal enrichment and fueled corruption, chaos, and kleptocracy everywhere. Out of that disorder, and out of the nostalgia for Soviet-era certainty, emerged the canny KGB operative who rules Russia today—who took personal control of the kleptocracy—and who later would help elect an *American* president who exploited *American* fears of lost greatness.

As that president might say: Sad.

But it truly is sad, because while President Clinton seemed psychologically astute and the rhetoric I wrote for him sounded the right notes, we—and I mean now the United States—did not in fact show the Russian people *respect*. Puffing them up about their greatness and then ignoring them was not the same as actual respect. Telling them that they could now have a junior version of the American Dream of free markets and free elections was not the same as respect. (Especially when it didn't happen.) A century after the Russian Revolution, that sickly nation is great mainly in its capacity to do harm.

And what's doubly sad is that we—President Clinton and his team—did not apply the same sensitivity to lost greatness and wounded pride to the swaths of our own country that were being de-industrialized by his Wall Street–friendly policies.

So: What could I have done? I had no hand in NAFTA or the Glass-Steagall repeal or the deregulation of commodities markets—policies that forcefully tilted our economy away from labor and toward capital. It wasn't my job. It was above my pay grade. And anyway, the economy was booming by the late '90s, the dot-com bubble was rising. While I didn't quite buy the notion that textile and steel workers who'd lost their jobs to Vietnam and Mexico could suddenly thrive selling stuff on eBay, it seemed at the time that things would work out for everyone.

But I was dreaming. Even after I left the White House, I didn't question the orthodoxies of unchecked free trade. I didn't *defend* the orthodoxies either. I just didn't pay attention. When the costs of free trade became clearer, I didn't think of it as my problem.

It was. When I think about what's happened in this country economically over my lifetime I think *I* was part of the problem, mainly because I was not a part of the solution. I could have been, had I been as awake as I am today. I should have been. It *was* my job, whatever my professional title. Because I was a citizen of the United States who had the social capital and the *connections* to speak and to be heard.

You can call me a product of the American Dream but in fact I am a product of the American meritocracy, which is not the same thing and in fact is often its enemy. The meritocracy of test-taking and selective colleges that made talented outsiders like Bill Clinton from Hope,

Arkansas, a Rhodes Scholar and a U.S. president, is about "merit" only in a narrow SAT sense and even then only at the front end, just to get in the door.

A friend of mine named Rocky told me once about his dad, who grew up in Appalachia but got out, got educated, and became a college professor—but never lost the aggrieved and mistrustful mindset of his Appalachian roots. As Rocky, the son of a professor, inherited the advantages that propelled him to a very selective Eastern college which then opened doors for a successful career, his dad always gave off an unspoken vibe that, as Rocky puts it, "connections are cheating."

If getting into the American meritocracy is mainly about a numerical score on a test, the preparation for which is itself influenced by inherited advantages, staying in is much more about who you know. This is the dirty little secret of the so-called meritocracy. And once you're in, you are of course motivated to believe that you get access to awesome opportunities because you *deserve* it.

The corollary to that, of course, is that anyone who doesn't have access to awesome opportunities *doesn't* deserve it. "Mistakes were made, but not by me."

This self-justifying myth of a deserving elite and an undeserving everyone else has fed inequality in the United States and helped people at the top rationalize why they should ignore it. It isn't necessarily surprising that the powerful have a strong instinct for self-justification. They need to defend their privilege, which is bound up with their identity, and they do so in ways both conscious and unconscious.

What *is* surprising is how often the powerless join them in defending it.

Psychologists call it "system justification theory," and it posits that people without power tend to blame themselves for their weak situation; worse, they often actively defend the system that renders them powerless. Why? Because it sometimes can be more bearable to make excuses for the system and its inequities than to admit the possibility that you are truly without agency. The latter is a greater threat to your dignity.

Underlying all these dynamics is the presence of cognitive dissonance—the tension between the image we want to have of ourselves and our actual circumstances. Humans always resolve cognitive dissonance in ways that reduce pain. That means explaining away—rationalizing—the embarrassment of being at the bottom. It means buying into legitimizing myths, the cultural narratives and ideologies that explain why the haves have and the have-nots have not.

In the words of one study, by Robb Willer of Stanford University and several other scholars, "The more participants reported feeling powerless, the more they believed that economic inequality was fair and legitimate."

Until now. What has made a moment like ours so tumultuous and exciting and dangerous is that meritocratic trickle-down legitimizing myths have lost their grip. People without power—or who feel in relative terms that they've lost power—have decided to reject elite rationalizations of the status quo. Trump supporters and Sanders supporters may not have shared a political style or a moral palette, but they did share in spades this readiness to "burn it all down."

People will tell themselves a self-blaming story as long as they possibly can if it helps keep cognitive dissonance at bay. And in America that is a very long time, because our hyperindividualistic culture blinds us to forces beyond the control of, well, an individual. But when enough evidence accumulates that the game is truly crony rigged, and that merit and effort have little to do with ascent, that justice is not blind but instead winks at the powerful, there comes a forceful snapback to reality. Literally, a dis-illusionment.

The pain of such disillusionment can be converted to action and reform—as during the American Revolution or the Civil Rights Movement—or it can lead to an utterly paralyzing cynicism. We are in a world of such pain today. The key variable now is whether citizens will wake up and remember how to claim power.

AWAKENING

What does it mean to be awakened?

Some activists I know have come to resent the way white Establishment liberals are bending over backwards these days to empathize with white Trump voters. When *whites* face a drug epidemic, they note, there are calls for compassion and treatment instead of mass incarceration and military-grade policing. When angry white voters elect a man who gives courage and cover to bigotry and hate, we are asked to understand the pain and fear that motivated *them* instead of the pain and fear they are now generating among nonwhite *others*.

It's a valid point. In fact, it's hard to deny. Yet I cannot shut down the impulse to understand. And I do not think that awakening or empathy need to be zero-sum. Because when I see a piece of art like *Sweat*—or when I read a similar work like my friend Robert Schenkkan's *The Kentucky Cycle*, a Pulitzer-winning set of nine short plays that take place between the 1770s and the 1970s on the same piece of ground in coal country—what I see is not white people getting too much coddling for having too many feelings of unrequited entitlement.

What I see is an opportunity to deliver on an unmet promise. What I see is a bright thick thread of a movement for renewal and reform. The desire to be seen, to be recognized, to not be overlooked or discarded or treated as a tool or an inert object or an obstacle— this desire is what connects Reading to Ferguson, rural opioid addicts to young urban gangsters, fast-food workers to coal miners, migrant farmworkers to Muslim refugees.

This desire is the stuff of an awakening. It is the stuff of a broad and diverse coalition of people united by their yearning to be *somebody*, to live the American promise of opportunity and reward for striving. Who can activate this desire in a way that elevates rather than scapegoats? Who can connect these isolated stories of disenfranchisement into an epic of empowerment?

We can.

Throughout American history, and especially in the eighteenth and nineteenth centuries, this land was set afire by religious revivalism. These Great Awakenings, as they were called, initially fire-and-brimstone and later more ecstatically evangelical, always tracked deep shifts in our society: the violent theft of Native lands; the consolidation of slavery; the urbanization and then the industrialization of the economy; the rise of speculative finance and the financial panics—mini-Depressions—that broke out every few decades.

All these tectonic shifts generated volcanic bursts of collective spiritual searching among white citizens. And all that religious seeking yielded massive social reforms every generation or two, from abolition to Prohibition to women's suffrage to the Progressive Era's curbing of monopolistic capitalism to the Civil Rights Movement.

In the twenty-first century we are a less churched nation. But all of us gathered here this morning are evidence that the human impulse for rebirth and renewal and great awakening is timeless, and it is secular as well as religious. Or, to use the language of Civic Saturdays, it is *civic religious*.

When I speak of American civic religion I mean not only the kinds of civic scripture read at the start of Civic Saturdays. What animates the text is the spirit. And what the spirits of Jefferson and Lincoln and King tell me today is that it's time to wake up. We are either going to die a slow national death, lost in the loops of our segregated self-justifying dreams, or we are going to set in motion a rejuvenation *together*.

Simply by showing up today you are saying you choose rebirth. You are part of a vanguard that will do the work of stitching movements and communities together into a bigger story. The greatness of America arises not when the people scrape for scraps beneath the indifferent gaze of a moneyed and merit-badged elite. The greatness of America arises when the people unite to push back to share in power and opportunity.

How do we convert this awakening into something coherent? Let me tell you what I've learned in the first week of travels on my book tour.

First, we've got to make a bigger story of us. Among my progressive friends, "intersectionality" is the buzzword these days: connecting self-identified causes like feminism and racial justice. But *deep* intersectionality expands that in-group to include white and black workers in the South who voted Trump but are literally getting chewed in the auto parts factories that moved from Mexico back to Mississippi and Alabama when corporations realized they could exploit Southern labor like Mexican labor.

I call this "Confederate capitalism," and there was a cover story in a recent issue of *Bloomberg Businessweek* that exposed its ravages: the pressure from foreign auto and auto parts companies, in complicity with union-busting state governments, to force low-wage workers to work extra shifts with no safety protections or recourse or remedy. When I read that, I thought *that's just wrong*. This is America. Then I thought: they should be allies with the people of Standing Rock and $15 Now and Black Lives Matter and others who are getting screwed by systems of concentrated power.

There's a big affirmative story of *us* that they—we—can all fit into. It's a story bigger than resistance. It's a story bigger than party or region. It's about work that means something and that makes you feel *you* mean something. It's about a sense of place. A sense of purpose that can carry you through hard times.

This story can have an obstacle—a self-serving elite—but it need not have an enemy. As the psychologist Gordon Allport observed in his classic book *The Nature of Prejudice,* the desire for security within a group can be achieved without hostility toward an out-group. We just have to make it safe inside.

Which brings me to my second lesson: We've got to show each other how to say what we are scared of and what we are ashamed of. To name our pain. This, and not scapegoating, is how we can build bonds that will truly liberate us. This point hit me last week when I was speaking at Civic Hall in New York. During the Q & A, a young African American woman asked for counsel on how to speak about politics to her relatives in Georgia who supported Trump and who were repelled by her liberal views.

My suggestion was not to speak about politics, at least politics as we know it, but rather to speak about her fears. To explain to her kin why she is afraid of persecution or condescension, to reveal in what ways she is insecure and where she is trying to shield a weakness or a wound, to own up to her own failings. This is to lead by example. To invite others to drop their guard. We all have been imprisoned by our histories, and we so often disrespect others to remedy the deficit of respect we have experienced.

The night I was at Civic Hall, I had to miss another event going on uptown at historic Riverside Church—a commemoration of the speech Martin Luther King Jr. had delivered there fifty years earlier, in which he spoke out for the first time against the Vietnam War, and tied the civil rights struggle to the antiwar struggle.

That speech made him immensely unpopular in many quarters— LBJ disinvited him from the White House—and that is part of why it is important. It laid the groundwork for the Poor People's Campaign that King set in motion the next year, in which civil rights and economic justice and peace would merge into a single revolutionary movement for *respect*. But then he was assassinated—a year to the day after his Riverside speech.

After his death, Americans came to sanctify a safer King, one who spoke of dreams in hopeful language and who could be used as a messenger of reconciliation and even colorblindness. The more radical, more fully awakened King that emerged late in life is less remembered but more necessary now. This King was unafraid to speak truth—both to power, and to his own allies in the fight against concentrated power.

And this is the third lesson I wish to share. Let's be brutally honest about the challenges we face so that we can be brutally honest in our demands. In recent weeks I've noticed big, visually arresting signs being pasted onto buildings and street structures in Seattle's Central District saying "WE DESERVE RENT CONTROL." Perhaps so. But the blunt truth is, to quote a line used both in the Clint Eastwood Western *Unforgiven* and in the HBO Baltimore crime series *The Wire*: "Deserve ain't got nothin' to do with it."

If you want change, don't make an appeal to just deserts. Make a map of who decides—whether it's about rent control or homelessness or taxes or health care. Make a plan to locate and pressure those deciders, or to replace them or become one of them. Then make an alliance with others to mobilize the crowds, the money, the media attention, the social norms pressure, and the state actors needed to execute that plan.

I met last week with Dale Ho, who directs voting rights litigation for the national ACLU. He has a degree from Yale. And he's using it to serve not himself but his Constitution.

His small but mighty team files lawsuits in every state where right-wing white insiders are trying to rig the rules to keep young and nonwhite outsiders from voting. It's a daunting task but Dale is a calm dude. He has a plan to re-rig the game, state by state. Power concedes nothing without a demand, Frederick Douglass told us. Let me add that a demand means nothing without a plan.

RISK AND REWARD

At the start of the sermon I asked, *What's the difference between a promise you've never kept and a lie?* I hope you've been pondering that as I've described this arc from dead sleep to willful dreaminess to full wakefulness.

I want to close now with another question: *What will you do to deliver on the American promise?*

All around us today, Americans young and old are getting acti-vated for the first time or the first time in a long time. We don't always know what we're doing. But the important thing is *that* we're doing. We can teach each other how to do it—how to practice power—with more skill and wisdom. We can read books of strategy like mine and many others. We can learn by trial and error with joy and fellowship.

One thing each of us must do first, though, is to be clear about what we're willing to lose. The risks of showing up and participating in times of upheaval are real: the risk of disappointment, of failure, of financial penalty or reputational damage or bodily harm.

But here's the reward: living as if you were wide awake, fully human, and not alone. For the sake of our country and the ideas for which it stands, let's take that chance.

7.

LEGITIMATE DOUBTS

Central Library · Seattle, WA
May 20, 2017

JUSTICE SONIA SOTOMAYOR
From My Beloved World
Published 2013

Until I arrived at Princeton, I had no idea how circumscribed my life had been, confined to a community that was essentially a village in the shadow of a great metropolis with so much to offer, of which I'd tasted almost nothing. I was enough of a realist not to fret about having missed summer camp, or travel abroad, or a casual familiarity with the language of wealth. I honestly felt no envy or resentment, only astonishment at how much of a world there was out there and how much of it others already knew. The agenda for self-cultivation that had been set for my classmates by their teachers and parents was something I'd have to develop for myself. And meanwhile, there could come at any moment the chagrin of discovering something else I was supposed to know. Once, I was trying to explain to my friend and later roommate Mary Cadette how out of place I sometimes felt at Princeton.

"It must be like Alice in Wonderland," she said sympathetically.

"Alice who?"

She was kind enough to salvage the moment with a quick grace: "It's a wonderful book, Sonia, you must read it!" In fact, she would guide me thoughtfully toward a long list of classics she had read while I'd been perusing *Reader's Digest*. What did my mother know of *Huckleberry Finn* or *Pride and Prejudice*?

PRESIDENT ABRAHAM LINCOLN
From his First Inaugural address
March 4, 1861

In *your* hands, my dissatisfied fellow countrymen, and not in *mine*, is the momentous issue of civil war. The government will not assail *you*. You can have no conflict, without being yourselves the aggressors. *You* have no oath registered in Heaven to destroy the government, while *I* shall have the most solemn one to "preserve, protect and defend" it.

I am loath to close. We are not enemies, but friends. We must not be enemies. Though passion may have strained, it must not break our bonds of affection. The mystic chords of memory, stretching from every battle-field and patriot grave, to every living heart and hearthstone, all over this broad land, will yet swell the chorus of the Union, when again touched, as surely they will be, by the better angels of our nature.

TERRY TEMPEST WILLIAMS
From When Women Were Birds
Published 2012

We wrote an impassioned letter to our friends. It began: "We need your help." The letter went on to say, "Utah's redrock wilderness is in jeopardy. Here's the political situation we are up against . . . We know you love Utah's wildlands. We are asking you to please write the most eloquent, beautiful essay or poem you have ever written. We cannot pay you, and we need your essay in three weeks." We mailed the letter to twenty-five western writers, each one with firsthand knowledge of America's redrock wilderness.

Miraculously, in three weeks we had twenty original pieces from a community of writers committed to language and landscape, essays as heartfelt as anything we had ever read. . . . We had to work quickly. We knew the biographies were important to show the standing of the writers involved. We wanted signatures from each of the writers to add solidarity and depth. . . . We included a map, with a list of all the proposed wilderness areas within the Citizens' Proposal for America's Red Rock Wilderness. In two weeks we had our book. We called this anthology *Testimony: Writers of the West Speak on Behalf of Utah Wilderness.*

Good work is a stay against despair.

Copies of *Testimony* were, in fact, passed throughout Congress. . . . Six months later, on September 18, 1996, President William Jefferson Clinton designated the new Grand Staircase–Escalante National Monument, protecting nearly two million acres of wilderness in Utah. . . . Afterward, President Clinton held up a copy of *Testimony* and said, "This little book made a difference."

One never knows the tangible effects of literature, but on that particular day, looking north into the vast wildlands of the Colorado Plateau, one could believe in the collective power of a chorus of voices.

It's so good to be with you all this morning at the Seattle Public Library.

This institution—the public library—represents everything that is vital in our democracy today, and everything that is under assault as well: fact, knowledge, curiosity, diversity, community, openness, stewardship. I was proud to serve for a decade as a trustee of this institution, and I would have served many years more if I hadn't been term-limited. I love the library, and I love the people who work here.

This building—designed by the daring Dutch architect Rem Koolhaas, hated by many Seattleites during the public comment period, and then, upon opening, celebrated for its light-filled, democratic boldness—this building reminds us how fickle public feeling can be. It shows us too that a cathedral makes the people as much as people make the cathedral. This building, imperfect but ambitiously unconventional, makes us better.

This morning at Civic Saturday, we have sung together. We have reflected silently. We have heard civic scripture. Well, here's another churchy component I'd like to add: confession.

Here you all have come, in search of meaning and purpose and some slender reeds of hope in a time when national politics obliterates and makes a mockery of all those things, and here I am, with the job of supplying such purpose or such hope.

Perhaps I will. But I want to confess to you first that I am full of doubts. That my faith in American civic religion is under stress. Maybe that's not surprising, given a crisis in Washington approaching Watergate depths and a simultaneous depth of ignorance and amnesia and inattention among giant swaths of the American public.

Still, I am usually Mr. Glass Half Full. And I am here to tell you today that, number one, I am doubting whether this government—and I do not only mean the Trump Administration—is legitimate. Number two, I am doubting whether democracy is, on balance, a good thing. And finally, I am doubting whether the Union is worth preserving.

I'd like to share my doubts on each of these three fronts, and see if we can come out the other side with something more than doubt. Let's begin with legitimacy.

LEGITIMACY

I recently realized that Donald Trump and I have something in common: neither of us can escape this nagging feeling that his presidency is illegitimate.

He is unfit mentally. He is dismissive of constitutional norms. He is in league with an American adversary to strengthen illiberal racist populists worldwide and to undermine the rule of law at home. He does not even remotely understand the rule of law. He wants people to take an oath to him and not to the Constitution.

And that's just from *yesterday's* Twitter feed.

His insecurity about being a popular-vote loser stuck at 38 percent approval, the fact of Russian manipulation in the election and his possible knowledge of collusion with Russia, compounded by his profound inability to regulate himself—all this makes Trump compulsively claim *as fact* what he knows is *in doubt*: that he's legit. It makes him lash out at anyone who could challenge him, from a free press to an independent FBI. He's a Pinocchio POTUS who wants to be a *real* boy and a *real president*.

But wishing doesn't make it so. Or let me amend that: *his* wishing it doesn't make it so. *Our* wishing it could. More on that in a moment.

Let's look first at what legitimacy means. Legitimacy is the widespread belief that institutions of power are just, both in their origins and operations, and should thus be respected. In the case of a president, it's the belief that he should be accepted and followed as the rightful holder of power.

But let's take that a layer deeper. How widespread must that belief be? How informed or active a belief? How much respect should such belief demand? How much is enough, and measured how?

One core theory is that legitimacy derives from consent of the people. As Madison wrote in *Federalist 49*, "the people are the only legitimate fountain of power." That is true when the alternative is, say, a king or emperor or self-proclaimed descendant of God. But taken on its own terms, "the people" is a problematic idea and always has been.

For most of this country's history most of its people had no opportunity to express consent. Today, when the Supreme Court and their *confederates* in Congress and the states gut the Voting Rights Act, making it harder for poor people and people of color to vote, how can we talk in earnest about the will of "the people"? And let's be honest: even absent active voter suppression, only three-fifths of our electorate bothers to vote in presidential elections, and far smaller percentages in every other election.

So is ignorance assent? Is apathy acceptance? Is a long habit of acquiescence enough to make our leaders legitimate?

Legitimacy has something to do with popularity and something to do with justice but it's not the same as either. Even at the depths of his unpopularity, Jimmy Carter was never seen as an illegitimate president. Richard Nixon became illegitimate well before he resigned in disgrace. And Jim Crow was plenty popular in the South and seen by the majority there as legitimate even if it was morally repugnant and unjust.

Well, then what about procedural legitimacy, the requirement that following legal procedures makes an institution or leader legitimate? By that standard, Trump's Electoral College win was legitimate. So was Hitler's rise to the Chancellorship in Germany. By that standard too, the United States Constitution is foundationally *illegitimate*, since it was created by a group of delegates told by the people they represented to shore up the Articles of Confederation, not replace them outright.

To borrow the title of a fascinating book by the historian Michael Klarman: the Constitution was the product of "a Framers' coup."

Most of us, of course, feel it is far too late to challenge the legitimacy of the Constitution itself. Heck, most of us rapidly acquiesced to the 2000 Bush-Gore presidential election, which some had described as a coup by the Supreme Court. Why? Because most of us feel it is better to pretend that the system is legitimate than to face the alternative of anarchy. Self-government in a democracy has always required a suspension of disbelief about public consent, a faith in the magic of unspoken trust to keep the system running.

But then Donald Trump came along. From the time he was a candidate, Trump ripped away the façade and gave us cause to wonder whether we should suspend disbelief any longer. By his ingrained instinct for disruption, by his attacks on the weakened and corrupted institutions of our democracy, and by his own reckless and feckless form of occupying the presidency these last 121 days, Trump has revealed the rot, and he has accelerated it. Those are separate things, and we shouldn't conflate them.

So let's thank him—and then contain him. Thank him for being the virus that got the immune system of the body politic to kick in. It took a made-for-TV, money-grubbing, self-dealing fraudster who thrives on inequality to prove that American democracy is now a made-for-TV, money-grubbing, self-dealing fraud-fest that thrives on inequality.

But after we thank Trump for making us face facts about how sick American politics is, for forcing us to admit how unworthy of trust our political institutions have become, we must contain him. As relentlessly as the U.S. contained Soviet communism during the Cold War. Because his brand of truth-warping illiberalism, ever anxious to justify itself and now weaponized by the state, poses a potentially fatal threat to freedom.

When South Carolina senator John C. Calhoun didn't like the drift of federal tariff laws in the 1840s, he proclaimed a right of "nullification"—the idea that states could nullify any federal law they didn't like. The U.S. Supreme Court repeatedly struck down the idea but the stance of nullification had staying power in the form of states' rights, all through the years before the Civil War and through the years of the Civil Rights Movement. Calhoun became a disunionist secessionist. But he and his kind had to yield, just as George Wallace and his kind did a century later, not because their claims were overruled by a court but because the United States used force to compel them to yield.

Push came to shove, bloodily.

Trump is a modern-day Calhoun but what he threatens to nullify is not just particular laws or statutes or treaties; he threatens, in his rhetoric and actions, to nullify the rule of law itself. The more he tries to delegitimize the FBI, the federal courts, the free press, the more he awakens America out of acquiescence. This is the origin of his illegitimacy. It is why he faces resistance at a scale that feels to his fragile ego like a witch hunt.

But consider this: Donald Trump could make himself more legitimate *today* if he started behaving like a grown man in control of his faculties who was respectful of the law and of the two-thirds of Americans who disapprove of him. He could. He could get a majority to root for him. Odds are, he won't. But the fact that he *could* tells us this: Donald Trump is not illegitimate because he is unpopular. He is unpopular because he is illegitimate.

Understandably, many people are unnerved by such talk. Indeed, some have suggested to me that the logical consequence of any questioning of a president's legitimacy must necessarily be armed rebellion against the government.

But that's simply wrong. Martin Luther King Jr. did not accept or respect the legitimacy of the governments of the former Confederate states. But he preached and practiced nonviolent resistance against their illegitimate systems of oppression. As did Gandhi, who had even less reason to accept the legitimacy of the British colonial government and even more numbers on his side had he wanted to foment armed rebellion.

There are nonviolent ways to challenge, hobble, change, or topple an administration that most people deem less than legitimate: protest, civil disobedience, organizing, and, of course, elections. Those, by the way, are the same tools for healing a democratic system that has been rigged by the privileged to reward the privileged.

In short, the alternative to blind acceptance of a leader's claim to legitimacy is not violent chaos; it is everyday politics. It is democratic argument.

But this then brings me to the second source of my doubts: democracy.

DEMOCRACY

About seven or eight years ago, a friend told Jená and me that we had to watch a movie called *Idiocracy*. Many of you have seen it. It's about someone who gets transported from present time to an America five hundred years from now when the society has become so lowest-common-denominator, so commercialized and entertainment-saturated, so obsessed with immediate gratification—in short, so democratic—that the public consists of lobotomized, manipulable fools who live among mounds of trash and broken cities while voting for idiots and watching a TV show called *Ow, My Balls*.

We hated it. It was so over the top and heavy-handed, so blunt in its satire and such a demonstration of the very thing it meant to satirize, that we could hardly finish it. Of course, this film today is understood as prophecy, a vision of the present. Mike Judge, the man who made the film and who's also the creator of *Beavis and Butthead* and more recently the much more subtle but equally biting satire *Silicon Valley*, has been quoted saying he could not have foreseen how quickly the nation's public life, online and off, would resemble *Idiocracy*.

I think that's overstated—but not by much. What concerns me today is not that so many people are civically uneducated and illiterate in power. What concerns me is that so many of those same people don't think they are. Tom Nichols, author of the new book *The Death of*

Expertise, has put it well. We have a culture today that doesn't just tolerate ignorance; it glorifies it. Nichols describes a *Washington Post* poll after the 2014 Russian invasion of Ukraine. Most Americans could not locate Ukraine on a map. No surprise. But what *was* surprising is that the more inaccurately people guessed Ukraine's location, the more certain they were that the U.S. should intervene militarily.

To be an expert is suspect because experts are elites, and elites are presumptively bad because elites are always looking down on non-elites. This was the view of many Trump voters. It was the view of Trump himself as he staffed his administration. But it's a view that precedes this president and is in evidence at the local level everywhere in the country. And of course, it expresses the essence of Jeffersonian equality and hypocrisy: no one's better than anyone else, so don't act like it if you are.

I know I keep coming back to the *Federalist Papers* but we live in times that underscore why Madison and Hamilton were always wary of both Jefferson and democracy. We live in times when Donald Trump can say he is the most persecuted politician in history, and while a thin layer of educated folks like us crack up and share memes mocking him, tens of millions of Americans who look to his Twitter feed as not just news but as truth believe him. And tens of millions more have no basis from which to question him.

With a democracy, as with almost any complex system, inputs are amplified as outputs. In that sense, our national government is highly representative. It's reflective of a populace that doesn't know history, doesn't know science, doesn't know ethics, doesn't know art, doesn't know math, and doesn't know civics. And doesn't know it doesn't know. The result is so-called leaders and citizens alike who do not know their own minds, who are fed thought patterns and talking points and rhetorical postures and who believe that participation means just regurgitating those patterns, points, and postures.

What I am saying is I have been doubting whether democracy works at this scale. Whether the people of the United States are capable of self-government.

One of the projects I've launched recently out of the Aspen Institute is called the Better Arguments Project. It's based on the premise that there are deep philosophical divides that define American civic life—between a Hamilton and a Jefferson view of the role of government, between equality and liberty, between *Pluribus* and *Unum*—and that what we need today is not fewer political arguments but *less stupid ones*. We're designing a framework for the six core American arguments, these enduring tensions, populated with history and science and ethics and art and math and civics. And we are building public events and educational partnerships to spread this idea of "better arguments."

The truth is, as we've been developing this project I have sometimes feared that it is too late. It seems a flimsy wall against a great wave of idiocracy. And I'm doing this from the Aspen Institute, for Pete's sake, a bastion of elitism if ever there was one. But I'll tell you what has pulled me out of doubt and back into belief. *Doing the work.* And remembering that while a democracy governs by majority rule, it is moved by minority will. In every instance of significant civic change, it is the *majority* that bends to a *minority*.

I've been on the road for many weeks on book tour, and I've met so many people who embody the best Whitmanesque possibilities of our country: a teenage activist from the Zuni Pueblo in New Mexico who's activating potterymakers and other artists to demand respect and a voice in local government; an intergenerational, interracial group of DC residents meeting in the basement of a Jewish Community Center to learn from the ACLU how to make sure city government protects refugees and immigrants; three eager millennials who are leading Appalshop, a historic center in Kentucky that uses filmmaking and media to unleash untapped creativity in these ravaged Appalachian communities; ex-gangbangers in Chicago who are organizing youth in the Back of the Yards to engage in city politics; sixtysomething activists in San Francisco's Chinatown who are mobilizing to preserve the clout of that community; Glenn Beck followers in Dallas who are committing, thanks in part to the example he and I have tried to set on air together, to rehumanizing politics one relationship at a time.

All the jeremiads about idiocracy and the dumbed-down American people are accurate about the current state and dangers of public ignorance. But what they don't take into account is that things change. They change when people are invited to *be* the change.

I'm reminded of a passage in Edmund Wilson's *To the Finland Station*, a sprawling intellectual history of the idea of revolution, from the storming of the Bastille in 1789 to Lenin's arrival at the Finland Station in St. Petersburg in 1917. Wilson describes how Karl Marx, who had been raised in authoritarian Prussia and who'd never really been among the workers he championed, based his catastrophic prophecy of a war between the proletariat and the bourgeoisie on a false assumption.

"The Armageddon that Karl Marx tended to expect," he wrote, "presupposed a situation in which the employer and the employee were unable to make any contact whatever. The former would not only be unable to sit down at the same table with the latter on the occasion of an industrial dispute; he would be inhibited from socking him in the jaw until the class lines had been definitely drawn and the proletarian army fully regimented.

"In other words," Wilson concluded, "Marx was incapable of imagining democracy at all."

What Wilson meant was that Marx was unable to imagine a contest for relative advantage among competing interests unfolding within a structure of laws and tribunals and elections and popular mobilizations that could change the game, the story, and the equation of power. He was unable to envision workers not as inert vessels for dialectical materialism, but as living citizens, exercising and demanding and wielding power.

Marx was unable to imagine democracy because he was blinded by his fixed and ultimately dehumanizing notion of what the proletariat was. Whenever I get down on my ignorant fellow Americans, I realize I too am sometimes unable to imagine democracy. I too can be blinded by a fixed dogmatic image of people in all their inglorious idiocy.

My condescension in those moments isn't worth a damn. The only thing that *is* is my willingness to grapple with the complexity of what I think is other people's simplicity. To see, as Mary Cadette did, what Sonia Sotomayor *was* and could be. Not what she'd read. What matters is my commitment to joining the work of facing ourselves and our deficits and giving others the space to do the same so that *from there, from that basis of equal humanity,* we can learn what we need to learn to argue better and to build better.

It only takes some of us, not all of us. We, who are more than a few, less than the many, and truly committed to living like citizens and not like idiots.

But it's hard. It's tempting just to retreat to like minds, and to minds of like levels or styles of cultivation. And it's not just me. Increasingly, so many of us are beginning in the age of Trump to indulge fantasies of secession, of self-segregation into safe and welcoming bubbles. Which brings me to the final object of my doubts: the Union itself.

UNION

Last month I saw the West Coast premiere of an imaginative satirical play called *Wellesley Girl*. It is set in the year 2465—around the time of *Idiocracy*, incidentally—and an environmental catastrophe has reduced the entire United States to four towns in the Boston suburbs, outside of which the water is undrinkable and it is assumed there is no life.

There are several hundred survivors, and so each one is a member of Congress. The one surviving lawyer is the Supreme Court.

There are humanoid robots among them but they don't vote. And the people are all at odds with each other because they have been contacted by someone on the outside—friend or foe, they do not know—and they can't decide whether to preemptively attack the outsiders or to welcome them.

One of the almost thrilling things about this ingenious play by Brendan Pelsue is that it forces us to imagine if we were each colonists in a small experimental society where every action and omission had life-and-death consequences. Even in what seems to be a homogenous setting, there is so much cause for discord and difference in aspiration, that the tiny nation—such as it is—can barely hold itself together.

That play reminds us again of the fiction of legitimacy and the imaginary nature of any nation. These people are acting out of a habit of obeying the Constitution and following parliamentary procedure, and it's funny and touching and pitiful all at once that they pretend to sustain the idea of the United States. Of the Union.

Anyone who has heard any of my prior Civic Saturday sermons knows that I worship at the altar of Lincoln. I believe deeply in the Union. And so when I tell you now that I have begun to doubt that faith, I hope you'll recognize how serious this is for me.

Why have I begun to doubt? Well, for one thing, postelection you can't get into a conversation among other progressives without someone making a sort-of joke about how the West Coast should secede or how Washington State should merge with British Columbia and become Cascadia or how blue cities should band together in an archipelago of progressivism and form their own federation separate from the rest of the country. I have hated such talk. I have never joined in. But it's everywhere.

I'm also influenced by the articles and polls showing that Trump voters, by and large, are just digging in despite the evidence of catastrophe and that the more he screws up or screws them over, the more they defend him—indeed, perversely, the more they seem to identify with him. When I see that, I sometimes have a deep visceral reaction: let them go, these fools who feel far more foreign to me than many foreigners.

And when I observe the bottomless cynicism of Congressional Republican leaders who are so committed to cutting taxes on the wealthy and deregulating the economy that they are willing to tolerate every single one of Donald Trump's threats to the republic, I must admit I sometimes think we still have a Confederacy. It's no longer all south of the Mason-Dixon line. It's in the Rust Belt and New England mill towns. It's in the Mountain West and inland California. It's in the United States Capitol. It exists wherever people are committed to a Confederate notion that capitalism is about reducing labor costs to as close to zero as possible, that white supremacy is a fine basis for a nation, that government is only an oppressor and never a liberator.

When I see these neo-Confederates I again think: *let them go*. Let them make their own nation and see how long they last. Let them try to play at independence and let them see how truly dependent they are, how deeply dysfunctional, how backward and lost they are without the Union.

And then I catch myself and I realize I am one million miles away from the man I worship. I am one million miles away from the self-control, the compassion, the capacity for forgiveness, the supple and profound humanity of Abraham Lincoln. I am one million miles away from the rigorous idea that Lincoln held of why the Union mattered.

Lincoln was not a fetishist. He didn't like the Union as a totem or a religious object. He believed in Union because he knew, as did the Framers of the Constitution before him, that disunion meant death for everyone. He believed in Union because he knew that the Civil War was not only a territorial conflict; it was, perhaps first and foremost, a conflict within each person's soul. He knew it was no more possible to cut off the South from the North than it is for a human to cut off hate from love, selfishness from altruism—that if we have honesty and *integrity* we know each of us is all these things.

And when I catch myself like that, I see articles like the one in today's *New York Times* about the removal of Confederate monuments, including a statue of Robert E. Lee, from the center of New Orleans. I read the words of Mayor Mitch Landrieu, who said, "To literally put the Confederacy on a pedestal in our most prominent places of honor is an inaccurate recitation of our past, it is an affront to our present, and it is a bad prescription for our future." And the article closes quoting an advocate for removal, a forty-three-year-old contractor who said as the Lee statue was taken down, "It happened just like that." That contractor's name, amazingly, is John Calhoun.

Of course, it didn't happen "just like that." It took 133 years. Disunion, like reunion, unfolds slowly. But the cascading effects of both can feel immediate.

Let's imagine that the West Coast secedes from red America. How soon before Bakersfield, California, and Wenatchee, Washington, and Pendleton, Oregon, start saying, "We're not part of the Left Coast. We want out." Imagine that Seattle secedes from the rest of Washington. What then? It will be just like *Wellesley Girl*. The differences *within* will be inescapable. Richer neighborhoods will want to secede from poorer ones. Denser, younger neighborhoods will want to secede from stodgier, leafy ones. What then? Madrona east of 34th Avenue will want to secede from Madrona west of 34th Avenue. North Capitol Hill from South Capitol Hill. Madison Park from Madison Valley. What then? People who own their homes will want to secede from people who rent. And so on and so on.

There is no end to the impulse for disunion. We can slice things in half infinitely, until we get to the living human heart. Then we will realize there is no achieving the dreams of purity and homogeneity that drive secession. The lesson of the entire American experiment is that it is far better to struggle with the difficulties and dissatisfactions of Union than to chase the illusory and unattainable safety of secession.

We live in a time of creeping disunion, and it remains possible that we will just fall apart rather than choose to come apart. But that possibility is what makes me shake off the blankets of doubt. That possibility—that our generation might, by simple neglect and fatigue, just let the United States come undone—is enough to get me to stand up.

RESOLUTION

And so this is my resolution: both in the sense of what I am *resolved* to do, and how I mean to *resolve* my doubts about the legitimacy of our democracy and our Union.

I hereby resolve to imagine my country and to do everything in my power to create it.

Among my teachers in this work are eighty high school students I met two weeks ago. They were mainly students of color from tough backgrounds in Boston-area schools, and all of them were participants in a program called Facing History and Ourselves. They, more than most, have reason to be cynical about the American idea and the American Dream. They, more than most, have cause to doubt the American promise. And they, more than most, have decided just to live it and challenge it and change it.

One student, a strong-voiced young black woman from TechBoston Academy, asked me how young people like her could claim their power in civic life. Then she told me about how in her history class, after reading Howard Zinn, she had to write an alternative history of her neighborhood and city, a history from the street level that includes all the people and lives and unsung stories and dissenting views that are usually excised from "legit" history.

I paused. I looked at her. And I told her she had just answered her own question. She is writing a new America, no less than Terry Tempest Williams did with *Testimony*. She is writing herself into the story. She *is* the story: of renewal, eyes wide open; of one nation, as indivisible as hope is from hurt and doubt from faith.

So are we all. And this is our time.

8

FEAR AND HOARDING

Town Hall · Seattle, WA
June 17, 2017

WILLIAM JENNINGS BRYAN
Democratic National Convention
Chicago, IL
July 8, 1896

There are two ideas of government. There are those who believe that, if you will only legislate to make the well-to-do prosperous, their prosperity will leak through on those below. The Democratic idea, however, has been that if you legislate to make the masses prosperous, their prosperity will find its way up through every class which rests upon them. . . .

Having behind us the producing masses of this nation and the world, supported by the commercial interests, the laboring interests, and the toilers everywhere, we will answer their demand for a gold standard by saying to them: You shall not press down upon the brow of labor this crown of thorns, you shall not crucify mankind upon a cross of gold.

RACHEL CARSON

From Silent Spring
Published 1962

We stand now where two roads diverge. But unlike the roads
in Robert Frost's familiar poem, they are not equally fair.
The road we have long been traveling is deceptively easy,
a smooth superhighway on which we progress with great
speed, but at its end lies disaster. The other fork of the road—
the one "less traveled by"—offers our last, our only chance to
reach a destination that assures the preservation of the earth.

This morning, we're going to change things up. As those of you
who have been to previous Civic Saturdays know, this is the part
where I give a sermon. The sermon is a key part of our civic analogue
to church—perhaps the churchiest part. But we at Citizen University
are always listening and creating and one of the things we sense is
that in this age of participation that we are experiencing today, it's not
enough just to do straight old-school sermons.

So today we are experimenting with a modified sermon, in which
I will share ideas in three chunks, and after each chunk we will pause
to reflect on a common question. The three topics I'd like to explore
today are fear, scarcity, and responsibility.

FEAR

I've mentioned at previous Civic Saturdays that in recent months I've
come to be friends with Glenn Beck. Well, because I have been on book

tour for much of the last twelve weeks, I had the chance recently to spend a day with Glenn in Dallas and went on his radio show and his television show.

As some of you know, Glenn has been making a very public pivot in recent months—not disavowing his positions on policy but taking responsibility for his role in making our political culture so toxic and for feeding the resentment and anxiety and raw hatred that helped elect Donald Trump. (Beck, to his credit, was never a Trump fan.) And as part of this responsibility-taking he's been engaging in public and on-air conversations with people like me, with whom he disagrees deeply on policy.

Over the course of our time on air we did disagree sharply, on everything from the minimum wage and trickle-down economics to transgender bathrooms to the Affordable Care Act. But what we did first, particularly on his long-form television interview, was talk on a different frequency.

I had observed that so much of our politics today is driven by fear. Trump voters voted their fear: of a globalizing economy that had stripped them of jobs and dignity, and of a demographic tide of young people of color and immigrants that is eroding the relative advantages of whiteness, straightness, and maleness. Of course, people who now resist Trump also are fueled by fear: fear of what he might do next to them—to us—or what he and his enablers in Congress are doing to our society and our planet.

And it's not just partisan fear. The police officer who killed Philando Castile was acquitted yesterday because the institutions of our country have enshrined a self-justifying story of anti-black fear: if black men are presumed dangerous, then dealing with a black man is inherently risky and perhaps life-threatening, and *therefore* killing a black man preemptively must be justified. This is the strange loop of racist logic by which juries determine what is "reasonable" fear.

It is also a reminder of why it must still be said: Black Lives Matter.

I was speaking about all these currents of fear flowing through and distorting our politics and Glenn Beck responded with a very simple question: *What are* you *afraid of?*

At first I answered in a political-civic mode, saying I was afraid that we are Rome, that the republic is done and we are collapsing in a heap of corruption and corrosion. But then he pressed me, really, to say what I was afraid of.

Because he pressed me, and because we had already spent some time together, I gave him a deeper answer the second time around. I told him that my father had died suddenly when I was twenty-two, and that I have lived most of my adult life with a fear that none of this adds up; that life is random and cruel and purposeless. And this fear has been a motor force, driving me to make meaning and to make something that'll outlive me.

As I said this, I saw Glenn's eyes well up. And he then described to me his own personal fears, and the complicated relationship he'd had with his father and family growing up not far from where I live in Seattle, and how so much of *his* desire to have a voice and to be part of something greater than himself had emerged from those circumstances.

We went on to argue, as I said, about many issues of the day. I am aware that he still runs a media empire that relies for revenue on fear and alarmism coupled with ignorance. My encounter with Glenn Beck did not make him a saint in my eyes. It only made him human. From then on it was not possible to demonize him when we disagreed because we had already humanized each other.

I give him all the credit because *he* invited *me* into that space of humanization. He asked me what I'm scared of, and I realized he meant it and wasn't setting up an ambush, and so I spoke from the heart. And now we are friends, not enemies, even if I am sure we will on many issues remain adversaries.

This is power. The power to set in motion a new normal. To turn the soil and weed the garden so that something better and healthier can grow in this plot. And now I'd like to ask you the same question Glenn asked me:

What are you afraid of?

I invite you to pause here and reflect on this question.

SCARCITY

One of the deep and often unspoken fears of our time, everywhere in the United States, is the fear of falling behind, and a sense that we are stuck in a zero-sum game where we must fight harder to get less. What's become clear from my travels is that it's not enough anymore to talk about how to boost opportunity. We also have to bust monopoly. And busting monopoly begins at home.

One of the positive developments of the last few years, at least compared to the years prior, is that we now have a national narrative of the 1 percent and the 99 percent. We are now paying attention to the fact that as a society we are experiencing the inevitable consequences of forty years of grinding inequality and concentration of wealth and the spread of episodic poverty deep into what used to be the solid middle class.

So it's good that today in our political lexicon we have the meme of the 1 percent and the 99 percent. But here's the thing. That meme lets most of us off far too easily. That meme makes it seem like only the 1 percent are blameworthy and the rest of us are innocent.

I've recently been very taken with a new book by the British scholar Richard Reeves called *Dream Hoarders*. You may have seen a piece he wrote in the *New York Times* called "Stop Pretending You're Not Rich." And his message is for most of the people in this room today.

In the United States today if your total annual household income is greater than $116,000 you are in the top 20 percent. And what Reeves said in that piece and at greater length in his book is that we of the top quintile are the real problem. Yes, the richest 1 percent, who, after all, have reaped 95 percent of the gains of the recovery, are the most visible and identifiable perpetrators of hoarding and beneficiaries of game-rigging. But we in the 20 percent—the educated upper-middle class—are not innocent bystanders, much less victims. We too are perpetrators and hoarders.

Reeves lists an array of policies that have been put in place, some by government and some by the private sector, that enable the upper-middle class to hoard privilege and opportunity and to create what he calls a "glass floor" beneath us and our children. Here are a few examples:

- The home mortgage interest deduction, which gets more valuable the richer you are, and which fundamentally rewards those already privileged enough to be homeowners—which is getting painfully hard in Seattle—for being so privileged.
- College admissions preferences for the children of alumni, which are justified nakedly as a way to extract more giving from those alumni, reward the already privileged for being privileged.
- Exclusionary zoning that makes it harder for density and new forms of affordable housing to be created in neighborhoods designated for single-family homes.
- The so-called "velvet-rope" economy that is spreading like a rash through every sector but is perhaps most palpable in the airline and hospitality industries, where people with the means to fly enough and lodge enough rack up points—well, let's call them what they are: privileges—to be able to move in comfort and with the little dignities that are denied to the masses.

I can hear the objections now. *I'm not rich! How dare you accuse me of hoarding—I am only doing what the law allows me to do, even encourages me to do. I know so many people who are so much more well-off than I am—why aren't you shaming them? And what about you, Eric? Aren't you just as guilty?*

Well, I am. But as I will say in the final chunk of this sermon, guilt isn't the issue. Responsibility is. And here's the thing. We live in a country where 38 percent of Americans say they could not pay for a $400 emergency without selling an asset or borrowing, and 14 percent could not pay at all; where 21 percent of children live in official poverty, which at $24,000 for a family of four is a shamefully low bar; and where you are less likely to advance from the bottom quintile to the top than you would be in England—a country that still has lords and an aristocracy!

We live in a country, moreover, where there aren't bright lines between the poor and nonpoor but where 94 percent of those who earn between 100 and 150 percent of the official poverty line still fall into poverty for at least a month—and where this perpetual insecurity and the sense that work no longer pays is changing the psychology and the will to fight of so many of our fellow Americans. We live in a country where people like those of us here, the great majority of whom have everything we need even if we don't yet have everything we might want, still remain stuck in a mentality of scarcity.

We are a long way from William Jennings Bryan and his loud warnings about plutocracy and being crucified on a cross of gold. But we are in danger of strangling ourselves silently with ropes of velvet.

Take inventory of your privilege, your capital, your wealth. I am not talking only about money and class. I am talking about white privilege, male privilege, heteronormative privilege, native-speaker privilege, college-educated privilege. I'm talking relationship capital, connections capital, reputation capital.

Be honest: we here today have so much.

And because we think we are products of a meritocracy in which hard work was justly rewarded by good schools and then good incomes, we feel not only the scarcity obsession and the fear of relative decline that unequal times generate generally, but also a very particular *defensiveness* and even righteousness about that scarcity mentality.

Here is the challenge that Reeves puts to me, and that we must now put to each other: to break this cycle. To lead by example. To do so not just in our individual and family choices, but in how we engage as citizens to change *norms* and *rules* and *laws*.

And that's the order of operations, by the way: norms first. Our norms are the material of which our hopes and dreams and fears in civic life are made. For over a generation, the people of the United States have internalized norms that accept inequality as a given and are consumed with the anxiety of being cut out of the deal.

So I'd like to pause again now and consider: How and when are you affected by a scarcity mentality?

RESPONSIBILITY

If you aren't actively unwinding the upper-middle class privilege matrix that Reeves laid out, then you are actively perpetuating it. There is no such thing as being a neutral unwitting beneficiary of privilege. Not in these times.

But you might want to ask a simple question now: *Why?* Why on earth should I willingly yield advantage and be the sucker who allows someone to take advantage of me?

I believe that the reason to take inventory and then responsibility is not to absolve oneself of guilt or to indulge in charity. The reason why we must face and deconstruct compounded power and privilege is so that the entire society does not come crashing down around us. This is not altruism. It is self-interest properly understood. When you take stock of what you have, and realize you are in the world of haves and not have-nots, you face a simple binary: shall I hoard or shall I circulate? Hoarding kills—first those who are denied resources, and eventually the hoarders themselves. Circulation saves, enabling us all to thrive. This is Frost's fork in the road, reimagined by Rachel Carson.

This is the logic of how the United States after World War II didn't say "America First" and didn't tell Germany and Japan to go fund themselves and didn't retreat into isolation—but how instead this country's leaders decided to bind ourselves to international agreements and alliances that limited our maneuverability, that funded the reconstruction of our defeated enemies, and that created our own competition. The logic was this: mutual aid makes both the giver and the recipient stronger and safer. We're all better off when we're all better off.

So what am I doing to circulate my privilege? Some things, and not enough. I've got to do more. I just spent many weeks on the road talking citizen power to audiences that frankly already have some. I need to spend many more weeks talking with and teaching people who don't and who can't buy my book. I've got to do more than bring my lessons of civic leadership to places like Yale. I need to spend time in prisons, with people who want to enter the circle of citizenship again, and among migrant workers, who want to enter it for the first time. I can't accept as a given the whiteness and agedness of so many civic engagement organizations. I need to bring more folks in, more new blood, more of my country.

Which is why beyond the circle of personal actions, I advocate as a citizen engaged in public policy for what I call a monopoly-busting agenda. Higher taxes on the incomes of the wealthy and the upper-middle class. Taxing capital at the same rates as labor. A robust estate tax. Baby bonds or a universal basic income to ensure that everyone starts life or career with a baseline of economic security. Flipping our upside-down system of tax breaks so that they don't disproportionately flow to the affluent. Making it easier for people to make a living wage, whether by boosting the minimum or cutting away licensure requirements that create occupational monopolies. An end to alumni preferences in admissions. A draft, for either military or civilian service.

You may or may not agree with the elements of such an agenda. Go make your own. You may or may not have been engaged in similar conversations about *white* privilege and how hard and complicated it will be to deconstruct the power structure that privileges whiteness and punishes various kinds of nonwhiteness. We are all at different stages of a journey of reckoning. But the reckoning is unavoidable.

So our final beat of reflection will center on this question: How can we take responsibility for making a more truly inclusive community?

CONCLUSION

It's commencement season, and so let me close today in that spirit.

We are called here to commence. We are called to make a passage. It is time for us in Seattle—this city that is becoming as unequal and technocratically self-satisfied as San Francisco—to grow up. To live like citizens. It is time for us in the United States—a nation whose elected leader is embarrassingly representative of our market-dominated, money-obsessed, soullessly self-dealing culture—to grow up.

And what does it mean for us, at this little moment of commencement, to grow up?

It means naming our fears and making it possible for others to name theirs—even those we claim not to like at all, those whom some in the United States proudly say they are ignorant of—so that we might learn to see each other and live together.

It means resisting the scarcity mindset and striving to become something bigger and more whole than a status-anxious petty hoarder.

Finally, it means taking responsibility for circulating power and tithing privilege at every fractal scale of our lives. It means having the wisdom to know that to yield some now is to advance more later. Together.

Let's begin. We have a city and a country and a future to set right.

9.

GRATITUDE, LUCK, RISK

Washington Hall · Seattle, WA
October 1, 2017

HENRY DAVID THOREAU
From his lecture "Civil Disobedience"
First delivered in Concord, MA
1848

I meet this American government, or its representative, the
State government, directly, and face to face, once a year—no
more—in the person of its tax-gatherer; this is the only
mode in which a man situated as I am necessarily meets it;
and it then says distinctly, Recognize me; and the simplest,
most effectual, and, in the present posture of affairs, the
indispensablest mode of treating with it on this head, of
expressing your little satisfaction with and love for it, is to
deny it then. . . .

I know this well, that if one thousand, if one hundred, if
ten men who I could name—if ten *honest* men only—ay, if *one*
HONEST man, in this State of Massachusetts, *ceasing to hold*

slaves, were actually to withdraw from this copartnership, and be locked up in the county jail therefor, it would be the abolition of slavery in America. For it matters not how small the beginning may seem to be: what is once well done is done forever.

I think it's rather fitting that we should be meeting on a Sunday today, at the time when many others are watching the NFL. Because on any given Sunday, as they say in pro football, anything can happen. Especially when the president of the United States is on Twitter. What I hope happens today is that we'll make a little sense out of all the nonsense, and a bit of hope out of the raw cynical hypocrisy of our times.

I'd like to reflect on three simple ideas this afternoon: gratitude, luck, and risk.

Let's start with gratitude.

My friend C. Terry Warner is an eightysomething retired professor of philosophy at Brigham Young University. Some of you have heard me talk about his classic book *Bonds That Make Us Free*. Its core insight is that at every scale of relationship, we fall into a cycle of collusion, in which I accuse *you* in order to excuse *me*. When in my heart I know I've done something wrong, I avoid blame by casting blame on you for something else. You then return the favor. Warner's book explains so much about our politics today. It explains almost all of Twitter, especially Twitter commentary about, say, the flag. And its core prescription is that the only way to break this cycle is to set in motion a counter-cycle of responsibility-taking rather than responsibility-shirking.

Well, earlier this year I decided, after quoting Terry Warner seemingly every other day, that I should reach out to him. I emailed him, told him how much my work and life have been shaped by his book, and asked if we could have a call. We did. It was nice. I sent him my new book on citizen power, which he read and sent me a letter about. Then this summer Jená and I were in Utah to visit Arches and Canyonlands National Parks and so we arranged to meet Terry and his wife, Susan, at their home in Provo.

They are a devout Mormon couple married for several decades, with ten kids and fifty-plus grandkids, and he's a former teacher of Mitt Romney. Jená and I are an irreligious Seattle couple married for three years, each with a daughter from a prior marriage, I a former speechwriter for Bill Clinton. We got on famously. We ate cookies and ice cream that Susan had made. We talked about art, acting, phenomenology, political philosophy, German and French intellectual history, missions and legacies both secular and spiritual.

We were there for just ninety minutes. But that face-to-face visit opened something up for which I am profoundly grateful. It has made Terry and me much more frequent correspondents. It has also made us mutual mentors. What a gift it is to learn from an elder—and to be told that he is learning from you. That is priceless.

Our friendship has gotten me thinking about the nature of gifts, and the meaning of gratitude. Gifts, properly understood, are not transactions. They are an exchange—a perpetual exchange, if you're lucky. In this sense, *power* is a gift. Every form of power we have as citizens—our voice, our presence, our ideas, our wealth, our beliefs, our creativity, our vote—exists not so that it can sit idle and inert but so that it can be circulated. Exchanged. Given—not thrown away heedlessly. And returned—gratefully.

In a healthy community, the circulation and exchange of power generates gratitude all around. In a healthy society, people remember that we're all better off when we're all better off. We give to get and we get to give. But in a sick society, it's not that way. In fact, one clear symptom of sickness is a corruption of the language and spirit of gift exchange and gratitude.

Let's go back to the NFL and black athletes taking a knee during the anthem. One of the most striking things about the media firestorm that followed Trump's tweets last weekend was how many white so-called conservatives, on cable shows and talk radio, brought up the topic of gratitude. They did so in a peculiar way. What they said was, "These millionaire athletes—instead of grandstanding, they should be *grateful* they get to play a game for a living. They should be *grateful* to the country that lets them do that."

This idea—that black people shouldn't protest racial injustice because they are just lucky to be here and, by the way, some of them are millionaires—is, in a word, un-American. It's as un-American as a U.S. president getting elected with the help of Russian disinformation. More than that, it's a weaponization of gratitude. It's a case of the entitled and privileged expecting, not getting, then eventually *demanding* tribute from those for whom they think they've done a favor. Colin Kaepernick may indeed feel blessed to live in the United States and to do what he is doing to push the United States closer to its stated creed of justice for all. But he owes no expression of gratitude to anyone but those who have taken a knee with him.

When gratitude is expected, it is no longer a gift. It becomes a tax. This spirit of smug oblivious entitlement animates the Trump proposal to cut income and estate and corporate taxes for the very wealthy. It's odd that white heirs to vast fortunes aren't subjected to lectures on Fox News about how grateful they should be just to be here, and how perhaps they might express that gratitude by being willing to pay a higher rate. Instead, we get from the trickle-down crowd this line: *I'm a job creator. You're lucky just to be in my presence; don't make demands of me. Don't ask me what I will do for others. Just thank me. Send me your tribute, your tax breaks, your bundled dollars.*

Well, I have no such gratitude to offer. Maybe the GOP will win this round, will apply their tools and sources of power effectively enough to enact unnecessary tax cuts for the rich. They will not be able to compel me to be thankful for it. I will feel lucky, though—lucky that I'm in a society where I can mobilize countervailing power—people power—to remedy the damage wrought by selfish, self-dealing plutocrats.

So now let's consider this topic of luck.

The white-privileged and the trickle-downers have a strange blindness when it comes to luck. Then again, we all do. Our profoundly unequal society, with meritocratic gold-star collectors like so many of us here today, conditions us to believe that what we have is what we earned. That individual hard work and virtue, or the lack thereof, explains our place in the world.

That's a bunch of crap.

Let me take inventory of my luck: I had the dumb luck to be born here in the latter third of the twentieth century, and to grow up in a time of peace and prosperity. I had the dumb luck of parents who, while immigrants, had social capital and education. I had the dumb luck that when my father became unlucky and was diagnosed in 1977 with end-stage kidney disease, he lived in the land of Medicare and therefore could get equipment and training for home dialysis. He lived another fourteen years and we were not bankrupted by those years. I had the dumb luck of being in an IBM family in an IBM company town when IBM was at its very peak: summer jobs for children of employees, college scholarships as well, health and dental insurance, pensions.

Yes, I worked hard. I worked hard enough to get into a college that then compounded my good fortune by opening the entire world to me, a world of unending dumb luck and connections. But countless others worked just as hard who didn't have the deck stacked in their favor this way. Some are teenagers in Tacoma today. Or single moms in Ohio. Or old men in Yemen. Talented but not connected. Talented but unlucky. I'm talented but stupidly lucky. I'd be an idiot if I didn't admit that—or if I were to resent you for pointing it out. And by that measure (among others), we are governed today by idiots.

During the so-called debate last week over the so-called plan to repeal and replace the Affordable Care Act, one Trump aide said to the media that he was offended that healthy people should have to subsidize sick people they didn't know. In other words, he was offended by the very moral and operational principle of insurance itself. The great thing was that this set off a cascade of commentary on social media in which everyday Americans began their tweets, "I was a healthy person subsidizing sick people until . . ." Until I broke my leg. Until my husband got diagnosed with cancer. Until my son was in a car accident. Until, in short, bad luck struck.

My dad loved the old 1930s comedian W. C. Fields. He loved to quote a piece of dialogue from a W. C. Fields movie called *My Little Chickadee*. "Is this a game of chance?" asks a newcomer. "Not the way I play it," answers the con man. We laugh at that, but that's the way it feels to most people today. Luck seems in short supply to the many. Education and health insurance are more costly and contingent. The line between holding on and falling apart is thin and ever shifting. There are no IBMs anymore, not in the sense of a social contract and safety net. You don't get a fair chance anymore. The game of social and economic opportunity, from tax breaks to college admissions, is rigged to favor those who already have opportunity.

So when I take inventory of my luck, am I agreeing with those righteous dog-whistling Fox News commentators who tell us Kaepernick and LeBron James should shut up and count their blessings? No. The reason I detest those dog-whistlers is that they do not see their own luck. They do not count their own blessings—their own unearned parcels of power, as subpar white men hired by a TV network to make subpar white men feel great again. They only want, in scolding the NFL players who take a knee, to pretend to be the source of *other* people's luck. They know nothing of true gratitude.

Robert Frank, in his book *Success and Luck*, describes a variety of social psychology studies that show the more self-aware you are about how chance and randomness have shaped your successes and opportunities, the more likely you are to find lasting happiness and purpose.

And the more likely you are to support and promote the common good, even at some personal cost.

Which brings me to the final topic for today, which is risk.

Thoreau wrote *Civil Disobedience* in 1848 after having spent a night in jail in Concord, Massachusetts, for refusing to pay a poll tax. He had refused to pay because he believed that to pay was to support a national government that tolerated and sustained slavery, and that had just gone to war in Mexico to build an empire. He could not abide complicity in such sins. The Civil War was still thirteen years away but the impending crisis of disunion was visible to anyone who cared to look. Thoreau looked, unflinchingly. He was fussy, self-righteous, cranky, inconvenient. But he was definitely woke. I want to share a passage in his talk about the push for abolitionism and reform in the late 1840s:

"Practically speaking, the opponents to a reform in Massachusetts are not a hundred thousand politicians at the South, but a hundred thousand merchants and farmers here, who are more interested in commerce and agriculture than they are in humanity, and are not prepared to do justice to the slave and to Mexico, *cost what it may*."

"Cost what it may." Those are four big words. Let them sink in. Ask yourself: What are you willing to spend for justice? What are you willing to risk?

Perhaps it is true that the United States today does not face as foundational a moral evil as slavery. But we do face a living legacy of white supremacy. I'm talking about the white supremacists who *don't* carry torches. Those who perpetuate the positioning of whiteness as the social default: in medicine, in law, in education, in art, in philanthropy, in health care, in media.

You may, if you are white, agree that the unearned and compounding advantages of being called white should eventually be wound down and dismantled. But imagine that "eventually" is now. What are you willing to give up? A promotion? An internship for your kid? A low marginal tax rate? The dividends from the family wealth that began to accumulate with your grandfather's GI Bill? A personal comfort level on your street?

But maybe "What are you willing to give up?" is the wrong question. Or only half the question. The other half is this: What can you imagine gaining? How can you imagine advancing by yielding? Because a system of white supremacy that must unrelentingly dehumanize nonwhites also unrelentingly dehumanizes *whites*. You have nothing but this emptiness to lose. You have your entire humanity to gain. The ending of whiteness as the default setting in America is not zero-sum. It is a positive-sum proposition.

"Cast your whole vote," Thoreau wrote, "not a strip of paper merely but your whole influence." Let me ask you: What is your whole influence? It is your art, your friendships, your privilege, your comfort, your assumptions, your reputation, your connections. Cast *that* vote for economic and social justice. Cost what it may.

Real justice is not cheap. We can argue about the pros and cons of Kaepernick's choice to kneel. But we cannot argue the fact that he has paid a price for his choice. He has been willing to risk his reputation, his wealth, his prospects for employment.

True gratitude costs something. Saying "Thank you for your service" to one of the million people who've done sixteen years of warfighting for us is gratitude on the cheap. So is letting them board the plane first or applauding them during the seventh-inning stretch. True gratitude means calling for a draft, or demanding higher taxes to pay for the "war on terror," or pushing, as GOP Senator Rand Paul did recently in a lonely gesture on the Senate floor, for an end to the open-ended authorization of military force enacted after 9/11. For an actual debate about what we're willing to spend in blood, treasure, and legitimacy for an endless war against an uneradicable tactic.

If you've seen the engrossing, heartbreaking Ken Burns and Lynn Novick documentary *The Vietnam War* on PBS, you realize how the absence of such a reckoning can be corrosive to a country. In that era, both the young people who answered the call to fight and those who organized protests against the war were willing to take great risks to uphold their ideas of true patriotism.

So what are *we* willing to risk?

The reason I believe in progressive taxation is not because I love taxes but because I believe in a higher principle of progressive *contribution*. Of time and talent. The more you have, the greater a share you should share. But unlike the taxman, I don't compel you. I *invite* you. And I want to let you in on a little secret: To pay your share is not a burden. It is a liberation. This is one of the many things I've learned from Terry Warner.

I was not raised in a church or in any faith tradition. And Terry and I have never spoken of his faith and his eldership in the Mormon Church. Except for this: when we were having ice cream and cookies, he and Susan described at length the missions they *still* go on, all over the world, serving and building and circulating their power and their know-how and relationships to benefit others. Not as charity but as responsibility. Not as a duty but as a *right*. As a form of *freedom*, properly understood. And he has pressed me since then to examine my own work in the world more closely. More intensely. He has done this so that he might press himself to do the same.

Let's make three commitments then, together, so that we can all navigate the game of chance we call life. To exchange gratitude like a gift. To circulate good luck rather than hoard it. To take a risk with your own capital so that it may help another prosper.

These are the acts of grown men and women. These are the choices *citizens* make. These are the bonds that make us free.

10

A THANKSGIVING RECIPE

Elliott Bay Book Company · Seattle, WA
November 18, 2017

WILLIAM CARLOS WILLIAMS

From Spring and All
Published 1923

Today where everything is being brought into sight the realism of art has bewildered us, confused us and forced us to re-invent in order to retain that which the older generations had without that effort.

Cézanne—

The only realism in art is of the imagination. It is only thus that the work escapes plagiarism after nature and becomes a creation

Invention of new forms to embody this reality of art, the one thing which art is, must occupy all serious minds concerned.

From the time of Poe in the U.S.—the first American poet had to be a man of great separation—with close identity with life. Poe could not have written a word without the violence of expulsive emotion combined with the in-driving force of a crudely repressive environment. Between the two his imagination was forced into being to keep him to that reality, completeness, sense of escape which is felt in his work—his topics. Typically American—accurately, even inevitably set in his time.

IDA B. WELLS
From "Lynch Law in All Its Phases" address
Tremont Temple, Boston, MA
February 13, 1893

I am before the American people today through no inclination of my own, but because of a deep-seated conviction that the country at large does not know the extent to which lynch law prevails in parts of the Republic, nor the conditions which force into exile those who speak the truth. I cannot believe that the apathy and indifference which so largely obtains regarding mob rule is other than the result of ignorance of the true situation. And yet, the observing and thoughtful must know that in one section, at least, of our common country, a government of the people, by the people, and for the people, means a government by the mob; where the land of the free and home of the brave means a land of lawlessness, murder and outrage; and where liberty of speech means the license of might to destroy the business and drive from home those who exercise the privilege contrary to the will of the mob. Repeated attacks on the life, liberty and happiness of any citizen or class of citizens are attacks on distinctive American institutions; such attacks imperiling as they do the foundation of government, law and order, merit the thoughtful consideration of far-sighted Americans; not from a standpoint of sentiment, not even so much from a standpoint of justice to a weak race, as from a desire to preserve our institutions.

It's five days before Thanksgiving and already I am so full. I am full of gratitude for our team and this community and my family. A year ago, we gathered here for the first-ever Civic Saturday. Together, through times of shock and awfulness, we have found power in persistence and resistance but also in affirmative, collective purpose and joy.

I am also overstuffed with impressions and new ideas. Over the last five weeks I have traveled for work to St. Paul, Minnesota. Camden, Maine. Paris, France. Then Chicago, Memphis, Austin, New Haven, DC, San Francisco, San Diego. Jená and I have met so many remarkable people, hundreds of them, most of whom you've never heard of, who are changing the frame of the possible in civic life.

My sermon today is an effort to make sense of all this learning and experience. And I've boiled it down to five simple notions I'd like to share with you.

1. Remembering requires forgetting.
2. Yearning requires yielding.
3. Seeing requires unseeing.
4. Believing requires skepticism.
5. Persuading requires being persuadable.

Let's start with *remembering requires forgetting*, about which I have the most to say.

At the start of my travels, at the PopTech conference in the old opera house of Camden, I heard a talk by Stephanie Coontz. She's a cultural historian at Evergreen State College and author of books like *The Way We Never Were*, which blows up the "Leave it to Beaver" image of the American nuclear family and 1950s suburban mythology. Stephanie's theme was nostalgia, but she surprised me. She didn't just criticize the politics of looking backward or mock "Make America Great Again." She instead distinguished between two kinds of nostalgia: a fruitless, unhealthy kind that tries to re-create a lost *environment*; and a potentially fruitful, healthy one that tries to re-create a lost *feeling*.

I say "potentially" because it all depends on the feeling. If the feeling is one of unchallenged privilege and unearned dominance, then wanting that feeling back—as millions of white men do today—is not healthy. But if the feeling is one of integrity and usefulness—if what you remember fondly is a time when you felt purposeful and whole— then that kind of nostalgia can be a prod to invention and creation.

My friend Jim Fallows grew up in Redlands, California, a small town in the Central Valley where people knew and trusted each other, where the Rotary and Optimists clubs were strong, where his dad was an esteemed doctor, where community pride was high. Jim has worked in the Carter White House, he's lived in Japan and China, he's been for years a national correspondent for *The Atlantic* and now is based in Europe. Throughout, he's remained attuned to that old Redlands feeling. In a new book he and his wife, Deb, are writing, Jim chronicles small towns across modern-day America where people are cultivating civic and economic renewal.

But in all these travels Jim is not trying to go back to Redlands. And he's not blind to the fact that Redlands then and now, ensconced in the heart of orange country, has only fitfully included Hispanic migrant workers in its "story of us." He's just trying to rekindle a feeling, of people knowing your name and your family and looking out for you, in constructive ways, in new and inclusive ways.

This kind of remembering requires a certain kind of forgetting. What you've got to forget, paradoxically, are the specific circumstances that you so fondly recall. You've got to recognize that environment not as universal but as particular. The Redlands of Jim's youth was not the Redlands of the nonwhite kid or even of the white kid whose dad wasn't town doctor. You've got to name this trick of memory—then release it. And preserve only the animating core of it, which was the feeling.

The feeling *is* universal; or, at least, universally desired. I went to Redlands recently. I got it. I felt it. The question is how to make a place where *everyone* gets that feeling. Where everyone feels seen and welcome.

When I was in Memphis, I stayed in the Peabody Hotel. I'd been told this was the place to stay; it was historic Memphis. Well, it was. A grand old Southern building with a long-standing tradition every morning in which an African American bellman walks a group of ducklings from a nearby pond into the magnificent lobby and back out. A family-friendly spectacle. But upon second glance, the hotel was a bit frayed at the edges, sticky on the surfaces, a place past its prime. When a fire alarm went off, forcing everyone to evacuate and huddle on the humid sidewalk in various states of dress, all the studied gentility and charm evaporated. And that bellman's face was tired.

From the hotel, I went to the local offices of Facing History and Ourselves, the great educational nonprofit that teaches high schoolers moral decision-making through curricula about the Holocaust and the Civil Rights Movement. The Memphis chapter of Facing History is located on the corner of Mulberry and Huling, and as I pulled up, I noticed across the street a sign I recognized: The Lorraine Motel. And as I turned the corner, what I saw took my breath away. A two-story 1950s motel, where the rooms of the second story were for some reason numbered in the 300s. And a giant fresh-flower wreath tied to the balcony railing in front of Room 306.

It was on this balcony that Martin Luther King Jr. took his last breath. It was from across the street, through a warehouse window, that James Earl Ray took King's life with a rifle shot. Today the Lorraine Motel has been remade into the National Civil Rights Museum. I confess I did not know this before I walked right up to its front door.

Standing on that sacred desecrated ground, the weight of our past came upon me heavily and suddenly.

The National Civil Rights Museum empowers remembrance but also forces a forgetting: it demands that we *discard* the narrative in which one man, MLK, was killed by another, James Earl Ray. It demands that we *replace* it with the narrative in which this assassin was birthed by America, was but one product of a centuries-old system of weaponized white supremacy and terror. Ida B. Wells, the fearless anti-lynching crusader, demanded that the country face this basic fact of its existence. That we set aside the creed and re-center the deed. Facing History and Ourselves has a new slogan: "People make choices. Choices make history." It is profoundly true. But so is the reverse. *History makes choices*: the past defines the set of options we think we have. *And choices make people*: we are, in the end, what we choose.

That evening in Memphis we went over to Kingsbury High School, where the student body was once predominantly black but where immigration from Yemen has now made the school a quarter Muslim. The principal told me he had gone into education to serve young African Americans and now he had the blessing and opportunity to stretch himself. We were there for the What Every American Should Know project that I run out of the Aspen Institute, and the evening was led beautifully by students.

Young people trained by Facing History facilitated workshops with parents, teachers, and elders about American identity. No one was an expert or a historian. But they chose to show up because their children had asked them to. The workshops revolved around three texts. One was a passage from my book *The Accidental Asian*, about being a child of immigrants hungry for a place to belong. A shy young woman in a hijab, not knowing I was the author of the passage, said four words that night: "I feel like him." And I wondered: What will she choose to do with that feeling in all her years to come?

That brings me to the second thing I learned on my travels: *yearning requires yielding*.

Pete Peterson is dean of the public policy school at Pepperdine University. He's a California Republican who has been beyond dismayed at Donald Trump's political pyromania. And he has decided to persuade other reform conservatives to get, well, *beyond dismay.* They've issued a manifesto called "A Way Forward," and because he's my collaborator on several projects, Pete asked me what I thought of it. I'll tell you what I told him: he's on to something profound.

The document contains plenty of things I quarrel with, like a broad caricature of the left as obsessed with ever-splintering identity politics and unable to think of bigger things. But it also excoriates the modern right for ignoring the deepest ailment of the body politic: an epidemic of alienation and social isolation, fed by unrestrained market thinking, that has made the people ripe for exploitation by hucksters. Pete and his coauthors call for a "conservatism of connection"—a philosophy that isn't about hating government but is about building community, about answering the yearning in so many people to be something other than involuntarily rugged individualists.

America is the land of the lonely. And loneliness is bad not just for the body politic but for the body. The former surgeon general Vivek Murthy has said that loneliness has the same effect on us as smoking fifteen cigarettes a day. The isolation, the stress of always trying to salve it, the temporariness of our distractions, the persistence of the isolation. All of it is wearing, and all of it is increasing in the United States. We yearn for company.

If we are to answer that yearning—and now I mean people of the left, right, and center—then we must give in to it. We must give up the pride that masks our aloneness. We must make friends. At the CityLab conference in Paris, I met a civic entrepreneur from Britain named Laura Alcock-Ferguson, who has launched something there called the Campaign to End Loneliness. It started by asking policymakers to do more to combat loneliness, especially among seniors; to destigmatize it. Now they're launching a public campaign of ads and events that can open more paths to friendship.

The day Pete asked me to read "A Way Forward" I was headed to a symposium in DC that was co-convened by the George W. Bush Institute. One of my jobs there was to interview Peter Wehner, who was a speechwriter and strategist for President Bush and is now a *New York Times* contributing columnist and, like Pete Peterson, a #NeverTrump conservative. The topic of our onstage conversation was "Civility in a Fractured Age," and Wehner ended up focusing on the "fractured" part. He spoke movingly about the friends he's lost by standing for principle against Trump and Trumpism. He spoke of how his faith has sustained him during these disorienting times. And he spoke of C. S. Lewis's beautiful notion of "first friends and second friends."

First friends are those who share your worldview completely, who are of your tribe and with whom things can be unspoken. Second friends are those with whom you argue on everything, who may share your interests but come at them from a different vantage. We need more second friends today, even if we might risk losing some first friends. We must yield to the fact that we see so very little of the truth and could benefit so very much from another's eyes.

Which brings me to the third takeaway from my travels: *seeing requires unseeing.*

When Jená and I were in France last month, we spent a few days in Aix-en-Provence, where my favorite painter, Paul Cézanne, lived the last years of his life. His studio was a kilometer or two up a gradual hill from the center of town. A few hundred meters farther up you come to a plateau from which you can see Mont Sainte-Victoire, off in the distance. If you know Cézanne, you know this mountain. It was his muse. He painted it over sixty times. And those sixty paintings are like a time-lapse series of his career, a window into the evolution of his sight. In the beginning, he saw like an Impressionist. By the end—and he *died* painting—he saw in the Cubism he was inventing. The planes flattened. The borders between trees and rocks were patched over by color. Some paintings consisted only of a few intersections, like the folds between two foothills, suggestions of continuing shapes, and otherwise just white space.

Cézanne cultivated a kind of blindness to see through to the essence of things. The less meticulously he tried to represent reality, the more truly he depicted it.

The modernist poet William Carlos Williams understood this. He wrote a generation after Cézanne died. Unlike Cézanne, Williams did not give his entire existence to art. He was a country doctor who wrote when he could. Maybe that binocular vision helped. His strange revolutionary volume *Spring and All* captures the essence of how best to depict reality: don't try to depict it literally. Break convention and cliché. Break lazy inherited scripts. Break prior modes of representation. Break the fake linearity of narrative. All that breaking cracks open a deeper truth. In this sense, Donald Trump, catastrophic president, isn't a half-bad performance artist.

I recently met a young African American high school teacher from Evanston, Illinois, which is a prosperous, largely white college town. We were talking about how polarized and uncivil our politics has become, about the disappearance of the center, and then he asked a powerfully disarming question: "Was there *ever* a center?"

In other words, what we thought was the vital center, to use the phrase coined by the historian Arthur Schlesinger after World War II, was perhaps just an illusion. It is true that American public life in the initial postwar years was notable for a broad moderate consensus. But it is also true that public life in those years excluded people who would have challenged that broad consensus: this teacher's parents and grandparents, who'd been redlined and crowbarred out of opportunity; Asian Americans perceived as foreign; closeted gay and lesbian Americans; and so on. Once those people began to step frankly into the square, to force themselves into visibility and recognition, the illusion of consensus dissolved. Reality, in its full complexity, emerged.

We are still struggling today to depict and to process that full complexity. If we are to make sense of that cacophonous, unordered reality, we must learn to see anew, which means we must unsee some things.

I practiced this kind of rewiring in a workshop I took with the celebrated illustrator Wendy MacNaughton. This was at the inaugural Obama Foundation Summit, where I was speaking, and where I had many extraordinary moments. But her workshop on how to see as citizens was perhaps the most useful part of my summit experience.

Wendy said that when most of us draw a face we draw not a face but an icon of a face: a circle with dots and a curved line that's a reflex. But when we draw from life, as she puts it, by actually looking at a face, we capture and express the true *feeling*. Especially if we commit to the act by using pens. ("Pencils suck" is one of her rules.) She had us pair up and draw blind contour drawings of our partner—no looking at your work and no lifting the pen off the page. You should have heard the laughter in that room, both as we were struggling to truly perceive the person across from us and then as we finally looked at our work products, which were unintentionally Picasso-esque in their distortions yet essentially accurate. Not looking had enabled us to see.

What does this art stuff have to do with real life? The poet Claudia Rankine told me recently about a comment by the African American scholar Fred Moten, who was addressing would-be white allies about how ending white supremacy would liberate not just him but *them*. Here's the Moten quote: "The coalition emerges out of your recognition that it's fucked up for you, in the same way that we've already recognized that it's fucked up for us. I don't need your help. I just need you to recognize that this shit is killing you too, however much more softly, you stupid motherfucker . . ."

Claudia quoted Moten perfectly in her calm, measured, resonant voice and when she was done we both guffawed. Don't see what you believe. Don't see what you already think our roles are. What you think you are. Unsee it. Blind yourself to it. Then see anew. You will realize then that the helper and the helped, the savior and the saved, the innocent and the culpable, are interchangeable parts of the same uninterrupted contour.

The fourth idea that struck me on my journey was this: *believing requires skepticism.*

At Logan Airport in Boston, as we were preparing to fly to Paris, I came upon an unlikely volume in the airport bookstore: Jean-Jacques Rousseau's *The Social Contract.* I hadn't read this since college, and I didn't know where that copy was, so I bought it.

Over the ensuing days, I read it and was reminded of two things: one, how revolutionary was Rousseau's notion of a social contract between the people and those who rule; and two, how his argument for the idea that the state always represents the "general will" of the people would pave the way not to democracy but to totalitarian dictatorships.

During the same trip, during the train ride to Provence, I read George Orwell's 1941 essay "The Lion and the Unicorn: Socialism and the English Genius." Again, I was struck by two things: first, how incisive and perceptive and subtle he was about the failings of England's ruling class in the interwar years; and two, how shockingly and clumsily naïve and wrong he was in predicting that socialism and the abolishment of private property would be humanity's salvation.

What my encounters on the page with Jean-Jacques and George taught me is be careful what you believe. Be careful of certainty. Skepticism about your own belief system is one of the citizen's highest obligations. Even people as logical as Rousseau and as sophisticated as Orwell could not always muster the skepticism they so valued and thus could not foresee where their beliefs, put into practice, might lead.

The best thing about the Obama summit, frankly, was escaping for a few days from the toxic air of Trumpistan. It was time spent in an alternate universe, where the decent people led us and where creative, idealistic activists were not the underground but the vanguard. We literally were in a bubble—an enclosed, secured two floors of a new Chicago hotel. Wow, it was nice.

And it took me a few days to regain my skeptical faculties. To remember Obama's shortcomings. To be reminded of his failures of imagination and execution. To remember that things hadn't been as great for everyone during the Obama years as I like to imagine—because if they had, we wouldn't be in the Trump years now.

Some might think that skepticism is the opposite of belief but it is not. It is its handmaiden. It is the resistance that makes the flame. Cynicism, on the other hand, is dangerous. And cynicism, even more than belief in an empirically failed ideology like trickle-down economics or state ownership of the means of production, is corrosive because it makes *all* beliefs fungible and it reduces a belief's worth to the question of whether it is, for the moment, espoused by people with power.

The white evangelical Alabamans whose support for Roy Moore has only *increased* since his apparent penchant for pedophilia became public—they are not believers in any sense of the word. They are cynics. And they, far more than their defrocked judge, are a danger to democracy. They also embody a core vulnerability of democracy, which Facebook fed and Putin's digital army exploited: tribal confirmation bias. Taking in only the evidence that reinforces the righteousness of your group's prior worldview.

And if you think only white Alabama evangelicals do this, you must be from Seattle.

This brings me to the fifth and final idea I want to share: *persuading requires being persuadable.*

At that symposium on civility in a fractured age where I met Peter Wehner, the dinner speaker was Stephen Carter of Yale Law School. Carter is a hard man to pigeonhole politically, and I say that as praise. His first book, over a quarter century ago, was called *Reflections of an Affirmative Action Baby*, and his candor about both the necessity of affirmative action and the psychic price one pays for it showed a mind at peace with nonbinaries. Many years earlier, he had clerked for Supreme Court Justice Thurgood Marshall and he was later entrusted by Justice Marshall to organize the oral history of his career and his catalytic role in the Civil Rights Movement.

What Carter learned in that project, and shared with me so that I might share with you, was this: in the depths of state-sanctioned segregation, amidst suffocating white customs of scorn that denied him social standing in the courtroom even though he had legal standing, young NAACP lawyer Thurgood Marshall never dehumanized the people who dehumanized him. He talked to them. He listened to them. He tried to persuade them, whether on the streets or in the jury box. He learned from them. Carter told this story to put the overheated fears today that speech is violence, that unfriendly ideas must be banned or banished, into proper perspective.

If Thurgood Marshall, who patiently built the legal foundation for his triumph in *Brown v. Board of Education*, could handle hearing from Jim Crow's finest in some very unsafe spaces, then we should toughen up and remember what it is *we* are trying to build.

Of course, it's more than a matter of toughening and being not fragile in the face of opposition. It's also a matter of loosening and being not closed in the face of the unfamiliar. And then making that openness reciprocal. As Carter put it: If I'm going to have a chance to change your mind, you've got to have a chance to change mine.

When I was in Austin recently, I spoke at the University of Texas to college and high school students who'd come in from across the state to learn about citizen power. There were liberals from Houston and conservatives from Abilene and many others from all points between who did not yet know their own minds. What I loved about my day with them was that they were practicing. Trying on stances. Removing them. Not being too quick to judge or to justify. In short: they changed each other. At the base of the Union Building on the UT campus is a great inscription: THE EYES OF TEXAS ARE ON YOU. I wish the adults of Texas had been able to watch their children at this symposium.

Not all persuasion, of course, is by argument. In fact, most of it is not. It is by example. Let me tell you about Christian Picciolini, whom I met last week in San Francisco at the Anti-Defamation League's summit on fighting anti-Semitism. Christian was fourteen when he was recruited into a white supremacist gang. He did not have an unhappy home life he was trying to escape. He was simply hungry for a tribe and for recognition. He rose in the neo-Nazi ranks as he became an adult. He opened a record store to sell white power heavy metal music.

And then his conversion began. He needed to expand his offerings to keep the store open and so he started selling hip-hop and other kinds of music. He began to be changed, he said, by his customers. Not by anything they said but by their presence. They knew who he was and who he associated with. They, like young Thurgood Marshall, chose not to dehumanize the dehumanizer. They didn't break his windows. They bought the music that they liked. They talked to him about it. And gradually, he let himself be persuaded by them. When he became a father, that opening expanded. Looking at his baby daughter, he faced anew the question that had first put him on this path: How can I find meaning and pride in a group? Now he had a different answer.

He needed to belong to a circle of decency. Today Christian's work is to turn Nazis into ex-Nazis. He is a recruiter for decency. I interpret the election results last week in this same spirit. This was a national referendum on the gross indecency of Trumpism. Not just in Virginia, where the tiki torches of Charlottesville served only to burn down a Republican legislative majority. But in Edison, New Jersey, where anonymous racist fliers against Chinese American and Indian American school board candidates did not prevent them from being the top two votegetters. And in our state's town of Burien, where an anti-immigrant group called Respect Washington had sent out fliers purportedly listing the names and addresses of undocumented immigrants, and where the voters just elected the city's first two Latino city council members.

In towns across the land on Election Day 2017 we saw a populism of the decent: a surge of everyday Americans who have no special connections or clout but who are now ready to elevate decency and dignity and who have persuaded others to do the same. Not by bad-gering or demonizing but by inviting. By example. And then by voting.

As you head to Thanksgiving, take these five ideas—that remem-bering requires forgetting, yearning requires yielding, seeing requires unseeing, believing requires skepticism, persuading requires being persuadable—as ingredients for the repast you are about to make with friends and family. Combine them in whatever proportions you see fit. Try different sequences. Make your own recipe for awakened citizen-ship. And make something *juicy*. Experience the joy of civic cooking.

I'll close with one last tidbit I was delighted to learn recently. The years before the Civil War saw the rise of the Know-Nothings, the nativist, populist, anti-immigrant, anti-antislavery thugs who were the proto-Klan and lineal ancestors of today's alt-right. We've all read about the Know-Nothings in our American history classes. What I didn't know about was the counter-group of young radical Republicans who organized a youth civic brigade to champion Abraham Lincoln and to take on the Know-Nothings. They used events, comic books, festive competitions. You know what they were called? The Wide-Awakes.

That is freaking awesome. Wokeness has been with us as long as slumber. Social justice warriors are as old as injustice.

So let's choose to be the new Wide-Awakes. Let's be eager to do every possible kind of nonviolent battle with the Know-Nothings of our day. Deploy history. Deploy decency. Deploy open-mindedness. Deploy the humility of the half-blind. Deploy an appropriate measure of doubt. Deploy love. And deploy a persistent and joyful faith that our cause is the cause that caused this country to be.

Then, my friends, let us give thanks that we are home.

11

A PRACTICING CITIZEN

Impact Hub · Seattle, WA
December 16, 2017

ALEXIS DE TOCQUEVILLE

From Democracy in America
Published 1835

Despotism, by its very nature suspicious, sees the isolation
of men as the best guarantee of its own permanence. So it
usually does all it can to isolate them. Of all the vices of the
human heart egoism is that which suits it best. A despot will
lightly forgive his subjects for not loving him, provided they
do not love one another. He does not ask them to help him
guide the state; it is enough if they do not claim to manage
it themselves. He calls those who try to unite their efforts to
create a general prosperity "turbulent and restless spirits," and
twisting the natural meaning of words, he calls those "good
citizens" who care for none but themselves.

GEORGE BAILEY

Speech during the bank run
From It's a Wonderful Life, *directed by Frank Capra*
Released 1946

You're thinking of this place all wrong. As if I had the money back in a safe. The money's not here. Your money's in Joe's house . . . right next to yours. And in the Kennedy house, and Mrs. Macklin's house, and a hundred others. Why, you're lending them the money to build, and then, they're going to pay it back to you as best they can. Now what are you going to do? Foreclose on them? . . . Now, we can get through this thing all right. We've got to stick together, though. We've got to have faith in each other.

DANIELLE ALLEN

From Our Declaration: A Reading of the Declaration
of Independence in Defense of Equality
Published 2014

Maybe we're born into a world, for instance, ancient Athens, where all the
men vote and move freely well beyond their homes, while all the women
are largely restricted to their households and play no role in politics.
Because things have been done one way for a long time, they seem
natural. Because we grow up with them, they seem given, even though
they might be changed.

Nature, in other words, isn't such an easy thing to grasp.

What happens, then, when what we know from abstract reflection
conflicts with what we know from habit, as it did for Jefferson?

The history of the world suggests that habit is the more powerful
source of knowledge. People are able to replace old habits with new
ones, based on ideas that show them the truth lies elsewhere, only with
great difficulty. Quite often they change only when forced by the people
who are worst off under reigning conditions.

We are in a season of miracles and faith.

It's the fifth day of Hanukkah, and still the oil burns. It's nine days till Christmas, when unto us a child will be born. And it's been four days since Doug Jones was elected United States Senator. Roy Moore is proof that the Lord works in mysterious ways. But the voters of Alabama—especially the African American voters who overrode every obstacle and deterrent—remind us that some miracles are wrought by women and men.

We are also in a season of traditions.

Festivals of lights, latkes and menorahs, *Messiah* and *Nutcracker* performances. I've always been attuned to the presence and absence of traditions. My immigrant parents didn't have a playbook for celebrating the holidays. We took our cues from TV specials and school concerts and advertisements. From popular culture. We were not Christian but every December we brought a big cardboard box up from the basement, assembled our tree, limb by color-coded limb, and decorated it. Then we had Chinese food. We were not Jewish but my Jewish neighbors and friends in suburban New York taught me to identify with persecuted underdogs nurturing their beliefs. Then we had Chinese food.

We are also today in a season of belief.

Or, at least, we should be. For as much reverence as Americans are taught to display toward the ancient miracles and traditions at this time of year, we spend precious little time during the shortening days of solstice asking just what we believe and why.

Eleven years ago, my friend Nick Hanauer and I asked ourselves that question, and the result many months later was two books, *The True Patriot* and *The Gardens of Democracy*. From those books emerged Citizen University. Yet those texts are not an ending; they are, like our Constitution, a never-ending beginning. The question—*what do you believe and why?*—should never be finally answered. If you and I are to live like citizens, we've got to ask the question anew each day.

When belief becomes a habit or a reflex, an unthinking, unfeeling reaction to other people's unthinking, unfeeling reactions, you get the politics of today. But when belief is a *practice*, a stretching and a straining, a stress test and an array of adjustments, you get something more like a yoga class: presence, confluence, and the certainty that you'll have to do it all again tomorrow to stay limber. This is the shape of a *new* politics.

Yoga is an interesting case. How many people do you know who say, "Yoga is my religion"? I know as many who say baseball is our religion. And three members of our team—Katherine, Arista, and Ben, who recently tied for first place at Harry Potter trivia night at Neumos bar on Capitol Hill—they might say Harry Potter is their religion.

But what do we mean when we say that?

A religion provides a moral framework for choice and an ethical standard for action. A religion provides shelter and respite from the suffering that suffuses human life. A religion offers a source of purpose and explanatory power in a world whose motor force is randomness. A religion provides a community and a set of rituals that root a rootless soul and that challenge the individual to be bigger than her self and her ego. A religion enshrines love and thus makes hope and human flourishing possible. A religion gives tangible institutional shape to an unseen spirit of connection and interdependence.

Humans are wired to seek belief and belonging. For billions of people, including some of you, religion takes the form of church or mosque or temple. It takes the form of prayer to a deity or deities. For others, including some of you, religion takes the form of the X when we say, "X is my religion." There is, of course, an infinite number of Xs.

But as the scholar Karen Armstrong wrote in her book *The Great Transformation: The Beginning of Our Religious Traditions*, every faith of what's called the Axial Age—the seven-century period of spiritual genius when Confucianism and Daoism took shape in China, Hinduism and Buddhism in India, and the three monotheistic faiths of Abraham in the Middle East—boiled down to the Golden Rule. To honoring the stranger. To the practice of compassion.

In the thirteen months since we started Civic Saturday, we've been asked from time to time why we talk about this gathering as a civic analogue to church, synagogue, or mosque. Why do we speak of civic religion, when some people are uncomfortable with any kind of religion? And what do we mean by that term, exactly?

I'd like to examine these questions with you today, and consider in turn the what, the why, and the how of civic religion.

WHAT IS CIVIC RELIGION?

Let's start with the what. Civic religion is the set of beliefs, texts, practices, rituals, and responsibilities that shape our ideal of civic life—that is, our best lives as citizens, as political actors and authors of our community and country.

It is not religion as God-centered worship. Nor is it what Jean-Jacques Rousseau called *civil* religion, by which he meant a generic theism under which the state would enforce a belief in God, reward virtue, punish vice, and promote tolerance. It's certainly not the tinpot theocracy of a Judge Roy Moore, who nailed the Ten Commandments to the wall of his Alabama courtroom like some idiot Luther.

Nor is it what the American scholar Robert Bellah described in a famous 1966 essay about the biblical roots of much of American political iconography: a city on a hill; Providence and Great Awakening and Manifest Destiny; first the colonists and then later the enslaved as Israelites in exodus from Egypt; and then Lincoln, a martyred Jesus who prophesied and made possible the rebirth of freedom. What Bellah calls American *civil* religion is the Christian leitmotif stretched across the frame of American myth.

What I call American *civic* religion is not about Christianity at all. It is about our secular creed, deeds, and rituals of citizenship. It is the *creed* of values and norms stated at the founding of this nation and restated whenever our fragile republican experiment has teetered toward failure (as it does now). It is the record of *deeds* that have fitfully and unevenly brought those values to life. It is the *rituals* that memorialize those deeds and that make the deeds repeatable across the generations.

That creed starts with the Declaration and the Constitution but it extends in every direction and dimension that evolution and inclusion have taken it. The proverbs of *Poor Richard's Almanac*. The psalms of Walt Whitman. The parables of Zora Neale Hurston and the lamentations of Nina Simone. The homilies of George Bailey.

Danielle Allen, in her many-layered book *Our Declaration*, performed an intensely close reading of the Declaration of Independence and the conclusion she came to is this: freedom and equality, so often seen as ideas in tension, are in fact the double helix of our civic DNA. True freedom requires equality, she argues. Equality not of means but of dignity and of recognition in the eyes of the law: what she calls "equality of agency." Without that, freedom is merely a shell. And equality doesn't come easily.

I've always believed that the most overlooked part of our country's civic creed wasn't written until after the Civil War, after the end of slavery but before the betrayal of emancipation. It's the Fourteenth Amendment, ratified in 1868.

Let's open our pocket Constitutions and read Section 1 aloud together:

All persons born or naturalized in the United States, and subject to the jurisdiction thereof, are citizens of the United States and of the State wherein they reside. No State shall make or enforce any law which shall abridge the privileges or immunities of citizens of the United States; nor shall any State deprive any person of life, liberty, or property, without due process of law; nor deny to any person within its jurisdiction the equal protection of the laws.

American civic religion is John Lewis girding himself as he crossed Edmund Pettus Bridge to ensure that no state, and certainly not Alabama, would deprive him of the privileges and immunities of citizenship of the United States, of his claim to equal protection of the laws. American civic religion is Lucretia Mott and Elizabeth Cady Stanton and all the women of the Seneca Falls Conference using the Declaration of Independence, with the words "men *and women*" in their Declaration of Sentiments for women's suffrage and full citizenship. American civic religion is Gordon Hirabayashi openly defying the order to register at an internment camp and welcoming prosecution so that his case could go all the way to the Supreme Court, where he lost, until his conviction was overturned by the U.S. District Court in Seattle in 1986. American civic religion is Edith Windsor successfully challenging the Defense of Marriage Act after her wife died and helping pave the way to marriage equality.

American civic religion is every time we march for justice. Every time we sing for justice. Every time we lie down in a die-in at city hall to protest the death of our homeless neighbors in Seattle. Every time we stand up at a town meeting with our member of Congress to show them who's boss. Every time we pick ourselves up after we lose an election or a policy fight. Every time we reclaim our agency and rediscover our power through acts of widening the circle. And every time we recall those acts in a catechism of historical reckoning.

I call this civic religion rather than just simple citizenship because our entire American experiment is an audacious statement of civic spirit and a continuous act of civic faith. We are nothing but promises on parchment and a willingness to keep things going. After their fateful actions, Lewis and Stanton and Hirabayashi and Windsor had no idea what would happen next, just as the signers of the original Declaration had no idea when they pledged their lives, their fortunes, their sacred honor. They each took leaps of faith.

Many who leapt were felled. Many who leapt were lynched. Many who leapt were deported. All who leapt leapt not alone but with others.

Not just with thoughts and prayers but with lawyers and organizers. And in none of their cases was that faith redeemed in a clean, immediate way. And still we leap. It takes years, sometimes decades, and we fight and lose and win and fight again.

As Donald Trump put it in a self-consoling tweet after Jones beat Moore, "It never ends!"

And this takes us to our second topic: why civic religion matters.

WHY CIVIC RELIGION MATTERS

Democracy, when it's working, is a game of infinite repeat play. It never ends! We believe that it's necessary in the face of such unending uncertainty to provide a ritual structure for belief in the possibility of democracy.

Why do we deliberately echo the elements of a faith gathering? Because that language, those forms, these rituals and habits all resonate on a deep level. We believe at Citizen University that all people—even unchurched Seattleites—*especially* unchurched Seattleites—yearn for the fellowship of neighbors and strangers. Isolation breeds despotism, as Tocqueville knew. When the soul of our country is threatened by hate, we invoke love. We kindle a connection to common purpose and a bigger story of *us*.

And we believe that those mystic chords of memory, stretching from every battlefield and patriot grave, to every living heart and hearthstone, all over this broad land, will yet swell the chorus of the Union when again touched, as surely as they will be, by the better angels of our nature.

If you recognize those words, you're in the right place. If you *don't* recognize those words, you're in the right place.

Civic Saturday has struck a chord and we are now taking it national with events around the country and with a new Civic Seminary that trains people to lead these gatherings and build these civic congregations in their own towns. In these darkest of days, in a time when politics is so fiercely polarized, when traditional religion fuels so much fundamentalist fanaticism, we want to appreciate anew the simple miracle of democratic citizenship. Look at the world. Self-government is a miracle.

This stuff matters not simply because it answers a universal and timeless yearning for shared purpose. It matters here because it locates us atomized, amnesiac Americans in the broad scheme of history and in a larger weave of morality. It matters because the norms and institutions of democracy are being corroded from within and without.

I recently got to know the Reverend William Barber, one of our generation's most fierce and effective civil rights leaders, who has been leading the Moral Mondays movement in North Carolina. That movement started with weekly mass citizen protests against the rigging of the legislature by Republicans and against the subsequent gutting of the state's safety net and voting rights and civil rights laws.

Those citizens have been fighting on many fronts. But beneath all those fights was the gerrymandered legislative map. So Barber helped to mobilize an army of everyday North Carolinians and activists and lawyers to get the rigged map overturned and to force a brand-new legislature into being next year. It has taken them six years.

With that kind of patience and persistence, Reverend Barber looks at what's going on nationally and says that this is hard but it is not new. He reminds us that Steve Bannon was around in 1877, when white supremacists took over Congress and put an end to Reconstruction. Richard Spencer and the tiki torchbearers of Charlottesville were there in 1921 when nativists rigged the immigration system to block almost everyone who wasn't from western Europe. And Donald Trump was in the Oval Office in 1942 when the internment of Japanese Americans got underway.

Putting today's fights in the context of history might make some people feel dispirited. *We're still fighting these same fights?* But Barber does it to give us heart: *we've fought and won these fights before.* And he does it to remind us that there's no quitting. Ever.

Barber is less interested in the language and tools of his professed Christian faith than he is in forcing his fellow Americans to live up to our civic religion. His is a deep, eyes-wide-open kind of patriotism. And perhaps the best statement of that kind of patriotism came a century and a quarter ago in another time of nativists and Know-Nothings, when Carl Schurz, a German immigrant who became a general in the Union Army and then a United States Senator from Missouri, took on the nationalists of his day. They were saying, "My country, right or wrong." Schurz replied that *true* patriotism is "My country—when right to be kept right, when wrong to be set right."

Think of that as the Golden Rule of Citizenship. And a never-ending obligation. A healthy American civic religion challenges us to live up to our creed, to reckon with the tensions and the hypocrisies, to do so with a knowledge of universal truths and the universality of human dignity, to be inclusive of every kind of person who is willing to abide by those truths and precepts, yet to maintain a sense of uncertainty about how best to do that. As Lincoln said in another part of his Second Inaugural, "with firmness in the right, as God gives us to see the right."

Which brings me to the final part of my sermon, about how to practice this civic religion.

HOW TO PRACTICE CIVIC RELIGION

William James was a pioneer in the new field of psychology at the turn of the twentieth century and part of the American philosophical school called pragmatism. The pragmatists held that the worth of a belief cannot be measured by its origins or its claimed origins; it can be measured best by its practical effects.

In his classic book *The Varieties of Religious Experience*, James applies the test of pragmatism to religion itself. Ask not whether a conversion experience originates in the chemistry of the brain; ask what it yields. Ask not whether you believe Joseph Smith had a vision in which an angel revealed golden plates that would become the Book of Mormon. Ask instead whether a belief in the Book of Mormon over subsequent generations has led to socially beneficial results. Many social scientists, looking at Mormon levels of service, family cohesion, and philanthropy, make the case that it has.

The idea that a religion is only as good as its effects can apply to American *civic* religion as well. The Constitution is worth caring about, the words and deeds of Lincoln and the like are worth venerating, only to the extent that they lead to a truly beloved community. James at one point observes that war can summon in a people common purpose and self-sacrifice and ingenuity and he says a society needs the "moral equivalent of war." I say we need the moral equivalent of religion, and that is what civic religion is.

So how do we practice it so that its effects are truly beneficial?

First, believe in tension. American civic life is a set of built-in tensions, of perpetual arguments that cannot and must not be resolved. Liberty and equality are in tension. Effective national government and strong local control are in tension. *Pluribus* and *Unum*, diversity and unity, are in tension. So are rights and responsibilities. Inhabit the tension. Know how to argue both sides. Know that elements of both are always necessary. Know that better arguments can bring us together.

Second, believe in doubt. Lincoln's phrase, "as God gives us to see the right," is a statement of humility, echoed half a century later by Judge Learned Hand, who spoke of the spirit of liberty as "a spirit that is not too sure that it is right," that seeks to understand the minds of others. We have too much righteous certainty now, too little understanding. There are no infallible original meanings and no inerrant interpretations. There are only broken, irrational, half-blind humans.

The Founders are proof. And they asked not for the idolatry of future generations but for our skeptical commitment.

Third, believe in gradations. Fundamentalism, whether of the left or right, is the greatest threat to American civic life today. Dismissing people as insufficiently woke or as fake conservatives—purging for purity—is both a cause and an effect of our contemporary tribalism. The writer Anand Giridharadas puts it powerfully: "Is there space among the woke for the still-waking?" We've got to make room. Otherwise, we silence and alienate too many bystanders. We stop too many journeys of mind-changing before they can start. And the only beneficiaries of that are Trumpian authoritarians, who depend on moral flattening, on this obliteration of a citizen's capacity to discern shades of gray.

Fourth, believe in coalition. The Alabama election, like the election nationwide a month ago, showed that a "coalition of the decent" is emerging. It took not just the heroic efforts of black Democrats, but the critical presence of some white Democrats and the calculated abstention of white Republicans to stop Roy Moore. When democracy is threatened by illiberal bigots at home and abroad, ideological litmus tests are a luxury. Coalition is a necessity.

Fifth and finally, believe in justice *for* all using methods *from* all. That means nurturing the spirit of mutuality and interdependence that George Bailey calls on in the middle of the bank panic. It means combining *your* civic power with that of others to change the systems and structures of law and policy so that more people can flourish and thrive.

Now, that may seem like a prescription for a progressive agenda. But it's not inherently one. Again, return to the effects test of the pragmatists. Empowering poor families of color to end their dependency on welfare and take more control of their economic and civic lives by activating social networks and using small financial incentives to change behavior—that may sound to you like an approach with right-wing origins, but it's a left-winger named Mauricio Lim Miller who's doing it, through an Oakland organization called the Family Independence Initiative.

Devising proposals for low-income workers in the gig economy to have a portable set of health and disability benefits—that may sound like it has left-wing origins, but it's a right-winger named Eli Lehrer who's doing it, through a libertarian think tank in Washington called the R Street Institute.

Origins do not matter as much as results. And results come only from trying, from thinking freely and enabling everyone to experiment, and from the hybrids that emerge from that liberty and those experiments. That's the lesson of pragmatism. It is the spirit of American civic religion. And it brings me to a concluding thought about practice.

CONCLUSION

I am not a practicing Christian. I am not a practicing Jew. I am not a practicing Muslim or Buddhist or Hindu. I am not a practicing atheist either.

I am a practicing citizen of the United States. I know my own mind. I know what part I have inherited from being Chinese, what part I have inherited from being American, and what part I have inherited from being Chinese American. I know what I believe and why. I know how to put those beliefs into action. And I know how to amend those beliefs and actions, as the evidence of my eyes and yours gives me to see the right.

All of us can do this, if we take seriously the opening words of the Constitution. And all of us must. Stand if you can and join me then in the reading of the Preamble:

We the People of the United States, in Order to form a more perfect Union, establish Justice, insure domestic Tranquility, provide for the common defence, promote the general Welfare, and secure the Blessings of Liberty to ourselves and our Posterity, do ordain and establish this Constitution for the United States of America.

We do it together. Our Union is imperfect. Justice comes first. We do it for posterity. *Imagine a society that operated on these principles. Imagine a country that lived by these ideals. We have the power to make such a miracle happen. It just takes practice.*

12

THE CITIZEN ARTIST

The Public Theater · New York, NY
January 20, 2018

SARAH RUHL

From 100 Essays I Don't Have Time to Write
Published 2014

Maria Irene Fornes was once my teacher. She objected to the language of intention in the method school of acting, to the constant refrain: "What does my character want in this scene?" One day she said to us, "Who always wants something from someone else? Only criminals. And Americans."

ROBERT F. KENNEDY

From remarks delivered in Indianapolis, IN
April 4, 1968

I have some very sad news for all of you, and, I think, sad
news for all of our fellow citizens, and people who love peace
all over the world; and that is that Martin Luther King was shot
and was killed tonight in Memphis, Tennessee.

Martin Luther King dedicated his life to love and to justice
between fellow human beings. He died in the cause of that
effort. In this difficult day, in this difficult time for the United
States, it's perhaps well to ask what kind of a nation we are
and what direction we want to move in. For those of you who
are black—considering the evidence evidently is that there
were white people who were responsible—you can be filled
with bitterness, and with hatred, and a desire for revenge.

We can move in that direction as a country, in greater
polarization—black people amongst blacks, and white
amongst whites, filled with hatred toward one another. Or we
can make an effort, as Martin Luther King did, to understand,
and to comprehend, and replace that violence, that stain of
bloodshed that has spread across our land, with an effort to
understand, compassion, and love.

For those of you who are black and are tempted to be
filled with hatred and mistrust of the injustice of such an act,
against all white people, I would only say that I can also feel in
my own heart the same kind of feeling. I had a member of my
family killed, but he was killed by a white man.

But we have to make an effort in the United States. We
have to make an effort to understand, to get beyond, or go
beyond these rather difficult times.

My favorite poet was Aeschylus. And he once wrote:
"Even in our sleep, pain which cannot forget falls drop by

drop upon the heart, until, in our own despair, against our will, comes wisdom through the awful grace of God."

What we need in the United States is not division; what we need in the United States is not hatred; what we need in the United States is not violence and lawlessness, but is love, and wisdom, and compassion toward one another, and a feeling of justice toward those who still suffer within our country, whether they be white or whether they be black.

THE UNITED STATES CONSTITUTION
Article II, Section 1, Clause 8

Before he enters the Execution of his Office, he shall take the following Oath or Affirmation:—"I do solemnly swear (or affirm) that I will faithfully execute the Office of President of the United States, and will to the best of my Ability, preserve, protect and defend the Constitution of the United States."

I'm not a preacher but I sometimes play one on TV. I've played one in a settlement house for immigrants. I've played one in a former Christian Science temple. I've played one in a multiracial Presbyterian church, in a steel-and-glass Rem Koolhaas library, in an exposed-beam, latte-scented coworking space, in a musty underground bookstore. And now, in the cabaret space of the greatest theater in the greatest city in the world.

Now you might say, "*Play* a preacher? You are one. You're preaching." It's true. I am. But it's also true that I'm playing. I mean this two ways. The first, of course, is that this is not church and I am not ordained. We are using the frame, the ritual, the raiments of a faith gathering to illuminate and activate our sense of civic religion in America today.

The other way I'm playing is that we're all playing—today, and every day, we play the social roles that circumstance and convention assign us, and, where circumstance and convention may be ambiguous, the roles we think or guess we ought to play.

This second sense of playing is fundamental to citizenship. You might say it *is* citizenship: playing a role in public with other people's eyes on you, when some of the parameters are clear but most aren't, and some of the script is legible but most isn't.

What are the norms in here? It's supposed to be church-ish but we're in a pub. It's supposed to be serious and deep but you're eating eggs Benedict and drinking Bloody Marys, for God's sake. We've got to figure it out together, what we're doing here. We've got to show each other respect and humility and curiosity and playfulness if we're going to figure it out.

And what a day for figuring things out.

A year ago today, I daresay most of us were marching. Now we are gathered in a dark, closed space and yet I submit to you we are still marching. We are here because we realized, during that glorious cascade of global marches last year, that to vote is also to march. To write is also to march. To sing is also to march. To organize is also to march. To persuade, or to be persuaded, is to march. To bring to bear people, money, ideas, customs, and every other form of power to unelect malefactors of great wealth and to contain white nationalists and their enablers. This, too, is to march.

For what *is* a march but a most stylized form of the sprawling, subtle theater of democracy? A march is to democracy as the Home Run Derby is to baseball: a distilled performance of the thing's most potent essence. So we *are* playing, all of us. We *are* performing. We *are* creating. Just by deciding to show up here and participate.

To make conversation in public is to make art. To make art in public is to make power. To make power in public is to make democracy.

The relationship of the citizen and the artist is what the Greeks puzzled over, until out of their puzzling poured forth both the theater and the republic. Today, Art Action Day 2018, I want to speak in some depth about this relationship of citizen and artist. I'll reflect first on the artist as citizen. Then on the citizen as artist. And I'll conclude with some thoughts about the meaning of civic imagination itself.

THE ARTIST AS CITIZEN

There are two ways of interpreting the term "citizen artist." One is simply the artist who is a good citizen. And that's the definition I'd like to explore first.

I should begin by pointing out that when I say "citizen" I am not speaking about documentation status under the immigration and naturalization laws of the United States. I mean the bigger, more capacious ethical notion of being a member of the body, a contributor to community. A non-sociopath.

Watching the current occupant of the presidency and some of the humans he is persecuting, we are reminded that there are plenty of people in this country who lack the documents but live like citizens— and plenty of people who have them but don't.

So the artist as citizen, in *this* sense, is someone who through her creations is a contributor to community—is, indeed, a catalyst for the transformation of community, real and imagined. Ava DuVernay. JR. Lynn Nottage. Lin-Manuel Miranda. Sarah Ruhl. Young Jean Lee. Carrie Mae Weems. Tony Kushner.

Each of these artists is making work that challenges us to live like citizens: to dismantle the prison-industrial complex; to reckon with staggering inequality; to empathize with working people of every color who've been displaced by globalized trade; to see in every black or brown orphan a possible Founding Father or Mother; to lift the burden of whiteness and to see just how heavily that burden falls on whites; and to know that every age will give us a new Roy Cohn and a new plague and a new thirst for angels.

Most importantly, they have taken risks: creative risks, reputational risks, power risks. And this presses the rest of us to ask, "What have I risked lately for the good of all?"

As we sit here, the fearless members of the Belarus Free Theatre are making secret plays in a nation where they have been threatened and imprisoned, where their work is censored, where theater itself is a threat to state security. The founders were smuggled to London for their own safety, and over Skype they continue to direct underground performances by their cast members.

Last fall, Jená and I and my stepdaughter, Zoey, were in Prague for what happened to be the annual Vaclav Havel Festival in the theater district. On that day the three founders of the Belarus Free Theatre were performing their work *Time of Women*, which describes the persecution, imprisonment, and exile of three journalists and activists who'd been leading the fight for democracy in Minsk. The performance was in Russian with supertitles promised in both Czech and English. But the English supertitles never appeared. So for two hours, in a tiny space about a quarter the size of this room, we three Americans sat in the dark a few feet from three Belarusian women enacting a perilous fight for freedom, with their gestures and glances and certain recurring cries the only keys we had for decoding the plot.

And it was thrilling. Because the plot was freedom. The protagonist was freedom. The motive was freedom. The inciting incident was freedom. The conflict was freedom. Freedom is not the mere absence of encumbrance. That's liberty. Freedom is the ability to create in the company of others; *because* of the company of others. That's *life*. Deprived of our language sense, we took in this play with a heightened moral sense. We left tasting our freedom acutely, like a bit tongue.

Can you taste *your* freedom? The folks here at The Public did when they staged *Julius Caesar* last summer with a vaguely Trumpian Caesar and incurred the wrath of the right-wing media. I happened to have been here that afternoon, talking to The Public Theater's Oskar Eustis and Stephanie Ybarra about this very series we have kicked off today. I was impressed by Oskar's clarity and calm amidst that shitstorm (a word, by the way, that should be making its way into the Times Style Guide any second now). The point, he said over and over again, was not the murder of a demagogue; it was the betrayal of the republic by those in the demagogue's circle. Which I imagine was not the response Fox News was looking for.

The folks here know their own minds. And they know how to make their minds known. Which is what an artist, a citizen, and an artist *as* citizen must always know.

In Washington Square Park, Ai Weiwei has constructed an immersive experience that invites us to realize how privileged are those who see cages as only art. In Seattle, an organization called Amplifier last year invited visual artists to create and donate images, then disseminated those images to tens of millions of people. If you marched last year, you held them up on placards. The marchers today are holding these and other images, and Amplifier has launched a Power to the Polls open call for new art from new artists that will spark new participation in politics.

In the Twin Cities, a nonprofit called Springboard for the Arts invites artists around the country to create playful "toolkits" in response to citizen requests. How can I get neighborhoods across the city to collaborate? How can I get to know the people on my street? The "answers" have ranged from pop-up galleries to five-hundred-person communal meals to sculptural bike racks—and the tools to replicate those projects anywhere.

In Wichita and Miami and Philadelphia and West Palm and Akron and Grand Forks and Charlotte and St. Paul and all around this country, my team at Citizen University has created a project called The Joy of Voting, in which we've invited visual artists, spoken word artists, theater artists, dancers, and musicians to generate local projects that rekindle a culture that once existed in cities across the country, before the advent of television: a culture of joyful, raucous participation in voting and elections. Street theater, open-air debates, dueling toasts, battles of the bands, competing parades, bonfires, and broadsides.

There is a common thread across these projects: invitation. Artists invite. Not just in the obvious way of inviting audiences and praying they show. (Bless you for being here, by the way.) But in the deeper sense of drawing us into places we wouldn't otherwise go to because we didn't know they were there or we did but were too scared to enter, or we were lost in our phones and we didn't know places was the point of being.

This is what artists who are civically awake show and teach all of us even when their work has not a trace of didacticism. They instruct us how to conjure from thin air the very real power of collective action. There is no better proof than an artist of my third law of power in civic life. Law number one: power compounds. Law number two: power justifies itself. See: white supremacy, male supremacy, trickle-down economics, divine right, and "because I said so." But law number three saves us and it is this:

Power is infinite.

Most of us most of the time forget this truth. But every artist who is awakened and participating in the life of her community and country reminds us of it. Forces us to see it. The artist is catalytic. And of course for this chemical reaction to happen there is a key component that is not the artist. It is us. We everyday citizens. We the people, who are to be ignited or transmuted. Yet we are more than inert. We are catalysts too. Which brings us to the second notion I want to explore today, the citizen as artist.

THE CITIZEN AS ARTIST

During the Women's March last year, the most palpable and memorable thing was not the numbers, impressive though they were. It was the staggeringly rich display of humor and ingenuity and beauty. The signs, the puppets, the posters, the icons, the costumes, the ballads, the chorales, the choreography. Our politics has been so devoid of such bottom-up creativity and imagination.

But when I speak of the citizen as artist, I'm not focusing on how everyday citizens perform as dancers, singers, painters, sculptors. I mean that citizenship itself is an art: a genre of generativity, a container for creativity. To be a citizen *is* to be an artist. Consider these six simple propositions:

1. To be a citizen is to put out a call and listen for who shouts it back.

Indivisible did this, when four young Hill staffers published a Google doc in 2017 about how to bend your member of Congress to the will of the people. That document went wildly viral, which its creators expected. Then the readers of the document decided to self-organize geographically, which was completely unexpected. Today there are over six thousand local Indivisible chapters across every congressional district in the land. Through call-and-response a movement breathed itself into existence. And by the way, that is exactly how the Tea Party movement emerged a decade ago—only they didn't have Google docs and Facebook. They used multi-thousand-person conference calls! But the fact that that movement sprang out of one man's rant on CNBC against federal bank bailouts is a good reminder that the left has no monopoly of civic artistry.

2. To be a citizen is to invent new hybrid forms out of what we find lying around.

Today's young libertarian activists are doing a pretty effective job of this, often out of view of older liberals and conservatives of the mainstream. They're mashing up Internet culture—short videos, memorable memes—with earnest interpretations of Hayek and from *Reason* magazine and the Cato Institute. Of course, the alt-right is also diabolically good at Internet culture, and its messages and methods mutate rapidly in online petri dishes. The earnest and well-meaning do not have a monopoly on civic artistry.

3. To be a citizen is to turn fragments of thought into poetry with the compact sharpness of arrowheads.

#BlackLivesMatter. #MeToo. #NeverthelessShePersisted. #NotYourAsianSidekick. #FightFor15. #DreamersUnite. War, said the famous Prussian strategist Clausewitz, is politics by other means. Each of these hashtags, crafted by no one you had ever heard of before, reminds us that poetry can be war by other means.

4. To be a citizen is to convert absolute awfulness into hope and hope into power.

When my friend Amanda Nguyen was sexually assaulted in college she could have given into self-centered despair. Instead she lobbied Congress tirelessly to create in 2014 the first federal bill of rights for survivors of sexual assault. She then created, out of nothing more than the power of her example, a national organization called Rise that's now working to pass similar bills in every state legislature in the country. She's twenty-six.

That's remarkable as an act of citizen organizing. It's in some ways even more remarkable as an act of moral re-creation. "Who always wants something from someone else?" asked the playwright Maria Irene Fornes. "Criminals and Americans," she said. But Amanda Nguyen complicates the picture. She is an American who, having suffered at the hands of a criminal, has wanted only to secure for *all* women basic justice and dignity.

5. To be a citizen is to use the barest frames of structure to spur improvisations.

The People's Supper is an organization that has been inviting folks to bring neighbors and strangers together for intentional meals that have only a few simple ground rules and some simple if profound conversation prompts. *Who are your people? How do you find strength when your cup is empty?* The results, in cities and small towns across the United States, have been transformative. Code for America has been sponsoring civic hack-a-thons in cities nationwide, inviting coders and developers to software-writing battles where the point is to come up with the most elegant, most beautiful solutions to the problems in the technology that local governments use.

Do you know who else operates like The People's Supper and Code for America? Jazz musicians. But the chord chart that yields the best possible, the most hard-to-anticipate, the most mind-blowing improvisational riffs you ever heard is not the B-minor blues. It's *E Pluribus Unum.*

6.   To be a citizen is to make the rituals that make a nation.

Five years ago, Jená and I attended several naturalization ceremonies. Nothing on any stage, even here at The Public, gets me choked up like the roll call of countries during this ceremony, when the immigrants are asked to rise as their nation of origin is named alphabetically, and after they have all been called they are told, "The next time you sit down you will be Americans." Then they take the oath of citizenship. One day Jená asked a simple question. What if all of us had a ritual like this? Not just naturalizing immigrants but also we who had done nothing to earn our citizenship but have the dumb luck to be born here. What if together the newcomer and the native-born could take part in a ceremony to renew our vows to the idea of this country? She started sketching a revival tent with a stage. Did I mention that Jená is a theater artist? "It's not being born-again," she said. "It's being *sworn-again.*" Did I mention that she is from Louisiana? And out of that inspiration emerged one of our projects, called Sworn-Again America. We created a downloadable template for a ceremony with a script, readings of iconic American texts, and a brand-new oath that is about citizenship not in the legal sense but in the moral sense: showing up for each other. Countless people have shown up for Sworn-Again America ceremonies in military bases, college campuses, public parks, concert halls, national museums, at *quinceaneras* and conference halls.

So let me recap: Put out a call so that it comes back amplified. Make hybrid forms out of the material you inherit. Weaponize poetry. Alchemize pain. Improvise like a pro. Create new rituals to create a new story of us.

That's a list of things citizens do. It's also a list of things artists do. *And I insist to you, these are the same thing.* Citizenship is art.

Many Americans, under the category "citizen," have the mental model of the janitor or the judge or the Scout or the Samaritan. But the model that fits best is the artist. I want you to leave today and tell the people you know that they are artists composing a community, devising a country, workshopping a *We* using nothing but a random pile of little *Me*'s and the flimsy wire frame of the Constitution. I want you to walk around your neighborhood tomorrow and look at it with the eyes of an artist, and ask, *Why is this not a park? Who decided the payday lender should be here? What if the subway opened out into something more alive? How could these old folks and these little kids be making something together?* Because every day is Art Action Day.

Citizenship, like *all* art, requires us to make something that coheres out of the tidal incoherence that is the world. Citizenship, like *all* art, demands that we take responsibility for our errors and acknowledge our debts and then transcend both. Citizenship, like *all* art, is only as useful as the imagination that animates it. And it's on this last notion—the limits of our imagination—that I want to close today.

CIVIC IMAGINATION

When Martin Luther King Jr. was assassinated, April 4, 1968, Robert Kennedy was en route to Indianapolis for a campaign rally. Many of you know the story that when Kennedy arrived, most of the large biracial crowd at the rally had not heard the news. And so he had to walk up onto this flatbed truck as his followers cheered and waved RFK signs and he had to ask them to be quiet and he had to tell them. And into that terrible silence, he extemporized one of the great American speeches.

There are three things notable about that speech, from the distance of a half century. One was the moral depth that Robert Kennedy summoned in that moment: his empathy for black Americans who might feel a murderous impulse for vengeance; his insistence that the assassination made King's call for love and nonviolence even more urgently necessary; and his candid admission that we might not be able to answer that call.

Second was his quotation of an ancient Greek dramatist. No political adviser would ever have counseled it but it's the authentic sound of a citizen artist. He was not showing off his erudition. He was sharing with the crowd the private source of poetic solace that had carried him through the preceding four and a half years. Most people aren't aware that this was the first time after November 22, 1963, that RFK had spoken in public about JFK's assassination. And even then, his awkwardly elliptical phrasing—"I had a member of my family killed"—is revealing both of his pain in saying it out loud and his desire to maximize the bond with all who grieved for King: after all, "a member of my family" is more general and relatable than "my brother John, the former president."

And this wholly unexpected speech did keep that rally that night from disintegrating into blind rage and violence. But here, alas, is the third thing that's important about the speech. It did not stop African American ghettos and college campuses and town squares across the rest of the nation from being consumed by uprising and flame the rest of that year. It did not speed the efforts of the United States government to address racial inequity. It did not slow the shedding of American blood at home or in Vietnam.

No speech quoting no poem can do that by itself. Moral imagination and civic imagination of the kind that late-stage RFK was demonstrating—remember, *early* RFK was a nepotistic, womanizing, entitled son of a bitch; but late RFK, grieving for his brother, sure that his own sins had fueled this tragedy, in a hurry to shed his privilege, was starting to see poor people and brown people as his brothers and his sisters—this kind of imagination is rare and special among leaders. And seeing it crystallized like this makes you realize it is not enough.

Imagination, especially in times of crisis, must be coupled with the practice of power. For it's only the practice of power that can make the imagined real. King had been in Memphis the day he was shot because he had recently expanded his imagination to lead not just a civil rights fight but a Poor People's Campaign. He had come to mobilize striking sanitation workers. RFK is a tragic and tantalizing figure—a human *What if?*—because he had long understood the exercise of power and he was lately coming into a wider moral awareness about beloved community. Had he lived and led this nation in its hour of peril, what might we be today?

Well, here's the thing. Though he did not live, we did. Though he did not govern us then, we govern ourselves now. In *this* hour of peril. One year ago, nearly at this very moment, Donald Trump swore an oath to uphold the Constitution, and nearly every day since he has broken it. As far as he's concerned, the Constitution is just words. He's right. All promises are just words. All covenants are just words. What animates them is not whether the words are in big black letters but whether we choose to honor them. And Trump's choice does not dictate ours.

So enough about presidents. The fact that we are here this day says we don't want our lives to revolve around a president or to be defined by resistance to that president. We want to create power, not just combat it. We remember that *creation* is the real long game. It is where art and citizenship are joined.

Uncle Tom's Cabin made it possible to imagine a day without slavery in America. Then John Brown and Wendell Phillips and William Lloyd Garrison sped the day and later Abraham Lincoln and U. S. Grant and William Tecumseh Sherman forced the dawn. *Will and Grace*—the first time around—helped change the narrative about gay relationships. Then thousands of loving couples and idealistic organizers and opportunistic politicians and dogged lawyers closed the deal at the Supreme Court, which did not make it the law of the land in *Obergefell v. Hodges* but only ratified it. *We* had made it.

When we get a Dream Act—and I believe we will—it will have happened not because a gang of six or eight senators cut a deal but because activists like Cristina Jimenez and Jose Antonio Vargas and Maru Mora Villalpando and Ravi Ragbir and thousands of other young undocumented neighbors and friends and coworkers of ours took the risk to tell their stories in public. And because we who have the documents stood beside them.

Let's imagine a society recommitted to inclusion, confident in its diversity, suffused with character and decency in every circle, nimble in the face of change, unafraid to hold ourselves as taxpayers and moral choicemakers to a creed that says we're all better off when we're all better off. And let's practice power to create that society—by organizing the people, the ideas, the money, the muscle, the norms, and the votes to make it so.

Citizen artists of New York, unite: we have a country to create.

13.

WHICH DREAM DO YOU DREAM?

Hillman City Collaboratory · Seattle, WA
February 3, 2018

JUDITH SHKLAR
From American Citizenship: The Quest for Inclusion
Published 1991

There is nothing equal about social standing in general. Nothing is more unequally distributed than social respect and prestige. It is only citizenship perceived as a natural right that bears a promise of equal political standing in a democracy.

FREDERICK DOUGLASS
From "The Composite Nation" speech
Delivered in Boston, MA
1869

I have said that the Chinese will come, and have given some reasons why we may expect them in very large numbers in no very distant future. Do you ask, if I favor such immigration,

I answer I would. Would you have them naturalized, and have them invested with all the rights of American citizenship? I would. Would you allow them to vote? I would. Would you allow them to hold office? I would.

But are there not reasons against all this? Is there not such a law or principle as that of self-preservation? Does not every race owe something to itself? Should it not attend to the dictates of common sense? Should not a superior race protect itself from contact with inferior ones? Are not the white people the owners of this continent? Have they not the right to say, what kind of people shall be allowed to come here and settle? Is there not such a thing as being more generous than wise? In the effort to promote civilization may we not corrupt and destroy what we have? Is it best to take on board more passengers than the ship will carry?

To all of this and more I have one among many answers, together satisfactory to me, though I cannot promise that it will be so to you. . . .

I want a home here not only for the Negro, the mulatto and the Latin races; but I want the Asiatic to find a home here in the United States, and feel at home here, both for his sake and for ours. Right wrongs no man. If respect is had to majorities, the fact that only one fifth of the population of the globe is white, the other four fifths are colored, ought to have some weight and influence in disposing of this and similar questions. It would be a sad reflection upon the laws of nature and upon the idea of justice, to say nothing of a common Creator, if four fifths of mankind were deprived of the rights of migration to make room for the one fifth. . . .

It's fitting that we gather today in a new-economy coworking space located in an old, proud South Seattle neighborhood that often gets overlooked. In its diversity, its traditions of mutual aid, its advancing gentrification, and its palpable tension between competing dreams of what life in Seattle can be, Hillman City is the whole of our city in microcosm.

This idea of competing dreams has been on my mind a lot lately. It's also clearly on the mind of the current occupant of the presidency. So, in my sermon today, I want first to explore who really is a dreamer in America. Second, I want to show how at every stage of this country's history and in every part of its territory now, two dreams have been competing for priority, for recognition, for the life force to bloom into reality. And finally, I want to make clear it's time to choose again between these dreams.

WHO'S A DREAMER?

Let me start with the question, "Who's a dreamer?"

On Tuesday, the day of Donald Trump's first State of the Union address, I did two notable things. First, I deleted Twitter and Facebook from my phone. Second, I watched the MLB Network instead of CNN during the speech. This was healthy on several levels. For one thing, with less than two weeks before pitchers and catchers report to spring training, I got a pretty good overview of the most promising young players in the game today. (If you're a Mariners fan, keep watching CNN. It'll be less depressing.)

More importantly, this choice of channels enabled me to regain something that some of you may remember, this thing people used to have and use all the time, called "perspective." With just one day's perspective, I managed to bypass all the microreactions that Trump triggered in real time, and by Wednesday I could see that there was only one important line in his eighty minutes of teleprompting.

The line was this: "Americans are dreamers too."

As a former White House speechwriter, I must say this was a very effective line. And it brings me no pleasure to say that.

What Trump was referring to are the young undocumented immigrants, blamelessly brought here as children, who remember only life in this country, who have been students and soldiers and contributors to this country, who under the DREAM Act would have been able to achieve a pathway to citizenship, and who have stepped out of the shadows, come out openly, and named themselves into existence as the Dreamers.

For all these many years of nativist, racist provocations on social media and elsewhere, Trump has rarely called these young people "Dreamers." He's called them "DACA," which of course is the administrative program President Obama created to exempt them temporarily from deportation. Trump intuited correctly that to call them Dreamers would be to legitimize their cause, to embed them in the iconography of the American Dream. It bugged him that the debate had been framed such that immigration restrictionists like him had to be against dreams and dreamers.

So on Tuesday he did in rhetoric what his followers want to do in real life: he grabbed back the American Dream. When Trump said those four words, "Americans are dreamers too," he did three big things. He re-alienized the young undocumented Dreamers, defining them as something other than American. He showed his base how to dress up resentment and scapegoating in the appealing garb of aspiration and fair play. And he gave permission to anyone feeling sympathy for the undocumented to care a bit less about them because, well, "America for Americans" and "America First."

Within minutes, white nationalists were making memes on social media with his four potent words and in every meme the image is of a clean-cut, smiling white family. They heard him loud and clear. To be fair, though, it's not just white supremacists and bigots who are motivated by the moral impulse to punish perceived line-cutters. The *New York Times* had a piece recently about legal immigrants from all over the world, people of color, who are fiercely opposed to any deal that would reward undocumented people for coming here illegally.

Yet I am reminded of a conversation I recently had with an immigrant in Minnesota whose whole family—him, his wife, his children—were in the United States illegally. He was describing hard conversations with white friends and neighbors who were adamant about deporting "all the illegals." When he reminded them that he was one of those "illegals," they replied, "Well, of course we don't mean people like you."

Did I mention he's from Iceland?

Let's get real. We are all dreamers. We all dream. Working-class whites without college degrees dream of a time when being white and high school educated was enough to get a ticket to prosperity. Prosperous whites who tolerate Trump's degradation of our republic as the price to pay for a big tax cut—they also dream. Of their own innocence.

African Americans dream too, of a day (not necessarily in February) when all Americans understand that you can't know American history without embracing African American history. As the son of immigrants who by coming here made citizenship my birthright, I also dream. I dream of a day when everyone lucky enough to be born a citizen thinks about what it would take to *earn* it.

And you know who else is a dreamer? A Dreamer. I think of a member of our Youth Power Project, a high school senior named Esmerelda who is undocumented and came to the United States as a child, who kept her undocumented status private until she could no longer stand the silence and secrecy and felt she had to speak out—not only for herself but for others in her position.

When Trump says, "Americans are dreamers too," I reply that "Dreamers are Americans too." Young undocumented immigrants are of course not citizens of the United States. But what are they if not Americans? Raised on American popular culture, schooled in American schools, serving American public institutions, buying and selling in the American economy, loving and being loved by their friends and neighbors and coworkers and classmates who are, in the most everyday sense, their fellow Americans.

These two statements—"Americans are dreamers too" and "Dreamers are Americans too"—capture the perpetual tension and interplay between two dreams that have shaped and warped this country from the start. That's what I'd like to turn to next.

INSIDER AND OUTSIDER DREAMS

When we talk about the American Dream, we ought to be more precise. There are in fact two variants of the dream: one for the insider and one for the outsider.

The insider is someone already in the circle, already a member of the society who holds some relative social standing and has a desire for more. He dreams of preserving and extending the status he currently holds. He prizes security. He is loss sensitive and risk averse. He sees things in a zero-sum way, and believes that an influx of newcomers threatens to dilute his relative power and standing.

The outsider stands on the other side of the circle. She dreams of entering it, of attaining the recognition and respect that comes with being included. She hungers for equal standing and because of that hunger and the promise of great gain she is willing to take risks and to challenge the status quo. She sees things in a positive-sum way, and believes that her arrival and her presence will make the whole stronger.

Now, you might think I'm stacking the deck. And it's true that one way to see the difference and the relationship between the insider and outsider dreams is to say that immigration restrictionists and white supremacists and male chauvinists and anti-Muslim and anti-Semitic scapegoaters dream the insider dream, while immigrants and people of color and women and religious minorities dream the outsider dream.

But that's too easy.

For one thing, think about those immigrants I mentioned earlier who came to the U.S. legally, often through arduous processes and dangerous circumstances. They see themselves as having earned insider status the hard way, the proper way. It would be foolish morally and politically to dismiss their point of view.

And let's bring it home. It's not just Trumpist right-wingers who dream the insider dream. It's liberal Seattleites too, people in neighborhoods from Hillman City to Columbia City to the Central District to Ballard. People who have progressive beliefs but resent the flood of tech newcomers who are upsetting the equilibrium of relationships and customs and relative clout. It's also people of color who resent the gentrification of what had been their neighborhoods and who resist displacement and the loss of place and identity.

On the other side, meanwhile, the outsider dream is not, per se, praiseworthy or wise. Trump himself came to power selling an outsider dream against establishment insiders of both parties, and his assault on the norms of democracy and the rule of law has been marked by the sense of righteous grievance that powers every outsider movement. And left-wing outsiders sometimes issue utopian calls for an end to borders and nations altogether, forgetting that nation-states, for all their failings, are the only institutions with the moral agency and capacity to defend the weak and the outsider. And forgetting too that if you owe the same duty of care to *everyone*, you will in the end be useful to *no one*. Nations do matter, and they have a right to decide who's in them.

The question is, on what basis? On the basis of whiteness or some other inherited characteristic? Or on the basis of proven fidelity to universal values and proven contribution? Here in the United States, at least for the time being, we get to decide.

Let's recognize that we are all at various times, and often at the *same* time, acting as insiders and outsiders. Trump, in fact, is proof that these two dreams are inseparable: from the start of his national political career, he has made white insiders feel like they had been made into outsiders by bad trade deals and bad immigration deals, and so he was able to activate both their desire to protect the advantages and entitlements of being white American citizens and yet, while doing so, to feel like innocent victims.

We all have felt both these impulses: to achieve an American Dream of a house with a fence that other people can't climb over; and to achieve an American Dream of hustling your way from being a nobody to being a somebody. One focuses on accumulating and protecting your gains; the other, on having nothing to lose.

But the oldest American story is that of outsiders who do manage to hustle their way into becoming insiders and then *almost immediately* turn around to keep out the next wave of outsiders. Every generation of immigrants after the *Mayflower* has tried to pull this trick. And I'll go further. The very idea of being American has from the start been defined negatively by who could be classified as not-American.

Twenty-seven years ago, a Harvard professor of government named Judith Shklar wrote a slim book called *American Citizenship: The Quest for Inclusion*. Don't let the dry title deceive you. It is one of the most electrifying volumes I've ever read. And what it says is this: citizenship in America has never been about the Constitution first; it's been about social standing and the social recognition that citizenship confers upon a person—and about how the value of what is conferred arises from how it is denied.

What has haunted and driven this quest for standing and recognition is the presence of slavery and the descendants of the enslaved. The poor white Virginian farmer in the 1700s, the poor white New York factory worker in the 1800s, the unlettered immigrant cobbler from Italy in the 1900s: all of them lived in fear of falling to the social status of a slave. And so for them, earning the right to vote and earning the right to earn, as a free laborer, was not about fulfilling the ideals of virtuous Athenian republican citizenship. It was about earning a badge that a black person (and, for a long stretch, a Chinese person) could never earn: the badge of citizen, first-class.

Shklar puts it well: "It was the denial of suffrage to large groups of Americans," she wrote, "that made the right to vote such a mark of social standing. To be refused the right was to be almost a slave, but once one possessed the right, it conferred no other personal advantages. Not the exercise, only the right, conferred deeply."

Not the exercise, only the right. This is key, and it is the same psychological dynamic at play in the minds and hearts of those who oppose so-called "amnesty" and who don't want a DREAM Act and who would be happy to deport eleven million of our neighbors.

The people who want to kick out or keep down the undocumented aren't primarily interested in developing their own skills and capacities as citizens, in serving more or voting more or learning more; they are primarily interested in maintaining their relative status by devaluing others. In fact, if you told them that since they are special enough to be citizens of the United States, they ought to serve more or vote more or learn more or contribute more, they'd likely reply with a profanity-laced version of "Don't tread on me."

As I've said often, there are many in this country who lack the documents but live like citizens—and many who have the documents but don't. In that latter category are plenty of people who are not hard-core anti-immigrant but are what I call interested bystanders. These interested bystanders are in the 80 percent who say in polls that they support a pathway to citizenship for the Dreamers. But when that 80 percent drops to 53 percent in a hypothetical where the choice is either a DREAM Act or a government shutdown, they are among the large numbers whose support for Dreamers evaporates. They want to signal support for the outsider, until there's a trade-off. Then not so much.

I don't mean to make fun of these people of squishy principle. These interested bystanders may be the most politically important group of Americans today. If they stand by silently while nativist authoritarians take control of the machinery of state, we're done. If they stand up for decency and inclusive democracy, we still have a shot.

And so what we are called to do is to understand how the insider dream and the outsider dream are at war in their hearts—and in our own. For only by starting there can we do what I want to talk about in my final segment today, and that is to move our country toward a healthy combination of dreams and a new basis for civic status.

WHO IS US?

I've long believed that one of the core American questions is "Who is us?" We are a nation that on paper is defined by a set of creedal values available to all, but that in practice is defined by our origins in whiteness and the original sins of slavery and genocide. So who is us *today*? All American politics is a contest over that question and is about defining circles of us that have the potency to win elections and change culture.

If Judith Shklar is right that citizenship is a form of currency in the economy of status—and I believe she is—then the question is whether we can imagine—whether we can *dream up*—a different basis for social standing and identity.

There are two ways to do this, two habits of mind and heart that we all can practice as members of the community. The first is to look at what we deem to be good as if it were bad, and vice versa.

Last weekend, when we were with the first cohort of our Civic Seminary, we had them do a simple exercise. There were two maps of the United States side by side. On one, we asked them to put sticky notes with their hopes and aspirations for America. On the other, their fears and concerns. As the notes on both maps were being read aloud, one seminarian asked a simple question. What if we swapped headers?

That is, what if we moved the Hopes and Aspirations sign above the map with all the fears and concerns, and moved the Fears and Concerns sign above the map with all the hopes and aspirations? This was mind-blowing. Because it forced us to stretch our conception of the good and the bad and the us for whom anything would be good or bad.

Under Hopes and Aspirations had been posted ideas like:

- The "Common Good" becomes a common idea
- Confronting our collective addiction to racism, sexism, and classism
- Accountability for the impact of our choices and actions on others and the environment

Seeing these ideas now as things to fear, as reasons for concern, made us step into the shoes of those who might see it that way. What was potentially oppressive about talk of the common good? How did people feel misunderstood, even attacked by the very premise that society is addicted to racism, sexism, and classism?

Conversely, under Fears and Concerns had been posted ideas like:

- Not being able to bring diverse voices to the table
- Historical amnesia
- Climate catastrophe

And here it wasn't just about trying to empathize with those who might actively welcome such things but also about seeing why, even believing these things to be threats, you too could reframe them as opportunities. A climate catastrophe, for example, might be the only thing that forces the widespread changes in policy and behavior that are needed to protect humanity.

What made the experiment of swapping our dreams and nightmares so useful was that it opened up possible ways to bring others into a sense of belonging and recognition. It opened up the possibility of asking the interested bystander who wants to be seen as inclusive but is also drawn to the politics of exclusion: What are you afraid will happen if we go down the path of inclusion? What do you mistrust about the outsider's dream? We can ask this at the level of our city and the level of our country.

From there it is possible to say to this other American dreamer: *We share a fear about not being respected. We share a fear of being taken advantage of. We share a fear about being isolated and picked off by those who have organized to exploit us.* And as we share fears so can we share hopes. The combination of your hope and mine diminishes neither. That was the message of Frederick Douglass's astonishing and little-appreciated speech in defense of Chinese immigration. "Right wrongs no man."

And this brings me to the second way to change the basis for standing and identity in America, which is to acknowledge the universal reflex to define oneself against others—and to channel that impulse in a more constructive direction. To put it simply, my message for people who want to scapegoat Mexican immigrants or Muslims for their troubles isn't "Stop scapegoating." It's "You've got the wrong scapegoat."

Massive corporations and monopolies that have punished local labor by globalizing capital, while rigging the compensation game for executives into a heads-I-win-tails-you-lose proposition—*that's* your scapegoat. Ten or eleven corporations and the members of Congress they own have done more damage to the American worker in the last few decades than ten or eleven million undocumented immigrants, the great bulk of whom are doing the work that most white and black Americans think is beneath them.

I don't see the former machinists of the Rust Belt or the former coal miners of Appalachia rushing to the Central Valley of California to pick the crops that are rotting on the vine now, thanks to a post-Trump shortage of migrant workers. Nor do I see them organizing at scale in labor unions or other worker-power associations to push back against organized corporate money.

You want standing and recognition? You don't get it on the cheap with a fraud like Trump promising walls built of bullshit. You earn it. It's time for any American who feels disenfranchised to stop acting like you are entitled by birth to be an insider and to bring an outsider's hustle to claim your place and to overcome the game-riggers. The game-rigging elites who preach trickle-down economics but practice upward distribution of wealth—*that's* your scapegoat. That's the proper focus for your fury.

Once we get the scapegoat right, it is possible to build a bigger, more inclusive circle of *us*. This *us* is made of people who work for a living, as opposed to those who move capital around and treat people as costs to be cut. This *us* is made of people who won't be divided and conquered by the old playbook of stoking white fear or zero-sum resentments among people of color. This *us* is also made of people who get out of the posture of learned helplessness and who choose to become literate in power—who understand how to move and change political and economic systems—and who take responsibility for building cross-racial coalitions of countervailing people power.

When Trump first started saying "Make America Great Again," people assumed he was looking back to the 1950s, before globalization, before the Civil Rights Movement and feminism and gay rights, before the apex of the American empire. But it turns out we had the decade wrong. His most malevolent advisers and allies admire the *1920s*. It was in the 1920s—after mass immigration from Southern and Eastern Europe, after a cataclysmic World War that highlighted the dangers of global engagement, after a surge of socialist and anarchist and revolutionary activism in the United States—it was then that the Klan came back strong, that nativists took over the United States government, and that a nakedly racist system of immigration quotas and exclusion became the law.

But cultural protectionism, like economic protectionism, buys its beneficiaries only a temporary and artificial sense that they've become better off. Then it collapses on itself. Walls will always get bypassed—from above, from below, from all around. In the twenties, everyone built a wall, from the domino sequence of national tariffs to the French folly of the Maginot Line, which Germany sidestepped by rolling through the Low Countries. By the thirties and forties, the entire world was on fire.

The 1820s teach us the same lesson. John C. Calhoun didn't live to see the fire but fire surely consumed his beloved slaveholding South. His views are repugnant and they are deeply American. Calhoun, whom the historian Richard Hofstadter dubbed "the Marx of the master class," perceived with Marxist acuity that the material and psychological stability of the South was dependent entirely on its peculiar solution to the problem of labor costs. But Calhoun had fooled himself into thinking this was actual stability and that it could last forever. It wasn't, and it couldn't. It was disturbed not by the interference of outsiders but by its own internal contradictions.

If we don't want the 2020s to look like the 1920s or 1820s, we'd better build a bigger story of us—one that combines the insider's dream of *security* and the outsider's dream of *opportunity* and both their desires for *dignity*. Where a populism of the left can counter a populism of the right and yield a populism of the decent, of the striving contributor, of those willing to earn their citizenship in every sense.

Let me close with another passage from Douglass's "The Composite Nation" speech:

We shall spread the network of our science and civilization over all who seek their shelter whether from Asia, Africa, or the Isles of the sea. We shall mold them all, each after his kind, into Americans; Indian and Celt; Negro and Saxon; Latin and Teuton; Mongolian and Caucasian; Jew and Gentile; all shall here bow to the same law, speak the same language, support the same Government, enjoy the same liberty, vibrate with the same national enthusiasm, and seek the same national ends.

Imagine an America where a fair shot has replaced a white face as the standard for participation, where contribution rather than consumption is the measure of civic status, and where the only individuals we treat as second class are those who want to treat entire groups as second class.

Or, in the alternative, imagine an America that is basically contemporary Russia or the old Confederacy: an oligarchy, with a thin crust of stolen wealth at the top and the deep rot of surrendered hopes and habituated obedience beneath.

Which nation do you dream of belonging to? Which kind of Dreamer do you want to be? Decide. Declare yourself. And with the people surrounding you now, and those you know who still stand on the sidelines, bring that country into being.

14.

BECOME AMERICA

The Basement East · Nashville, TN
March 31, 2018

EXCERPTS FROM THE RECONSTRUCTION
AMENDMENTS TO THE UNITED STATES CONSTITUTION

Thirteenth Amendment
Ratified on December 6, 1865

Section 1. Neither slavery nor involuntary servitude, except as a
punishment for crime whereof the party shall have been duly
convicted, shall exist within the United States, or any place
subject to their jurisdiction.

Fourteenth Amendment
Ratified on July 9, 1868

Section 1. All persons born or naturalized in the United States, and subject to the jurisdiction thereof, are citizens of the United States and of the State wherein they reside. . . .

Fifteenth Amendment
Ratified on February 3, 1870

Section 1. The right of citizens of the United States to vote shall not be denied or abridged by the United States or by any State on account of race, color, or previous condition of servitude.

W. E. B. DU BOIS
Excerpt from The Souls of Black Folk
Published 1903

Your country? How came it yours? Before the Pilgrims landed we were here. Here we have brought our three gifts and mingled them with yours: a gift of story and song—soft, stirring melody in an ill-harmonized and unmelodious land; the gift of sweat and brawn to beat back the wilderness, conquer the soil, and lay the foundations of this vast economic empire two hundred years earlier than your weak hands could have done it; the third, a gift of the Spirit. . . . Actively we have woven ourselves with the very warp and woof of this nation,—we fought their battles, shared their sorrow, mingled our blood with theirs, and generation after generation have pleaded with a headstrong, careless people to despise not Justice, Mercy, and Truth, lest the nation be smitten with a curse. Our song, our toil, our cheer, and warning have been given to this nation in blood-brotherhood. Are not these gifts worth the giving? Is not this work and striving? Would America have been America without her Negro people?

ANN PATCHETT
Excerpt from This Is the Story of a Happy Marriage
Published 2013

Forgiveness. The ability to forgive oneself. Stop here for a few breaths and think about this because it is the key to making art, and very possibly the key to finding any semblance of happiness in life. Every time I have set out to translate the book (or story, or hopelessly long essay) that exists in such brilliant detail on the big screen of my limbic system onto a piece of paper (which, let's face it, was once a towering tree crowned with leaves and a home to birds), I grieve for my own lack of talent and intelligence. Every. Single. Time. Were I smarter, more gifted, I could pin down a closer facsimile of the wonders I see. I believe, more than anything, that this grief of constantly having to face down our own inadequacies is what keeps people from being writers. Forgiveness, therefore, is key. I can't write the book I want to write, but I can and will write the book I am capable of writing. Again and again throughout the course of my life I will forgive myself.

My parents were immigrants who came from China by way of Taiwan. I'm from New York by way of Seattle. But I know a thing or two about the Volunteer State. I know, for instance, why your flag has three stars—for East, Middle, and West Tennessee; each region with its own folkways and feeling and topography. And while this is my first time in Middle Tennessee, it occurs to me that on my last two trips to the state I went to some significant sites in East and West Tennessee. Let me tell you about them.

Six years ago, the University of Tennessee chose my book *The Accidental Asian* to be the text that all incoming first-year students had to read and discuss. It's not every day that an SEC school makes everyone read a Chinese American's reflections on race and identity. The best part of that visit was speaking to the five or six thousand students in Thompson-Boling Arena, that cathedral of hoops where the Volunteers and Lady Vols have made sports history so many times. I tried to get those young men and women to channel their pride for Tennessee and for America into a vision of our country's purpose that's about inclusion and diversity not as kindness or political correctness but as the way to field the strongest possible team. To win on the court. They were into it. By the end, they were cheering for these ideas. It's the closest this five-foot-four dude is ever going to get to basketball glory.

Then last year, across the state in Memphis, I had a very different experience. I was meeting with educators from a nonprofit called Facing History and Ourselves. Facing History is based in Boston but their Memphis offices, I discovered, are across from the Lorraine Motel, where Martin Luther King Jr. was assassinated. He was on the balcony of Room 306 when James Earl Ray murdered him at 6:05 pm on April 4, 1968: fifty years ago, next Wednesday. As some of you know, when you stand before the Lorraine Motel on a quiet afternoon, you are transported: not to the past but to a future that was also assassinated that night; an alternate reality that never got to unfurl. The motel is now the National Civil Rights Museum and to stand there on Mulberry Street is to stand on ground that is civically sacred: sacralized by sacrifice, by bloody loss, but also by the promise, unmet but still unextinguished, a promise of rebirth and redemption.

When I say "civically sacred," I mean it. We are gathered here today in this hip venue for something we call Civic Saturday, which we describe, perhaps unhiply, as a civic analogue to church or synagogue. And because we are gathering on what turns out to be Holy Saturday and the second day of Passover, I want to say a word about what this is and isn't. Civic Saturday is *not* church or synagogue or mosque. But it is about American *civic* religion: the *creed* of liberty and equal justice stated at the founding of this nation; the record of *deeds* that have fitfully, unevenly brought those values to fruition; and *rituals* that memorialize and revivify those deeds.

We give Civic Saturday the shape of a faith gathering because democracy itself is an act of faith. We believe that in American civic life, as much as in anyone's faith life, it's vital not just to revere words on a page but to live up to them. To *embody* in practice a professed *spirit* of love and responsibility. This is why we sing together, why we talk with the strangers beside us, why we hear spoken word and readings of what you might call civic scripture, and why, with a music stand as my pulpit, I call this talk a sermon.

We've launched a Civic Seminary to train dozens of people from small towns and large to lead their own Civic Saturdays. And for weeks, I've been excited to be in this town and in this joint. Nashville is not just the capital of country music. It's a repository of American *memory*, encoded in song and Grand Ole structures. It's powered by a *motivation* to convert pain and longing into beauty and glory. And it's a place where people can reinvent themselves—be reborn, or at least get a *makeover*.

Well, today I'd like to reflect on these three themes—memory, motives, and makeovers—and how they shape our sense of civic purpose in America.

MEMORY

My father, Chao-hua Liu, was born in Nanjing, China, in 1936. He and his family fled to Taiwan in 1949, when the Communists won the Chinese civil war. He came to the United States in 1958 to go to college at the University of Illinois. He worked for IBM his entire career, climbing up middle management in Poughkeepsie, New York. He was diagnosed with end-stage kidney disease in 1976 and began home dialysis in 1977. He did that for fourteen years until he died suddenly in 1991 at the age of fifty-four. All those years, he had let only a few people know he was ill.

My dad had often been sick as a kid too, and spent long childhood days in the sickbed reading Chinese poetry and the Chinese classics. When he came to America, he was a sponge for new texts: the texts of American culture. And he passed down to me everything he had absorbed. Though I was the one born here, *he* introduced *me* to Hank Williams and Elvis. He taught me the rules of basketball and boxing, and led me to admire Dr. J and Muhammad Ali but not Isiah Thomas and Sugar Ray Leonard, whom he mistrusted. Dale Carnegie and Donald Trump were on his bookshelf, alongside those Chinese classics. He delighted in Rodney Dangerfield. He shared late-night jokes about Gerald Ford and Jimmy Carter and Dan Quayle.

My primary memories of my dad are of him laughing uproariously—he had a mischievous, corny sense of humor—or of him thinking hard before explaining something—he had a clarity of thought and expression that was layers deeper than English or Mandarin. This was a gift. For most of our time together, he was profoundly sick and he knew that his sickness would shorten his life. Yet my memories are not of his sickness or sadness or bitterness. He almost never showed any despair and he left no evidence of it—except, perhaps, one ambiguous fragment. After he died, I was going through his old jackets and found in the inner pocket of one a folded sheet of paper on which he had scribbled the lyrics of Hank Williams's "I'm So Lonesome I Could Cry."

What was the meaning of that? My eye went immediately to the line: "That means he's lost the will to live." Was this his private, folded-up cry of anguish? But then my eye went to another line: "The silence of a falling star/Lights up a purple sky." And I remembered Hank Williams originally wrote this song as a spoken word piece, without a melody. And I realized that the poet and wordsmith in my father might have appreciated the song just for its spare beauty and craft.

I don't know. I won't ever know. If I wanted to, I could construct from that secondhand material an elaborate narrative about how the loneliness of American life made my father recall the pangs of the old Chinese poets, and that Hank Williams sang that echo aloud for him. But that would be my story. It'd be a monument to my emotions and perceptions, not his. The true way to honor my father's memory is not to enshrine it in a myth that reveals more about me than about him. It is to live my life and inform my child's life with the useful and helpful parts of my father's ethical DNA—his determination, yes, but maybe not the denialism that left our family unprepared when he passed; his courage, yes, but maybe not his prideful secrecy.

How do we prune and splice our ethical DNA? I've been thinking about this because Nashville has been reckoning with memory, personal and collective, and with the meaning of monuments. I am inspired by your new mayor's proposal to nix a private development at Fort Negley and instead create a public park that would honor the enslaved African Americans conscripted by the Union Army into building a Union fort there. Hundreds of black men died in that endeavor, not as freedmen or heroes but as confiscated property. As slaves whose labor was commandeered by their would-be liberators. Complicated, isn't it? This planned park would do more than counterbalance the Confederate statues or street names elsewhere in town; it would rewrite and redraw in more than black and white what Toni Morrison called "rememory"—the memory of a memory, which is another way of saying *identity*.

You know that this state was divided from east to west on whether to join the Confederacy. You know that more battles of the Civil War were fought in Tennessee than in any other state. You know that the Battle of Nashville essentially ended the war in this state and that after the war Tennessee became the first Southern state to ratify the Fourteenth Amendment and the first to rejoin the Union. You know that Andrew Johnson was a senator from this state and, as a War Democrat, became military governor here and then Lincoln's vice president. You know that *President* Johnson, in a rush to reunion with the South, undermined Reconstruction and betrayed the freedmen and vetoed the Civil Rights Act of 1866 and was overridden and then impeached—150 years ago this very week, in fact—by a Republican Congress frustrated that Lincoln's former deputy would turn out to be such a friend of the unreconstructed Confederacy and a foe of black aspirations to citizenship. You know that in 1869 Tennessee rejected the Fifteenth Amendment, which gave ex-slaves the vote—and didn't ratify it until *1997.* You know that Tennessee put the Nineteenth Amendment over the top in 1920, and that women in the United States got the vote because a young state legislator, Harry Burn from McMinn County, got a call from his mother telling him to change his vote.

You do know all this, right?

What do you do then with this knowledge, with all this rememory? This state is soaked in blood and self-justification. Some of you can draw family trees right through that blood. Others of you are immigrants here, whether from abroad or from, say, San Francisco. What do you choose to remember? What song do you mix out of these cacophonous samples? Some in the White House want to weaponize nostalgia in the service of white supremacy. Some in white households want memory to be a swaddling blanket of racial innocence, so that they can continue to enjoy the privilege of not having to confront their privilege. But others, like your white male mayor, want Nashville and Tennessee and the South and the North to grow up. To face history and ourselves.

That starts with letting go of some things. Recently I read a moving essay by Sallie Tisdale about what caring for Alzheimer's patients has taught her. She's learned that when loved ones of the demented (that's the word she uses) get angry or frustrated with their demented mother, for instance, they are ignoring what's truly happening. That mother may be losing her memory and her patterns of behavior may be shifting but she is not losing her capacity for feeling or awareness or consciousness. She is simply becoming something else, *which was always happening anyway.* The child drew security and identity from the illusion that the parent was unchanging. The end of that illusion makes the child sad. But the mother isn't necessarily sad. She just is. She is experiencing life *now.* And if the child could let go of her fixed story of what the parent was and must forever be—the way, for instance, a caregiver is able to—then perhaps that child can find some grace in watching how this transformed, newborn adult moves and learns and communicates.

As it is with a family, so it is with a polity. Tisdale writes: "When we say *She's not my mother anymore,* we mean she is not the mother she used to be, the mother we remember." Before us is ambiguity and flux. Do we see only catastrophe or can we imagine creation? We choose how to see. That is the case with an aging elder. It is true of a region like Middle Tennessee that either will or will not bring itself to break out of the patterns of a segregated, stratified past. It is true for a diversifying nation that must decide whether making itself great again means welcoming or punishing immigrants, including or excluding people of color, seeing or not seeing religious minorities, LGBTQ people, the poor and disabled and the disfavored. Who is the *we* in *we the people?*

This is why what Mayor Briley is doing to create this new park is more than a mere gesture of compensatory justice. It is an invitation to every citizen of Nashville to let go of a zero-sum way of thinking—the mindset that says if black lives matter then white lives must not; that the only alternative to domination must be subjugation. It is a reminder that a bigger story of us is possible, one that contains the past in all its complexity and faces the future in all *its* complexity and simplifies that complexity with the throughline that is neither domination nor subjugation but is *equality of dignity.*

Can we deal with that? To grow up civically means being candid about our own deep emotional drives. Why do we act as we do? What are we afraid of? Are we trying to hide pain? To avoid responsibility? To hoard power and authority? To shirk shame? To sabotage ourselves or others? The ardent defenders of the statues of Sam Davis or Nathan Bedford Forrest, Confederate soldier and general, respectively, are often guilty of acting out like adolescents. But so sometimes are their critics. In politics today, we don't really see or fight each other. Whether trolling on Facebook or shouting across a square at the capitol, it's more like we have avatars in a video game who are engaged in ritual combat, where the weapons are narratives and the goal is annihilation, while we, the actual humans playing this game at a virtual remove, don't know our own minds and can't plumb our own hearts.

Which brings me to my second theme this morning: naming our motives.

MOTIVES

The three Reconstruction Amendments to the Constitution of the United States form a pretty good case study of clouded and manipulated motivations. The standard history textbook tells a simple story about the intentions behind each. The Thirteenth Amendment was meant to end slavery. The Fourteenth Amendment was meant to give ex-slaves citizenship. The Fifteenth Amendment was to give ex-slaves the franchise.

Those readings are true, as far as they go. But they don't go far enough.

The Thirteenth Amendment, as the filmmaker Ava DuVernay points out in her documentary *13th*, banned involuntary servitude (Yay!) "except as a punishment for crime" (What?) and through that clause came the Black Codes and the Jim Crow laws and the perfectly legal systems for prosecuting the formerly enslaved on trumped-up charges like "vagrancy" and sending them back into systems of industrial bondage that gave rise to the modern-day complex of mass incarceration. Out of that clause—"except as a punishment for crime"—bloomed the malevolent motivations of white supremacists to remain supreme and to enact slavery by another name.

Well, how about the Fourteenth Amendment? It says that "all persons born or naturalized in the United States, and subject to the jurisdiction thereof, are citizens of the United States." Correct. But not just them. A generation after the Civil War, a laborer named Wong Kim Ark, born in San Francisco to Chinese immigrant parents, went to China to visit relatives and when he tried to come back to San Francisco the authorities barred him because the Chinese Exclusion Act of 1882 was in effect. But Wong said, "I'm not a foreigner. I'm an American. I was born here and the Fourteenth Amendment makes me a citizen." And the Supreme Court reluctantly had to agree. The plain language of the amendment was clear: birthright citizenship for all.

Except. Except for that phrase "subject to the jurisdiction thereof." At the time, the Reconstruction Republicans who drafted that language explained that this phrase was meant to exclude from birthright citizenship Native Americans and foreign diplomats or visitors, all of whom had allegiances to other sovereign jurisdictions. But today, nativist anti-immigrant activists, haunted by the specter of so-called "anchor babies" and "chain migration," want to repeal birthright citizenship for the children of undocumented immigrants. They argue that immigrants who came here illegally, no matter how long they have lived and worked here and raised families here, remain subject to the jurisdiction of, say, Mexico, and that their children born here cannot count as citizens. They argue, in short, that the sin and stigma of the father must be passed on to the son.

Today that is a minority view in the legal community. But there is a right-wing legal and political machine dedicated to making it mainstream. And the question for everyday Americans now is not so much how to decode legislative history and constitutional law but rather whether we like the basic motives behind this push. Is the motive to define American narrowly around a white core—a motive of fear and scarcity and chauvinism—itself un-American?

A cynic might say, no, it's as American as motherhood and apple pie. There were many mothers who thought that when the Fifteenth Amendment was being debated. Here too is a case of hidden meanings and lawyerly silences. The right to vote "shall not be denied or abridged . . . on account of race, color, or previous condition of servitude." Sounds like an unimpeachably good thing. We hear it as a guarantee to ex-slaves that they'll have the right to vote. But it's not. Nowhere in the Constitution is there any affirmative right to vote. The Fifteenth Amendment says the right to vote can't be denied because of race. But it *can* be denied for plenty of other reasons. It *can* be denied, for instance, because of failure to pass a literacy test or to make the poll tax payments that became the preferred legal method of Southern states to keep blacks out of the ballot box. And guess what else: it could be denied on the basis of sex.

There was a great debate about this in 1869. The wording of the Fifteenth was crafted intentionally to allow states to keep women from voting. Suffragists pushed Congress to add, after "on account of race or color," the words "or sex." They failed. They were laughed out of the chamber. Which is why some of them resented and even resisted the extension of the franchise to blacks. And that's why suffrage activists had to spend *fifty* more years organizing and advocating until they could push through their own amendment, the Nineteenth, in 1920.

The most remarkable thing about U.S. citizenship is that it has never been defined. The Constitution uses the word "citizen" but never explains it. The Fourteenth Amendment created a new status called "citizens of the United States"—superior to citizenship of a state—and made it a birthright with "privileges and immunities." But it did not spell out what that meant. And even these vague protections were undermined right away by the Gilded Age Supreme Court and a Congress weary of Reconstruction. From that time onward, citizenship has been defined mainly in the negative. By exclusion. By saying, *This person cannot claim citizenship. This person "has no rights a white man is bound to respect,"* to use the infamous words of the *Dred Scott* decision.

In short, to be a citizen of the United States has mainly meant to be not *not* a citizen. It's a club whose sole apparent purpose is to deny certain people membership. It's a club in another sense as well—a cudgel to keep certain people down.

Consider the current controversy about the Census. As you may have heard, the Trump administration announced this week that for the first time in seventy years, the U.S. Census is going to ask people whether they are citizens. Now, many of you might think, what's wrong with that? Seems reasonable.

What's wrong is the motive behind the question. That motive is intimidation. Intimidate immigrants, documented or not, and make them hide from the Census. Which means there will be an undercount of Hispanics and Asians and Muslims. Which means Congressional apportionment and state legislative redistricting can proceed as if America were whiter and older and more Republican than it is or may ever be again. This president and his enablers among the GOP leadership look at the changing demographics of our nation, look at the rising progressivism of young people, and figure, *If you can't beat 'em and you don't want to join 'em, then don't count 'em.*

Do I have proof of this motive? Not in a smoking gun statement from the commerce secretary, who's responsible for managing the Census. But I have it in the way he overruled experts from both parties who warn that asking the citizenship question will distort the results. I have it in the record of the words and deeds of his boss, the president. I have it in the sympathy that Donald Trump expresses for those who seek a blood-and-soil American identity based on whiteness and Christianity and origins on our territory. I have it in the bad faith way he makes promises.

Some of my friends on the right say I'm overstating the danger. But I invite them to consider how they'd respond if the Census were suddenly to ask about gun ownership. Then they will sympathize rather quickly with the fear that the machinery of state might be deployed to intimidate and stigmatize and to create a registry of who and what can be rounded up and confiscated on a moment's notice.

Motive matters. And it is all pretty simple. If your motive is to exclude, to hoard, to try to block the future from happening, then you should lose. American history is a record of groups of people fighting that exclusion, challenging that hoarding, opening the gates to the future. American history is a record of small groups of people who keep remaking this country over and over, and who reveal to us all that the perpetual remaking is the greatest statement of fidelity to our creed and our national purpose, which is not to be like Russia, white and stagnant and oligarchic, or like China, monoethnic and authoritarian and centralized, but to be more like America, hybrid and dynamic and democratic and free to be remade.

You know how we do that? We show up. We join clubs. We start clubs. We build citizen muscle. We learn how to read and write power, starting in our local communities. We learn how to practice civic character in gatherings like this. We register. We register others. We vote. Because there is no such thing as not voting. Not voting *is* voting to hand your power to someone who despises and will use it against you. We ask disarming questions. We listen. We make friends. We make trouble, what John Lewis calls *good* trouble. We make this country live up to its promises by starting with ourselves. We *realize* this country by making it more possible for more people more of the time to participate in and contribute to the simple miracle of self-government.

That's my motive. What's yours? Do you live to exclude or include, to hoard or to circulate, to leech or to feed? Be honest. Do you believe it's every man for himself—or do you believe we're all better off when we're all better off? Careful: both beliefs are self-fulfilling. You behave like you believe. Then society becomes how you behave. It's only by looking with clear eyes at what really drives our choices—not what we say, what we will tell a pollster or a neighbor—that we open the possibility of truth, reconciliation, and civic renewal. And that's my third theme today: how to make ourselves anew.

MAKEOVERS

So, the other day my wife and I watched an episode of *Queer Eye* on Netflix. It's a revival of the series from the early 2000s in which a quintet of stereotypically stylish gay men perform an extreme makeover on a hetero man who needs serious help with his wardrobe, home furnishings, diet, and grooming. Jená was watching it and as I walked through the TV room I scoffed at her and the whole idea and then I sat down and then I stayed and forty minutes later we were both wiping tears off our faces.

This episode featured Tom, a fifty-seven-year-old, thrice-divorced man from Dallas, Georgia—a guy with a ZZ Top beard, a uniform of baseball cap and red shirt and jean shorts, and a diet of beef burritos and what he called "redneck margaritas." His warning at the start was, "You can't fix ugly." But gradually, and cheerfully, Tom changed. He traded the cap for a knit hat, the jean shorts for khakis, the stained recliner for a his-and-hers pair of chairs, ZZ Top for Ulysses S. Grant. In the end, he wooed a woman named Abby—his most recent ex-wife, whom he said he had never stopped loving—and she responded.

I cried, not so much at Tom's physical transformation, which was great, but at his openhearted willingness to be transformed. To make friends. His readiness to being guided by his Fab Five counselors, and his readiness—when they asked without judgment—to acknowledge his pain and fear and loneliness and shame, all of which had led him to be stuck for twelve years in a loop of numbed avoidance and beef burritos. I realized, that's most of America. That's most of us here today. In a lonely habit of numbed avoidance.

That episode of that silly show moved me so deeply because it showed me a man willing to forgive himself. It's like your Nashville neighbor Ann Patchett says: there's a chasm between the life we imagine on the big screen of our limbic system and the life that unfolds in our measurable little habits. That applies to the nation as it does to the person. Forgive the gap. Then we might have a shot at closing it.

But remember: extreme makeovers are temporary made-for-TV spectacles. The slog, the shift by degrees, is what most of life is. Tom's time on *Queer Eye* reminded me that a citizenship based on feeling and admitting grief is better than one based on avoiding and stifling it. A citizenship based on reckoning with the ugly, whether it's fixable or not, is what we are called to practice now. And our ancestors can show us how.

In 1885, a bright young man from Great Barrington, Massachusetts, came down to Nashville to study at Fisk University. He would graduate in three years and go on from there to Harvard for graduate school and to Germany, where he studied further, and then to Atlanta, where he taught and helped found the National Association for the Advancement of Colored People. His name was William Edward Burghardt Du Bois.

The years that W. E. B. Du Bois spent in Tennessee changed his life. His time at Fisk planted in his mind the idea of the "talented tenth"— that a black elite had a responsibility to serve all black Americans. His time here also gave a sheltered Northern boy his first exposure to Jim Crow in the raw, and to the daily degradations most blacks in the South had to bear. He left feeling more responsible for the deliverance of this nation.

Du Bois would come to renown as a great social scientist, pioneering methods of studying the African American experience that are still influential today. But his time in Tennessee shaped him on the spirit level. It was out of this experience—at Fisk, and in the small towns outside Nashville where he taught unlettered, unshod black kids how to read and write—that he wrote his classic work *The Souls of Black Folk*. What made that book a classic is that he told a story of resilience and persistence and claiming and unacknowledged authorship of the country—and he told that tale using a prose that was like poetry, using music instead of math.

This was a work of American civic religion. A work that promises no makeovers, only the slog. And maybe a reason or two to keep slogging.

At the head of every chapter Du Bois printed a few bars of the "sorrow songs," spirituals and other ancient songs that black Americans had used as a salve for their suffering and a source of hope for the possibility of rebirth and liberation. But in the text of every chapter he made clear just how hard liberation would be—how liberation from old ways and old identities had failed at the institutional level after the Civil War because it had failed at the imaginative level. The fatigue that set in, the way that the Freedmen's Bureau lost its will and its way as Reconstruction crumbled, the way the Confederacy struck back, was not a failure of bureaucracy. It was a failure of empathy.

As the century closed, white Americans North and South just wanted to get rich. New European immigrants arrived and figured out that the way to be called white instead of foreign was to put down blacks. None of them wanted to imagine the formerly enslaved as people like them. And through it all, black women and men kept living and dying and remaking Nashville and Davidson County and Tennessee and the United States.

"Through all the sorrow of the Sorrow Songs," writes Du Bois, "there breathes a hope—a faith in the ultimate justice of things. The minor cadences of despair change often to triumph and calm confidence. Sometimes it is faith in life, sometimes a faith in death, sometimes assurance of boundless justice in some fair world beyond. But whichever it is, the meaning is always clear: that sometime, somewhere, men will judge men by their souls and not by their skins. Is such a hope justified? Do the Sorrow Songs sing true?"

We haven't yet answered those questions. Trumpian nationalists want an America that is whiter and more Anglo and less foreign. And in the near term they may be able to deport Salvadorans and Liberians and Syrians and Iranians and to demonize black and Mexican and Chinese people. But sooner or later, as the sorrow songs teach us, they will not be able to stem the tide of diversity and impurity that is America and that has been America for "thrice a hundred years," as Du Bois put it.

There is no such thing as an extreme makeover, though we pretend for the sake of narrative that there is. Trump's America is still, to a large extent, Obama's America. *Roseanne* 2018 is deeply like *Roseanne* 1998. When the *Queer Eye* cameras left, some of Tom's bad habits surely returned. Yet his original willingness to grow and be vulnerable—I bet that remains. Deep structure, like it or not, endures. A structural tilt toward racism. A structural bent for justice. All that was good about yesterday has not been extinguished and all that is bad about today didn't just arrive.

BECOME AMERICA

Let me close with a note about music. My wife and I recently went to hear the Seattle Symphony perform the world premiere of a piece by John Luther Adams called *Become Desert*. It was the companion to a piece he'd composed in 2014 called *Become Ocean*, which won the Pulitzer Prize. Neither piece has traditional musical narrative or structure; they are more like sound baths of rolling thunder and dew drops with whorls of water and fauna unfolding. They are like nature itself: immersive, random, patterned, and chaotic. I felt this music in my body, the way I felt democracy in my body when I was marching with half a hundred thousand others in the March for Our Lives last Saturday. If Walt Whitman could score symphonies about the self-regenerating multitudes of American life, it might sound like these compositions.

I tell you about *Become Ocean* and *Become Desert* because it is Easter tomorrow. It is Passover now. It is four days before Dr. King dies again. Listen. Open your hearts, your ears, your eyes. Question your memories, your motives, your impulse to make yourself over. The souls of American folk will be saved not by church or synagogue or mosque alone. They will be saved also by simple civic habits of forbearance and friendship and openness and love. It's time to become humble.

To become responsible. To become faithful to our creed. To become curious about what else, what other music, we might make together.

It is time—it is long past time—to become America.

15.

TIME TRAVEL

Northwest African American Museum · Seattle, WA
April 28, 2018

BRYAN STEVENSON
From Just Mercy
Published 2014

Proximity has taught me some basic and humbling truths, including this vital lesson: Each of us is more than the worst thing we've ever done. My work with the poor and the incarcerated has persuaded me that the opposite of poverty is not wealth; the opposite of poverty is justice. Finally, I've come to believe that the true measure of our commitment to justice, the character of our society, our commitment to the rule of law, fairness, and equality cannot be measured by how we treat the rich, the powerful, the privileged, and the respected among us. The true measure of our character is how we treat the poor, the disfavored, the accused, the incarcerated, and the condemned.

JAMES WELDON JOHNSON

"Lift Every Voice and Sing"
Written 1900, set to music 1902

Lift every voice and sing
Till earth and heaven ring,
Ring with the harmonies of Liberty;
Let our rejoicing rise
High as the listening skies,
Let it resound loud as the rolling sea.
Sing a song full of the faith that the dark past has taught us,
Sing a song full of the hope that the present has brought us.
Facing the rising sun of our new day begun
Let us march on till victory is won.

Stony the road we trod,
Bitter the chastening rod,
Felt in the days when hope unborn had died;
Yet with a steady beat,
Have not our weary feet
Come to the place for which our fathers sighed?
We have come over a way that with tears has been watered,
We have come, treading our path through the blood of the
slaughtered,
Out from the gloomy past,
Till now we stand at last
Where the white gleam of our bright star is cast.

God of our weary years,
God of our silent tears,
Thou who has brought us thus far on the way;
Thou who has by Thy might
Led us into the light,
Keep us forever in the path, we pray.

Lest our feet stray from the places, our God, where we met
Thee,
Lest, our hearts drunk with the wine of the world, we forget
Thee;
Shadowed beneath Thy hand,
May we forever stand.
True to our God,
True to our native land.

PAULI MURRAY
From "An American Credo"
Published 1945

I do not intend to destroy segregation by physical force. I
hope to see it destroyed by a power greater than all the robot
bombs and explosives of human creation—by a power of the
spirit, an appeal to the intelligence of man, a laying hold of the
creative and dynamic impulses within the minds of men. The
great poets and prophets have heralded this method; Christ,
Thoreau, and Gandhi have demonstrated it. I intend to do my
part through the power of persuasion, by spiritual resistance,
by the power of the pen, and by inviting the violence upon
my own body.

I am so moved to be here today at the Northwest African American Museum because two days ago in Montgomery, Alabama, a remarkable cousin to this institution opened its gates to the public. It's called the National Memorial for Peace and Justice but everyone has been referring to it as "the lynching museum."

The National Memorial is the brainchild of the lawyer Bryan Stevenson, founder of the Equal Justice Initiative and celebrated defender of death row inmates. It honors the thousands of African American men and women lynched by white citizens in the nineteenth and twentieth centuries. It forces our country to see that white supremacy is a system not only of laws but of social norms, and that for every white American who ever put a noose around the neck of an innocent black American or set that swinging body on fire or sliced off its appendages, there were hundreds more white bystanders who stood in the crowd in their Sunday best smiling for the camera.

Many of them still walk the earth today.

That memorial in Montgomery, like this museum here in Seattle, is testament to the fact that in the journey of truth and reconciliation, truth must come first. That memorial, like this museum, challenges us not just to face the past truthfully but also to see, as Faulkner said, that the past is not even past. It is with us, like a second self.

I've been thinking a lot about how truth travels through time. This morning, in fact, I was thinking about how it has become something of a convention, almost a cliché, at least in more progressive spaces, to open gatherings like this with a solemn statement of acknowledgment that we stand on Native lands and we remember the Duwamish and the other first peoples who claimed this place long before us.

When this started happening at events and conferences a few years ago, I thought it was stirring and appropriate. Lately, though, I am finding this gesture to be unsatisfying. And a little bit dishonest. This land is not in fact Native land anymore. It is land that was appropriated—let's say it plainly—*stolen* by white people, through force and legal subterfuge, from the Native peoples who were its earliest inhabitants.

That's the truth. And the question is: What, if anything, are we going to do with the truth? Most of the time, the solemn acknowledgment is followed by a quiet pause and then on to the business at hand. The better way to honor Native communities, I think, is not to say for show that this is still their land; it is to acknowledge that their ancestors were dispossessed of this land and that all of us who live here today have some obligation beyond words to address that. To make amends. To help reduce the inequities of health, education, and opportunity that have flowed from that history of dispossession.

This is the spirit of what Bryan Stevenson has created in Alabama. He draws a thick, unbroken line between the state-sponsored terrorism that was the Jim Crow lynch mob and the system of mass incarceration of black and brown people today. His day job is about repairing today's system of mass incarceration. And the memorial he and his team have created invites us to consider whether we, either in our day jobs or simply in our lives as citizens, might also be willing to step from remembrance to repair.

This is a year of so many fiftieth anniversaries in American social and political history. In the room next door, an exhibit commemorates the fiftieth anniversary of the Seattle Black Panther Party. Recently, we observed the moment fifty years ago when Martin Luther King Jr. was assassinated on the balcony of the Lorraine Motel. I myself will be hitting the half-century mark in November. Which is why I have been eager to ensure that you and I don't just saunter self-indulgently along memory lane. Rather, you and I this year, this moment, must articulate a philosophy of memory that is aligned with a philosophy of action. What shall we *do* with our memory?

Most of the time, we Americans don't even bother to remember. How many Americans know that *Black Panther* is a top-grossing, mega-phenomenon of a comic-book film but have no idea what the Black Panther Party was or did? How many Seattleites posted commentary online about the movie's magical society of Wakanda yet have no idea that the Carolyn Downs Clinic just a few blocks from here was born of the Black Panthers' community activism and is the nation's only remaining such clinic from that era? How few of us in this room know that "Lift Every Voice and Sing" started its life as a poem written for another anniversary—the one-hundredth birthday of Abraham Lincoln—but became a cherished civil rights anthem and is considered today the black national anthem?

This tendency toward amnesia is why we Americans often presume the mere act of remembrance is an achievement deserving of a prize. But it isn't. It's just the price of the ticket. You've earned the right to shape civic and political life if you know something about what came before and what people endured. That's why my theme today is time travel: literally and figuratively, politically and culturally, individually and collectively.

Imagine that we were jumping back in history, one decade at a time. What would you tell people if you—the *you* you are now—were transported in the blink of an eye back to 2008, then after a while to 1998, to '88, to '78, and finally back to 1968? This thought experiment is occasioned by this fiftieth-anniversary year. But it's inspired by Octavia Butler, whose great novel, *Kindred*, imagined a black woman and her white husband becoming transported, without warning, back and forth between their apartment in California in 1976 and the Maryland plantation where her enslaved and enslaving ancestors lived during the nineteenth century.

Though Butler is often called a science fiction author, she insisted that *Kindred* should be read not as science fiction but as a "grim fantasy" that would enable people to know more than the facts of the history of this nation and instead to feel that history in their gut. So come with me now as I unspool the decades in a journey of revelation.

All at once, it's 2008. I'm in my house in Seattle. I see my reflection in the window and my face has fewer lines, my glasses are not my current glasses, and I'm wearing a sweatshirt I thought I'd given away years ago. Yet it's me inside. I still know what I know, have experienced what I've experienced, as if it were 2018. Everything has been rewound but my soul. I look at my daughter, who isn't in college as I think she should be but is not yet nine and is doing homework in the kitchen, and at my wife, Jená, who won't be my wife for six more years and only just moved in with me and Olivia.

They don't notice that I am stunned and disoriented to be suddenly a decade younger, so I slip downstairs to the office. I open my old clunky laptop and instinctively go to social media to find out what's happening, except that it's still three months before I will join Facebook and a year and a half before I sign up for Twitter. When I go to the *New York Times* website I see that it is April 28, 2008.

Who knows how long I'll be in this state, in this time? I ask myself: What should I tell people? What should I warn others about? Can I prevent anything bad? Is there something I did in this time, in the spring of 2008, that I have always regretted and now I can do differently or not at all?

The possibilities are paralyzing. Now that I have the chance, it seems, to redo and undo, I am newly aware that I don't know what it really is that I *did* do. It's hard to untangle the skein of action and omission in my personal life and to know what strands to snip or to savor. What about my life as a citizen, then? Are cause and effect any easier to untangle here? The main front-page headline of the *Times* that day is "Lenders Fight Stricter Rules on Mortgages." Who do I tell, where do I go to ring the bell, to say, *Stop futzing around! The economy is going to melt down in a few months and you are going to unleash a global tsunami of populist anger and racist scapegoating unless you curb these banks and stop giving mortgages to anyone with a pulse!*

I could warn the people I know who work for John McCain that if he chooses Sarah Palin as his running mate this summer he will release a strand of paranoid, nativist, anti-intellectualism into Republican politics that will destroy their party in all but name. Or I could go around and tell people to watch out for Donald Trump—yes, the *Celebrity Apprentice* star—to curb him now so he can't build a nihilist, reactionary movement to become the president of the United States who follows the dignified, decent, two-term President Barack Obama. But who would believe me? Well, then what? Should I at least tell people not to join Facebook—that they'll regret the addiction, that our country will regret the manipulation this platform makes possible?

I'm contemplating all this when suddenly the screen of my laptop gets fuzzy and then the room around me dematerializes and now I've fallen further back in time.

It's April 1998. I'm in midtown Manhattan, near Rockefeller Center. It's still me inside but it's definitely the late '90s outside. Everyone around me looks like they're extras on the set of *Friends*. My clothes are impossibly baggy and my hair looks like a Chia Pet version of my hair in 2018. People walking down the street and waiting at crosswalks and standing at bus stops are looking at other people, at the sky, at the windows of cafés. They have no smartphones. They have no idea what just happened in the world. "Breaking news" is not yet a sad description of the state of American journalism. It is something that happens, not very often, that you'll hear about later, possibly not until the next day, unless you are watching one of these new twenty-four-hour cable networks.

As it happens, I work for one of these networks in 1998. I'm a new pundit at the new network called MSNBC, and three times a week, I'm thrown together with several other young pundits of all races and all political persuasions to debate the news of the day in politics and culture. Nobody's watching this new channel but we're having a blast. I am marveling at the game of it all, at how I can be having a heated debate on-air with Ann Coulter in which it occurs to me she is the very face of evil and then once the cameras are off she's warmly asking about my family and talking about plans for the weekend.

I know, standing there with my MSNBC colleagues, that even though it'll be for a brief moment and for a mere flicker of public attention, I have a platform. And I know how all this is going to end.

Should I use that platform like Howard Beale did in *Network*, to go off on a live in-studio rant about how much the United States at the very peak of its global power is getting ready to squander all of what made it truly great?

The Monica Lewinsky scandal is blooming and the president will be impeached before the year is out and the dot-com boom is becoming a bubble but how do you know when a boom is a bubble and everyone has become a day trader and a stock picker and the hustle is intoxicating and meanwhile Boris Yeltsin's Russian democracy is curdling into kleptocracy and Osama Bin Laden is planning the bombings of the U.S. Embassy in Nairobi that will kill hundreds and wound thousands and most Americans won't notice. We are all looking at the wrong things. And we will all learn the wrong lessons.

I sit in the TV studio, I clear my throat, and I am about to use my twenty years of foresight to tell my fellow Americans to get their shit together, when—*bam*—another decade has been obliterated. It is April 1988.

My mind, which is already scrambled by this unpredictably predictable march backward in time, struggles to recall what the world was like when I was nineteen going on twenty. As I get my bearings, every cell in my body screams to call my father. My father, who will be dead in three years, dead suddenly without a proper chance to say goodbye. If it's April 28, 1988, I have three years, two months, nine days, and six hours to call him and see him as often as possible and to bring a notebook so I can record his answers to all the questions I've been wanting to ask him for the last twenty-eight years of *my* life. There is so much I want to say to him, and will have to find a way to say without revealing that I have come from the future and know his fate and ours.

And to my country? What do I want to say to my country now that I've traveled back thirty years? I am in college. It is my sophomore spring. I am nineteen and have yet to cast my first vote. George H. W. Bush and his Southern henchman Lee Atwater will run a campaign that is more than ruthless enough to dispatch nice Mike Dukakis. President Bush will expel Saddam Hussein from Kuwait in a couple of years and make possible another President Bush who will think he's finishing the job in Iraq but instead will commit the greatest unforced error in the history of American foreign policy.

But that's not what I want to turn around and tell my classmates in 1988. What I really want to tell them is that thirty years from now Barbara Bush will have passed, George Bush the elder will be frail, the Bush dynasty will be at an end, and with it the WASP Establishment way of being American. Because I am at Yale in 1988, forty years after young war hero Poppy Bush was there, I will be able to see that the WASP Establishment, for all its clubby insularity and hypocrisy and obliviousness to the rest of America, did get some things right. I will be able to warn everyone I encounter—classmates, professors, visiting dignitaries—that the United States had better come up with an affirmative alternative to the WASP ethic of service before self, institutions over individuals, party above country, and no crying just because the world is cruel.

I will tell them that in years to come the nation will rediscover African American activists like Pauli Murray from the early civil rights fights, who through the force of her words and deeds integrated American life more deeply—and that in fact, the newest residential college at Yale will be named after Pauli Murray in 2017. I will tell folks that young Chinese New Yorkers like me, or young Kenyan Kansans like Barack Obama, will want to inject into that WASP ethic our abiding belief in American hybridity. But I will tell them also that the torch will be passed, if I may defile JFK's language, to a new generation of white supremacists: born in this century, tainted by war, deformed by a hard and bitter peace, and proud of what they mistakenly take to be their heritage.

The first time through the year 1988 I was just a kid. I didn't yet know how to convey all this to the world. But in my return trip now, knowing all that I know, I just want to help my country accelerate its readiness to deal with the day when America is white no longer. And part of what I know now is that even a kid—especially a kid—has the moral authority and the clarity of imagination to call forth a new story of us. Now I know that the teens in Parkland and Seattle and all points between—some of whom are here today—organized the March for Our Lives with just a few weeks' notice and grabbed hold of the national narrative to make gun reform more likely. I know now—and I'll tell my nineteen-year-old friends in 1988—that being young is no bar to being a big citizen.

But just as I start organizing, as I start to find my voice—which is to say, to give my younger self my older voice—the elm trees of the Old Campus start pixelating into patches of abstract color, and with one dizzying turn I now find myself thrust back ten more years. Next thing I know I'm in the family room of my childhood home in Wappingers Falls, in the Hudson Valley of New York. It is April 1978. I'm wearing a bowl haircut. In fact, I'm six years away from accepting my buddies' dare to get my head shaved, which then set me onto a lifetime of crew cuts. And though I am not yet ten, my mind and my spirit somehow carry the hard-won wisdom of nearly fifty years of being.

So the first thing I do, of course, is to run down the street and tell my pals playing baseball not to lose faith—that the Yankees will fall fourteen and a half games behind the Red Sox by July and still, *still* they will triumph: they will come back and win the division in a one-game playoff against the Sox and then win the World Series against the Dodgers. I tell them that it will be a glorious and life-shaping season, and that they must suffer the sting of every early season loss to appreciate the full glory of what's to come. And I tell them to savor it for another reason: it will be eighteen more years—a whole generation—before the Yanks will win another Series.

Now, I know you Mariner fans are thinking, *A World Series win every eighteen years? I'll take that.* But my pals in Wappingers Falls are looking at me like the kids in *Stranger Things* and thinking, *Eighteen years, fourteen and a half games—you're being weirdly specific. How do you know this?* To throw them off, I tell them to have faith in something else: in New York. The City in 1978 felt at best adrift and at worst condemned. A year earlier the Bronx had burned, there were blackouts and riots, the Son of Sam was on the loose. Even in my outer suburb there was a creeping sense, certainly among the adults, that not just the city but the entire world was unraveling.

With the hindsight that time travel makes into foresight, I know that New York will bounce back, for just the reason that if I can ever get back to 2018 I will tell folks then and there that *America* will bounce back: the resilient chaos of a complex system that no single person can control or destroy, the capillaries and axons of immigrant hustle that cause the society to repair itself, the unrelenting will to reinvent, and the annoying habit of waiting until things are really broken before patching them for a while longer.

I'll tell it to anyone who will listen. I'll quote my friend Jim Fallows, who will write a book in eleven years, in 1989, called *More Like Us*, explaining why nurturing those qualities—acting more like us and not trying to mimic a rising Japan—will enable America to stave off decline; and then another book in forty years with his wife, Deb, called *Our Towns*, explaining why for every visible, palpable dysfunction of national politics in 2018 there are many more invisible, intangible things that work in San Bernardino and Sioux Falls and Greenville and that a bottom-up renewal of civic life is underway in our towns.

I believe it. I have faith in it. And I am aware that only by believing in the possibility of renewal can I make that renewal possible. Of course, these complicated feelings filling the heart of a nine-year-old, son-of-immigrants Little Leaguer can hardly make their way through the narrow canal of language out into the world. So much belief, so much feeling and faith and fear, never gets spoken.

And this is what I am thinking when the final burst of chronological energy blinds me and sends me back to April 28, 1968. I am in the womb of my mother, Julia Liu. I won't be born for another six months and three days. I am the reason for my mother to have faith. I am the gut feeling she has and will always have. If my forty-nine-year-old consciousness could express itself now I would tell my mom to pay attention when Dr. King is slain and to support the Poor People's Campaign he had launched before his death, to ask why the U.S. keeps slogging on after the Tet Offensive in Vietnam, to ache when Bobby Kennedy's eyes lose their light on the floor of that California hotel, to become a citizen sooner than 1977 so she can vote in this pivotal year.

But my mother is not paying attention. She is just being. She is breathing, circulating blood, converting food into energy, taking long, quiet rests, and believing . . . and that breath, blood, energy, and unspoken belief are making me ready to face the world one day.

And here I am. Here we all are, born to so many different mothers, born of so many different worlds, traveling so many curved and broken arcs of time and space to arrive here at this museum on this morning.

It's been quite a journey. Now imagine taking your own decade-by-decade trip back in time. Imagine knowing then what you know now. In this final portion of my sermon, I want to share five truths that this thought experiment of time travel has revealed to me.

First, we should spend less time preserving forms and more time preserving values. Only values should endure. The Congress of the United States exists in roughly the form it took in 1789 but the values that animated it then have nearly evaporated. It is not obvious we need a Congress constituted as it is today but we do need a working system of representative democracy unrigged by money power. The Black Panther Party is not here anymore in structure yet its values of self-help and mutual aid, of independence and interdependence, endure in many social movements today, both on the left and the right. Nurturing spirit is better than worshipping institutions.

Second, it is too easy to read into our history a single straight-line story of rise or fall or a single personality. We are all things at once. We contain Whitman's multitudes, and we won't know for at least fifty more years whether we are done. When I was born in 1968 America sure looked done. It was not. Or, rather, it was and it wasn't all at once.

Earlier this week, Ben Phillips from our team at Citizen University performed in a brilliant production of *Hamlet* at the Stimson-Green Mansion on First Hill in Seattle, in which there are two casts in two tracks that merge and split from room to room. Hamlet the character, we all know, is divided. But by having two actors play Hamlet at once he is also doubled. The genius of expressing our division as a doubling is something to take from the stage to the civic arena. I'm not myself. Am I? Is America itself, or at war with itself? The answer is *yes*: we elected Obama and we elected Trump. *To be and not to be.*

Third, our patterns betray us. Whatever we say we are, what we do over time tells. We Americans say we believe in individual liberty but we have let an imperial trickle-down market mentality march through our society and obliterate the middle class that in the end is liberty's greatest guarantor. We say we believe in equal justice but the majority does not honor the three words "black lives matter," just as it did not honor fifty years ago the four words "I AM a man," because then, as now, the majority saw such assertions of equality of dignity as an attack on their identity. Our patterns betray us.

Fourth, nothing great happens by individual action. Pauli Murray was willing, in an unconscious echo of Nathan Hale, to give her "one small life" for the cause of desegregation but it took decades of collective action for that cause to prevail. At no time could she have stopped Jim Crow alone. She might have stopped a single lynching with superhuman courage and extraordinary luck. But it would take all of us to undo the system that made lynching as routine and special as a big football game. Because it takes all of us, whether we are awake or not, to make and maintain such a system.

Fifth, and finally, we are all time traveling right now, so we should learn to do it better. At this very moment there are things from the '60s—the 1860s—still happening in our country. Indentured servitude. Caste and color lines that cannot be crossed. Sexual slavery.

Underground sanctuaries for people without papers. Seattle itself is twenty-first-century splendor and nineteenth-century squalor, and you can travel across the span of centuries by walking down a single block in Pioneer Square or South Lake Union.

Hindsight is foresight if we know how to see. The cultural movement that yielded Octavia Butler and her novelistic universes, as well as the Black Panther comics and film characters, is called Afrofuturism. It weaves diasporan dreams with fantastic technologies to make people here and now see that the technology for transformation already exists. It is in our hearts. It is in our willingness to organize and to make power out of thin air. We could all stand to learn from Afrofuturism. We need a futurism for us all that is dedicated to the proposition that if we are all created equal we should start acting like it. We need a futurism that uses superheroes and comic-book villains to teach us how to see what's right in front of us.

And you know what? If you pay attention, you'll notice that we have the raw material for such a futurism. The superheroes and their foils are all around us. Teenagers across the country are organizing some of the greatest social protests and direct civic actions this country has seen in, well, half a century. Meanwhile the occupant of the White House and the occupant of Kanye West's mansion are tweeting that they are spirit brothers because indeed they are: brothers in narcissism, in a talent for attention-getting, in ignorant certitude that wealth equals wisdom, in a flattened ahistorical belief that what is now is all that is.

Civic Saturday exists so that together we can remember that no condition in our country was created yesterday and no citizen of this country will live forever. Civic Saturday exists so that we can teach each other how not just to tell the truth about our history but also to reckon with it. Civic Saturday exists to remind us that to reckon means to calculate, to count up and tally. To prepare ourselves and others to pay the price of reconciliation.

So, here at the Northwest African American Museum, where the Central District meets South Seattle, I want to close by acknowledging that we stand on land that was once inhabited by aspiring African American families, whose elders migrated here as hopeful young people three generations ago from the segregated South and who found a foothold here for a while—for a blink of an eye—and who now have been displaced by gentrification and by the compounding inequity of wealth that has left them unable to withstand the tide of gentrification.

I want to acknowledge further that we must give our time and votes and money to people and organizations and institutions that are working to remedy that underlying inequity and injustice. Some are here today, registering people to vote or working to put universal health care on the ballot in our state or sharing art made by and for activists or teaching the basics of community organizing and empowerment.

And I want to acknowledge the long line of civic superheroes who built this museum: who built it by building it or built it by designing it or built it by justifying it, by living the history that is told within these walls.

Many of them still walk the earth today.

Let us honor them by living like grown-up citizens who know our own minds, who know our place in time, and who will join with others to ensure that the spirit of the struggle for liberty and justice outlives its fragile bodily forms.

16

A TEST OF OUR CITIZENSHIP

Grand View University · Des Moines, IA
May 5, 2018

JANE SMILEY
From A Thousand Acres
Published 1991

There was no way to tell by looking that the land beneath my childish feet wasn't the primeval mold I read about at school, but it was new, created by magic lines of tile my father would talk about with pleasure and reverence. Tile "drew" the water, warmed the soil, and made it easy to work, enabled him to get into the fields with his machinery a mere twenty-four hours after the heaviest storm. Most magically, tile produced prosperity—more bushels per acre of a better crop, year after year, wet or dry. I knew what the tile looked like . . . but for years, I imagined a floor beneath the topsoil, checkered aqua and yellow like the floor in the girls' bathroom at the elementary school, a hard shiny floor you could not sink beneath, better than a trust fund, more reliable than crop insurance, a farmer's best patrimony. It took John and Sam and, at the end, my father, a generation, twenty-five years, to lay the tile lines and dig the drainage wells and cisterns. I in my Sunday dress and hat, driving in the Buick to church, was a beneficiary of this grand effort, someone who would always have a floor to walk on. However much these acres looked like a gift of nature, or of God, they were not. We went to church to pay our respects, not to give thanks.

MARILYNNE ROBINSON
From What Are We Doing Here?
Published 2018

Our sample of existence—that is, the growing sum of whatever we can observe, test, describe, derive, or know in any meaningful sense—is too small and untypical, too contaminated with error and assumption, too prejudiced by accident and limitation to yield a metaphysics. Yet we need a metaphysics, an uncomfortable parallel reality able to support such essential concepts as mind, conscience, and soul, if we are to sustain the civilization culture and history created for us. To quote Flavel, "The soul of the poorest child is of equal dignity with the soul of Adam." All men are created equal. Nothing about these statements is self-evident. Yet they can shape and create institutions, and they can testify against them when they fail. They have only their own beauty and the beauty of their influence to affirm them.

NATURALIZATION OATH OF ALLEGIANCE TO THE
UNITED STATES OF AMERICA
Modified as part of the Immigration Act of September 23, 1950

I hereby declare, on oath, that I absolutely and entirely renounce and abjure all allegiance and fidelity to any foreign prince, potentate, state, or sovereignty, of whom or which I have heretofore been a subject or citizen; that I will support and defend the Constitution and laws of the United States of America against all enemies, foreign and domestic; that I will bear true faith and allegiance to the same; that I will bear arms on behalf of the United States when required by the law; that I will perform noncombatant service in the Armed Forces of the United States when required by the law; that I will perform work of national importance under civilian direction when required by the law; and that I take this obligation freely, without any mental reservation or purpose of evasion; so help me God.

I am the son of immigrants. I am the great-grandson of a farmer. His son—my paternal grandfather—left the farm to become a fighter pilot in the new air force of the new Republic of China eighty years ago. His name was Liu Guo-yun, meaning "deliverance of the nation." (No pressure.) My maternal grandfather was a history professor, on the move from university to university across a China wracked by war and revolution.

So, I feel particularly at home here at Grand View, at this university founded by Danish Lutheran immigrants 122 years ago to make morally sound citizens who could deliver their new nation from darkness.

What does it mean to live like a citizen? In our work, and in the name of our organization, we don't only or even primarily mean documentation status under U.S. immigration laws. We're talking about a more capacious ethical notion of being a member of the body, a contributor to the health of the community. A nonsociopath.

It's worth saying that these days. Because sociopathy is contagious. It trickles down. But decency is contagious too. It emerges from the middle out. From our hearts to those nearby. From neighbor to neighbor, congregation to congregation, campus to campus.

I am of course stating something self-evident in this part of the country, with its reputation for decency. But just as New Englanders tire of Puritan stereotypes, and Californians tire of their reputation for New Age flakiness, maybe you here in the heartland tire of the very word "heartland" and all its virtuous connotations. I, a Yankee of the New York suburbs and eighteen years a Seattleite, am not here to pander or puff you up. I don't think everyone in Des Moines is decent. I don't think all Midwesterners are nice. I don't assume that being rooted to the land makes Iowans inherently more responsible or virtuous than anyone else. I believe you are simply human: a kind of human called American and a kind of American called Iowan.

The true measure of a person's moral and civic worth in American life is not what region's label you carry or even what nation's passport. It is whether you live up to the ideals upon which the American experiment has been constructed and reconstructed.

I've been thinking about this topic, the content of our citizenship and how to measure it, because in our culture today there is a lot of anxiety over who deserves to belong. You hear it in the debates about immigration, if you can call them debates, and how people like Iowa's own Steve King proudly stir up nativist fears about drug-running rapists and murderers from Mexico overrunning your corn fields. You also hear it in proposals in several states, including Iowa, to require high school students to pass the citizenship exam that immigrants take to become naturalized citizens.

The idea seems at first to be unobjectionable. But then you realize what it says about the state of civic education in America. The citizenship exam, consisting of one hundred questions, most at the level of "Who is the president?" and "How many branches of government are there?" sets a pretty low bar. Yet large numbers of students, and equally large numbers of their parents, could not pass it today. Only a third of Americans can name even one branch of the federal government. More than a third have no idea what rights the First Amendment protects.

When people aren't prepared to get over a low bar, the problem isn't with the bar; it's with the preparation. Across the country there's been a disinvestment in the teaching of civics over the last four decades. Only an idiot would be surprised by the idiocracy that follows. Making students memorize answers to one hundred questions won't solve that.

But there's a deeper problem with the proposal to use the citizenship test as a graduation requirement. It exposes our hypocrisy about who belongs in America. If you are an immigrant, failing the test is enough to keep you out of the circle of U.S. citizenship. But if you are an Iowa-born eighteen-year-old with the lifelong benefit of being steeped in American institutions, failing the same test would deprive you at most of a diploma. No one is going to grab your citizenship papers. No one is going to deport you.

To be clear, I'm not proposing deportation for dummies. But I am suggesting that we who had the dumb luck to be born here shouldn't get off easy when it comes to being citizens. So this morning I'd like to explore three questions from the actual naturalization test. I've picked what I think are the hardest three—questions that have straightforward official answers but that are in fact surprisingly complex, even profound.

Here's the first one: "What does the Constitution do?"

The approved answers are: "sets up the government," "defines the government," or "protects basic rights of Americans." Naturalizing citizens studying for the test learn to memorize one of those three responses.

My answer is different. My answer is, "Nothing." The Constitution by itself does nothing. My longer answer is, "It does nothing but challenge us to make it mean something."

In 1965, Mary Beth Tinker was a thirteen-year-old student at Warren Harding Junior High School here in Des Moines. She and her siblings decided to wear black armbands to school to protest the Vietnam War. They were suspended. Their family got death threats. The ACLU took up their case and helped Mary Beth sue the school district for infringing on her First Amendment rights. Four years later, in *Tinker v. Des Moines Independent School District*, the Supreme Court ruled in her favor and severely curtailed the ability of schools to punish student speech. You can mark a straight line from Mary Beth Tinker to the March for Our Lives led by a new generation of students. Tinker, by the way, is still advocating and teaching the meaning of her youthful act.

But what the *Tinker* case teaches us is that the words of the Constitution are not self-executing. We enact them by confronting injustice, by electing people who will uphold the spirit of the words, and by exercising power—people power, ideas power, money power, reputational power—to make the words take form in policy and institutional practice. Until we do, it's just words. Unless we do, it's just words.

And I don't say "just words" casually. I'm in the word business, after all. I know that words are powerful tools of action, words shape the stories that shape our sense of who we are. But when we are flooded by fake news and when politicians think they should be called honest because they lie so brazenly, we realize words untethered from values are worse than useless. They are useful to the worst kind of people.

What does the Constitution do? It warns us to keep up our institutions. It mocks us when we don't. It challenges us to practice power. It stands mute when we betray it.

My friend Mark Meckler, one of the original founders of the Tea Party Patriots and now head of an organization called Citizens for Self-Governance, believes fervently in the Second and the Tenth Amendments. We all know what the Second Amendment is about: the right to bear arms. But few of us remember the Tenth. It says, "The powers not delegated to the United States by the Constitution, nor prohibited by it to the States, are reserved to the States respectively, or to the people."

Mark and I don't agree on many policy questions or on the necessity of a strong federal government, but we do agree that the words of the Tenth Amendment come to life only to the extent that we breathe life into them. In his case, he's organizing people patiently and relentlessly to get enough state legislatures to call a new constitutional convention—a convention of states, provided for in Article V of the Constitution—that would curtail the scope of the federal government and restore the spirit of the Tenth Amendment.

If that were ever to happen, we would have to reckon with what we are willing to give up to live up to the rhetoric about less government. Crop insurance, anyone? Ethanol subsidies? As some of Mark's own followers said during the health care debates, *Get your government hands off my Medicare!* We would also receive a vivid reminder that constitutions depend upon conventions, in another meaning of the word "convention," which is *norms*: what we think is normal and conventional.

What seems normal is determined, for better and worse, by you and me. Is it normal to attack a free press? Is it normal to threaten to lock up your political opponents? Is it normal to undermine the integrity of the judiciary or to call FBI agents Storm Troopers?

All laws—including constitutions, which are just laws about laws—rest on a foundation of social norms. When that foundation is weak, the laws are wobbly and can be knocked aside by a single strong man. By a strongman. Russia today has a constitution. So does the People's Republic of China. So does Turkey. Those constitutions are filled with words and nods to due process that we Americans would recognize. But none of those autocratic nations has a deep enough foundation of norms—social practices, habits of the heart, political traditions, civic clubs—to sustain democratic self-government.

If I had to choose between constitutions and democratic norms I'd choose the norms every time. Consider our friends in England. They don't have a written constitution. They lack a single document to organize their government or protect their rights. What they have is centuries of history of conflicts between monarchs and citizens that led to an accumulation of settlements that incrementally institutionalized self-government and protected citizens against arbitrary state power.

Those settlements took various forms along the way, like the Magna Carta in 1215, in which irritated noblemen reined in an abusive monarch, and the Declaration of Rights after the 1688 Glorious Revolution in which Parliament booted out one king and invited in a new one from the Netherlands. A century later ornery American colonists, using the 1689 Declaration of Right as their model, started publishing local declarations of independence from Great Britain and it was those town- and county- and colony-level declarations that provided the seed for Thomas Jefferson's nation-birthing masterpiece. The recent British prime minister Gordon Brown summed it up nicely: "In establishing the rule of law," he said, "the first five hundred years are always the hardest."

Which brings us to the second sample question from the U.S. citizenship exam. It's another doozy: "What is the rule of law?"

In uneventful times, most Americans would have a hard time answering this. But even in tumultuous times like these, when many more people are worrying about the fragility of the rule of law, many of us would have at best a fuzzy reply to the question.

The approved answers, according to the government exammakers, are:

- Everyone must follow the law
- Leaders must obey the law
- Government must obey the law
- No one is above the law

One way to summarize these four approved answers is to say we are a government of laws and not of men. The exercise of public power should follow neutral rules to be applied in all cases, not the arbitrary whims and appetites of a single leader. It is necessary—more necessary than it's been since Watergate—to say this.

But it's not sufficient. The enslavement of Africans, and then the segregation of their descendants who were free citizens of the United States, all occurred under color of law, according to neutrally worded rules. Those systems of degradation had not only statute but also constitutional precedent behind them. The suspension of the German constitution to make Hitler chancellor in 1933 and grant him emergency powers—that too was done in strict observance of required legal procedure. And the Nazis, once in power, studied the American system of Jim Crow to learn how to build a perfectly legal system to turn some groups into second-class subhuman outcasts.

To put it simply, just because something is legal does not make it just. And just because something is unjust does not make it illegal.

In Jane Smiley's tragic novel *A Thousand Acres*, which she modeled after Shakespeare's *King Lear*, a patriarchal Iowa farmer decides impulsively to divvy up his farm among his three daughters, who eventually go to war with each other and with him. In the end, the entire patrimony—the legacy of a thousand acres that were tiled and drained and tilled and planted over the course of generations, during which the wealth of the land compounded—was squandered and cast to the winds. And worst of all, the patriarch's crime at the heart of the whole saga (I won't spoil it for those of you who haven't read it yet) is never named and never punished.

"No one is above the law. Leaders must obey the law." Do we mean it? We may be tested soon. We are being tested now.

When Richard Nixon abused the powers of his office to cover up a petty burglary, the tenets of the rule of law were upheld by a press that was trusted, a judiciary that was unassailable, a Congress in which the president's party was willing to put country above party, and a citizenry that paid attention and watched a single, unifying television screen.

If Donald Trump forces a constitutional crisis—by firing the special counsel investigating him, say—few of those conditions will obtain. He will face a press that is mistrusted, a judiciary he has maligned, a Congress in which his own party's leaders will not stand up to him, and a citizenry that is fragmented, distracted, and unable to look up from the phone to get any perspective.

Yet if I sound pessimistic, I am not. The reason why is that there is another dimension to the rule of law that is timeless and that can make itself felt even in times of great dysfunction. That is the dimension of conscience. The conscience of a citizen is what actually makes or breaks a republic.

Let me quote another Iowa writer, Marilynne Robinson, who in addition to her great novels like *Gilead* and *Home*, about the quiet tensions of rural ministers and their flocks, has also published essays that express her deep Calvinist faith and her desire to rehabilitate the Puritans not as dour witch-burners but as the original idealistic reformers who gave every American afterward the DNA of idealism and reformism.

In her recent book *What Are We Doing Here?* Robinson tells us "the center of Puritan individualism was the conscience, so sacred that it was the foundation of their definition of freedom." Conscience was an internalized voice of God, with the irresistible power of the will of God. To disregard conscience was to sin. She adds, drily: "To bring such seriousness to the negotiations of one's moral and ethical life might interfere with good times as currently defined." But this notion of conscience was at the heart of what Robinson calls "the strenuous drama of Puritan life."

When I read that line, I thought of Teddy Roosevelt and his obsession with "the strenuous life" and its virtues. I also thought of *Finding Nemo*. Remember when the amnesiac Dory is in the pitch-black sea and hears Marlin telling her what to do? She asks: "Are you my conscience?" I am here today not to preach Puritan or Pixar notions of faith. I am here to say that just as the Puritans and their descendants put great stock in a godly notion of conscience, we today must put great vigor and rigor into a *civic* notion of conscience.

When you see someone berate a woman on the bus for wearing a head scarf or speaking Arabic, your civic conscience is awakened. When you learn that neo-Nazis are meeting in your town, your civic conscience stirs. When you notice that the cops have swooped into Starbucks to arrest two customers for waiting while black, your civic conscience speaks. We gather like this to make sure that after our conscience speaks, we say out loud that no one is above the law. After it stirs, we act. After it awakens, we move. Together. As citizens responsible for the rule of law. Conscience precedes institutions; it then becomes the magnetism binding the atoms of those institutions.

Our republic is a little like that thousand-acre farm in Jane Smiley's novel. Claimed and tamed long ago by some hard-hearted SOBs who never owned up to the misdeeds that fertilized the fields; populated next by their childish descendants who didn't realize how much they were taking for granted as they wasted their inheritance; then appropriated by numbers of people who don't know or care about what came before but want to maximize the yield and treat the place as a monetizable asset to be worked not just *by* machines but *as* a machine.

Here's the thing, though: a farm is not a machine. It is a kind of garden. And a democracy is not a machine. It too is a kind of garden. Machines operate by rules that are programmed to perpetuate themselves. Gardens unfold as chaos in chaos. Gardens require gardeners: to weed, to seed, to feed, to notice at all times the emerging patterns of erosion or overuse or neglect or overgrowth.

What is the rule of law? It is you and me tending the garden of democracy. More than that, it is you and me knowing that we *owe* it to each other to tend the garden. The rule of law is civic conscience, activated collectively.

So now let's explore the third and final sample question from the citizenship exam: "What is one promise you make when you become a United States citizen?"

Well, this is sort of a trick question. Most of you didn't have to promise anything to become a citizen because most of you were born here. But it's in the trick that a larger truth comes out. The correct answer, according to the Citizenship and Immigration Services, is any of the following six:

- Give up loyalty to other countries
- Defend the Constitution and laws of the United States
- Obey the laws of the United States
- Serve in the U.S. military (if needed)
- Serve (do important work for) the nation (if needed)
- Be loyal to the United States

All six of these promises are drawn from the oath that naturalizing citizens must take to make it official. That oath, as you heard, is a clunky old-fashioned thing that drains the poetry and inspiration out of the moment. But it means something. I've been to many naturalization ceremonies. If you haven't gone to one, I urge you to go. It's one of the most moving civic experiences you can have. All the immigrants, who have already passed the test, stand up as a roll of their native countries is called, and then they are told, "*The next time you sit down, you will be Americans.*" Goosebumps.

After we'd been to several of these naturalization ceremonies, my wife, Jená, the cofounder of Citizen University, had a brilliant idea. What if we created something like that, but for everyone? Not just immigrants becoming citizens but people born here too, folks who never have been asked to reflect on the content of their citizenship. It would be like renewing their vows. And because she has a theater background, she started sketching a stage and a revival tent and said, "We'll call it a Sworn-Again American ceremony."

So we did. We created a template for a ceremony, with a script and readings and of course our own Sworn-Again American oath. It goes like this:

I pledge to be an active American.
To show up for others,
To govern myself,
To help govern my community.
I recommit myself to my country's creed:
To cherish liberty as a responsibility.
I pledge to serve and to push my country:
When right, to be kept right; when wrong, to be set right.
Wherever my ancestors and I were born,
I claim America
And I pledge to live like a citizen.

People have taken this oath and held Sworn-Again American ceremonies in towns all across the United States—on campuses and military bases, public libraries and convention halls, theaters and parks, from Alabama to Arizona. You can do it too. The template is on our website. Doing it makes you notice the everyday heroes around you.

In Seattle, our Mary Beth Tinker is named is Gordon Hirabayashi. In 1942 Gordon was a student at the University of Washington. He, like all Japanese American citizens in the aftermath of Pearl Harbor, had been made subject to curfew and incarceration under FDR's Executive Order 9066. He, unlike most Japanese Americans, resisted the order. He violated the curfew, refused induction into the armed services, turned himself in to the FBI, and sued the United States with a little help from his friends—literally: the Quakers' Friends Service Committee took up his case. He lost—in *Hirabayashi v. United States* the Supreme Court ruled that the internment order was constitutional in a time of emergency—and he spent over a year in federal prison.

We wrote the Sworn-Again American oath with people like Gordon Hirabayashi and Mary Beth Tinker in mind. They cherished liberty as a responsibility. They knew their own minds and knew how to govern themselves. They didn't say *My country, right or wrong.* They pushed their country, when wrong, to be set right.

If you measure Hirabayashi against the six promises of the actual citizenship oath, he went four for six. He did not serve in the military when called. He did not obey the laws of the United States. But the reason why is he was too busy living up to the other four tenets: it was by challenging the U.S. government that he showed his loyalty to the U.S., renounced any other loyalty, served his nation, and upheld the Constitution.

Forty-five years after his trial, his conviction was overturned and the Court of Appeals disavowed the *Hirabayashi* decision. Twenty-five years after that, President Obama awarded Gordon Hirabayashi the Presidential Medal of Freedom.

What is one promise you make to become a United States citizen? What I love about the question is that it implies that citizenship isn't just a status or a bundle of rights and privileges. It is a covenant. To be a citizen is to live an implied promise and others may act in reliance of the expectation that you will keep the promise. If you are faithful to the nation's creed, you can demand that the nation keep faith with you.

If I were a student again—if I were doing my history thesis here— I'd want to do it on the topic of oaths. I would recount how Americans once put great stock in oaths and were afraid to take them if they weren't sure they could live up to them; and I would examine how and when it became OK to not really mean it. Or to mean it at the time but not later, when inconvenient, which is of course the same as not really meaning it.

Then I remember: I *am* a student. So are you, whether you are enrolled at Grand View or not. We are called to learn and practice the art of powerful citizenship. For most of us, the tests of citizenship will not be pen-and-paper quizzes or oral exams. They won't even be the obvious occasions like Election Day. They will be small moments that sneak up on you without warning like a tap on the shoulder or a tweet in the dark. When suddenly a passerby or a president forces you to be more than a bystander.

Are you ready to live up to your promises?

I said at the outset I wasn't going to pander to you Iowans. But as I close, I can't resist. You know how much the rest of the country hates the outsized role your caucuses play in picking presidents. Folks say the caucus is an outmoded, unrepresentative format. They say that white rural Iowa is an outmoded, unrepresentative state. Well, I say they're wrong. I love the caucus, because it's a school of citizenship open to all. And I believe Iowa is representative of the Union in two deep and important ways.

First, this state contains all the polarized contradictions of the rest of the country. What is Iowa? Is it the land of right-wing nativist Steve King or the land of left-wing Calvinist Marilynne Robinson? Is it where state legislators eviscerate health-care coverage for the poor or where the *Des Moines Register* wins a Pulitzer Prize for exposing that act? Is it a place where young people are feeling powerless or a place where groups like the Iowa Student Learning Initiative are teaching a new generation to find their voice? The answer, of course, is *yes*. To live here is to live with that complexity and contradiction.

This state reflects the United States in one other respect: character. Herman Melville wrote in *Moby-Dick* that only being at sea made a man a man. "In landlessness alone," he wrote, "resides the highest truth, shoreless, indefinite as God." I think that's pretty much crap. But like Melville, you know that the appearance of stasis and stability is always a mirage. You know better than to think that you can just sail back in time and make everything great again. You know, as Jane Smiley put it in *A Thousand Acres*, that "the seemingly stationary fields are always flowing toward one farmer and away from another." And you know that the grown-up thing to do is prepare, and face the changes and the storms that are as relentless as if you were at sea.

That's what a citizen would do. In these tumultuous times, that is what a citizen must do. Serve. Listen. Forgive. Organize. Advocate. Vote. *Tend the garden.* My friends—my fellow descendants of farmers and immigrants—let's recommit to our country's creed. Let's live like Sworn-Again Americans.

17.

ARE WE ENOUGH?

El Centro De La Raza · Seattle, WA
June 2, 2018

ELLA BAKER
Quoted in Moving the Mountain:
Women Working for Social Change
By Ellen Cantarow, Susan O'Malley, et al.
Published 1980

First, there is a prerequisite: the recognition on the part of the established powers that people have a right to participate in the decisions that affect their lives. And it doesn't matter whether those decisions have to do with schools or housing or some other aspect of their lives. There is a corollary to this prerequisite: the citizens themselves must be conscious of the fact that this is their right. Then comes the question, how do you reach the people if they aren't already conscious of this right? And how do you break down resistance on the part of the powers that be toward citizens becoming participants in decision making?

I don't have any cut pattern, except that I believe that people, when informed about the things they are concerned with, will find a way to react. . . . In organizing a community, you start with people where they are. . . .

You didn't see me on television, you didn't see news stories about me. The kind of role that I tried to play was to pick up pieces or put together pieces out of which I hoped organization might come. My theory is, strong people don't need strong leaders.

JAMES AGEE
From Let Us Now Praise Famous Men
Published 1941

Human beings, with the assistance of mules, worked this land so that they might live. The sphere of power of a single human family and a mule is small; and within the limits of each of these small spheres the essential human frailty, the ultimately mortal wound which is living and the indignant strength not to perish, had erected against its hostile surroundings this scab, this shelter for a family and its animals: so that the fields, the houses, the towns, the cities, expressed themselves upon the grieved membrane of the earth in the symmetry of a disease: the literal symmetry of the literal disease of which they were literally so essentially a part.

The prime generic inescapable stage of this disease is being. A special complication is life. A malignant variant of this complication is consciousness. The most complex and malignant form of it known to us is human consciousness.

PETE PETERSON, RICH TAFEL, ET AL.
From "A Way Forward: A Conservatism of Connection"
Published 2017

Authentic conservatism is essentially about three connections: 1. Connection to the Past: We retain from our heritage what is valuable and worth cherishing, 2. Connection to Our Future: We innovate as conditions change to adapt inherited ways to new conditions, 3. Connection to One Another: Through America's famed mediating institutions, we connect to one another in achieving the common good.

American conservatism recognizes that today's crisis of spirit has repeated itself throughout our history. Episodes of alienation and estrangement not only punctuate our history, but also reveal our deepest ongoing challenge. America's gradual incorporation of an astonishing array of peoples and cultures into a common civilization is a true, powerful, and profoundly important story, even as each stage of that development as a nation has required us to overcome tragic periods of exclusion, particularly racial and ethnic exclusion. This too is an "identity politics" of a very dangerous sort, which must be rejected.

We must restore the American Project by repairing the three conservative connections that demonstrate our principles and draw us into the risky but rewarding work of active citizenship.

**EQUAL RIGHTS AMENDMENT TO THE
UNITED STATES CONSTITUTION**

Passed by the U.S. Senate and submitted to the states
March 22, 1972

SECTION 1. Equality of rights under the law shall not be denied or abridged by the United States or by any State on account of sex.

SECTION 2. The Congress shall have the power to enforce, by appropriate legislation, the provisions of this article.

SECTION 3. This amendment shall take effect two years after the date of ratification.

I'm so gratified to be here with you this morning at El Centro de la Raza, and especially to be here at Plaza Roberto Maestas.

Roberto has been gone eight years now but he remains so vivid to me in his gestures, the texture of his voice, his knowing and mischievous laugh. I feel like I could call him for coffee later today and we would sit out on Beacon Avenue and he'd riff on all that's happening in our city. For those of you who never met him or have no idea who he was or why this place is named for him, let me tell you about Roberto Maestas.

Roberto was one of the best civic improvisers I ever knew. Born into poverty in Depression-era New Mexico and raised by his grandparents, he ran away at fourteen and became a migrant farmworker in eastern Washington. Eventually he hustled his way west to Seattle and got himself through high school while working odd industrial jobs on late shifts. He eventually earned a degree in Spanish at the University of Washington, and became a teacher at Seattle's Franklin High School.

It was there, during the 1960s, that his evolution into a firebrand revolutionary began. He became a vocal leader in the emerging

Chicano movement. He joined black student activist Larry Gossett, Native American leader Bernie Whitebear, and Asian American leader Bob Santos to create multiracial coalitions for justice in education, policing, immigration, and other issues. Together they became masters of organizing and direct action. These so-called "Four Amigos" were bonded by personal chemistry. But they also recognized that in predominantly white Seattle they were stronger together.

This was particularly the case for Seattle's small, dispersed Latino community. Maestas sought a way to galvanize Latinos into a visible sense of shared fate. So in October 1972, he and over seventy other activists entered and took over the abandoned Beacon Hill School, which had been shuttered because of declining enrollments. The aging building lacked heat, electricity, running water, or supplies. But it now had occupants (or at least occupiers). The activists proclaimed it "El Centro De La Raza"—which they translated, strategically, as the Center for People of *All* Races, not *the* race.

They secured a commitment from the school superintendent that they would not be forcibly evicted, and from there they began to negotiate. As the talks got underway, the activists organized educational and artistic projects in the building, from English lessons to mural-making, to show what El Centro could be. They also organized rallies at the city council and in the streets. Along the way, Maestas and a young fellow occupier named Estela Ortega were married, in the unheated school gymnasium. Three months later, the district agreed to lease the property to the activists for $1 a year.

From that point on, El Centro became a civic hub and a political force. Combining the spirit of the urban crusader Jane Addams and the revolutionary Cuban poet Jose Martí, with a dose of the Black Panther Party, El Centro created a space for low-income immigrant families that was equal parts settlement house, people's school, childcare center, free breakfast program, and activist proving ground.

Maestas led with zest and swagger. He was unafraid to confront community leaders he felt weren't moving quickly enough to include poor and brown people. He marched and protested, often with the other Four Amigos. But he mastered the inside game as well. Fiesty public challenges would be followed by subtle private negotiations. He cultivated working relationships with business and philanthropic insiders. His office became a necessary stop for aspiring political candidates.

By the time of its thirty-fifth anniversary celebration in 2007, El Centro de la Raza was serving many thousands of people annually through more than forty-five different programs. It had a strong presence as an advocate for immigrants and poor communities of color. It had become a key conduit of the local power structure. Governors, mayors, and councilmembers all paid homage at the anniversary, as the restless Maestas worked the room all night.

Roberto died in 2010 of lung cancer. Estela Ortega, who had been running things day to day, took over formally as El Centro's executive director. She would never say it, but Estela has become a full-fledged member of the city power structure. She is wired into city hall. She doesn't have to raise her voice to get things done in this town.

Estela decided after taking over to launch a legacy project: a festive plaza, adjacent to the old schoolhouse she and Roberto had once occupied, with street-level retail, a community center, light rail, and affordable housing for hundreds of low-income residents. The project opened in 2017. It's called Plaza Roberto Maestas, and here we are.

Now, why did I tell you so much about this place and this person? Because I believe that memory matters, and that it's important to honor our elders and those who build our institutions. And because at *every* Civic Saturday, whether here in Seattle or in Nashville or Des Moines, Iowa, or in Atlanta, our approach is to name the layers of history beneath our feet and to remind ourselves that there is never in America a truly blank canvas, never a second act that was not corrupted by the first.

But another reason why I tell you about Roberto and Estela is that they embody the spirit of perpetual revolution, which is of course the essence of the American idea. Coming out of the liberation movements of the 1960s, they were at the practical, useful cutting edge of the counterculture.

And I submit to you that we gathered here today are the new counterculture. In a culture of celebrity worship and consumerism, we stand for service and citizenship. In an age of hyperindividualism, we practice collective action and common cause. In a time of fundamentalism and showy righteousness, we stand for discernment and humility. In the smog of hypocrisy and situational ethics, we still live and breathe the universal timeless values and ideals of the Tao, of the Golden Rule, of the Declaration.

That is radical. We who choose to show up on a Saturday morning for fellowship and friend-making and skill-honing and power-building, we are at the cutting edge of the counterculture now. If we do our jobs right, we will spark a great civic awakening all across this country. A renewal of people power and a replenishment of civic character. If we don't, we may realize that the decades we have been alive will turn out to have been the blip, the exception, and that American political life is returning to the nasty, brutish, corrupt condition of the 1820s or the 1850s or the 1880s.

So today, in the countercultural spirit of Roberto—a spirit of play, of war, of art, and of love—I want to ask a simple question.

Are we enough?

Are we who gather here and others like us who show up for Civic Saturdays, are we enough to undo the toxic effects of concentrating wealth and the culture of hoarding? Are we enough to fight the imperialism of the market and the addiction of narcissism? Are we enough to make our country live up to its promise as a city upon a hill? And what about *this* city, built upon seven hills?

Let me tell you first why I worry whether we are enough, then let me tell you why I still have hope.

WHY I WORRY

When the great civil rights organizer Ella Baker said, "Strong people don't need strong leaders," she was referring obliquely to MLK, with whom she often disagreed over how hierarchical or decentralized the movement ought to be. She is not famous today but she was right. The corollary, of course, is that weak people do need strong leaders.

One measure of whether we the people are strong or weak is how susceptible we are to viruses. How robust is the civic immune system, and how resistant to infection? The infection is called racism or white nationalism or misogyny or nativist scapegoating populism. But the precursor virus now deeply rooted in the body politic is absolutism.

Absolutism kills. And our viral load of absolutism is high and getting higher.

On Monday Jeff Sessions, the attorney general of the United States, detailed a "zero tolerance" policy for people attempting illegally to cross the border into the U.S. Every such migrant, he said, would now be subject to immediate prosecution.

That got me angry, because many of these migrants are seeking asylum, which is not a crime; because migrant parents who are being detained as criminals are thus being separated from their children; and because it was the cold-blooded goal of this administration to use well-publicized separations to deter future migration.

But then I got to thinking about all the ways "zero tolerance" appears in American life, in law and norms, and I realized that it's not just in this president's immigration policies. It's everywhere. It started with zero-tolerance policies in schools in the mid-1990s. Bring a gun to school, or drugs, and you'd be suspended. Boom. Bring a gun-shaped key chain to school, or ibuprofen for cramps, and you might be suspended too. Wait, what?

This absolutist logic was a response to the anxieties of the day about crime and delinquency. About law and order—and race. It found its way into three-strikes-you're-out criminal laws and sentencing guidelines that made imprisonment without parole automatic. And even though many people now admit that these policies have resulted in a school-to-prison pipeline that has fed a new Jim Crow system of mass incarceration of brown and black men, Americans have not fallen out of love with zero tolerance.

To the contrary. Our society has doubled down on it—and often in the name of social justice. Colleges, corporations, government agencies, and media outlets have adopted zero-tolerance policies against sexual harassment and assault, racism, bullying, hate speech. The omnipresence of iPhones and the contagious righteousness of social media mean that every single day brings forth a new moral outrage, a new occasion for us to declare, "There should be zero tolerance for this!"

As a mode of justice, zero tolerance has primordial appeal. It simplifies. It sends a clear message about where moral norms stand. It creates solidarity and power among those who assert and enforce those norms. When Roseanne tweets racist tweets or when the video emerges of the Starbucks manager calling the cops, or when it comes out that Harvey Weinstein is a power-abusing sexual predator, and then we share our outrage about the incidents on social media, it can feel immensely satisfying to have a hand in administering the real-time punishment of shaming and social banishment.

But if you've ever seen an episode of *Black Mirror*, the show on Netflix that depicts an eerie near future in which the state does not need to be authoritarian because the *crowd* is, you will know that that feeling should be a warning.

The absolutism of our political culture today flattens the moral landscape. It smashes proportion and perspective and priority. Al Franken was not Donald Trump. Samantha Bee, who called Ivanka Trump the c-word, is not Roseanne—although MSNBC's Joy Reid, who has peddled 9/11 truther conspiracies about and cheered Iran's proposal to kick the Jews out of Israel, appears to be far more problematic than liberals want to admit. Meanwhile, on the day the Internet went crazy about Roseanne a report was published that over

4,600 American citizens died in Puerto Rico because of Hurricane Maria and the administration's half-hearted response to it. Who noticed?

This unwillingness to make distinctions becomes an *inability* to make distinctions, which then clears the field for moral relativism—indeed, for malevolent moral relativism.

Enter Donald Trump. One of his savant-like gifts is that he intuits that he more than anyone will benefit from the obliteration of moral proportion and perspective. That's why his response to the Roseanne flap was to pardon the bigoted, outrage-spewing felon Dinesh D'Souza. Cue the outrage to blunt the previous outrage! Our troll-in-chief is both the product and the creator of a culture of blind moral fury. And the blindness of it all—the reflexive contagious response of fury—makes authoritarianism ever more likely.

In part that's because in this kind of culture a hard callus forms over the nerve endings of our moral sense. John Kelly, the White House chief of staff, assured the public recently that the migrant children separated from their parents at the border would be just fine, that they'd be "put into foster care or whatever."

No phrase better captures the casual indifference and savage ignorance, the dehumanizing sociopathy that trickles down from John Kelly's boss. To them and their base, the prime threat is migration of nonwhite people from shithole countries into the United States and if deterring that threat means demonizing Central American migrants as criminals and misplacing children who shouldn't be here anyway, well, whatever.

Callousness is not just about cruelty, though. It is about shamelessness. Shame is a necessary part of a moral repertoire, and the absence of shame is sociopathy. But when our discourse—I'm sorry; our media-entertainment mob of instant weaponized judgment—is dominated by shame and attempts to shame, then eventually some proportion of the people will stop responding to shame altogether. They may even adopt an identity that takes pride in the thing meant to be shamed.

The overuse of shame has an effect like the overuse of antibiotics and antibacterial hand sanitizers: eventually, a resistant strain of angry, righteous hate emerges, and we become defenseless against far more vicious infections than we see in normal times.

The worst part of a culture of absolutism is that it absolves us of the responsibility to know our own minds—and then it strips us of that responsibility. Zero tolerance for unaccepted views is the mantra of a people who do not trust themselves to make good judgments. So they automate it. On/off. One/zero. Black/white. Zero tolerance is the perfect mantra for an age when more and more of our social interactions are automated, mediated by algorithm, unthinking and undiscerning.

We don't have to know what we think. We just need to know what we're supposed to think. This isn't just about national politics. Consider the debate about taxes and homelessness in Seattle. If you support the head tax you despise business. If you oppose the head tax you despise the homeless. Whichever tribe you are in, you despise the other. You should be ashamed to admit it when the other has a point. So you won't.

But isn't it possible *both* that Amazon and other big employers should be contributing more to address the consequences of unchecked growth *and* that our city government should be more effective at spending public money? Absolutist politics make pawns and symbols of people in a ping-pong game of whataboutism. Trump separates migrant parents and kids. But what about Obama—didn't he separate migrant siblings? Back and forth, on and on, while children remain lost or abandoned or trafficked into hell. Now that Seattle business leaders are pushing a referendum to repeal the head tax, we will argue back and forth, on and on, over whether we want taxes or jobs, while the number of homeless families and homeless deaths keeps rising.

I ask again: Are we enough?

You can see why I worry. I go around the country telling a story that as dysfunctional as DC has become, at least at the local level people are resisting tribalism and the Manichean moral absolutism of national politics; that at the local level there is no time for the Kabuki posturing and virtue signaling of national politics because you either are or are not going to get the problem fixed; and that, in fact, it will be practical problem-solvers from towns across America who will save America.

I confess to you that I tell that story these days with slightly less conviction. Adam Smith wrote about the "moral sentiments" that hold a society together. Tocqueville described the "habits of the heart" that held a young America together. But here's the thing: self-righteousness is as much a moral sentiment as duty and benevolence; dehumanizing rage can be as much a habit of the heart as compassion. Habits are nothing more than what we keep doing and keep indulging.

And here in Seattle, because we have now become the most unequal city in the United States, surpassing San Francisco recently, we have developed the *bad* habits, the *unhealthy* moral sentiments of an ailing society. Our civic immune system is faltering. When you see the chanting and counter-chanting at neighborhood meetings, or the ironworkers shouting down socialist city councilmember Kshama Sawant, whose followers are often doing the shouting, you realize we have been infected.

But let me tell you why, despite all this, I still have hope.

WHY I HOPE

I still have hope because last month our team went to New Orleans to lead our first CitizenFEST, a learning summit on civic power and civic character. We learned with and from so many unsung big citizens from the African American community who have been taking down Confederate monuments, forming story circles to face the everyday traumas of life in the Big Easy, creating mutual-aid networks to lift each other out of poverty, and using step dance and chair fitness to boost physical and civic health. Most were invited by Denise Graves, a faith leader and organizer who is honored and respected among the poor families of the city and who has seen so much and who, just when it seems she has grown weary, will say something simple and loving in quiet response to someone's pain or another's ignorance that works like acupuncture for everyone. Reverend Denise is the furthest possible opposite of President Donald.

I still have hope because when we were in Des Moines, Iowa, to lead a Civic Saturday in May, we met with educators who are organizing and persisting even though they live in a state that forty years ago outlawed teachers' strikes and that forty days ago stripped unions of their leverage in collective bargaining by giving school districts and not arbitrators the final say in contract negotiations. They know the fight now is to convince rural and small-town school boards not to abuse that power—that Iowa must not go the way of Kansas and try to cut its way to quality teachers and schools. They labor under labor laws that remind you what a relative paradise for workers Washington State is. We in Washington have the right to have rights—which is the heart of citizenship.

I still have hope because I recently went to Oakland and in a single afternoon I got together with Wendy MacNaughton, an illustrator -journalist and citizen artist, and we discovered that both of us had recently read *Let Us Now Praise Famous Men* and we asked what if we collaborated the way Walker Evans and James Agee did for that pioneering, uncategorizable book of text and image about the sharecropping South, and now she is traveling the country for a month to harvest stories; and then with Ann O'Leary, who was Hillary Clinton's top policy aide throughout the campaign and in the wake of that upheaval has replanted herself in Oakland, refastened herself to civic purpose, and found new ways to be of service; and later with Mia Birdsong, a teacher and activist and urban farmer who keeps three hives of bees in her yard and shares honey with her neighbors on her block which has changed in eight years from 60 percent black to 10 percent but remains a place where her black children feel free and safe to play outside until suppertime, who organizes circles of black women who push each other to work on what they need to work on, and who is writing a book about how young people of color are reimagining family; and then with Jen Pahlka, who founded Code for America and convened a summit with one thousand citizen technologists who are using their digital savvy to help ordinary citizens build power, fight for justice, and make government more responsive to people. I told Jen and her Code for America Brigades, with Wendy in mind, that they were technologists and coders but what they had to offer wasn't coding skills so much as artist skills—the skills of seeing patterns, improvising solutions out of limited resources, experimenting and adapting perpetually—which are, of course, citizen skills. Wendy and Ann and Mia and Jen will give anyone hope.

I have hope because Illinois has become the thirty-seventh state of the Union to ratify the Equal Rights Amendment. And this means only one more state is needed to cross the constitutional threshold for ratification. Now, yes, the thirteen remaining states are the former Confederacy plus Arizona, Utah, and Oklahoma. So, not the most fertile ground. And, yes, there is debate about whether too much time has elapsed since most of the states ratified. But remember, in 1982 and for the next thirty-five years the ERA was as dead as disco, the Pinto, and seventies hairdos. Until it wasn't anymore. Until Hillary Clinton became the nominee and almost POTUS. Until record numbers of women decided to run for office. Until #MeToo. Until a few citizens in Nevada in 2017 and in Illinois in 2018 imagined what it'd be like to get the ERA across the finish line.

I also have hope because my colleague Pete Peterson, who's the dean of the public policy school at Pepperdine, a Republican and former candidate for California secretary of state, has been organizing thoughtful reformers on the right for a movement called "a conservatism of connection"—a conservatism that does not worship the market, does not demonize government, does not scapegoat immigrants, but does make an affirmative case for why citizens empowered to help each other should be the solvers of problems of first resort. Pete and I part ways on many policy questions. But his conservativism of connection, like our civic counterculture, is about a shared civic spirit and civic purpose that materialism and immediate gratification can never satisfy.

But let me bring it home now.

I still have hope because the improvisation and occupation that became El Centro de la Raza in 1972, is now, nearly a half-century later, the magnificent centerpiece of a vibrant Beacon Hill and a beacon for immigrants and people of all races. The murals painted on the walls back then have become the beloved community in the plaza today.

I still have hope because with us here today are some of the high school students from Bothell and Seattle and Kent who made the March for Our Lives happen nearly spontaneously and are now organizing the Vote for Our Lives campaign to get high school students statewide to register and vote. They are living proof of my third law of civic power, which is that power is infinite. In even the most seemingly stuck and rigged situations, it is entirely possible to generate brand-new power out of thin air and to reset the equation of power—through the magic act of organizing.

I have hope because the other night I gave a talk at the University of Washington convened by the American Academy of Arts and Sciences. The Academy was founded in 1780, by John Adams during the Revolutionary War, and this was the 2,068th Stated Meeting of the American Academy, and because I'm a sucker for lineages, this gave me goosebumps. And after my lecture one of the most thoughtful questions came from a man who, it turns out, is running against my friend Jamie Pedersen, the state senator from the forty-third district. This fellow, Dan, is a conservative, a label he emphasized over Republican, and he realizes just how outnumbered he is in this district that centers around the Capitol Hill neighborhood. But he thinks Seattle has gone tax-crazy. He thinks local government is out of control. And unlike others who might think so too, he is putting himself forward to challenge an incumbent because he believes that's what a citizen should do.

I want to be clear. All these people from our city and others don't make me *optimistic*. They give me *hope*. There's a difference. Optimism is appropriate for situations where you have no hand in the outcome. I'm optimistic that the Yankees and the Mariners will be in the play-off hunt all season long. But in my optimism, I am only a spectator. Hope is appropriate for situations where you have something to do with how things turn out. I am hopeful that our country and our city will not collapse into the hyper-inequities of an extractive Third World society—but that's only because I can help shape the course of events. Hope implies agency. Hope demands that we not waste our power.

Our agency, our authorship of the city and the nation yet to be written, depends on our mutual commitment to pledge our lives, our fortunes, our sacred honor to an ideal that says we are all better off when we are all better off, that treats liberty as a responsibility and not as a way out of responsibility. Our agency is expressed in whether we will live like citizens or like customers, as an active people or a passive mass.

Will we love one another enough? Earlier this year our team launched a Civic Seminary, through which we're training and shaping two dozen leaders in 2018, ranging in age from their early twenties to their late sixties, and coming from towns across the country, to lead their own Civic Saturdays and build their own congregations. From their time together, from our collective questioning of the texts and the creed that compose the foundation of America's civic charter, they came to see that just as all great faith traditions reduce finally to love, American *civic* religion can be distilled to *civic* love. Whenever we are in group messages, we usually sign off with #CivicLove.

To love your neighbor can be very difficult whether your neighbor is a selfish jerk who resists change or a crusading ideologue who is forcing change on others. To love your enemy can be difficult when you are arguing about what one of you thinks is a double standard and the other thinks is a single truth. To love a stranger can be difficult when radical inequality creates status anxiety creates scarcity thinking creates scapegoating.

I am telling you this to remind *myself*. Because I do not automatically love my neighbor or my enemy or a stranger as myself. "With malice toward none and charity for all" is not my default setting. Let's be honest; that's true for most of us. Even Lincoln said those words only after having made clear to the Confederacy in his Second Inaugural that he was quite willing to see that "every drop of blood drawn with the lash shall be paid by another drawn with the sword." His morality was as much Old Testament as New.

Will we hold ourselves and each other to account, lovingly, when we are lapsing into absolutist binary ways of being? That takes commitment. It takes a social contract. We hope that you have come here today or will leave here today with someone who can enter into a pact with you: a pact to call each other out when you start acting like cable and Twitter provocateurs—even when you agree with them. Especially when you do.

Will we know how to discern among shades of gray, even if doing so makes us seem insufficiently woke or unfashionably out of line with the party or the tribe?

Will we learn to listen to the people and will we remember we *are* the people and so we must each find our own voice and must know our own mind and our own heart without cues or scripts supplied by others?

Will we remember that democracy is no guarantee of freedom or equality—only liberal democracy is, and only with the spirit of a republic, which is to say, the spirit that says I claim this, I must lead this, I must *be* this, I *am* the public?

Will we be a strong people? Strong enough to keep our republic?

I am hopeful. I believe we are enough. But I have no illusions. When you drive around our churning city and see so many homes being torn down or built up, when the staircase to the oversized mansion isn't finished and the ugly retaining wall and drainage pipes are exposed, when gentrification knocks down the slanted bungalow and the sad beauty of the land is revealed anew—in such moments of phase shift we pierce the illusion generated by finished buildings with finished trim: the illusion of stability. Nothing is stable. Nothing is fixed except as we fix it.

And that is our opportunity. If Maestas were here, he would remind us: let's not get too attached to this shiny new place. Let's keep on the lookout for another abandoned school to occupy, without permission—and let's teach each other anew how to govern ourselves.

18

TOO BUSY TO LOVE

Center for Civic Innovation · Atlanta, GA
June 23, 2018

FLANNERY O'CONNOR
From Mystery and Manners
Published 1969

There is something in us, as storytellers and as listeners to stories, that demands the redemptive act, that demands that what falls at least be offered the chance to be restored. The reader of today looks for this motion, and rightly so, but what he has forgotten is the cost of it. His sense of evil is diluted or lacking altogether, and so he has forgotten the price of restoration. When he reads a novel, he wants either his senses tormented or his spirits raised. He wants to be transported, instantly, either to mock damnation or a mock innocence.

FOURTEEN PRINCIPLES OF
MARINE CORPS LEADERSHIP

From Marine Corps Values: A User's Guide for Discussion Leaders
2016 edition

BEARING: Creating a favorable impression in carriage, appearance, and personal conduct at all times.

COURAGE: Courage is a mental quality that recognizes fear of danger or criticism, but enables a Marine to proceed in the face of danger with calmness and firmness.

DECISIVENESS: Ability to make decisions promptly and to announce them in a clear, forceful manner.

DEPENDABILITY: The certainty of proper performance of duty.

ENDURANCE: The mental and physical stamina measured by the ability to withstand pain, fatigue, stress, and hardship.

ENTHUSIASM: The display of sincere interest and exuberance in the performance of duty.

INITIATIVE: Taking action in the absence of orders.

INTEGRITY: Uprightness of character and soundness of moral principles. The quality of truthfulness and honesty.

JUDGMENT: The ability to weigh facts and possible courses of action in order to make sound decisions.

JUSTICE: Giving reward and punishment according to the merits of the case in question. The ability to administer a system of rewards and punishments impartially and consistently.

KNOWLEDGE: Understanding of a science or an art. The range of one's information, including professional knowledge and understanding of your Marines.

LOYALTY: Faithfulness to country, Corps, unit, seniors, subordinates, and peers.

TACT: The ability to deal with others in a manner that will maintain good relations and avoid offense. More simply stated, tact is the ability to say and do the right thing at the right time.

UNSELFISHNESS: Avoidance of providing for one's own comfort and personal advancement at the expense of others.

FREDERICK DOUGLASS

From a speech before the British and Foreign Anti-Slavery Society
Delivered in Finsbury Chapel, London
1846

Instead of preaching the gospel against this tyranny, rebuke, and wrong, ministers of religion have sought, by all and every means, to throw in the background whatever in the Bible could be construed into opposition to slavery, and to bring forward that which they could torture into its support. This I conceive to be the darkest feature of slavery, and the most difficult to attack, because it is identified with religion, and exposes those who denounce it to the charge of infidelity. . . .

I love that religion that sends its votaries to bind up the wounds of him that has fallen among thieves. I love that religion that makes it the duty of its disciples to visit the fatherless and the widow in their affliction. I love that religion that is based upon the glorious principle, of love to God and love to man; which makes its followers do unto others as they themselves would be done by. If you demand liberty to yourself, it says, grant it to your neighbors. If you claim a right to think for yourself, it says, allow your neighbors the same right. . . .

It is because I love this religion that I hate the slaveholding, the woman-whipping, the mind-darkening, the soul-destroying religion that exists in the Southern states of America. It is because I regard the one as good, and pure, and holy, that I cannot but regard the other as bad, corrupt, and wicked. Loving the one I must hate the other; holding to the one I must reject the other.

I'm so grateful to you for inviting us to Atlanta and for showing up this morning for Civic Saturday. You all embody a spirit—some call it the Atlanta Spirit—that is more than can-do; it is *must*-do. More than self-help, it's *selves*-help.

Atlanta, I have come to realize, is like America in all its complexity and contradiction.

It is, as W. E. B. Du Bois said, south of the North but north of the South, challenging the assumptions and mores of each half of the nation. It's a city that General Sherman had to burn to the ground so that Dr. King could rise from it a century later. A capital of slavery and a hub of black liberation. A city of rising prosperity and inequality, of suburban sprawl and status anxiety and immigrant influx and persistent poverty—and beneath it all, a web of faith communities and a corporate power structure that dominates civic life. This is a city with global cultural clout, where *Queer Eye* and Donald Glover's *Atlanta* and *The Real Housewives of Atlanta*, to say nothing of Coke and Home Depot, all feed and form the American public imagination.

Taste the feeling. More saving, more doing. You all made that.

This is a city with boosterism and salesmanship in its DNA, a place defined by ambitious slogans that become narratives that become agendas that become the actual ambitions of the people of the place.

Though it was founded a century after Savannah and other ports of the region, Atlanta even as a small town claimed to be "Gate City." After Reconstruction failed, it named itself the capital of the New South. In the 1920s, your chamber of commerce launched a national ad campaign called "Forward Atlanta" that led national corporations to locate here. Then in the 1960s, as other Southern cities became infamous for resisting civil rights violently, Atlanta came up with its most famous slogan yet: "The City Too Busy to Hate."

The pragmatism and tolerance of that slogan are deeply American. It could've been the slogan for the Dutch and English who built the polyglot markets of New Amsterdam and New York. It's more realistic than "The City of Brotherly Love," which Philadelphia truly was in the age of Franklin—but we're not in that age anymore. And relative to cities like Selma that found *plenty* of time to hate in the 1960s, it's downright admirable. It was admirable in January 1965 when Atlanta mayor Ivan Allen and J. Paul Austin, the CEO of Coca-Cola, pushed a reluctant white business community to host a gala to honor the newly minted Nobel Laureate Martin Luther King Jr.

"It's embarrassing for Coca-Cola to be located in a city that refuses to honor its Nobel Prize winner," Austin told his peers. "We are an international business. The Coca-Cola Company does not need Atlanta. You all need to decide whether Atlanta needs the Coca-Cola Company." The elite fell in line and the gala was sold out and made national news. Some say that was the night Atlanta truly became too busy to hate.

But let's be honest. "Too busy to hate," admirable though it may be, still sets a pretty low bar. It sets the same low bar that the idea of tolerance does. Tolerance, after all, implies irritation or distaste— some *other* to be suffered, overcome, and *tolerated*. Being too busy to hate doesn't mean the desire to hate has been eradicated. It just means we don't have time to indulge it. We are prioritizing busyness— business—over hate.

There is a higher bar. And a place like Atlanta, that has so often led the South and the nation to face its flaws and fears, should lead us over that bar. The question in Atlanta and America is not whether we're too busy to hate. It's whether we are too busy to love.

I've been thinking about this question the last few weeks and especially the last few days as we've all been awash in images of agents of the United States government separating infants and toddlers from their mothers and fathers and incarcerating them.

Are we too busy to love? Some have hardened their hearts, either because they think there's too much pain and too little power in this situation or because, as some Trumpists believe, the images are fake and photoshopped and can be ignored.

Are we too busy to love? I've marveled at the commentary from the president on up in which these children, whose immigrant parents seek asylum or yearn for a chance to pick your lettuce or empty your mother's bedpan, are described not as humans but as an infestation, as animals subject to "catch-and-release," to be caged and kenneled.

Are we too busy to love? What strikes me as I travel the country doing this work of fostering powerful citizenship is how many people flat out don't have time for this. They are at Terminal B in Hartsfield-Jackson walking past the CNN screen about migrant children being separated from their mothers and incarcerated. They are on a MARTA train to go work their second job and there is no CNN. They are stuck in Atlanta traffic trying to get their own kids—not some foreign law-breaker's kids—to soccer practice.

Citizen University started organizing Civic Saturday gatherings in Seattle in 2016 because we sensed that people in this age of radical inequality and social fragmentation *are* too busy to love—but that people will respond to an invitation to make the time for love. And here we are. We've organized such gatherings in other places that asked for them, and we've started a Civic Seminary to prepare other Americans to lead Civic Saturdays and build these communities.

Our first class of Civic Seminarians learned all about the American creed, about what young Abraham Lincoln called America's "political religion" and what I call civic religion, about the teaching and practice of power and character in public life, and they boiled down all their learning into a simple compact idea: *civic love.*

This morning I want to explore this idea of civic love with you. What does it mean to love like a citizen? To love your country. To love your neighbor. To love your enemies. I want to probe beneath these three ideas—clichés, really—to ask what choices we make or avoid when we practice civic love. What does it cost to love—to choose to love even when you don't have time for it or when no one really cares whether you do or don't?

I.

Let's start with love of country.

Thirty years ago, when I was nineteen, my father drove me to LaGuardia Airport and he put me on a Delta Shuttle to National Airport in Washington. From there I boarded a bus that took me an hour and a half to Quantico, Virginia. The moment I got off that bus that night, large, muscle-bound men began screaming at me and the other passengers, pushing us around and making us dump our bags to get in line and get our heads shaved. So began my embarkation into Marine Corps Officer Candidates School.

I spent six weeks that summer at OCS in what was called Platoon Leaders Class (Junior) and I went back the next summer for six more weeks of PLC (Senior). Those twelve weeks shaped me profoundly. I learned so much—about the history and culture of the Marine Corps, of course, but also about what it felt like to be part of something greater than oneself, connected to a line of service that goes back to the creation of the nation. The red and the gold, the anchor and the globe, the cadence calls, the tales of uncommon valor, the brutally honest leadership coaching we'd get from peers and instructors alike, the physical and mental hardships that I endured with a group of other students from south and north, rural towns and inner cities, rich and poor families.

I was the only Asian American in my company, the only Ivy Leaguer, one of two with glasses, and definitely the smallest. In that swamp crucible, I did more than survive. My unit the second summer, Fox Company, Second Platoon, began with forty-three candidates and after attrition ended with twenty-five. I ranked eighth. And when I graduated from OCS in August 1989 and marched with the battalion across the parade deck, snapping EYES RIGHT at the brass in the reviewing stand with my immigrant parents in the bleachers, listening to the band play the Marine Corps Hymn, I thought what a miracle this country is.

Later that year, when I was back at college, I chose to decline the second lieutenant's commission I had earned. I chose instead to serve in government, where I came to work with leaders like Georgia's Senator Sam Nunn on foreign policy and later with his daughter and my friend Michelle Nunn on volunteerism and national service. I've never regretted my choice. But I often marvel at how much my sense of patriotism was shaped by the Marines—and how little of it is about the military or warfighting and how much of it is about core ethics and values. About a set of ideals.

To love this country is to love its ideals. And to love its ideals is not to shout about them, to have a parade about them, to wave or hug the flag. To love the ideals of this country is to force the country, in the company of others, to live up to those ideals.

This week many citizens are swarming to LaGuardia Airport, not to send their sons and daughters off to OCS like my father did in 1988 but to show support to the terrified undocumented parents and toddlers who've been separated and dispersed to various holding facilities across the nation. These citizens are swarming to airports and detention centers, just as they did after the first Muslim travel ban, to make what John Lewis calls "good trouble": to warn the government of the United States and of the several states that we the people, using freedom of the press and freedom of assembly and freedom of speech, will keep defending the disfavored.

The body politic has an immune system. People of conscience are the antibodies. And we will keep swarming the virus of hate that is loose in the land and we will contain it.

All these years later, I don't remember how to take apart an M-16A2 rifle. I don't recall the ins and outs of small-unit infantry tactics. But my idea of what it means to be a citizen was formed by that list of leadership principles for Marine officers that I learned in 1988. I took that list seriously. I internalized it and retain it to this day.

So when I observe people today, whether it's a high school student in our YouthPower Project who emigrated from Guatemala last year and is still learning English, or whether it's the president of the United States, who is also still learning English, or his chief of staff or secretary of defense, both former Marine generals, I judge them by their bearing, yes, but more by their bent for justice, which means not justice for the strong but justice for the weak. I judge them by their moral courage, which the Marines taught me is harder to sustain than physical courage, especially when the crowd encourages cowardice. By their unselfishness, which is not only about letting the men and women in your charge eat before you eat, but is also about leading in a way that does not increase their fear of scarcity and their every-man-for-himself scapegoating of outsiders.

To love this country, in short, is to lead and to live with a sense of humanity, humility, responsibility, and decency that is in short supply in national politics and utterly absent in this administration's execution of the laws. A nation must have borders and be able to regulate them. There must be consequences for those who evade those borders and the law of entry. And nothing in those two statements permits, much less requires, the intentional tearing apart of families and the intentional traumatization of children calculated to gain negotiating leverage or to please the base or trig the libs or *whatever*.

We've heard often in the last week the earnest claim, "This is not who we are." I beg to differ. Our history—from the Thomas Frazer and Company slave auction house that once stood on the site of the Five Points MARTA station a block from here to the expulsion of the Cherokee from Georgia to the abusive assimilation practiced at Indian boarding schools to the Fugitive Slave Act to the incarceration of Japanese American citizens after Pearl Harbor—our history shakes its head and replies, "This is *exactly* who we are." The more plausible claim, then, is that this is not who are called to be.

We are called to be bigger. We are called by the creed we profess to believe. The creed of the Declaration and the Preamble of the Constitution and the Fourteenth Amendment and young King's "Letter from a Birmingham Jail" and Reagan's speech at the Berlin Wall and Susan B. Anthony's speech at her trial for the crime of attempted voting. That creed is not blind reverence for law, for evil is often legal. The creed is liberty and justice for all.

We are called to renounce any religious institution, as Frederick Douglass did, that contorts itself to rationalize hatred and weaponize bigotry. And the same is true of our American civic religion. Any movement or party that contorts itself to become an authoritarian cult of personality is one that true patriots must challenge and reclaim. We are called to do this—to live up to this creed—not just as faithful citizens of the United States, for those of us lucky enough to have that status, but as citizens of our towns.

2.

This brings me to the second dimension of civic love I want to explore today: to love your neighbor. That is the injunction of Scripture and it is a decent starting point for any notion of civic love. We can convince ourselves we believe it. Then we take note of life in the city and we face ourselves more candidly.

Last week I was in Kansas City, Missouri, and I saw a man die. I was on the fifteenth floor of the Holiday Inn Aladdin Hotel. It was Thursday around 3:30 p.m. I was working on my laptop—actually, I was writing a tweet about Romans 13, the part of the Bible that Jeff Sessions and Sarah Sanders cited as authority for their policy of separating migrant families, which, it turns out, is the part of the Bible that slavery advocates cited as authority for the Fugitive Slave Act. Getting that tweet phrased just right seemed so important in that moment. Then I heard a sound outside like a gunshot. It was midafternoon in the heart of downtown. Must've been construction in the big plaza across the street by the convention center. I kept on crafting my tweet. Twenty seconds later, BANG BANG BANG BANG. There was no mistaking the noise now. I ran across the room to the window overlooking that plaza and saw four cops in tactical formation, handguns drawn, approaching a person who was on the ground and on his back.

The plaza is a wide-open concrete space divided like a grid by small shade trees every twenty feet or so, and near some of the trees are little tables and chairs. The man who had been shot was partially in the shade of one of those trees. His face was obscured but his right arm was not and I will confess to you that in that instant of realizing what I was witnessing, one of my first thoughts was to see whether that arm was white or black, and then immediately after that, I felt a flash of something like relief, ashamed relief, that it was not black. This is where we are today. The policemen approached him cautiously, then nudged him with their feet, at which point his arm began to move, as if he were weakly reaching for something. Or waving something away.

I walked back to the desk to get my phone, unsure of what I was present for but sensing I should document it, and by the time I came back to the window a few seconds later the man was receiving CPR. A few minutes later he was dead. So many emotions washed over me. Shock. Sadness, profound sadness that this person had lost his life looking up at scraggly branches and a hazy sky in ninety-six-degree heat as men with guns and armor stood over him and strangers behind the curtains of hotel windows watched. A feeling of impropriety, even *impiety*, a sense that I should not have seen that—that someone this man knew should have witnessed his body's last movement and the passing of his soul.

I say all this without knowing who this man was except, as a police officer later told me when they were taking down the crime scene tape, that he was a "bad guy." There were in fact two men, as the local TV news would soon report, who'd gotten into a loud fight about a stolen golf cart. One had a gun and was pistol-whipping the other. An observer called the police. The police say that when they arrived on the scene the one with the gun fired at them. That was the first bang. The cops fired back. The next four bangs. And in that blaze they killed not just the man with the gun but the other man too. I never even saw the other man, who was entirely obscured by the tree, and didn't realize there was a second body until two separate tarps were laid on the ground.

What was the fight about? Were they both, as the cop said, bad guys? Or only one of them? Did they both have to die? Who knew them? Who mourns them? These are the kinds of issues that local news did not probe on Twitter or TV or in the *Kansas City Star*. It was just another day in America. In fact, that was the second police-involved killing of the day in KC: that morning a woman wielding a sword in a residential neighborhood had been shot by police. A few days later both stories were swept from the headlines by an inmate who escaped transfer and killed two sheriff's deputies.

The next morning, I saw something nearly as chilling as the death of a stranger. I pushed aside the thin curtain and looked down into the plaza, and where that unnamed man had bled and breathed his last, there was now just an irregular patch of sand on the gray surface of this plaza. Right by that patch of sand, under that same shade tree and in one of those dinky little chairs, sat a man in a dress shirt and khakis sipping his morning joe and looking at his phone. He had no idea what had happened there less than a day before. No one did. The plaza was its near-empty prosaic self.

This story is not just about how we've normalized the epidemic levels of gun violence in our country. It is about the overall coarseness of civic life. We take that for granted in America now, the same way we accept strip malls and billboards everywhere selling us crap. This state of degradation long precedes Trump, though it also begat Trump.

After fifteen years of war fought by a subcontracted 1 percent of us, after forty years of concentration of wealth into the hands of a very different 1 percent, after the thinning out of Elks and Rotary Clubs, after twenty years of reality TV and cage fighting, after ten years of social media narcissism, while despair and addiction have shortened the average American lifespan and white lifespans in particular, what we have is a civic culture in which we don't know our neighbors except as they might irritate us and we don't know ourselves except as Facebook friends might validate us. We don't serve together. We don't play together. We don't sing together. We don't fix things together.

To love your neighbors doesn't require that you like them. It does require that you know them. Gentrification makes that harder. Politics makes that harder. Busyness makes that harder. Which is why we have to be the ones to make a habit of neighborly love.

Neighborly love is well below MLK's exalted ideal of *agape*, the Greek word he favored describing selfless, all-inclusive love. Neighborly love has some of what Ben Franklin would have promoted, a reciprocal spirit of mutual interest. It also has some of what the social scientist Mark Granovetter called two centuries later "the strength of weak ties"— bonds of trust and affection strong enough to make you care about common concerns but not so strong that they become blindly tribal. It is an agreement to see each other: to recognize and be recognized, to not let another human fall into the anonymity of a message board or the grim grid of that concrete plaza in Kansas City. Do you *see* your neighbor? And I don't mean just the person next door. I mean the homeless man on the sidewalk. The immigrant woman cleaning your bathroom or preparing your lunch.

There's a new documentary out about Mister Rogers called *Won't You Be My Neighbor?* Those of you who do remember the PBS children's show, and Fred Rogers's soothing and subtly radical message that you are loved and capable of loving, will recall that when white Americans did not want black Americans to put their black bodies in the blue waters of public swimming pools, Mister Rogers and Officer Clemmons, the black police officer character, took their shoes off and sat in lawn chairs with their feet in a wading pool, and spoke as friends. And a generation watched and learned.

To love your neighbor is to see them. To humanize them. To share the gift of believing in their dignity. To rescue them from the noisy loneliness that plagues American life. To save them from the social death that often leads to actual death. This may seem a long way from the troubles of our democratic institutions in Washington and the assaults of today's angry populists against the rule of law. But it's not a long way. It is right there. You get neo-Nazi and white supremacist rallies—and you get masked antifa activists—when nobody knows your name or nobody loves their neighbors. You fall into the habit of justifying evil when evil is the nearest path to belonging.

3.

Let me come now to the third and final dimension of civic love, and maybe the hardest: loving your enemies. Recently I was at a very interesting two-day meeting with many homeless conservatives. I don't mean they are without physical shelter. I mean they have been left without a party now that their party has become a cult of Trump.

One of them was the columnist Mona Charen, who had the guts at CPAC, the annual conservative conference, to call out the hypocrites there who had defended Roy Moore and embraced French neo-Nazi

Marine Le Pen. She was booed forcefully, threatened, and needed a security escort to leave the building. Another was David French, a writer for the conservative magazine *National Review*, a devout Calvinist who grew up in small-town Tennessee and still lives there, who served in Iraq as an Army JAG, and who has had friends and neighbors literally turn their backs on him at church and social gatherings because he has had the temerity to warn that Trumpism is at odds with true conservativism. A third was Sarah Longwell of the Log Cabin Republicans, who knew she was conservative long before she knew she was gay and who has fiercely argued that an embrace of liberty should mean an embrace of her and her wife. And she has watched one GOP operative after another capitulate to bigotry.

What struck me most about these folks was their courage. They have paid a price for their stance. They have been ostracized socially and professionally and are reviled by many Trumpian true believers who regard them as infidels. They've been forced to hang out with the likes of *me*. Which then made me think: Who are *their* enemies?

There was a time not long ago when I might have been their enemy. I've been a Democrat all my life and I generally have progressive views. Mona and I disagree on affirmative action. David and I disagree on the Colorado baker who refused to make a wedding cake for a gay couple. Sarah and I don't see eye to eye on tax cuts for the rich.

But we've been brought together by a shared concern for the health of the republic and a shared commitment to defending democracy against rising authoritarianism and tribalism and polarization. We've been brought together by a crisis. And because we are at the same table now with some common purpose, we have humanized each other. Mona and David have kids about the age of my daughter and stepdaughter. Sarah has a fighting spirit, a solid core, a get-it-done attitude, and I just want to be more like her. David's wife has written books with Sarah Palin, which you literally could not pay me enough to do, yet we discovered we have a dear friend and colleague in common.

I can tell you that if the United States ever gets to a saner politics, where it's just about arguing over our philosophies and recognizing that democracy is meant to be a game of infinite repeat play, not a finite scorched-earth contest—if we get to that saner place, where I'll be debating with David and Sarah and Mona and others like them, winning some and losing some, I can tell you these people will not be my enemies. Not because I love everything about them or everything about their beliefs. But because I found *something* about them and *something* about their beliefs to love.

Most of us don't get a chance to engage like this. Think about the countless missed connections in our lives as citizens, missed chances to make friends out of enemies. Let me close now with a tale of two drivers.

The week before last I was in Wichita, with the folks at the Kansas Health Foundation and the Kansas Leadership Center. The man who gave me a ride to the airport was about sixty-five years old. White, Kansas native, Air Force veteran, used to have a good job in aircraft maintenance. When he learned that I ran an organization called Citizen University, he could not wait to share his views about how "illegals" had taken away jobs at the factories. He told me about a woman he knows who is here illegally and had gotten free tuition to get certified in phlebotomy, the field he had once hoped to enter. He said he'd told her she should get U.S. citizenship. When I explained that there is no way for her just to "get" citizenship, he was unmoved. I said Congress needs to create a pathway to citizenship for the eleven million undocumented people because, among other reasons, we could not possibly deport them all at once. He replied, "Not all at once."

Then on my way to the airport yesterday, I met his opposite number. A woman who grew up in the Seattle exurbs, got herself emancipated at sixteen so she could live on her own in the city, was a voter and a left-wing activist from the get-go, marching against Vietnam, against Reagan's embrace of the religious right, against the Iraq War, and now against the people who put immigrants in concentration camps and who, as she put it, hate dykes like her. She is an artist and photographer and she and her partner dream of retiring to the Oregon Coast. But she is over sixty and is barely breaking even as a Lyft driver. After a long career in telecom, she encountered the silent ageism of the tech workplace. She took English and math courses to get her AA but says that unless her degree can take her back in time forty years, it's not going to help her. So, after years of applying for jobs and not getting interviews, for her final English 106 assignment she wrote a break-up letter to corporate America. She posted it to her LinkedIn page. A big FU to the big businesses she says have screwed Seattle.

These two Americans have never met and likely never will. But they think they know each other. They have pictures in their minds of each other: the coiled racist who wants to build a wall and take us back to the Fifties; the pierced-nose socialist who cares about everyone but Americans. Their minds are set to Enemymode and Enemymode makes two-dimensional characters out of three-dimensional humans. Enemymode is flattening and blinding and all-consuming. Like a good video game, it trains you to focus and filter out complication and just keep score. I am naturally good at Enemymode. You are too.

But if I could bring these two American enemies to the same town and introduce them, they would discover they are living the same story. They would recognize the sadness, the disappointment in each other's stories, as well as the determination and resilience. They would see that they face a common adversary of free market fundamentalism and of globalized capital that's free to exploit local labor. They would discover they both have been treated as outsiders in their own land. They would see that they don't have to pass down that pain to other outsiders, that they can help each other and not fall for demagogues of either the right or the left. They would realize they are not alone. They would discover civic power—and the possibility of civic love.

Here's the thing: I *can* bring these two Americans together. So can you. We are surrounded by them. We *are* them. We just need to make the time to listen to their stories—and each of us to our own conscience. We cannot be too busy to love in Atlanta or America. In fact, we've got to be in a hurry to love. There are migrant babies in cages screaming for their mothers. Be in a hurry to love. There are angry white men blaming nearby immigrants for the sins of faraway capitalists. Search for something in them to love. Be in a hurry to love. There are inflamed liberals who cannot or will not distinguish between a conservative and a Nazi. Love them still. Be in a hurry to love.

Flannery O'Connor, daughter of Georgia and great storyteller of the South, warned us to resist tidy redemptive narratives. I offer no promise of redemption. Our country's soul is on fire the way this city was at the end of the Civil War, and what will douse the flames is not more hating but more loving. That is our only hope. To love like citizens: to cherish our creed, our neighbors, our enemies.

Hurry up and love. Our country calls us.

19

READING OUR COUNTRY

Hillman City Collaboratory · Seattle, WA
August 4, 2018

TOM WOLFE

From The Right Stuff
Published 1979

It was as if the press in America, for all its vaunted
independence, were a great colonial animal, an animal made
up of countless clustered organisms responding to a single
nervous system. In the late 1950s (as in the late 1970s) the
animal seemed determined that in all matters of national
importance the *proper emotion*, the *seemly sentiment*, the
fitting moral tone should be established and should prevail;
and all information that muddied the tone and weakened the
feeling should simply be thrown down the memory hole. In
a later period this impulse of the animal would take the form
of blazing indignation about corruption, abuses of power, and
even minor ethical lapses, among public officials; here, in April

of 1959, it took the form of a blazing patriotic passion for the seven test pilots who had volunteered to go into space. In either case, the animal's fundamental concern remained the same: the public, the populace, the citizenry, must be provided with *the correct feelings*! One might regard this animal as the consummate hypocritical Victorian gent. Sentiments that one scarcely gives a second thought to in one's private life are nevertheless insisted upon in all public utterances.

LAYLI LONG SOLDIER
From Whereas: *"38"*
Published 2017

You may or may not have heard about the Dakota 38.

If this is the first time you've heard of it, you might wonder, "What is the Dakota 38?"

The Dakota 38 refers to thirty-eight Dakota men who were executed by hanging, under orders from President Abraham Lincoln.

To date, this is the largest "legal" mass execution in US history.

The hanging took place on December 26, 1862—the day after Christmas.

This was the *same week* that President Lincoln signed the Emancipation Proclamation.

In the preceding sentence, I italicize "same week" for emphasis.

There was a movie titled *Lincoln* about the presidency of Abraham Lincoln.

The signing of the Emancipation Proclamation was included in the film *Lincoln*; the hanging of the Dakota 38 was not.

In any case, you might be asking, "Why were thirty-eight Dakota men hung?"

As a side note, the past tense of hang is *hung*, but when referring to the capital punishment of hanging, the correct past tense is *hanged*.

So it's possible that you're asking, "Why were thirty-eight Dakota men hanged?"

They were hanged for the Sioux Uprising.

I want to tell you about the Sioux Uprising, but I don't know where to begin.

SUZAN-LORI PARKS

From the play Father Comes Home from the Wars: Parts 1, 2 & 3
Published 2015

COLONEL: I am grateful every day that God made me white. As a white I stand on the summit and all the other colors reside beneath me, down below. For me, no matter how much money I've got or don't got, if my farm is failing or my horse is dead, if my woman is sour or my child has passed on, I can at least rest in the grace that God made me white. And I don't ever have to fight the Battle of Darkness. What difficulties I may encounter will at least never be those. Life might bring me low but not that low. And I know that I will be received in most any quarter. And if the Lord should choose to further advance my economics, then I will be received in all the great houses. Not so with the lower ones. The lower ones will always be lowly. No matter how high they climb. There is a kind of comfort in that. And I take that comfort. For no matter how low I fall, and no matter how thoroughly I fail, I will always be white.

It's Seafair weekend in Seattle, which I liken to an intraseason solstice: the point of peak ripeness of that sensation of summer. For me, that sensation has always been bound up in books. Books in sunshine. When my daughter, Olivia, was six and seven, we would go to the downtown Central Library at the start of summer, receive a blank form for the Summer Reading Challenge, and check out a stack of *Goosebumps* books. And in the ensuing weeks she would joyfully fill in the lines of the form with the titles of the texts that she'd devoured while sitting in the yard, laying in our tent, or spread out on the couch. If you read ten books you'd get a certificate and maybe a T-shirt. I don't remember what the reward was exactly because it wasn't the point.

The point was that Olivia, now nineteen, is a voracious reader to this day.

On this midsummer's morning, I'd like to reflect on what it means to read like a citizen. To decode, to make sense, to cohere patterns from chaos. To read, in short, is to know how to live among others. It is to know ourselves and our nation. It's why in a great city, public life is dense with reading and readers: at bus stops, on the trolleys, in the cafes.

Harry Truman said, "Not all readers are leaders, but all leaders are readers." Truman's line rings deeply true. A love of reading is central to deep citizenship. Reading novels. Reading histories. Reading plays. Reading poems. These habits, in turn, make us better at reading people.

Reading situations. Reading trends. Reading trouble. Virginia Woolf put it this way: "One has only to read, to look, to listen, to remember."

The ambiguity of this single line of text is arrestingly beautiful. Let me say it again: "One has only to read, to look, to listen, to remember."

Does she mean that one needs to read, look, and listen *in order* to remember? Or is she saying that to read, look, listen, and remember—to do these four discrete things—is sufficient for a happy life? The text, like that of the Second Amendment or the phrase "all men are created equal," is forever open to interpretation.

I usually have several books on my nightstand or on our coffee table or on the end table. I like having those texts interweave in my waking and sleeping imagination. I love connecting dots from one to another, between memory and aspiration. And so today I want to share with you some ideas, images, emotions, and interpretations that four books have stirred in me during this summer of reading and sense-making.

I.

A couple of months ago I finally saw *Hidden Figures*, the film about three African American women mathematicians who were the unsung heroes of America's early space program. Their complex calculations made it possible for the rocket launches of the Mercury missions to succeed. It was the age before supercomputers—and before racial integration had become a norm, which is what makes this a double overcoming-the-odds story. The movie was as neatly inspiring as I expected it to be.

When I saw *Hidden Figures*, the novelist and journalist Tom Wolfe had recently died, so I decided to re-read his classic book about the space program called *The Right Stuff*. That book, in Wolfe's distinctive hyperkinetic prose, describes how the first American astronauts arose from the 1950s culture of military fighter pilots. They were daring young Americans who, as JFK put it in his inaugural address, were "tempered by war, disciplined by a hard and bitter peace." Men of the new generation to whom the torch had been passed, like Chuck Yeager of West Virginia and the Air Force, the first human to break the sound barrier, and John Glenn of Ohio and the Marine Corps, the first American to orbit the earth. That culture was all about "pushing the envelope," a term coined by the pilots who were testing the limits of their experimental aircraft. It was a culture bound up with the sparkly optimism of Kennedy's New Frontier and the existential anxiety of the Cold War. Fundamentally, it was about living fast: in Wolfe's capitalized mantra, "Flying & Drinking and Drinking & Driving."

The Blue Angels of the U.S. Navy roaring overhead this weekend in F/A-18s are also daring fighter jocks who are ice-cold under pressure—but over the generations the homespun roughness of test pilot culture has been polished away. Here's my favorite story from *The Right Stuff*: two nights before Chuck Yeager was to attempt the first supersonic flight, he and his fellow pilots and his wife, Glennis, were at the bar near the airfield, and after many beers he and Glennis decided to get on a couple of horses and race each other through the Joshua trees in the moonlit desert. Yeager never saw the gate that catapulted him at full speed; when he got up, his right side hurt like hell. He'd broken a couple of ribs. He soon realized there was no way he'd be able to use his right arm to close the cockpit door of his X-1 rocket plane. But there was also no way he was going to tell his commanders or beg out of the flight. So, he confided in another pilot, Jack Ridley, an Oklahoma-born engineer who sawed nine inches off the end of a broomstick and made a lever that Yeager could use with his *left* hand to turn the handle that would secure the door. The next morning, Chuck Yeager broke the sound barrier.

That's a story about American ingenuity. It's a story about having the right stuff: a willingness to take great risks—even reckless risks—on frontiers old and new. It is a story about American character. But what *is* American character? Shall we measure it by the acts of heroes or of everyday people? By the worst among us or by the best? By patterns over time or by signature moments? By the traits of the long-dominant group or of the long-subordinated?

Those African American female mathematicians working in the basement also had the right stuff, but until their story was told the American people didn't know it. Didn't know they had lived, didn't know their names: Katherine Johnson of West Virginia, Dorothy Vaughan of Missouri, Mary Jackson of Virginia. American character is a *fable*, told by some to stand for all: a narrative that may have basis in fact but is not historical so much as aspirational. That's what *Hidden Figures* was too: based on a true story, but tidied up, with only a nod to the messiness of the world and to the unhappy beginnings and endings that existed in real life outside the frame of the film. It exists as legend. A tale we like to tell about ourselves.

Tom Wolfe's often manic prose can mislead a reader into thinking he was a booster, a true believer in the frenzied patriotism that he chronicles and a full participant in the primal mass yearning in 1959 and '60 and '61 to make heroes of those astronauts because they were willing to race the godless Soviets and sit on top of exploding rockets and die for our glory, and so when they came back alive they needed to be turned into *gods*. But read *The Right Stuff* closely and you realize Wolfe is questioning that worshipful exuberance, revealing its manic brittleness; he is, in exaggerating the great American narrative about the rugged individualist cowboy flyboy American hero, asking whether we doth protest too much. Whether we are nervous conformists at heart. Whether we are more scared and empty and godless than we want to admit.

And when he talks about how the third and seventh and tenth missions to space became routine and the public grew bored, and the long-suffering wives of those flyboys and spacemen felt cheated out of the parades and adulation that had been part of the social contract of being the wife of an astronaut, Wolfe is describing a coming back to earth: a routinization of the thrill, yes, but also a reminder that it is impossible to sustain a fever pitch of anything—and that myths, even necessary myths, will lose their force if you stare at them too long.

2.

Which brings me to the second book of my summer. It's called *The Death of Democracy*, by Benjamin Carter Hett, and it's an absorbing and alarming history of Germany's Weimar Republic and the rise of Adolf Hitler.

I've long known the outlines of this period between the world wars: the way the German people resented having to pay reparations; the hyperinflation and constant economic upheavals long before the Great Depression; the exploitation of democratic institutions by demagogues; the iron partisanship that became weaponized and violent; the fateful miscalculations by establishment right-wing leaders who thought they could control Hitler by bringing him to power.

Do you get now why I'm alarmed?

But until reading this book I did not appreciate the degree to which two myths, about August and November, had shaped the politics of Weimar Germany. The first myth said that in August 1914 the nation was unified and joyful as it went to war. Everybody's memories of that time were as warm and sun-dappled as the month itself. The reality, though, was that the nation was divided; there were as many demonstrations against the war as for it. The other myth said that in gray, cold November 1919, the nation was betrayed by liberal politicians who ended the war too soon.

Both myths were made possible by the fact that the fighting in World War I never touched German soil. And because Germans were fed a steady diet of fake news that stoked the passions of August, most were shocked when the November armistice came five years later. How could it be that Germany had given up: their armies were on the move! How could its politicians accept such humiliating terms? Yes, many young men had died—there was no denying it—but not a single shell had landed on the fatherland.

There was only one way for millions of Germans to close this gap of cognitive dissonance and that was to buy into the myth of the "stab in the back": a nationalist narrative that said the generals were doing their jobs and the war was still winnable except that left-wing politicians and Jews had conspired to deny the army its final chance and had betrayed the nation at Versailles in November 1919.

Perhaps the most powerful exponent of the "stab in the back" lie was Field Marshal Paul von Hindenburg, the supreme commander who had not been able to prevail in the fields of France but who was unwilling to take responsibility for his failure or for the truce that he knew was Germany's only way out. He kept his distance from the armistice signing, and when he returned from the war all he did was cast blame and legitimatize the stab-in-the-back conspiracy theories that fueled right-wing revanchism.

That's enough to put the man in the Hall of Infamy. But he wasn't done. Later, as a still-revered military man, Hindenburg was elected president. He hastened the death of democracy by collaborating with one right-wing nationalist politician after another to gut the Constitution in the name of staving off communism. The proud Prussian general was always scornful of Hitler, whom he called "the Bohemian private." But as the Nazi party reached critical mass during the depths of the Depression, Hindenburg chose to make Hitler chancellor, thinking that he could control him, rather than form an anti-fascist coalition with parties of the left and center. The rest, as they say, is history.

The United States today is not Weimar-era Germany. But moral cowardice is timeless. And so is the desire to believe in stories where you are both the victim and the hero. Millions of white Americans today cannot abide a reality in which they think they are losing relative power and privilege. They will not consider the possibility of coalition with long-disfavored minorities. They see life as zero-sum. They don't believe that we are all better off when we're all better off. So they nurse two myths, akin to the myths of August and November. The first myth says America was greatest when whites dominated. The second says we can keep it that way forever.

You can't blame Donald Trump for exploiting these anxieties any more than you can blame a virus for infecting the body. You *can* blame every Republican elected leader who knows better and stays silent or, worse, pulls a Hindenburg and calculates that this demagoguery and degradation of our institutions is worth a corporate tax cut and a Supreme Court pick or two. And you *can* blame every Democrat who would rather resist than persuade, who cannot explain to someone who feels otherwise that life is more than zero-sum and that we *can* be better together.

And that's something else this book has reminded me: the desire to be both the victim and the hero of one's own story is as strong on the left as it is on the right.

That was true a hundred years ago in Germany and it is true today in the United States. It is true in over-righteous Seattle. One cautionary lesson of the Weimar years is how factional divisions—in that case, between reactionary Protestants and centrist Catholics, between nationalists and democrats, capitalists and communists—made for a dehumanized politics in which *everyone* evaded responsibility for the good of the realm. Compromise evaporated. Everyone weaponized identity and the winners killed the losers. The socialists and the conservative nationalists had their own militia-gangs like the Nazi SS. But because the winners killed the losers, today we know only the SS.

Winners killing losers. Some might say that's life. Or that's politics. Maybe. But it wasn't supposed to be the American way. Or maybe it was always the American way but it wasn't supposed to be the American story. Either way, for better and for worse, no matter who kills whom, nothing is ever truly dead. Germany's chancellor today, Angela Merkel, put it chillingly well in a recent interview: "When the generation that survived the war is no longer with us," she said, "we'll find out whether we have learned from history." We are always two or three generations away from repeating our catastrophes.

You and I gathered together on this August morning, looking to Novembers past and yet to come, must take on the doubly against-the-odds task of fighting those who want to undermine democratic institutions while also checking our own tendencies to become that which we fight. That is why we are here. To do what may be impossible. To keep each other honest about our hypocrisies.

What could be more American?

3.

I said nothing is ever dead, *for better and for worse*. A body falls, it becomes grass, it feeds another. Was it a villain's body or a hero's body? It is grass. Is the one who now feeds aware of the chains of sin and saintliness that soak the soil? It is grass.

The thought is Whitmanesque. But the third book I want to tell you about is a slender volume of poetry not by Walt Whitman but by the contemporary Native American poet Layli Long Soldier. It is called *Whereas*. It opens with these lines:

Now
make room in the mouth
for grassesgrassesgrasses

It is composed in two parts—"These Being the Concerns" and "Whereas"—a structure that echoes the litany of wrongs that opens the Declaration of Independence and the concise statement of resolution that closes it. But the text Long Soldier is riffing off of is not the Declaration of Independence. It is the Congressional Resolution of Apology to Native Americans, S.J. Res. 14, of the 111th Congress.

I confess I had not heard of this resolution. That's perhaps unsurprising, since it passed in December 2009 as an amendment to a massive defense appropriations bill and was signed by President Obama in January 2010 with no fanfare or ceremony. It includes some blunt language about the wrongs done to Native Peoples and "the breaking of covenants." It apologizes for "many instances of violence, mistreatment, and neglect." It expresses regret "for the ramifications of former wrongs." But it closes with a disclaimer that says, "Nothing in this Resolution 1) authorizes or supports any claim against the United States; or 2) serves as a settlement of any claim against the United States."

What eats at Layli Long Soldier is pretty much all of it. The sorry-not-sorry disclaimer. The disrespectful silence that surrounded the resolution's enactment. (If an apology is issued in a forest and nobody hears it, did it issue?) Her form-twisting, time-looping poems meditate in anger and in sorrow on the circuits of history and the way that history—even history we are not aware of—enters the body. In the habits of her daughter who tries not to cry, tries in fact to smile, when her knees are skinned and bleeding. In the habits of accepting and rejecting, simultaneously hating and needing, the boxes of language that the people and government of the United States have long placed Native Americans into: treaties, resolutions, reservations, coffins. She resolves to reject this so-called apology and its caveats. To declare herself.

The poem excerpted here, about the Dakota 38, closes with these lines:

Sometimes, when in a circle, if I wish to exit, I must leap.
And let the body   swing.
From the platform
                    Out
                              to the grasses.

As it happens, the day I read these poems I was in Aspen, Colorado, and in the bathroom of the Western chic log-cabin mansion I was visiting was a 1948 photograph of the remaining American Indian survivors of the Battle of Little Bighorn. Eight aging men, dressed in full feather, sitting and crouching in a field of grass.

I stood staring at this photograph, taken less than a year after Chuck Yeager flew faster than sound, and I had to wonder. What if the Native Americans had won? What if in the lavish homes of modern-day Pueblo or Plains Indians, the restrooms were adorned with collectors' item photos of white warriors who had fallen during Little Bighorn or, better yet, had survived to live out their years as traveling curiosities and kitschy icons? How would white people today feel about that?

Then I started thinking: What if Union veterans who returned home from the Civil War to build their lives and their fortunes decided to adorn their parlors and powder rooms with images of the white Confederate soldiers they'd defeated? Why didn't they? Why didn't they make those brave fallen adversaries into good-luck totems or symbols of a self-congratulatory tolerance?

Oh right—because they were white. They were brothers, to be reunited after the war. The enemies became once again "us," and the people formerly enslaved by those enemies became once again "them."

And this is the topic of the fourth and final book I want to share with you.

4.

This book is a recent play by Suzan-Lori Parks. It is called *Father Comes Home from the Wars: Parts 1, 2 & 3*. Everything about the title is deliberately Civil War–era clunky. The rapid cadence and jagged syntax of the dialogue is at once Victorian, jazzy, and something else more distant that you can't quite identify until you realize—wait, the main character is named Hero, his rival is Homer, the woman he leaves behind is Penny, his cross-eyed dog is Odd-see. This is the *Odyssey*.

The play is about a loyal and honest slave, Hero, who decides to leave his wife, Penny, to be by the side of his master, a colonel in the

Confederate Army. Colonel has promised Hero his freedom for his service. During the war, Colonel and Hero get lost in the woods. Along the way they capture a wounded Union officer named Smith. The three of them hear an approaching army and they wait, as if for Godot. Smith, it turns out, is a light-skinned black soldier in the Colored Regiment passing for a white officer. He wears the coat of his dead captain on top of his own private's coat. When Colonel steps away, Smith shares his secret with Hero and offers him one of his coats so they can flee together to the Union army. Hero frees Smith but chooses not to join him. Later, after Colonel dies in battle, Hero returns to the farm. He has renamed himself Ulysses. The remaining slaves are preparing to run away. Ulysses stays. And he forgets to mention a piece of paper folded in his pocket: a proclamation of emancipation.

Who is us? Who is them? What does it mean to change coats? Who is empowered to liberate whom? Should we be loyal to people or to ideas? And if to people, to people now before us or to people in our memories? Who gets to call this act fidelity to the nation and that act betrayal? And who is truly ready to handle the burdens of freedom?

I had my answers to these questions, and *Father Comes Home from the Wars* made me rethink every one of them.

This is a play every American should read. I mean read. I would love to see it performed. In the original production in 2014, at the Public Theater in New York, Sterling K. Brown, now of *This Is Us* and *Black Panther* fame, played Hero. *That* I would have loved to have seen. But to read this work is to appreciate the genius of its devices. One device Parks invents is a distinction between a rest and a spell. A rest is a breath, a pause for transition. A spell is "elongated and heightened," as she puts it in her author's note. It's signified by a stacking of characters' names with no dialogue:

Homer

Hero

Homer

Hero

That stacking signifies a pregnant silence between the characters, to be staged at the director's discretion. When I read the play and saw where Parks chose to use this device, I imagined the actors freezing, their eyes locked in deep unspoken emotion. Casting a spell on each other and the audience.

This three-part play, this triptych tale of losing oneself while finding one's way home, is a story that's in our bones. It's older than Homer and as fresh as this morning. We reenact it every time we migrate. Every time we reinvent ourselves. Every time we amputate the appendages of inconvenient memory, only to learn that the phantom limb haunts us more. A play like this can make North act as if it were South, Asian as if black or white, born here as if brought here, free to go as if free to stay. A play like this is a garden of empathy. But not moral relativism: you don't come to see the Colonel's praise song to whiteness as morally praiseworthy. You do come to realize what a man like that thinks he has to lose. And that is helpful in the United States today.

I don't know how many of you still indulge in this Civil War–era habit called "reading a newspaper," but the other day I was indulging at my kitchen table with the New York Times. Actually, I was procrastinating on this sermon. You could tell I was procrastinating because I had gotten to the Thursday Styles section and was still reading. Lo and behold, with a half-page photograph of soldiers in blue and gray, was a long article about Civil War reenactors. It was called "Fading Into History."

Reenactments happen at famous battlefields like Gettysburg and Manassas. Middle-aged men, mainly white and mainly conservative, don Union and Confederate uniforms and camp out using only period implements and firearms and food, and then in the searing heat pretend to kill each other by the tens of thousands. Or at least it used to be tens of thousands. The problem is that turnout for reenactments has been on a steady decline for decades. Now only a few thousand show up to participate or watch.

Why? Well, as with so many collective experiences, the younger generation isn't into it. So the participants are aging and getting hurt and getting heat stroke and deciding to return home from the wars and hang it up. But it's more than that. Reenactment has come to seem increasingly out of step with today's moral and political climate because while it is about re-creating battles it is also about not taking sides.

Civil War reenactment grows out of a culture that honors the dead on both sides. That says there were fine people on both sides and worthy causes all around. Innocence everywhere, guilt nowhere. Reenactment is about fidelity to the finest detail—the Confederate battle flag, the insignia, the precise times and locations of cavalry charges—fidelity to everything except *why* the Civil War was fought.

And in the age of Black Lives Matter and torchlight parades in Charlottesville and kneeling NFL players and still-standing Confederate monuments, the why of the Civil War and the why of Reconstruction and the Civil Rights Movement cannot be avoided, and certainly not to provide for the emotional comfort of a group of Civil War reenactors. The *why* of the war is the *why* of why we say all persons are created equal.

But does that mean we should demonize and stereotype the people who are afraid to go there, whose identity as reenactors is bound up in a myth of innocence? What good will that do? They are human characters, each with motivations and self-stories as complicated and contradictory as those of Hero and Ulysses, who were the same man after all, or of Smith the white captain and Smith the black private, one man in two coats. In this year's Gettysburg reenactment there was a group of younger African American men who came dressed as members of a black Union unit. As professional actors like to ask: What's their motivation? We can find out best by asking.

If we must argue, let's argue to understand rather than to win. Understanding is real and lasting; winning is illusory and temporary. I don't know how many of you still indulge in this modern habit called "going on Twitter," but if you spend a few minutes on any trending political topic you realize we are all arguing to win instead of to understand. In the process, we are all enacting a Second Civil War into existence.

But remember: we are not actors. We must not be actors, blindly following someone else's script. We are authors of *this* play. This play does not have an ending. It almost certainly won't unfold in a triptych or in a four-part sermon or in a hip-hop libretto. Because it is not the kind of art that's made after the event. It is the kind of art that's made *out of* events. In short, it is citizenship in a democracy. It is participation in a complex adaptive system influenced by some more than others but controlled by no one and moveable by anyone. It is the quantum unpredictability of life itself. That's the scary and urgent thing about the Weimar Republic: there were people then as committed to liberal democracy as we are now.

Do we have the right stuff to save our Union? People love quoting Martin Luther King on how "the arc of the moral universe is long, but it bends toward justice." Yet they often forget the arc doesn't self-bend; it is *bent*. And they forget the words of John Maynard Keynes, who said, "In the long run, we are all dead." Here we are now, the living, called to read and write our nation back into existence—and this time, into an existence that is not premised on male domination or on white supremacy or on stealing the labor and land of the nonwhite or on a failure to apologize that curdles into shame and blame.

If you have had a hand in our troubles—and you have, as have I— then don't be like Paul von Hindenburg. Don't shirk responsibility and scapegoat others. Own your piece of it. If you have any modicum of privilege—and you do—then don't be like the Congress and President Obama in 2010. Don't be afraid of who you might lose when you try to set things right. Just set things right.

We must fight for Union: a union based not on avoiding our divisions but reckoning with them. We must fight for civic love: love that judges *and* forgives. We must bring this fight home now. You and I and Suzan-Lori Parks and Layli Long Soldier, we all get to decide the matter right alongside Mitch McConnell and Roseanne Barr and Sean Hannity. We get to reconstruct the script by including new characters and new lines as the play unfolds. Or by reading the old lines with new feeling. We get to commit to each other to do that. We've got to, from one hill in Seattle to another, from this Washington to the other one, from sea to shining sea.

Look at one another for a spell. Read each other's eyes and, through them, see what our country can be.

ACKNOWLEDGMENTS

I may have written the sermons you've just read, but this book is the product of both a team and a community.

The team, at its core, consists of all the people who over the last few years have worked at Citizen University to make Civic Saturdays a reality: Tera Beach, Arista Burwell-Chen, Jená Cane, Kayla DeMonte, Taneum Fotheringill, Ben Phillips, Taelore Rhoden, Katherine Sims, and Grace Stephenson. Their creativity and savvy are the "secret sauce" of everything we do. The team also includes the committed and passionate professionals at Sasquatch Books and Penguin Random House who immediately saw the promise of this idea for a book and brought it to market with skill and speed: Sarah Hanson, Gary Luke, Shari Miranda, and Jill Saginario. It's a joy to be doing another project with the smart and nimble Sasquatch. Rafe Sagalyn has been not just my trusted counselor and literary agent, but also my friend for over a quarter century. He and his colleague at Sagalyn/ICM, Brandon Coward, made this book a reality.

The community that begat this book begins with our many partners in Seattle, New York, Nashville, Des Moines, Atlanta, Los Angeles, and across the United States who've hosted Civic Saturdays thus far. (Special thanks to Karen Maeda Allman and her colleagues at Elliott Bay Book Company in Seattle, for hosting our very first Civic Saturday and partnering in many others, and to our Seattle artists-in-residence, poet Naa Akua and musician Michael Feldman.) Our community centers around the thousands of people in communities nationwide who've participated in our gatherings. And it now extends to the leaders who've gone through our Civic Seminary program to bring Civic Saturdays to their own small towns and big cities and to build dozens of new congregations of committed citizens. I am grateful to all these partners, participants, and colleagues for showing up. We together are part of a movement to rekindle the spirit of American civic religion—a movement that I hope you will join.

My wife, Jená Cane, is the cofounder of Citizen University. We developed the idea for Civic Saturday together in one of our frequent kitchen-table civic jam sessions. It is one of my life's greatest blessings to be able to create with her.

READING GROUP GUIDE

1. **A Divided Heart**
    Do you want to engage in the work of political reconciliation? What would that look like to you?

2. **Present at the Creation**
    What is a belief that shapes your life—and what if you released it?

3. **If We Can Keep It**
    For whom and what are you responsible, and in what ways?

4. **Alternate Realities**
    Think of an adversary who could be an ally if political and cultural circumstances were different.

5. **Where Is America?**
    Where does your family's American story begin?

6. **A Great Awakening**
    What illusions about our country have you shed? Are you glad to have shed them?

7. **Legitimate Doubts**
    Tell about a time when you lost faith—be it in our leaders, our country, or a belief system.

8. **Fear and Hoarding**
    What are you most afraid of in these times?

9. **Gratitude, Luck, Risk**
    How have you been fortunate in your life and how do you try to circulate your fortune?

10. A Thanksgiving Recipe
What are you willing to change your mind about?

11. A Practicing Citizen
How do you live up to the ideals of the American creed?

12. The Citizen Artist
Who inspires you to imagine something better than the status quo?

13. Which Dream Do You Dream?
What does the American Dream mean to you and why?

14. Become America
How does historical memory shape your identity as an American?

15. Time Travel
If you could travel to another time in American history, would you? If so, when and why?

16. A Test of Our Citizenship
What does it mean to be a citizen?

17. Are We Enough?
What gives you hope for our democracy?

18. Too Busy to Love
Do people in your community practice civic love? In what ways?

19. Reading Our Country
Who is 'us'?

TEXT CREDITS

ABOUT THE AUTHOR

Eric Liu is cofounder and CEO of Citizen University, which fosters a culture of powerful citizenship in the United States. He also directs the Aspen Institute Citizenship and American Identity Program. He is author of several books, including most recently *You're More Powerful Than You Think: A Citizen's Guide to Making Change Happen.*

N. Fechin

Published with the
assistance of a grant from the
Cooper Foundation
in honor of Virginia Faulkner
and Bernice Slote,
in recognition of their unique
contributions to
the study of Willa Cather

Frontispiece: After a drawing of Willa Cather
by Nicolai Fechin. Courtesy of Paul Beigelman

☉ Joan Crane

Willa
Cather

A Bibliography

Foreword by Frederick B. Adams

University of Nebraska Press: Lincoln and London

Copyright 1982 by the
University of Nebraska Press.
All rights reserved.
Manufactured in the United
States of America.
The paper in this book meets
the guidelines for
permanence and durability
of the Committee on
Production Guidelines for
Book Longevity of the
Council on Library Resources.

Library of Congress
Cataloging in Publication Data

Crane, Joan, 1927-
Willa Cather: a bibliography.

Includes index.
1. Cather, Willa, 1873-1947—
Bibliography. I. Title
Z8155.65.C73 [PS3505.A87]
016.813'52 81-23134
ISBN 0-8032-1415-4 AACR2

For
Josiah Quincy Bennett
and
John S. Van E. Kohn
1906–1976
Robert F. Metzdorf
1913–1975

Contents

Foreword

It may seem surprising that an author of Willa Cather's stature should still await detailed bibliographical study more than three decades after her death. This is not due to a diminution of her literary reputation, but rather to special conditions arising from Miss Cather's own attitudes. She shunned publicity and controlled it as carefully as possible, even beyond the grave. She did not encourage bibliographical probing, although she was more concerned than most authors with correctness of text and proper presentation. She resented investigation of her youthful writings, pseudonymous or acknowledged, on the basis that they were apprentice work (she began to publish at the age of fifteen) and chiefly a means of livelihood. According to Edith Lewis, she went so far as to consider that proposals for publishing her early work were "merely an attempt to exploit her name for purposes of self-interest." The difficulty of finding sure evidence to resolve bibliographical problems has daunted bibliographers; as Professor Bernice Slote commented in her preface to *The Kingdom of Art*, "The field sometimes seems made of quicksilver."

Nevertheless, there have been useful precursors of the present work. Two numbers of *The Colophon* (New Graphic Series) in 1939 carried my "mongrel assortment of biography, bibliography and criticism" on Willa Cather's writings up to 1920. John P. Hinz contributed to *The New Colophon* in 1950 an article listing more than a hundred titles from Pittsburgh newspapers and periodicals, written by Miss Cather under her own name and many pseudonyms. Three summer issues of the *Bulletin of the New York Public Library* in 1956 carried serially Mrs. Phyllis Martin Hutchinson's "The Writings of Willa Cather: A List of Works by and about Her." This was specifically "directed to readers and students of her work, rather than to the collector,"

and was not intended to be a definitive bibliography. It will continue to be a useful reference to reviews and critical articles about Miss Cather's work, with quotations of essential passages.

In 1950, the University of Nebraska Press inaugurated a series of volumes recording and reprinting the often pseudonymous writings that Miss Cather did not consider worth resurrecting, principally literary journalism and drama and music criticism, but including a scattering of stories of the sort that their author dismissed as "bald, clumsy, and emotional." These collections, the assiduous work of James R. Shively, William M. Curtin, Mildred R. Bennett, and especially Bernice Slote (see Section AA), have more than an archeological interest. One must moderate the author's disclaimers of their value. The freshness of her approach, her independence of spirit and youthful zest—the evidence of her wide reading, not only in the masters of her own language—her early attempts to deal with the raw material of the Nebraska frontier—should be taken into account by any inquirer into the works of her golden years, 1913 to 1931.

These precursors have eased the way for Miss Crane in preparing her bibliography, without providing solutions for some of her most difficult problems. A number of the clues that forwarded her investigations have come from collectors, notably Benjamin D. Hitz, whose Cather collection and valuable documentation are now in the Newberry Library, and C. Waller Barrett, whose remarkable library is in the vigilant care of Miss Crane in the Alderman Library at the University of Virginia. Some have come from booksellers, especially the late John Kohn, whose Cather expertise was generously available for four decades. Some have come from other bibliographers, not least from Jacob Blanck. And other clues have been supplied, as is evident, from the files and correspondence of Miss Cather's publishers.

Suffice it to say that Miss Crane has now provided the answers to questions that have long perplexed Cather scholars and collectors, for example:

In the first issue of *The Troll Garden*, the story title leaf for "The Marriage of Phaedra" is always a cancel; no example of the original cancelland has ever been reported.

The first state and issue of *Alexander's Bridge* is distinguished from later issues both by the gilt-stamped lettering on the binding and by the order of the preliminaries, which is confirmed to have been originally the habitual order by the set of advance-copy gatherings in the Barrett Collection.

O Pioneers! was issued first in bindings of vertically ribbed cloth, later in cheaper linen cloth.

The extent of and reason for Willa Cather's participation in the preparation of Georgine Milmine's *Life of Mary Baker Eddy* are established beyond question, justifying Miss Cather's resentment of exaggerated claims about her "responsibility" for the text.

Her ghost-written S. S. McClure *Autobiography*, for which she cheerfully acknowledged authorship but not invention, was first issued with the copyright reservation date of September, 1914, and a line repeated on page 239. The copyright date of May, 1914, found in the second printing, is an error for May, 1915.

The first issue of *The Song of the Lark* is easily distinguished by an advertisement notice of previous books by Willa Sibert Cather on the copyright page and a misprint at the foot of page 8.

The first state of *My Ántonia* has the inserted Benda illustrations on coated stock; in the second state they are on text paper stock. No priority of issue can be proven.

Contrary to common belief and natural expectations, in the first state of *A Lost Lady*, line 19 on page 174 has the correct printing 'of'. Since this is the state occurring in advance review copies, it is also the first issue. The preposition is misprinted 'af' in later states and issues, including the limited issue on special paper.

The typographical error on page 20 of *Death Comes for the Archbishop*, 'happned' for 'happened', often noted by "point-maniacs" and "issue-mongers," was not corrected until the third printing, and another error on page 57 remained uncorrected for many years.

Copies of *Shadows on the Rock* with the reading 'Second Edition' on the copyright page actually constitute the first issue (advance copies sent to the book trade and reviewers).

The priority, or lack of it, of the limited, signed issues on special paper is carefully explained and justified.

There is much important information of other kinds to be found in Miss Crane's bibliography. The rise and fall in popularity of the various titles can be followed in the size and frequency of the reprintings. Significant textual variants are described, and some of them verge on the farcical, such as the proposal to change the name of the bull 'Brigham Young' for a special Utah printing of *My Ántonia*, and the elimination, in the English edition of *The Song of the Lark*, of a passage associating Lillie Langtry with Edward VII as Prince of Wales.

Willa Cather was faithful, in succession, to two publishers, Houghton Mifflin through the person of Ferris Greenslet, and Alfred A. Knopf. In the former, she found a textual editor of extraordinary competence; in the latter, a publisher who cared almost passionately about the appearance of his books. As Miss Crane brings out, both served her well and faithfully with their respective abilities. Greenslet might not have permitted water to run uphill in an open trough in *Death Comes for the Archbishop*, and Knopf would probably have handled with greater finesse the problems that arose with the Benda illustrations for *My Ántonia*. It must be added that when agreement was reached for Houghton Mifflin to publish their definitive Autograph Edition in 1937, they engaged Bruce Rogers to design it, with impeccable results. These volumes entice us to reread Willa Cather's novels and stories, and now, following the clear signposts provided in this bibliography, we may proceed to do so.

FREDERICK B. ADAMS

Acknowledgments

The existence of this bibliography results from a decision by Bernice Slote and the late Virginia Faulkner to recommend me for the job to the University of Nebraska Press. These two pre-eminent Cather scholars placed confidence in my ability to add another Nebraska volume to the important series devoted to Willa Cather's work. Having made the recommendation, they backed it unreservedly with help, encouragement, and practical assurances of faith in my work. Without their earlier research, however, the bibliography of Willa Cather would have been impossible to complete in a mere four years.

As prime movers, I thank Donald Jackson, former editor of the George Washington Papers, University of Virginia, and Fredson Bowers for putting my name and qualifications forward to Professors Slote and Faulkner.

I owe a special debt of thanks to Clifton Waller Barrett, whose great collection at the University of Virginia provided the nucleus for this project. Mr. Barrett gallantly relinquished his prior right to a catalog already in progress of his own Cather collection in favor of its contribution to the definitive bibliography.

The publishing firm of Alfred A. Knopf, Inc., gave invaluable cooperation through the most obliging person of William A. Koshland, who made available to me the production records of Willa Cather's Knopf publications and engaged in a correspondence which continuously demonstrated his good nature and forbearance.

Austin Olney made possible consultation of similar records from the Houghton Mifflin Company retired files.

By courtesy of an introduction from Warren Chappell and William Koshland, I had the privileged opportunity of personal exchange with Alfred A. Knopf. Mr. Knopf, in a busy and peripatetic retirement, found time to answer questions, correct errors, and exercise his prodigious powers of recollection. He and Mr. Koshland also put me in touch with one of the most reliable sources of information on Knopf publication, Sydney Jacobs, head of book production in the Knopf firm for many years prior to his retirement.

Funds for travel and photocopying and the inestimable gift of time are essential to the accomplishment of a bibliographical project. Thus I was greatly aided by a University of Virginia appointment to a Sesquicentennial Associateship which allowed a full semester of unhindered work. The Library Research Committee of the University of Virginia Library supplemented this compensated period with travel and photocopying funds. When photocopying demands became more pressing, the Willa Cather Pioneer Memorial and Educational Foundation assumed that expense with good grace. Latterly, a grant from the Center for Great Plains Studies of the University of Nebraska–Lincoln has provided for major expenses with regard to the work in hand. Mrs. Rosemary Bergstrom of the Center for Great Plains Studies fulfilled every request with cheerful ease and lack of delay quite unprecedented in the usually complicated *apparat* of grant bestowals. If there was red tape and paperwork, I never knew of it—such was the consideration and generosity of the center.

The most important repository of bibliographical information on the works of Willa Cather is the private collection of the former head of the Pierpont Morgan Library, Frederick B. Adams, Jr., now in retirement in France. Mr. Adams permitted me full access to forty years' accumulation of correspondence and notes. Furthermore, he gave me the benefit of his own solutions to many problems that occur in an analysis of Willa Cather's books. Mr. Adams's contributions to this bibliography are pervasive—far beyond the foreword he kindly supplied for the front matter. For these and other favors extended to me by both Mr.

and Mrs. Adams in their beautiful part of the Touraine, my gratitude is in excess of mere manners to express.

During a visit to Nebraska in 1977, I was made abundantly welcome in Lincoln by Professors Slote and Faulkner and, in turn, by Robert Boyce, Special Collections librarian, University of Nebraska, and Ann Reinhart, librarian of the Nebraska State Historical Society. L. Brent Bohlke, instructor in English at the University of Nebraska–Lincoln and chaplain of St. Mark's on the Campus, Lincoln, acted as a discerning guide to my first experience of the Nebraska plains. In Red Cloud, Mrs. Mildred R. Bennett, chairman of the board of the Willa Cather Pioneer Memorial and Educational Foundation, was kind in sharing with me her wide knowledge; and I received sensitive and thoughtful assistance from the erstwhile director of the foundation, JoAnna Lathrop, who, together with Miriam Mountford, president of the foundation, allowed me freedom of the collection there. To Ms. Lathrop, too, a debt is gladly acknowledged for her *Willa Cather: A Checklist of Her Published Writing* (Lincoln: University of Nebraska Press, 1975). It was an essential tool in my research and stands as precursor to this volume.

In more recent years, Viola Borton, currently director of the WCPM, has continued to·give help as required, and Mrs. Bennett has many times proved herself a source of information available nowhere else.

I have been fortunate in a close association with members of the antiquarian book trade. These former colleagues have made special efforts to acquire for me or bring to my attention unusual material significant to this work. Hence, my duty to Bart Auerbach, John Brett-Smith, Marguerite Cohn, Duff Gilfond, Peter Howard, the late John S. Van E. Kohn, Gillian Kyles, Judith Lowry, Philip Lyman, Bradford Morrow, Howard Mott, the late Michael Papantonio, J. Howard Woolmer, and Jacob Zeitlin.

In any bibliographical work, librarians and archivists all over the world, collectors, and people of other professions with a special interest in one's subject are altruistic in their efforts to be of help. I am indebted to many for contributions of importance:

Josiah Q. Bennett (Lilly Library, Indiana University), Paul M. Beigelman, M.D. (for permitting use of the Fechin drawing as frontispiece to this volume), Matthew J. Bruccoli (University of South Carolina), Judith Bucke (the Queen's University Library, Belfast), Herbert Cahoon (the Pierpont Morgan Library, New York), the Reverend Morris Cather, Cyril Clemens, William M. Curtin (University of Connecticut), Frank K. Cylke and his staff (National Library Service for the Blind and Physically Handicapped, Library of Congress), the Colby College Library staff, Donald Gallup (the Beinecke Library, Yale University), Claude Gibson (College English Association), Doris Grumbach, Diana Haskell (Newberry Library, Chicago), Edwin Honig, Richard Layman (BC Research, Columbia, S.C.), Sally Leach (Humanities Research Center, University of Texas), Lucia Woods Lindley, J. William Matheson (chief, Rare Books and Special Collections Division, Library of Congress), Yehudi Menuhin, James B. Meriwether (University of South Carolina), Patrick Miehe (Harvard University Library), the University of Nebraska Library staff, Neil A. G. Nicholls (North-Eastern Education and Library Board, Ballymena, County Antrim, Ireland), Norman O'Connor (Literary Guild of America), Noel Polk (University of Southern Mississippi), Paul R. Rugen (keeper of manuscripts, Library of Congress), Patrick Samway, S.J. (chairman, English Department, Le Moyne College, Syracuse, N.Y.), Mary Lee Settle, Clinton Sisson (University of Virginia Library), Mrs. Philip L. Southwick, Kendon L. Stubbs (associate librarian, University of Virginia Library), Kyoko Suyama (the National Diet Library, Tokyo), Peter Van Wingen (Rare Books Division, Library of Congress), Michael Winship (Bibliography of American Literature, Houghton Library, Harvard University), and Wilhelm Zacharasiewicz (Vienna, Austria).

My particular thanks to the Houghton Library, Harvard University, and the Houghton Mifflin Company for permission to consult and use here the correspondence between Willa Cather and her Houghton Mifflin editor, Ferris Greenslet, from the Houghton Mifflin Company archives at Harvard. It is to be regretted that the strict terms of Willa Cather's will do not permit direct quotation; hence, the use of paraphrase where necessary.

The index for this volume was compiled by Barbara MacAdam.

Introduction

Apologia pro Opere Suo

The style of this volume generally follows established principles of bibliographical description—an objective discipline to which modern bibliographers are obliged to adhere. It was my intention that the letter of the rule be observed; but, inevitably, I have strayed into proscribed bypaths. With no desire to give scandal to the orthodoxy of my profession, I wished nevertheless to express something beyond the mere accidence of books. This bibliography exceeds the limits of a rigorous litany of facts and, therefore, the current ideal of bibliographical austerity.

I am of a generation of bookmen educated in the trade who trained on works like Charles F. Heartman and James R. Canny's *Edgar Allan Poe*, Stuart Mason's gossipy *Oscar Wilde*, Whitman Bennett's opinionated *American Rare Book Guide*, and the notorious Ashley Catalogue with its T. J. Wise forgeries and locks of Robert Browning's hair. To consult these references placed one in peril of fascinating distraction, but the information sought usually turned up in one form or other along the way. In that era of free-wheeling, loosely ordered, idiosyncratic bibliographies characterized by quixotic methods of description, a nimble wit needed to be developed to use them at all. One was often sidetracked, but much was learned that frequently proved useful later on.

If, therefore, some backsliding has occurred here, it must be taken as instinctive to my background and training. It may also be taken as a subliminal tribute to those eccentric reference tools of my early years in the profession.

On the Treatment of Circumstantial Evidence

Several enigmas make Willa Cather's published works an exercise in speculative detection to the bibliographer: the extent of her involvement in the writing of the Mary Baker Eddy biography, authorship and correct dating of the S. S. McClure biography, the complex and fascinating permutations in the plates of *A Lost Lady*, the disordering of texts in *Death Comes for the Archbishop*, the author's influence on the first edition format of *My Ántonia*, and the unsolved mystery of the nonsectarian bull in the third edition, fourth printing, of that title.

In addressing these puzzles, I have permitted myself occasional legitimate assumptions, which I believe, within limits of reason, to be allowable. These I defend with a personal conviction that one privilege of the analytical bibliographer is the practice of deductive opinion where no hard evidence exists. Right or wrong, it makes the sport worth the candle and serves a practical purpose of opening lines of conjecture for later critics to prove or refute.

Color Identification

I have come to doubt the possibility of exact color designation in book description. Aids like the Nickerson Color Fan with its chroma of 40 hues and the more complex color chart of the Royal Horticultural Society notwithstanding, color description of a binding or dust jacket can never be objective. It is only as accurate as the ability of the eye to perceive color—an ability that varies greatly from one set of eyes to another. In books of a certain age, other factors must also be taken into account: the effects of time, light, and dust on original binding colors, inevitable variance between the smooth surface of a color chip and the irregular texture of binding fabric which distorts a perceived likeness of color, and the quality of light under which the book is examined. The need for precise color description is evident, but it cannot be other than approximate and subjective until more sophisticated spectroscopic tools are developed.

For purposes of color identification in this bibliography, ISCC-NBS (Inter-Society Color Council—National Bureau of Stan-

dards) Centroid numbers are used as a guide to the colors of bindings, dust jackets, and significant color printed elsewhere in the book. If the shade, hue, or color value is not essential to identification, a simple subjective color designation is provided. Where 2 varying colors are seen in different copies of the same edition, Centroid numbers are used; otherwise, not.

In quasi-facsimile transcriptions of matter printed in more than one color, the initial lettering is black unless otherwise designated. Varying colors are identified in brackets preceding the lettering in that color, and a return to black is similarly identified in brackets.

Blackletter and the Use of Rules

No attempt is made at type facsimile where gothic type occurs in a title or elsewhere. Gothic type is indicated by note "blackletter" in brackets preceding the passage, and a return to Roman type is so indicated in brackets.

Single vertical rules represent line endings in quasi-facsimile transcription. More than one rule signals the appearance of a rule or rules printed on the page. An initial or terminal rule also signals a rule on the printed page. If an ornamental rule is present, it is described in brackets.

Locations

Locations of copies examined by me or reported by bibliographers in other institutions are cited in the A-section entries for the earliest printings and issues of works published before 1920 and secondary books of unusual importance or scarcity. By 1920, Willa Cather's books were so well known, printed in such large numbers, and so widely purchased that numerous copies are to be found in virtually every institutional library of American literature. To avoid unnecessary repetition, location notes are not provided in descriptions after 1920. It may be assumed that no fewer than 4 (and frequently more) examples of each major entry have been physically and textually compared for the descriptions of ideal copies. Multiple copies were seen in the Clifton Waller Barrett Library rare book collection and the Rob-

ert C. Taylor Collection of the University of Virginia Library; the holdings of the University of Nebraska and the Willa Cather Pioneer Memorial; and in the private collections of Frederick B. Adams, Bernice Slote, and Virginia Faulkner. Accurate information on specific items has been supplied to me for comparison by Peter Van Wingen of the Library of Congress; Sally S. Leach of the Humanities Research Center, University of Texas; Donald Gallup of the Beinecke Library; Josiah Q. Bennett of the Lilly Library; James B. Meriwether of the University of South Carolina; and others. It may, therefore, be taken as stated that most or all of the following symbols are locations for all of the first and limited editions after 1920 and have been seen in or reported from those repositories: FBA, CWB, DLC, VF, ICN, InU, MeWC, MH, NbU, PPiU, BS, RCT, TxU, and WCPM. (For a key to abbreviations, see page xxv). Exceptions are enumerated, usually in the publication note.

Dating of Printings after the First and Presswork

The date of a printing which appears in the publisher's production record occasionally differs—sometimes by as much as 4 weeks—from the date printed beneath the copyright. In the case of a discrepancy, both dates are given if a copy of that printing has been seen. If not, the date supplied is taken from the Knopf and Houghton Mifflin production records only.

Information about the presswork of various printings is given when available in the production records; otherwise, not.

Treatment of Secondary Editions

The texts of some of Willa Cather's books were newly set and printed in inexpensive format long after the original publications. I refer specifically to the wartime Armed Services editions, the Signet paperback of *The Troll Garden* (1961), the Bantam paperback of *Alexander's Bridge* (1962), the Random House Vintage paperbacks of *My Mortal Enemy* (1961) and *One of Ours* (1971), and, more significantly, volumes in the series published by the University of Nebraska Press: *April Twilights* (1962, 1968) and *Alexander's Bridge* (1977). Although these are secondary publications in the hierarchical sense, they must be accorded

the bibliographical rank of new editions in spite of lateness of date, popular format, wide availability, and low price.

To emphasize the distinction between these derivative editions and the progenitor editions, they are given major entry numbers, but treated to a less detailed physical description appropriate to their status. This reduced style does not imply inferiority, nor should it be seen as a gratuitous snub to the legitimacy of these late offspring—especially to such worthy descendants as the admirable and scholarly Nebraska Press books—but, rather, as a rule of familial protocol which establishes proper relationship, bibliographically speaking, to the clearly more venerable antecedent editions.

Thus 3 styles of description are used for true edition entries in Section A. The original editions are described in full, formal bibliographical style: quasi-facsimile title page transcription, collation by gatherings, pagination and leaf count; separate notes for illustration, contents, text content, paper, binding, dust jacket; and a discursive history of publication followed by a chronological listing of ancillary and subsequent printings.

Later editions set from new plates receive condensed treatment after the title page transcription, in which physical characteristics of the book and publication notes are abbreviated and combined in a single paragraph.

In the third category, books owing their origin to a previous edition, but having the distinction of wide distribution under a new imprint (such as the Hamish Hamilton English editions of the novels, published in the sixties and early seventies, which are uniformly in photo-offset from the American editions), a simple calendar listing is used under a major entry number.

English and Canadian Editions

If an English edition is made up of American sheets or set from American plates, it is briefly identified as a part of the American printing from which it derives in the chronological sequence of the parent edition. A separate section for English editions follows each American title grouping in the A section. There, a

full descriptive and analytical entry, further identifying it as the first English "edition," is provided. This and subsequent English editions are differentiated by a separate numerical chronology in italic followed by "(e)".

The Canadian "edition" is always of American first printing sheets, usually bound in the United States. It is briefly described in a note following the publication note of the first American printing that designates it as an integral particular of that entry.

Textual Collations

The interjection of lengthy text comparisons is generally inappropriate to a descriptive bibliography and its primary functions. Properly, such textual apparatus should be reserved for the definitive text edition (which will be undertaken in due course by a team of qualified textual scholars). However, alterations in the texts of several of Willa Cather's books have important bearing on the history of publication, especially in the case of *Death Comes for the Archbishop*. Here, presentation of a textual collation informs the chronological relationship of the stages of revision from edition to edition. These are not omnibus lists swelled to repetitious proportions by the inclusion of minutiae, as would be mandatory for definitive comparisons of texts. Instead, they show only substantive alterations, intended as a guide to identification of texts in the physical life of the book.

Format

Section A is a chronological listing of all books by Willa Cather in first and subsequent editions and the states, issues, and printings deriving therefrom. The system of numbering indicates the major title entry (in letter cap and arabic number) followed by the edition (in lower case roman letter) and printing (in lower case roman number). Where an edition exists in one printing only, the entry number is not extended to include the number of the printing (as in *April Twilights* [1903], which is designated simply A1.a. rather than A1.a.i.). The abbreviation acts as an indicator that the original plates were used once and never again. States and issues are described within the numerical designation (always in the first printing) under a separate heading.

In 3 instances (all in the *Death Comes for the Archbishop* entry), related secondary editions of excerpted text printed in book form are listed following the entry and differentiated by the addition of subscript numbers to the main title entry number ($A16_1$, $A16_2$ and $A16_3$).

Subsections AA (collected works) and AAA (works edited by Willa Cather) follow the same style of major entry.

Section B contains an abbreviated calendar, numbered chronologically, of the poems with first and subsequent appearances in print listed numerically in arabic after the title. Musical settings of poems are included in this listing.

Section C (short fiction) follows the same style as Section B. Similar treatment for anthologized excerpted fiction is used in Subsection CC and for novels published first in periodicals in Subsection CCC.

Section D contains a numbered chronological calendar of articles, reviews, and essays in newspapers and periodicals with reprintings enumerated after the title. A preliminary listing in the D section, differentiated by the use of lowercase "d" preceding the number, consists of Willa Cather's student writing (other than stories and poems) printed in the University of Nebraska *Hesperian*. This group is necessarily incomplete and gives only a sampling of her juvenilia, which was far more extensive. The complete information on this difficult area exists in the notes and continuing research of Bernice Slote.

In this section, as in sections B, C, and E (translations, below), many of the entries have not been seen, but are reported from other repositories or located from standard reference sources which, in many cases, do not contain complete information. For this reason, some entries lack full names of editors, translators, publishers, places of publication, or pagination. In deference to the reader's need, I have elected to supply as much information as was available to me rather than truncate the style to conform to those entries with incomplete information; hence, an inconsistency in the listings.

Subsection DD (introductions, prefaces, and contributions to books) and Subsection DDD (printed personal letters, statements, and quotations) follow the calendar style. Two appendix entries follow the DD subsection, providing more extended description of particularly important items that are listed and numbered in the calendar chronology of DD.

Section E contains translations of novels and stories into foreign languages. These are arranged alphabetically by language, numerically and chronologically listed within the language category. Phonetic transliterations in the language of the translation are provided in most cases. In some, the title in English is supplied in brackets. Initials of the original book titles or full story titles precede each entry in brackets. Subsection EE is a listing of Tauchnitz English language editions, and Subsection EEE contains other foreign editions in English.

Section F (large-type books), Section G (books for the blind in Braille), Section H (recorded books for the blind) and sections I and J (adaptations on film and for theater) conform to the calendar style, allowing for greater or less detail as required.

Terminology

Edition: All copies of a book printed from a single setting of type, including all printings from standing type or from plates or by photo-offset reproduction.

Printing: All copies of a book printed at a specifically ordered interval from other copies within the same edition.

State: Copies within a single printing differentiated from each other by alterations in the binding, paper, typesetting, or makeup of one or more sheets during the process of manufacture.

Issue: Copies within a single printing which exhibit physical evidence of priority or separateness of distribution in the binding, paper, typesetting, or makeup.

Note: In general, the "limited edition" of Knopf's Cather publications constitutes a separate state or issue from the regular "trade edition," but forms part of the same edition and printing.

O⊙

Abbreviations

Symbols indicating location in institutions are taken from *The National Union Catalogue*:

CtY
Yale University (Beinecke Library), New Haven, Connecticut.

DLC
United States Library of Congress, Washington, D.C.

ICN
Newberry Library, Chicago.

InU
Indiana University (Lilly Library), Bloomington.

MH
Harvard University (Houghton Library), Cambridge, Massachusetts.

MeWC
Colby College, Waterville, Maine.

NbU
University of Nebraska–Lincoln.

PPiU
University of Pittsburgh.

TxU
University of Texas (Humanities Research Center), Austin.

ViU
University of Virginia, Charlottesville.

Location symbols for private and special collections:

FBA
Frederick B. Adams, Jr., Chisseaux, France.

CWB
Clifton Waller Barrett (ViU).

VF
Virginia Faulkner, Lincoln, Nebraska.

AHG
Adrian Homer Goldstone
(TxU).

AAK
Alfred A. Knopf (TxU).

BS
Bernice Slote, Lincoln,
Nebraska.

RCT
Robert C. Taylor (ViU).

WCPM
Willa Cather Pioneer
Memorial, Red Cloud,
Nebraska.

Publications:

AB
Alexander's Bridge.

AE
Autograph Edition of the
Works of Willa Cather,
13 vols. (Boston: Houghton
Mifflin Co., 1937–1941).

ALL
A Lost Lady.

AT
April Twilights.

ATOP
*April Twilights and Other
Poems.*

Courier
Lincoln (Nebr.) *Courier.*

DCA
Death Comes for the Archbishop.

Early Stories
Early Stories of Willa Cather,
sel. and with commentary by
Mildred R. Bennett (New
York: Dodd, Mead & Co.,
1957).

Five Stories
*Five Stories with an Article by
George N. Kates on Miss Cather's
Last, Unfinished, and Unpub-
lished Avignon Story* (New
York: Vintage Books, 1956).

HM
Home Monthly (Pittsburgh).

IPL
Index of Pittsburgh Life.

KA
*The Kingdom of Art: Willa
Cather's First Principles and
Critical Statements*, sel. and ed.
with two essays and a com-
mentary by Bernice Slote (Lin-
coln: University of Nebraska
Press, 1966).

LG
Lucy Gayheart.

MA
My Ántonia.

MME
My Mortal Enemy.

NSJ
Nebraska State Journal
(Lincoln).

NUF
Not under Forty.

OB
The Old Beauty and Others.

OD
Obscure Destinies.

OO
One of Ours.

OP
O Pioneers!

OW
Willa Cather on Writing.

PG
Pittsburgh Gazette.

PH
The Professor's House.

PL
Pittsburgh Leader.

PW
Publishers Weekly.

SOL
The Song of the Lark.

SOR
Shadows on the Rock.

SSG
Sapphira and the Slave Girl.

TG
The Troll Garden.

TLS
Times (London) Literary
Supplement.

UV
Uncle Valentine and Other Stories, ed. and introd. Bernice
Slote (Lincoln: University of
Nebraska Press, 1965).

WCCSF
Willa Cather's Collected Short
Fiction, 1892–1912, ed. Virginia Faulkner, introd.
Mildred R. Bennett (Lincoln:
University of Nebraska Press,
1965; 1970).

WCCY
Writings from Willa Cather's
Campus Years, ed., James R.
Shively (Lincoln: University of
Nebraska Press, 1950).

WCE
Willa Cather in Europe (New
York: Knopf, 1956).

WCPM
Newsletter
The Willa Cather Pioneer Memo-
rial Newsletter.

W & P
The World and the Parish:
Willa Cather's Articles and
Reviews, 1893–1902, 2 vols.,
sel. and ed. with a com-
mentary by William M. Cur-
tin (Lincoln: University of
Nebraska Press, 1970).

YBM
Youth and the Bright Medusa.

Other Abbreviations:

FG
Ferris Greenslet

H M Co.
Houghton Mifflin Company

UNP
University of Nebraska Press

W C
Willa Cather

Part One

27.13   ON CYNDUS] On Cydnus (*title head*)
30.26   dewey-dim] dewy-dim (Lament for Marsyas)
 33.8   cried,] cried. (I Sought the Wood in Winter)
39.17   mist clad] mist-clad (The Night Express)
41.14   Absolom] Absalom (Thine Advocate)
42.10   ivys] ivies (Poppies on Ludlow Castle)
 47.7   demense] demesne (I Have No House for Love to Shelter Him)
47.10   spicéd] spicèd (I Have No House for Love to Shelter Him)
48.13   pluméd] plumèd (The Poor Minstrel)
51.1,13   Troubador] Troubadour (Song)

b.i.)   Second edition, first printing, 1962

April Twilights (1903) | Poems by | WILLA CATHER | Edited
with an introduction by | BERNICE SLOTE | University of
Nebraska Press • Lincoln

The true second edition of the first edition text. *Collation:* [1-2]⁸
[3-5]¹⁶; pp.[i-iv] v-xxxxviii, [1-2] 3-72 [73-80] = 64 leaves. 2
inserted plates. Blue cloth, dust jacket, $3.50. 202 x 134 mm.

Typographical and orthographical emendations to the first
edition listed by the editor in notes. A bibliography of the
published poems (pp.59-72). An error, 'Duckworth' (corrected
to 'Ducker' in the third printing), at p.vi, l.27. 'The Night
Express', 'Dedicatory', 'White Birch in Wyoming', and 'Thine
Advocate' are reprinted here for the first time since the first
edition of 1903.

b.ii.)   Second printing (Bison Books paperback). Second edition plates
with the University of Nebraska Press Bison Books device added
to the title page. Simultaneous publication.

Paperback, perfect binding; pagination as the first printing.
2 inserted plates. Decorated wrappers, $1.50. 202 x 134
mm. Bison Book BB150. At p.vi, third line from bottom:
'Duckworth' (corrected to 'Ducker' in third printing).

b.iii.)   Third printing (Bison Books paperback [1964]). '*Second
Printing, 1964*' on copyright page. Collation, pagination, and
physical format as in the first Bison printing (second printing);

Reviewed in the *New York Times*, 20 June 1903.

In 1908, Willa Cather bought the remainder of the first edition and destroyed it. She permitted Knopf to publish a new edition in 1923 after removing 13 poems from the original contents and adding 12 new ones. Chronologically, the collected Autograph Edition volume (1937; A3) followed with 2 more poems removed. Of the poems withdrawn, 2 were not reprinted until 1962, in the true second edition of the original contents, published by the University of Nebraska Press (A1.b.i., below).

Note 1: For a full critical exposition of the first edition, see Bernice Slote's introduction in A1.c.

Note 2: American Book Prices Current for 1930 contains an auction record for a copy of *April Twilights* with a tipped-in 'Literary Note' sold at the Ritter-Hopson Galleries, 6 November 1930. The insertion is noted by Merle Johnson in *American First Editions,* but had never been seen by Jacob Blanck or Frederick B. Adams, who mentions it in his Cather article in *Colophon* (New Graphic Series 1, no.3 [1939], p.94) as being "obviously more authentic than the purple cow" on the evidence of the Ritter-Hopson Galleries copy.

It is reasonably safe to conclude that the 'Literary Note' was, in fact, an announcement flyer for the book in the form of an advertisement and order form issued by the publisher, Richard Badger, in April 1903. The front cover has a photographic portrait of WC at the upper left corner. Lettered: 'April | Twilights | BY | *Willa Sibert Cather* | [14-line blurb]'. The announcement is illustrated in *April Twilights (1903)* (Lincoln: University of Nebraska Press, 1962 [A1.b.i.]).

Locations: CWB (3 copies), AHG, FBA

Textual Errata: Typographical and orthographical errors in the 1903 edition, corrected in the University of Nebraska editions of 1962 and 1968 (A1.b.i-c.) and in later editions that include the poems in which errors occur. Corrections by page and line:

5.15   *On Cyndus*] On Cydnus (*title listing in* Contents)
9.27   As They] An' they ("Grandmither, Think Not I Forget")
22.13   least] lest (Antinous)
23.10   insistant] insistent (Paradox)

Antinous. B41
Paradox. B42
Provençal Legend. B43
Winter at Delphi. *Critic* 39 (September 1901). B30
On Cyndus [*sic*]. B44
The Namesake. *Lippincott's* 69 (April 1902). B32
Lament for Marsyas. B45
White Birch in Wyoming. B46
I Sought the Wood in Winter. B47
Evening Song. B48
Eurydice. B49
The Encore. *Lippincott's* [with the title 'The Poet to His Public']
    66 (December 1900). B27
London Roses. B51
The Night Express. *Youth's Companion* 76 (26 June 1902). B33
Prairie Dawn. B52
Aftermath. B53
Thine Advocate. B54
Poppies on Ludlow Castle. B55
Sonnet. B56
Thou Art the Pearl. *Library* 1 (24 March 1900). B18
From the Valley. B57
I Have No House for Love to Shelter Him. B58
The Poor Minstrel. B59
Paris. *The Garden of the Heart* . . . (Boston: Badger, 1903). B60
Song. B61
L'Envoi. B62

Paper: Heavy wove stock, no watermark. 191 x 131 mm.; edges
uncut. End papers of the same stock.

Binding: Drab boards with cream paper label (64 x 68 mm.)
mounted on the front cover, '*April Twilights* | [orange floral orn.
rule] | *Willa Sibert* | *Cather*'. Cream paper spine label: 'APRIL
TWILIGHTS — CATHER'.

Publication: Badger's Gorham Press was a vanity press. The
author contributed a substantial part of the cost for publication.
The copyright copy was received at the Library of Congress on
30 April 1903. Listed in the *PW* spring announcements for 21
March 1903 under the name "Willie Sibert Cather," at $1.00.

A

Separate Publications

A1.   APRIL TWILIGHTS

a.)   First edition, 1903

[rule of 7 green (137) 5-petaled rose orn.] | APRIL |
TWILIGHTS | POEMS BY | *Willa Sibert Cather* | [green (137)
Gorham Press device] | Boston: Richard G. Badger | The
Gorham Press: 1903 | [orn. rule as above]

Collation: [1-3]⁸ [4]⁴; pp.[1-8] 9-52 [53-56] = 28 leaves.

Contents: P.1: title page; p.2: 'Copyright 1903 by Willa Sibert
Cather | [rule] | *All Rights Reserved* | *Printed at* | *The Gorham
Press,* | *Boston, U.S.A.*'; p.3: 'DEDICATORY | To R. C. C.
AND C. D. C. | [25-line poem in italic]'; p.4: blank; pp.5-6:
contents; p.7: half title; p.8: blank; pp.9-52: text; pp.53-56:
blank.

Text Contents (first publication as noted):
Dedicatory. B35
"Grandmither, Think Not I Forget". *Critic* 36 (April 1900).
   B19
In Rose Time. *Lippincott's* 70 (July 1902). B34
Asphodel. *Critic* 37 (December 1900). B28
Mills of Montmartre. B36
Arcadian Winter. *Harper's*, 4 January 1902. B31
The Hawthorn Tree. B37
Sleep, Minstrel, Sleep. B38
Fides, Spes. B39
The Tavern. B40
In Media Vita. *Lippincott's* 67 (May 1901). B29

on p.vi, 'Duckworth' is corrected to 'Ducker'. A 23-line note 'ABOUT BERNICE SLOTE' has been added on p.74. The UNP logo removed from the copyright page.

c.)   Third edition (first edition of this selection), 1968

April Twilights (1903) | Poems by | WILLA CATHER | Edited with an introduction by | BERNICE SLOTE | UNIVERSITY OF NEBRASKA PRESS · LINCOLN

Collation: [1-3]^{16} [4]^{4} [5]^{16}; pp.[i-iv] v-xlviii, [1-2] 3-88 = 68 leaves. 2 inserted plates. 2-tone blue cloth, dust jacket, $5.50. 241 x 155 mm.

Revised and amplified introduction, checklist, text content as in A1.b.i., with the addition of an appendix of 9 previously uncollected poems (all published):
Shakespeare. *Hesperian*, 1 June 1892. B1
Columbus. *Hesperian*, 1 November 1892. B2
My Little Boy. *HM*, August 1896. B6
"Thine Eyes So Blue and Tender". *HM*, October 1896. B7
Bobby Shafto. *HM*, October 1896. B8
My Horseman. *HM*, November 1896. B9
[Then Back to Ancient France Again]. *Courier*, 22 April 1899.
     B15
Broncho Bill's Valedictory. *Library*, 30 June 1900. B24
Are You Sleeping, Little Brother? *Library*, 4 August 1900. B26

A2.   APRIL TWILIGHTS AND OTHER POEMS

a.)   First edition (limited), 1923

[within a dec. light olive (94) rule-frame and a single black rule-frame with small orn. inside corners] APRIL | TWILIGHTS | AND OTHER POEMS | BY WILLA CATHER | [olive (94) oval Knopf device within a single black rule panel with floral orn. on vertical sides] | ALFRED · A · KNOPF | NEW YORK · MCMXXIII

Collation: [1-9]⁴; pp.[π1-2, 1-12] 13-66 [67-70] = 36 leaves.

Contents: Pp.π1-2: blank; p.1: half title; p.2: blank; p.3: title page; p.4: '*Copyright, 1923, by Alfred A. Knopf, Inc.*'; p.5: dedication, 'TO | MY | FATHER | FOR | A | VALENTINE | [orn.]'; p.6: blank; p.7: 7-line statement of acknowledgment, subscribed 'WILLA CATHER'; p.8: blank; pp.9-10: contents; p.11: part title, 'PART I'; p.12: blank; pp.13-44: text of part 1; p.45: part title, 'PART II'; p.46: blank; pp.47-66: text of part 2; p.67: blank; p.68: colophon, '*Of this book, there were printed | in February, nineteen hundred & twenty three, | four hundred and fifty numbered copies, each | signed by the author, of which this is* NO. [space supplied for number] | [author's holograph signature]'; pp.69-70: blank.

Text Content: Thirteen poems have been withdrawn from the text of the 1903 edition:
Dedicatory
Asphodel
Mills of Montmartre
On Cydnus
The Namesake
White Birch in Wyoming
Eurydice
The Night Express
Thine Advocate
Sonnet
From the Valley
I Have No House For Love to Shelter Him
Paris

The new poems (first published as indicated) comprising Part 2:

The Palatine. *McClure's* 33 (June 1909). B65
The Gaul in the Capitol. B76
A Likeness. *Scribner's* 54 (December 1913). B69
The Swedish Mother. *McClure's* 37 (September 1911). B66
Spanish Johnny. *McClure's* 39 (June 1912). B67
Autumn Melody. *McClure's* 30 (November 1907). B63
Prairie Spring. *McClure's* 40 (December 1912). B68

Macon Prairie. B74
Street in Packingtown. *Century* 90 (May 1915). B72
A Silver Cup. B77
Recognition. B73
Going Home. B75

Paper: Heavy white laid stock with vertical chain lines 33 mm.
apart. 227 x 145 mm.; edges uncut. Watermark: 'LITTLE
CHART | ENGLAND' with countermark of horned crown and
shield over initials 'B J'. End papers of the same stock.

Binding: Decorated paper over boards; cream vellum paper
shelfback lettered, '[orn. in yellow] | APRIL | TWI-|
LIGHTS | [yellow orn.]'. The paper is a mottled tan oriental
rice paper with an overall design of small brown butterflies,
bright red-orange petaled flowers and smaller yellow and green
flowers. In a black paper-covered box with cream label on the
spine, '*April Twilights and Other Poems*'.

Publication: 450 signed and numbered copies. Published 20
February 1923, 2 months before the trade edition, which is in a
different setting and format. Presswork for the limited edition
was by the Pynson Printers. Trade edition presswork was by
Vail-Ballou. The limited edition is listed in the *PW* monthly
announcement for 3 February 1923 at $7.50.

Locations: CWB, ViU, NbU, WCPM, AHG, AAK.

Textual Changes and Emendations: Pagination and line are keyed
to the 1923 limited edition revised text with the 1903 text
supplied after. Poem title follows in parentheses. These changes
are reflected in all succeeding edition texts which include these
poems.

15.11	of lovers] of the lovers (Fides, Spes)
15.21	of love] o' love (Fides, Spes)
16.23	despoil] defile (The Tavern)
25.2	of the] o' the (In Media Vita)
25.10	cleft of] cleft o' (In Media Vita)
25.11	that are hushed] that hushed (In Media Vita)
25.19	Young lads] Hot lads (In Media Vita)

27.[29-41]   *omit] third stanza of 13 lines* (Lament for Marsyas)
   30.6   clouds a] clouds the (Sleep, Minstrel, Sleep)
33.[21-23]   *omit] 3-line footnote* (Poppies on Ludlow Castle)
   37.21   in the market-place] of the market place (Thou Art the Pearl)
 38.19,20   Calls the . . . Of an] Calls a . . . From an (Arcadian Winter)

   b.i.)   Second edition (trade), first printing, 1923

   [within a thin-thick-thin rule-frame] APRIL TWILIGHTS |
   AND OTHER POEMS | BY | WILLA CATHER | [Knopf oval
   device within a floriated panel] | ALFRED A KNOPF | NEW
   YORK · MCMXXIII

   Collation: [1-3]⁸ [4]¹⁰; pp.[1-12] 13-66 [67-68] = 34 leaves.

   Contents: P.1: half title; p.2: advt. '[within a thin-thick-thin
   rule] BOOKS BY WILLA CATHER | [orn.] ALEXANDER'S
   BRIDGE | O PIONEERS | THE SONG OF THE LARK | MY
   ANTONIA | YOUTH AND THE BRIGHT MEDUSA | ONE
   OF OURS | A LOST LADY | *(in preparation)* | [orn.]'; p.3: title
   page; p.4: 'COPYRIGHT, 1923, | BY ALFRED A. KNOPF,
   INC. | Published, April, 1923 | MANUFACTURED IN THE
   UNITED STATES OF AMERICA'; p.5: dedication, '*To my
   Father | for a Valentine*'; p.6: blank; p.7: statement (as in A2.a.);
   p.8: blank; pp.9-10: contents; p.11: part title, 'PART I'; p.12:
   blank; pp.13-44: text of part 1; p.45: part title, 'PART II';
   p.46: blank; pp.47-66: text of part 2; pp.67-68: blank.

   Text Contents: As in A2.a.

   Paper: Cream wove without watermark. 218 x 140 mm.; top
   edge trimmed and stained orange, fore edge rough-cut, bottom
   edge uncut. End papers of smoother wove stock.

   Binding: Decorated paper-covered boards, green-gray spine
   lettered in green, '[orn. rule] | APRIL | TWILIGHTS |
   [orn.] | WILLA | CATHER | [orn. rule]'. Cover paper with
   a regular pattern of gray-blue flowers on an orange field,
   intertwined with green berries.

Publication: Published 23 April 1923 in a first printing of 1,500 copies priced at $2.50, 2 months after the limited edition in an entirely different setting and format. The trade edition plates were set by Vail-Ballou; the limited, by the Pynson Printers. A Knopf *PW* advertisement (10 February 1923) announces the publication date and price of the trade edition as $2.00. A later advertisement on 10 March also has the $2.00 price, but the *PW* weekly record on 12 May lists the price as $2.50.

Locations: CWB, ViU, WCPM, AHG, AAK.

b.ii.)   Second printing, 1924

[title and collation as in the first printing]

Contents: On p.2, in the advertisement for *A Lost Lady*, the line *'(in preparation)'* is removed (*ALL* was published in September 1923). The copyright (p.4) is reset: 'COPYRIGHT, 1923, BY WILLA CATHER | *Published, April, 1923* | *Second Printing, January, 1924* | MANUFACTURED IN THE UNITED STATES OF AMERICA'.

Text contents, paper, binding as in the first printing; the binding differs only in the cover paper (regular blue and green figures on a cream ground).

Publication: January 1924 in a printing of 610 copies. Three hundred ninety sets of sheets of this printing were sent to Heinemann for the first English edition (*A2.a.i.*[e]).

b.iii.)   Third printing, 1933

[title as in the first printing, with new date, 'MCMXXXIII']

Collation: [1-4]⁸ [5]⁴; pp.[1-12] 13-70 [71-72] = 36 leaves.

Contents: As in the first and second printings with the following changes: the advertisement has been removed from p.2, which is blank; the copyright (p.4) is altered to read 'COPYRIGHT, 1923, BY WILLA CATHER | *All rights reserved. No part of this*

book may be reproduced | *in any form without permission in writing* *from the publisher,* | *except by a reviewer who may quote brief passages in a review* | *to be printed in a magazine or newspaper.* | *Published, April, 1923* | *Second Printing, January, 1924* | *Third Printing, January, 1933* | MANUFACTURED IN THE UNITED STATES OF AMERICA'; pp.67-70: the added poem 'Poor Marty'; p.71: blank; p.72: 'A NOTE ON THE TYPE IN | WHICH THIS BOOK IS SET | [10 lines in italic on the history of Bodoni type] | [Knopf oval borzoi device] | SET UP BY VAIL-BALLOU PRESS, | BINGHAMTON, N. Y. · PRINTED | AND BOUND BY THE PLIMPTON | PRESS, NORWOOD, MASS. | PAPER MADE BY S. D. | WARREN CO., BOSTON'.

Text Contents: As in A2.a-bii. with the addition of the new poem, 'Poor Marty', which was printed first in the *Atlantic Monthly* 147 (May 1931): 585-587 (B78).

Paper: Cream laid, watermark '[unicorn orn.] | UNICORN | 100% RAG'. Vertical chain lines 40 mm. apart. Leaves 219 x 144 mm.; top edge trimmed and stained orange, other edges uncut. End papers of the same stock.

Binding: Decorated cloth-covered boards, light yellow-green cloth shelfback with spine lettered in gilt, '[orn. rule] APRIL | TWI- | LIGHTS | [orn.] | WILLA | CATHER | [orn. rule]'.

Publication: Published 5 May 1933 in a printing of 725 copies. Set from the plates of the second edition, to which minor batter repairs were made, with the addition of the new poem, 'Poor Marty'. Presswork for this printing was transferred from Vail-Ballou to the Plimpton Press. Described in *PW* (spring index, 20 May 1933) as a "new edition" priced at $2.00.

b.iv.)   Fourth printing. 800 copies, June 1933. Plimpton Press.

b.v.)   Fifth printing. 750 copies, August 1951. Plimpton Press.

b.vi.)   Sixth printing. 1,000 copies, January 1961. According to the Knopf production records, this printing was not satisfactory,

and the presswork was done over at the expense of the Plimpton Press.

b.vii.)   Seventh printing. 723 copies, August 1969. In July 1969, the Edectro plastic plates (from the original Vail-Ballou first printing plates), used by the Plimpton Press since the 1933 third printing, were purchased by Random House / Knopf. The plates were sent to the Book Press, Brattleboro, Vermont, who printed the seventh printing.

English Edition

A2.*a.i.*(e)   First English edition (American sheets of A2.b.ii), 1924

[within a thin-thick-thin rule frame] APRIL TWILIGHTS | AND OTHER POEMS | BY | WILLA CATHER | 19[Heinemann device]24 || LONDON: WILLIAM HEINEMANN

Collation: [1-3]⁸ [4]¹⁰; pp.[1-12] 13-66 [67-68] = 34 leaves.

Contents: P.1: half title; p.2: advt. as in A2.b.ii.; p.3: title page; p.4: 'PRINTED IN THE UNITED STATES OF AMERICA'; p.5: dedication as in A2.b.i.; p.6: blank; p.7: statement as in A2.a-b.ii.; pp.9-68: as in A2.a-b.ii.

Text Contents: As in A2.a-b.ii.

Paper: As in A2.b.ii. 216x140mm. Top edge trimmed and unstained, other edges uncut. End papers of heavy smooth cream wove stock.

Binding: Light blue-gray (191) linen cloth. Front cover: '[within a blind-stamped border rule, with 3 panels outlined in blind; in the first 15 mm. panel:] APRIL TWILIGHTS | [154x127mm. blank panel] | [23 mm. panel:] WILLA CATHER'. Spine: '[blind rule] APRIL | TWILIGHTS | WILLA | CATHER | HEINEMANN [blind rule]'. Back cover: Heinemann device stamped in blind on the lower right corner.

Publication: 390 sets of American trade second printing of *April Twilights and Other Poems*, bound in England, supplied with the

Heinemann imprint on the title page and altered text of the copyright. Published September 1924 at 5s. The statement '*(in preparation)*', referring to *A Lost Lady*, has been removed from p.2. Heinemann published *ALL* in England a month before this edition of *ATOP*.

A3.   APRIL TWILIGHTS
(with *Alexander's Bridge;* Autograph Edition, vol. 3)

a.)   First edition of this selection, 1937

[dec. rule] | WILLA CATHER | [dec. rule] | Alexander's Bridge | & | April Twilights | [dec. rule] | [orange-brown: 'H M Co' cipher] | BOSTON | HOUGHTON MIFFLIN COMPANY | 1937

Collation: [1-14]⁸; pp.[i-iv, 1-2] 3-216 [217-220] = 112 leaves.

Illustration: Facsimile of the first page of the original MS of "The Palatine," inserted between pp.186-187 with a protective facing sheet of lighter paper.

Contents: P.i: half title, 'THE NOVELS AND STORIES | OF | WILLA CATHER | [orn.] 3 [orn.] | AUTOGRAPH EDITION'; p.ii: limitation notice, 'NINE HUNDRED AND SEVENTY COPIES OF THIS EDITION | HAVE BEEN PRINTED FROM TYPE AT THE RIVERSIDE PRESS, | CAMBRIDGE, MASSACHUSETTS, OF WHICH NINE HUNDRED | AND FIFTY SIGNED AND NUMBERED COPIES ARE FOR SALE. | THIS COPY IS NUMBER [number in ink]'; p.iii: title page; p.iv: 'COPYRIGHT, 1912 AND 1922, BY WILLA SIBERT CATHER | COPYRIGHT, 1903 AND 1923, BY WILLA CATHER | ALL RIGHTS. . . .'; p.1: half title, 'Alexander's Bridge'; p.2: blank; pp.3-137: text of *AB;* p.138: blank; p.139: half title, 'April Twilights'; p.140: blank; pp.141-142: contents; p.143: part title, 'PART I | *EARLY VERSES*'; p.144: blank; pp.145-182: text of part 1; p.183: part title, 'PART II | *LATER VERSES*'; p.184: blank; pp.185-217: text of part 2; p.218: blank; p.219: Riverside Press device; p.220: blank.

Text Contents: Two poems, 'In Media Vita' and 'Song', have been withdrawn in addition to the 13 removed in 1923 (A2.b.i.); otherwise, as in A2.b.iii.

Notes on paper, binding, dust jacket and publication with the entry for the entire Autograph Edition (AA1).

Textual Changes and Emendations: Pagination and line are keyed to the 1937 Autograph Edition revised text with the 1923 and 1933 texts supplied after. Poem title follows in parentheses. These changes reflect Willa Cather's final text revision.

158.1	heart] arms (Winter at Delphi)
164.15	or] nor (I Sought the Wood in Winter)
166.2	your] thy (Sleep, Minstrel, Sleep)
172.5	purple shadows rising, and the flash] purple mists ascending, and the flare (Prairie Dawn)
175.3	Could] Can (Thou Art the Pearl)
176.9	Now the] And the (Arcadian Winter)
193.10[2]	*omit*] Then all sheep come over de hills, / Big white dust, an' old dog Nils. (The Swedish Mother)
199.15	skirmishers who] skirmishers that (Macon Prairie)
212.3	were] was (Poor Marty)

A4. THE TROLL GARDEN

a.) First edition, 1905

FIRST ISSUE

THE | TROLL GARDEN | BY | WILLA SIBERT CATHER | [orange (48) publisher's device] | A FAIRY PALACE, WITH A FAIRY GARDEN; . . . . . | INSIDE THE TROLLS DWELL, ... WORKING AT | THEIR MAGIC FORGES, MAKING AND MAKING ALWAYS | THINGS RARE AND STRANGE [space] CHARLES KINGSLEY | NEW YORK | McCLURE, PHILLIPS & CO. | MCMV

Collation: [1]^4 [2-10]^8 [11]^8 ($\pm$ 11$_6$) [12-17]^8; pp.[i-viii, 1-3] 4-253 [254-256] = 132 leaves.

Contents: P.i: half title; p.ii: epigraph, ' *"We must not look at Goblin men,* | *We must not buy their fruits;* | *Who knows upon what soil they fed* | *Their hungry thirsty roots?"* | GOBLIN MARKET.'; p.iii: title page; p.iv: '*Copyright, 1905, by* | McCLURE, PHILLIPS & CO. | *Published March, 1905* | [page foot] Copyright, 1904-05, by The S. S. McClure Co. Copyright, 1905, by | Charles Scribner's Sons. Copyright, 1904, by The Ridgway-Thayer Co.'; p.v: dedication, '*To* | *Isabelle McClung*'; p.vi: blank; p.vii: contents; p.viii: blank; pp.1-253: text (at the foot of p.253: 'THE McCLURE PRESS, NEW YORK'); pp.254-256: blank.

Text Contents (first published as indicated):
Flavia and Her Artists. C34
The Sculptor's Funeral. *McClure's* 24 (January 1905). C33
The Garden Lodge. C35
"A Death in the Desert". *Scribner's* 33 (January 1903). C31
The Marriage of Phædra. C36
A Wagner Matinée. *Everybody's Magazine* 10 (February 1904). C32
Paul's Case. C37

'Paul's Case' appeared in *McClure's* 25 (May 1905) 2 months after book publication. 'Flavia and Her Artists', 'The Garden Lodge', and 'The Marriage of Phædra' were never reprinted in WC's lifetime. '"A Death in the Desert"' and 'A Wagner Matinée' were extensively reworked by WC for inclusion in *The Troll Garden*.

Paper: Cream wove stock without watermark. 183 x 119 mm.; top edge trimmed, other edges uncut. Cream end papers of a smoother stock.

Binding: Red (16) vertical rib cloth. Front cover: '[gilt lettering] THE | TROLL | GARDEN | WILLA | SIBERT | CATHER'. The title is within a blind-stamped romanesque border with 4 stylized flowers on each side (the upper 4 flanking the lettering); beneath the lettering is a stylized floral decoration. In the lower left corner are initials 'W J' [William Jordan] with 'J' upright and 'W' lying on its back with the perpendicular ascender in a horizontal position. Spine: '[gilt] THE | TROLL | GARDEN |

WILLA | SIBERT | CATHER | [at foot] McCLURE |
PHILLIPS | [orn.] & CO. [orn.]'. Back cover blank. *Note:*
William Jordan (fl. 1898-1914) also designed the Aldine
colophon for McClure Phillips.

Dust Jacket: Pale gray-green (154) wove paper. Overall lettering
is light yellow-green (117). Front cover decoration is chartreuse
(99). Front cover jacket design exactly duplicates the front cover
of the book. Spine: 'THE | TROLL | GARDEN | WILLA |
SIBERT | CATHER | [McClure's device] | *McClure* | *Phillips* |
& Co.' Back cover: Advt. for *McClure's Magazine*, headed by the
publisher's device; the whole within a single rule frame. Inner
flaps blank.

Publication: 5 April 1905. $1.25. Of 2 copies deposited for
copyright in the Library of Congress on that date, one has
disappeared. The surviving copy (PZ3.C2858T, Copy 2) has the
copyright deposit stamp, 'Two copies received | 5 April 1905',
on the verso of the title page.

In all copies examined, including the DLC deposit copy, the
story title leaf for 'The Marriage of Phædra' (11_6, pp.155-156) is
a cancel. No example of the original cancellans has ever been
noted in the first issue. See Frederick B. Adams's notes in
Colophon (New Graphic Series 1, no.3 [1939], 94-95) regarding
this title. The firm of McClure, Phillips & Co. was dissolved in
1906, and the remainder of the edition was bought by Doubleday, Page & Co., who issued the original McClure, Phillips
sheets (including the McClure, Phillips title page) in a new
binding with their firm name at the foot of the spine (see
"Second Issue").

The misspelling 'exculsive' for 'exclusive' at p.21, l.2, is
corrected in later editions. On p.120, in either l.1 or 2, the
word 'more' has been omitted in error from the sentence, 'There
are many reasons why I am concerned than I can tell you.' The
Signet paperback (second edition, A4.b.i-iii.) silently revises to
read 'There are more reasons why I am concerned than I can tell
you.' The third edition (*Willa Cather's Collected Short Fiction,
1892-1912,* A4.c.) fills the lacuna in brackets as an adverb

modifying 'concerned' rather than as an adjective modifying 'reasons': 'There are many reasons why I am [more] concerned than I can tell you.'

Locations: CWB (3 copies; d.j.), DLC (copyright deposit copy 2), NbU, FBA, AHG, AAK.

SECOND ISSUE

Differs from the first issue only in the binding, which has the name of Doubleday, Page & Co. at the foot of the spine. This binding is of coarse mesh cloth. The story title leaf for 'The Marriage of Phædra' (11_6, pp. 155-156) is integral and not a cancel in these copies. The DLC copy, acquired 28 September 1931, has an ownership inscription, 'Anna Washington Croton, / Northhampton'.

Locations: FBA, DLC.

b.i.)   Second edition, first printing (Signet paperback), 1961

The | TROLL | GARDEN | [orn.] BY [orn.] | WILLA CATHER | *With an Afterword by* | Katherine Anne Porter | A SIGNET [Signet Classics cipher] CLASSIC | *Published by* | The New American Library

Paperback, perfect binding; pp.[1-6] 7-152 = 76 leaves. Signet Classic CD31. $0.50. Decorated wrappers. 178 x 107 mm.

'First Printing, August, 1961'. Approximately 700 silent alterations and corrections. No note to acknowledge editing. Katherine Anne Porter's afterword is copyrighted 1952 and 1961. It was first published as "Critical Reflections on Willa Cather" in *Mademoiselle* (July 1952) and collected in *The Days Before* (New York: Harcourt, Brace, 1952). This version has a 'Note' added in 1961 to the 1952 text. Biographical sketch of WC on p. 1.

b.ii.)   Second printing (English edition), 1966

As the first printing with the imprint of the New English Library (Signet Books). Published November 1966 at 3s.6d.

b.iii.)   Third printing (Plume paperback), 1971

The | Troll | Garden | [orn.] BY Willa Cather, WITH AN | AFTERWORD BY KATHERINE ANNE PORTER | [Plume Books cipher] | A PLUME BOOK from | NEW AMERICAN LIBRARY | TIMES MIRROR | New York, London, and Scarborough, Ontario

Paperback, perfect binding; pp.[1-6] 7-151 [152-160] = 80 leaves. Plume Books Z5049. $2.95. Decorated wrappers. 202 x 136 mm.

'First PLUME Printing, December, 1971' on the copyright. A photographically enlarged setting of the 1961 Signet Classics plates. Only the biographical sketch on p. 1 and the preliminaries have been reset. List of Plume books at pp. 158-159.

c.)   Third edition, 1965

See AA7, *Willa Cather's Collected Short Fiction, 1892-1912.* Pp. 147-261 comprise the 7 stories from the 1905 edition of *The Troll Garden* with 40 obvious textual emendations; otherwise, un-copy-edited.

A5.   ALEXANDER'S BRIDGE

a.i.)   First edition, first printing, 1912

FIRST ISSUE

ALEXANDER'S BRIDGE | BY | WILLA SIBERT CATHER | [publisher's device] | BOSTON AND NEW YORK | HOUGHTON MIFFLIN COMPANY | [black letter] The Riverside Press Cambridge | [roman] 1912

Collation: [1-11]⁸ [12]⁴; pp.[i-iv] 1-174 [175-180] = 92 leaves.

Contents: P.i: half title; p.ii: blank; p.iii: title page; p.iv: 'COPYRIGHT, 1912, BY WILLA SIBERT CATHER | ALL RIGHTS RESERVED | *Published April 1912*'; pp.1-175: text; p.176: '[black letter] The Riverside Press | [roman] CAMBRIDGE · MASSACHUSETTS | U. S. A.'; pp.177-180: Houghton Mifflin advts. for H. J. Smith's *Enchanted Ground*, Ian Hay's *A Man's Man*, Alice Brown's *John Winterbourne's Family*, and Peter Harding's *The Corner of Harley Street*. *Note:* Placement of the half title preceding the title page is the point of issue.

Paper: Cream wove, no watermark. 186x124 mm.; edges trimmed. End papers of the same stock.

Binding: Coarse blue (182) or purple (245) mesh cloth, gilt-stamped lettering overall. Front cover: '[within a blind-stamped border rule; lettering within a gilt-stamped 38x85 mm. panel rule] ALEXANDER'S | BRIDGE | BY WILLA S. CATHER'. Spine: 'ALEXANDER'S | BRIDGE | WILLA S. | CATHER | HOUGHTON | MIFFLIN CO.' Back cover blank. *Note:* The Library of Congress copyright deposit copy binding and a copy in the private collection of Frederick B. Adams are the only copies located with the author's name inside the front cover panel. The DLC copy is in purple cloth.

SECOND ISSUE

[title and collation as in the first issue]

Contents: P.i: title page; p.ii: copyright; p.iii: half title; p.iv: blank; pp.1-180: as in the first issue. *Note:* Placement of the half title after the title page–copyright leaf is the second issue point.

Paper: As in the first issue.

Bindings (no priority established):
a: Smooth blue (182) cloth, gilt-stamped lettering overall. Front cover: '[within a blind-stamped border rule; title within a gilt-stamped 38 x 85 mm. panel rule] ALEXANDER'S | BRIDGE | [beneath the panel] WILLA S. CATHER'. Spine as on the first issue binding.

b: Rough purple (245) cloth, gilt-stamped as a.
c: Gray-green (150) vertical rib cloth, gilt-stamped as a.
d: Coarse blue (182) mesh cloth, gilt-stamped as a.

Note: Bindings after 1918 are distinguished by the removal of middle initial 'S' from the author's name on front cover and spine. Ink stamping replaces gilt, and a variety of cloths have been seen or reported: lavender mesh, smooth cream tan, blue-gray mesh with blue ink stamping. White cloth copies with blue ink stamping are said to be associated with 300 sets of sheets sold by the publishers in 1919 to the Syndicate Trading Company. A letter from John S. Van E. Kohn to Frederick B. Adams, 3 July 1940, reports "the copy of AB in white cloth with blue lettering" sold to Benjamin D. Hitz, 'Willa Cather' on front cover and spine. "There is not the slightest evidence that the white copy was bound by the Syndicate Trading Company."
A ViU copy (CWB 599340) contains a note in WC's hand: "This book was bound up in odds and ends of cloth, as the publishers did not think much of it. . . . I have seen copies bound in brown, yellow, and purple cloth, but none in white."

Dust Jackets: AB appeared in 2 different jackets within a few weeks of publication. The second is announced in an advertisement in *PW* (20 April 1912, p.1346): "A special Cootes poster and jacket is now in preparation and copies will be sent on application." The second jacket with pictorial embellishments supplanted the first at the end of April 1912. F. Graham Cootes's illustrations were made for the *McClure's* serialization (February–April 1912) and were also used in the English edition (*A5.a.i.*[e]).

a: Pale green-gray wove paper with dark blue lettering overall. Front cover: '[within a 150x89mm. border panel] ALEXANDER'S | BRIDGE | [short rule] | BY WILLA S. CATHER || [Riverside Press device inset in vertical rules] || [13-line blurb, refers to 'A Troll Garden']'. Spine: 'ALEXAN-| DER'S | BRIDGE | WILLA S. | CATHER | $1.00 *net* | HOUGHTON | MIFFLIN CO.' Back cover: '[within a border rule, heading flanked by mirror-image Riverside Press devices] HOUGHTON MIFFLIN CO.'S | LATEST FICTION | [list of

11 publications, beginning with Meredith Nicholson's *A Hoosier Chronicle*, ending with Mary Rogers Bangs's *High Bradford*]'. Inner flaps blank.

b.: An illustration by F. Graham Cootes in a panel above the title and author's name: Bartley Alexander and Hilda at a small table (used in the March 1912 number of the *McClure's* serialization). Beneath is the 13-line blurb. Spine and back cover as on jacket a. Front inner flap: advt. for Henry Sydnor Harrison's *Queed*. Back inner flap: advt. for Meredith Nicholson's *A Hoosier Chronicle*.

Note: A later jacket (associated with copies after 1918) has the Cootes illustration, title, and author's name as on jacket b. The 13-line front cover blurb has been removed, and the space is blank. The price is removed from the spine, and the new price, $1.50, is printed on the front inner flap, which also contains 5 review excerpts and lists *MA, SOL, OP,* and *AB.* The back cover lists 20 titles of 'New Fiction,' beginning with Katharine Newlin Burt's *Quest* and ending with Denis MacKail's *Greenery Street.* The back inner flap is an advertisement for Anne Douglas Sedgwick's *The Little French Girl.*

Publication: Published first with the title *Alexander's Masquerade* in *McClure's Magazine* (38, nos.4, 5, 6 [February, March, April 1912]) (CCC1). The book was published on 20 April 1912 at $1.00 in a total edition of 5,270 copies. It was reissued by Houghton Mifflin in about 1918 using surplus sheets of the original printing. Later copies are identified only by variant bindings (see above). A typographical error on p.74, l.17: 'low' for 'blow' is corrected in the 1912 English edition and the 1922 second printing (A5.a.ii.).

Of all copies examined and noted, the Library of Congress copyright copy and the Frederick B. Adams copy are the only ones that combine features that characterize the first issue: arrangement of preliminaries with half title preceding the title page, coarse blue or purple mesh cloth with title and author's name within a gilt rule, cover lettering in the same typeface as on the 2 early dust jackets. The University of Virginia Barrett

Library has a set of loose, unbound gatherings—a so-called advance copy—with the same arrangement of the preliminaries.

Rearrangement of the preliminaries, effecting the placement of the half title after the title page—copyright leaf, may have occurred in the second pressrun from the standing plates. Scarcity of the first issue arrangement, however, indicates that the change was made earlier in the first run, probably a stop-press correction.

The contract for Willa Cather's first novel was signed on 1 December 1911 with Houghton Mifflin. Terms stipulated 10% royalty to 3,000 copies sold, 12.5% to 5,000 copies, and 15% above that number, with the publisher's option of refusal for the next book. A preliminary dummy was ordered on 19 December 1911. The composition order was placed at the Riverside Press on 28 December, and the book was in press on 3 January 1912 for a first impression of 2,270 sets of sheets. A $200 advertising allowance was approved. Presswork was completed in March, and 2 copies of the book were sent to Heinemann in London on 25 March for the purpose of securing British copyright. The title was registered in England on the same date as the American copyright (20 April 1912). Heinemann was offered 270 sets of the original sheets by Houghton Mifflin for the English edition, but elected to reprint the text in England (see *A5.a.i.*[e]).

A second printing from standing type of 3,000 sets of sheets, bound as required until 1922.

Locations: CWB (first issue, unbound; second issue, 4 copies, bindings a–d; d.j. a and b), FBA (first issue, binding a; d.j. a), DLC (first issue, binding a), ViU (second issue, 3 copies).

b.i.) Second edition, 1922

ALEXANDER'S BRIDGE | BY | WILLA SIBERT CATHER | NEW EDITION WITH A PREFACE | [Riverside Press device in oval] | BOSTON AND NEW YORK | HOUGHTON MIFFLIN COMPANY | [black letter] The Riverside Press Cambridge | [roman] 1922

Collation: [1-11]⁸ [12]⁶; pp.[π1-2, i-iv] v-viii [ix-x], 1-174 [175-176] = 94 leaves.

Contents: P.π1: blank; p.π2: '[black letter] Books by Willa Sibert Cather | [short rule] | [roman] ALEXANDER'S BRIDGE | O PIONEERS! | THE SONG OF THE LARK | MY ÁNTONIA | YOUTH AND THE BRIGHT MEDUSA | ONE OF OURS'; p.i: half title; p.ii: blank; p.iii: title page; p.iv: 'COPYRIGHT, 1912 AND 1922, BY WILLA SIBERT CATHER | ALL RIGHTS RESERVED | [black letter] The Riverside Press | [roman] CAMBRIDGE · MASSACHUSETTS | PRINTED IN THE U. S. A.'; pp.v-ix: preface, signed in print and ending, 'WHALE COVE COTTAGE | GRAND MANAN, N. B. | *September*, 1922'; p.x: blank; pp.1-175: text; p.176: blank.

Paper: Heavy cream wove. 185 x 125 mm.; edges trimmed. End papers of smoother cream wove stock.

Binding: Blue (182) linen cloth, gilt-stamped lettering overall. Front: '[title within a 38 x 86 mm. single gilt rule panel] ALEXANDER'S | BRIDGE | [beneath the panel] WILLA CATHER'. Spine: 'ALEXANDER'S | BRIDGE | WILLA | CATHER | HOUGHTON | MIFFLIN CO.' Back cover blank.

Dust Jacket: Coated cream wove paper printed in dark brown. Front: '[within a single rule frame: 65 x 104 mm. illus. by F. G. Cootes] | ALEXANDER'S | BRIDGE | [short rule] | BY WILLA S. CATHER || [9-line excerpt from a critical review by H. L. Mencken] | New Edition | with an introduction by the author'. Spine: 'ALEXANDER'S | BRIDGE | WILLA S. | CATHER | HOUGHTON | MIFFLIN CO.' Back cover: 'NEW FICTION || [14 titles, beginning with Sabatini's *Captain Blood* and ending with his *The Snare*]'. Front inner flap: '$1.50 | WILLA SIBERT CATHER | [excerpts from 5 critical reviews] | Books by Miss Cather | MY ANTONIA | THE SONG OF THE LARK | O PIONEERS! | ALEXANDER'S BRIDGE'. Back inner flap: 'MY ANTONIA | *By* | WILLA SIBERT CATHER | [31-line blurb] | *With illustrations by Benda.*'

Publication: January 1922 at $1.50. The text is set from the original 1912 plates to which is added the new front matter. Printer's imprint and 1912 advertisements removed from the back and the typographical error on p.74 ('low' for 'blow') corrected.

b.ii.)   Second printing, October 1922.

b.iii.)   Third printing, July 1925.

b.iv.)   Fourth printing, June 1933.

c.)   Third edition (with *April Twilights;* Autograph Edition, vol.3), 1937

See A3. Text of *AB*, pp.3-137. Notes on paper, binding, and publication with the entry for the entire Autograph Edition (AA1).

d.)   Fourth edition (Bantam paperback), 1962

ALEXANDER'S BRIDGE | by | WILLA SIBERT CATHER | NEW EDITION | WITH A PREFACE | [orn.] | BANTAM BOOKS / NEW YORK

Paperback, perfect binding; pp.[i-iv] v-viii [ix-x], 1-112 [113-118] = 64 leaves.

Contents: P.i: Bantam Classics device above 21-line biographical sketch; p.ii: large Bantam Classics device; p.iii: title page; p.iv: copyright, '. . . *Bantam Classic edition published June 1962* . . .'; pp.v-viii: preface, signed on p.viii and dated September 1922; p.ix: half title; p.x: blank; pp.1-112: text; p.113: 'The photograph of Willa Cather on the | cover is from the Picture Collection | of the New York Public Library. | [Bantam Classics device] | BANTAM CLASSICS | [7-line blurb for Bantam Classics]'; pp.114-117: advts. for Bantam Classics; p.118: blank.

Paper: Cheap wove stock. 176 x 108 mm., edges trimmed.

Binding: Gilt heavy paper cut flush with edges. Front cover: '[upper left corner] HC161 60¢ | [heavy black lettering] Alexander's Bridge | [in a 50 mm. panel with lettering in white on orange and deep pink ground; to the left, a photograph of WC] WILLA | CATHER | [8-line blurb in black italic] | *complete and unabridged.*' In the right margin, lettered bottom to top and surmounted by a Bantam device in deep pink on a white 16x8 mm. panel: 'a bantam classic'. Spine: 'Hc161 || 60¢ | [Bantam device in deep pink on white 16x8 mm. panel] | BANTAM | CLASSIC | [lettered top to bottom] *alexander's bridge* [red slash] willa cather'. Back cover: '[20-line blurb in black italic] | [white orn.] | *willa cather* | Alexander's Bridge'. In the left margin, lettered bottom to top and surmounted by the Bantam device] *a bantam classic* [3 leaf orn. in black]'.

Publication: June 1962 at $0.60.

e.)   Fifth edition (Bison Books paperback), 1977

WILLA CATHER | ALEXANDER'S BRIDGE | Introduction by Bernice Slote | [Bison Books device] | UNIVERSITY OF NEBRASKA PRESS | LINCOLN [space] LONDON

Paperback, perfect binding; pp. [i-iv] v-xxviii [xxix-xxx], 1-138 = 84 leaves. Photographic wrappers cut flush with the leaves. 202 x 134 mm. Bison Book BB635. $2.95. First printing indicated by digital code '1'. A new setting of the text, published by arrangement with Houghton Mifflin Co. Bernice Slote's introduction, pp. v-xxvi.

The Bison Books edition bound in peach (26) library buckram was offered for sale by Windsor House, a subsidiary of Queens House, Larchmont, New York. The listing in *Books in Print* indicates Windsor House as the publisher and the list price as $10.00. Nowhere inside or outside the book does the Windsor House imprint occur. This distribution was unauthorized either by the University of Nebraska Press or Houghton Mifflin. The title is included, however, in a brochure listing the "publications" of Queens House, which also states, "All editions limited to 450 copies."

English Editions

***A5.a.i.*(e).**   First English edition, 1912

[within a single rule frame:] [red-brown] ALEXANDER'S |
BRIDGES | [black] BY | WILLA SIBERT CATHER |
ILLUSTRATED | [publisher's device in black and red-brown] |
[black] LONDON | [red-brown] WILLIAM HEINEMANN |
[black] 1912

Collation: [A]⁴ B-M⁸; pp.[i-viii, 1] 2-10, 13-72, 75-138,
141-182 = 92 leaves. *Note:* The breaks in pagination are
accounted for by 3 illustrations tipped into the text and implied
in the pagination as pp.11-12, 73-74 and 139-140. Versos
blank.

Illustrations: Frontispiece and 3 illustrations by F. Graham
Cootes on coated paper, tipped in preceding the title page and
as indicated in the collation note. These illustrations were used
first in the periodical publication of *Alexander's Masquerade*
(*McClure's*, February, March, April 1912). The third illustration
(p.73), with the caption 'How jolly it was being young, Hilda!
Do you remember that first walk we took together in Paris?',
was used on the second dust jacket of the American first edition.

Contents: Pp.i-ii: blank; p.iii: half title; p.iv: advt. for Heinemann publications, printed in black and red-brown; p.v: title
page; p.vi: '[lower left corner] *Copyright, 1912.*'; p.vii: list of
illus.; p.viii: blank; pp.1-182: text. At the foot of p.182, ' |
J. Miles & Co. Ltd., 68-70, Wardour Street, W.'

Paper: Heavy cream laid, vertical chain lines 25 mm. apart; no
watermark. 183 x 120 mm.; edges trimmed. End papers of a
smoother wove cream paper.

Binding: Light brown (77) linen cloth. Front cover: '[within a
blind-stamped border rule; title within a 29 x 78 mm. panel rule
in black, black lettering] ALEXANDER'S | BRIDGES | [at
foot] WILLA S. CATHER'. Spine: '[gilt-stamped lettering]
ALEXANDER'S | BRIDGES | WILLA S. | CATHER |

HEINEMANN'. The Heinemann device stamped in blind in the center of the back cover.

Publication: Copyrighted in England on 20 April 1912 from 2 copies of the American edition. Reprinted by J. Miles & Co. for Heinemann and published in August 1912 at 2s. The error 'low' for 'blow' (p.79, l.7) is corrected.

A6. O PIONEERS!

a.i.) First edition, first printing, 1913

O PIONEERS! | BY | WILLA SIBERT CATHER | "Those fields, colored by various grain!" | MICKIEWICZ | [oval publisher's device] | BOSTON AND NEW YORK | HOUGHTON MIFFLIN COMPANY | [black letter] The Riverside Press Cambridge | [roman] 1913

Collation: [1-20]^8 [21]$_1$; pp.[i-xii, 1-2] 3-308 [309-310] = 161 leaves.

Illustration: Frontispiece portrait captioned 'Alexandra', in color, by Clarence F. Underwood. On coated paper, inserted facing the title page, stub between pp.xii and 1.

Contents: P.i: blank; p.ii: '[within a 26x52 mm. single rule panel] [black letter] By Willa Sibert Cather | [short rule] | [roman] O PIONEERS! With colored frontispiece. | ALEXANDER'S BRIDGE. | HOUGHTON MIFFLIN COMPANY | BOSTON AND NEW YORK'; p.iii: half title; p.iv: blank; p.v: title page; p.vi: 'COPYRIGHT, 1913, BY WILLA SIBERT CATHER | ALL RIGHTS RESERVED | *Published June 1913*'; p.vii: dedication 'TO THE MEMORY OF | SARAH ORNE JEWETT | IN WHOSE BEAUTIFUL AND DELICATE WORK | THERE IS THE PERFECTION | THAT ENDURES'; p.viii: blank; p.ix: 'PRAIRIE SPRING | [19-line poem]'; p.x: blank; p.xi: contents; p.xii: blank; p.1: part title, 'PART I | THE WILD LAND'; p.2: blank; pp.3-71: text of part 1; p.72: blank; p.73: part title, 'PART II |

NEIGHBORING FIELDS'; p.74: blank; pp.75-183: text of
part 2; p.184: blank; p.185: part title, 'PART III | WINTER
MEMORIES'; p.186: blank; pp.187-207: text of part 3; p.208:
blank; p.209: part title, 'PART IV | THE WHITE
MULBERRY TREE'; p.210: blank; pp.211-271: text of part 4;
p.272: blank; p.273: part title, 'PART V | ALEXANDRA';
p.274: blank; pp.275-309: text of part 5; p.310: '[black letter]
The Riverside Press | [roman] CAMBRIDGE ·
MASSACHUSETTS | U · S · A'.

Paper: Heavy cream wove, no watermark. Leaves 185 x 123 mm.;
edges trimmed. End papers of heavier smooth stock.

Binding: Priority is based on the presence of an advance publisher's notice tipped into an examined copy (ViU) of binding a and
the use of cheaper materials for the third binding:

a: Light yellow-brown (76) vertical rib cloth, lettering stamped
in dark brown. Front cover: 'O PIONEERS! | WILLA S.
CATHER'. Spine: 'O PIONEERS! | [short rule] | WILLA S. |
CATHER | HOUGHTON | MIFFLIN CO.' Back cover blank.
The period following 'CO' on the spine touches the 'O'.

b: Pale cream yellow (89) vertical rib cloth, lettering stamped in
dark brown. Lettering as on binding a. The period following
'CO' on the spine touches the 'O'. Possibly a trial binding.

c: Light yellow-brown (76) linen cloth, lettering in dark brown,
but stamped lightly. Lettering as on a and b. The period
following 'CO' on the spine is separated from the 'O'.

Dust Jacket: White coated paper, lettering black overall;
illustration in colors. Front cover: '[bust detail of the
frontispiece portrait by Clarence F. Underwood in horizontal
oval] | O PIONEERS! | [10-line blurb] | By Willa Sibert
Cather'. Spine: 'O PIONEERS! | [short rule] | WILLA S. |
CATHER | $1.25 net | HOUGHTON | MIFFLIN CO'. Back
cover: '[within a border rule, heading flanked by 2 publisher's
devices] The Latest Fiction || [advt. for HM Co., listing 8
titles, beginning with H. S. Harrison's *V. V.'s Eyes* and ending
with Charles McEvoy's *Brass Faces*]'. Front inner flap: advt. for

Mary Johnston's *The Long Roll* and *Cease Firing*, within a border
rule. Back inner flap: 'NOVELS BY | RICHARD PRYCE | [5
titles]'.

Publication: 28 June 1913 in a first printing of 2,000 copies
at $1.25. Announced in the 5 July *PW* weekly record, listed
in the *New York Times* on 6 July and reviewed there on 14 September. *OP* was named one of the 100 best books of 1913 in the
New York Times on 30 November.

In all examined copies of the first printing, the final leaf (21_1) is
tipped in. Benjamin D. Hitz (*Papers of the Bibliographical Society
of America* 35, no.2 [1941]: 161) reports a copy, apparently in
binding c, in which a blank leaf follows the last leaf of text. The
final gathering, including the blank, consists of 10 integral
leaves. This is undoubtedly a later printing.

Post-1918 reprints are identified by the removal of the middle
initial from the author's name on front cover and spine, the use
of variant cloth bindings, and the presence of post-*OP* titles on
the advertisement page.

The contract for Willa Cather's second novel was signed with
Houghton Mifflin on 29 March 1913. The terms were slightly
more advantageous to the author than the contract for *AB:* 10%
to 5,000, 15% to 25,000, and 20% thereafter. A preliminary
dummy was ordered on 18 March. The composition order went
to the Riverside Press on 1 April, and presswork was completed
on 14 April. The allowance for advertising was $300. Galleys
sent to Heinemann on 25 April were used to secure the English
copyright on the same day as the American, 28 June 1913.
Subsequently, 1,050 sets of sheets were sent to Heinemann for
the English edition on 11 July.

Records of the second through thirteenth printings of *OP* are
lacking from the Houghton Mifflin files, nor were they to be
found among the Houghton Mifflin papers at the Houghton
Library, Harvard; hence, the lacuna between first and fourteenth
printings.

The plates of the first edition have been used (latterly in photo-offset) for all reprintings of *OP* to date, including the paperback Sentry Edition (thirty-first printing, 1962, A6.a.xxxi). Houghton Mifflin did not, as in the cases of *The Song of the Lark* and *My Ántonia*, retire the first edition plates and set all printings after 1937 from the Autograph Edition (A6.b.i.) resetting of the text.

An advance review copy is located in the Lilly Library, Indiana University. Josiah Q. Bennett kindly supplied this information about it: "The wrappers [plain drab paper with a bluish cast] are cut flush with the text. It is a millimeter shorter and narrower than the bound copy. It bulks 3 mm. thicker and does not appear to have been pressed except for folding, which would account for the greater bulk. It is folded like the cloth copy, but not sewn through the folds. It has been pierced with three holes and side-sewn through them, the cords being knotted front and back. There are no endpapers and the frontispiece portrait of Alexandra is omitted. The spine was not treated to any backing when the cover went on." An oblong paper label lettered 'O PIONEERS!' is pasted on the spine.

A typographical error on p.60, l.8, "chince-bugs", for "chinch-bugs", persists through all Houghton Mifflin printings (including the Sentry Edition) to date. It was corrected in the Autograph Edition (second edition, A6.b.i.).

Locations: CWB (3 copies; bindings a-c, d.j.), FBA, InU (advance review copy), AHG, AAK.

a.ii-a.xiii.)   Second through thirteenth printings. Between August 1913 and January 1925. Records not available.

a.xiv.)   Fourteenth printing. 1,000 copies, July 1926.

a.xv.)   Fifteenth printing. 1,000 copies, January 1928.

a.xvi.)   Sixteenth printing (Riverside Library Star Books). Number of copies not known, 1929. In larger format on cheap paper. Pictorial dust jacket by J. Perkins. $1.00. WC disapproved of

this cheap edition, which was made with her reluctant consent. It was discontinued in 1932.

a.xvii.)   Seventeenth printing. 2,500 copies, January 1933.

a.xviii.)   Eighteenth printing. 2,500 copies, July 1934.

a.xix.)   Nineteenth printing. 2,500 copies, December 1936.

a.xx.)   Twentieth printing. 2,500 copies, November 1938.

a.xxi.)   Twenty-first printing. 2,500 copies, July 1941.

a.xxii.)   Twenty-second printing. 1,000 copies, October 1943.

a.xxiii.)   Twenty-third printing. 1,500 copies, July 1944.

a.xxiv.)   Twenty-fourth printing. 2,000 copies, April 1946.

a.xxv.)   Twenty-fifth printing. 1,500 copies, September 1947.

a.xxvi.)   Twenty-sixth printing. 2,500 copies, November 1948.

a.xxvii.)   Twenty-seventh printing. 5,000 copies, July 1950.

a.xxviii.)   Twenty-eighth printing. 4,000 copies, March 1954.

a.xxix.)   Twenty-ninth printing. 3,500 copies, September 1957.

a.xxx.)   Thirtieth printing. 4,000 copies, May 1959.

a.xxxi.)   Thirty-first printing (first Sentry paperback edition, SE 16). 12,500 copies, January 1962.

a.xxxii.)   Thirty-second printing (second Sentry printing). 5,000 copies, July 1962.

a.xxxiii.)   Thirty-third printing (third Sentry printing). 10,000 copies, July 1963.

a.xxxiv.)   Thirty-fourth printing (fourth Sentry printing and thirty-first regular trade printing). 9,000 copies (Sentry: 6,000; regular trade: 3,000), January 1966. Bound separately using the same setting of sheets.

a.xxxv.)   Thirty-fifth printing (Keith Jennison Books Large Type edition. New York: Franklin Watts [1966]). Number of copies not known. Published by Watts, a division of Grolier Corporation, by arrangement with Houghton Mifflin. See F3.

a.xxxvi.)   Thirty-sixth printing (fifth Sentry printing and thirty-second regular trade printing). 12,000 copies (Sentry: 10,000; regular trade: 2,000), January 1967.

a.xxxvii.)   Thirty-seventh printing (sixth Sentry printing). 12,000 copies, January 1969.

a.xxxviii.)   Thirty-eighth printing (seventh Sentry printing and thirty-third regular trade printing). 9,500 copies (Sentry: 8,000; regular trade: 1,500), May 1972.

a.xxxix.)   Thirty-ninth printing (eighth Sentry printing and thirty-fourth regular trade printing). 11,000 copies (Sentry: 10,000; regular trade: 1,000), January 1973.

a.xl.)   Fortieth printing (ninth Sentry printing and thirty-fifth regular trade printing). 11,000 copies (Sentry: 10,000; regular trade: 1,000), December 1975.

a.xli.)   Forty-first printing (tenth Sentry printing). 10,000 copies, April 1977.

a.xlii.)   Forty-second printing (eleventh Sentry printing). 12,500 copies, September 1978.

b.i.)   Second edition, first printing (Autograph Edition, vol. 1), 1937

[dec. rule] | WILLA CATHER | [dec. rule] | O Pioneers! | [dec. rule] | *'Those fields, coloured by various grain!'* | MICKIEWICZ | [orange-brown: 'H M Co' cipher] | BOSTON | HOUGHTON MIFFLIN COMPANY | 1937

Collation: [1-16]⁸ [17]¹⁰; pp.[i-x, 1-2] 3-261 [262-266] = 138 leaves.

Illustration: Frontispiece portrait inserted facing the title page with a protective leaf of China paper; stub pasted to 1₇ᵥ. Caption: '*Willa Cather* | FROM A PASSPORT PHOTOGRAPH TAKEN IN 1920'.

Contents: P.i: half title 'THE NOVELS AND STORIES | OF | WILLA CATHER | [orn.] I [orn.] | AUTOGRAPH EDITION'; p.ii: limitation notice 'NINE HUNDRED AND SEVENTY COPIES OF THIS EDITION | HAVE BEEN PRINTED FROM TYPE AT THE RIVERSIDE PRESS, | CAMBRIDGE, MASSACHUSETTS, OF WHICH NINE HUNDRED | AND FIFTY SIGNED AND NUMBERED COPIES ARE FOR SALE. | THIS COPY IS NUMBER [number in ink] | [WC signature in black ink]'; p.iii: title page; p.iv: 'COPYRIGHT, 1913, BY WILLA SIBERT CATHER | ALL RIGHTS RESERVED INCLUDING THE RIGHT | TO REPRODUCE THIS BOOK OR PARTS THEREOF | IN ANY FORM | PRINTED IN THE U. S. A.'; p.v: dedication, '[orn. rule] TO THE MEMORY OF | SARAH ORNE JEWETT [orn. rule]'; p.vi: blank; p.vii: '[orn. rule] PRAIRIE SPRING | [19-line poem in italic]'; p.viii: blank; p.ix: contents; p.x: blank; p.1: part title, 'PART I | The Wild Land'; p.2: blank; pp.3-62: text of part 1; p.63: part title, 'PART II | Neighbouring Fields'; p.64: blank; pp.65-155: text of part 2; p.156: blank; p.157: part title, 'PART III | Winter Memories'; p.158: blank; pp.159-176: text of part 3; p.177: part title, 'PART IV | The White Mulberry Tree'; p.178: blank; pp.179-229: text of part 4; p.230: blank; p.231: part title, 'PART V | Alexandra'; p.232: blank; pp.233-262: text of part 5; p.263: Riverside Press device; pp.264-266: blank.

The error 'chince-bugs', which persists through the HM Co. first edition, p.60, has been corrected on p.52, l.13, to 'chinch-bugs'.

Notes on paper, binding, dust jacket, and publication with the entry for the entire Autograph Edition (AA1).

c.)   Third edition (Armed Services edition), 1945

[within a dash-rule border, beneath the border on the left,
'823'; title set in 2 panels. Left panel:] PUBLISHED BY
ARRANGEMENT WITH | HOUGHTON MIFFLIN
COMPANY, BOSTON | *All rights reserved* | COPYRIGHT,
1913, | BY WILLA SIBERT CATHER [right panel:] O
Pioneers! | *By* | WILLA CATHER | *Editions for the Armed
Services, Inc.* | A NON-PROFIT ORGANIZATION
ESTABLISHED BY | THE COUNCIL ON BOOKS IN
WARTIME, NEW YORK

Paperback perfect binding, glued at the spine and text leaves
secured with a single staple; pp.[1-4] 5-223 [224]. Text set in
double columns. Cheap wove paper; leaves measure 99 x 140
mm.; edges trimmed flush with the cover. Pictorial stiff paper
wrapper. No.823 of the Armed Services Editions, published in
September 1945.

English Editions

A6.a.i.(e)   First English edition (American sheets), 1913

O PIONEERS! | By | Willa Sibert Cather | "Those fields,
colored by various grain!" | MICKIEWICZ | [Heinemann device] |
London | William Heinemann | 1913

Collation: [1-20]^8 [21]$_1$, [χ]^8; pp.[i-xii, 1-2] 3-308 [309-310,
1] 2-16 = 169 leaves. *Note:* Terminal gathering χ^8 is 16 pages
of Heinemann advertisements, 'A List of Current Fiction', on
lighter paper.

Illustration: Frontispiece portrait in color, captioned 'Alexandra',
by Clarence F. Underwood. On coated paper, tipped in facing
the title page.

Contents: P.i: blank; p.ii: Heinemann advt. 'New 6s. Novels [13
titles]'; p.iii: half title, 'O PIONEERS!'; p.iv: blank; p.v: title
page; p.vi: 'COPYRIGHT, 1913, BY WILLA SIBERT
CATHER | ALL RIGHTS RESERVED'; p.vii: dedication as in

a.i.; p.viii: blank; p.ix: 'PRAIRIE SPRING | [19-line poem]';
p.x: blank; p.xi: contents; pp.1-309: as in A6.a.i.; p.310:
[black letter] 'The Riverside Press | [roman] PRINTED BY
H. O. HOUGHTON & CO. | CAMBRIDGE, MASS. |
U. S. A.'; pp.1-16: Heinemann advts.

Paper: As in A6.a.i. 187 x 118 mm.; top and fore edges
trimmed, bottom edge rough-cut. End papers of smoother
cream paper.

Binding: Dark purple (229) linen cloth. Front cover: '[gilt-
stamped within a 39 x 115 mm. gilt-rule panel; flanked by
2 gilt-stamped floral orns.] O PIONEERS! | [3 gilt-stamped
dots] | W. S. CATHER'. Spine (gilt-stamped): ' | O
PIONEERS! | [3 dots] | W. S. CATHER ||| HEINEMANN |'.
Back cover: Heinemann device stamped in blind at the lower
right corner.

Dust Jacket: Not seen.

Publication: English copyright secured 28 June 1913 from the
galleys of the American edition; published in August in an
edition of 1,050 copies at 6s. American sheets of the first
printing bound in England.

b.i.(e)   Second English edition. London: Hamish Hamilton, 1963.
Printed by photo-offset from the American plates. Remained in
print until 1976.

A7. MY AUTOBIOGRAPHY – S. S. McCLURE

a.i.)   First edition, first printing, 1914

FIRST ISSUE

MY | AUTOBIOGRAPHY | BY | S. S. McCLURE |
FOUNDER OF "McCLURE'S MAGAZINE" | *WITH MANY
ILLUSTRATIONS* | [publisher's device] | NEW YORK |
FREDERICK A. STOKES COMPANY | PUBLISHERS

Collation: [1]^{10} [2-17]^8 [18]^6; pp.[π1-4, i-iv] v-xii [xiii-xiv], 1-266 [267-270] = 144 leaves.

Illustrations: Frontispiece portrait of S. S. McClure (photograph by Arnold Genthe) on coated paper inserted facing the title page with a protective tissue; 31 illustrations on 15 inserted leaves of coated paper, printed on rectos and versos.

Contents: Pp.π1-4: blank; p.i: half title, 'MY AUTOBIOGRAPHY'; p.ii: blank; p.iii: title page; p.iv: 'COPYRIGHT, 1914, BY | FREDERICK A. STOKES COMPANY | [short rule] | COPYRIGHT, 1913, 1914, BY | THE MCCLURE PUBLICATIONS, INC. | [short rule] | *All rights reserved* | [within a 7 x 38 mm. panel rule, the publisher's initials in a decorative cipher at left] *September, 1914*'; pp.v-vi: untitled foreword, signed in print, 'S. S. McCLURE.'; pp.vii-ix: contents; p.x: blank; pp.xi-xii: list of illus.; p.xiii: second half title (as the first); p.xiv: blank; pp.1-266: text; pp.267-270: blank.

Note 1: The first issue has 2 points of identification: (1) '*September, 1914*' on the copyright (p.iv). (2) An extraneous l.13 on p.239, 'H. H. Rogers for his comment and suggestions.' The page contains 28 lines. The extra line is in the original periodical text. See full publication note following the second printing description (A7.a.ii).

Note 2: McClure acknowledges his debt to WC in the first paragraph of the foreword: 'It will be seen from this narrative that to my | mother and to my wife I owe much. I am in- | debted to the coöperation of Miss Willa Sibert | Cather for the very existence of this book.'

Note 3: An error on p.195, l.6, 'friend' for 'friends', was never corrected and persists through all printings.

Paper: Rough cream wove stock. 204 x 127 mm.; edges trimmed. End papers of heavier smooth wove stock. A front flyleaf of endpaper stock.

Binding: Maroon (14) linen cloth, measuring 210 mm. tall and 128 mm. wide at the front cover from hinge to fore edge. Front cover: '[within a single gilt rule panel 50 x 117 mm., gilt-stamped lettering] MY | AUTOBIOGRAPHY | [short gilt rule] | S. S. McCLURE | [a second gilt rule panel, 34 x 117 mm., directly beneath, on which is mounted a sepia illus. of 2 boys tramping a moonlit country road]'. Spine: '[gilt-stamped] MY | AUTOBIOGRAPHY | [short gilt rule] | S. S. McCLURE | [in letters 3 mm. high] STOKES'. Back cover blank.

Dust Jacket: Not seen.

Publication: See publication note for the second printing.

Locations: CWB, ViU, InU, FBA.

SECOND ISSUE

[title as in the first issue]

Collation: [1]^{10} [2-15]^8 [16]^8 ($\pm$16$_7$) [17]^8 [18]^6; pp.[π1-4, i-iv] v-xii [xiii-xiv], 1-266 [267-270] = 144 leaves.

Contents: As in the first issue ('*September, 1914*' on copyright); however, a cancel (16$_7$) corrects the text of p.239, resulting in a page of 27 lines.

Illustrations, paper and binding as in the first issue, but without the front flyleaf (see A7.a.i paper note).

Dust Jacket: Not seen.

Publication: See publication note for the second printing.

Locations: CWB, ViU, FBA.

a.ii.)   Second printing, **1915**

[title as in the first printing]

Collation: [1-18]⁸; pp.[π1-4, i-iv] v-xii [xiii-xiv], 1-266 [267-270] = 144 leaves.

Contents: The notice on the copyright (p.iv) has been changed to '*May, 1914*'; otherwise, as in the first printing, second issue, with corrected p.239 integral.

Illustrations: As in the first printing.

Paper: As of the first printing, but leaves measure 203 x 129 mm.; end papers of wove, semismooth stock.

Binding: As on the first printing, but 208 mm. tall and 130 mm. wide at the front cover measured from the hinge. Publisher's name on the spine 4 mm. in height.

Dust Jacket: Cream coated paper, printed in brown. Front cover: '[within a single border rule] MY | AUTOBIOGRAPHY | [short rule] | S. S. McCLURE | [illus. as on binding] | [5-line blurb, 8-line blurb in smaller font] | BOOTH TARKINGTON has said of McClure's story: | [6-line quote] | *$2.00 net* || Publishers — FREDERICK A. STOKES COMPANY — New York'. Spine: '[heavy rule] | MY AUTOBIOGRAPHY | [short rule] | McCLURE | STOKES | [heavy rule]'. Back cover: '[within a single border rule] YASHKA | My Life as Peasant, Officer and Exile || By MARIA BOTCHKAREVA || *As set down by* Isaac Don Levine | [28-line blurb]. . . .'. Front inner flap: advt. for E. Cooper's *My Lady of the Chinese Courtyard*. Back inner flap: advt. for John Roland's *The Good Shepherd*.

Of the 3 books advertised on the dust jacket, the Cooper title was published in 1914, the Roland in 1915, and Botchkareva's *Yashka* in 1919. Two copies of the second printing have been seen in this dust jacket (CWB, InU). It is possible that this is the first jacket, printed and supplied to the books in 1919, and that earlier copies were issued without dust jackets—at least, no example has been seen or reported.

Publication: 5 September 1914 at $1.75. Several puzzles attend the publication history of McClure's *My Autobiography* (actually

written by Willa Cather). Two variant states of the copyright
page exist: one with the notice 'May, 1914' and the other with
'September, 1914'. Jacob Blanck's "News from the Rare Book
Sellers" in *PW* (25 April 1942, p.1610) reports 2 copies of
the 'May, 1914' copyright noted by Gabriel Engel. Engel's
conclusion, based on a Stokes advertisement in the June 1914
issue of *McClure's Magazine* (where *My Autobiography* ran serially
from October 1913 to May 1914 [see below]) which announced
the book as "Just published in Book Form," was that the 'May'
copies were of the true first issue in spite of the fact that copies
deposited for copyright in September at the Library of Congress
carry the September notice. The only other point of differenti-
ation noted by Engel is a larger typeface used for the gilt-
stamped publisher's name at the foot of the spine on May copies.

In fact, the American edition exists in 2 printings, 9 months
apart, and in 2 issues of the first printing. *First issue:* 'September, 1914' on the copyright, first gathering of 10 leaves and
final gathering of 6 leaves (the rest in eights), 210 x 128 mm. at
the front cover, publisher's name on the spine 3 mm. in height,
a thirteenth line 'H. H. Rogers for his comment and suggestions.' on p.239 resulting in a page of 28 lines. *Second issue:* leaf
7 of 16^8 (pp.239-240) is a cancel with the text of p.239
corrected by removal of the extraneous line, resulting in a 27-
line page of text; otherwise, identical with the first issue.

The second printing has 'May, 1914' on the copyright, is gathered entirely in eights (a more regular collation by gatherings
usually implies later issue), 208 x 130 mm. on the front cover,
publisher's name on the spine 4 mm. in height. Leaf 17$_1$
(pp.239-240) is integral, and the text of p.239 is corrected.

'May, 1914' is a printer's error. The date should have been
1915. The September copyright combined with uncorrected text
of p.239 constitutes the true first issue of the first printing.

It seems apparent that publication by Stokes was originally
intended for earlier in 1914. A Stokes advertisement in *PW* (21
February 1914, p.622) carries an announcement for the book,
though it is not listed in the spring announcements until
14 March. It is not advertised again until 2 May (*PW*, p.1423),

and then in terms that indicate the book is already available. A similar advertisement appeared in the June issue of *McClure's*. Nevertheless, it is not in the *PW* weekly record until 12 September, having been again advertised in another Stokes *PW* ad (5 September 1914, p.610) as published on 4 September, a date that tallies with the copyright deposit copies.

My Autobiography was serialized in 8 numbers of *McClure's Magazine* before book publication:

October 1913, pp.33-45 (on p.33: 'I wish to express my indebtedness to Miss Willa Sibert Cather for her invaluable assistance in the preparation of these memoirs.'). D568
November 1913, pp.78-87. D570
December 1913, pp.95-106. D572
January 1914, pp.96-108. D573
February 1914, pp.76-87. D575
March 1914, pp.95-108. D576
April 1914, pp.85-95. D577
May 1914, pp.137-154. D578
A concluding section, not contained in the published book, is in *McClure's*, June 1914, pp.120-128, titled 'Letters About My Autobiography'.

Some minor changes (not included in the textual collation below) occur in the text between periodical and book publications. The 12 major changes and additions to the book text are as follows, keyed to page and line of the first printing, second issue (where cited, first issue is designated 'FI'). Periodical text follows, designated by month, page, and column (in roman):

15.23-17.13	I have . . . Boyd."] *omit* (Oct., 39.i)
52.24-53.12	school. A friend. . . . school." ¶This] school. I stayed with the Kellogs again, but this (Nov., 85.i)
70.10-72.20	To give . . . woman."*] *omit* (Dec., 98.ii)
75.10-77.14	My grandfather, . . . I did." . . .] *omit* (Dec., 99.ii)
103.14-104.17	My cousin . . . incident."] *omit* (Jan., 97.ii)
114.3-19	Dr. F. J. Scott, . . . is this.] *omit* (Jan., 101.ii)
121.7-125.18	Imagine . . . of her death.] *omit* (Jan., 104.i)
137.23-138.11	Just at . . . tender history."] *omit* (Jan., 108.i)
239.9-13[FI]	history. Miss Tarbell . . . interested. ¶H. H. Rogers for his comment and suggestions.

[¶ After these] history; for which offer we were duly thankful. Up to the fourteenth article, Miss Tarbell took each article, as it was written to Mr. H. H. Rogers for his comment and suggestions (May, 137.ii)

239.9-12   history. Miss Tarbell . . . interested. ¶After these] *as preceding entry*

257.12   In the winter of 1906-1907] In the winter of 1905-1906 (May, 146.ii)

258.3-6   course. They . . . dark. From] course. ¶From (May, 148.i)

258.18-23   article. This . . . Mr. Kennan's] article. ¶Mr. Kennan's (May, 148.i)

The nature of these changes suggests a reason for postponement of publication. Originally, Willa Cather's text for the book may have duplicated exactly that of the periodical publication. If that were so, the text could already have been set in galleys by Stokes at the conclusion of the part publication in May or even before. Reader response to the *McClure's* serialization was beyond expectation, and S. S. McClure incorporated some of the letters he received into the book text. Resetting to include approximately 14 pages of new material would have been required, an alteration which, in itself, would not have taken 3 months to effect. Two of the letters (Ramsay and Tichenor) were already published in the June issue of *McClure's* in a "Letters about My Autobiography" section. McClure may have delayed book publication in anticipation of more letters or in order to give the correspondents whose letters were to be included time to expand and detail their relevant information. Whatever the circumstances, official publication seems to have been postponed, giving credence to an incorrect theory of priority in favor of the 'May, 1914' copyright notice.

The autobiography was also published in the *Ballymena Observer* (County Antrim, Ireland) in 24 weekly installments between 26 December 1913 and 26 June 1914. See D568, 570, 572-73, 575-78.

Locations: CWB (2 copies), ViU (*McClure's; Ballymena Observer*), InU (in d.j.).

a.iii.   Third printing, 1924

Title page imprint, replacing Stokes imprint of A7.a.i.:
'SPECIAL EDITION | Published for the Inspiration of the Field
Secretaries of | LEWIS E. MYERS & COMPANY | Valparaiso,
Indiana, U. S. A. [short rule] MAGAZINE PUBLISHERS, INC., |
NEW YORK.

Sheets of the second issue with altered title page copyright
notice centered on p.iv with the Stokes date panel removed,
p.239 corrected, and the leaf on which the correction occurs
integral. The illustration panel on the front cover has been
removed. Spine imprint is 'MAGAZINE | PUBLISHERS |
INCORPORATED'.

Note: For the historical background of this printing, see Peter
Lyon's Success Story: The Life and Times of S. S. McClure ([New
York: Scribners, 1963], pp.395-396, 399). Lewis Myers was the
last owner of McClure's Magazine to retain S. S. McClure as
editor. This printing was part of an extravagant promotion
scheme to sell subscriptions and inspire Myers's salesmen ("Field
Secretaries") when Myers took over the magazine and set up
Magazine Publishers, Inc., in New York. The venture survived
9 issues of McClure's, when Myers, who had sustained damaging
losses, sold his interests to Hearst's International Publications in
early 1925 and S. S. McClure's association with the magazine
ended.

Locations: CWB, CtY, InU.

a.iv.)   Fourth printing, 1963

AMERICAN CLASSICS || MY | AUTOBIOGRAPHY | S. S.
McCLURE | Introduction by | LOUIS FILLER | Antioch
College || FREDERICK UNGAR PUBLISHING CO. | NEW
YORK

Reproduced by photo-offset from the text of the first printing,
first issue, retaining the error on p.239. Frontispiece and 15
leaves of illustrations are integral, but not included in the

pagination. Blue-green cloth, dust jacket. $4.50. 202 x 133 mm. LC Catalog Card No. 63-11334. Louis Filler's introduction mentions WC's collaboration on the autobiography, but the book was reprinted for its association with S. S. McClure, not Willa Cather.

English Edition

A7.*a*.*i*.(e)   First English edition (American sheets), 1914

MY | AUTOBIOGRAPHY | BY S. S. McCLURE | FOUNDER OF "McCLURE'S MAGAZINE" | WITH ILLUSTRATIONS | LONDON | JOHN MURRAY, ALBEMARLE STREET, W. | 1914

Collation: [1]^8 2-18^8; pp.[i-iv] v-xi [xii] 1-226 [267-276] = 144 leaves.

Illustrations: Genthe's McClure portrait frontispiece with caption 'Frontispiece', on coated paper facing the title page with a protective tissue. Seven illustrations on coated paper (printed on rectos only) in the text.

Contents: P.i: half title; p.ii: blank; p.iii: title page; p.iv: copyright, '*All rights reserved*'; pp.v-vi: preface; pp.vii-ix: contents; p.x: blank; p.xi: list of illus.; p.xii: blank; pp.1-266: text; pp.267-276: catalog of Murray publications.

Paper: Rough cream wove stock (as in A7.a.i.). 203 x 140 mm.; top edge trimmed and gilt, fore edge rough-cut, bottom edge uncut. End papers of slightly smoother wove stock. *Note:* A copy noted in a variant binding (see binding note below) has uncut fore and bottom edges, and leaves measure 204 x 145 mm.; top edge stained red-orange.

Binding: Dull red (16) linen cloth. Front cover: '[within a blind-rule frame; gilt-stamped] MY AUTOBIOGRAPHY | S. S. McCLURE'. Spine: '[gilt] MY | AUTOBIOGRAPHY | McCLURE | JOHN MURRAY'. Back cover blank.

Note: A later variant binding noted is of cheaper red-orange (37) linen cloth. Front cover lettering stamped in brown. Spine gilt-stamped as above, but 'JOHN MURRAY' at the foot measures 3 mm. in height as against 4 mm. on the earlier binding.

Publication: October 1914 at 10s.6d. American sheets of the first edition, first issue (retaining the additional line on p.239) were used for the English edition. Nevertheless, one copy examined has on the copyright page a purple ink-stamp introduced by hand, 'MADE AND PRINTED IN GREAT BRITAIN.' The binding was done in England, and possibly the preliminaries were printed there as well, but the sheets are demonstrably American.

The book was reviewed in *TLS* on 29 October 1914.

Location: ViU.

A8.   THE SONG OF THE LARK

a.i.)   First edition, first printing, 1915

THE SONG OF | THE LARK | BY | WILLA SIBERT CATHER | *"It was a wond'rous lovely storm that drove me!"* | LENAU'S *"Don Juan."* | [oval publisher's device] | BOSTON AND NEW YORK | HOUGHTON MIFFLIN COMPANY | [black letter] The Riverside Press Cambridge | [roman] 1915

FIRST ISSUE

Collation: [1-31]^8 [32]^4; pp.[π1-2, i-viii, 1-2] 3-489 [490-494] = 252 leaves.

Contents: Pp.π1-2: blank; p.i: half title 'THE SONG OF THE LARK'; p.ii: blank; p.iii: title page; p.iv: 'COPYRIGHT, 1915, BY WILLA SIBERT CATHER | ALL RIGHTS RESERVED | *Published October 1915* | [within a 30 x 51 mm. panel rule] [black letter] By Willa Sibert Cather |

[short rule] | [roman] THE SONG OF THE LARK. | O
PIONEERS! With colored frontispiece. | ALEXANDER'S
BRIDGE. | HOUGHTON MIFFLIN COMPANY | BOSTON
AND NEW YORK'; p.v: dedication 'TO | ISABELLE MCCLUNG |
On uplands, | *At morning,* | *The world was young, the winds were*
free; | *A garden fair,* | *In that blue desert air,* | *Its guest invited me*
to be.'; p.vi: blank; p.vii: contents; p.viii: blank; p.1: part
title, 'THE SONG OF THE LARK | PART I | FRIENDS OF
CHILDHOOD'; p.2: blank; pp.3-157: text of part 1; p.158:
blank; p.159: part title, 'PART II | THE SONG OF THE
LARK'; p.160: blank; pp.161-246: text of part 2; p.247: part
title, 'PART III | STUPID FACES'; p.248: blank; pp.249-291:
text of part 3; p.292: blank; p.293: part title, 'PART IV | THE
ANCIENT PEOPLE'; p.294: blank; pp.295-342: text of part 4;
p.343: part title, 'PART V | DR. ARCHIE'S VENTURE';
p.344: blank; pp.345-381: text of part 5; p.382: blank; p.383:
part title, 'PART VI | KRONBORG | *Ten Years Later*'; p.384:
blank; pp.385-480: text of part 6; p.481: 'EPILOGUE'; p.482:
blank; pp.483-490: text of epilogue; p.491: blank; p.492:
[black letter] 'The Riverside Press | [roman] CAMBRIDGE ·
MASSACHUSETTS | U. S. A.'; pp.493-494: blank.

Note: The first issue has 2 points of identification: (1) The advertisement notice of 3 books by WC in a panel rule is on the
copyright page. In the second issue, the notice is on the verso of
the second leaf, facing the half title. (2) A misprint, 'moment'
for 'moments', on p.8, third line from the bottom, is corrected
in the second issue.

Paper: Cream wove, no watermark. 189 x 126 mm., edges
trimmed. End papers of heavy smoother stock.

Bindings: Of 2 bindings noted, priority assigned is inconclu-
sively based on the location of the ad notice in the greater
number of copies seen.

a: Identified with the first issue. Blue (182) smooth cloth, gilt-
stamped lettering overall. Front: '[within a 2 mm. thick single
gilt rule panel measuring 37 x 117 mm., divided into 3 panels;
title at center, flanked by orns.] THE SONG OF | THE LARK |
[3 dots] | W. S. CATHER'. Spine: '[2 mm. thick gilt rule] |

THE SONG | OF THE | LARK | [3 dots] | W. S. CATHER |
[2 mm. gilt rule] | HOUGHTON | MIFFLIN CO.' Back cover
blank. One copy of the second issue seen in this binding.

b: Identified with the second issue. Blue (182) vertical rib cloth.
Otherwise, as binding a. All copies seen in this binding were of
the second issue.

Dust Jacket: White coated paper, lettering and decoration overall
in gray-blue (174) and shadings thereof (185, 186, 190). Front:
'THE SONG OF | THE LARK | [stylized silhouette of Jules
Breton's painting, *The Song of the Lark*] | [lower left] *By* |
WILLA | SIBERT | CATHER'. Spine: '[thick rule] | THE
SONG | OF THE | LARK | [3 dots] | W. S. CATHER | [thick
rule] | *$1.40 net* | HOUGHTON | MIFFLIN CO.' Back cover:
'[within a dec. border rule; the heading flanked by publisher's
devices] NEW FICTION || [9 titles, beginning with Mary
Roberts Rinehart's *"K."* and ending with Mary Hallock Foote's
The Valley Road] | [short rule] | HOUGHTON MIFFLIN
COMPANY'. Front inner flap: '[within a single rule frame]
THE SONG OF | THE LARK | BY | WILLA S. CATHER |
[14-line blurb] | *$1.40 net. Postpaid.*' Back inner flap: '[within a
single rule frame] A New Woman! A New Country! A New
Idea! | O PIONEERS! | BY | WILLA SIBERT | CATHER | [30
lines of review excerpts] | *$1.25 net.*'

SECOND ISSUE

The misprint, 'moment' for 'moments', is corrected on p.8. A
note from the papers of Frederick B. Adams, Jr.: "Jake Blanck
told me in 12/24/43 that my deduction about copies with ads
on c/r page being first was substantiated by misprint 'moment'
for 'moments,' p.8, l.3 from bottom (same sig. as preliminaries)
which is uncorrected in all copies examined with notice on c/r
page—corrected in others."

The advertisement panel (on copyright page in the first issue) is
on p.π2 verso facing the half title; otherwise, the second issue is
physically identical to the first. Priority is based on the publisher's records for August 1915, where a charge is noted for
"duplicating the panel [advt.] and attaching it to the copyright

page." The second issue seems usually to be in combination
with binding b (vertical rib cloth, see above).

Publication: 2 October 1915 in a first printing of 3,000 copies
at $1.40. Listed in the *PW* fall announcement index (25
September 1915); in the *PW* weekly record on 2 October 1915.

SOL was contracted with Houghton Mifflin on 16 April 1915
with royalty terms of 15% to 25,000 and 20% thereafter. A
preliminary dummy was ordered 30 April, composition order
sent to the Riverside Press 11 May, and presswork for 3,000 sets
of sheets completed on 28 May. An allowance of $1,000 was
allocated for advertising. A 12-page prospectus in booklet form
was printed for distribution with text written by Willa Cather
(DD Appendix 1). Proofs were sent to William Heinemann on
29 July, but Heinemann declined to publish *SOL* in England.
In September, an offer of English publication was made to John
Murray, who agreed to be the English publisher, and 1,000
American first printing sheets were shipped on 23 November.
Published in England in March 1916.

The original plates were used for 19 printings before the text
was extensively revised by the author for the Autograph Edition
of 1937 (A8.b.i.). A full textual collation of the alterations
is too lengthy for inclusion here. Useful collations may be
consulted in P. R. R. Heyeck's "Willa Cather's *The Song of the
Lark:* The 1937 Revisions and Their Significance" (M.A. thesis,
Stanford University, 1965) and in an unpublished paper by Noel
Polk, "Willa Cather's *The Song of the Lark:* A Textual Study
Based upon a Collation of Two Editions," written in 1967 as a
term paper at the University of South Carolina.

After publication of the Autograph Edition revised text with its
subsequent trade printings, the original 1915 text was not
available in print until 1978, when it was reprinted by photo-
offset by the University of Nebraska Press from the first edition
plates (A8.a.xx).

Locations: CWB (first issue, bindings a-b, d.j.; second issue,
d.j.), FBA (first issue, binding a, d.j.), WCPM (first issue),
InU (first issue), AHG (first issue), AAK (first issue).

a.ii-xi.)   Second through eleventh printings. Publisher's production records are not available for the first 10 reprintings.

a.xii.)   Twelfth printing. 1,000 copies, June 1926.

a.xiii.)   Thirteenth printing. 1,000 copies, November 1927.

a.xiv.)   Fourteenth printing. 1,500 copies, January 1929.

a.xv.)   Fifteenth printing. 1,000 copies, January 1931.

a.xvi.)   Sixteenth printing. 2,500 copies, January 1932. The poem is removed from the dedication page.

a.xvii.)   Seventeenth printing. 1,000 copies, June 1932.

a.xviii.)   Eighteenth printing. 2,500 copies, June 1933.

a.xix.)   Nineteenth printing. 2,500 copies, March 1936.

a.xx.)   Twentieth printing (Bison Books edition, BB670). Lincoln: University of Nebraska Press, 1978. Printed by photo-offset from the 1915 plates by arrangement with Houghton Mifflin. Publisher's preface (pp.vii-xiv) by Virginia Faulkner for the University of Nebraska Press. Paperback format. $4.95.

b.i.)   Second edition, first printing (Autograph Edition, vol. 2), 1937

[dec. rule] | WILLA CATHER | [dec. rule] | The Song of the | Lark | [dec. rule] | '*It was a wondrous lovely storm that drove me!*' | LENAU'S 'DON JUAN' | [orange-brown: 'H M Co' cipher] | BOSTON | HOUGHTON MIFFLIN COMPANY | 1937

Collation: [1-36]⁸ [37]¹⁰; pp.[i-xii, 1-2] 3-580 [581-584] = 298 leaves.

Illustration: Frontispiece portrait inserted facing title page with a protective leaf of China paper, captioned '*Willa Cather* | PHOTOGRAPH BY HOLLINGER 1915'. Stub pasted to 1₇ᵥ.

Contents: P.i: half title, 'THE NOVELS AND STORIES | OF | WILLA CATHER | [orn.] 2 [orn.] | AUTOGRAPH EDITION'; p.ii: limitation notice as in A3 and A5.c; p.iii: title page; p.iv: 'COPYRIGHT, 1915 AND 1937, BY WILLA SIBERT CATHER | ALL RIGHTS RESERVED INCLUDING THE RIGHT TO REPRODUCE THIS BOOK OR PARTS THEREOF | IN ANY FORM | PRINTED IN THE U. S. A.'; p.v: dedication '[orn. rule] TO | ISABELLE McCLUNG [orn. rule]'; p.vi: blank; pp.vii-ix: preface, signed in print 'WILLA CATHER | NEW BRUNSWICK, CANADA | *July* 16, 1932'; p.x: blank; p.xi: contents; p.xii: blank; p.1: part title, 'PART I | Friends of Childhood'; p.2: blank; pp.3-199: text of part 1; p.200: blank; p.201: part title, 'PART II | The Song of the Lark'; p.202: blank; pp.203-310: text of part 2; p.311: part title, 'PART III | Stupid Faces'; p.312: blank; pp.313-363: text of part 3; p.364: blank; p.365: part title, 'PART IV | The Ancient People'; p.366: blank; pp.367-425: text of part 4; p.426: blank; p.427: part title, 'PART V | Doctor Archie's Venture'; p.428: blank; pp.429-467: text of part 5; p.468: blank; p.469: part title, 'PART VI | Kronborg | *Ten Years Later*'; p.470: blank; pp.471-573: text of part 6; p.574: blank; pp.575-581: 'Epilogue [at heading of p.575]'; p.582: blank; p.583: Riverside Press device; p.584: blank.

Notes on paper, binding, dust jacket, and publication are with the entry for the entire Autograph Edition (AA1).

Note: After the original Autograph Edition first printing of 1937, 18 printings were made from these plates between 1938 and 1974. Of these, 3 were the Sentry edition paperback (1963, 1966, and 1968). The rest were regular trade edition printings numbered by the publisher consecutively from the first edition, first printing of 1915; hence the 1968 seventeenth printing of this edition is designated on the copyright 'Thirty-fourth printing.' The second printing of this edition (A8.b.ii) states 'Twentieth impression' on the copyright page. To add to the confusion, the Sentry printings are not counted in Houghton Mifflin's sequence. According to their calculation, therefore, the seventeenth printing is reckoned to be the thirty-fourth.

b.ii.)   Second printing. 2,500 copies, September 1938. 'Twentieth impression, August 1938' on the copyright. On the dusk jacket: 'New Edition.' $2.50.

b.iii.)   Third printing. 2,500 copies, March 1941. Copyright: 'New edition containing revisions made by the author in 1937, twenty-first impression'.

b.iv.)   Fourth printing. 1,000 copies, August 1943.

b.v.)   Fifth printing. 2,000 copies, January 1944.

b.vi.)   Sixth printing. 1,000 copies, October 1945.

b.vii.)   Seventh printing. 2,000 copies, July 1946.

b.viii.)   Eighth printing. 2,500 copies, July 1948.

b.ix.)   Ninth printing. 2,500 copies, July 1951.

b.x.)   Tenth printing. 2,500 copies, May 1954.

b.xi.)   Eleventh printing. 2,000 copies, April 1958.

b.xii.)   Twelfth printing. 3,000 copies, April 1960.

b.xiii.)   Thirteenth printing. 3,000 copies, October 1962.

b.xiv.)   Fourteenth printing. 1,500 copies, June 1963.

b.xv.)   Fifteenth printing (first Sentry edition paperback [SE28]). 10,000 copies, June 1963. Copyright: 'FIRST PRINTING, SENTRY EDITION C'.

b.xvi.)   Sixteenth printing (second Sentry edition paperback [SE28]). 7,500 copies, September 1966.

b.xvii.)   Seventeenth printing. 3,000 copies, August 1968. Copyright: 'THIRTY-FOURTH PRINTING C'.

b.xviii.) Eighteenth printing (third Sentry edition paperback [SE28]).
4,000 copies, April 1971. A note in the HM Co. production
record: "10/19/72–Sentry voted OP, refer to reg."

b.xix.) Nineteenth printing. 1,500 copies, August 1974. A note in the
HM Co. production record: "Letterpress text plates, binder's
dies moved to American Book 5/10/77."

English Editions

A8.a.8.i.(e) First English edition (American sheets), 1916

THE SONG OF | THE LARK | BY | WILLA SIBERT
CATHER | *"It was a wond'rous lovely storm that drove me!"* |
LENAU's *"Don Juan."* | LONDON: | JOHN MURRAY,
ALBEMARLE STREET, W. | 1916

Collation: As in the first American printing.

Contents: The copyright page (p.iv) is blank and the advertisement is not present; otherwise, as in the first American printing
with altered title page. P.8, third line from bottom: 'moments'.

Paper: As in the first American printing.

Binding: Blue (182) coarse linen cloth, covers blank. Spine
lettered in gilt: 'THE | SONG OF | THE LARK | [dot] |
W.S. | CATHER | JOHN MURRAY'.

Publication: Bound in England using 1,000 sets of the American
first printing sheets, published in March 1916 at 6s. Murray
requested that the passage about Lillie Langtry and the Prince of
Wales on p.111 (ll.21-27) be removed for the English edition.
WC agreed to the alteration in a letter to Ferris Greenslet on
25 October 1915, and the change was made in the plates for the
Murray edition. The leaf is integral and not a cancel. *SOL* remained in print under the Murray imprint until 1928, with a
price rise to 7s.6d. in 1924. It was not thereafter available in
print in England until the 1932 Jonathan Cape Travellers' Library edition (see below).

a.ii.(e).   Second printing (Travellers' Library), 1932

THE SONG OF THE LARK | by | WILLA CATHER | With a new Preface by the Author | [publisher's device] | LONDON | JONATHAN CAPE 30 BEDFORD SQUARE

Collation: [1-15]¹⁶ [16]¹²; pp.[i-xii, 1-2] 3-489 [490-492] = 252 leaves.

Contents: Pp.i-ii: blank; p.iii: half title, 'THE TRAVELLERS' LIBRARY | [star] | THE SONG OF THE LARK'; p.iv: advt. for Travellers' Library; p.v: title page; p.vi: copyright 'FIRST PUBLISHED OCTOBER 1915 | FIRST ISSUED IN THE TRAVELLERS' LIBRARY 1932 | JONATHAN CAPE LTD. 30 BEDFORD SQUARE LONDON | AND 91 WELLINGTON STREET WEST TORONTO | PRINTED IN GREAT BRITAIN BY | KIMBLE & BRADFORD, LONDON, W.I. | PAPER MADE BY MESSRS. JOHN | DICKINSON & CO. LTD. BOUND BY THE GARDEN CITY PRESS LTD.'; p.vii: contents; p.viii: blank; pp.ix-x: preface, subscribed 'WILLA CATHER | July 16, 1932, | New Brunswick, | Canada'; p.xi: dedication 'TO | ISABELLE MCCLUNG'; p.xii: "It was a wond'rous lovely storm that drove me!' | LENAU'S *'Don Juan.'*";
p.1: part title 'PART I | FRIENDS OF CHILDHOOD'; p.2: blank; pp.3-490: as in the first printing (A8.a.i.), but with the running heads and printer's imprint at back removed.

Paper: Thin cream wove stock, 170x114 mm.; edges trimmed. End papers of heavier wove stock.

Binding: Dark blue (179) smooth fine linen cloth. Front cover blank. Spine gilt-stamped: '[orn. rule] | *The* | SONG | OF THE | LARK | [star orn.] | WILLA | CATHER | [publisher's device] | JONATHAN | CAPE | [orn. rule]'. Back cover has the Cape cipher, 'J' superimposed on 'C', stamped in blind at center.

Dust Jacket: Yellow (67) wove paper printed overall in black ink. Front cover: '[within a dec. border rule] THE TRAVELLERS' LIBRARY | [star orn.] | THE SONG OF THE LARK | by |

WILLA CATHER | [publisher's device] | WITH A NEW
PREFACE | BY THE AUTHOR'. Spine: '[orn. rule] | THE
SONG | OF | THE LARK | [star orn.] | WILLA | CATHER |
[publisher's device] | THE | TRAVELLERS' | LIBRARY |
No. 183 | JONATHAN | CAPE | [orn. rule]'. Back cover: 34-
line biographical note on WC. Front inner flap: blurb for *SOL*
with the price, 3s.6d. net. Back inner flap blank.

Publication: Reproduced photographically, slightly reduced, in
1932 from the American first printing; hence it contains the
passage on p.111 about Lillie Langtry and has the corrected
state, 'moments', on p.8, l.3 from bottom. The second
'impression' was printed in 1936. *SOL* was available in this
edition until the Cassell revised edition of 1938 (see below).

A note in the Houghton Mifflin production record: "4-14-32
520/500 at .62 1/4 offered to John Murray flat sheets inc.
royalty. Cape has arranged with Murray to include book in their
Travellers' Library edition–6-7-32." Murray declined to publish
the second English edition, but permitted Cape to add the title
to the Travellers' Library.

Willa Cather did not approve Murray's sale of *SOL* to Cape for
this cheap reprint. In a letter to her former Houghton Mifflin
editor Ferris Greenslet (17 July 1932), she says that Cape has
asked her for a new preface. She is sending him one because she
does not want this book to come out in England as a new book.
The preface appears in this Travellers' Library printing for the
first time.

WC was never pleased with the arrangement whereby Cape paid
royalties to Murray on the sales of the Travellers' Library edition, and Murray, in turn, deducted one-third of the amounts
paid before remitting them to America. In 1938, she succeeded
in transferring the British rights of *SOL* to Cassell for the second
English edition (see below).

b.i.(e)   Second English edition, 1938

THE | SONG OF THE | LARK | By | WILLA CATHER | '*It
was a wondrous lovely storm that drove me!*' | LENAU'S 'DON

JUAN' | [publisher's device] | CASSELL AND COMPANY
LTD. | LONDON, TORONTO, MELBOURNE AND SYDNEY

Collation: [1-36]^8 [37]^{10}; pp.[i-vi] vii-viii [ix-xii, 1-2] 3-580
[581-584] = 298 leaves.

Contents: P.i: half title, 'THE SONG OF THE LARK'; p.ii: *'BY
THE SAME AUTHOR* || LUCY GAYHEART | OBSCURE
DESTINIES | SHADOWS ON THE ROCK | NOT UNDER
FORTY'; p.iii: title page; p.iv: copyright, 'First published in
Great Britain 1938 | Printed in Great Britain by Jarrold & Sons,
Limited, Norwich | F.938'; p.v: dedication '| TO | ISABELLE
McCLUNG ||'; p.vi: blank; pp.vii-ix: preface, signed in print
'WILLA CATHER | NEW BRUNSWICK, CANADA'; p.x: blank; p.xi:
contents; p.xii: blank; p.1: part title, 'PART I | Friends of
Childhood'; p.2: blank; pp.3-581: text; pp.582-584: blank.

Paper: Cream wove stock; 215 x 137mm., edges trimmed. End
papers of heavier cream wove stock.

Binding: Light red (15) linen cloth, covers blank. Spine
gilt-stamped: 'THE | SONG OF | THE | LARK | WILLA |
CATHER | CASSELL'.

Dust Jacket: Cream wove paper, lettering in black, decorations in
pink (26). Front cover: '[within a dec. border rule] THE |
SONG OF | THE | LARK | *By* | WILLA | CATHER'. Spine:
[within 2 pink-black-pink triple-line vertical rules] [dec. pink
panel] | THE | SONG OF | THE | LARK | *By* WILLA |
CATHER | [dec. pink panel] | 8/6 net | CASSELL'. Back cover:
'THE SONG OF THE LARK | [15-line blurb] | WILLA
CATHER'. Front inner flap: *'Other Books by* | WILLA
CATHER | [swelling rule] | [*SOR, LG, OD, NUF* listed; each
with a statement from a review]'. Back inner flap blank.

Publication: The revised text, published in 1938 at 8s.6d. Set
photographically in England from the plates of the Autograph
Edition. When WC transferred the British rights of *SOL* from
Jonathan Cape to Cassell, Ferris Greenslet of Houghton Mifflin
arranged to send Cassell's Newman Flower a complete set of the
corrected proofs of the Autograph Edition text from which to set

the new English edition (FG to WC, 13 April 1938). Neither
the Autograph Edition nor this English second edition contains
the passage about Lillie Langtry first excised from the 1916
Murray English edition.

b.ii.(e)   The Hamish Hamilton (London, 1963) edition, printed by
photo-offset from the Autograph Edition plates, remained in
print until 1974.

A9. MY ÁNTONIA

a.i.)   First edition, first printing, 1918

MY ÁNTONIA | BY | WILLA SIBERT CATHER | *Optima dies
. . . prima fugit* | VIRGIL | WITH ILLUSTRATIONS BY |
W. T. BENDA | [Riverside Press device] | BOSTON AND
NEW YORK | HOUGHTON MIFFLIN COMPANY | [black
letter] The Riverside Press Cambridge | [roman] 1918

FIRST STATE

Collation: [1-26]⁸ χ₁ [27]⁸; pp.[π1-2, i-viii] ix-xiii [xiv] 3-418
[419-420] = 217 leaves. *Note:* Leaf χ₁ (pp.403-404) is inserted,
pasted to 27₁ᵣ.

Illustrations: 8 illustrations on coated paper inserted following
pp.6, 46, 88, 98, 142, 158, 188, and 358. *Note:* The second
state illustrations are on text stock. In neither state are they
included in the pagination.

Contents: P.π1: blank; p.π2: advt. for Cather novels in a single
rule panel; p.i: half title; p.ii: blank; p.iii: title page; p.iv:
'COPYRIGHT, 1918, BY WILLA SIBERT CATHER | ALL
RIGHTS RESERVED | *Published October 1918*'; p.v: dedication
'TO | CARRIE AND IRENE MINER | *In memory of affections
old and true*'; p.vi: blank; p.vii: contents; p.viii: blank;
pp.ix-xiv: introduction; pp.3-159: text of book 1 ('The
Shimerdas'); p.160: blank; p.161: part title, 'BOOK II | THE
HIRED GIRLS'; p.162: blank; pp.163-288: text of book 2;

p.289: part title, 'BOOK III | LENA LINGARD'; p.290: blank;
pp.291-332: text of book 3; p.333: part title, 'BOOK IV | THE
PIONEER WOMAN'S STORY'; p.334: blank; pp.335-365:
text of book 4; p.366: blank; p.367: part title, 'BOOK V |
CUZAK'S BOYS'; p.368: blank; pp.369-419: text of book 5;
p.420: printer's imprint, '[black letter] The Riverside Press |
[roman] CAMBRIDGE · MASSACHUSETTS | U. S. A'.

Note: The reason for the hiatus in preliminary pagination
(lacking pp.1-2) is given in a letter from WC to Ferris Greenslet
(20 June 1918): "Here is the Introduction, which ought to
come directly before the first page of the narrative proper. . . .
That would mean no blank page with 'Book I The Shimerdas'
on it, but merely the first page of text." The first divisional half
title, which would have occupied pp.1-2, was removed to ac-
commodate the introduction, which was not in the makeup
when the pages were numbered.

Paper: Cream wove, no watermark. 185 x 120mm.; edges
trimmed. End papers of a smoother stock. A finer stock of text
paper is noted in some copies.

Binding: Brown (77) coarse linen cloth, lettering stamped in
light yellow-orange (70). Front cover: '[thick rule] | MY
ÁNTONIA | [thick rule] | WILLA CATHER'. Spine: '[thick
rule] | MY | ÁNTONIA | [thick rule] | WILLA | CATHER |
HOUGHTON | MIFFLIN CO.' Back cover blank.

Dust Jacket: Orange-yellow (71) coated paper, lettering in
brown (78). Front cover: 'MY ÁNTONIA | *BY* | WILLA S.
CATHER | *Author of* | THE SONG OF THE LARK, O
PIONEERS! *etc* | [orn.] | [13-line blurb, signed beneath in
facsimile autograph, 'Houghton Mifflin Company']'. Spine:
'[thick rule] | MY | ÁNTONIA | [thick rule] | WILLA
CATHER | [Riverside Press device] | *$1.60 net* | HOUGHTON
| MIFFLIN CO.' Back cover: '[thick-thin rule] | NEW
NOVELS YOU WILL ENJOY || [advt. for Houghton Mifflin
books; 10 titles, beginning with *My Ántonia* and ending with
Clara Endicott Sears's *The Bell-Ringer*]'. Front inner flap:
'[within a single-line border rule] MY ÁNTONIA | *By* | WILLA
SIBERT CATHER | [31-line blurb] | *With illustrations by Benda*.

$1.60 *net* | [beneath the border rule: a War Savings Stamps circular device]'. Back inner flap: 'RECENT FICTION | [12 titles, beginning with Eleanor H. Porter's *Oh, Money! Money!* and ending with Archie P. McKishnie's *Willow, the Wisp*] | [War Savings Stamps circular device]'.

A later jacket, associated with a copy of the first printing at the University of Texas, has excerpts from 4 reviews on the front cover: *Reedy's St. Louis Mirror*, H. L. Mencken in the *Smart Set*, *Detroit Saturday Night*, and the *Chicago Daily News*. The back cover lists 13 books published in 1919, starting with Eleanor H. Porter's *Dawn* and ending with Arthur Hodges's *The Bounder*. If this jacket is one in which the book was issued, it indicates that copies of the first printing were still available late in 1919. It is possible, of course, that the jacket was supplied from a later printing.

Publication: 21 September 1918 in a first printing of 3,500 copies at $1.60. The contract was signed on 24 January 1918 with the same royalty terms as *SOL:* 15% to 25,000 copies and 20% thereafter. A dummy was ordered in November 1917, the composition order went to the Riverside Press on 6 January 1918, and composition was completed in February. An advertising allowance of only $300 ($700 less than *SOL*) was allocated. An order for 3,000 sets of the Benda illustrations was placed on 12 December 1917. These were on coated paper, as would be normal for delicate drawings to be inserted. WC was later most specific about requesting text paper for the illustrations (see below). The publisher, wishing to accommodate her preference, ordered the additional sets on text paper, but would have been unlikely to discard those already printed on coated paper. It was wartime, and such waste was out of the question. Copies with illustrations on coated and text paper are of the same printing. Assignment of priority is based on the conclusions reached in the historical note following the second state description.

The English edition was not contracted until April 1919, when Heinemann ordered 1,000 copies bound in America with their imprint, but without dust jackets. The jacket was printed in England.

Historical Note on the Publication of My Ántonia

Willa Cather was deeply involved in the physical production of *MA*. Her close participation is clearly revealed in correspondence with her Houghton Mifflin editor, Ferris Greenslet. These letters are part of the Houghton Mifflin Company archive in the Houghton Library, Harvard University.

Completion and production of *MA* took much longer than was originally anticipated. As early as 8 March 1917, WC wrote to Greenslet that she was half way through the first writing, but would not have it finished by the end of April. She optimistically thought that it might be ready for the printers by the end of May or the middle of June. Illness and travel intervened before she sent Greenslet copy for the first 2 chapters (12 pages) on 14 November 1917 and 50 more pages on 26 December. By 28 February 1918, she was writing that there was no sufficient reason why the story should take two winters to finish. She wondered whether it would not be better to wait until fall for publication unless Greenslet wanted her to try to get through by the end of March.

Intermittently, from the fall of 1917 until March 1918, she concerned herself personally with the conception, execution, and printing of the Benda illustrations. On 18 October 1917, she told Greenslet that she was going to ask Benda to dinner and talk to him about head and tail-pieces. If Benda did not get the idea, no one else would, and she would prefer to go unillustrated. She admitted to having tried to make head and tail-pieces in the text herself, but wanted a professional artist who could echo her conceptions.

Originally, she had wanted pictorial line cuts to be used as headpieces and tailpieces at the beginnings and ends of chapters. It was she who chose W. T. Benda for the art work and commissioned the drawings in direct consultation with him. When Benda had completed 3 drawings, a problem over the amount to be paid him for the work prompted WC to write to Houghton Mifflin (on 7 March 1918) that, if he were not paid more, she would prefer to forgo illustrations altogether. Ten trial drawings were executed and submitted to her, of which she rejected 2. It

was decided that the drawings be used as full-page illustrations rather than headpieces and tailpieces (which would, of course, have been printed in the forms with the text). In a letter to R. L. Scaife, Houghton Mifflin production manager (9 December 1917), she gave directions on how they were to be used: on recto pages, printed small in black on a liberal page without captions. She was also specific about where she wanted them placed in the text: not at uniform intervals throughout the book, but precisely facing the text section they illustrated. She oversaw proofs of the cuts and offered to assume the cost of remaking one that did not please her, giving instructions on how she wanted it recut (WC to FG, 10 December 1917). In these letters concerning the illustrations, she mentions everything but the type of paper on which the illustrations are to be printed. It is, therefore, likely that she had taken it for granted they were to be integral and not inserted. It was 2 days later on 12 December that Houghton Mifflin placed its order for 3,000 sets of coated paper illustrations.

On 20 June 1918, she sent Houghton Mifflin the manuscript of the introduction and the final chapters. With the MS, she also returned 27 corrected galleys and requested to see page proofs to ensure that her galley corrections were made. This letter too indicates that she still assumed that the illustrations were to be integral with the text. She asks to be sent at once proofs of Benda's 8 drawings so she can mark each one where it will come in relation to the text so that the makeup man will be able to place them "before the page printing begins."

In July 1918, when she received page proofs, she was perplexed to find that blank space for the cuts had not been provided in the proof text. She asked Greenslet (11 July 1918) whether it would not be cheaper to print the illustrations in the 4-page forms with the text (that is, as integral leaves in the gatherings), rather than bind them in as inserts. She was "particularly anxious" that the cuts be printed on the same paper as the text, not on coated paper.

For the book format, she requested a square type, larger than that used for SOL, rough cream paper that would take the line cuts well, a "strong navy blue" (later changed to brown cloth

with "pumpkin-colored ink") binding and a bright yellow jacket with very black type (later changed to "pumpkin color") and no front cover illustration (13 March 1917; HM Co. memo, 6 November 1917). She rejected a dummy with 'WILLA S. CATHER' on the front cover and asked that the 'S.' be removed as it looked "too business-like for the queer title above it" (WC to FG, February 1918).

While reading galleys in June 1918, she complained to Ferris Greenslet (2 July 1918) of changes made between manuscript and galley by the copy editor, especially in her use of the subjunctive mood. She suspected the copy editor to be of that "ferocious band who are out to exterminate [the subjunctive] along with the brown-tailed moth." In reinstating the subjunctives, she asked that the Riverside Press not charge her for those corrections. She was again concerned that the illustrations were to be inserted and worried that they would not be placed in the text as she had indicated (17 July 1918). The first copies of the completed book reached her in Red Cloud, Nebraska, on 30 September. She wrote immediately to Scaife expressing her pleasure with the appearance of the books and the placing of the illustrations.

She was not, however, pleased with Houghton Mifflin's promotion and handling of the book. Between the publication date in September and the year following, her letters are filled with promptings for wider advertising, urgings for the use of quotations from favorable reviews, complaints that booksellers are not receiving orders, and general annoyance at the uninspired publicity provided for the book. The tardiness in negotiating for an English edition was also a source of dissatisfaction. Frequent remarks to Greenslet in the correspondence indicate that she was casting about for a new publisher. On 19 May 1919, the matter came to a head in a private letter to Greenslet in which all of her discontent is expressed. Comparisons are made between Knopf's and Houghton Mifflin's promotion policies. Negotiations with Knopf are implied, though a definite commitment had not yet been made.

At this time, it was still assumed that Houghton Mifflin would publish *One of Ours* (referred to in the correspondence as *Claude*)

on which she had begun work in January 1919. Knopf, however, had agreed to publish a book of stories, *Youth and the Bright Medusa*, which would include some of the stories from *The Troll Garden*—a publication that WC had suggested to Houghton Mifflin and they declined. On 28 December 1919 (WC to FG), permission had been given to Knopf for *YBM*. WC promised Greenslet that if he were to bring out *Claude*, the Knopf book would not be published until 6 weeks after in fairness to Houghton Mifflin, so that the "impetus of 'Antonia'" would pass directly to the new novel, rather than to the book of early stories.

The final break with Houghton Mifflin came in January 1921. WC writes to Greenslet (12 January) that she has decided to let Alfred Knopf publish *One of Ours* after seeing the results of his promotion campaign for *YBM*. Thus she turned to Knopf as the publisher with whom she maintained a successful professional relationship for the rest of her working life. Houghton Mifflin, who held the copyrights for her first 4 novels, continued to issue reprints of the early books, frequently coinciding with publication of her later books under the Borzoi imprint.

SECOND STATE

The second state conforms to the physical characteristics of the first except for the use of text paper rather than coated paper for the illustrations. As in the first state, the illustrations are inserted and not included in the pagination. Copies of later printings with the date removed from the title page have been noted with inserted illustrations on coated paper or text paper.

Historical Note on the Benda Illustrations for My Ántonia

It cannot be stated with certainty how many copies of the first printing were issued with illustrations on text paper and how many with coated paper. If the publisher's cost records are interpreted correctly, 3,000 sets of illustrations were ordered on 12 December 1917. These were undoubtedly on the coated paper, as WC's insistence upon text paper for the illustrations was not clearly understood until it was emphasized in her 11 July 1918 letter, in which she states, "You know I am partic-

ularly anxious" to have cuts on the same paper as the text. If the book had been planned with illustrations on text paper, it would have been cheaper to run cuts with the text in the same forms with consecutive pagination, as WC apparently thought was to be done until 11 July. Three thousand sets were already printed on coated paper, and the book past page proofs. Houghton Mifflin had no alternative but to order the additional sets of illustrations on text paper. With publication date only a few weeks away, copies with coated illustrations were probably bound by early August and ready to be shipped to reviewers and booksellers–possibly as many as 2,500 copies. In theory, the remaining 500 sets of coated paper illustrations could have been reserved for the second and third printings and enough sets on text paper printed to fill out the first printing in deference to WC's wishes with an overrun to be used in subsequent print-ings. Both states of the inserted plates were used until it was possible to switch to integral illustrations. It is, therefore, suggested here that the first printing contains approximately 2,500 copies with coated paper illustrations and 1,000 with text paper illustrations. The second and third printings (without date on the title page) have mixed states of the inserted plates.

Locations: CWB (first state, d.j.; second state, d.j.), ViU (first state, 2 copies), FBA (first state, d.j.), InU (first and second states), AHG (first state), AAK (first state), RCT (first state, d.j.), WCPM (first state), NbU (first state).

a.ii.)   Second printing, 1918. Date removed from the title page. Inserted illustrations on coated or text paper.

a.iii.)   Third printing, 1918. Date removed from title page. Inserted illustrations on coated or text paper. Indistinguishable from second printing.

a.iv.)   Fourth printing, 1919. Date removed from the title page. The illustrations, on text paper, are integral leaves of the gatherings. *Collation:* [1-27]^8 χ$_1$ [28]^8; pp.[π1-2, i-viii] ix-xiii [xiv], 3-6 [a2], 7-46 [b2], 47-88 [c2], 89-98 [d2], 99-142 [e2], 143-158 [f2], 159-188 [g2], 189-358 [h2], 359-418 [419-420]=225 leaves.

Note: The additional unpaged leaves are the 8 integral text paper illustrations with blank versos. Leaf χ_1, preceding the final gathering, is inserted pasted to 28_{1r}. The first English edition (*A9.a.i.*[e]) also has integral illustrations on text paper. The English sheets were printed in this country by H. O. Houghton & Co. and were, therefore, of this printing of 1919. The only copy of the American fourth printing located with integral illustrations is at the University of Texas, Austin (reported, not seen).

a.v.) Fifth printing. 2,000 copies, October 1921 (mentioned in a letter from FG to WC, 27 October 1921).

a.vi.) Sixth printing. No records available.

a.vii.) Seventh printing. No records available.

a.viii.) Eighth printing. 2,000 copies, June 1922.

a.ix.) Ninth printing. No records available. 'NINTH IMPRESSION' on the copyright page.

b.i.) Second edition, first printing, 1926

MY ÁNTONIA | BY | WILLA CATHER | *Optima dies . . . prima fugit* | VIRGIL | WITH ILLUSTRATIONS BY | W. T. BENDA | *New Edition* | [Riverside Press device] | BOSTON AND NEW YORK | HOUGHTON MIFFLIN COMPANY | [black letter] The Riverside Press Cambridge | [roman] 1926

Collation: $[1-13]^{16}$ $[14]^{18}$; pp. $[\pi 1-2,$ i-viii] ix-x [xi-xii, 1-2] 3-6 [a2], 7-46 [b2], 47-88 [c2], 89-98 [d2], 99-142 [e2], 143-158 [f2], 159-188 [g2], 189-358 [h2], 359-418 [419-422] = 226 leaves. *Note:* Pages designated a2-h2 are 8 integral illustrations not included in the pagination.

Contents: P.π1: blank; p.π2: '[black letter] Books by Willa Sibert Cather | [short rule] | [roman] ALEXANDER'S BRIDGE | O PIONEERS! | THE SONG OF THE LARK | MY ÁNTONIA | YOUTH AND THE BRIGHT MEDUSA | ONE

OF OURS | APRIL TWILIGHTS | A LOST LADY | THE
PROFESSOR'S HOUSE'; p.i: half title; p.ii: blank; p.iii: title
page; p.iv: 'COPYRIGHT, 1918 and 1926, BY WILLA
SIBERT CATHER | ALL RIGHTS RESERVED | [black letter]
The Riverside Press | [roman] CAMBRIDGE ·
MASSACHUSETTS | PRINTED IN THE U. S. A.'; p.v:
dedication, 'TO | CARRIE AND IRENE MINER | *In memory of
affections old and true*'; p.vi: blank; p.vii: contents; p.viii: blank;
pp.ix-xi: 'Introduction'; p.xii: blank; p.1: part title, 'BOOK I |
THE SHIMERDAS'; p.2: blank; pp.3-419: as in the first
edition, fourth printing (A9.a.iv); pp.420-422: blank. *Note:*
Lettering of the part titles is placed in the upper right corner
rather than center page as in previous printings.

Paper: Cream wove, no watermark. 191 x 129mm.; top edge
trimmed and stained brick red, fore edge uncut, bottom edge
rough-cut. End papers of a heavier stock.

Binding: Brown (77) cloth, gilt-stamped lettering and
decoration. Front cover: '[thick rule] | MY ÁNTONIA | [thick
rule] | [oval Riverside Press device] | WILLA CATHER'. Spine:
'[thick rule] | MY | ÁNTONIA | [thick rule] | WILLA |
CATHER | HOUGHTON | MIFFLIN CO.' Back cover blank.
Copies in red-brown (43) with orange lettering are a later
binding of this edition.

Dust Jacket: Light orange-brown (57) heavy laid paper with
horizontal chain lines 38 mm. apart; watermarked '*Italian
Pressed*' in italic script. Lettering and decoration are in black.
Front cover: 'MY ÁNTONIA [a small black square level with
the apex of the final 'A' and forming a corner of the overall cover
decoration] | [illus. of a man plowing uphill with a 2-horse
team, signed 'W. T. Benda'] | BY WILLA CATHER'. Spine:
'MY ÁNTONIA | WILLA CATHER | [Riverside Press device] |
HOUGHTON | MIFFLIN | COMPANY'. Back cover: 'NEW
FICTION || [list of 15 titles, beginning with Sabatini's *The
Lion's Skin* and ending with Albert Kinross's *God and Tony
Hewitt*]'. Front inner flap: $2.50 | MY ÁNTONIA | *By* | WILLA
SIBERT CATHER | [31-line blurb] | *With illustrations by Benda.*'
Back inner flap: '*WILLA SIBERT CATHER* | [5 critical
quotations] | *Books by Miss Cather* | MY ÁNTONIA | THE

SONG OF THE LARK | O PIONEERS! | ALEXANDER'S
BRIDGE'. A later jacket has advertisements on the back cover
for books published in 1933.

Publication: 23 July 1926 in a first printing of 5,000 copies
at $2.50. Although the first chapter, 'Introduction', was
substantially rewritten by Willa Cather (see textual collation
below), the book was set from the plates of the first edition text
and is not a "new edition" (as advertised by Houghton Mifflin)
in the strict bibliographical sense. To avoid confusion that could
occur by listing this important late printing and its subsequent
thirteen reprintings briefly as appendages to the first edition of
1918, it is here given the status of a new edition on the basis of
its existence as a different book in a different format, containing
authorial revisions of the text.

While revising the 'Introduction', Willa Cather wrote to Ferris
Greenslet (May 1926), requesting a correction on p.156:

156.13   each other] the silk

The first printing only has the date on the title page. This is the
only respect in which it differs from the next 4 printings. On
20 February 1930, WC wrote to Greenslet asking for 2 text
corrections in the next printing (the sixth in April 1930):

121.14   Austrians] Prussians
311.19-20   *"misterioso, misterioso!"*] *"misterios' altero!"*

Printings after the fifth contain the corrected readings. These
plates remained in use until publication of the Autograph
Edition (A9.c.i.) in 1937.

Textual Collation of the 'Introduction'. The preliminary section,
'Introduction' (pp.ix-xi), was extensively revised and shortened
by Willa Cather for this edition. The variant texts are supplied
below with page and line reference to the first edition (A9.a.i):

ix.1-5   Last . . . West.] Last summer, in a season of intense heat, Jim
          Burden and I happened to be crossing Iowa on the same train.
          (ix.1-2)
ix.6   friends—] friends, (ix.3)
ix.7   town—] town, (ix.4)
ix.7   much] a great deal (ix.5)

x.4   and are old friends,] *omit*

x.6   railways, and is sometimes] railways and is often (x.3-4)

x.7   New York] *omit*

x.8   do not often] seldom (x.5)

x.9   wife. ¶] wife. She (x.6)

x.10-29   When . . . interest.] *omit*

xi.9-xii.7   no disappointments. . . . American.] disappointments have not changed him. The romantic disposition which often made him seem very funny as a boy, has been one of the strongest elements in his success. He loves with a personal passion the great country through which his railroad runs and branches. His faith in it and his knowledge of it have played an important part in its development. (x.16-23)

xii.11   and whom both of us admired.] *omit*

xii.14-15   To speak . . . brain.] *omit*

xii.18   had] and had (xi.3)

xii.19   him,] him. (xi.4)

xii.19-21   and . . . friendship.] *omit*

xii.24-   "I can't. . . . to me.] "From time to time I've been writing

xiv.18   down what I remember about Ántonia," he told me. "On my long trips across the country, I amuse myself like that, in my stateroom." ¶When I told him that I would like to read his account of her, he said I should certainly see it,—if it were ever finished. ¶Months afterward, Jim called at my apartment one stormy winter afternoon, carrying a legal portfolio. He brought it into the sitting-room with him, and said, as he stood warming his hands, ¶"Here is the thing about Ántonia. Do you still want to read it? I finished it last night. I didn't take time to arrange it; I simply wrote down pretty much all that her name recalls to me. I suppose it hasn't any form. It hasn't any title, either." He went into the next room, sat down at my desk and wrote across the face of the portfolio the word, "Ántonia." He frowned at this a moment, then prefixed another word, making it "My Ántonia." That seemed to satisfy him. (xi.7-29)

b.ii.)   Second printing. 5,000 copies, December 1926.

b.iii.)   Third printing. 3,000 copies, January 1928.

b.iv.)   Fourth printing. 2,500 copies, January 1929.

b.v.)   Fifth printing. 2,500 copies, June 1929. No illustrations.

b.vi.)   Sixth printing. 3,000 copies, April 1930. Textual corrections on pp.121 and 311 (see publication note). No illustrations.

b.vii.)   Seventh printing. 3,000 copies, February 1931. No illustrations.

b.viii.)   Eighth printing. 3,000 copies, November 1931. No illustrations.

b.ix.)   Ninth printing. 2,500 copies, September 1932. The Benda illustrations were reinstated in this printing.

b.x.)   Tenth printing. 2,500 copies, September 1933.

b.xi.)   Eleventh printing. 2,500 copies, October 1934.

b.xii.)   Twelfth printing. 3,000 copies, September 1935.

b.xiii.)   Thirteenth printing. 3,000 copies, October 1936.

b.xiv.)   Fourteenth printing. 5,000 copies, May 1937.

c.i.)   Third edition, first printing (Autograph edition, vol. 4), 1937

[dec. rule] | WILLA CATHER | [dec. rule] | My Ántonia | [dec. rule] | 'Optima dies . . . prima fugit.' | VIRGIL | [orange brown: 'H M Co' cipher] | BOSTON | HOUGHTON MIFFLIN COMPANY | 1937

Collation: [1-23]⁸ [24]¹⁰; pp.[i-viii] ix-xi [xii, 1-2] 3-371 [372-376] = 194 leaves.

Illustration: Inserted facing the first page of text (p.3) is the Benda drawing of Bohemians at a train station with the caption, "From a drawing by W. T. Benda | which appeared in the first edition of 'My Ántonia'". Printed on text paper.

Contents: P.i: half title, 'THE NOVELS AND STORIES | OF | WILLA CATHER | [orn.] 4 [orn.] | AUTOGRAPH EDITION'; p.ii: limitation notice; p.iii: title page; p.iv:

'COPYRIGHT, 1918 and 1926, BY WILLA SIBERT
CATHER | ALL RIGHTS RESERVED INCLUDING THE
RIGHT TO REPRODUCE THIS BOOK OR PARTS
THEREOF IN ANY FORM | PRINTED IN THE U. S. A.';
p.v: dedication, '[dec. rule] | TO CARRIE AND IRENE
MINER | *In memory of affections old and true* | [dec. rule]'; p.vi:
blank; p.vii: contents; p.viii: blank; pp.ix-xi: 'Introduction';
p.xii: blank; p.1: part title, 'BOOK I | The Shimerdas'; p.2:
blank; pp.3-140: text of book 1; p.141: part title, 'BOOK II |
The Hired Girls'; p.142: blank; pp.143-253: text of book 2;
p.254: blank; p.255: part title, 'BOOK III | Lena Lingard';
p.256: blank; pp.257-293: text of book 3; p.294: blank; p.295:
part title, 'BOOK IV | The Pioneer Woman's Story'; p.296:
blank; pp.297-323: text of book 4; p.324: blank; p.325: part
title, 'BOOK V | Cuzak's Boys'; p.326: blank; pp.327-372: text
of book 5; p.373: Riverside Press device; pp.374-376: blank.

Notes on paper, binding, dust jacket, and publication with the
entry for the entire Autograph Edition (AA1).

c.ii.)   Second printing (trade printing). 5,000 copies, November
1938. Though the setting is from the 1937 Autograph Edition
plates, some plate alterations were made for the trade printing:
the Benda illustration plates are incorporated into the text, part-
title pages are reset, running heads are reset in roman between
rules, page numbering is moved from page-foot center to nearer
the outer margin. The large initial letters of each part in the
Autograph Edition have been removed and replaced by capital
letters of the text font. This required resetting first lines of each
part and, in 23 instances, resetting of the entire first paragraphs
on pp.19, 28, 38, 43, 62, 70, 80, 88, 94, 104, 114, 119,
120, 137, 143, 159, 172, 180, 193, 197, 209, 271, and 278.

c.iii.)   Third printing. 3,500 copies, September 1940.

c.iv.)   Fourth printing. 5,000 copies, October 1941. A curious
exchange of letters between WC and Ferris Greenslet on 20 February and 24 February 1940 prompts a note on this printing.
Greenslet tells WC that a bookseller in Utah wishes to buy, for
a special market, 1,000 copies of *MA* at the full wholesale
price, but that he will be unable to make the purchase unless

the name of the bull on p.91 is changed from 'Brigham Young' to another name that would not give offense to Mormons. Greenslet assumes that 'Joseph Smith' would be equally unsatisfactory, but asks whether WC would be willing to make the change to 'George Washington', 'Woodrow Wilson', or another. In WC's reply, she first says, "Why not Ferdinand?" and then agrees to change the name of her bull to 'Andrew Jackson' for the special edition. She asks Greenslet to write her an agreement to the effect that the bull's name is to be changed for 1,000 copies only and will then revert to 'Brigham Young' for future printings. She explains that her father's 2 bulls were named Gladstone and Brigham Young—one referring to a stubborn disposition and the other to "physical adequacy." No further reference to this textual alteration or to the special Utah sale occurs in the correspondence, and the arrangement may have been canceled. No copy containing the altered name on p.91 has been seen; however, the size of this printing suggests that the 1,000 altered copies could have been included in it.

If this alteration was made, the fourth printing would actually constitute 2 separate printings.

It is of some interest to note that Alexandra's horse in *O Pioneers!* is also named Brigham.

c.v.)   Fifth printing. 2,500 copies, September 1943.

c.vi.)   Sixth printing. 3,000 copies, July 1944.

c.vii.)   Seventh printing. 3,500 copies, February 1945.

c.viii.)   Eighth printing. 5,000 copies, December 1945.

c.ix.)   Ninth printing. 5,000 copies, October 1946.

c.x.)   Tenth printing. 5,000 copies, October 1947.

c.xi.)   Eleventh printing. 6,000 copies, October 1948.

c.xii.)   Twelfth printing. 5,000 copies, October 1950.

c.xiii.)   Thirteenth printing. 5,000 copies, May 1952.

c.xiv.)   Fourteenth printing. 5,000 copies, April 1954.

c.xv.)   Fifteenth printing. 5,000 copies, August 1956.

c.xvi.)   Sixteenth printing. 3,500 copies, June 1958.

c.xvii.)   Seventeenth printing. 5,000 copies, June 1959.

c.xviii.)   Eighteenth printing (first paperback Sentry edition printing [SE 7]). 7,500 copies, September 1961. Originally intended as a first printing of 10,000 copies, the first run sheets were considered too bulky for the Sentry paperback and were used instead to supply sheets for the hardbound book as needed until 1963. A note in the Houghton Mifflin production record: "First Sentry run of 10,000 on 50# Novel Antique too bulky. Sheets set aside to be bound as hardbound. Sentry re-run on Eggshell to give bulk 15/16. . . . First run was 10,500 of which 500 for special dummies. The 10,000 was to be part hard, part Sentry. Order dated 3-7-61. The second run actually the first Sentry run was 7,500 ordered 4-28-61." In some of the Sentry entries that follow, the printings contain a specified number of hardbound copies deriving from the same Sentry setting. Presswork was by photo-offset by the Riverside Press until 1962; then by the Colonial Press until 1977, when the offset films were sent to Vail-Ballou.

c.xix.)   Nineteenth printing (second Sentry only). 5,000 copies, April 1962.

c.xx.)   Twentieth printing (third Sentry only). 5,000 copies, May 1962.

c.xxi.)   Twenty-first printing (fourth Sentry only). 10,000 copies, September 1962.

c.xxii.)   Twenty-second printing (fifth Sentry only). 10,000 copies, February 1963.

c.xxiii.)   Twenty-third printing (sixth Sentry / part hardbound). 15,000 Sentry, 4,000 hardbound; September 1963.

c.xxiv.)   Twenty-fourth printing (seventh Sentry only). 15,000 copies, December 1963.

c.xxv.)   Twenty-fifth printing (hardbound only). 5,000 copies, August 1964.

c.xxvi.)   Twenty-sixth printing (eighth Sentry only). 16,400 copies, September 1964.

c.xxvii.)   Twenty-seventh printing (ninth Sentry only). 15,000 copies, April 1965.

c.xxviii.)   Twenty-eighth printing (hardbound only). 5,000 copies, December 1965.

c.xxix.)   Twenty-ninth printing (tenth Sentry only). 25,000 copies, April 1966.

c.xxx.)   Thirtieth printing (hardbound only). 7,500 copies, October 1966.

c.xxxi.)   Thirty-first printing (eleventh Sentry / part hardbound). 30,000 Sentry, 3,500 hardbound; February 1967.

c.xxxii.)   Thirty-second printing (twelfth Sentry / part hardbound). 30,000 Sentry, 1,250 hardbound; May 1969.

c.xxxiii.)   Thirty-third printing (hardbound only). 3,000 copies, November 1970.

c.xxxiv.)   Thirty-fourth printing (thirteenth Sentry only). 15,000 copies, August 1971.

c.xxxv.)   Thirty-fifth printing (fourteenth Sentry / part hardbound). 20,000 Sentry, 1,500 hardbound; November 1972.

c.xxxvi.)   Thirty-sixth printing (fifteenth Sentry / part hardbound). 20,000 Sentry, 1,500 hardbound; November 1973.

c.xxxvii.)   Thirty-seventh printing (sixteenth Sentry only). 25,000 copies, July 1974.

c.xxxviii.)   Thirty-eighth printing (seventeenth Sentry only). 25,000 copies, June 1975.

c.xxxix.)   Thirty-ninth printing (eighteenth Sentry / part hardbound). 25,000 Sentry, 1,500 hardbound; March 1976.

c.xl.)   Fortieth printing (nineteenth Sentry / part hardbound). 30,000 Sentry, 2,500 hardbound; February 1977. On 13 May 1977 the offset text films and binder's dies were moved to Vail-Ballou from the Colonial Press.

c.xli.   Forty-first printing (twentieth Sentry only) 30,000 copies, May 1978.

c.xlii.   Forty-second printing (twenty-first Sentry only). 30,000 copies, March 1979.

c.xliii.)   Forty-third printing (twenty-second Sentry only). New, smaller format (196 x 124mm.) with full color pictorial illustration on front and back covers and spine. On the back cover, a quote from H. L. Mencken. Spring 1981.

d.)   Fourth edition (Armed Services Edition), 1944

[within a double-rule border, title set in 2 panels. Left panel:] PUBLISHED BY ARRANGEMENT WITH | HOUGHTON MIFFLIN COMPANY, BOSTON | DEDICATION: | TO CARRIE AND IRENE MINER | *In memory of affections old and true* | *All rights reserved, including the right to reproduce this book or* | *parts thereof in any form.* | COPYRIGHT, 1918 and 1926, BY WILLA SIBERT CATHER [right panel:] MY | ÁNTONIA | *By* WILLA CATHER | *Optima dies . . . prima fugit* | VIRGIL | *Editions for the Armed Services, Inc.* | A NON-PROFIT ORGANIZATION ESTABLISHED | BY THE COUNCIL ON BOOKS IN WARTIME | NEW YORK

Paperback perfect binding, glued at the spine, text leaves secured by a single staple; pp.[i-vi, 1] 2-313 [314]. Text set in

double columns. Cheap wove paper; leaves measure 95 x
138mm.; edges trimmed flush with the cover. Pictorial stiff
paper wrapper. No.G-185 of the Armed Services Editions,
published in March 1944.

These pocket editions were sold to members of the armed forces
at cost. WC received a royalty of $0.01 per copy. Her first roy-
alty check was for $803.38, which meant that 80,338 copies of
MA had been sold.

e.i.)   Fifth edition, first printing, 1949

[title-page extends over 2 facing pages; right page:] *Willa
Cather* | [left:] MY [right:] ÁNTONIA | [within a single
rule panel] *Optima dies . . . prima fugit* | VIRGIL | [beneath
the panel, left page:] *With an Introduction by* WALTER
HAVIGHURST, | *Professor of English, Miami University* | [orn.]
Suggestions for Reading and Discussion by | BERTHA HANDLAN,
Acting Consultant in English | *to the Denver Public Schools, formerly
of the* | *Department of English, University of Colorado.* | [left page:]
HOUGHTON MIFFLIN [right page:] COMPANY · *Boston* ·
New York · *Chicago* · *Dallas* | *Atlanta* · *San Francisco* [black
letter] The Riverside Press Cambridge

Originally called the Student Edition, revised in 1961 for the
Riverside Literature Series, no.19, which remains available in
hardbound and soft covers.

A new setting of the text by the Riverside Press for the Houghton Mifflin Educational Department by arrangement with the
trade department. Pp.[i-v] vi-xvi [xvii-xx, 1] 2-266 [267-268].
P.iv: dedication, 5-line acknowledgment to E. K. Brown and
copyright: 'COPYRIGHT, 1949, BY HOUGHTON MIFFLIN
COMPANY | COPYRIGHT, 1918, 1926, AND 1946, BY
WILLA SIBERT CATHER | ALL RIGHTS RESERVED
INCLUDING THE RIGHT TO REPRODUCE | THIS
BOOK OR PARTS THEREOF IN ANY FORM | [orn.] [black
letter] The Riverside Press | [roman] CAMBRIDGE,
MASSACHUSETTS | PRINTED IN THE U. S. A.' The Benda
illustration plates in the text; part-title illus. by Bruce Adams.
Intended for use in schools. The Havighurst introductory essay,

'Prairie Life in My Ántonia' (pp.v-xvi) at front; the 'Suggestions for Reading and Discussion' section (pp.241-266) at back by Bertha Handlan (in later printings, Bertha Handlan Campbell).

In recent Riverside printings, the half title is replaced by a Riverside Literature Series title on recto of the left title page. Kenneth S. Lynn and Arno Jewett are the general editors. The Riverside Press imprint is removed from the copyright and 'New York, Atlanta, Geneva, Ill., Dallas and Palo Alto' are printed in the title page publisher's imprint.

f.)   Sixth edition (International Collectors Library), 1975

MY | ÁNTONIA | [orn.] | *by Willa Cather* | *Optima dies . . . prima fugit* | VIRGIL | INTERNATIONAL COLLECTORS LIBRARY | *Garden City, New York*

Collation: [1] ^{12} 2-5 ^{12} [6-10] ^{12}; pp.[i-viii] ix-x [1-2] 3-228 [229-230] = 120 leaves.

Contents: P.i: half title; p.ii: blank; p.iii: title page; p.iv: copyright, '. . . *This edition by arrangement with* | *Houghton Mifflin Company, Boston* | *Printed in the United States of America*'; p.v: contents; p.vi: blank; p.vii: dedication; p.viii: blank; pp.ix-x: 'INTRODUCTION'; p.1: 'BOOK ONE | *The Shimerdas*'; p.2: blank; pp.3-228: text; pp.229-230: blank.

Paper: White laid stock; vertical chain lines 20mm. apart. 207 x 137mm.; top and bottom edges trimmed, fore edge uncut. End papers of heavy white wove stock embedded with fiber hairs.

Binding: Dark blue composition fabric gilt- and blind-stamped in simulation of leather; a so-called William Morris Binding. Covers decorated in gilt and blind. Spine: 'MY | ANTONIA | WILLA | CATHER | INTERNATIONAL | COLLECTORS | LIBRARY'.

Publication: The title was first offered to International Collectors Library book club members as the selection for Fall 1975. International Collectors Library operates on a 14-month year. The

extra 2 months, or cycles, are given the designations of Spring,
Fall, Winter, or Summer, depending upon where they occur
when the yearly schedule is made up. In this instance, Fall 1975
came between November and December; the actual date of
shipping to members was probably late October. The date of
shipment would constitute the book club's publication date.
Between 25,000 and 30,000 copies were printed. The book is
still available to members.

English Editions

A9.*a.i.*(e)   First English edition (American sheets), 1919

MY ÁNTONIA | BY | WILLA S. CATHER | *Author of*
"O Pioneers!" Etc. | ILLUSTRATED BY W. T. BENDA |
[Heinemann device] || LONDON: WILLIAM HEINEMANN |
1919

Collation: As in the first American edition, fourth printing, with
unpaged leaves comprising the 8 illustrations (blank versos)
integral with the text and the inserted leaf pasted to the recto of
28_{1r}.

Illustrations: As in the first American edition, fourth printing.

Contents: P.π1: '[within a single rule panel] [black letter] Novels
by Willa S. Cather | [short rule] | [roman] O PIONEERS! |
ALEXANDER'S BRIDGE'; p.π2: blank; p.i: half title; p.ii:
advt. for 9 Heinemann novels; p.iii: title page; p.iv: blank; p.v:
dedication (as in A9.a.i.); p.vi: blank; p.vii: contents; p.viii:
blank; pp.ix-xiv: introduction; pp.3-6: text of book 1; pp.a1-2:
illus.; pp.7-46: text of book 1; pp.b1-2: illus.; pp.47-88: text
of book 1; pp.c1-2: illus.; pp.89-98: text of book 1; pp.d1-2:
illus.; pp.99-142: text of book 1; pp.e1-2: illus.; pp.143-158:
text of book 1; pp.f1-2: illus.; p.159: final page of book 1 text;
p.160: blank; p.161: part title, 'BOOK II | THE HIRED
GIRLS'; p.162: blank; pp.163-188: text of book 2; pp.g1-2:
illus.; pp.189-288: text of book 2; p.289: part title, 'BOOK III |
LENA LINGARD'; p.290: blank; pp.291-332: text of book 3;
p.333: part title, 'BOOK IV | THE PIONEER WOMAN'S
STORY'; p.334: blank; pp.335-358: text of book 4; p.366:

blank; p.367: part title, 'BOOK V | CUZAK'S BOYS'; p.368: blank; pp.369-419: text of book 5; p.420: printer's imprint, '[black letter] The Riverside Press | [roman] PRINTED BY H. O. HOUGHTON & CO. | CAMBRIDGE, MASS. | U. S. A.'

Paper: Cream wove, no watermark. 185 x 124mm.; edges trimmed. End papers of heavier, smoother stock.

Binding: Brown (77) coarse linen cloth, lettering stamped in light yellow-orange (70) as on the American edition. Front cover: '[thick rule] | MY ÁNTONIA | [thick rule] | WILLA CATHER'. Spine: '[thick rule] | MY | ÁNTONIA | [thick rule] | WILLA | CATHER | HEINEMANN'. Back cover blank.

Dust Jacket: Light brown (57) wove paper, lettering and decoration in black. Front cover: 'MY ÁNTONIA | [Benda illus. of horseman with Christmas tree] | A NEW NOVEL | By WILLA CATHER'. Spine: 'MY | ÁNTONIA | WILLA | CATHER | 7/- NET | Heinemann'. Back cover: '[within a single rule border] NEW & FORTHCOMING FICTION || [8 titles] || London: WILLIAM HEINEMANN, 21 Bedford St., W. C. 2.' Front inner flap: '[thick-thin rule] MY | ÁNTONIA | BY | WILLA S. CATHER | [thin-thick-thin rule] | [13-line blurb] | [thin-thick rule]'. Back inner flap: '[triple dec. rule] | CHEAP FICTION | [triple dec. rule | [27 titles] | [rule] | WM. HEINEMANN, 21 Bedford Street, W. C. 2.'

Publication: 1,000 copies of the American fourth printing (integral illustrations), bound in America with the Heinemann imprint and sent to England in April 1919, published in October 1919 at 7s. The printer's imprint has been altered to 'Printed by H. O. Houghton & Co.' Leaf χ₁ (pp.403-404) is still inserted, although the illustrations are integral. The dust jacket was printed in England.

a.ii.(e)   Second printing (Windmill Library), 1930

[within a single rule frame] MY ÁNTONIA | *By Willa Cather* | *Optima dies . . . prima fugit* | VIRGIL | [Heinemann device] | London | William Heinemann, Ltd. | 1930

Collation: [A]⁸ B-S⁸ T¹⁰ (T₁ unsigned; T₂ signed 'T*'); pp.
[π1-8] i-iii [iv, 1-2] 3-295 [296] = 154 leaves.

The Heinemann Windmill Library edition; the first printed in
England photographically from the plates of the first English
edition (that is, first American edition, fourth printing). Laid
paper, vertical chain lines; edges trimmed, top edge stained
brick red. 167 x 110mm. End papers of heavy cream wove stock.
Light brown-orange cloth, gilt-stamped lettering and decoration
on front cover and spine. The Heinemann device stamped in
blind on the lower right corner of the back cover. Published at
3s.6d.

***b.i.*(e)**   Second English edition (American sheets), 1927

No copy of this edition has been seen, but its existence is
verified by an entry in Houghton Mifflin's production record for
the 1926 revised printing of *MA* (A9.b.i.; second edition). On
28 March 1927, 250 copies of the American edition, supplied
with the Heinemann imprint and bound in America, were
shipped to Heinemann. The title is listed in Heinemann's
catalogue for 1928 at 7s.6d.

***c.i.*(e)**   Third English edition (Readers Union), 1943

OPTIMA DIES . . . PRIMA FUGIT—*VIRGIL* || *My Án-
tonia* || *Willa Cather* | READERS UNION LTD | WILLIAM
HEINEMANN LTD

Collation: [A]¹² χ₁ 2χ₁ B-F¹⁶ G²⁰ (-G₂₀); pp.[i-iv] v-viii, 1-217
[218] = 113 leaves. *Note:* χ₁ and 2χ₁ are 2 text leaves inserted
after the first gathering. The final leaf present in some copies,
G₁₉ (last text page), is pasted down on the inside back cover.
G₂₀, presumed a blank, is excised.

The first edition set and printed in England. A wartime edition
for sale only to members of the Readers Union. Printed at
Kingswood, Surrey, by the Windmill Press and bound by the
Temple Press bindery, Letchworth. Wove paper, edges trimmed,
top edge stained green. 183 x 119mm. Front end paper of coarse

wove paper. Orange cloth binding, covers blank. Spine:
'WILLA || My | Ántonia || CATHER | [white: 'R U' cipher
within a circle]'. Five illustrations, placed in the text at section
headings, are adapted from the original Benda drawings by
L. M. Vernon.

d.i.(e)   Fourth English edition. London: Hamish Hamilton, 1962.
Reproduced by photo-offset from the American plates. C8. 16s.
Continued available in print until 1975.

e.i.(e)   Fifth English edition. London: Virago Modern Classics, 1980.
New introduction by A. S. Byatt. Not seen. The publisher's
catalogue: 'February 1980 | Fiction | 400 pp | Paperback 1254 |
£2.50 Not for sale in the USA or Canada'.

A10.   YOUTH AND THE BRIGHT MEDUSA

a.i.)   First edition, first printing, 1920

TRADE ISSUE

YOUTH | AND THE BRIGHT MEDUSA | *BY* | WILLA
CATHER | *"We must not look at Goblin men,* | *We must not buy*
their fruits; | *Who knows upon what soil they fed* | *Their hungry,*
thirsty roots?" | *Goblin Market* | [oval borzoi device] | NEW
YORK | ALFRED [orn. dot] A [orn. dot] KNOPF | MCMXX

Collation: [1-19]⁸; pp.[1-10] 11-303 [304]= 152 leaves.

Contents: P. 1: half title; p.2: '[within a double border rule,
within a panel rule] BOOKS BY | *WILLA CATHER* | [5 titles]';
p.3: title page; p.4: 'COPYRIGHT, 1920, BY | WILLA
CATHER | PRINTED IN THE UNITED STATES OF
AMERICA'; p.5: contents; p.6: blank; p.7: 9-line author's
acknowledgment of republication rights; p.8: blank; p.9: second
half title; p.10: blank; pp.11-78: text of 'Coming, Aphrodite!';
pp.79-139: text of 'The Diamond Mine'; pp.140-168: text of 'A
Gold Slipper'; pp.169-198: text of 'Scandal'; pp.199-234: text
of 'Paul's Case'; pp.235-247: text of 'A Wagner Matinée';

pp.248-272: text of 'The Sculptor's Funeral'; pp.273-303: text of '"A Death in the Desert"'; p.304: blank.

Note: The text has italic running heads of story titles on rectos, book title on versos.

Text Contents (previously published as noted):
Coming, Aphrodite! *Smart Set* 92 (August 1920), with the title 'Coming, Eden Bower!'. Variant text. C54
The Diamond Mine. *McClure's* 47 (October 1916). C49
A Gold Slipper. *Harper's* (January 1917). C50
Scandal. *Century* 98 (August 1919). C52
Paul's Case. *McClure's* 25 (May 1905); *The Troll Garden.* C37
A Wagner Matinée. *Everybody's Magazine* 10 (February 1904); *The Troll Garden.* C32
The Sculptor's Funeral. *McClure's* 24 (January 1905); *The Troll Garden.* C33
"A Death in the Desert." *Scribner's* 33 (January 1903); *The Troll Garden.* C31

Paper: Cream wove, no watermark. 189x129mm.; top edge trimmed and stained purple-blue (200), other edges uncut. End papers of heavier cream wove stock.

Binding: Bright yellow-green (131) fine linen cloth, lettering and decoration in dark blue. Front cover: '[within a dec. 4-line rule supported by a Medusa head] YOUTH · AND · THE | BRIGHT · MEDUSA | [below:] WILLA · CATHER'. Spine: ' || [first 4 lines flanked by a floriated dec.] YOUTH | AND · THE | BRIGHT | MEDUSA | WILLA · CATHER |||| ALFRED · A · KNOPF ||'. Back cover: '[16x22mm. panel stamped in dark blue] BORZOI | [borzoi logo in green] | BOOKS'. Measurement from the top rule of the front cover panel to the bottom of the author's name line is 169mm. Measurement from the top rule to the bottom rule on the spine is 184mm. (See comparative measurements for the limited issue.)

Dust Jacket: Bright yellow-green (130) laid paper with horizontal chain lines 30mm. apart; lettering and decoration in black overall. Front cover: 'A New Book of Stories by the Author of |

"My Antonia" | [title within a dec. 4-line rule panel supported by a Medusa head] YOUTH · AND · THE | BRIGHT · MEDUSA | By WILLA CATHER | [11 lines of a blurb that ends with the line: '[continued on back of wrapper]'] | ALFRED A. KNOPF [publisher's device] PUBLISHER, N. Y.' Spine: '|| [first 4 lines flanked by a floriated dec.] YOUTH | AND · THE | BRIGHT | MEDUSA | WILLA · CATHER | [borzoi device] | ALFRED A. | KNOPF'. Back cover: 27-line continuation of the front cover blurb with heading, '[continued from front of jacket]'. Front inner flap: '$2.25 net | WILLA CATHER | [22-line blurb]'. Back inner flap blank.

Publication: Copyright secured 15 September 1920. A first printing of 3,500 copies at $2.25. Plates set by Vail-Ballou (who also printed the galleys); presswork by the Plimpton Press. A Knopf *PW* ad (25 September) announces *YBM* as "already published." Listed in the *PW* weekly record on 2 October 1920. Copies of the American edition were available in England by October (reviewed in *TLS* on 14 October 1920), although the Heinemann English edition (made up of the American fourth printing sheets) was not published in London until 1921 (*A10.a.i.*[e]).

LIMITED ISSUE

Thirty-five copies of the first edition, first printing were bound with untrimmed top edge and signed on the front open end paper recto by Willa Cather. These copies are 8mm. taller than the trade issue. Measurement from the top rule of the front cover panel to the bottom of the author's name line is 176mm. Measurement from the top rule to the bottom rule of the spine is 190mm. The 2 issues are otherwise identical.

a.ii.)   Second printing. 1,000 copies. 'COPYRIGHT, 1920, BY | WILLA CATHER | [short rule] | *First Printing, September,* *1920* | *Second Printing, December, 1920* | PRINTED IN THE UNITED STATES OF AMERICA'. Presswork: the Plimpton Press.

a.iii.)   Third printing. 500 copies. Title page has title and oval borzoi device printed in bright orange-red. '*Third Printing, April,*

1921'. Collational formula is altered to make the half-title-advertisement leaf a single-leaf insert preceding the first 8vo gathering. This arrangement results in a single terminal blank leaf following the text. Presswork: the Plimpton Press.

a.iv.)   Fourth printing. 1,530 sets of sheets printed; 750 copies bound for the American trade. 2-color title page, collational format as in the third printing. *'Fourth Printing, June, 1921'* added to the copyright. Presswork: the Plimpton Press. Of this printing, 780 sets of sewn sheets were sent to Heinemann for the English edition (*A10.a.i*.[e]).

a.v.)   Fifth printing. 1,500 copies. *'Fifth Printing, January, 1923'* added to copyright. Reset title page has title, epigraph, and publisher's name in black; author's name, borzoi oval device, place and new date ('MCMXXIII') in bright yellow-orange. New binding: tan (91) cloth with gilt-stamped and bright orange lettering. Knopf device stamped in blind at lower right corner of back cover. Top edge trimmed and stained orange; end papers of bright orange paper patterned in white. Presswork: the Plimpton Press / Vail-Ballou.

a.vi.)   Sixth printing (Borzoi Pocket Book series, no.29). 3,000 sets of sheets printed, 1,500 bound April 1925. Copyright: 'COPYRIGHT, 1920, BY WILLA CATHER · SET | UP, ELECTROTYPED AND PRINTED BY THE | VAIL-BALLOU PRESS, INC., BINGHAMTON, | N. Y. · PAPER FURNISHED BY W. F. ETHER-|INGTON & CO., NEW YORK · BOUND BY THE | H. WOLFF ESTATE, NEW YORK. · | [First through fifth printings listed in small caps] | POCKET BOOK EDITION, PUBLISHED APRIL, 1925 | MANUFACTURED IN THE UNITED STATES OF | AMERICA'. $1.25. Presswork: Vail-Ballou.

a.vii.)   Seventh printing. 750 sets of sheets printed, 250 bound January 1928. The sixth regular trade edition printing with *'Sixth Printing, January, 1928'* on the copyright. The remainder of the sheets bound as required through 1937. Presswork: Vail-Ballou.

a.viii.)   Eighth printing (Borzoi Pocket Book series, no.30). 3,000 sets of sheets printed, 1,500 bound March 1929. The second Bor-

zoi Pocket Book edition with copyright: 'PUBLISHED
SEPTEMBER, 1920 | REPRINTED FIVE TIMES | NEW
POCKET BOOK EDITION, MARCH, 1929'. $1.00. Press-
work: H. Wolff.

a.ix.)   Ninth printing. 1,000 sets of sheets printed, 500 bound
October 1938. The seventh regular trade printing. Copyright:
'PUBLISHED SEPTEMBER 15, 1920 | REPRINTED FIVE
TIMES | SEVENTH PRINTING, October 1938'. $2.50. Of
this printing, 233 copies were bound in 1942 and 202 in 1944.
Presswork: H. Wolff.

b.)   Second edition (Autograph Edition, vol.6), 1937

[dec. rule]| WILLA CATHER | [dec. rule] | Youth and the
Bright | Medusa | [dec. rule] | [orange brown: 'H M Co'
cipher] | BOSTON | HOUGHTON MIFFLIN COMPANY |
1937

Collation: [1-18]^8 [19]^6; pp.[i-vi, 1-2] 3-288 [289-294]= 150
leaves.

Illustration: Frontispiece facsimile page of the original first draft
of *Coming, Aphrodite!*, facing the title page.

Contents: P.i: half title; p.ii: limitation notice; p.iii: title page;
p.iv: copyright, 'COPYRIGHT, 1920, BY WILLA
CATHER | . . .'; p.v: contents; p.vi: blank; p.1: part title,
'Coming, Aphrodite!'; p.2: blank; pp.3-74: text of story, dated
'New York, 1920' on p.74; p.75: part title, 'The Diamond
Mine'; p.76: blank; pp.77-140: text of story, dated 'New York,
1916' on p.140; p.141: part title, 'A Gold Slipper'; p.142:
blank; pp.143-172: text of story, dated 'Red Cloud, Nebraska,
1916' on p.172; p. 173: part title, 'Scandal'; p.174: blank;
pp.175-205: text of story, dated 'Denver, Colorado, 1916' on
p.205; p.206: blank; p.207: part title, 'Paul's Case'; p.208:
blank; pp.209-245: text of story, dated 'Pittsburgh, 1904' on
p.245; p.246: blank; p.247: part title, 'A Wagner Matinée';
p.248: blank; pp.249-261: text of story, dated 'Pittsburgh,
1903' on p.261; p.262: blank; p.263: part title, 'The Sculptor's
Funeral'; p.264: blank; pp.265-289: text of story, dated

'Pittsburgh, 1903' on p.289; p.290: blank; p.291: Riverside
Press device; pp.292-294: blank.

Text Content: Of the 8 stories in the first edition (1920), '"A
Death in the Desert"' has not been included in this edition.

Notes on paper, binding, dust jacket, and publication with the
entry for the entire Autograph Edition (AA1).

Textual Collation: Willa Cather made numerous corrections in
the 1920 story texts for the Autograph Edition. Many of these
were corrections of punctuation, spelling, capitalization, and so
forth. Only the substantive changes are given here. Pagination
and line are keyed to *Youth and the Bright Medusa* (1920)
(A10.a.i.).

29.4	box] package
64.5	Buddah] Buddha
74.25	Williams] William
78.8	the street] the new street
94.1	reached] felt
94.9	go at] go on at
99.1	, and no other,] *omit*
103.6-7	else] but that
107.14	bony finger] long finger
107.21	very much] somewhat
107.22	later] *omit*
107.23	were just] were then just
108.17	grab] catch
109.15	to a page] to the page
109.22	*fôrets] forêts*
111.2	very] fairly
111.6	gaunt] slender
132.7	large] long
140.3	Carnegie] Pittsburgh Carnegie
141.4	no one could] one could not
142.25	, carried away by] with
144.21	Mozart and Handel and Beethoven.] Pergolesi and Mozart and Handel.
145.11	Beethoven and] *omit*
148.12	*Faust] La Bohème*

153.20	creatures] *omit*
154.29	care less?"] care still less?"
155.17-18	as he came toward them] *omit*
157.7	that] whom
161.28	me and] me or
164.17	that] which
168.1	often] sometimes
169.10	wintry] dreary
169.11	they] she
169.11-12	upon. She] upon. It was the wet, raw winter of 1915. She
169.29	that] which
172.7	and disquieting] and the disquieting
179.20	, that was] *omit*
180.2	Petrograd] St. Petersburg
180.5	the province of Moscow] St. Petersburg
181.29	from stages.] upon the public.
182.9	candy] box of sweets
183.20	admiration."] friendship."
188.18	She worked] She once worked
203.9	wildly] *omit*
206.29	the city] Pittsburgh
217.10	blue] *omit*
217.22	autograph] autographed
219.12	long] tall
219.29	nonce] time
222.10	that] which
226.3	Opera] Metropolitan
233.12	all] *omit*
235.4	village.] town.
236.29	latter] late
240.18	for a] for more than a
240.24	Brown hotel] Brown Palace
242.11-16	With the battle . . . combat; and] *omit*
242.29	staring dully] quietly looking
243.22	pelting] *omit*
243.3-4	sat silent . . . Darien. She] *omit*
243.27	this] her
244.9	with quivering eyelids] *omit*
244.20-22	She wept . . . of the melody.] *omit*
245.15-16	as though . . . of illness.] during the intermission.
245.19	queried] asked

245.26-29   My aunt wept . . . rain-storm.] Throughout these I felt that my
Aunt had drifted quite away from me.

245.29   dim] *omit*

246.4-6   She burst into . . . want to go!"] She turned to me with a sad
little smile. "I don't want to go, Clark. I suppose we must."

248.11   open, their] open (they never buttoned them), their

251.15   body.] remains.

252.2   Bostonian] stranger

253.17   casket] coffin

255.19   conspicuous for . . . knuckles,] *omit*

256.2   unkept] unkempt

256.7   orgy of grief] behaviour

257.18   ever] just

258.9   into the master's] at the sculptor's

260.11-13   Oh, he . . . lips!] *omit*

260.15   feeling and] *omit*

260.23   thin, tired] woman's

262.1-6   ; liberated it . . . his own] *omit*

264.20   dozen] *omit*

264.21   cattle-farms] cattle-ranch

267.17   also variegated,] *omit*

269.17   ; and a] . A

270.18   their annuities] *omit*

271.4   big,] *omit*

271.10-12   Harvey Merrick . . . know it.] *omit*

271.14   a genius] a man like Harvey

c.i.)   Third edition, first printing, 1945

[within a dec. blue rule frame] Youth and the | Bright Medusa |
BY | WILLA CATHER | *"We must not look at Goblin men,* | *We*
must not buy their fruits; | *Who knows upon what soil they fed* | *Their*
hungry, thirsty roots?" | —GOBLIN MARKET |
ALFRED · A · KNOPF | *New York* [oval Borzoi device] mcmxlv

Collation: [1-9]¹⁶; pp.[i-viii, 1-2] 3-279 [280] = 144 leaves.

Contents: Pp.i-ii: blank; p.iii: half title, 'YOUTH AND | THE
BRIGHT MEDUSA | [short rule]'; p.iv: '*The Novels of* | WILLA
CATHER | [12 titles]'; p.v: title page; p.vi: copyright,

'*Copyright 1920 by Willa Cather* | [5-line italic rights reserved statement] | PUBLISHED SEPTEMBER 15, 1920 | REPRINTED SIX TIMES | EIGHTH PRINTING, OCTOBER 1945'; p.vii: contents; p.viii: 8-line author's note; p.1: story title, '*COMING, APHRODITE!*'; p.2: blank; pp.3-279: text; p.280: '*A NOTE ON THE TYPE* | *in which this book is set* | [11-line italic note] | [borzoi hound orn.] | COMPOSED, PRINTED, AND BOUND BY | THE PLIMPTON PRESS, NORWOOD, MASS.'

Note: On p.280, the type is identified as one adapted from a type designed by Pierre Simon Fournier the younger in the eighteenth century.

Text Content: As in the first edition.

Paper: Fine cream wove stock watermarked '*Ticonderoga*'; 191 x 128mm., top edge trimmed and stained orange, other edges rough cut. End papers of heavier cream wove stock.

Binding: Bright yellow-green (131) linen cloth. A gray paper label, 51 x 83mm., on the front cover: '[within a bright orange dec. border rule] YOUTH | AND THE BRIGHT | MEDUSA | WILLA CATHER'. A gray paper label on the spine, 67 x 24 mm.: '[bright orange orn.] YOUTH | AND THE | BRIGHT | MEDUSA | [bright orange triangle] | CATHER'. Back cover blank.

Dust Jacket: Not seen.

Publication: The text was reset and printed from new plates in October 1945. All subsequent printings were from these plates, including the Vintage paperback of 1975, reproduced by photo-offset.

c.ii.)   Second printing. July 1951. Publisher's records not available for this printing. Presswork: Plimpton Press.

c.iii.)   Third printing. December 1956. Publisher's records not available for this printing. Presswork: Plimpton Press.

c.iv.)   Fourth printing. September 1961. Publisher's records are not available for this printing. Presswork: Plimpton Press.

c.v.)   Fifth printing. 700 copies, June 1971. By this date Knopf and Random House were affiliates. Random House bought the plates from the Plimpton Press and ordered the presswork from H. Wolff.

c.vi.)   Sixth printing (first Vintage Books edition, V-684). Set by photo-offset from the third edition plates, September 1975. Under the imprint of Vintage Books, a division of Random House. First printing of 700 copies. Presswork by H. Wolff; subsequent printings by American Book-Stratford Press.

English Editions

A10.a.i.(e)   First English edition (American sheets), 1921

YOUTH | AND THE BRIGHT MEDUSA | *BY* | WILLA CATHER | [4 line quotation in italic] | *Goblin Market* | 19[Heinemann device]21 || LONDON: WILLIAM HEINEMANN

Collation: As in the first American edition A10.a.i.

Contents: As in A10.a.i., but with p.2 blank and the copyright notice removed from p.4.

Text Contents: As in A10.a.i.

Paper: As in the American first edition, fourth printing, A10.a.iv., 198x125mm.; edges trimmed, top edge unstained.

Binding: Dull brown orange (54) smooth linen cloth, lettered in black. Front cover: '[within a 3-paneled oblong thick rule, title flanked by 2 thistle orns.] YOUTH AND THE | BRIGHT MEDUSA | · · · | WILLA CATHER'. Spine: '[thick rule] | YOUTH | AND THE | BRIGHT | MEDUSA | · · · | WILLA CATHER | [thick rule] | [thick rule] | HEINEMANN | [thick rule]'. Back cover: the Heinemann device stamped in black at the lower right corner.

Publication: Published in England in August 1921. 780 sets of sewn sheets from the American fourth printing, bound in England.

A11.   ONE OF OURS

a.i.)   First edition, first printing, 1922

LIMITED ISSUE

ONE OF OURS | [orange (50)] WILLA CATHER | [black] *"Bidding the eagles of the West fly on . . ."* | *Vachel Lindsay* | [orange (50) oval borzoi device] | [orange (50)] NEW YORK | [black] ALFRED · A · KNOPF | [orange (50)] MCMXXII

Collation: [1-29]⁸ [30]⁴; pp.[i-x] 1-459 [460-462] = 236 leaves.

Contents: P.i: half title; p.ii: limitation notice, 'THE FIRST EDITION OF "ONE OF OURS" | CONSISTS OF THREE HUNDRED AND | FORTY-FIVE COPIES AS FOLLOWS: THIRTY-|FIVE ON IMPERIAL JAPAN VELLUM (OF | WHICH FIVE ARE NOT FOR SALE) NUM-|BERED FROM I TO 35; AND THREE | HUNDRED AND TEN COPIES ON PERUSIA | HANDMADE ITALIAN PAPER (OF WHICH | FIFTEEN ARE NOT FOR SALE) NUMBERED | 36 TO 345. EACH COPY IS SIGNED BY | THE AUTHOR. | [number in red ink] | [holograph signature in black ink]'; p.iii: title page; p.iv: 'COPYRIGHT, 1922, BY | WILLA CATHER | *Published, September, 1922* | *Set up and electrotyped by the Vail-Ballou Co., Binghamton, N.Y.* | *Paper furnished by the Japan Paper Co., New York, N.Y.* | *Printed and bound by the Plimpton Press, Norwood, Mass.* | MANUFACTURED IN THE UNITED STATES OF AMERICA'; p.v: dedication, *'For my mother* | VIRGINIA CATHER'; p.vi: blank; p.vii: contents; p.viii: blank; p.ix: part title, 'BOOK ONE: | ON LOVELY CREEK'; p.x: blank; pp.1-113: text of book 1; p.114: blank; p.115: part title, 'BOOK TWO: | ENID'; p.116: blank; pp.117-198: text of book 2; p.199: part title, 'BOOK THREE: | SUNRISE ON THE PRAIRIE'; p.200: blank; pp.201-263: text of book 3;

p.264: blank; p.265: part title, 'BOOK FOUR: | THE
VOYAGE OF THE ANCHISES'; p.266: blank; pp.267-319:
text of book 4; p.320: blank; p.321: part title, 'BOOK FIVE: |
"BIDDING THE EAGLES | OF THE WEST FLY ON"';
p.322: blank; pp.323-459: text of book 5; pp.460-462: blank.

Paper: 310 copies: cream laid stock with horizontal chain
lines 26mm. apart, watermarked '[crowned lion rampant] |
PERVSIA | ITALY', with countermark 'P M | FABRIANO'.
233x152mm.; edges uncut. End papers of the same stock.

35 copies: Japan vellum. 224x148mm.; top edge gilt, other
edges uncut.

Binding: 310 copies: pale green and purple batik rough paper
over boards, cream rough linen shelfback with a 62x44mm.
printed paper label, '|| ONE OF | OURS | *by* | *Willa* | *Cather* ||
FIRST EDITION ||'. In a gray-blue linen-textured board box
with the same label on the spine. The copy number is supplied
in red ink beneath the double rules of the label.

35 copies: ivory vellum, gilt-stamped on the front cover,
'[within a single gilt border rule] *WILLA CATHER* | *ONE OF*
OURS | [circular orn.]'. Spine: '*Willa* | *Cather* | *ONE* | *OF* |
OURS | [short wavy rule] | *Alfred A. Knopf* ||'. The Knopf
borzoi device is stamped in gilt on the lower right corner of the
back cover. In a transparent glassine wrapper; a white satin place
marker attached to the cording at the top inner spine.

Publication: 8 September 1922, 345 copies: 310 at $10.00 on
Perusia paper, of which 15 were not for sale, and 35 on Imperial
Japan vellum at $25.00, of which 5 were not for sale. Presswork
was done by the Plimpton Press from plates set and electrotyped
by Vail-Ballou. Each copy is numbered in red ink on the limitation page and signed by the author. The trade issue is designated 'second printing' by the publisher. As it was printed at
the same time from the same press setting, it is here designated
the "trade issue" (see below).

TRADE ISSUE

[title and collation as in the limited issue]

Contents: P.i: half title, 'ONE OF OURS'; p.ii: advt., '[within a double-rule border frame, within a single-rule panel] *BOOKS BY* | *WILLA CATHER* | [6 titles]'; p.iii: title page; p.iv: 'COPYRIGHT, 1922, BY | ALFRED A. KNOPF, INC. | *First printing, September, 1922, consisted of thirty-five* | *copies on Imperial Japan Vellum and three hundred and* | *ten copies on Perusia handmade Italian paper, num-|bered and signed by the author.* | *Second Printing, September, 1922* | [printer's imprint as in the limited issue] | MANUFACTURED IN THE UNITED STATES OF AMERICA'; pp.v-x, 1-462: as in the limited issue.

Paper: Cream wove stock, 190x128mm.; top edge trimmed and stained orange, other edges rough-cut. End papers of heavier cream stock.

Binding: Smooth olive-tan (approx. 91) linen cloth. Front cover: '[gilt-stamped] *WILLA CATHER* | [orange:] *ONE OF OURS* | [gilt circular orn.]'. Spine: '[gilt-stamped] *Willa* | *Cather* | [orange:] *ONE* | *OF* | *OURS* | [gilt short wavy rule] | [gilt:] *Alfred A. Knopf*'. Back cover: Borzoi Books device stamped in blind on the lower right corner.

Dust Jacket: Deep orange (51) coated paper, lettering and decoration in black overall. Front cover: '[within a geometrical pattern border frame] ONE OF OURS | By WILLA CATHER | *Author of* "YOUTH AND THE BRIGHT MEDUSA" | [orn.] | [23-line blurb, signed in facsimile holograph, 'Alfred A. Knopf'] | ALFRED A. KNOPF [Borzoi Books device] PUBLISHER, N. Y.' Spine: '[geometrical pattern rule] ONE OF | OURS | *By* | WILLA | CATHER | *Author of* | "*Youth and the* | *Bright Medusa*" | [orn.] | [Borzoi Books device] | ALFRED A. | KNOPF | [geometrical pattern rule]'. Back cover: '[within a geometrical pattern border rule] BY THE SAME AUTHOR | YOUTH AND THE | BRIGHT MEDUSA | [orn.] | [excerpts from critical reviews] | ALFRED A. KNOPF [Borzoi Books device] PUBLISHER, N. Y.' Front inner flap: 12-line advt. for

Borzoi Books. Back inner flap: 'BORZOI BOOKS | [27-line
advt.] | [an order blank beneath a thick-thin rule]'.

Publication: 8 September 1922 in a first printing of 12,000
copies at $2.50. Plates set by Vail-Ballou, printed and bound by
the Plimpton Press from the same press-setting as the limited
issue. '*Second Printing, September, 1922*' on the copyright.

The entire first printing was of 15,000 sets of sheets. Of these,
3,000 were supplied with the title page imprint of the Macmillan Co., Toronto, for the Canadian edition.

Special Issue (Advance Review Copies)

Two hundred fifty copies of the trade issue were specially
bound in mottled gray paper-covered boards with lettering and
decoration stamped in orange. Internally, these copies differ only
in the insertion of a single leaf preceding the title page, printed
on the verso, 'THIS IS ONE OF AN EDITION | OF TWO
HUNDRED AND | FIFTY COPIES SPECIALLY | MADE
FOR BOOKSELLER | FRIENDS OF BORZOI BOOKS'.

Ninety-five copies in this binding, without the insert leaf and
with the Canadian title page Macmillan imprint, were sent to
Canada in advance of the regular Canadian edition copies. The
copyright notice has been entirely removed, save for the
statement 'MANUFACTURED IN THE UNITED STATES OF
AMERICA' at the foot of the page. The Macmillan imprint
replaces the Knopf imprint at the foot of the binding spine, but
the Borzoi Books device is still present on the back cover. These
copies are in a red (12) dust jacket that duplicates the American
dust jacket, but with the Macmillan imprint supplanting the
Knopf at the foot of the front and back cover and the spine. The
inner flaps still carry the Knopf advertisements. This is the
standard jacket for the Canadian edition.

Canadian edition: Toronto: Macmillan Co., American sheets of
the first printing, 1922. Macmillan imprint, 'TORONTO:
THE MACMILLAN COMPANY OF | CANADA, LTD., AT
ST. MARTIN'S HOUSE | 1922', on the title page; first

American trade edition binding with the Macmillan name
stamped at the foot of the spine replacing 'Alfred A. Knopf'.

a.ii.)   Second printing. 10,000 copies, 21 September 1922. Copyright
extended: 'Third Printing, September, 1922'. Some copies were
manually supplied with a typewritten paste-over, lettered 'First
Regular Edition | for public distribution' covering the copyright
notice.

a.iii.)   Third printing. 12,500 copies, 28 September 1922. (Knopf
'fourth printing'). Presswork: the Plimpton Press. In this
printing, 5 important substantive textual alterations were made:

241.27   dismissed,] concluded,
272.21-22   A man in a smart uniform appeared on the bridge and began
talking] A few moments later a man appeared on the bridge and
began to talk
278.18   battle ships.] destroyers.
336.16   Chateau Thierry] Belleau Wood
390.18   Chateau Thierry] Belleau Wood

Historical note: These changes were suggested to WC by her
Houghton Mifflin editor, Ferris Greenslet, in a letter on 22
August 1922. He had been sent a copy of the newly published
novel by Alfred Knopf and made these criticisms: (1) a court
case untried for lack of evidence is "dismissed"; a case which has
been heard is "concluded." (2) It is an inviolable custom in their
profession that the pilot's "uniform" consists of a black suit,
overcoat, and bowler hat, rather than a "smart uniform." (3)
Battle ships were not used in convoy service. (4) "Chateau
Thierry" is used to designate the Allied offensive beginning 15
July 1918; WC's references are to the fighting of the marines
and the First Division at Belleau Wood northwest of Chateau
Thierry early in June, 1918.

a.iv.)   Fourth printing. 6,000 copies, November 1922. Knopf 'fifth
printing'. Presswork: the Plimpton Press.

a.v.)   Fifth printing. 3,000 copies, 28 May 1923. Knopf 'sixth
printing'. Presswork: the Plimpton Press.

a.vi.)   Sixth printing. 6,000 copies, June 1923. Knopf 'seventh printing'. Presswork: the Plimpton Press.

a.vii.)   Seventh printing. 4,700 copies, August 1923. Knopf 'eighth printing'. Presswork: the Plimpton Press.

a.viii.)   Eighth printing. 6,700 copies, November 1923. Knopf 'ninth printing'. Presswork: the Plimpton Press.

a.ix.)   Ninth printing (Students' Library of Contemporary Fiction text edition). 2,500 copies, June 1926. Introduction by Stanley T. Williams (pp.vii-xx). Cheap green (131) smooth cloth binding with black lettering; cipher 'A K' incorporated in decorative blind-stamped rules above and below the cover title. Presswork: Vail-Ballou.

a.x.)   Tenth printing. 2,000 copies, December 1931. Presswork: the Plimpton Press.

a.xi.)   Eleventh printing. 2,350 copies, September 1934. Presswork: the Plimpton Press.

a.xii.)   Twelfth printing. 3,000 sets of sheets printed, February (copyright states 'January') 1940. 500 bound in February 1940, 500 bound in July 1941, 524 in October 1942, 411 in November 1943, 943 in December 1944. Presswork: the Plimpton Press.

a.xiii.)   Thirteenth printing. 1,500 copies, February 1949. Presswork: the Plimpton Press. Corrections in the text by WC were incorporated in this printing:
6.19   loaned] lent (5 *lines reset*)
20.16   very much] *omit* (5 *lines reset*)

a.xiv.)   Fourteenth printing. 2,055 copies, March 1953.

a.xv.)   Fifteenth printing. 2,840 copies, May 1960. 1,340 additional sets of sheets printed to be bound as needed through 1964. Presswork: the Plimpton Press.

a.xvi.)   Sixteenth printing. 2,500 copies, November 1965. New plates
set photographically from the first edition plates by the Haddon
Craftsmen.

a.xvii.)   Seventeenth printing. 2,800 copies, August 1968. Presswork:
Haddon Craftsmen.

a.xviii.)   Eighteenth printing. 1,900 copies, October 1970. Presswork:
Haddon Craftsmen.

a.xix.)   Nineteenth printing. 786 copies, March 1976. Presswork:
American Book-Stratford Press.

b.)   Second edition (Autograph Edition, vol.5), 1937

[dec. rule] | WILLA CATHER | [dec. rule] | One of Ours |
[dec. rule] | 'Bidding the eagles of the West fly on . . .' |
VACHEL LINDSAY | [brown-orange: 'H M Co' cipher] |
BOSTON | HOUGHTON MIFFLIN COMPANY | 1937

Collation: [1-32]^8 [33]^6; pp.[i-vi, 1-2] 3-513 [514-518]= 262
leaves.

Illustration: Photographic frontispiece of WC and a dog,
captioned '*In the Garden at Ville d'Avray, France* | 1922'. On
heavy wove paper, inserted facing the title page, protective
tissue.

Contents: P.i: edition title; p.ii: limitation notice; p.iii: title
page; p.iv: copyright; p.v: contents; p.vi: blank; p.1: part title,
'BOOK ONE | On Lively Creek'; p.2: blank; pp.3-514: text;
p.515: Riverside Press device; pp.516-518: blank.

Notes on paper, binding, dust jacket, and publication with the
entry for the entire Autograph Edition (AA1).

c.i.)   Third edition, first printing (Random House Vintage Books
[V-252]), 1971

· WILLA CATHER · *One* | *of* | *Ours* | *"Bidding the eagles of the West* | *fly on . . ."* | VACHEL LINDSAY | [sun orn.] | *Vintage Books* | A DIVISION OF RANDOM HOUSE | NEW YORK

Paperback, adhesive perfect binding; pp.[i-x, 1-2] 3-391 [392-406] = 208 leaves. The final page of text is p.391; on p.393 is a biographical note on WC followed by a listing of Vintage paperbacks (pp.395-406). Copyright: *'Vintage Books Edition, November 1971'*. Decorative wrappers; book design by Charlotte Staub, cover artwork by Guy Fleming. 184x119mm. $1.95.

A new setting of the text. Plates set by H. Wolff. First printing of 10,000 copies. Typographical errors: 'him' for 'his' (193.26), 'still' for 'till' (269.32).

Subsequent printings by American Book-Stratford Press and the Longacre Press. In 1974 the cover was redesigned with artwork by J. K. Lambert. The price was raised to $2.45.

c.ii.)   Second printing. 5,000 copies, November 1974.

c.iii.)   Third printing. 5,600 copies, December 1974.

c.iv.)   Fourth printing. 5,118 copies, January 1975.

c.v.)   Fifth printing. 5,160 copies, December 1977.

English Editions

AII.a.i.(e)   First English edition, 1923

ONE OF OURS | BY | WILLA CATHER | *"Bidding the eagles of the West fly on . . ."* | VACHEL LINDSAY | 19[Heinemann device]23 || LONDON : WILLIAM HEINEMANN LTD.

Collation: [A]⁴ B-I⁸ K-U⁸ X-Z⁸ AA⁸ BB² ($₂ signed); pp.[i-viii] 1-372 = 190 leaves.

Contents: P.i: half title 'ONE OF OURS'; p.ii: '[within a single rule panel] BOOKS BY | *WILLA CATHER* | [6 titles: *AB, OP,*

SOL, MA, YBM, 00]'; p.iii: title page; p.iv: *'First Published 1923. | Printed in Great Britain by The Whitefriars Press, Ltd., | London and Tonbridge'*; p.v: dedication, 'FOR MY MOTHER | VIRGINIA CATHER'; p.vi: blank; p.vii: contents; p.viii: blank; p.1: part title, 'BOOK ONE | ON LOVELY CREEK'; p.2: blank; pp.3-95: text of book 1; p.96: blank; p.97: part title, 'BOOK TWO | ENID'; p.98: blank; pp.99-162: text of book 2; p.163: part title, 'BOOK THREE | SUNRISE ON THE PRAIRIE'; p.164: blank; pp.165-216: text of book 3; p.217: part title, 'BOOK FOUR | THE VOYAGE OF THE *ANCHISES*'; p.218: blank; pp.219-260: text of book 4; p.261: part title, 'BOOK FIVE | "BIDDING THE EAGLES OF THE WEST | FLY ON"'; p.262: blank; pp.263-372: text of book 5.

Paper: Cream wove, 182 x 121mm.; edges trimmed. End papers of heavier cream wove stock.

Binding: 2 bindings noted. Priority is assumed from the more elaborate decoration of the first listed:

a: Red (12) linen cloth stamped in glossy black. Front cover: '[within a thick single rule panel flanked by mirror-image identical flowering bush orns.] ONE OF OURS | [three dots] | WILLA CATHER'. Spine: '[thick rule] | ONE OF | OURS | [three dots] | WILLA CATHER | [thick rule]'. Back cover: the Heinemann windmill device on the lower right corner.

b: Salmon (approx. 27) crisscross cloth stamped in dull black. Front cover: 'ONE OF OURS | [three dots] | WILLA CATHER'. Spine: 'ONE OF | OURS | [three dots] | WILLA CATHER | HEINEMANN'. Back cover: the Heinemann windmill device stamped in blind on the lower right corner.

Publication: Printed in England and published in October 1923 at 7s. 6d. Listed in *TLS* on 18 October 1923 and reviewed favorably in the same number.

b.i.(e).   Second English edition. London: Hamish Hamilton, 1967. Photo-offset from the first American edition plates.

A12.   VERSE BY WILLA CATHER ["Grandmither, Think Not I Forget"]

a.)   First separate printing, 1922

[cover title; within a dec. tan frame rule and smaller black single rule with orn. at inner corners] V E R S E | BY | WILLA CATHER | [tan oval borzoi hound device within a dec. black panel rule] | ALFRED A. KNOPF | NEW YORK · MCMXXII

Single-fold sheet, 215 x 163mm., beige wove paper; 4pp.: p. 1: cover title; p. 2: blank; p. 3 [signed '4']: poem text; p. 4: blank. Text heading: '[orn. rule] | V E R S E | BY WILLA CATHER | [orn.] | "GRANDMITHER, THINK NOT I FORGET"'. Text consists of the first 2 stanzas (of 4) only. The typography is the same as that designed by Elmer Adler for the Knopf 1923 edition of *April Twilights and Other Poems* (A2.a). Commas following ll.8 and 17 in the 1923 edition are not present in this separate printing.

This has the appearance of a keepsake, but was printed as a promotional circular announcing *April Twilights and Other Poems* (1923) before publication.

Also listed as B19.(13).

A13.   A LOST LADY

a.i.)   First edition, first printing, 1923

TRADE ISSUE (State A)

[within a green decorative border rule] A LOST LADY | BY | WILLA CATHER | [green rule] | ". . . . . Come, my coach! | Good night, ladies; good night, sweet ladies; | Good night, good night." | [green rule] | [oval borzoi device flanked by four green orns.] | [green rule] | MCMXXIII | ALFRED · A · KNOPF | New York

Collation: [1-11]⁸; pp.[1-8] 9-173 [174-176] = 88 leaves.

Contents: P. 1: half title; p.2: 'Books by | *WILLA CATHER* |
[8 titles, including *ALL*]'; p.3: title page; p.4: 'COPYRIGHT,
1923, BY WILLA CATHER | *The first edition of* A LOST LADY
consists of | *twenty thousand two hundred and twenty copies as* |
follows: twenty on Borzoi all rag paper signed by | *the author and*
numbered A to T; two hundred | *copies on Borzoi all rag paper signed*
by the author | *and numbered 1 to 200; and twenty thousand* | *copies*
on English featherweight paper. | *Published September, 1923* | [below]
Set up and electrotyped by the Vail-Ballou Co., Binghamton, N. Y. |
Paper furnished by W. F. Etherington & Co., New York. |
Printed and bound by the Plimpton Press, Norwood, Mass. |
MANUFACTURED IN THE UNITED STATES OF
AMERICA'; p.5: dedication, '*For* | *Jan Hambourg*'; p.6: blank;
p.7: part title, 'PART | ONE'; p.8: blank; pp.9-100: text of
part 1; p.101: part title, 'PART | TWO'; p.102: blank;
pp.103-174: text of part 2; pp.175-176: blank.

Note: State A of the text (see note on textual states below) with
unaltered texts on pp.164, 171, 173 and 174. P.174, l.19 is
correctly printed 'of .

Paper: Cream wove. 190 x 127mm.; top edge trimmed and
stained dull red, other edges rough-cut. End papers of a
decorative lozenge-and-web pattern in pale green and mauve on
the facing side only; verso light gray.

Binding: Pale green (135) fine linen cloth, stamped in gilt
overall. Front: '[facsimile of WC holograph] A Lost Lady'.
Spine: 'A | *LOST* | *LADY* | [short wavy rule] | *Willa* | *Cather* |
[below] *Alfred A. Knopf* '. Back: rectangular Borzoi Books device
stamped in blind on the lower right corner.

Dust Jacket: Laid paper with heavy vertical chain lines 30mm.
apart. The lines are light green (144) on a paler green ground.
With 2 exceptions noted, lettering and decoration are black
overall. Front cover: '[within a decorative border rule] *A LOST*
LADY | *by* WILLA CATHER | *Author of* ONE OF OURS |
[yellow-brown (74): vignette of a tree-lined drive leading to a

large house in the distance, signed 'K' (Bernhardt Kleboe)] |
Publisher | ALFRED · A · KNOPF | *New York*'. Spine: '[orn.
rule] *A* | *LOST* | *LADY* | *by* | WILLA | CATHER | [orn.] |
[Borzoi Books device in yellow-brown (74)] | [orn.] | ALFRED
A | KNOPF | [orn. rule]'. Back cover: '[within a decorative
border rule] *A LOST LADY by* WILLA CATHER | [orn.] |
[22-line blurb] | ALFRED·A·KNOPF [Borzoi Books device]
PUBLISHER·N·Y'. Front inner flap: '*By the same Author* | ONE
OF OURS | [6-line announcement of the Pulitzer Prize for *One
of Ours*, followed by 32 lines of critical opinion by Dorothy
Canfield, N. P. Dawson, William Allen White, Llewellyn Jones,
Burton Rascoe, and Harry Hansen]'. Back inner flap: '*By the
same Author* | YOUTH AND | THE BRIGHT MEDUSA |
[orn.] | [12-line review excerpt from the *New York Times:* 15-
line review excerpt from the *Nation*]'.

Publication: 14 September 1923 in a first printing of 20,000
copies at $1.75. *ALL* was serialized before book publication in
Century 105, no.6 (April 1923); 106, 1 (May 1923); 106, no.2
(June 1923) [CCC2]. The first printing was ready at the Plimpton Press on 31 July 1923 (a month and a half before publication date), and 2 subsequent printings of 6,000 copies each were
ordered before 14 September. Knopf advertisements first appear
in *PW* on 4 August 1923 (p.416). In an 18 August (p.535)
advertisement, Knopf states that the first printing is "the largest
edition I have ever printed of any book, and I have already
ordered a second printing of 6000 copies." An advertisement on
1 September confirms that 32,000 copies were printed before
publication date.

Advance review copies are in paper wrappers duplicating the
front cover, spine, and back cover of the dust jacket. The advance review copies are also in state A of the text. The note on
textual states below suggests the hypothesis that states A and B
were both of the first printing. The numbers of each state are
not known.

TRADE ISSUE (State B)

Title, collation, contents, paper and dust jacket as in state A.
This is a mixed state of the first printing alterations in which

p.164 and 173 are reset (see note on textual states below). Two bindings are noted: the green cloth of state A and also tan linen cloth. Front cover: '[gilt] *WILLA CATHER* | [orange] *A LOST LADY* | [circular gilt orn.]'. Spine: '[gilt] *Willa* | *Cather* | [orange] *A* | *LOST* | *LADY* | [gilt short swash rule] | [below, gilt] *Alfred A. Knopf* '. Back cover: Borzoi Books square device stamped in blind at the lower right corner. This binding is in combination with end papers of a regular stylized marbled pattern in pale blue on a ground of orange-brown (54) on the facing side only, verso white.

The Canadian edition of 1,050 copies, published in September 1923, is also of state B. American sheets with altered title page imprint: 'TORONTO: THE MACMILLAN COMPANY OF | CANADA, LTD., AT ST. MARTIN'S HOUSE | 1923'. The limitation notice is removed from the copyright page. In the American state A trade issue binding with the Macmillan imprint on the spine, but without the Borzoi Books blind stamp on the back cover. Page 174.19, 'of'.

a.ii.)   Second printing. 6,000 copies, August 1923. State C of the text; a mixed state with pp.171 and 174 only reset and the error 'af' for 'of' on p.174.19. This printing is otherwise identical with the first.

LIMITED ISSUE (State D)

[title as in the trade issue]

Collation: [1]² [2-11]⁸ [12]⁶; pp.[1-8] 9-173 [174-176] = 88 leaves.

Contents: P.1: half title, 'A LOST LADY'; p.2: limitation notice, *'The first edition of* A LOST LADY *consists of* | *twenty thousand two hundred* . . . [as in the trade issue] . . . *featherweight paper.* | *This is Number* [space for hand-supplied letter or number in red ink] | [author's signature in blue ink]'; p.3: title page; p.4: 'COPYRIGHT, 1923, BY WILLA CATHER | MANUFACTURED IN THE UNITED STATES OF AMERICA'; pp.5-176: as in the trade issue.

Note: State D of the text (see note on textual states below) with alterations on pp. 164, 171, 173 and 174. The error 'af' for 'of' on p. 174.19.

Paper: Heavy cream laid with vertical chain lines 20mm. apart. Borzoi Books rectangular watermark '[within a single panel rule] BORZOI | [borzoi hound] | BOOKS'. 240 x 147mm., edges uncut. End papers of the same stock.

Binding: Light blue (182) laid paper over boards. Horizontal chain lines 28mm. apart. Watermark 'Ingres' in large script. Wheat-colored rough linen shelfback with a paper label of the same blue paper, 74 x 28mm., pasted on the spine, '[orn.] | A | LOST | LADY | [square dot] | *Willa* | *Cather* | [orn.]'. A duplicate label is tipped in on the final pastedown end paper. In a gray-blue linen-textured board box with the same label on the spine. The copy number is supplied in ink beneath the lettering.

Publication: 14 September 1923, printed at the Plimpton Press from plates set by Vail-Ballou in an edition of 220 copies: 20 lettered A-T, signed; 200 numbered 1-200, signed. $10.00. The text state, as described in the note below, indicates that the limited issue was not put into press until the first and second printings had been printed.

Locations: State A: CWB, InU, AHG, AAK. State B: FBA, CWB, RCT. State C: FBA, CWB, ViU. State D: CWB, InU, CtY, WCPM. State E: ViU.

Textual States in A LOST LADY

The chronology of textual states in the publishing history of the first 2 trade printings of *A Lost Lady* is extremely complex to determine. For the purpose of creating more space between words in passages too closely crammed (p. 164, l. 20; p. 171, ll. 18, 19; p. 173, ll. 7-23; p. 174, ll. 16-20), 4 pages in the last gathering were partially reset in 2 separate stop-press operations during the first and second printings. Until now, these changes have generally been thought to constitute points of differentia-

tion between the trade and limited issues only. In fact, 3 variant states of the text were effected before the limited issue was put into work at the Plimpton Press. Another confusion has been caused by the assumption that the misprint 'af' for 'of' (174.19) is the earliest state of the text because it occurs in the limited issue (though, curiously, not in advance review copies or the first trade printing); hence, the conclusion that the limited issue preceded the trade. The misprint persists through the tenth printing (May 1930). It was corrected in the eleventh printing (July 1931). A more logical conclusion, therefore, is that this error was introduced when ll. 16-20 of p. 174 were reset for the second printing.

The text changes occur on 2 conjugate leaf pages (164 and 173) of the outer form and 2 head-attached leaf pages (171 and 174) of the inner form. P. 173 is also the outer form recto of inner form p. 174 (verso). While major adjustment of lines was being made in the outer form plate on p. 173, a minor alteration was simultaneously made on p. 164. In the same manner, when major word-spacing changes were made on inner form p. 174, the appearance of p. 171 was also slightly improved by resetting 2 lines.

Chronology is determined in the apparatus provided below, which follows the progression of textual changes through the entire edition. The variants are designated states A, B, C, D, and E:

A: Advance review copies and first state of the first printing.

B: Mixed state of alterations in the first printing (also, the Canadian edition). Pp. 164 and 173 only are reset.

C: Second printing (mixed state). Pp. 171 and 174 only reset. The error 'af' for 'of' introduced on p. 174.

D: Limited issue (all above alterations effected) and all subsequent printings until 1930. Error 'af' for 'of' on p. 174.

E: Eleventh and following printings (July 1931). The error on p. 174 is corrected to 'of'.

164.20   (last word) sandal- (A, C)] san- (B, D, E)

171.18,19   (last words) clever/she (A, B)] and/as (C-E)

173.7-23   (last words) cranky/name. / met / a / car / and / had /
Brazilian / quarrel- / have / fine / along, / changed / deal /
down / I / re- (A, C)] rich, / his / me, / they / in / inquiries /
a / to / but / to / a / maid / hadn't / good / women / red, /
I (B, D, E)

173.11   ranch, (A, C)] ranch, (B, D, E)

174.16-20   Day. / old / of / *late* / *Collins.'"* (A, B)] Decoration / letter /

(last words)   the / *mem-* / *Collins.'"* (C-E)

174.19   of (A, B, E)] af (C, D)

If this chronology is correct, alterations were made first on the
outer form pp. 164 and 173, for which an overrun of the first
state had probably already been printed. When alterations were
made in the inner form pp. 171 and 174, some of the first state
sheets of the outer form were put through the press in combination with the corrected inner form, and, conversely, the new
outer form was combined with sheets already printed of the old
inner form; hence, the mixed states of B and C. The first
alteration seems to have occurred at some time during the first
printing run, and the second for the second printing. The first
and second printings are not identified on the copyright page. It
was not until the third printing (September 1923) that the
statement '*First and second printings before publication*' appeared on
the copyright. For this reason, priority of state B over state C
cannot be definitely affirmed, and it is also possible that copies
of the second printing exist in the same state (D) as the limited
issue.

a.iii.)   Third printing. 6,000 copies, September 1923. Copyright:
'*First and second printings before publication* | *Published September,
1923* | *Third Printing, September, 1923*'. State D of the text. Tan
linen cloth like first printing, state B. Presswork through 1963
by the Plimpton Press.

a.iv.)   Fourth printing. 6,000 copies, November 1923.

a.v.)   Fifth printing. 6,000 copies, November 1923. State D. Tan
linen binding like first printing, state B.

a.vi.)   Sixth printing. 6,000 copies, December 1923. A cheap ($0.75)
Grosset & Dunlap edition, with the sixth printing copyright
notice, was published in February 1925 with a new title page:
'[within a thick-thin border rule] A LOST LADY| BY | WILLA
CATHER | AUTHOR OF | ONE OF OURS, ETC. | [quotation
in italics] | ILLUSTRATED WITH SCENES | FROM THE
PHOTOPLAY | A WARNER BROS'. SCREEN CLASSIC |
[orn.] | GROSSET & DUNLAP | PUBLISHERS NEW YORK |
[beneath the border rule:] Made in the United States of
America'. State D.

The book is illustrated with 6 inserted photographs on coated
paper. These are still shots from the 1925 Warner Brothers film.
The Grosset & Dunlap volume was a spin-off from Knopf's sale
of the movie rights to *ALL* in early 1924 for $12,000. WC's
disenchantment with this film and a second unauthorized version in 1934 precipitated her lifelong determination to prevent
further adaptation of her works to theater, film, or radio. She
was adamant in her refusal of many offers—among them, one
from Orson Welles, who wanted to produce a radio adaptation
of *My Ántonia* for his Mercury Theater. (See II-2.)

a.vii.)   Seventh printing. 1,000 copies, August 1924.

a.viii.)   Eighth printing. 500 copies, August 1926.

a.ix.)   Ninth printing. 1,000 copies, November 1927.

a.x.)   Tenth printing. 1,000 copies, May 1930.

a.xi.)   Eleventh printing. 1,000 copies, September 1931. Text state E
with 'af' corrected to 'of' on p.174.19. In the Knopf production
record is a notation for this printing, "correction in text."

a.xii.)   Twelfth printing. 1,000 copies, September 1932.

a.xiii.)   Thirteenth printing. 1,000 copies, October 1934.

a.xiv.)   Fourteenth printing. 1,000 copies, August 1936.

a.xv.) Fifteenth printing. 1,430 sets of sheets printed in January 1939, of which 250 were bound in January 1939, 350 in January 1940, 500 in February 1941, and 303 in September 1942.

a.xvi.) Sixteenth printing. 1,500 copies, January 1943.

a.xvii.) Seventeenth printing. 1,500 copies, September 1944. The dedication to Jan Hambourg was removed from this and subsequent printings.

a.xviii.) Eighteenth printing. 2,000 copies, August 1945.

a.xix.) Nineteenth printing. 2,000 copies, December 1949.

a.xx.) Twentieth printing. 2,000 copies, October 1952.

a.xxi.) Twenty-first printing. 2,500 copies, May 1956.

a.xxii.) Twenty-second printing. 2,500 copies, February 1958.

a.xxiii.) Twenty-third printing. 3,300 copies, April 1961

a.xxiv.) Twenty-fourth printing. 3,000 copies, December 1963.

a.xxv.) Twenty-fifth printing (Random House Vintage Books [V-705]). 7,500 copies, May 1972. Photo-offset presswork by American Book-Stratford Press. Design and cover artwork by Guy Fleming. $1.95.

b.) Second edition (Autograph Edition, vol.7), 1938

[dec. rule] | WILLA CATHER | [dec. rule] | A Lost Lady | [dec. rule] | '. . . . . *Come, my coach!* | *Goodnight, ladies; good-night, sweet ladies,* | *Good-night, good-night.'* | [brown-orange: 'H M Co' cipher] | BOSTON | HOUGHTON MIFFLIN COMPANY | 1938

Collation: [1-10]^8 [11]^{10}; pp.[i-iv, 1-2] 3-172 [173-176]= 90 leaves.

Illustration: Portrait photograph of WC, captioned '*Willa Cather* | FROM A PHOTOGRAPH BY NICHOLAS MURAY, 1924'. On heavy wove paper, inserted facing the title page with a protective tissue.

Contents: P.i: edition title; p.ii: limitation notice; p.iii: title page; p.iv: copyright notice; p.1: part title, 'PART ONE'; p.2: blank; pp.3-95: text of part 1; p.96: blank; p.97: part title, 'PART TWO'; p.98: blank; pp.99-173: text of part 2; p.174: blank; p.175: Riverside Press device; p.176: blank.

Notes on paper, binding, dust jacket, and publication are with the entry for the entire Autograph Edition (AA1).

c.)   Third edition (First Centennial Edition), 1973

[dark red (16)] A Lost | Lady | [black] WILLA CATHER | [within thick-thin red oval rules: borzoi orn. in black on a red oval] | [black] *New York:* Alfred · A · Knopf | [swelling red rule] | [black] 1973

Collation: [1-6]^{16}; pp.[i-x, 1-2] 3-177 [178-182]=96 leaves.

Contents: P.i: blank; p.ii: '[swelling rule] | THE WORKS OF Willa Cather | [18 titles listed with publication dates]'; p.iii: half title; p.iv: blank; p.v: title page; p.vi: '[swelling rule] THIS IS A BORZOI BOOK | PUBLISHED BY ALFRED A. KNOPF, INC. | [swelling rule] | Copyright 1923 by Willa Cather. | Copyright renewed 1951 by the executors of the estate of | Willa Cather | [5-line reserved rights notice] | [5-line Library of Congress publication data] | First Knopf Edition published September 14, 1923. | Reprinted twenty-six times. | First Centennial Edition, September 1973. | Manufactured in the United States of America'; p.vii: epigraph, '[swelling rule] | ". . . . . Come, my coach! | Good night, ladies; good night, sweet ladies, | Good night, good night."'; p.viii: blank; p.ix: '[swelling rule] | [dark red] 1873 ['W C' in white on a dark red oval within black thick-thin rules] 1973 | [black] IT HAS SEEMED to me . . . [8-line statement above the facsimile signature of Alfred A. Knopf]'; p.x: blank; p.1 part title,

'[swelling rule] | Part One'; p.2: blank; pp.3-97: text of part 1;
p.98: blank; p.99: part title, '[swelling rule] Part Two'; p.100:
blank; pp.101-177: text of part 2; p.178: blank; p.179:
'[swelling rule] | A *Note on the Type* | [13-line note in roman] |
The book was composed, printed, and bound by | Kingsport
Press, Inc., Kingsport, Tennessee. | *Typography and binding
design by* | WARREN [logogram of W. Chappell] CHAPPELL';
p.180: blank.

Note: The 'Note on the Type' on p.179 identifies the type as
Janson, set on the Linotype; a recutting made direct from type
cast from matrices made by Nicholas Kis (1650-1702).

Paper: Cream laid stock with vertical chain lines 22mm. apart.
No watermark. 208x131mm.; top edge trimmed and stained
yellow-green (115), other edges trimmed. End papers of heavy
deep yellow (85) laid stock with vertical chain lines 20mm.
apart, watermarked 'TW'.

Binding: Rough light beige cloth; deep brown (56) shelf-
back. Front cover: '[lettering in very dark brown] WILLA |
CATHER | [bright red swelling rule] | MDCCC | LXXIII'.
Spine: '[bright red flower orn.] | [gilt perpendicular lettering,
top to bottom, within a bright red single-rule panel] A LOST
LADY [bright red dot] Willa Cather | [bright red flower orn.] |
[gilt] Knopf'. Back cover: Borzoi Books device stamped in blind
on the lower right corner.

Dust Jacket: Ground of heavy wove cream stock, faced with an
overground of bright yellow-green (115) with a regular pattern
of initials 'WC' in black alternating with red floral ornaments.
Front cover: at center, a cream panel in a thick red (12) rule
frame, 'A | LOST | LADY | [red swelling rule] | Willa | Cather'.
Spine: '[within a single red rule on a black panel, perpendicular
lettering in white] A LOST LADY [red dot] Willa Cather |
[horizontal white lettering] Knopf | [beneath the panel, a
circular Borzoi Books device in white on black with red letter-
ing]'. Back cover: patterned yellow-green overground. On the
lower left corner, perpendicular lettering, 'PRINTED IN
U. S. A.' On the lower right corner, '394-48558-0'. Front inner
flap: '$7.50 | [32-line blurb] | *Complete centennial edition* | *designed*

by Warren Chappell'. Back inner flap: '[within 2 red single rules: the Steichen portrait photograph of WC] | [18-line blurb] | [borzoi hound in bright green] | Alfred A. Knopf, *Publisher, New York* | 8/73'. In a bright green (115) paper-over-board box; top and bottom of red (12) paper. Front cover: '[within a red line rule on a black panel, lettering in white] A LOST | LADY | [rule of 12 floral orns. in red] | Willa Cather'. Spine: '[on a black panel, within a red rule, printed in red] 1873 | 1973 | [white] A | LOST | LADY | [rule of 3 floral orns. in red] | Willa | Cather | [red] KNOPF | [red rule]'. Back cover: as the front cover.

Publication: 24 September 1973 at $7.50. Distributed by Random House. Alfred A. Knopf's complete statement on p.ix: 'It has seemed to me for a long time that *A Lost Lady* deserved a better dress than we gave it on its first appearance half a century ago and that no one was so suited as Warren Chappell to design in its entirety the book which you now hold in your hands and which is our small contribution to the celebration of the centennial of Willa Cather's birth.' Warren Chappell, the noted calligrapher, illustrator, and typographer, designed 125 volumes for Knopf from 1940 to the present.

English Editions

A13.a.i.(e)   First English edition, 1924

A Lost Lady | *by* | WILLA CATHER | [orn.] | ". . . . . . .
. . . . . Come, my coach! | Good night, ladies; good night, sweet ladies, | Good night, good night." | [orn.] | London | WILLIAM HEINEMANN | 1924

Collation: [A]⁴ B-L⁸ M⁴; pp.[i-viii], 1 [2] 3-166 [167-168] = 88 leaves.

Contents: Pp.i-ii: blank; p.iii: half title 'A | *Lost Lady* | [orn.]'; p.iv: 'RECENT FICTION | [9 titles] | WILLIAM HEINEMANN, LTD.'; p.v: title page; p.vi: 'First published 1924 | Printed in Great Britain by R. & R. CLARK, LIMITED, Edinburgh.'; p.vii: dedication 'for | JAN HAMBOURG | [orn.]'; p.viii: blank; p.1: part title, 'Part One'; p.2: blank; pp.

3-94: text of part 1; p.95: part title 'Part Two'; p.96: blank; pp.97-167: text of part 2; p.168: blank.

Paper: Cheap wove stock; 182 x 106mm., edges trimmed. End papers of light tan wove stock.

Binding: Dull light green linen cloth, lettering in dark green. Front cover: '[within a triple border rule with triple fleurs-de-lys at the corners] A Lost Lady | by | Willa Cather | [orn.]'. Spine: '[within a double border rule with single fleur-de-lys at corners] A | Lost | Lady | by | Willa | Cather | [orn.] | Heinemann'.

Dust Jacket: Not seen.

Publication: Printed in England in a new setting; published in August 1924, a month before the English edition of *April Twilights and Other Poems* (A2.*a.i.*[e]).

a.ii.(e)   Second English 'edition'. London: Heinemann Windmill edition, 1928. Photographically set from the first English edition plates. 3s.6d. Available in print until 1936.

b.i.(e)   Third English edition. London: Hamish Hamilton, 1961. Photo offset from the American plates. Introduction by J. B. Priestley.

c.i.(e)   Fourth English edition. London: Virago Modern Classics, 1980. New introduction by A. S. Byatt.

Not seen. The publisher's catalogue: 'February 1980 | Fiction | 192 pp | Paperback 126 2 | £2.50 Not for sale in the USA or Canada'.

A14.   THE PROFESSOR'S HOUSE

a.i.)   First edition, first printing, 1925

LIMITED ISSUE

[within an orn. blue (179) border] THE | PROFESSOR'S | HOUSE | by | WILLA CATHER | "A turquoise set in silver, | wasn't it? . . Yes, a turquoise | set in dull silver." | —LOUIE

MARSELLUS | ALFRED · A · KNOPF | *New York* [borzoi device in blue (179)] *mcmxxv*

Collation: [1-18]⁸; pp.[i-ii, 1-10] 11-283 [284-286]= 144 leaves.

Contents: P.i: blank; p.ii: limitation notice, 'THE FIRST EDITION OF "THE PROFESSOR'S | HOUSE" CONSISTS OF TWO HUNDRED | TWENTY FIVE COPIES, SIGNED BY THE | AUTHOR, AS FOLLOWS: FORTY ON IMPERIAL JAPAN VELLUM (OF WHICH FIVE | ARE NOT FOR SALE) NUMBERED FROM I | TO 40; AND ONE HUNDRED EIGHTY FIVE | COPIES (OF WHICH TEN ARE NOT FOR | SALE) NUMBERED 41 TO 225. | THIS BOOK IS NUMBER | [space for hand-supplied number in ink] | [author's holograph signature]'; p.1: half title, 'THE PROFESSOR'S | HOUSE'; p.2: '[within the orn. blue border as on title page] BOOKS BY | Willa Cather | [orn.] | ALEXANDER'S BRIDGE | O PIONEERS! | THE SONG OF THE LARK | MY ÁNTONIA | YOUTH AND THE BRIGHT MEDUSA | ONE OF OURS | APRIL TWILIGHTS and other verses | A LOST LADY | THE PROFESSOR'S HOUSE'; p.3: title page; p.4: 'COPYRIGHT, 1925, BY WILLA CATHER | MANUFACTURED IN THE UNITED STATES OF AMERICA'; p.5: dedication, '*For Jan, because he likes narrative*'; p.6: blank; p.7: contents; p.8: blank; p.9: part title, 'BOOK ONE | THE FAMILY'; p.10: blank; pp.11-176: text of book 1; p.177: part title, 'BOOK TWO | TOM OUTLAND'S STORY'; p.178: blank; pp.179-253: text of book 2; p.254: blank; p.255: part title, 'BOOK THREE | THE PROFESSOR'; p.256: blank; p.257-283: text of book 3; p.284: 'A NOTE ON THE TYPE IN | WHICH THIS BOOK IS SET | [12 lines in italic] | [borzoi oval device] | [10-line printer and binder's note in small caps]'; pp.285-286: blank.

Note: According to the information on p.284 ('A NOTE ON THE TYPE . . .'), the book is set in Caslon Old Face; was set up and electrotyped by the Vail-Ballou Press, Binghamton, New York; and was printed and bound by the Plimpton Press, Norwood, Massachusetts.

Paper: The paper of the 185 copies is Esparto, manufactured in Scotland for W. F. Etherington & Co., New York. Heavy cream laid with vertical chain lines 20mm. apart. 234×150mm., edges uncut. Watermark with the rectangular Borzoi Books device. End papers of the same stock.

The paper of the 40 copies is Imperial Japan vellum; wove, unwatermarked. 230×147mm.; top edge trimmed and gilt, other edges uncut. End papers of the same stock.

Bindings: Laid paper with horizontal chain lines 27mm. apart over boards on the 185 copies. Paper decorated with an over-all pattern of flowers and leaves in pink, light green and blue-green; pale sand-yellow ground. Dull yellow-green (136) coarse linen shelfback with a pink (262) printed paper label, 61×31mm., on the upper spine, '|| THE | PROFESSOR'S | HOUSE | *by* | *Willa* | *Cather* || FIRST EDITION ||'. In a board box covered with light gray-brown laid paper with horizontal chain lines 28mm. apart; the same pink spine label on the back with copy number supplied in ink beneath. A duplicate spine label is tipped in on the final pastedown end paper.

The 40 copies are bound in heavy cream vellum over boards. Front cover: thick-thin border rules with corner and center decoration gilt-stamped. Spine: '[gilt] *THE* | *PROFESSOR'S* | *HOUSE* | [short wavy dash] | *Willa Cather* | [orn.] | ALFRED A KNOPF'. Back cover: rectangular Borzoi Books device stamped in gilt at the lower right corner.

Publication: Published 4 September at $10.00 for the 185 (10 not for sale) on laid paper and $25.00 for the 40 (5 not for sale) on Japan vellum. The limited edition was advertised by Knopf only in the first *PW* ad for *The Professor's House* (18 July 1925, p.152).

TRADE ISSUE

[title as in the limited issue]

Collation: [1-18]⁸; pp.[1-10] 11-283 [284-288]= 144 leaves.

Contents: P.1: half title, 'THE PROFESSOR'S | HOUSE';
p.2: advt. as in the limited issue; p.3: title page;
p.4: 'COPYRIGHT, 1925, BY WILLA CATHER |
MANUFACTURED IN THE UNITED STATES OF
AMERICA'; pp.5-284: as in the limited issue; pp.285-288:
blank.

Paper: Cream wove. 191 x 127mm.; top edge trimmed and
stained red-orange, other edges rough-cut. End papers of the
same stock.

Note: The trade issue, on different paper, nevertheless has the
same note at p.284, stating that the book is on 'Esparto paper
manufactured in Scotland and furnished by W. F. Etherington &
Co., New York.' The paper of the trade issue is of a common
wove type. The 'Esparto' paper refers only to that used for the
limited issue.

Binding: Orange (35) fine linen cloth; purple-blue (196) fine
linen cloth shelfback. Front cover blank. Spine: '[gilt-stamped]
Willa | Cather | THE | PROFESSOR'S | HOUSE | [short wavy
rule]'. Back cover: the Borzoi Books device stamped in blind on
the lower right corner.

Dust Jacket: White wove coated paper; lettering in dark blue
(179) except as noted. Front cover: 'The | Professor's | House |
[88 x 85mm. illus. panel of a mountain cave delineated in dark
blue (179), two Indian pots in foreground; facing across a
wooded canyon to a pueblo in the distance. Distant cliffs in
orange (52), pueblo shadowing in purple (222), foliage in green
(118)] | Willa Cather'. Spine: 'The | Professor's | House | [arrow
orn.] | Willa | Cather | [orange (52) Borzoi Books device] |
Alfred A. Knopf'. Back cover: '[within a green fine leaf design
border rule] [orange (52)] THE | PROFESSOR'S | HOUSE |
[dark blue (179)] BY WILLA CATHER | AUTHOR OF ONE OF
OURS AND A LOST LADY | [19-line blurb] | *Alfred A. Knopf*
[orange (52) Borzoi Books device] *Publisher, N. Y.*' Front inner
flap: '*By the same author* | [purple (222)] ONE OF OURS | [blue
(179): 6-line notice of the Pulitzer Prize; 4 excerpts from critical
reviews by Dorothy Canfield, Llewellyn Jones, Burton Rascoe,
and Harry Hansen] | [purple (222)] YOUTH AND | THE

BRIGHT MEDUSA | [blue (179): 13-line review excerpt from the *Nation*]'. Back inner flap: 'By the same author | [purple (222)] A LOST LADY | [blue (179): 4 excerpts from reviews by Henry Seidel Canby, Joseph Wood Krutch, Zoë Akins, and Harry Hansen]'.

Publication: 4 September 1925 in a first printing of 20,000 copies at $2.00. Plates set by Vail-Ballou; printing by the Plimpton Press. Knopf announced that the first printing was sold out 3 weeks before publication date. Shipments started on 7 August (*PW* advt., 18 July 1925, p.152). By late October, the book was "already in its 55th thousand and more copies have been sold than have ever been sold in a similar period—ten weeks—of any book by Willa Cather" (*PW* advt., 31 October 1925).

PH was serialized before book publication in 9 weekly installments of *Collier's* (23 June to 5 August 1925) [CCC 3].

Advance review copies are in paper wrappers identical to the dust jacket.

Canadian edition: September 1925. American sheets of the first printing with altered title page imprint beneath (rather than above, as in the American title page) the publisher's device: 'TORONTO: THE MACMILLAN COMPANY OF | CANADA, LTD., AT ST. MARTIN'S HOUSE | MCMXXV'. Copyright notice removed; at the foot of the copyright page, 'MANUFACTURED IN THE UNITED STATES OF AMERICA'. American trade issue binding with Macmillan spine imprint and lacking the blind-stamp device on the back cover.

a.ii.)   Second printing. 10,000 copies, August 1925. Copyright: 'FIRST AND SECOND PRINTINGS BEFORE PUBLICATION'. Tan linen cloth binding like the trade issue of *One of Ours*. Presswork for all printings until the thirteenth (December 1963) was by the Plimpton Press.

a.iii.) Third printing. 5,000 copies, September 1925. Copyright: 'THIRD PRINTING, SEPTEMBER, 1925'.

a.iv.)   Fourth printing. 5,000 copies, September 1925. Copyright: 'FOURTH PRINTING, SEPTEMBER, 1925'.

a.v.)   Fifth printing. 10,000 copies, 'FIFTH PRINTING, OCTOBER, 1925'.

a.vi.)   Sixth printing. 5,000 copies, '. . . SIXTH PRINTING, OCTOBER, 1925'. Of these, 2,500 were specially bound as a "holiday gift edition" in "Brilliant green and blue cloth backs stamped in gold and orange Borzoi Batik sides in a handsome slip case with a gay label, $2.50" (*PW* Knopf advt., 31 October 1925).

a.vii.)   Seventh printing. 5,000 copies, 'SEVENTH PRINTING, NOVEMBER, 1925'.

a.viii.)   Eighth printing. 5,000 copies, '. . . EIGHTH PRINTING, DECEMBER, 1925'. Of these, 2,383 were bound on 22 December 1925 and 2,056 on 1 January 1926. Two hundred eighty sets of the sheets were bound in August 1940 (publisher's production file note: "green cloth; labels—uniform with *Death Comes* 8/21/40"; order duplicated 5/18/42) and 280 in May 1942. Of the 2,383 bound in December, copies seen are in tan linen cloth binding.

A cheap Grosset & Dunlap edition ($1.00) was published in September 1927, offset from the original Vail-Ballou plates with altered title page imprint: 'NEW YORK | GROSSET & DUNLAP | PUBLISHERS | By Arrangement with Alfred A. Knopf'. The copyright notice is for the eighth printing, and the note on type is removed from p.284.

a.ix.)   Ninth printing. 785 copies, October 1942. Textual corrections were made in this printing which required resetting 2 pages and making 6 other alterations:

40.26-27   bulkheaded vacuum] Outland engine
40.27-29   *resetting of same text*
41.1-4   *resetting of same text*
41.7   vacuum] engine
41.25   vacuum] engine
115.22   moved] mover

135.19   vacuum] patent
147.8   vacuum] patent

a.x.)   Tenth printing. 1,500 copies, January 1949. The dedication to Jan Hambourg was removed from this and subsequent printings.

a.xi.)   Eleventh printing. 2,000 copies, March 1953.

a.xii.)   Twelfth printing. 3,000 copies, May 1959.

a.xiii.)   Thirteenth printing. 2,500 copies, December 1963.

a.xiv.)   Fourteenth printing. 2,487 copies, March 1967. Presswork (a.xiv-xvii): H. Wolff.

a.xv.)   Fifteenth printing. 1,911 copies, September 1969.

a.xvi.)   Sixteenth printing. 1,505 copies, December 1970.

a.xvii.)   Seventeenth printing. 1,021 copies, August 1973.

a.xvii.)   Eighteenth printing (Random House Vintage Books [V-913]). First Vintage printing of 5,000 copies, May 1973. Photo-offset presswork by American Book-Stratford Press. $2.45.

b.i.)   Second edition (Autograph Edition, vol. 8), 1938

[dec. rule] | WILLA CATHER | [dec. rule] | The Professor's House | [dec. rule] | 'A turquoise set in silver, wasn't it?' | . . . Yes, a turquoise set in dull silver.' | LOUIE MARSELLUS | [brown-orange: 'HM Co' cipher] | BOSTON | HOUGHTON MIFFLIN COMPANY | 1938

Collation: [1-17]^8 [18]^{10}; pp. [i-viii, 1-2] 3-280 [281-284] = 146 leaves.

Illustration: On text paper, inserted facing the title page with a protective tissue. Caption: *'Reduced facsimile of page I of the original manuscript of "The Professor's House"'*.

Contents: P.i: edition title; p.ii: limitation notice; p.iii: title page; p.iv: copyright; p.v: dedication '*For Jan because he likes narrative*'; p.vi: blank; p.vii: contents; p.viii: blank; p.1: part title, 'BOOK ONE | The Family'; p.2: blank; pp.3-172: text of book 1; p.173: part title, 'BOOK TWO | Tom Outland's Story'; p.174: blank; pp.175-252: text of book 2; p.253: part title, 'BOOK THREE | The Professor'; p.254: blank; pp.255-281: text of book 3; p.282: blank; p.283: Riverside Press device; p.284: blank.

Notes on paper, binding, dust jacket, and publication with the entry for the entire Autograph Edition (AA1).

English Editions

A14.a.i.(e)   First English edition, 1925

THE PROFESSOR'S | HOUSE | *by* | WILLA CATHER | [Heinemann windmill device] | LONDON | WILLIAM HEINEMANN LTD.

Collation: [A]⁸ B-S⁸; pp.[i-viii, 1-2] 3-275 [276-280] = 144 leaves.

Contents: Pp.i-ii: blank; p.iii: half title, 'THE PROFESSOR'S HOUSE'; p.iv: 'New and Recent Fiction || [8 titles] || LONDON | WILLIAM HEINEMANN LTD.'; p.v: title page; p.vi: '*First published in 1925* | PRINTED IN GREAT BRITAIN BY | THE LONDON AND NORWICH PRESS, LIMITED, ST. GILES' WORKS, NORWICH'; p.vii: contents; p.viii: blank; p.1: part title, 'BOOK ONE | THE FAMILY'; p.2: blank; pp.3-168: text of book 1; p.169: part title, 'BOOK TWO | TOM OUTLAND'S STORY'; p.170: blank; pp.171-245: text of book 2; p.246: blank; p.247: part title, 'BOOK THREE | THE PROFESSOR'; p.248: blank; pp.249-275: text of book 3 (at the foot of p.275: '[short rule] | THE LONDON AND NORWICH PRESS, LIMITED, ST. GILES' WORKS, NORWICH.'); pp.276-280: blank.

Note: Pp. 277-280 are used as the terminal open and pastedown end papers. They are integral with the final gathering.

Paper: White laid, vertical chain lines 25mm. apart. 186x122mm.; top and fore edges trimmed, bottom edge rough-cut. Front end papers of heavier wove stock; terminal end papers of text stock.

Binding: Light brown (80) linen cloth. Front cover blank. Spine: '[gilt-stamped] [orn. panel rule] | THE | PROFESSOR'S | HOUSE | WILLA | CATHER | HEINEMANN | [orn. panel rule]'. Back cover has the blind-stamped Heinemann windmill device at the lower right corner.

Dust Jacket: Not seen.

Publication: Printed in England and published in November 1925. 7s.6d. Reviewed in *TLS* on 19 November 1925 (p.779).

On page 250, l.2: 'baritone' ('barytone' in the American edition, p.258, l.1).

b.i.(e)   Second English edition. London: Hamish Hamilton, 1961. Photo-offset from the first American edition (1925) plates. Introduction by J. B. Priestley. Printed in London by Lowe and Brydone. Available in print until 1973.

A15.   MY MORTAL ENEMY

a.i.)   First edition, first printing (limited), 1926

MY | MORTAL ENEMY | WILLA CATHER | [oval borzoi device set in green geometric frame] | ALFRED A. KNOPF | NEW YORK | 1926

Collation: [1-17]^4; pp.[1-7] 8-132 [133-136]= 68 leaves.

Illustration: 13 line illustrations on panels in varying pastel colors by W. A. Dwiggins, placed at the head of each chapter at pp.7, 17, 30, 44, 51, 65, 75, 89, 99, 107, 115, 123 and 129. Pagination is contained in decorative panels at the top of each page.

Contents: P. 1: half title, 'MY | MORTAL ENEMY'; p. 2: blank;
p. 3: title page; p. 4: *'Printed in the United States of America |
Copyright 1926 · Alfred A. Knopf, Inc.'*; p. 5: part title, 'PART I';
p. 6: blank; pp. 7-71: text of part 1; p. 72: blank; p. 73: part
title, 'PART II'; p. 74: blank; pp. 75-132: text of part 2; p. 133:
blank; p. 134: limitation notice, '[square black-outline vignette
of Pegasus and Hermes on a larger panel of pale yellow] | THE
FIRST EDITION OF | MY MORTAL ENEMY | CONSISTS
OF TWO HUNDRED AND | TWENTY COPIES, OF
WHICH TWENTY | ARE NOT FOR SALE | THE FORMAT
AND DESIGNS WERE | MADE BY W. A. DWIGGINS |
AND THE BOOKS WERE MADE BY | THE PYNSON
PRINTERS OF NEW YORK | EACH COPY IS SIGNED BY
THE AUTHOR | THIS BEING NUMBER [space for hand-
supplied number] | [author's holograph signature]';
pp. 135-136: blank.

Paper: Heavy white wove stock. 233 x 162mm.; edges uncut.
End papers of the same stock.

Binding: Black paper over boards. Paper with a regular pattern
of dull gold squares and silver dots on the diagonal. A variant
black paper with silver-leaved gold roses has been noted. Cream
buckram shelfback with white paper label (78 x 21mm.) pasted
at the top of the spine, '[thick-thin bright green rules] | MY |
MORTAL | ENEMY | CATHER | [green stylized flower orn.]'.
In a board box covered with black wove paper.

Publication: 20 October 1926; 220 copies (20 not for sale) at
$15.00.

a.ii.)   Second printing (trade)

[title as in the limited printing with yellow rather than green
ornamental geometric frame around the borzoi device]

Collation: [1-8]⁸; pp.[1-9] 10-122 [123-128]= 64 leaves.

Illustration: 13 line illustrations on pale yellow panels, by
W. A. Dwiggins, at the head of each chapter at pp. 9, 18, 29,
42, 49, 62, 71, 84, 93, 100, 107, 114 and 119. Pagination,

varying from the limited printing, is contained in decorative
yellow panels at the top of each page.

Contents: Pp.1-2: blank; p.3: half title; p.4: blank; p.5: title
page; p.6: copyright as in A15.a.i.; p.7: part 1 part title; p.8:
blank; pp.9-68: text of part 1; p.69: part 2 part title; p.70:
blank; pp.71-122: text of part 2; p.123: blank; p.124: '*This
book is set in a type called Scotch*. . . . [8-line note in large italic
on the type] | THE FORMAT, . . . [6-line note in small italic
on the format]'; pp.125-128: blank.

Note: Type identified as 'Scotch' on p.124, which also states that
the book was manufactured under the supervision of the Pynson
Printers of New York; presswork and binding by the Plimpton
Press, paper made by the H.C. Chalfant Mill, decorations and
illustrations by W.A. Dwiggins.

Paper: Heavy cream wove. 208 x 127mm.; top edge trimmed,
other edges rough-cut. End papers of the same stock.

Binding: Pale yellow-green (104) paper over boards, black cloth
shelfback. Front cover (printed in light blue-green): '[within a
dec. floriated rhombus panel, in a rectangular thick-line frame]
MY | MORTAL ENEMY | WILLA CATHER'. Spine (stamped
in gilt): '[thick-thin rule] | [lettered from top to bottom] MY
MORTAL ENEMY || *CATHER* | [thin-thick rule] || [horizontal
lettering] ALFRED A. | KNOPF'. Back cover blank. In a paper
covered box. The paper is very light green-blue (greener than
171); lettering is black overall, decoration is yellow-orange (69).
Front cover: duplicates the front cover of the book. Box spine:
'MY | MORTAL | ENEMY | [dec. panel extending 156mm.
down the spine] | ALFRED A KNOPF | NEW YORK'. Back
cover: '[within a dec. border rule, a single black line-rule] MY
MORTAL ENEMY | BY WILLA CATHER | [16-line blurb] |
Publisher ALFRED A KNOPF New York'.

Dust Jacket: Very light gray-green (154) wove paper. Front
cover, spine, and back cover repeat the lettering, decoration,
and printed colors of the binding. Front inner flap: 'Also by
Willa Cather | ONE OF OURS | [6 lines in italic announcing
the Pulitzer Prize award to WC; beneath, review excerpts from

Dorothy Canfield and Harry Hansen and a review excerpt of
YBM from the *Nation*]'. Back inner flap: 'Also by Willa
Cather | THE | PROFESSOR'S HOUSE | *Stuart P. Sherman
says:* | [12-line review excerpt] | A LOST LADY | *Henry Seidel
Canby, in|* the *Literary Review:* | [8-line review excerpt] |
ALFRED · A · KNOPF | PUBLISHER | NEW YORK |
[yellow-orange Borzoi Books device]'.

Publication: 20 October 1926 in a printing of 10,000 copies.
$2.50. Knopf announced 'First, second and third printings
before publication' with the 'fourth' (actually, the fifth printing
in November 1926 and 5 (that is, 6) printings by the end of the
year. A *PW* Knopf advertisement on 2 October 1926 notes a
change in publication date. Advance review copies carry a notice
of publication for 15 October. A copy inscribed by WC to
Isabelle McClung (CWB 700651) is dated 6 October.

Though set from the plates of the limited printing, the trade
printing is in a different collational format with differing
pagination; hence, a new printing.

Advance review copies are in paper wrappers identical to the
dust jacket, but with added front cover lettering: 'THE NEW
NOVEL *by* | *America's* | *Greatest* | *Woman* | *Author* | *Publisher* |
ALFRED · A · KNOPF NEW YORK'. A notice slip tipped in
on the front cover is dated 15 October.

The available Knopf production records for *MME* were
incomplete. Information on the subsequent printings is,
therefore, lacking for the seventh and tenth printings.

Canadian edition: Published in Canada in October 1926. The
American sheets with altered title page imprint, 'THE
MACMILLIAN CO. OF CANADA, LTD. | AT ST. MARTIN'S
HOUSE | TORONTO · 1926'. Copyright as in the American
edition. Binding as on the American trade edition with the
publisher's name removed from the spine, but not replaced with
the Macmillan name. Dust jacket as on the American trade
edition; the Macmillan name at the foot of the spine replacing
Knopf's, but the Knopf imprint on the back inner flap.

a.iii.)   Third printing. October 1926. Copyright: *'First and Second printing before publication'*. Presswork (a.iii-xi.): the Plimpton Press.

a.iv.)   Fourth printing. October 1926. Copyright: *'First, Second and Third printing before publication'*.

a.v.)   Fifth printing. November 1926. Copyright: *'First, Second and Third printings before publication | Published October, 1926 | Fourth Printing November, 1926'*.

a.vi.)   Sixth printing. December 1926.

a.vii.)   Seventh printing.

a.viii.)   Eighth printing. 1,140 copies, April 1950.

a.ix.)   Ninth printing. 1,690 copies, October 1957.

a.x.)   Tenth printing.

a.xi.)   Eleventh printing. 1,810 copies, January 1967.

b.)   Second edition (with *Lucy Gayheart;* Autograph Edition, vol. 11), 1938

[dec. rule] | WILLA CATHER | [dec. rule] | Lucy Gayheart | & | My Mortal Enemy | [dec. rule] | [brown-orange: 'HMCo' cipher] | BOSTON | HOUGHTON MIFFLIN COMPANY | 1938

Collation: [21]⁸; pp.[i-iv, 1-2] 3-328 [329-332]= 168 leaves.

Illustration: On text paper, inserted facing the title page with a protective tissue. Caption: *'Reduced facsimile of a page of the original manuscript of "Lucy Gayheart"'*.

Contents: P.i: edition title; p.ii: limitation notice; p.iii: title page; p.iv: copyright; pp.1-234: *Lucy Gayheart;* p.235: part title, 'My Mortal Enemy | PART I'; p.236: blank; pp.237-283: text of part 1; p.284: blank; p.285: part title, 'PART II';

p.286: blank; pp.287-329: text of part 2; p.330: blank; p.331: Riverside Press device; p.332: blank.

Notes on paper, binding, dust jacket, and publication with the entry for the entire Autograph Edition (AA1).

c.i.)   Third edition, first printing (Random House Vintage Book [V-200]), 1961

MY | MORTAL | ENEMY | [thick-thin short rule] | Willa Cather | [thin-thick short rule] | [sun orn.] | Vintage Books | A DIVISION OF RANDOM HOUSE | NEW YORK

Paperback, perfect binding; pp.[i-v] vi-xxii [1-3] 4-105 [106]. 184x110mm. A new setting of the text in 'Fairfield,' a typeface designed by Rudolph Ruzicka. Copyright: 'FIRST VINTAGE EDITION, September, 1961'. The copyright page also has the statement, 'VINTAGE BOOKS | are published by ALFRED A. KNOPF, INC. | and RANDOM HOUSE, INC.' Text ends on p.105; on p.106 is a biographical note on WC and a note on the type and design. Introduction by Marcus Klein (pp.v-xxii). Cover design by Antonio Frasconi.

First printing of 15,000 copies by the Colonial Press. $1.95. The Canadian Vintage edition was published simultaneously in Toronto.

c.ii.)   Second printing. 3,000 copies, September 1965. Presswork (c.ii-c.vi): Colonial Press.

c.iii.)   Third printing. 1,000 copies, April 1967.

c.iv.)   Fourth printing. 2,000 copies, March 1968.

c.v.)   Fifth printing. 2,100 copies, February 1970.

c.vi.)   Sixth printing. 3,000 copies, May 1972.

c.vii.)   Seventh printing. 2,500 copies, May 1974. Presswork (c.vii-c.x): American Book-Stratford Press.

c.viii.)   Eighth printing. 2,368 copies, April 1975.

c.ix.)   Ninth printing. 3,500 copies, May 1976.

c.x.)   Tenth printing. 4,913 copies, August 1978.

English Editions

A15.a.i.(e)   First English edition (American sheets), 1928

MY | MORTAL ENEMY | WILLA CATHER | [pale yellow: Heinemann device incorporating the date] | LONDON: WILLIAM HEINEMANN

Collation: [1-7]^8 [8]^8 (-8$_7$, 8$_8$); pp.[1-9] 10-122 [123-124] = 62 leaves. *Note:* 8$_7$ and 8$_8$ are excised terminal blanks.

Illustration: As in the American trade printing.

Contents: As in the American trade printing, but with 2 excised terminal blank leaves. The copyright page (p.6) deletes the line '*Copyright 1926 · Alfred A. Knopf, Inc.*'

Paper: Heavy cream wove as in the American trade printing. 208 x 127mm.; top edge trimmed, fore edge uncut, bottom edge rough cut. End papers of rough cream wove stock.

Binding: Sand-yellow (73) laid paper over boards, black fine linen shelfback. Covers blank, spine gilt, '| MY | MORTAL | ENEMY | [small circle] | WILLA | CATHER | HEINEMANN |'.

Dust Jacket: Sand (73) laid paper with vertical chain lines 26mm. apart; printed overall in dark brown. Front cover as on the American trade printing. Spine: '| MY | MORTAL | ENEMY | [dot] | WILLA | CATHER | 2/6 | NET | HEINEMANN |'. Back cover: 'DEATH COMES FOR THE | ARCHBISHOP | *By WILLA CATHER   PRICE 3s.6d. NET* | [vignette illus.] | [review excerpt from the *Observer* and *TLS*] | WILLIAM HEINEMANN LTD'. Front inner flap: 11-line

blurb for *My Mortal Enemy*. Back inner flap: 'BY THE SAME AUTHOR | DEATH COMES FOR THE | ARCHBISHOP | *3s. 6d. net* | YOUTH AND THE BRIGHT MEDUSA | *7s.6d. net* | A LOST LADY (The Windmill Library) | *3s.6d. net* | WILLIAM HEINEMANN LTD.'

Publication: Though the English edition consists of American trade sheets, the book was not published in England until April 1928 at 5s. after Heinemann had also published the English edition of *Death Comes for the Archbishop*. *My Mortal Enemy* was announced in *TLS* on 10 May 1928.

a.ii.(e)   Second printing. Heinemann Windmill Library edition, February 1930. 2s.6d.

a.iii.(e)   Third printing. Heinemann regular trade edition, November 1948. 7s.6d.

a.iv.(e)   Fourth printing. Heinemann regular trade edition, January 1949. 7s.6d.

a.v.(e)   Fifth printing (second English 'edition'). London: Hamish Hamilton, 1963. Printed by photo-offset from the American first-trade-printing plates. This "edition" remained available in England until 1976.

A16.   DEATH COMES FOR THE ARCHBISHOP

a.i.)   First edition, first printing, 1927

LIMITED ISSUE

[within a dec. dark blue rule frame] BY WILLA CATHER | [dark blue:] Death comes | for the | Archbishop | [black:] *"Auspice Maria!"* | Father Vaillant's signet-ring | [blue oval borzoi device] | [black:] NEW YORK | ALFRED A KNOPF · MCMXXVII

Collation: π_1 [1-19]⁸ [20]⁴; pp.[i-x] 1-303 [304]= 157 leaves.
Note: The first leaf, π_1, is the inserted signed limitation notice
on verso; recto blank.

Contents: P.i: blank; p.ii: limitation notice, '*The first edition of*
DEATH COMES FOR | THE ARCHBISHOP *consists of twenty*
thou-|sand two hundred twenty-five copies as follows: | *fifty on Japan*
Vellum signed by the author | *and numbered 1 to 50; one hundred*
seventy-|five on Borzoi all rag paper signed by the author | *and*
numbered 1 to 175; and twenty thou-|sand copies on Mellow Book
Laid paper. | *This is Number* [number supplied by hand] |
[author's signature]'; p.iii: half title; p.iv: '[within a dec. dark
blue rule frame] *The Works of* | WILLA CATHER | [10 titles]';
p.v: title page; p.vi: 'COPYRIGHT 1926, 1927, BY WILLA
CATHER | MANUFACTURED IN THE UNITED STATES
OF AMERICA'; p.vii: contents; p.viii: blank; p.ix: second half
title (as first); p.x: blank; pp.1-303: text; p.304: 'A NOTE ON
THE TYPE IN WHICH | THIS BOOK IS SET. . . . | [13
lines in italic] | [oval borzoi orn.] | set up, ELECTROTYPED,
PRINTED AND | BOUND BY THE PLIMPTON PRESS, |
NORWOOD, MASS.'

Note: The type face is identified on p.304 as Old Style No.31,
composed on the monotype.

Paper: Cream Japan vellum, 228 x 147mm.; top edge trimmed
and gilt, other edges uncut. End papers of the same stock.

Binding: Olive brown (94), bright green (131), white and dark
brown curl marbled paper over boards; green (141) cloth
shelfback. A black leather label, 39 x 49mm., on the spine with
gilt-stamped lettering, 'WILLA | CATHER || DEATH |
COMES FOR | THE ARCH-|BISHOP'. In a board box covered
with yellow-green (120) laid paper with horizontal chain lines
30mm. apart; black leather label (as on the binding spine) on
the back of the box.

The 50 copies on Japan vellum are bound in full cream vellum
paper with gilt-stamped decoration on the front cover. Spine
gilt-stamped: 'WILLA | CATHER || DEATH | COMES FOR |

THE ARCH-|BISHOP | [orn.] | ALFRED A. KNOPF'. Back cover blank. Top edge trimmed and gilt, other edges uncut.

Publication: 2 September 1927. $10.00 for the 175 copies on laid paper; $25.00 for the 50 copies on Japan vellum.

TRADE ISSUE

[title-page as in the limited issue]

Collation: [1-19]⁸ [20]⁴; pp.[i-viii] 1-303 [304] = 156 leaves.

Contents: P. i: as in limited issue; p.ii: advts. as in limited issue; p.iii: title page; p.iv: copyright as in limited issue; p.v: contents; p.vi: blank; p.vii: second half title (as first); p.viii: blank; pp. 1-303: text; p.304: 'A NOTE ON THE TYPE IN WHICH | THIS BOOK IS SET | [13 lines in italic] | [oval borzoi orn.] | SET UP, ELECTROTYPED, PRINTED AND | BOUND BY THE PLIMPTON PRESS, | NORWOOD, MASS. · PAPER FUR-|NISHED BY W. F. ETHERINGTON | & CO., NEW YORK'.

Note: Differs textually from the limited issue only in the addition of 2 lines to the printer's imprint on p. 304 and the removal of the limitation leaf, which alters preliminary pagination.

Paper: Cream laid stock (identified as 'Mellow Book Laid') with vertical chain lines 21mm. apart. No visible watermark. 190×127mm.; top edge trimmed and stained ochre, other edges rough-cut. End papers of cream wove stock.

Note: Copies in the second and third printing binding (see below) have the top edge stained red-orange and end papers with an overall Borzoi Books device pattern of alternating light yellow and gray-blue.

Binding: Green (131) linen cloth. Front cover: a very pale gray paper label, 52×83mm., mounted on the cover, 'within a dec. yellow border rule] DEATH | COMES FOR THE |

ARCHBISHOP | WILLA CATHER'. Spine: a very pale gray label, 68 x 32mm., mounted at the top of the spine, '[yellow orn.] | DEATH | COMES | FOR THE | ARCH-|BISHOP | [yellow inverted triangle] | CATHER | [yellow inverted triangle]'. Back cover blank.

The second and third printings with copyright notices, 'FIRST AND SECOND PRINTINGS BEFORE PUBLICATION' and 'FIRST, SECOND AND THIRD PRINTINGS | BEFORE PUBLICATION' are bound in smooth olive-tan (95) cloth. Front cover: '[gilt-stamped] WILLA CATHER | [orange:] DEATH COMES FOR | THE ARCHBISHOP | [gilt circular orn.]'. Spine: '[gilt] Willa | Cather | [orange:] DEATH COMES | FOR THE | ARCHBISHOP | [gilt short wavy rule] [gilt:] Alfred A. Knopf'. Back cover: rectangular Borzoi Books device stamped in blind on the lower right corner. This binding conforms with the trade binding of One of Ours.

Dust Jacket: Light tan coated paper. Front cover: 'BY WILLA CATHER | [rough rule] | [red-brown:] Death comes for the | Archbishop | [rough rule] | [black:] · ALFRED A KNOPF · [space] · [space] NEW YORK · | [von Schmidt illus. in black of the bishop on horseback]'. Spine: 'WILLA | CATHER | [rough rule] | [red-brown:] Death | comes | for the | Arch-|bishop | [rough rule] | [black:] Alfred A Knopf | [black Borzoi Books device]'. Back cover: 'BY WILLA CATHER | [rough rule] | [red-brown:] Death comes for the | Archbishop | [rough rule] | [black:] Price $2.50 | ALSO BY MISS CATHER | A Lost Lady   One of Ours | [excerpts from critical reviews beneath each title] | [oval borzoi orn.] | Alfred A Knopf PUBLISHER New York'. Front inner flap: '[rough rule] | [red-brown: Borzoi Books device] | ALFRED A KNOPF | Publisher | 730 Fifth Avenue | NEW YORK | [rough rule] | [black:] ALSO BY MISS CATHER | My Mortal Enemy | [2 excerpts from critical reviews] | $2.50 | The Professor's House | [2 excerpts from critical reviews] | $2.50'. Back inner flap: as the front inner flap, but advertising Youth and the Bright Medusa and April Twilights.

Publication: 2 September 1927 at $2.50. The first 3 printings had been bound and distributed before publication date. Advance review copies are of the first printing in paper wrappers

with front and back covers and spine of the first trade issue dust jacket. A notice is tipped in on the front cover with the publication date.

The first printing was of 25,000 sets of sheets, of which 20,000 copies were bound in green cloth in July 1927. Of these, 1,040 copies were uniformly bound but imprinted for Macmillan (Knopf's Canadian representative) on title page and spine for the Canadian edition. In August, 5,000 more copies of the first printing were bound in the green cloth.

In the first 2 printings (therefore, also in the limited issue and Canadian edition), a typographical error on p.20, l.16, 'happned' for 'happened', occurs, which was corrected in the third and all subsequent printings. Another error, 'suppper' for 'supper' (57.15) persisted through all printings until the text was reset in 1945.

DCA was first published serially in the *Forum* 77, nos.1-6 (January-June 1927) [CCC 4] before book publication. The periodical publication was illustrated with drawings by Harold von Schmidt, who illustrated the second edition (A16.b.i). Though the serial text is essentially the same as that of the first book printing and no major revision occurs, over 200 alterations were made before the book plates were set, and, of these, at least 100 are substantive. Three sections of the book text are not in the serial publication: book 5, 'Padre Martinez' (pp.139-174), part 1 of book 7, 'The Month of *Mary*' (pp.198-211), and part 1 of book 8, 'Cathedral' (pp.239-245). The greater number of changes are simple ones of spelling, punctuation, capitalization, italicization, hyphenation, and rearrangement of paragraph breaks. Examples: 'cañon' is changed to 'canyon', 'sand hills,—' to 'sand-hills—', 'procathedral' to 'pro-cathedral', '*compote*' to 'compote', 'Vicario' to 'vicario', 'Saint Joseph' to 'St. Joseph'. For purposes of economy, most of these minor corrections are not included in the textual collation that follows. Significant changes only are noted. Page and line reference is to the first printing, with passages from the *Forum* serial publication located by page and line number or page and column number (in roman) as appropriate.

1.13-14	the balustrade] the low balustrade (23.5)
1.14	was the drop . . . below] *omit* (23)
2.9	motion. The] motion; the (23.16)
2.19	their heads] *omit* (23)
2.19	them] their heads (23.24-25)
4.4-6	Lawn tennis . . . played.] Considering the outdoor game unfitting in a churchman, he now played a formidable game of indoor tennis. (24.21-22)
8.14	*serpents à sonnettes*] *serpents des sonnettes* (27.6)
10.2	the Bishop] your Grace (28.4)
12.1-3	I have noticed . . . reserved.] He is very reserved; but I have noticed that he is a man of severe and refined tastes. (29.10-11)
19.22	last!] last. (132.i)
20.5	young] *omit* (132.i)
20.15-16	On his arrival . . . there] That was a long story. The Mexican priests at Santa Fé (132.i)
22.20	before; it] before. It (133.i)
23.3-5	—which, he . . . Water] *omit* (133.i)
23.5	were] was (133.i)
23.6	the] his (133.i)
23.6	two] two of his (133.i)
23.10	pot] great pot (133.i)
24.1	declared] was sure (133.i)
24.19	their] *omit* (133.ii)
28.7	pathless sand-hills] sand hills (134.ii)
28.9-31.8	In the late. . . . almost over.] *omit* (134)
32.3	there] *omit* (134.ii)
34.9-11	(sent . . . suggestion).], sent . . . suggestion. (135.ii)
37.13	("Whitney")] *omit* (136.i)
42.12-13	after his . . . residence,] the first night he spent in his Episcopal residence (286.ii)
52.3	*rancho*] *ranchero* (289.i)
53.17	twenty to thirty] thirty to forty (289.ii)
55.25	children?] children, (290.i)
65.12	Puy-de-Dôm] Puy-de-Dom (293.i)
67.23	ridges] layers (293.ii)
67.24	layers] ridges (293.ii)
81.14	diocese; the] Diocese. The (451.i)
81.24	El Paso del Norte] El Paso (451.i)
84.23	paths,—with] paths,—each with (452.i)

88.6-14   patches of wild pumpkin—. . . . by fear. ¶As the] sometimes a
           little dry white grass. As the (453.i)
89.3-9   The sun set. . . . that afternoon] Toward night the wind grew
           intensely cold, the red sun set in an atmosphere murky with
           sand. The travelers made a dry camp and slept behind a clump
           of greasewood bushes. It was not until the next afternoon that
           (453.i)
91.20-27   Jacinto usually. . . . perhaps.] *omit* (453.ii)
97.4   these] their (455.i)
99.3   Ácomas] Ácoma (456.i)
104.6   Built upon] At the (457.ii)
104.6   of the cloister] of the upper cloister (457.ii)
104.18   Through all] All (457.ii)
104.18   that] in which (457.ii)
105.6   Spaniards] Castilians (457.ii)
108.19   became] grew (458.ii)
108.26   Baltazar's] His (459.i)
119.26   When his man] Tranquilino (613.i)
119.27   door, Father Latour, already in his] door. Father Latour, in his
           (613.i)
121.25   dry and clean,] still under a roof. It was dry and clean, (613.ii)
121.26   to] that he would (613.ii)
136.28   certain] so sure (618.ii)
139.1-174.21 *Book 5, 'Padre Martinez'*] *omit* (619.i)
178.17-18 San Antonio] El Paso (620.i)
183.7   Tonight] And tonight (621.ii)
184.23   shot. With] shot, but with (622.i)
184.24   rival; he] rival. He (622.i)
186.5   the boy] he (622.i)
186.20-21 creature, he] creature, red or yellow, he (622.ii)
189.20   kept; there] kept. There (623.i)
191.27   pallid] blue (624.i)
196.18   Everyone] Every one (625.ii)
198.1-221.4 *Book 7, part 1, 'The Month of Mary'*] *omit* (770)
213.21   Roman] Catholic (771.ii)
221.25   velvet and] *omit* (774.i)
221.26   wore] *omit* (774.i)
223.13   which were] *omit* (774.i)
223.27   the main trunk] *omit* (774.ii)
223.28   a strong] one (774.ii)

224.7   leaves—] foliage, (774.ii)
230.19-20 for his . . . Holy City] to visit the Holy City for the first time (776.ii)
232.4   Bishop Latour] The Bishop (777.i)
232.17   EUSABIO (*section heading*)] omit (777.i)
232.26   of his visit with Eusabio,] *omit* (777.i)
233.4   he] Father Latour (777.i)
233.26-28 a crimson . . . black hair] his hair done up in a red banda (777.ii)
235.2   sky. The] upper blue,—(777.ii)
237.23   demeanour: an] demeanor. An (778.ii)
239.1-245.28 *Book 8, part 1, 'Cathedral'*] omit (778)
246.1-7   The day. . . . Leavenworth.] One evening, about a fortnight after Father Vaillant had returned to Santa Fé in response to his Bishop's summons, Father Latour told him that he would require his company in his study after dinner. The weekly post which arrived that morning, brought him a letter of great importance from the Bishop of Leavenworth, which he and his Vicar must consider together. (778.ii-779.i)
247.27   -rooms; and] -rooms. And (779.i)
248.25   In the evening after dinner,] *omit* (779.ii)
254.28   flash, how the] flash that his (781.ii)
258.3   graces; Virgin-daughter,] graces. Virgin-daughter (782.i)
266.5   the growing of fruit.] growing fruit. (930.ii)
267.7   In his retirement] After his retirement, (931.i)
268.16   , Bernard Ducrot,] named Bernard, (931.ii)
269.1   Throughout] During (931.ii)
269.5   performed] sang (931.ii)
269.7   resident] *omit* (931.ii)
272.12   before the door] in front (932.ii)
275.10   towering] *omit* (933.ii)
275.11   *omit*] the comeliness of the villages, (933.ii)
275.15   old gardens] garden (933.ii)
276.25   it; one] it. One (934.i)
278.5   Sevigné] Sévigny (934.i)
279.7   without food or water] eating herbs and roots (934.ii)
279.25   *Hunger, Thirst, Cold, Nakedness*] hunger, thirst, cold, nakedness (934.ii)
280.20   Junípero Serra] Junipero (935.i)
282.17   called aloud,] called (935.ii)
285.1-2   a pretense] a great pretense (936.ii)

285.8   wavy white] *omit* (936.ii)
285.19   as boys] as students (936.ii)
286.27-28 at dawn in a] at dawn on the fateful day, in a (937.i)
289.18-19 the Church. He was . . . money,] for very little money,—
           (937.ii)
296.20   Canyon de Chelly] Cañon de Chelly (939.ii)
298.18   desert. Seen at] desert. To the white man's eye, seen at (940.ii)
298.21   the white man named it accordingly] he named it so (940.ii)
300.6   unforeseen] strange (941.i)
300.25   ruins; once] ruins. Once (941.i)
302.17   listening] waiting (941.ii)

a.ii.)   Second printing (before publication). 10,000 copies bound in
         olive-tan linen cloth (uniform with the first trade issue binding
         of *One of Ours*) on 11 August 1927. Copyright: 'FIRST AND
         SECOND PRINTINGS BEFORE PUBLICATION'.
         Typographical error 'happned' for 'happened' (20.16). Presswork
         (a.iii-xxvii, xxix, xxxi, xxxiv): Plimpton Press.

a.iii.) Third printing (before publication). 5,000 copies bound in
         olive-tan linen cloth on 19 August 1927. Copyright: 'FIRST,
         SECOND AND THIRD PRINTINGS | BEFORE
         PUBLICATION'. Error on p.20 corrected. Presswork (a.iii-
         xxvii, xxix, xxxi, xxxiv): Plimpton Press.

a.iv.)   Fourth printing. 5,500 sets of sheets in October 1927, of which
         2,000 were bound in olive-tan and the remainder in the bright
         green cloth with paper labels of the first printing.

a.v.)   Fifth printing. 1,500 copies, December 1927. Green cloth.

a.vi.)   Sixth printing. 3,500 copies, December 1927. Green cloth on
         all printings henceforth, except as noted.

a.vii.) Seventh printing. 3,000 copies. December 1927.

a.viii.) Eighth printing. 5,000 copies, December 1927.

a.ix.)   Ninth printing. 2,000 copies, December 1927.

a.x.)   Tenth printing. 3,000 copies, December 1927.

a.xi.)   Eleventh printing. 5,000 copies, January 1928.

a.xii.)   Twelfth printing. 5,000 copies, February 1928.

a.xiii.)   Thirteenth printing. 2,000 copies, May 1928.

a.xiv.)   Fourteenth printing. 2,500 copies, June 1928.

a.xv.)   Fifteenth printing. 2,500 copies, July 1928.

a.xvi.)   Sixteenth printing. 2,000 copies, September 1928.

a.xvii.)   Seventeenth printing. 2,000 copies, November 1928.

a.xviii.)   Eighteenth printing. 2,000 copies, December 1928.

a.xix.)   Nineteenth printing. 1,000 copies, March 1929.

a.xx.)   Twentieth printing. 1,500 copies, June 1929.

a.xxi.)   Twenty-first printing. 1,000 copies, September 1929.

a.xxii.)   Twenty-second printing. 1,000 copies, November 1929.

a.xxiii.)   Twenty-third printing. 2,000 copies, February 1930.

a.xxiv.)   Twenty-fourth printing. 1,750 copies, August 1930.

a.xxv.)   Twenty-fifth printing. 1,000 copies, November 1930.

a.xxvi.)   Twenty-sixth printing. 1,500 copies, February 1931.

a.xxvii.)   Twenty-seventh printing. 1,500 copies, July 1931.

a.xxviii.)   Twenty-eighth printing (the Modern Library edition).
September 1931. Plates sent to Parkway Printing Co. on 31
July for the Modern Library first printing, returned to the
Plimpton Press on 2 September. Title page imprint:
'BENNETT A. CERF · DONALD S. KLOPFER | THE
MODERN LIBRARY | NEW YORK'. Bound by H. Wolff.

a.xxix.)   Twenty-ninth printing. 1,000 copies, October 1931.

a.xxx.)   Thirtieth printing (second Modern Library printing). November 1931. Plates sent to Parkway Printing Co. on 19 October, returned to the Plimpton Press on 9 November.

a.xxxi.)   Thirty-first printing. 2,000 copies, January 1932. Batter repairs were made to the plates after use for the Modern Library printings. Corrections were made on pp. 156, 171, 200, 247, and a new plate made for p. 113.

a.xxxii.)   Thirty-second printing (third Modern Library printing). December 1932. Plates sent to Parkway Printing Co. on 17 November.

a.xxxiii.)   Thirty-third printing (fourth Modern Library printing). July 1933. Plates sent to Parkway Printing Co. on 6 June, returned to the Plimpton Press on 12 July 1933.

a.xxxiv.)   Thirty-fourth printing. 3,300 sets of sheets printed. 2,000 copies, January 1934. 1,300 copies of this printing were not bound until December 1934. Some of these latter copies were held in reserve until 1936 and were listed in the *PW* weekly record (12 September 1936) with the note, "In this issue the size is smaller than in the $5 illustrated edition."

b.i.)   Second edition, first printing, 1929

LIMITED ISSUE

[within a frame of irregular horizontal rules] WILLA CATHER | DEATH COMES | FOR | THE ARCHBISHOP | *With drawings and designs by Harold Von Schmidt* | ALFRED · A · KNOPF · NEW YORK | MCM[borzoi orn.]XXIX

Collation: π_1 [1]^8 ($1_3 + \chi_1$) [2-22]^8; pp.[i-x, 1-3] 4-343 [344-346] = 178 leaves. Note: π_1 is an inserted blank flyleaf; χ_1 is the inserted contents leaf.

Illustrations: 10 full-page black-on-white illustrations by Harold von Schmidt at pp.2, 18, 60, 92, 134, 158, 198, 224, 270 and 300. 48 black-on-white vignette illus. throughout the text. The half-title vignette is of the archbishop on horseback.

Contents: Pp.i-ii: blank; p.iii: blank; p.iv: limitation, 'OF THIS EDITION OF | *DEATH COMES FOR THE ARCHBISHOP* | ONE HUNDRED AND SEVENTY COPIES | OF WHICH ONE HUNDRED AND SIXTY ARE FOR SALE | HAVE BEEN PRINTED ON | *RIVES CREAM PLATE PAPER* | NUMBERED FROM 1 to 170 | EACH COPY IS SIGNED BY THE AUTHOR | THIS IS NUMBER | [space for number] | [author's signature]'; p.v: half title, '[vignette] | DEATH COMES | FOR THE ARCHBISHOP | *"Auspice Maria," Father Valliant's signet ring*'; p.vi: 'The Works of | WILLA CATHER | [11 titles]'; p.vii: title page; p.viii: '*Copyright 1926, 1927, 1929, by Willa Cather* | All rights reserved including the right to reproduce | this book or parts thereof in any form | *Manufactured in the United States of America*'; p.ix: contents; p.x: blank; p.1: part title, '*PROLOGUE: AT ROME*'; p.2: illus.; pp.3-15: text of part 1; p.16: blank; p.17: part title, '*THE VICAR APOSTOLIC*'; p.18: illus.; pp.19-58: text of part 2; p.59: part title, '*MISSIONARY JOURNEYS*'; p.60: illus.; pp.61-89: text of part 3; p.90: blank; p.91: part title, '*THE MASS AT ÁCOMA*'; p.92: illus.; pp.93-131: text of part 4; p.132: blank; p.133: part title, '*SNAKE ROOT*'; p.134: illus.; pp.135-156: text of part 5; p.157: part title, '*PADRE MARTINEZ*'; p.158: illus.; pp.159-196: text of part 6; p.197: part title, '*DONA ISABELLA*'; p.198: illus.; pp.199-222: text of part 7; p.223: part title, '*THE GREAT DIOCESE*'; p.224: illus.; pp.225-267: text of part 8; p.268: part title, '*GOLD UNDER PIKE'S PEAK*'; p.269: illus.; pp.270-298: text of part 9; p.299: part title, '*DEATH COMES | FOR THE ARCHBISHOP*'; p.300: illus.; pp.301-343: text of part 10; p.344: colophon, 'THIS BOOK, DESIGNED BY | ELMER ADLER, WAS SET ON | THE MONOTYPE IN POLIPHILUS, | ELECTROTYPED, PRINTED AND | BOUND BY THE PLIMPTON PRESS OF | NORWOOD, MASSACHUSETTS. THE | JAPAN PAPER COMPANY OF NEW YORK | SUPPLIED THE PAPER. THE

ILLUSTRATIONS WERE REPRODUCED | BY FEDERAL
PHOTO-ENGRAVING | CORPORATION OF NEW YORK';
pp.345-346: blank.

Paper: Heavy cream wove paper, watermarked 'RIVES',
'FRANCE', and 'BFK'. 290x200mm.; top edge rough-
trimmed and silvered, other edges uncut. End papers of the
same stock.

Binding: Full cream vellum paper over limp boards; fore edge
beveled. Front cover: a broken Indian pot stamped in silver.
Spine: '[silver-stamped] DEATH | COMES | FOR THE |
ARCHBISHOP | [thick silver rule] | WILLA | CATHER |
ALFRED A. | KNOPF'. Back cover: the Borzoi Books device
stamped in blind on the lower right corner. In a board box
covered with light brown (76) laid paper with vertical chain
lines 26mm. apart. A lighter tan paper label, 75x44mm.,
'DEATH | COMES | FOR THE | ARCHBISHOP | [heavy black
rule] | WILLA | CATHER', on the spine. At the foot of the box
spine, the limitation number is supplied by hand.

Dust Jacket: Light tan laid paper with vertical chain lines 30mm.
apart; Borzoi Books watermark. Front and back covers blank.
Spine: 'DEATH | COMES | FOR THE | ARCHBISHOP |
[heavy black rule] | WILLA | CATHER | ALFRED A. |
KNOPF'. The jacket is a full-wrap type with flaps over top and
bottom of the volume.

Publication: 9 November 1929. $25.00. 170 copies (10 not for
sale).

TRADE ISSUE

[title as in the limited issue]

Collation: [1-22]^8 χ_1; pp.[i-viii, 1-3] 4-343 [344-346]= 177
leaves. *Note:* Terminal χ_1 is a blank on laid paper like text
paper.

Illustrations: As in the limited issue.

Contents: Pp. i-ii: blank; p.iii: half title; p.iv: advt. as in limited issue; p.v: title page; p.vi: copyright as in limited issue; p.vii: contents; p.viii: blank; pp.1-346: as in the limited issue.

Paper: Cream laid paper with vertical chain lines 31mm. apart. The Borzoi Books watermark. 225 x 178mm.; top edge trimmed and stained brown, other edges rough-cut. Illustrative end papers of a desert scene in light brown by von Schmidt on the same stock.

Binding: Light yellow-brown (77) cloth, lettering and decoration overall brown (58). Front cover: 'DEATH COMES FOR | THE ARCHBISHOP | WILLA CATHER | [broken Indian pot]'. Spine: 'DEATH | COMES | FOR THE | ARCHBISHOP | [heavy brown rule] | WILLA | CATHER | ALFRED A. | KNOPF'. Back cover: the Borzoi Books device stamped in blind on the lower right corner.

Dust Jacket: Heavy cream laid paper with horizontal chain lines 31mm. apart. Watermark: '[circular orn.] | *Utopian*'. Front cover: 'BY WILLA CATHER | [brown rule] | [black:] DEATH COMES FOR | THE ARCHBISHOP | [brown rule] | *DRAWINGS BY HAROLD VON SCHMIDT* | [enlarged detail in brown of von Schmidt's illus. of the bishop on horseback] | [brown rule] | ALFRED · A · KNOPF · NEW YORK'. Spine: 'DEATH COMES | FOR THE | ARCHBISHOP | *by* | *WILLA CATHER* | [olive-green rule] | [black:] *DRAWINGS* | *by* | *HAROLD* | *VON SCHMIDT* | [detail in olive-green of the von Schmidt illus., 'The Cruciform Tree'] | [olive-green rule] | [black:] ALFRED · A · KNOPF'. Back cover: 'BY WILLA CATHER | [brown rule] | [black:] *DRAWINGS BY HAROLD VON SCHMIDT* | [20 lines of review excerpts] | [brown rule] | ALFRED · A · KNOPF · NEW YORK'. Front inner flap: '$5.00 | *How Willa Cather came to write* | DEATH COMES FOR THE ARCHBISHOP | *Condensation of a letter from Willa Cather to the* | *Editor of the Commonweal:* | [35 lines] | *(Continued on back flap)*'. Back inner flap: '*(Continued from front flap)* | [35 lines]'. In a board box covered with red-orange Japanese paper decorated in blue, green, and white leaf and flower pattern.

Publication: 9 November 1929 at $5.00. First printing of 2,500 copies. This new edition was originally intended for the 1929 Christmas trade and is called the "holiday edition" in the Knopf production records. The black-on-white illustrations and text drawings are by Harold von Schmidt, who illustrated the *Forum* periodical publication of 1927.

As early as 11 September 1933, Knopf considered making the illustrated edition the standard text. On that date, Alfred Knopf wrote to WC suggesting that "it would be a good idea for us not to reprint the regular edition, of which our stock was low— the book was then available in the Modern Library edition—but to reprint the illustrated edition and sell only it . . . this was based on the assumption that we could make the price of the illustrated edition $2.50" (personal communication, Knopf to author, 29 July 1980). Although WC agreed, the price reduction proved unfeasible.

The plates were not reactivated until 1936 for the second printing. A note inserted in the production record of the third printing (October 1937) indicates that Knopf was thinking of resetting the text in a new unillustrated edition: "Before reprinting consult Mr. Knopf on the possibility of resetting the regular edition (without illustrations). See correspondence in folder regarding condition of the plates of the regular edition." The first edition plates showed marked deterioration after use for 30 Knopf printings in 8 years and 4 Modern Library printings for the cheap popular edition. Although a new edition of *DCA* had been under consideration since 1937, the plates were not, in fact, reset until the new edition of 1945.

Sydney Jacobs (Knopf chief of production) wrote to WC on 24 March 1937: "In January you gave me several corrections to be made in *Death Comes for the Archbishop*. Two of the corrections in the text were made but you never gave me copy to replace the material deleted from page 189 of the illustrated edition and 167 of the regular edition [see collation following A16.e.]. There is no immediate need for this material, but if you can get it to me sometime soon, I would appreciate it" (private archive of Alfred A. Knopf in Purchase, N.Y.). In 1937, WC was

making revisions in the text of *DCA* for the ninth volume of Houghton Mifflin's Autograph Edition (A16.c.; AA1). Sixty-two of the text changes she considered sufficiently important to be incorporated in the text of the illustrated edition. A note in the Knopf production record, dated 14 December 1938: "Miss Cather has some important corrections to make in the plates of DEATH COMES FOR THE ARCHBISHOP and this book is under no circumstances to be reprinted until these corrections are made in the plates. She will deliver them after Christmas." These corrections were made in the fifth printing of 1940. A textual collation comparing the texts of all editions of *DCA* is appended to the 1945 fifth edition entry (A16.e.).

b.ii.)   Second printing. 2,500 copies, July 1936. Copyright: '*Copyright 1926, 1927, 1929, by Willa Cather* | [extended 4-line rights notice] | *Manufactured in the United States of America* | *Published September, 1927* | *Reprinted twenty-nine times* | *Illustrated edition published November, 1929* | *Reprinted July, 1936*'. Presswork for all printings: the Plimpton Press.

b.iii.)   Third printing. 3,500 copies, October 1937.

b.iv.)   Fourth printing. 1,775 copies, August 1939.

b.v.)   Fifth printing. 5,860 copies, May 1940. This printing incorporates the changes made by WC for the Autograph Edition, vol. 9 (see textual collation following A16.e.).

b.vi.)   Sixth printing. 7,700 copies, June 1942.

c.)   Third edition (Autograph Edition, vol. 9), 1938

[dec. rule] | WILLA CATHER | [dec. rule] | Death comes for the Archbishop | [dec. rule] | '*Auspice Maria!*' | FATHER VAILLANT'S SIGNET-RING | [brown-orange: 'H M Co' cipher] | BOSTON | HOUGHTON MIFFLIN COMPANY | 1938

Collation: [1-21]^8 [22]^{10}; pp.[i-vi, 1-2] 3-347 [348-350]= 178 leaves.

Illustrations: On text paper, inserted facing the title page with a protective tissue. Caption: *'Reduced facsimile of page 1 of the original first draft of "Death Comes for the Archbishop"'*.

Contents: P.i: edition title; p.ii: limitation notice; p.iii: title page; p.iv: copyright; p.v: contents; p.vi: blank; p.1: half title; p.2: blank; pp.3-348: text; p.349: Riverside Press device; p.350: blank.

Note: Willa Cather made 64 corrections and revisions for the text of this edition. A full listing of the changes is made in the textual collation of all editions following the entry for the fifth edition (A16.e.i.).

Notes on paper, binding, dust jacket, and publication with the entry for the entire Autograph Edition (AA1).

d.)   Fourth edition (Armed Services edition), 1943

[within a double-rule border, title set in 2 panels. Left panel:] PUBLISHED BY ARRANGEMENT WITH | ALFRED A. KNOPF, INC., NEW YORK | [9-line copyright notice in italic and caps] [right panel:] DEATH COMES | FOR THE | ARCHBISHOP | *By* WILLA CATHER | *Armed Services Editions* | COUNCIL ON BOOKS IN WARTIME, INC. | NEW YORK

Paperback in a single gathering of 128 leaves stapled at the center fold; pp.[1-5] 6-255 [256]. Text set in double columns. Cheap wove paper, 95 x 138mm., edges trimmed flush with cover. Pictorial stiff paper wrapper. No.D-97 of the Armed Services Editions published in December 1943.

This edition used as copy-text the second edition (illustrated), fifth printing. It reflects all the corrections made by Willa Cather for the Autograph Edition (third edition) that were incorporated into the fifth printing of the Knopf illustrated edition in 1940.

e.i.)   Fifth edition, first printing, 1945

[within a dec. border rule] BY WILLA CATHER | DEATH
COMES | FOR THE | ARCHBISHOP | *"Auspice Maria!"*
Father Vaillant's | signet ring | [oval borzoi device] | NEW
YORK | ALFRED A KNOPF · MCMXLV

Collation: [1-8]^{16} [9]^{12} [10]^{16}; pp.[i-viii, 1-2] 3-299
[300-304] = 156 leaves.

Contents: Pp.i-ii: blank; p.iii: half title, 'DEATH COMES FOR
THE | ARCHBISHOP | [short rule]; p.iv: advt. '[within a dec.
border rule] *The Novels of* | *WILLA CATHER* | [12 titles]';
p.v: title page; p.vi: copyright 'THIS BOOK HAS BEEN
PRODUCED | IN FULL COMPLIANCE | WITH ALL
GOVERNMENT REGULATIONS | FOR THE
CONSERVATION OF PAPER, METAL | AND OTHER
ESSENTIAL MATERIALS | *Copyright 1926, 1927 by Willa
Cather* | [4-line statement in italic of reserved rights] |
PUBLISHED SEPTEMBER 1927 | REPRINTED TWENTY-
NINE TIMES | RESET AND PRINTED FROM NEW
PLATES 1945'; p.vii: contents; p.viii: blank; p.1: part title
'*PROLOGUE: AT ROME*'; p.2: blank; pp.3-299: text; p.300:
'*A NOTE ON THE TYPE* | *in which this book is set* | [26 lines in
italic] | [Borzoi hound device] | COMPOSED, PRINTED AND
BOUND BY | THE PLIMPTON PRESS, NORWOOD,
MASS.'; pp.301-304: blank.

Note: On p.300, the type is identified as having been adapted
from a typeface originally designed by Pierre Simon Fournier the
younger (1712-1768).

Paper: Cream wove, 190x128mm.; top edge trimmed and
stained red, fore edge rough-cut, bottom edge trimmed. End
papers of a heavier wove stock.

Binding: Green (131) linen cloth. Front cover: a pale blue paper
label mounted in a blind panel, lettered as the first edition trade
issue. Spine: as in the first edition trade issue. The Borzoi Books
device stamped in blind on the lower right corner of the back
cover.

Dust Jacket: Not seen.

Publication: January 1945 in a first printing of 5,000 copies. An error occurred in this printing on p.239 in the chapter heading line, which reads '||| BOOK SEVEN | *GOLD UNDER PIKE'S PEAK* ||'. This was corrected in the second printing to '||| BOOK EIGHT | *GOLD UNDER PIKE'S PEAK* ||'. The part title on the recto of the preceding leaf (p.237) is correctly printed '*BOOK VIII*'.

On 14 September 1944, Alfred Knopf sent a telegram to WC in Boston: "PAPER SHORTAGE MAKES IT IMPOSSIBLE REPRINT ARCHBISHOP ILLUSTRATED FORMAT CONSEQUENTLY MUST RESET MAKING NEW PLATES STOP WOULD GREATLY PREFER FOLLOW TYPOGRAPHY SHADOWS ROCK IF YOU WILLING STOP IF NOT WILL FOLLOW TYPOGRAPHY ORIGINAL EDITION WILL YOU PLEASE TELEGRAPH IMMEDIATELY AS OFFICE CLOSED SATURDAY TO WEDNESDAY AFFECTIONATE GREETINGS ALFRED." WC replied by wire the next day: "AGREE WITH YOU IN PREFERRING TYPOGRAPHY OF SHADOWS ROCK W S CATHER" (from the Knopf archive in Purchase, N.Y.).

On 2 October 1944, WC received a letter from the Knopf production department: "I find that a long time ago you gave Mr. Preston some special corrections for THE ARCHBISHOP—taken, I think, from the Bruce Rogers edition [HM Co. Autograph Edition]. This corrected text is the one we are setting from. I hope this is all right" (the carbon of this letter from the Knopf archives, kindly supplied for use here by William Koshland, is unsigned).

Though the plan was clearly to use the Autograph Edition as copy-text, this edition instead follows the first edition text. It therefore revives and perpetuates the usages that WC eliminated in her text revisions for the Autograph Edition which had been carefully incorporated into the Knopf second (illustrated) edition, fifth printing, in 1940. How this happened can perhaps be explained by wartime replacements of key personnel in the production department (Sydney Jacobs was away in war service). Although specific passages that had been particularly earmarked for alteration are changed (see textual collation), in every other instance the new setting reflects the first edition text, and every

reprint to date is set or photographically reproduced from the same plates.

The texts collated are:

1: First edition, first printing, September 1927.

2: Second edition (illustrated), first printing, November 1929.

3: Second edition (illustrated), fifth printing, May 1940 (and the Armed Services fourth edition which used the second edition, fifth printing as copy-text).

4: Third edition (Autograph Edition, vol. 9, 1938).

5: Fifth edition, January 1945. Page and line reference is to 2 in order to emphasize Willa Cather's corrections in the Autograph Edition and the illustrated edition.

3.11	ilex (1, 5)] *omit* (3, 4)
8.18	gold seekers (1, 5)] gold-seekers (3, 4)
10.14	Hudson (1, 5)] Hudson's (3, 4)
11.6	Padre (1, 5)] Padre, (3, 4)
14.5	happened (5)] happen (1, 3, 4)
24.19	colors (1)] colours (3, 4, 5)
26.10	horse-back (1, 5)] horseback (3, 4)
27.13	acacias, (1, 5)] locust trees, (3, 4)
34.21	thrashing-floor (1, 5)] threshing-floor (3, 4)
42.13	evening-star (1, 5)] evening star (3, 4)
44.18	nearly (1, 5)], perhaps, (3, 4)
52.7	oriental (1, 5)] Oriental (3, 4)
53.3	Guadaloupe (1)] Guadalupe (3, 5)] Guadeloupe (4)
55.17	Guadaloupe (1)] Guadalupe (3, 5)] Guadeloupe (4)
56.17	hill-side (1, 5)] hillside (3, 4)
75.14	Puy-de-Dôm (1)] Puy-de-Dôme (3, 4, 5)
86.3, 7	Christobal (1, 3, 4)] Christóbal (5)
93.4	Plenary (1, 3, 5)] Provincial (4)
93.4	at (1, 4, 5)] of (3)
98.7	him, (1, 5)] him; (3, 4)
101.4	rabbit brush (1, 5)] rabbit-brush (3, 4)
105.21	evening-star (1, 5)] evening star (3, 4)
109.6	rabbit brush (1, 5)] rabbit-brush (3, 4)
109.24	oriental (1, 5)] Oriental (3, 4)
117.19	drouth (1, 5)] drought (3, 4)
123.9	drouth (1, 5)] drought (3, 4)

124.4   water jars (1, 5)] water-jars (3, 4)

154.10   neighborhood (1, 5)] neighbourhood (3, 4)

179.9   Guadeloupe (1, 4)] Guadalupe (3, 5)

186.2   theft, (1, 5)] theft͵ (3, 4)

188.8   Hondo (1, 5)] Hondo; (3, 4)

189.1   flowed a rushing stream (1, 4, 5)] rushed a foaming creek (3)

189.2-11 Its original source. . . . hill like that. ¶The water (1)] By merely laying. . . . the Hondo lay. The water (3)] Its original source. . . . the Hondo began. The water (5)] Its original source. . . . the Hondo began. ¶The water (4)

190.7, 10 Conçeption (1)] Conception (3, 4)] Conçeptión (5)

193.7, 8, 10   Christobal (1, 3, 4)] Christóbal (5)

211.1, 8 mountain (1, 5)] mountains (3)] Mountains (4)

218.1   icy cold (1, 5)] limp, (3)] icy-cold (4)

218.13   Olivares's (1, 5)] Olivares' (3, 4)

219.18   court room (1, 5)] courtroom (3, 4)

230.7   Puy-de-Dôm (1)] Puy-de-Dôme (3, 4, 5)

232.3   road-side (1, 5)] roadside (3, 4)

254.8   Puy-de-Dôm (1)] Puy-de-Dôme (3, 4, 5)

258.6   hem-stitching (1, 5)] hemstitching (3, 4)

260.5   missionaries, (1, 5)] missionaries͵ (3, 4)

263.15   drum-head (1, 5)] drumhead (3, 4)

286.2   his breviary and the ordinary of the Mass. (1)] his breviary and his missal. (3)] his breviary. (4, 5)

289.5   his (1, 5)] His (3, 4)

293.16   road builders (1, 5)] road-builders (3, 4)

301.7   *death* (1, 5)] *Death* (3)] Death (4)

302.12   hill-side, (1, 5)] hillside, (3, 4)

302.24   acacia (1, 5)] locust (3, 4)

303.2   hill-side (1, 5)] hillside (3, 4)

304.4   hill-side (1, 5)] hillside (3, 4)

308.18   acacia (1, 5)] locust (3, 4)

312.1-2   Puy-de-Dôm (1)] Puy-de-Dôme (3, 4, 5)

313.16   plowed (1, 5)] ploughed (3, 4)

315.7   Sevigné (1, 5)] Sévigné (3, 4)

325.24   road-side (1, 5)] roadside (3, 4)

326.5   Puy-de-Dôm (1)] Puy-de-Dôme (3, 4, 5)

335.23   their life. (1, 5)] their tribal life. (3, 4)

Preliminary Note to the Chronology of Printings

On the copyright notices for printings of this 1945 edition, Knopf did not differentiate between the 29 printings made from the plates of the original 1927 edition and those from the plates of the new edition. They were numbered in sequence from 1927 through 1978; hence, for example, the copyright statement for the thirteenth printing of this edition (e.xiii.) designates it the forty-second printing: 'PUBLISHED SEPTEMBER 1927 | REPRINTED TWENTY-NINE TIMES | RESET AND PRINTED FROM NEW PLATES JANUARY 1945 | REPRINTED TEN TIMES | FORTY-SECOND PRINTING, MAY 1966'. The actual number of the printing of this edition is reckoned by subtracting the 29 printings of the first edition from the number stated on the copyright after 1946.

e.ii.) Second printing. 5,250 copies, May 1946. P.239 corrected: ' ||| BOOK EIGHT | *GOLD UNDER PIKE'S PEAK* ||'. Presswork for all Knopf printings: the Plimpton Press.

e.iii.) Third printing. 5,000 copies, August 1947.

e.iv.) Fourth printing. 5,000 copies, January 1949.

e.v.) Fifth printing. 6,000 copies, March 1950.

e.vi.) Sixth printing. 10,000 copies, December 1951.

e.vii.) Seventh printing. 10,000 copies, February 1955.

e.viii.) Eighth printing. 10,000 copies, August 1957.

e.ix.) Ninth printing. 15,000 copies, November 1959.

e.x.) Tenth printing. 6,000 copies, October 1961.

e.xi.) Eleventh printing. 6,385 copies, August 1963.

e.xii.) Twelfth printing. 12,450 copies, May 1964.

e.xiii.)   Thirteenth printing. 12,000 copies, June 1966.

e.xiv.)   Fourteenth printing. 7,500 copies, October 1967.

e.xv.)   Fifteenth printing. 7,500 copies, October 1968.

e.xvi.)   Sixteenth printing. 4,000 copies, October 1970.

e.xvii.)   Seventeenth printing (Random House Vintage Books [V-679]). First printing of 10,000 copies, April 1971. $2.45. The Vintage paperback continues to be reprinted by Random House in quantity as required. No further accounting will be made of these photo-offset reprints.

e.xviii.)   Eighteenth printing. 2,000 copies, March 1974.

e.xix.)   Nineteenth printing. 1,500 copies, June 1976.

e.xx.)   Twentieth printing. 1,000 copies, June 1978.

English Editions

A16.a.i.(e)   First English edition, 1927

DEATH COMES FOR | THE ARCHBISHOP | *by* | WILLA CATHER | [publisher's device] | LONDON | WILLIAM HEINEMANN LTD | MCMXXVII

Collation: [A]⁴ B-T⁸ U⁴ R²; pp.[i-vi] vii-viii, 1-298 [299-300] = 154 leaves.

Contents: Pp.i-ii: blank; p.iii: half title 'DEATH COMES FOR THE ARCHBISHOP'; p.iv: '*By the same Author* | My Ántonia | One of Ours | Youth and the Bright Medusa | The Professor's House | April Twilights (Poems)'; p.v: title page; p.vi: '[bottom of page] Printed in England | at The Westminster Press | 411a Harrow Road | London, W.9'; pp.vii-viii: contents; pp.1-299: text; p.300: '[printer's device] | The Westminster Press | 411a Harrow Road | London, W.9'.

Paper: White laid stock, vertical chain lines 27mm. apart. 190×120mm.; top and fore edges trimmed, bottom edge uncut. End papers of white wove stock.

Binding: Smooth black cloth, gilt-stamped. Front cover: 'DEATH COMES FOR THE ARCHBISHOP'. Spine: 'DEATH COMES | FOR THE | ARCHBISHOP | WILLA | CATHER | HEINEMANN'. Back cover: Heinemann device stamped in blind at the lower right corner.

Dust Jacket: Cream wove paper. Front cover: '{illus. in black ink on yellow-gold ground of Latour on horseback, signed 'Pinker Davis'} | {heavy irregular rule} | · Death comes for the | Archbishop · | {heavy irregular rule} | · By Willa Cather ·'. Spine: 'WILLA | CATHER | {heavy irregular rule} | Death | comes | for the | Arch- | bishop | {heavy irregular rule} | 7s. 6d. | NET | {Heinemann device} | HEINEMANN'. Back cover: 'Also by Willa Cather || {ads for ALL, OO, and PH'. Front inner flap: blurb for *DCA* (18 lines). Back inner flap: advts. for Robert Nathan's *Fiddler in Barley* and K. Pleydell-Bouverie's *The Inn in the Valley*.

Publication: Printed in England and published in November 1927, 2 months after American publication. Noted in *TLS* on 1 December 1927. 7s.6d.

Reprinted in December 1927; January, February, May, October 1928. The Windmill Library popular edition (set from the same plates) published in April 1929 at 3s.6d. The standard edition reprinted in April and October 1929, October 1930, February 1931, December 1933, March 1935. A copy of the 1935 printing has been seen with the spine stamped 'DEATH COMES | TO THE | ARCHBISHOP'.

A16.b.i.(e)   Second English edition (1929 American sheets), 1930

{title-page as in the American second edition (A16.b.i.), but with the imprint 'LONDON | WILLIAM HEINEMANN'}

Collation: [1]^8 (-1$_{2,3}$; 1$_1$ + χ^2) [2-22]^8 [23]^2 (-23$_1$); pp.[i-viii, 1-3] 4-343 [344-346] = 177 leaves. *Note:* Inserted χ^2 is tipped in on the stub of excised 1$_2$.

Illustrations: As in the American second edition.

Contents: Pp.i-ii: blank; p.iii: half title as in A16.b.i.; p.iv: blank; p.v: title page; p.vi: '[at the foot] *Printed in the United States of America*'; p.vii: contents; p.viii: blank; pp.1-343: text as in A16.b.i.; pp.344-346: blank.

Paper: As in A16.b.i. (trade issue). 235 x 177mm.; edges uncut. End papers as in A16.b.i.

Binding: Light brown (74-77) buckram. Front cover blank. Spine: '[gilt-stamped] DEATH COMES | FOR THE | ARCHBISHOP | WILLA | CATHER | HEINEMANN'. Back cover: the Heinemann windmill device stamped in blind on the lower right corner.

Dust Jacket: Heavy mottled cream wove stock, printed overall in green. Front cover: '[within a decorative panel rule] Death Comes | for the | Archbishop | [short swelling rule] | WILLA CATHER'. Spine: 'Death | Comes | for the | Archbishop | [orn.] | Willa | Cather | [orn.] | 15/- | NET | [Heinemann device] | HEINEMANN'. Back cover: the Heinemann device at center. Front inner flap: a 17-line blurb for the book. Back inner flap: 'BY THE SAME AUTHOR | A LOST LADY | *In the Windmill Library* | MY MORTAL ENEMY | *2s. 6d. net* | YOUTH AND THE | BRIGHT MEDUSA | *7s. 6d. net* | DEATH COMES FOR | THE ARCHBISHOP | *Cr. 8vo. 3s. 6d. net* [orn.]'.

Publication: May 1930 at 15s. American second edition sheets with altered title page imprint, bound in England.

c.i.(e)   Third English edition. London: Hamish Hamilton, 1961. Photo-offset from the American fifth edition (A16.e.i.) plates. Available in print until 1972.

A16₁.   DECEMBER NIGHT (first separate edition of chapter 7 from *Death Comes for the Archbishop*,) 1933

[cover title within a cruciform design] A SCENE FROM | "DEATH COMES FOR | THE ARCHBISHOP" | DECEMBER | NIGHT | BY WILLA | CATHER

Collation: [1]⁸; pp.[1-16] = 8 leaves.

Illustrations: Text illustrations and decoration by Harold von Schmidt.

Contents: P. 1: blank (pastedown end paper recto); p. 2: pastedown end paper verso '[within a red-orange elaborate decorative border] [black] December Night | A Scene from Willa Cather's Novel | "Death Comes for the Archbishop" | Place | The episcopal residence and adobe pro-Cathedral | at Santa Fé | Time | About seventy-five years ago | Characters | Jean Baptiste Lamy ("Father Latour") | first Archbishop of New Mexico | Sada, a poor Mexican woman | First Edition in this format | Copyright 1926 · 1927 · 1933 by Willa Cather | No part of this book may be reproduced in any form | without permission in writing from the publisher | Manufactured in the United States of America'; pp. 3-14: unnumbered text pages set in decorative ornamental borders printed in red-orange and black, decorative initials in red-orange and black, catchwords and religious text phrases in red orange; p. 15: terminal pastedown end paper recto, '[within a red-orange decorative border] [black] The special designs | for this book were done with ink | by Harold von Schmidt | The type face, Freehand, was designed | to resemble letters made by a quill pen | & | the book was set by hand | and made by Pynson Printers | under the direction of Elmer Adler | The all rag paper was made in Massachusetts | by the Worthy Paper Company and | the binding by George McKibbin & Son | Published by | Alfred A. Knopf · New York | in November, mcmxxxiii'; p. 16: blank (terminal pastedown end paper verso).

Paper: Cream wove stock. 228 x 177mm.; edges trimmed.

Binding: Very smooth light brown (76) coated paper over boards; lettering deep-stamped in slightly darker light brown (deeper 76) as in the title. Spine blank. Back cover: the cruciform lines only, as on the front cover, in light brown (57).

Dust Jacket: Heavy wove tan (73) paper, printed in light brown (57). Front cover: text as on the binding front cover, but set in the Freehand type face; elaborate floriated decorations in the 4 corner panels and above and beneath the title. Spine blank. Back cover repeats the front cover cruciform decoration without the lettering.

Publication: December 1933 at $1.00 in a first printing of 10,000 copies. Listed as "Christmas Story" in *PW* fall index (16 September 1933) and as "December Night" in the weekly record for 9 December. Reprinted from chapter 7, 'The Great Diocese', of *Death Comes for the Archbishop* (first edition, pp.211-220). Insignificant changes occur in the text: italicized quotations in the first edition are in roman printed in red, the words 'patio' and 'casa' are italic in the first edition, roman in this printing; 'bondwoman' for 'bond-woman' (first ed.) and the ending, 'Here ends the story of that December night', is not in the first edition. 'December Night' was reprinted for the Christmas trade by Knopf in 1934 and 1935. The text, jacket plates, and lettering dies were melted in September 1942.

A16₂. **FATHER JUNIPERO'S HOLY FAMILY** (first separate edition of chapter 9 from *Death Comes for the Archbishop*), 1955

[cover title:] [Green cross outlined in blue-green] | [red] [black letter] Father Junipero's Holy Family | [black] [roman] BY WILLA CATHER | PRESENTED AS A NEW YEAR GREETING | BY | [blue-green] IRVING W. ROBBINS, JR. | [black] NUMBER IV | IN THE AMERICANA SERIES

Collation: [1]⁶; pp.[1-12] = 6 leaves.

Contents: Pp.1-2: blank; pp.3-7: text, headed by a blue-green Greek cross and the title in red black-letter; p.8: blank; p.9:

'"Father Junipero's Holy Family" | Reprinted from Death
Comes for the Archbishop by Willa Cather, | by permission of
Alfred A. Knopf, Inc. Copyright 1926, | 1927 by Willa Cather.
Renewal copyright 1954, 1955 | by the Executors of the Estate
of Willa Cather. | DESIGNED AND PRINTED BY LAWTON
KENNEDY'; pp. 10-12: blank.

Paper: White laid text with vertical chain lines 26mm. apart,
watermarked 'STRATHMORE TEXT U.S.A.' 237 x 158mm.;
edges trimmed, fore edges of the preliminary and terminal
blanks uncut.

Binding: Heavy rough white wove stock, printed as above on the
front cover. Top and bottom edges trimmed, front fore edge
deckled. Stapled at the center fold.

Publication: A New Year's keepsake printed by Lawton Kennedy
of San Francisco for the California collector, Irving W. Robbins,
in a limited edition for private distribution. Reprinted from
chapter 9, 'Death Comes for the Archbishop', of the novel (first
edition; p. 279, 1.8–p. 284, 1.26). The Americana Series were
pamphlets commissioned by Robbins.

A16₃.   **FATHER JUNIPERO'S HOLY FAMILY** (second separate
edition of chapter 9 from *Death Comes for the Archbishop*,) **1956**

[red] FATHER JUNIPERO'S HOLY FAMILY | [black] by
Willa Cather | [signature in red at foot left] a

Collation: π⁴ a-c⁴; pp. [1-32] = 16 leaves.

Contents: Pp. 1-6: blank; p. 7: '"Father Junipero's Holy Family"
[orn.] Reprinted from | Death Comes for the Archbishop by
Willa Cather, | by permission of Alfred A. Knopf, Inc. Copy-
right 1926, | 1927 by Willa Cather. Renewal copyright 1954,
1955 | by the Executors of the Estate of Willa Cather.'; p. 8:
blank; p. 9: title page; p. 10: blank; pp. 11-23: text printed in a
red and black uncial font. A 7-line biographical note on Fr.

Junipero Serra in red precedes the story text. Beneath the text on p.23, '[red] A[d] + M[aiorem] + D[ei] + G[loriam]'; p.24: '"Father Junipero's Holy Family" is reprinted from Death | Comes for the Archbishop by Willa Cather, Book Nine; | set in American Uncial type and two hundred copies printed by | Carolyn Reading Hammer at The Anvil Press in | Lexington, Kentucky, m.cm.lvi.'; pp.25-32: blank.

Note: The preliminary and terminal blank leaves are used as pastedown end papers.

Paper: Rough white wove rag paper, watermarked 'J WHATMAN'. 151 x 124mm.; edges uncut.

Binding: Rough oatmeal paper over boards. Front cover: '[red] father | [black] juni | [red] peros | [black] holy | [red] family'. Spine: '[lettered perpendicularly, reading from bottom to top between two red Maltese crosses] WILLA CATHER'. Back cover blank.

Publication: 200 copies printed by Carolyn Reading Hammer at the Anvil Press, Lexington, Ky., 1956. This text reprints the short biographical paragraph on Father Junipero Serra that appears in A16$_2$.

A17.   SHADOWS ON THE ROCK

a.i.)   First edition, first printing, 1931

TRADE ISSUE

[within a double-rule frame] *BY WILLA CATHER* | [within a single-rule panel] [a shadow image in gray of each title letter behind the individual letters] SHADOWS | ON | THE | ROCK | [beneath the panel] NEW YORK [borzoi oval orn. in gray] MCM XXXI | ALFRED · A · KNOPF

Collation: [1-18]^8; pp.i-vi, 1-2] 3-280 [281-282] = 144 leaves.

Contents: P.i: half title, 'SHADOWS ON THE ROCK | [short rule]'; p.ii: '[within a double-rule frame] *The Works of* | WILLA CATHER | [11 titles listed with dates of publication]'; p.iii: title page; p.iv: 'COPYRIGHT 1931 BY WILLA CATHER | *All rights reserved—no part of this book may be reprinted* | *in any form without permission in writing from the publisher* | FIRST EDITION | MANUFACTURED IN THE UNITED STATES OF AMERICA'; p.v: contents; p.vi: blank; p.1: part title, 'BOOK I | THE APOTHECARY'; p.2: epigraph, '*Vous me demandez des graines de fleurs de ce pays.* | *Nous en faisons venir de France pour notre jardin, n'y en* | *ayant pas ici de fort rares ni de fort belles. Tout y est sauvage, les fleurs aussi bien que les hommes.* | *Marie de l'Incarnation* | (LETTRE À UNE DE SES SOEURS) | *Québec, le 12 août, 1653*'; pp.3-42: text of book 1; p.43: part title, '*BOOK II* | *CÉCILE AND JACQUES*'; p.44: blank; pp.45-113: text of book 2; p.114: blank; p.115: part title, '*BOOK III* | *THE LONG WINTER*'; p.116: blank; pp.117-166: text of book 3; p.167: part title, '*BOOK IV* | *PIERRE CHARRON*'; p.168: blank; pp.169-198: text of book 4; p.199: part title, '*BOOK V* | *THE SHIPS FROM FRANCE*'; p.200: blank; pp.201-234: text of book 5; p.235: part title, '*BOOK VI* | *THE DYING COUNT*'; p.236: blank; pp.237-268: text of book 6; pp.269-280: epilogue; p.281: blank; p.282: '[within a double-rule frame] A NOTE ON THE TYPE | *in which this book is set* | [12 lines in italic] | [borzoi oval orn.] | SET UP, | ELECTROTYPED, PRINTED | AND BOUND BY THE PLIMPTON PRESS, NORWOOD, MASS. | PAPER MADE BY | TICONDEROGA PULP & PAPER CO., | TICONDEROGA, N. Y.'.

Note: The note on type (p.282) describes the type as a font adapted from one designed by Pierre Simon Fournier the younger.

Paper: Cream laid paper with vertical chain lines 18mm. apart. No visible watermark. 190 x 127mm.; top edge trimmed and stained yellow-orange, other edges rough-cut. End papers of the same stock.

Binding: Bright green (131) cloth. A light blue-gray paper label, 52 x 84mm., is mounted on the front cover, '[within a

bright orange decorative frame] SHADOWS | ON THE
ROCK | WILLA CATHER'. A light blue-gray paper label,
68x30mm., is mounted on the spine, '[bright orange decorative
orn.] | SHADOWS | ON THE | ROCK | [bright orange
inverted triangle] | CATHER | [bright orange inverted tri-
angle]'. Back cover blank.

Dust Jacket: 2 jacket colors noted in wove fiber (containing
minute threads that effect an overall mottled appearance) paper:
pale green (134) and rose (2). Both are printed in dark red
overall. Front cover: '[within decorative border rule]
SHADOWS | ON | THE ROCK | [short thick rule] | *WILLA
CATHER* | [short thick rule] | Seldom has any novel been as |
widely bought and as dearly loved as | *Death Comes for the
Archbishop*. I assure | Miss Cather's readers that *Shadows on | the
Rock* is of the same superb vintage | [facsimile signature] Alfred
A. Knopf | ALFRED · A · KNOPF [Borzoi Books device]
NEW YORK'. Spine: '[dec. rule] | SHADOWS | ON | THE
ROCK | A | *New Novel* | *by* | *WILLA CATHER* | *Author of* |
DEATH COMES | FOR THE | ARCHBISHOP | [Borzoi Books
device] | ALFRED A. KNOPF | [dec. rule]'. Back cover:
'[within dec. border rule] {14-line blurb, with Knopf's facsimile
signature beneath}'. Front inner flap: '*By Miss Cather* | [short
swelling rule] | [excerpts from critical reviews for *Death Comes
for the Archbishop*, *My Mortal Enemy*, and *The Professor's House*]'.
Back inner flap: '*By Miss Cather* | [short swelling rule] |
[excerpts from critical reviews for *A Lost Lady*, *One of Ours*,
Youth and the Bright Medusa, and *April Twilights*]'.

Two later dust jackets have been noted:

a: Associated with a copy of the fifth printing (September
1931). The front cover has a stylized mountain scene extending
over the spine; a church on the mountain top and village at the
foot, lettering in white on the front cover: 'SHADOWS | ON
THE | ROCK | *WILLA CATHER* | *Author of* DEATH COMES
FOR THE ARCHBISHOP | ALFRED · A · KNOPF ·
PUBLISHER · N Y'. Spine: 'SHADOWS | ON | THE ROCK |
WILLA | CATHER | *Author of* | DEATH COMES | FOR THE |
ARCHBISHOP | [Borzoi Books device in white] | [white]
ALFRED · A · KNOPF'. Front flap: 'WILBUR CROSS |

Governor of Connecticut | *in the Saturday Review of Literature* |
[text of Cross review] | *(Continued on back of jacket)*'. Back cover:
continuation of Cross review and a 4-line excerpt from Fanny
Butcher's review in the *Chicago Tribune*. Back flap: advt. for WC
Knopf publications.

b: Associated with a copy of the seventh printing (October
1931). Pink wove fiber and decorative format of the first issue
dust jacket, printed in red overall. Front cover: as in the first
issue, but the Knopf statement and facsimile signature are
replaced by 'WILBUR CROSS, Governor of Connecticut, | in *The
Saturday Review of Literature:* | [11-line quote] | *(Continued on
front flap of jacket)*'. Spine: as in the first issue. Back cover:
'*(Continued from front flap of jacket)* | [25 lines of excerpted
reviews in the *San Francisco Chronicle, New York Sun* (Laurence
Stallings), and the *Atlantic Monthly*]'. Front inner flap: '*(Con-
tinued from front of jacket)* | [15-line conclusion of Cross quote, 15
lines of excerpted reviews in the *Chicago Tribune* (Fanny Butcher)
and the *Cleveland Plain Dealer*] | *(Continued on back of jacket)*'.
Back inner flap: '*Some other books by Willa Cather.* | *Have you read
them all?* | [swelling rule] | [list of 7 Knopf titles] | [swelling
rule] | ALFRED · A · KNOPF · PUBLISHER · N · Y ·'.

Note 1: The Santa Barbara rare book dealer, Bradford Morrow,
generously permitted me to borrow the dust jacket described
above for examination and description.

Note 2: Copies of the first printing were sent out to dealers
wrapped in sealed cellophane. Beneath the transparent wrap was
inserted a printed note: 'This is a copy of the First Edition'. No
example of this special wrapping has been seen, but a sealed
copy is offered in a catalog by the Casanova Booksellers,
Milwaukee, Wisconsin, fall, 1932 (no. 85).

Publication: 1 August 1931 at $2.50. The first printing was
announced in *PW* (2 May 1931 and 25 July 1931) as 25,000
copies. Publisher's cost records for the first printing show that
the Plimpton Press delivered 25,700 bound copies between May
and June 1931. Of these, 24,700 were bound in the standard
green trade cloth and 300 in library buckram for H. C. Huntting
and the Library Book House, distributing houses for institutional collections. The overrun of 700 copies were bound in

wrappers made up of a trial dust jacket for distribution as advance review copies. In all review copies examined, the copyright notice is 'SECOND EDITION', and this statement is seen in no other printing. This was an error, rectified by a stop-press correction, early in the pressrun. It may be argued that the advance review copy, therefore, is the true first issue.

Statements of limitation in the limited issues of most of Cather's books show that Knopf intended the limited to be considered the first edition (for collectors), and the trade, though also a part of the first edition, was not always clearly identified as such. The trade and limited issues are almost invariably printed from the same press-setting, and a muddle about bibliographical identification frequently ensues. In a letter from Sidney R. Jacobs, for many years head of Knopf's production department, the Knopf policy is stated in this way: "Knopf never intended that the trade edition of any title, for which a limited number of copies were printed on special paper and numbered and signed, should be anything other than a first edition. In fact . . . different presses and make-readies were needed, and frequently the two printings were performed side by side with different sections of the text being on press at the same moment on the two presses. The trade edition was always considered a first edition, or at least part of a first edition" (Jacobs to author, November 1978).

In the case of the 'SECOND EDITION' review copies, it appears that the printer may have interpreted literally the logic implied by the limited issue notice and set up 'SECOND EDITION' in error for the trade issue copyright page. The error was apparently noticed early in the pressrun, and the 700 sets of sheets so printed, rather than be wasted, were bound in dust jacket wrappers and distributed as review copies. A piece of minor evidence exists to support the chronological precedence of 'SECOND EDITION' copies over 'FIRST EDITION' copies: the back cover of the jacket wrapper has a 14-line blurb with Alfred A. Knopf's name in print rather than facsimile signature as it appears on the trade issue jackets. Also, the wrapper is printed in black rather than red, as were the later jackets—obviously an earlier trial jacket.

The copyright is correctly 'FIRST EDITION' on all examined copies of the trade issue and the title-page–copyright leaf is integral, not a cancel.

Only the limited issue and the first trade printing were worked by Plimpton. On 27 June 1931 (a month before publication), the plates were sent to the Haddon Craftsmen for the second through sixteenth printings. Haddon was the Book-of-the-Month Club's printer and binder, better equipped for the volume of the book club and later printings.

For the advertising campaign in *PW* during the first year of publication, Knopf was at pains to be explicit on numbers of copies shipped each month. A *PW* ad for 16 January 1932 states that 167,679 copies (comprising 10 printings) were shipped in 1931, and the figures are broken down thus:

Book-of-the-Month Club / Catholic Book Club	51,800
before publication	47,290
after publication	21,366
September	14,557
October	8,933
November	7,356
December	10,097
to Canada	5,600
shipped before 10 Jan. 1932	680

These figures show that, although the eleventh printing was completed (5,000 copies; December 1931), orders were still being supplied from the tenth printing. The twelfth printing was not until October 1932, so orders for the greater part of the year were filled from the eleventh printing.

The Canadian edition (Macmillan, 5,600 copies) is of the first trade printing sheets with altered title page imprint and copyright and with the Macmillan name stamped at the foot of the spine.

A textual error, resulting from plate degeneration, occurs on p.250, l.18, of the limited issue and the trade issue, first printing: 'hay-bale' for 'hay-bales'. This was corrected in the

second printing. The 'SECOND EDITION' review copies contain the error.

SOR was reprinted 19 times from the original plates. After the sixteenth printing, the work reverted to the Plimpton Press for the seventeenth to thirtieth printings. New plates were made by the Plimpton Press in April 1946. The copyright states: 'RESET AND PRINTED FROM NEW PLATES'. These plates were electrotyped from the original plates of 1931; hence, not a new edition, but the twenty-first printing.

LIMITED ISSUE

[title as in the trade issue]

Collation: [1]^{10} (1_1 + χ_1) [2-18]^8; pp.[i-x, 1-2] 3-180 [281-284] = 147 leaves. *Note:* Leaf χ_1 is the inserted limitation leaf.

Contents: Pp.i-iii: blank; p.iv: limitation, 'OF THE FIRST EDITION OF | *SHADOWS ON THE ROCK* | SIX HUNDRED NINETEEN COPIES | (OF WHICH SIX HUNDRED SEVEN ARE | FOR SALE) | HAVE BEEN PRINTED ON | *CROXLEY HAND MADE PAPER* | EACH COPY IS SIGNED BY THE AUTHOR | THIS IS NUMBER | [space for number] | [author's signature]' (see note below); pp.v-x: half title (verso blank), title page, copyright, and contents (verso blank) as in the trade issue; pp.1-281: as in trade issue; p.282: as in trade issue, save for the last 2 lines, 'JOHN DICKINSON & CO. LTD., | OF LONDON'; pp.283-284: blank.

Note: The limitation notice in vellum copies: 'OF THE FIRST EDITION OF | *SHADOWS ON THE ROCK* | ONE HUNDRED NINETY-NINE COPIES | (OF WHICH ONE HUNDRED NINETY-FOUR | ARE FOR SALE) | HAVE BEEN PRINTED ON | *SHIDZUOKA JAPAN VELLUM* | EACH COPY IS SIGNED BY THE AUTHOR | THIS IS NUMBER | [space for number] | [author's signature]'.

Paper: 619 copies on cream laid stock with vertical chain lines 28mm. apart (Croxley hand-made paper). Rectangular Borzoi

Books watermark. 234×149mm.; top edge rough-cut and gilt, other edges uncut. End papers of the same stock. 199 copies on Japan vellum (Shidzuoka). 232×148mm.; edges rough-cut, top edge gilt. End papers of the same stock.

Binding: 619 copies in fine linen marbled curl cloth in green-blue, dark blue, red-brown and ochre. Beveled edges. Red-brown leather label on the spine, lettering stamped in gilt, 'WILLA | CATHER || SHADOWS | ON THE | ROCK'. A red ribbon place marker attached at the center of the top inner spine. In a board box covered with red (12) wove paper.

Copies of the 619 limitation have also been noted in cloth of the same marbled pattern in dark and light gray, and red-brown and ochre.

199 copies in full orange (34) limp vellum with beveled edges. Front cover with gilt-stamped decoration. Spine stamped in gilt: 'WILLA | CATHER || SHADOWS | ON THE | ROCK | [orn.]'. Back cover with gilt-stamped rectangular Borzoi Books device at the lower right corner. In a dull green (128) board box with the limitation number in red ink at the foot of the spine. Red ribbon place marker.

Dust Jacket: All copies in heavy cream laid stock with vertical chain lines 30mm. apart. Rectangular Borzoi Books watermark. A full-wrap jacket with flaps folding over the edges. Covers blank. Spine lettered in black as on the binding spine. The limitation number supplied in ink at the foot of the spine.

Publication: 1 August 1931 at $10.00 for the 619 copies on laid paper, and $25.00 for the 199 on Japan vellum. Priority of the limited issue over the trade or vice versa is difficult to establish in any Cather title published by Knopf. The limited issue follows the trade here because of a new policy stated in a Knopf *PW* ad (16 January 1932, p.474): "In keeping with the policy instituted with the limited edition of *Shadows on the Rock*, the exact number of copies printed will depend on orders received." It is reasonably certain that a large part of the first printing of the trade issue had already come off the presses when the numbers of the limited issue were determined and put in work,

especially as Knopf announced that 47,290 trade copies had been shipped before publication and Willa Cather had her own copies by 24 June (CWB copy 700653, inscribed to the Hambourgs on that date), over a month before publication date. As the limited and trade issues were printed from the same setting of plates and frequently simultaneously, it is splitting hairs to make too fine a point of priority.

A note on Book-of-the-Month Club printings of Knopf publications in the thirties: In the 1930s, Haddon Craftsmen was the Book-of-the-Month Club's printer and binder. The club preferred to have their work done in the Haddon plant (at a later date, H. Wolff shared the production of the club, and, later still, Kingsport was allocated a part of Book-of-the-Month Club's production business). One set of plates was expected to take care of BOMC's and Knopf's needs, and Knopf sent their plates to Haddon for their own later printings as well as the club's. This resulted in cost saving to both the club and the publisher because the printings were either combined or run sequentially to share make-ready costs.

Book club bindings differed from the publisher's in that the top edge of the book usually remained unstained, the colophon was sometimes omitted, and a large dot was stamped in blind at the bottom right of the back cover. Otherwise, the bindings were the same.

The paper sometimes varied. Book-of-the-Month Club tried to match the publisher's paper, but customarily used the Glatfelter mill. Most of Knopf's paper came from the Warren mill, with small quantities from Ticonderoga and Curtis.

Book-of-the-Month Club did not carry a club edition notice on the copyright or elsewhere in the book. Despite numerous printings, subscribers were not to know whether their copies were part of the first printing or a later one. (This information is kindly supplied by Sidney R. Jacobs.)

a.ii.1.)   Second printing, first impression. 40,000 copies, June 1931. Copyright: '*Published August 1931 | First and Second Printings*

before Publication'. The colophon (p.282) has been patched to incorporate the statement 'PRINTED AND BOUND BY THE HADDON CRAFTSMEN, INC., CAMDEN, N. J.'. Plate correction made in p.250, replacing the 's' in l.18. Presswork for the second through sixteenth printings (November 1938) is by the Haddon Craftsmen.

a.ii.2.)   Second printing, second impression (Book-of-the-Month Club / Catholic Book Club). 51,800 copies, July 1931. No production record available in the Knopf files.

Variant title page: [within a dark blue single-line arch surmounted by a line-and-dot cross; within a dark blue scalloped dec. rule arch] *SHADOWS* | *on the* | *ROCK* | WILLA CATHER | New York | ALFRED A. KNOPF | 1931

The double rules are removed from the advertisement (p.ii) and p.282 (colophon). Second printing copyright and printer's colophon.

a.iii.)   Third printing. 10,000 copies, August 1931. Copyright adds *'Third Printing, August, 1931'*.

a.iv.)   Fourth printing. 10,000 copies, August 1931. Copyright patched.

a.v.)   Fifth printing. 10,000 copies, September 1931.

a.vi.)   Sixth printing. 5,000 copies, October 1931.

a.vii.)   Seventh printing. 5,000 copies, October 1931.

a.viii.)   Eighth printing. 5,000 copies, November 1931.

a.ix.)   Ninth printing. 5,000 copies, November 1931.

a.x.)   Tenth printing. 5,000 copies, December 1931.

a.xi.)   Eleventh printing. 5,000 copies, December 1931.

a.xii.)   Twelfth printing. 5,000 copies, October 1932.

a.xiii.)   Thirteenth printing. 3,000 copies, October 1934.

a.xiv.)   Fourteenth printing. 2,500 copies, February 1936.

a.xv.)   Fifteenth printing. 3,000 copies, April 1937.

a.xvi.)   Sixteenth printing. 3,000 copies, November 1938.

a.xvii.)   Seventeenth printing. 3,000 copies, October 1940. Presswork for the seventeenth through twenty-eighth (December 1963) printings is by the Plimpton Press.

a.xviii.)   Eighteenth printing. 3,020 copies, September 1942.

a.xix.)   Nineteenth printing. 2,000 copies, December 1943.

a.xx.)   Twentieth printing. 3,000 copies, December 1944.

a.xxi.)   Twenty-first printing. 5,000 copies, April 1946. Copyright: '. . . RESET AND PRINTED FROM NEW PLATES | APRIL 1946'. Actually, not a new edition, but electrotype plates from the same setting. Although the copyright states 'Reprinted eighteen times' before this printing, evidence in the production records indicates that there were 19 reprintings prior to this.

a.xxii.)   Twenty-second printing. 5,000 copies, February 1949. Copyright: 'SECOND PRINTING'.

a.xxiii.)   Twenty-third printing. 5,500 copies, December 1951. Copyright: 'THIRD PRINTING'.

a.xxiv.)   Twenty-fourth printing. 6,000 copies, May 1955. Copyright: 'FOURTH PRINTING'.

a.xxv.)   Twenty-fifth printing. 5,110 copies, August 1958. Copyright: 'FIFTH PRINTING'.

a.xxvi.)   Twenty-sixth printing. 4,840 copies, June 1960. Copyright: 'SIXTH PRINTING'.

a.xxvii.)   Twenty-seventh printing. 6,000 copies, January 1962. Copyright: 'SEVENTH PRINTING'.

a.xxviii.)   Twenty-eighth printing. 6,435 copies, December 1963. Copyright: 'EIGHTH PRINTING'.

a.xxix.)   Twenty-ninth printing. 6,000 copies, April 1966. Presswork: Haddon Craftsmen. Copyright: 'NINTH PRINTING'.

a.xxx.)   Thirtieth printing. 8,000 copies, June 1967. Presswork: H. Wolff. Copyright: 'TENTH PRINTING'.

a.xxxi.)   Thirty-first printing. 3,000 copies, January 1970. Presswork: H. Wolff. Copyright: 'ELEVENTH PRINTING'.

a.xxxii.)   Thirty-second printing (Random House Vintage Books [V-680]). First Vintage printing of 10,000 copies, April 1971. Book design by Charlotte Staub, cover art work by Guy Fleming. Presswork: H. Wolff. The Vintage paperback is not included in Knopf's chronological sequence of printings.

a.xxxiii.)   Thirty-third printing (Second Vintage). 5,000 copies, October 1971. Presswork: H. Wolff.

a.xxxiv.)   Thirty-fourth printing. 1,000 copies, June 1973. Presswork: American Book-Stratford Press. Copyright: 'TWELFTH PRINTING'.

a.xxxv.)   Thirty-fifth printing (Third Vintage). 5,000 copies, May 1974. Presswork: American Book-Stratford Press.

a.xxxvi.)   Thirty-sixth printing (Fourth Vintage). 5,000 copies, November 1975. Presswork: American Book-Stratford Press.

a.xxxvii.)   Thirty-seventh printing (Fifth Vintage). 5,000 copies, May 1976. Presswork: American Book-Stratford Press.

a.xxxviii.   Thirty-eighth printing. 1,000 copies, September 1976. Presswork: Haddon Craftsmen. Copyright: 'THIRTEENTH PRINTING'.

a.xxxix.)   Thirty-ninth printing. 1,000 copies, May 1977. Presswork: Haddon Craftsmen. Copyright: 'FOURTEENTH PRINTING'.

b.)   Second edition (Autograph Edition, vol. 10), 1938

[dec. rule] | WILLA CATHER | [dec. rule] | Shadows on the | Rock | [dec. rule] | [brown-orange: 'H M Co' cipher] | BOSTON | HOUGHTON MIFFLIN COMPANY | 1938

Collation: [1-21]⁸; pp.[i-vi, 1-2] 3-324 [325-330] = 168 leaves.

Illustration: On text paper, inserted facing the title page with a protective tissue. Caption: '*Reduced facsimile of a page of original typescript, with Author's corrections, of "Shadows on the Rock"*'.

Contents: P.i: edition title; p.ii: limitation notice; p.iii: title page; p.iv: copyright; p.v: contents; p.vi: blank; pp.1-325: text with part titles; p.326: blank; p.327: Riverside Press device; pp.328-330: blank.

Notes on paper, binding, dust jacket, and publication with the entry for the entire Autograph Edition (AA1).

English Editions

A17.a.i.(e)   First English edition, 1932

SHADOWS | ON THE | ROCK | By | WILLA | CATHER | [publisher's device] | CASSELL | AND COMPANY, LIMITED | London, Toronto, Melbourne | and Sydney

Collation: [A]⁸ B-I, K-S⁸; pp.[i-viii, 1-2] 3-277 [278-280] = 144 leaves.

Contents: Pp.i-ii: blank; p.iii: half title, 'SHADOWS ON THE | ROCK'; p.iv: '*By the same Author* | [8 titles]'; p.v: title page; p.vi: copyright 'First published 1932 | PRINTED IN GREAT BRITAIN'; p.vii: contents; p.viii: blank; p.1: part title '*BOOK I | THE APOTHECARY* | [epigraph as on p.2 of A17.a.i.]'; p.2: blank; pp.3-42: text of book 1; p.43: part title '*BOOK II* |

CÉCILE AND JACQUES'; p.44: blank; pp.45-112: text of book 2; p.113: part title '*BOOK III* | *THE LONG WINTER*'; p.114: blank; pp.115-163: text of book 3; p.164: blank; p.165: part title '*BOOK IV* | *PIERRE CHARRON*'; p.166: blank; pp.167-196: text of book 4; p.197: part title '*BOOK V* | *THE SHIPS FROM FRANCE*'; p.198: blank; pp.199-231: text of book 5; p.232: blank; p.233: part title '*BOOK VI* | *THE DYING COUNT*'; p.234: blank; pp.235-265: text of book 6; p.266: blank; pp.267-278: epilogue. At the foot of p.278, 'Printed in Great Britain by Butler & Tanner Ltd., Frome and London | F100.1131'; pp.279-280: blank.

Paper: Cream laid stock, vertical chain lines 25mm. apart. Leaves measure 185 x 120mm., edges trimmed. End papers of cream wove stock.

Binding: Tan (77) linen cloth; front and back covers blank. Spine stamped in gilt: 'SHADOWS | ON THE | ROCK | WILLA | CATHER | CASSELL'.

Dust Jacket: Not seen.

Publication: January 1932, 7s.6d. Reviewed in *TLS* on 21 January 1932.

a.ii.(e).   Cassell Pocket Library edition. London, 1936. Available in print until 1961.

b.i.(e).   Second English edition. London: Hamish Hamilton, 1961. Photo-offset from the American plates. Available in print until 1977.

A18.   THE FEAR THAT WALKS BY NOONDAY, 1931

a.)   First separate printing

[within an olive-green rule within an olive-green dec. border rule] [olive-green orn.] [black] THE FEAR | THAT WALKS |

BY NOONDAY | [olive-green swelling rule] | [black] BY |
WILLA CATHER | AND | DOROTHY CANFIELD | NEW
YORK | PHOENIX BOOK SHOP | 1931

Collation: [1]¹²; pp.[i-vi, 1] 2-13 [14-18] = 12 leaves.

Contents: Pp. i-ii: blank; p.iii: title page; p.iv: blank; p.v:
'FOREWORD', signed in print 'Ralph Allan | *October 9th,*
1931'; p.vi: blank; pp. 1-13: text; p.14: 'This edition is strictly
limited to 30 numbered | copies, 25 of which are for sale by the
Phoenix | Book Shop, 41 East 49th Street, New York. | This is
copy number [number supplied in ink]'; pp. 15-18: blank.

Paper: Cream wove; 230 x 154mm., edges uncut. End papers of
the same stock.

Binding: Dark olive-green (128) mottled paper over boards.
Covers blank. Cream paper spine label, 52 x 7mm., '[orn.] |
The | Fear | That | Walks | by | Noon-|day | [orn.] | *Willa* |
Cather | *&* | *Dorothy* | *Canfield* | [orn.]'.

Publication: October 1931; 30 copies printed for the Phoenix
Book Shop. Printed first in the University of Nebraska yearbook
Sombrero ('Quarter-Centennial Edition', vol. 3, 1895), of which
Willa Cather was an associate editor. In his foreword for the
present volume, Ralph Allan states, "It is here reprinted from
the files of a now unobtainable college magazine with the gra-
cious permission of Willa Cather and Dorothy Canfield." The
story was again reprinted in *Willa Cather's Collected Short Fiction,*
1892-1912 [AA7].

A letter from WC to Dorothy Canfield Fisher (4 September
1931) indicates that she is willing to permit the publication in
a very small edition for collectors in order to retrieve the story
from the public domain. She wishes Allan to keep the edition
away from reviewers and newspapers.

A letter from Dorothy Canfield to Ralph Allan (28 August
1931) candidly states that, although the original idea was her
own, the story was written by WC, who generously insisted

that both their names be listed as authors. (These 2 letters are in the private collection of Frederick B. Adams, Jr.)

A19.   OBSCURE DESTINIES

a.i.)   First edition, first printing, 1932

TRADE ISSUE

[green rule] | [black] WILLA CATHER | [green rule] | OBSCURE | DESTINIES | [vignette of an ear of corn in green within a green scalloped oval frame] | [borzoi hound in black] | *New York* ALFRED · A · KNOPF Mcmxxxii

Collation: [1-13]⁸ [14]¹⁰ [15]⁸; pp.[i-x, 1-3] 4-229 [230-234] = 122 leaves.

Contents: Pp.i-iii: blank; p.iv: '*The Works of* | WILLA CATHER | [12 titles with publication dates]'; p.v: half title, '| OBSCURE DESTINIES |'; p.vi: blank; p.vii: title page; p.viii: 'COPYRIGHT 1930, 1932 BY WILLA CATHER | All rights reserved—no part of this book may be reprinted | in any form without permission in writing from the publisher | FIRST EDITION | MANUFACTURED IN THE UNITED STATES OF AMERICA'; p.ix: contents; p.x: blank; p.1: part title, '*NEIGHBOUR ROSICKY*'; p.2: blank; pp.3-71: text of 'Neighbour Rosicky' (a vignette headpiece of a sunflower in green on p.3); p.72: blank; p.73: part title, '*OLD MRS. HARRIS*'; p.74: blank; pp.75-190: text of 'Old Mrs. Harris'; p.191: part title, '*TWO FRIENDS*'; p.192: blank; pp.193-230: text of 'Two Friends'; p.231: blank; p.232: 'A NOTE ON THE TYPE IN | WHICH THIS BOOK IS SET | [15 lines in italic] | [oval borzoi device] | COMPOSED, PRINTED, AND BOUND BY THE | PLIMPTON PRESS, NORWOOD, MASS. PAPER | MADE BY TICONDEROGA PULP & PAPER CO., | TICONDEROGA, N. Y.'

Note: The note on type (p.232) describes the type as Scotch, deriving from an early Scottish type called Modern Roman.

Text Contents (previous publication as noted):
Neighbour Rosicky. *Woman's Home Companion* 57 (April, May
    1930). Title: 'Neighbor Rosicky'. C57
Old Mrs. Harris. *Ladies' Home Journal* 49 (September, October,
    November 1932). Title: 'Three Women'. C59
Two Friends. *Woman's Home Companion* 59 (July 1932). C58

Paper: Cream laid paper with vertical chain lines 18mm. apart.
189 x 127mm.; top edge trimmed and stained dull orange, other
edges rough-cut. End papers of the same stock.

Binding: Green (136) cloth. A pale blue printed paper label
mounted on the front cover, 52 x 83mm., '[within a bright
orange decorative rule frame] [black] OBSCURE | DESTINIES |
WILLA CATHER'. A pale blue printed paper label mounted on
the spine, 68 x 25mm., '[bright orange decorative orn.] |
OBSCURE | DESTINIES | [inverted bright orange triangle] |
CATHER | [inverted bright orange triangle]'. Back cover
blank.

Dust Jacket: Jackets in 2 colors with no priority. Gray-pink fiber
wove paper. Front cover: '[red decorative leaf rule] | [blue]
WILLA CATHER | [red] OBSCURE | DESTINIES | [blue]
Three | *New Stories of* | *the West* | [red leaf rule] | [double red
rules] | [on a 20mm. wide red band, lettered in blue] ALFRED
A. KNOPF [Borzoi Books device] PUBLISHER N. Y.' Spine:
'[red leaf rule] | [red] OBSCURE | DESTINIES | [blue] *Three* |
New Stories | *of the West* | *by* | [red] WILLA | CATHER | [blue]
Author of | SHADOWS ON | THE ROCK | ALFRED A. | KNOPF |
[red leaf rule] | [double red rules] | [on a 20mm. wide red band,
in blue: Borzoi Books device]'. Back cover: '[red leaf rule] |
[blue] *"Among the permanent treasures of American literature"* |
WILLA CATHER'S latest novel | [red] SHADOWS ON THE ROCK |
[21-line blurb in blue] | $2.50 Net | [red leaf rule] | [double
red rule] | [on a 20mm. wide red band, lettered in blue]
ALFRED A. KNOPF [Borzoi Books device] PUBLISHER
N. Y.' Front inner flap: a 41-line blurb printed in blue; red leaf
rule at top, leaf rule at bottom with double red rules and blank
red band. Back inner flap: '[red leaf rule] | [blue] *Some other books
by* | [red] WILLA CATHER | [blue] *Have you read them all?* |
[advts. for 7 titles]'.

The other dust jacket noted is of bright yellow (83) paper with
lettering and decoration as on the first described, but with front
cover title, rules, bands, and decorations in green; other lettering in dark red. On all copies of both jackets, a corner is cut
away from the front inner flap where the price was printed (see
publication note below).

Publication: 5 August 1932 at $2.00 in a first printing of
25,000 copies. First listed in the *PW* weekly record (30 July
1932) at $2.00; in the *PW* fall index (17 September 1932) at
$2.50. The dust jacket was imprinted with the higher price on
the front inner flap. When the lower price was decided upon,
the corner of the flap containing the price was clipped. A note
in the Knopf publication record for the first printing states,
"When jacket is reprinted, price on flap should be changed to
$2.00." Forty-one thousand jackets were printed with the
higher price and were used for the first 5 printings.

A salesman's dummy in first edition trade binding (with red-
printed yellow dust jacket printed on the front cover only) contains title page, copyright, contents page, part titles for the 3
stories, and text from pp.3-9 of 'Neighbour Rosicky', pp.75-81
of 'Old Mrs. Harris', and pp.193-198 of 'Two Friends'. The rest
of the full-size book consists of blank leaves. Back cover and
inner flaps of the dust jacket are blank.

LIMITED ISSUE

[title as in the trade edition]

Collation: $[1]^8 (1_2 + \chi_1) [2-14]^8 [15]^8 [15_8 + 2\chi_1) [16]^2$;
pp.[i-xiv, 1-3] 4-229 [230-234] = 124 leaves. *Note:* Leaf χ_1 is
the inserted limitation leaf; $2\chi_1$ is the final 2 pages of text.

Contents: Pp.i-v: blank; p.vi: 'OF THE FIRST EDITION OF |
OBSCURE DESTINIES | TWO HUNDRED AND SIXTY
COPIES | (OF WHICH TWO HUNDRED AND
THIRTY-|FIVE ARE FOR SALE) | HAVE BEEN PRINTED
ON | *NIHON JAPAN VELLUM* | EACH COPY IS SIGNED
BY THE AUTHOR | THIS IS NUMBER [space for the hand-

supplied number] | [author's signature]'; p.vii: blank; p.viii: advertisement as in trade edition; p.ix: half title as in trade edition; p.x: blank; p.xi: title page; p.xii: copyright as in trade edition; p.xiii: contents; p.xiv: blank; pp.1-230: text as in trade edition; p.231: blank; p.232: note on type and printer's imprint as in trade edition.

Paper: Japan vellum without watermark. 235 x 148mm.; top edge rough-trimmed and gilt, other edges uncut. End papers of the same stock.

Binding: Bright green (131), black- and gold-flecked, Chinese paper over boards. White vellum paper shelfback. A gold paper label, 68 x 93mm., lettered and decorated in black, mounted on the front cover, '[within a border rule decorated with a leaf motif] OBSCURE | DESTINIES | [small 6-pointed star] | WILLA CATHER'. Spine lettered in gilt: '[leaf rule] | OBSCURE | DESTINIES | [small gilt 6-pointed star] | WILLA | CATHER | [leaf rule]'. Back cover: Borzoi Books device stamped in gilt on the lower right corner. A green satin ribbon place marker is attached at the top of the inner spine.

Dust Jacket: Cream laid paper with vertical chain lines 30mm. apart. The Borzoi Book watermark. Covers blank. Spine lettered in black as on the binding spine with the limitation number supplied by hand in ink at the foot of the spine. A full-wrap jacket. In a board box covered with bright yellow (83) paper. Covers and spine are blank. The limitation number is supplied by hand in ink at the foot of the spine.

Publication: 5 August 1932; 260 copies (235 for sale) at $15.00 the copy. The custom of 2 separate limited issues at different prices as in previous years was curtailed to a single limited issue.

a.ii.)   Second printing. 5,000 copies, August 1932. Overrun of first printing jackets with clipped corners used. Presswork for the first 9 printings was by the Plimpton Press.

a.iii.)   Third printing. 3,000 copies, September 1932. First printing jackets used.

a.iv.) Fourth printing. 5,000 copies, October 1932. First printing jackets used.

a.v.) Fifth printing. 2,500 copies, December 1932. Remainder of 1,500 first printing jackets used up and 1,200 new jackets with corrected price printed.

a.vi.) Sixth printing. 1,500 copies, September 1941.

a.vii.) Seventh printing. 1,200 copies, November 1949.

a.viii.) Eighth printing. 1,000 copies, April 1953.

a.ix.) Ninth printing. 2,000 copies, May 1960.

a.x.) Tenth printing. 2,000 copies, May 1966. Presswork: Haddon Craftsmen.

a.xi.) Eleventh printing (Random House Vintage Books, V-179). 10,000 copies, September 1974. Offset printing: American Book-Stratford Press.

b.) Second edition (Autograph Edition, vol. 12), **1938**

[dec. rule] | WILLA CATHER | [dec. rule] | Obscure Destinies | & | Literary Encounters | [dec. rule] | [brown-orange: 'H M Co' cipher] | BOSTON | HOUGHTON MIFFLIN COMPANY | 1938

Collation: [1-21]⁸; pp.[i-iv, 1-6] 7-327 [328-332] = 168 leaves.

Contents: P.i: edition title; p.ii: limitation notice; p.iii: title page; p.iv: copyright; p.1: half title 'OBSCURE DESTINIES'; p.2: blank; p.3: contents; p.4: blank; p.5: part title, 'Neighbour Rosicky'; p.6: blank; pp.7-62: text of 'Neighbour Rosicky'; p.63: part title, 'Old Mrs. Harris'; p.64: blank; pp.65-158: text of 'Old Mrs. Harris'; p.159: part title, 'Two Friends'; p.160: blank; pp.161-191: text of 'Two Friends'; p.192: blank; pp.193-328: *Literary Encounters* (i.e., *Not Under Forty*); p.329: Riverside Press device; pp.330-332: blank.

Notes on paper, binding, dust jacket, and publication will be found with the entry for the entire Autograph Edition (AA1).

English Editions

A19.a.i.(e)   First English edition, 1932

OBSCURE | DESTINIES | *by* | WILLA CATHER | [pub. device] | CASSELL | and Company Limited | London, Toronto, Melbourne | and Sydney

Collation: [A]⁸ B-O⁸; pp.[1-4] 5 [6-8] 9-223 [224] = 112 leaves.

Contents: P.1: half title, 'OBSCURE DESTINIES'; p.2: blank; p.3: title page; p.4: copyright, 'First published 1932 | *Printed in Great Britain*'; p.5: contents; p.6: blank; p.7: part title, 'NEIGHBOUR ROSICKY'; p.8: blank; pp.9-73: text of 'Neighbour Rosicky', subscribed '*New York*, 1928'; p.74: blank; p.75: part title, 'OLD MRS. HARRIS'; p.76: blank; pp.77-186: text of 'Old Mrs. Harris', subscribed '*New Brunswick*, 1931'; p.187: part title, 'TWO FRIENDS'; p.188: blank; pp.189-223: text of 'Two Friends', subscribed '*Pasadena*, 1931'; p.224: '*Printed in Great Britain by* | *Hazell, Watson & Viney Ltd.* | *London and Aylesbury*'.

Paper: Smooth cream wove stock, 184 x 120mm.; edges trimmed. End papers of smoother wove stock.

Binding: Bright green cloth. Covers blank; front cover with a blind border rule. Spine: '[gilt-stamped] OBSCURE | DESTINIES | WILLA | CATHER | CASSELL'.

Dust Jacket: Not seen.

Publication: December 1932. Printed and bound in England by Hazell, Watson & Viney for Cassell.

b.i.(e).   Second English edition. London: Hamish Hamilton, 1967. Offset from the American plates. Available in print until 1970.

A20.   LUCY GAYHEART

a.i.)   First edition, first printing, 1935

TRADE ISSUE

[within a double rule frame] BY | WILLA CATHER | [orange-
brown] Lucy Gayheart | [black] ALFRED A. KNOPF New York
1935 | [borzoi hound orn.]

Collation: [1-15]⁸; pp.[i-vi, 1-2] 3-231 [232-234] = 120 leaves.

Contents: Pp.i-ii: blank; p.iii: half title, 'LUCY GAYHEART';
p.iv: 'THE WORKS OF | WILLA CATHER | [15 titles with
publication dates]'; p.v: title page; p.vi: 'COPYRIGHT 1935
BY WILLA CATHER | ALL RIGHTS RESERVED. NO PART
OF THIS BOOK | MAY BE REPRODUCED IN ANY FORM
WITHOUT | PERMISSION IN WRITING FROM THE
PUBLISHER, | EXCEPT BY A REVIEWER WHO MAY
QUOTE BRIEF | PASSAGES IN A REVIEW TO BE
PRINTED IN A MAGA-|ZINE OR NEWSPAPER. | FIRST
EDITION | MANUFACTURED IN THE UNITED STATES';
p.1: part title, '|| *Lucy Gayheart* | BOOK I |'; p.2: blank;
pp.3-139: text of book 1; p.140: blank; p.141: part title, '||
BOOK II |'; p.142: blank; pp.143-201: text of book 2; p.202:
blank; p.203: part title, '|| BOOK III |'; p.204: blank;
pp.205-231: text of book 3; p.232: blank; p.233: '*The characters
and situations in this work are | wholly fictional and imaginary, and
do not portray | and are not intended to portray any actual persons | or
parties.*'; p.234: 'DESIGNER'S NOTE | [17-line note in roman
signed, "W. A. D[wiggins].] | SET UP, ELECTROTYPED,
PRINTED, AND BOUND | BY THE PLIMPTON PRESS,
NORWOOD, | MASSACHUSETTS | PAPER MADE BY
S. D. WARREN CO., | BOSTON, MASSACHUSETTS'.

Note: The designer's note (p.234) describes the font as 11-point
Linotype Caslon with long descenders on 13-point body, with
running heads in Linotype Janson Italic.

Paper: Cream laid stock with vertical chain lines 24mm. apart.
No visible watermark. 190x125mm.; top edge trimmed and

stained dull yellow-orange, other edges rough-cut. End papers of the same stock.

Binding: Yellowish green (136) cloth. A gray-blue paper label, 53x84mm., mounted on the front cover, '[within a bright orange decorative border] LUCY | GAYHEART | WILLA CATHER'. A gray-blue paper label, 68x31mm., on the spine, '[bright orange orn.] | LUCY | GAY-|HEART | [bright orange inverted triangle] | CATHER | [bright orange inverted triangle]'. Back cover blank.

Dust Jacket: Dull coated wove paper with the ground colors in descending panels of blue-green (162), greenish blue (168), and black. Lettering and decoration on the front cover are white: '[title letters with black 'shadow'] Lucy | Gayheart | WILLA CATHER'S | NEW NOVEL [flying bird outline]'. Spine: '[in a black panel, lettering in white] *Lucy* | *Gayheart* | WILLA | CATHER'S | NEW | NOVEL | [8 orn. on a greenish blue (168) panel] | [black lettering on a blue-green panel (162)] *Alfred A. Knopf* | [Borzoi Books rectangular device]'. Back cover: '[orn. of 4 short vertical rules in greenish blue] | [black] WILLA CATHER'S PREVIOUS NOVEL | SHADOWS ON THE ROCK | [orn. of 4 short vertical rules in greenish blue] | [13-line excerpt from a review by Henry Seidel Canby | [rectangular Borzoi Books device] ALFRED · A · KNOPF · PUBLISHER · N. Y.' Front inner flap: '[greenish blue] $2.00 NET | [black] Lucy Gayheart | [greenish blue orn.] | [8-line blurb, signed in facsimile 'Alfred A. Knopf'] | [greenish blue orn.] | Jacket Drawing by Rudolph Rusicka'. Back inner flap: '[lettered vertically from bottom to top] SOME OTHER BOOKS BY WILLA CATHER—HAVE YOU READ THEM ALL? [horizontal lettering] [green-blue] NOVELS | [8 titles listed, printed in black] | ALFRED · A · KNOPF · PUBLISHER. N.Y.'

Publication: 1 August 1935 at $2.00 in a first printing of 25,000 copies with 'FIRST EDITION' on the copyright. The first and second printings were printed and bound at the same time by the Plimpton Press. The second printing of 27,500 copies has the copyright notice, 'PUBLISHED AUGUST 1, 1935 | FIRST AND SECOND PRINTINGS | BEFORE PUBLICATION' and has the title page printed in black. Use of

color on the title page is only in the limited issue and the first
trade printing.

LG was serialized before book publication in *Woman's Home
Companion* 62 (March-July 1935) in 5 parts. [CCC5]

In a *PW* ad for 4 May 1935 (p.1725), Knopf states the policy,
"Since I anticipate a sale of at least 50,000 copies, the first
printing will have to be pro-rated among booksellers according
to the total of their individual orders." Knopf may have received
complaints from booksellers about prepublication orders for previous Cather titles which bore copyright notices for printings
later than the first.

A salesman's dummy, containing no text, is in first edition
binding and dust jacket. It has a notice printed on the open
endpaper recto: '[Triple rule] | *This new novel by* | WILLA
CATHER | —her first since SHADOWS ON THE ROCK, | pub-
lished in 1931—is Romantic, West-|ern, Modern, a story of the
passionate | enthusiasms of youth, which triumph | even when
they seem to fail | TO BE PUBLISHED AUGUST I | 240
PAGES, $2.00 NET |||'. The only other printed matter in the
book is a title page followed by 6 pages of lined spaces for
subscription orders under the heading '*Place your order now for a
copy of* | Lucy Gayheart | *Your signature below will guarantee* | *your
getting a copy as soon as it is published*'.

The advance reading copies are of the second printing (A20.a.ii.).
The plain tan jacket has on the front cover, 'advance copy | for |
READING ONLY | [dot] | not for sale'. On the title page is a
purple ink rubber-stamp: 'Reading Copy | Not For Sale'.

LIMITED ISSUE

[title as in the trade issue]

Collation: [1]^8 (1_2 + χ_1) [2-13]^8 [14]^4 [15-16]^8; pp.[i-xii, 1-2]
3-231 [232-238]= 125 leaves. *Note:* Leaf χ_1 is the inserted
limitation leaf; the stub is pasted to the inner margin of 1_{7r}.

Contents: Pp.i-v: blank; p.vi: limitation notice, *'Of the first edition of* | LUCY GAYHEART | SEVEN HUNDRED AND FORTY-NINE COPIES | (OF WHICH SEVEN HUNDRED AND TWENTY-| FOUR ARE FOR SALE) HAVE BEEN PRINTED | ON CROXLEY RAG PAPER · EACH COPY IS | SIGNED BY THE AUTHOR | THIS IS NUMBER [space for hand-supplied number] | [author's signature]'; p.vii: blank; p.viii: advt. as in trade issue; p.ix: half title, 'LUCY GAYHEART'; p.x: blank; p.xi: title page; p.xii: copyright as in the trade issue; pp.1-233: as in the trade issue; p.234: 'DESIGNER'S NOTE | [17 lines in roman, signed 'W. A. D[wiggins].'] | SET UP, ELECTROTYPED, PRINTED, AND BOUND | BY THE PLIMPTON PRESS, NORWOOD, | MASSACHUSETTS | PAPER MADE BY JOHN DICKINSON & CO., LTD., | OF LONDON'; pp.235-238: blank.

Paper: Heavy cream laid, vertical chain lines 30mm. apart. Borzoi Books rectangular watermark. 227 x 148mm.; top edge trimmed and gilt, other edges uncut. End papers of the same stock.

Binding: Blue (182) buckram, beveled edges. Front cover blank. Spine lettered and decorated in gilt stamp: '[double orn. rule] | Lucy | Gayheart | [orn. rule] | WILLA | CATHER | [double orn. rule] | ALFRED·A· | KNOPF'. Back cover with the Borzoi Books device stamped in blind on the lower right corner. In a board box covered with light gray wove paper; covers and spine blank. The limitation number is supplied in ink by hand at the foot of the spine. A blue ribbon place marker attached at the top inner spine.

Dust Jacket: Cream laid stock (like the text paper, but with more regular horizontal chain lines 30mm. apart). The Borzoi Books watermark. Covers blank. Spine printed in black; lettered and decorated as the binding. A full-wrap jacket.

Publication: 1 August 1935 in a limitation of 749 copies (25 not for sale) at $10.00. Knopf stated in a *PW* ad (27 April 1935, p.1651) that the exact number of limited copies would depend on orders received by 1 June.

Canadian edition: Toronto: the Ryerson Press, 1935. 2,500 sets of the American second printing sheets (see A20.a.ii. below) bound by the Plimpton Press with the Ryerson imprint and special copyright.

a.ii.)   Second printing. 27,500 copies, August 1953. Printed simultaneously with the first printing with patched copyright, '. . . FIRST AND SECOND PRINTINGS | BEFORE PUBLICATION' and title page printed in black only. 2,500 copies bound for the Canadian edition. Presswork (a.ii-iv.): the Plimpton Press.

a.iii.)   Third printing. 10,000 copies, August 1935. 5,000 copies only were bound and distributed in 1935. The remainder of the printing was bound as required until 1942.

a.iv.)   Fourth printing. 3,000 copies, December 1961.

a.v.)   Fifth printing. 3,000 copies, September 1966. Presswork: H. Wolff.

a.vi.)   Sixth printing. 1,500 copies, September 1969. Presswork: H. Wolff.

a.vii.)   Seventh printing. 1,000 copies, January 1973. Presswork: H. Wolff.

a.viii.)   Eighth printing (Random House Vintage Book, V-756). 7,500 copies, June 1976. Offset printing: American Book-Stratford Press.

b.)   Second edition (with *My Mortal Enemy;* Autograph Edition, vol. 11), 1938

See A15.b. *Lucy Gayheart* comprises pp. 1-234 of vol. 11. Notes on paper, binding, dust jacket, and publication with the entry for the entire Autograph Edition (AA1).

English Editions

A20.a.i.(e)   First English edition, 1935

[within a double-line rule frame] LUCY GAYHEART | By | WILLA CATHER | [publisher's device] | CASSELL AND COMPANY, LTD. | LONDON, TORONTO, MELBOURNE AND SYDNEY'

Collation: [A]⁸ B-Q⁸; [1-8] 9-254 [255-256] = 128 leaves.

Contents: Pp. 1-2: blank; p.3: half title, 'LUCY GAYHEART'; p.4: 'By the SAME AUTHOR | OBSCURE DESTINIES | SHADOWS ON THE ROCK'; p.5: title page; p.6: 'FIRST PUBLISHED . . . 1935 | *Printed in Great Britain by* | *Hazell, Watson & Viney, Ltd., London and Aylesbury.* | F50.635.'; p.6: part title, 'BOOK I'; p.8: blank; pp.9-156: text of book 1; p.157: part title, 'BOOK II'; p.158: blank; pp.159-221: text of book 2; p.222: blank; p.223: part title, 'BOOK III'; p.224: blank; pp.225-254: text of book 3; pp.255-256: blank.

Paper: White wove stock. Leaves measure 185 x 121mm.; all edges trimmed. End papers of heavier cream wove stock.

Binding: Light blue-green (163) cloth. Covers blank. Spine stamped in gilt: '[orn. rule] LUCY | GAYHEART | [orn.] | WILLA | CATHER | CASSELL | [orn. rule]'.

Dust Jacket: White wove paper. Front cover: at top and bottom are alternating rules of red leaves, red circles separated by triple black rules, '*LUCY GAYHEART* | *BY* | *WILLA CATHER* | [orn.]'. Spine: '[rules as on front cover] | *LUCY* | *GAYHEART* | *BY* | *WILLA* | *CATHER* | *7s.6d. net* | *CASSELL* | [rules as on front cover]'. Back cover: '*LUCY GAYHEART* | [12-line blurb] | *WILLA CATHER* | [at foot] *Curwen Press*'. Front inner flap: 'BY THE SAME AUTHOR | SHADOWS ON | THE ROCK | [excerpts from 2 English reviews] | 3s.6d. net | *Pocket Edition* | Leather 5s. net Cloth 3s.6d. net | OBSCURE DESTINIES | [excerpts from 2 English reviews] | 3s.6d. net'. Back inner flap blank.

Publication: 25 July 1935 at 7s.6d. Printed in England. Reviewed in *TLS*, 25 July 1935.

b.i.(e).   Second English edition. London: Hamish Hamilton, 1962. Set photographically from the American first edition plates.

A21.   NOT UNDER FORTY

a.i.)   First edition, first printing, 1936

TRADE ISSUE

[bright red-orange] Not Under Forty | [black] *BY* | WILLA CATHER | [red-orange rule] | [within a double black rule frame] 1 9 [red-orange borzoi hound] 3 6 | NEW YORK | ALFRED A KNOPF

Collation: [1-10]⁸; pp.[i-x, 1-2] 3-147 [148-150] = 80 leaves.

Contents: P.i: blank; p.ii: 'THE WORKS OF | WILLA CATHER | [16 titles with publication dates]'; p.iii: half title, 'NOT UNDER FORTY'; p.iv: blank; p.v: title page; p.vi: 'COPYRIGHT 1922, 1933, 1936 BY WILLA CATHER | [5-line 'rights reserved' notice in caps] | FIRST EDITION | MANUFACTURED IN THE UNITED STATES OF AMERICA'; p.vii (designated 'v'): prefatory note; p.viii: blank; p.ix: contents; p.x: blank; p.1: second half title (as p.iii); p.2: blank; pp.3-147: text; p.148: 'DESIGNER'S NOTE | [22 lines in italic] | W. A. DWIGGINS'; pp.149-150: blank.

Note: In the 'Designer's Note' (p.148), the type fonts used are identified as Electra for the body matter and page numbers, Linotype Janson for the running heads. Also, 'The book was set up, printed and bound by The Plimpton Press. . . . The paper was made by Curtis & Brother, Newark, Delaware.' This note is altered in the limited issue.

Text Contents (previously published as noted):
A Chance Meeting. *Atlantic Monthly* 252 (February 1933).
   D591
The Novel Démeublé. *The New Republic*, 12 April 1922. D583
148 Charles Street. *New York Evening Post, Literary Review,* 4

November 1922. With the title, 'The House on Charles
Street'. D584

Miss Jewett. In *The Best Stories of Sarah Orne Jewett* (Boston:
Houghton Mifflin, 1925). Preface. DD7

"Joseph and His Brothers." *Saturday Review of Literature* 14
(6 June 1936). Title: 'The Birth of Personality: An
Appreciation of Thomas Mann's Trilogy'. D593

Katherine Mansfield. In *The Borzoi 1925* (New York: Knopf,
1925). This version was expanded and developed for inclusion
in *NUF*. DD6

Paper: Cream laid stock, vertical chain lines 30mm. apart.;
Borzoi Books rectangular watermark. 227 x 137mm.; top edge
trimmed and stained gray-brown, other edges rough-cut. End
papers of the same stock.

Binding: Light yellow-green (119) cloth stamped on the front
cover in gray-brown with a stylized floral device, surmounted by
'W S C'. Spine stamped in gray-brown: '[orn. rule] | NOT |
UNDER | FORTY | BY | *Willa* | *Cather* | [orn. rule] |
KNOPF'. Borzoi Books device stamped at the lower right
corner of the back cover in gray-brown.

Dust Jacket: Coated laid paper with vertical chain lines 28mm.
apart. Ground color is cream, overprinted in colors. Front cover:
'[within a deep pink (248) panel rule, lettering in red-orange
(35)] Not | Under Forty | [blue-green (164) thick rule] | [blue-
green (164)] *by Willa Cather* | [within a solid panel of red-
orange (35), quasi-floral geometric design in cream, pink (248)
and blue-green (164)] | [deep pink (248) thick rule] | [blue-
green lettering on cream panel] *Studies of Literary Personalities
and Certain* | *Aspects of Literature.* | [4-line blurb in roman] |
[red-orange (35) thick rule]'. Spine: '[orn. panel rule in pink
(248) and red-orange (35)] | [blue-green (164)] Not | Under |
Forty | BY | WILLA | CATHER | [orn. panel rule in same
colors] | [Borzoi Books device in cream on blue-green (164)] |
[thick pink (248) rule] | [blue-green (164)] KNOPF | [thick
red-orange (35) rule]'. Back cover: '[red-orange (35)] *also* | *by*
Miss Cather || [advts., printed in blue-green (164), for 6 titles,
arranged in 2 columns] | [red-orange] *Alfred A. Knopf* [space]
NEW YORK'. Front inner flap: '[red-orange (35)] *Not Under*

Forty $2.00 *net* | [double blue-green rule] | [blue-green] *also by Miss Cather* | Death comes for | the Archbishop | *With Drawings by* | HAROLD VON SCHMIDT | [2 excerpts from reviews printed in blue-green]'. Back inner flap: '[double blue-green rule, lettering in blue-green] *also by Miss Cather* | [review excerpts for 3 titles]'.

Publication: 23 November 1936 at $2.00 in a first printing of 6,200 copies designated 'FIRST EDITION' on the copyright. Presswork for the first 5 printings was by the Plimpton Press, later printings by the Haddon Craftsmen.

LIMITED ISSUE

[title-page as in the first edition, trade issue]

Collation: π_1 [1-10]^8; pp.[i-xii, 1-2] 3-147 [148-150] = 81 leaves. *Note:* Leaf π_1 is the inserted limitation leaf.

Contents: P.i: blank; p.ii: limitation notice, 'OF THE FIRST EDITION OF | NOT UNDER FORTY | THREE HUNDRED AND THIRTY-THREE COPIES (OF | WHICH THREE HUNDRED AND THIRTEEN ARE FOR | SALE) HAVE BEEN PRINTED ON NIHON JAPAN | VELLUM. | EACH COPY IS SIGNED BY THE AUTHOR. THIS | IS NUMBER [space for hand-supplied number] | [author's signature]'; p.iii: blank; p.iv: advt. as in trade issue; p.v: half title; p.vi: blank; p.vii: title page; p.viii: copyright as in trade issue; p.ix (numbered 'v'): prefatory note; p.x: blank; p.xi: contents; p.xii: blank; pp.1-147: as in trade issue; p.148: 'DESIGNER'S NOTE. . . .'; pp.149-150: blank.

Note: P.148 (designer's note) is altered in the 2 final lines: '*Paper supplied by Thomas N. Fairbanks, New* | *York.*' The prefatory note (p.ix) is numbered 'v' because Knopf's pagination did not include the limitation leaf or the integral advertisement leaf (pp.iii-iv).

Paper: Heavy wove Japan vellum. 229 x 147mm.; top edge trimmed and gilt, other edges uncut. End papers of the same stock.

Binding: Blue (182) buckram, beveled edges. Front cover gilt-stamped 'W · S · C | [elaborate geometric floral orn.]'. Spine gilt-stamped, '|[5 thick-thin rules] | NOT | UNDER | FORTY | BY | WILLA | CATHER | [5 thick-thin rules] |'. Back cover: Borzoi rectangular device stamped in blind on the lower right corner. A blue ribbon place marker attached at the top inner spine.

Dust Jacket: Cream wove paper printed in black as on the binding front cover and spine. Limitation number supplied by hand at the foot of the spine. Back cover and inner flaps blank. A full-wrap jacket. In a plain gray paper-covered box.

Publication: 23 November 1936; 333 copies (20 not for sale) at $7.50. The exact number of limited copies depended on orders received by 1 October (Knopf *PW* advt. 19 September 1936, p.1035).

a.ii.) Second printing. 2,500 copies, November 1936. Presswork (a.ii-v): Plimpton Press.

a.iii.) Third printing. 2,500 copies, November 1936.

a.iv.) Fourth printing. 2,500 copies, December 1936.

a.v.) Fifth printing. 940 copies, March 1953.

a.vi.) Sixth printing. 750 copies, January 1964. Presswork (a.vi-viii): Haddon Craftsmen.

a.vii.) Seventh printing. 1,000 copies, January 1967.

a.viii.) Eighth printing. 1,100 copies, January 1971.

b.) Second edition (with *Obscure Destinies;* Autograph Edition, vol.12), 1938

See A19.b. *Not Under Forty*, with the title *Literary Encounters*, comprises pp.193-328 of vol.12, preceded by *Obscure Destinies* text. Notes on paper, binding, dust jacket and publication with the entry for the entire Autograph Edition (AA1).

English Editions

A21.a.i.(e).   First English edition, 1936

NOT UNDER FORTY | by | WILLA CATHER | [pub.
device] | CASSELL | *and Company Limited* | *London, Toronto,*
Melbourne | *and Sydney*

Collation: [1]⁸ 2-11⁸; pp.[i-iv] v [vi-viii], 1-165 [166-168] = 88
leaves.

Contents: P.i: half title, 'NOT UNDER FORTY'; p.ii: '*By Willa*
Cather || LUCY GAYHEART | OBSCURE DESTINIES |
SHADOWS ON THE ROCK | DEATH COMES FOR THE
ARCHBISHOP'; p.iii: title page; p.iv: copyright, '*First*
published in 1936 | PRINTED IN GREAT BRITAIN BY |
EBENEZER BAYLIS AND SON, LTD., THE | TRINITY
PRESS, WORCESTER, AND LONDON | F.1036'; p.v:
'PREFATORY NOTE | [15 lines] | THE AUTHOR.'; p.vi: blank;
p.vii: contents; p.viii: blank; pp.1-166: text; p.167-168: blank.

Text content: As in A20.a.i. (first American edition).

Paper: Cream wove stock; 185 x 121mm., edges trimmed. End
papers of a heavier cream wove stock.

Binding: Blue (duller than 179) linen cloth, covers blank. Spine
stamped in gilt: '[orn. rule] NOT | UNDER | FORTY | [star
orn.] | WILLA | CATHER [orn. rule] | CASSELL'.

Dust Jacket: Smooth cream wove stock. Front cover: '*NOT*
UNDER | *FORTY* | [bright yellow green (131) calligraphic
orn.] | *WILLA CATHER*'. Back cover: 'NOT UNDER
FORTY | [24-line blurb] | WILLA CATHER'. Spine: 'NOT |
UNDER | FORTY | WILLA | CATHER | 5S. | net |
CASSELL'. Front inner flap: 5 review excerpts for *Lucy Gayheart*.
Back inner flap: 2 review excerpts for *Shadows on the Rock* and 2
for *Obscure Destinies*.

Publication: Printed in England by the Trinity Press, Ebenezer Baylis and Son, Ltd., Worcester and London. Published in December 1936 at 5s.

A22.   SAPPHIRA AND THE SLAVE GIRL

a.i.)   First edition, first printing, 1940

TRADE ISSUE

[within a double rule-frame] BY | [bright red-orange] WILLA CATHER | [black] Sapphira | *and the* | Slave Girl | ALFRED A. KNOPF *New York* 1940 | [borzoi hound in bright red-orange]

Collation: [1-19]⁸ x₁; pp.[i-vii] viii [1-2] 3-295 [296-298] = 153 leaves. *Note:* Terminal leaf χ₁ is an inserted blank.

Contents: P.i: blank; p.ii: 'THE WORKS OF | WILLA CATHER | [18 titles with publication dates]'; p.iii: half title; p.iv: blank; p.v: title page; p.vi: 'COPYRIGHT 1940 BY WILLA CATHER | [6-line reserved rights statement in caps] | FIRST EDITION | MANUFACTURED IN THE UNITED STATES'; pp.vii-viii: contents; p.1: part title, '|| *Book I* | SAPPHIRA AND HER HOUSEHOLD |'; p.2: blank; pp.3-54: text of book 1; p.55: part title, '||*Book II* | NANCY AND TILL |'; p.56: blank; pp.57-82: text of book 2; p.83: part title, '|| *Book III* | OLD JEZEBEL |'; p.84: blank; pp.85-112: text of book 3; p.113: part title, '|| *Book IV* | SAPPHIRA'S DAUGHTER |'; p.114: blank; pp.115-145: text of book 4; p.146: blank; p.147: part title, '|| *Book V* | MARTIN COLBERT |'; p.148: blank; pp.149-186: text of book 5; p.187: part title, '|| *Book VI* | SAMPSON SPEAKS TO THE MASTER |'; p.188: blank; pp.189-211: text of book 6; p.212: blank; p.213: part title, '|| *Book VII* | NANCY'S FLIGHT |'; p.214: blank; pp.215-239: text of book 7; p.240: blank; p.241: part title, '|| *Book VIII* | THE DARK AUTUMN |'; p.242: blank; pp.243-269: text of book 8; p.270: blank; p.271: part title, '|| *Book IX* | NANCY'S RETURN | *(Epilogue—Twenty-five years later)* |'; p.272: blank; pp.273-295: text of book 9 with 13

lines in italic, signed in print 'WILLA CATHER' at the end of
p.295; p.296: 'A NOTE ON THE DESIGN | [17 lines in
roman] | COMPOSED, PRINTED, AND BOUND | BY THE
PLIMPTON PRESS, NORWOOD, | MASSACHUSETTS |
PAPER MADE BY S. D. WARREN CO., | BOSTON,
MASSACHUSETTS | THE TYPOGRAPHY IS BASED ON |
DESIGNS BY W. A. DWIGGINS'; pp.297-298: blank.

Note: The note on p.296 identifies the text type as 11-point
Linotype Caslon with long descenders on 13-point body, with
running heads in Linotype Janson Italic.

Paper: Cream laid stock with vertical chain lines 24mm. apart.
190×127mm.; top edge trimmed and stained dull orange, other
edges rough-cut. End papers of the same stock.

Binding: Grass-green (117) cloth with pale blue printed paper
labels mounted on the front cover and spine. Front cover: label
54×87mm., '[within an orange decorative rule, lettered in
black] SAPPHIRA | AND THE | SLAVE GIRL | WILLA
CATHER'. Spine: label 70×31mm., '[orange decorative rule] |
[black] SAPPHIRA | AND THE | SLAVE | GIRL | [inverted
orange triangle] | CATHER | [inverted orange triangle]'. The
Borzoi Books rectangular device is stamped in blind on the
lower right corner of the back cover.

Dust Jacket: Cream laid paper with vertical chain lines 30mm.
apart. Front cover and spine over-printed with a ground design
of dusty pink (30) roses with blue-green (163) stems and leaves.
The jacket design is by Rudolph Ruzicka. Front cover: '[on a
large black oval within a blue-green (163) basket pattern frame,
lettered in white:] Sapphira | and the | slave girl | A NEW
NOVEL BY | WILLA CATHER'. Spine: '[on a black
rectangular panel having a blue-green basket pattern rule at top
and bottom, lettered in white within the panel:] Sapphira | and
the | slave girl | [black, beneath the panel:] WILLA |
CATHER | [borzoi oval device in white on black] | *Alfred A.
Knopf*'. Back cover: '[display italic *s*] *SAPPHIRA AND THE
SLAVE GIRL* | *is* MISS CATHER'S *first novel* | *in five years. Her
last previous novel was* | LUCY GAYHEART | [rose orn.] |
[excerpts from 2 critical reviews] | [Borzoi Books device in rose]

[rose:] ALFRED · A · KNOPF · PUBLISHER · N · Y'. Front inner flap: '[rose] *Sapphira and the Slave Girl* [black] $2.50 | *net* | [double rules in rose] | [37-line blurb] | [rose] JACKET DRAWING BY RUDOLPH RUZICKA'. Back inner flap: '*Other Books by* | [rose] WILLA CATHER || [12 titles listed] || [borzoi hound in rose] | [black] THESE ARE BORZOI BOOKS'.

Publication: 7 December 1940 at $2.50 in a first printing of 50,000 copies. Knopf production records are not available for the first 6 printings, but much of the publication history can be reconstructed from the advertising campaign in *Publisher's Weekly*. A Knopf advertisement in *PW* on 14 September (pp.908-909) announced an initial printing of 25,000 copies on 2 December with first printing copies prorated by individual dealers' orders received. A month later, a *PW* advertisement (26 October 1940, p.1642) states that, because of advance orders, the initial printing is 50,000 rather than 25,000 and publication date is advanced 5 days to 7 December.

The first printing has 'FIRST EDITION' on the copyright, and the colophon (p.296) states, 'COMPOSED, PRINTED, AND BOUND | BY THE PLIMPTON PRESS . . .'

SSG was the Book-of-the-Month Club dual selection for January 1941. According to Knopf's statement, 219,806 copies were printed for that distribution. Book-of-the-Month Club copies have 'FIRST EDITION' removed from the copyright and a variant colophon patched to read, 'COMPOSED BY THE PLIMPTON PRESS, | NORWOOD, MASSACHUSETTS | PRINTED AND BOUND BY H. WOLFF, NEW YORK | PAPER MADE BY P. H. GLATFELTER CO., | SPRING GROVE, PA. . . .' The jacket has a Book-of-the Month Club device in rose on the back cover in place of the Borzoi device.

By 15 March 1941 (*PW* advt., p.1178), Knopf announced that, in addition to Book-of-the-Month Club copies, 65,194 copies had been sold to the trade.

A salesman's dummy was available before September 1940 (when Willa Cather was finishing the novel at Grand Manan

Island), if the contents page of the dummy can be counted as evidence. Books 1-7 are listed, but not books 8 and 9. The dummy consists of title page (printed in black only) with blank verso, 2 pages of contents, and 12 pages in a variant setting of the beginning text of book 1. The following variant readings are keyed to the text of the first printing:

10.2   Then] When he came back
10.6   dining-room,] dining-room‸
10.7   hall,] hall‸
12.5   thirty feet or so)] forty feet or more)

The body of the dummy is made up of blank leaves of wove paper to the bulk and dimensions of the completed books with top edge trimmed and stained orange. It has the first edition trade binding save for the blind-stamped device on the back cover, which is absent. Dust jacket is printed only on the front cover and spine. The printer's color register at the outer corners of the front inner flap and on the back cover.

Advance review copies, identical in every other respect to the first printing, have '*Complimentary Advance Copy* | [borzoi hound]' printed on the front open endpaper recto.

An interesting binding variant exists of some copies of the first printing bound for libraries by the Joseph Ruzicka Bindery of Baltimore. These are in heavy blue (182) cloth with pale salmon (28) lettering on dark blue (197) panels on the front cover and spine. The lettering and design is identical with the Rudolph Ruzicka dust jacket. Rudolph and Joseph Ruzicka were brothers, and these library bindings were probably executed as a gesture of homage by the binder to his designer brother.

LIMITED ISSUE

[title-page as in the trade issue]

Collation: [1]^8 (1_2 + χ_1) [2-19]^8 [20]^4; pp.[i-xii, 1-2] 3-295 [296-302] = 157 leaves. *Note:* Leaf χ_1 is the inserted limitation leaf. The stub is pasted to the gutter of 1_{7r}.

Contents: Pp. i-iii: blank; p.iv: advt. as in trade issue; p.v: blank; p.vi: limitation notice, 'OF THE FIRST EDITION OF | *SAPPHIRA AND THE SLAVE GIRL* | FIVE HUNDRED AND TWENTY COPIES | (OF WHICH FOUR HUNDRED AND NINETY-EIGHT COPIES | ARE FOR SALE) HAVE BEEN PRINTED ON RIVES LIAMPRE ALL-RAG PAPER. | EACH COPY IS SIGNED BY THE AUTHOR. | THIS IS NUMBER [space for hand-supplied number] | [author's signature]'; p.vii: half title; p.viii: blank; p.ix: title page; p.x: copyright notice as in trade issue; pp.xi-xii [p.xii designated 'viii']: contents; pp.1-295: as in trade issue; p.296: 'A NOTE ON THE DESIGN | [as in the trade issue, except as noted below]'; pp.297-302: blank.

Note: The text of the note on p.296 has been altered to read 'PAPER SUPPLIED BY | THOMAS N. FAIRBANKS COMPANY, INC., | NEW YORK' in lines 4-6 of the printer's notice.

Paper: White laid stock with vertical chain lines 28mm. apart. Watermarks: '*RIVES*', 'FRANCE', 'LIAMPRE', and 'B F K'. 245 x 156mm.; top edge rough-cut and gilt, other edges uncut. End papers of the same stock.

Binding: Bright green (140) paper over boards, beveled edges. Dark yellow-green (137) cloth shelfback. All lettering and decoration gilt-stamped. Front cover: 'W · S · C | [Dwiggins / Cather orn.]'. Spine: '[orn. rule] | SAPPHIRA | AND THE | SLAVE | GIRL | *Willa* | *Cather* | [orn. rule] | KNOPF'. Back cover: the Borzoi Books rectangular device stamped in blind on the lower right corner. A yellow ribbon place marker is attached at the top inner spine. In a plain light gray paper-covered board box with the limitation number supplied in ink by hand at the foot of the spine.

Dust Jacket: Cream laid paper with horizontal chain lines 28mm. apart. No visible watermark. Covers blank, the spine printed in black duplicating the binding spine. A full-wrap jacket.

Publication: 7 December 1940; 520 copies (498 for sale) at
$10.00. The number of limited copies printed depended on
orders received by press date, 10 October.

a.ii.)   Second printing. Copyright: 'FIRST AND SECOND
PRINTINGS | BEFORE PUBLICATION'. First printing
colophon (p.296). Presswork (aii-vii): Plimpton Press.

a.iii.)   Third printing. Copyright: 'FIRST, SECOND, AND THIRD
PRINTINGS | BEFORE PUBLICATION'. First printing
colophon (p.296).

a.iv.-a.vi.)   Fourth, fifth, and sixth printings. December 1940 to 1965. The
title is listed as available in print up to the date of the seventh
printing in *Books in Print*.

a.vii.)   Seventh printing. 2,000 copies, March 1967.

a.viii.)   Eighth printing. 1,500 copies, January 1970. Presswork:
H. Wolff.

a.ix.)   Ninth printing. 1,000 copies, August 1973. Presswork:
American Book-Stratford Press.

a.x.)   Tenth printing (Random House Vintage Book, V-434). 7,414
copies, June 1975. Offset printing: American Book-Stratford
Press.

a.xi.)   Eleventh printing. 1,000 copies, September 1976. 'TENTH
PRINTING, SEPTEMBER 1976'. Knopf's reckoning does not
include the Vintage paperback (A22.a.x.). Presswork: Haddon
Craftsmen.

b.)   Second edition (Autograph Edition, vol.13), **1941**

[dec. rule] | WILLA CATHER | [dec. rule] | Sapphira and the |
Slave Girl | [dec. rule] | [brown-orange: 'HMCo' cipher] |
BOSTON | HOUGHTON MIFFLIN COMPANY | 1941

Collation: [1-18]⁸ [19]⁴; pp.[i-viii, 1-2] 3-284 [285-288]= 148
leaves.

Contents: P.i: edition title; p.ii: limitation notice; p.iii: title page; p.iv: copyright; p.v: contents; p.vi: blank; p.vii: 11-line note in italic, subscribed 'WILLA CATHER'; p.viii: blank; pp.1-285: text with part titles; p.286: blank; p.287: Riverside Press device; p.288: blank.

Notes on paper, binding, dust jacket, and publication with the entry for the entire Autograph Edition (AA1).

Willa Cather's note on Frederick County surnames, which is placed directly following the end of the text on p.295 in the Knopf first edition, has been moved in this edition to the front of the book on p.vii, preceding the text. The change of position was made at the suggestion of Ferris Greenslet, who thought its original position at the end, following hard upon the moving death of Sapphira, was "a little off the key," as he writes to WC on 20 November 1940. He considers the normal place for such a statement to be in the preliminaries preceding the text. "I can see the undesirability of putting it there in this case, with the effectiveness of keeping from the reader the revelation of the autobiographic, nostalgic basis of the book until the epilogue." He first asks her to consider placing it on a separate page following 'THE END', "in the position which is always used by Alfred for his 'Note on the Design.'" They agreed finally upon the relocation of the note to the front of the book.

English Editions

A22.*a.i*.(e)   First English edition, 1941

[within a double rule frame] Sapphira | *and the* | Slave Girl | BY | WILLA CATHER | [publisher's device] | Cassell and Company, Ltd. | LONDON, TORONTO, MELBOURNE AND SYDNEY

Collation: [A]^8 B-T^8; pp.[i-v] vi, [1-2] 3-295 [296-298] = 152 leaves.

Contents: P.i: half title; p.ii: '*BY THE SAME AUTHOR* | [4 titles]'; p.iii: title page; p.iv: 'FIRST PUBLISHED IN GREAT BRITAIN, 1941 | PRINTED IN GREAT BRITAIN BY |

LOWE AND BRYDONE PRINTERS LIMITED, LONDON,
S. W.10 | F. 441'; pp.v-vi: contents; pp.1-295: part titles and
text (at the foot of p.295 is a 13-line note in italic subscribed
'WILLA CATHER'); pp.296-298: blank. *Note:* Part titles (with
blank versos) are at pp.1, 55, 83, 113, 147, 187, 213, 241,
and 271.

Paper: White wove stock. 185 x 120mm.; edges trimmed. End
papers of heavier cream wove stock.

Binding: Light gray-blue linen cloth. Covers blank. Spine:
'[lettering in gray-blue within a black panel] *Sapphira* | *and the* |
slave girl | [beneath the panel, lettered in black] WILLA
CATHER | CASSELL'. The spine panel duplicates the Ruzicka
design of the American edition.

Dust Jacket: Not seen.

Publication: August 1941 at 7s.6d. Printed and bound in
England. Reviewed in *TLS*, 2 August 1941.

b.i.(e)   Second English edition. London: Hamish Hamilton, 1963.
Photographic offset from the American plates. On the copyright: 'First published in this edition 1963'.

A23. THE OLD BEAUTY AND OTHERS

a.i.)   First edition, first printing, 1948

[bright red] The Old Beauty | and Others | [black] *BY* |
WILLA CATHER | [bright red rule] | [within a black double
rule frame] 1 9 [bright red borzoi device] 4 8 | NEW YORK |
ALFRED A KNOPF

Collation: [1-11]^8; pp.[i-viii, 1-2] 3-166 [167-168] = 88 leaves.

Contents: P.i: blank; p.ii: 'THE WORKS OF | WILLA
CATHER | [list of 19 titles]'; p.iii: half title, 'THE OLD
BEAUTY | AND OTHERS'; p.iv: blank; p.v: title page;

p.vi: 'COPYRIGHT 1948 BY ALFRED A. KNOPF, INC. |
[5-line 'rights reserved' statement in caps] | FIRST EDITION |
[within a panel consisting of thick-thin rule at top, thin-thick
rule at bottom, uprights of leaf orn.] THIS IS A BORZOI
BOOK, | PUBLISHED BY ALFRED A. KNOPF, INC. |
COPYRIGHT IN CANADA BY ALFRED A. KNOPF,
INC. | MANUFACTURED IN THE UNITED STATES OF
AMERICA'; p.vii: contents; p.viii: blank; p.1: part title,
'THE OLD BEAUTY'; p.2: blank; pp.3-72: text of 'The Old
Beauty'; p.73: part title, 'THE BEST YEARS'; p.74: blank;
pp.75-138: text of 'The Best Years'; p.139: part title, 'BEFORE
BREAKFAST'; p.140: blank; pp.141-166: text of 'Before
Breakfast'; p.167: blank; p.168: '[borzoi device in oval] |
PRINTER'S NOTE | [11 lines in italic, stating that the book is
set in Electra Linotype face by W. A. Dwiggins; composed,
printed, and bound by the Plimpton Press, Norwood, Mass.
Typography and binding based on designs by Dwiggins]'.

Text Content:
The Old Beauty
The Best Years
Before Breakfast

Paper: Laid cream stock with vertical chain lines 24mm. apart.
Watermark: 'WARREN'S | OLDE STYLE'. 205 x 137mm. Top
edge trimmed and stained brown, other edges rough-cut. End
papers of heavier wove cream stock.

Binding: Light red-orange (37) cloth, lettering and decoration
stamped in green-gray. Front cover: the Dwiggins stylized plant
design with 'W S C' above. Spine: '[orn. and thick rule] |
THE | OLD | BEAUTY | AND | OTHERS | BY | *Willa* |
Cather | [thick rule and orn.] K N O P F'. Back cover: borzoi
device at the lower right corner.

Dust Jacket: Cream wove coated paper. Front cover: '[within a
light blue-green rule panel] [light blue (181)] THE Old
Beauty | And Others | [thick brown rule] | [brown] *by Willa*
Cather | [large decorative orn. in cream, blue-green and brown
on a light blue (181) panel] | [blue-green thick rule] | [brown]
The last three stories | of a writer who has given us some of the

greatest | literary creations of our time | [thick light blue rule]'.
Spine: '[orn. in light blue and blue-green] | [brown] THE |
Old | Beauty | and | Others | BY | WILLA | CATHER | [light
blue and blue green orn.] | [borzoi books device in brown] |
[blue-green thick rule] | [brown] KNOPF | [light blue rule]'.
Back cover, lettered in brown: '[light blue orn.] *Willa Cather*
[the Steichen photograph printed in brown] | [34-line bio-
graphical sketch of Willa Cather | [light blue rule]'. Front inner
flap: '[brown] $2.50 | net | [light blue] *Announcement* | [42-line
blurb in brown] | [light blue] *Typography, binding, and jacket
based on designs by* | *W.A. Dwiggins.*' Back inner flap: '[brown]
THE WORKS OF | *Willa Cather* [18 titles listed]'.

Publication: 13 September 1948 at $2.50 in a first printing of
20,300 copies. Presswork by the Plimpton Press, first through
fifth printings. 'FIRST EDITION' on the copyright.

Advance review copies, made up of loosely sewn gatherings of
the first printing with plain covers pasted on front and back,
were received as early as 28 June 1948.

a.ii.)   Second printing. 3,000 copies, October 1948.

a.iii.)   Third printing. 3,500 copies, November 1948.

a.iv.)   Fourth printing. 940 copies, March 1953.

a.v.)   Fifth printing. 1,000 copies, December 1963.

a.vi.)   Sixth printing. 1,500 copies, September 1967. Presswork:
Kingsport Press.

a.vii.)   Seventh printing. 750 copies, May 1974. Presswork: American
Book-Stratford Press.

a.viii.)   Eighth printing. 750 copies, August 1974. Presswork: American Book-Stratford Press.

a.ix.)   Ninth printing (Random House Vintage Book, V-122). 7,636

copies, October 1976. Offset printing: American Book-Stratford Press.

English Editions

A23.1.*i*.(e)   First English edition, 1956

[within a dec. border rule] The Old Beauty | and Others | by WILLA CATHER | [publisher's device | CASSELL & COMPANY LTD | LONDON

Collation: [A]⁸ Bob-Kob⁸; pp.[1-8] 9-160 = 80 leaves

Contents: P.1: half title; p.2: 'THE WORKS OF | WILLA CATHER | [19 titles listed]'; p.3: title page; p.4: 'CASSELL & CO. LTD | 37/38 St. Andrew's Hill, Queen Victoria Street, | London, E. C. 4 | and at [11-line list of other addresses] | *First published in Great Britain 1956 | All rights reserved | Printed in Great Britain by | The Camelot Press Ltd., London and South-ampton | F. 155*'; p.5: contents; p.6: blank; p.7: part title, 'THE OLD BEAUTY'; p.8: blank; pp.9-73: text of 'The Old Beauty'; p.74: blank; p.75: part title, 'THE BEST YEARS'; p.76: blank; pp.77-134: text of 'The Best Years'; p.135: part title, 'BEFORE BREAKFAST'; p.136: blank; pp.137-160: text of 'Before Breakfast'.

Text Content: As in a.1.

Paper: White wove. 184x121mm.; edges trimmed. End papers of the same stock.

Binding: Black cloth, covers blank. Spine lettered in gilt: 'The | Old | Beauty | and | Others | WILLA | CATHER | CASSELL'.

Dust Jacket: Not seen.

Publication: Printed in England 22 March 1956 at 9s.6d.

Collections

AA1. AUTOGRAPH EDITION; LIBRARY EDITION, 1937-1941

FIRST ISSUE *(Autograph Edition)*

Title transcriptions, collations, and contents are described in entries for the individual volumes:
 1. *O Pioneers!* (A6.b.)
 2. *The Song of the Lark* (A8.b.)
 3. *Alexander's Bridge & April Twilights* (A3, A5.c.)
 4. *My Ántonia* (A9.c.i.)
 5. *One of Ours* (A11.b.)
 6. *Youth and the Bright Medusa* (A10.b.)
 7. *A Lost Lady* (A13.b.)
 8. *The Professor's House* (A14.b.)
 9. *Death Comes for the Archbishop* (A16.c.)
 10. *Shadows on the Rock* (A17.b.)
 11. *Lucy Gayheart & My Mortal Enemy* (A15.b., A20.b.)
 12. *Obscure Destinies & Literary Encounters [Not under Forty]* (A19.b., A21.b.)
 13. *Sapphira and the Slave Girl* (A22.b.)

Paper: Fine cream laid stock with vertical chain lines 21mm. apart; top edge trimmed and gilt, other edges uncut. No visible watermark. 227 x 152mm. End papers of the same stock.

Binding: Dark gray-blue (187) linen cloth, cream linen cloth shelfback with horizontal bands in a blind pattern. Front cover: the author's initials in a gilt-stamped decorative cipher. Spine: stamped in gilt on a leather label 60 x 32mm., '[dec. rule] | CATHER | [dotted rule] | [title] | [dotted rule] | [thistle orn.] |

[dec. rule]'. Back cover: the Willa Cather cipher repeated in gilt.

Dust Jacket: A full-wrap jacket, with flaps folding over all open cover edges, in pale blue-green (163) wove paper, printed overall in black. Front cover: the Cather cipher. Spine: as on the binding label. Back cover: the Cather cipher. Inner flaps blank.

Publication: Vols. 1 and 2 were published 11 November 1937; volumes 3-6 on 15 December 1937; volumes 7-12 on 15 March 1938. Volume 13 (*Sapphira and the Slave Girl*) was published in 1941. The edition was limited to 970 copies, of which 20 copies were not for sale. These 20 were reserved for the author and the publisher and were not numbered, but designated by hand 'Author's Copy' or 'Publisher's Copy' on the limitation leaf in the space provided for the number. Though the limitation notices gives the impression that all copies of all titles in the edition were signed, Willa Cather signed only the first volume (*O Pioneers!*) of each set. Set price was $120.

The Houghton Mifflin prospectus for the edition states, "The Autograph Edition, as corrected and revised by the Author, is printed from type on an octavo sheet, with wide margins, folded to a page size 6″x9″. A natural rag paper, with deckle edge, was made after consultation between the designer, printer and paper-maker, to show the type to advantage. The type is Janson, with long descenders, as newly adapted by Sol. Hess for composition on the 'Monotype.' . . . The Autograph Edition is also available, on order in three-quarter and full French levant, hand bound, and tooled as desired, according to the best traditions of taste and workmanship for which The Riverside Press is justly famous." Bruce Rogers was the designer of the edition for Houghton Mifflin. The Riverside Press device is at the end of each volume.

A Japanese facsimile of the Autograph Edition was published in Kyoto in 1973. Title page verso: 'Reproduced by Rinsen Book Co. | in 1973 from the 1937 edition of Houghton | Mifflin Co., Boston, Mass., U. S. A. Offset Reprint | rights arranged through Japan Uni Agency, Inc., Tokyo.' Colophon: 'This autograph edition has been reprinted | from the original type

of the Riverside Press, | Cambridge, Massachusetts. The
publication | is limited to two hundred numbered copies. | This
copy is number [supplied in orange ink] | [facsimile WSC
signature]'.

SECOND ISSUE *(Library Edition)*

The cheaper Library Edition, on wove paper and of less elaborate
materials, differs textually only in the substitution of LIBRARY
EDITION for AUTOGRAPH EDITION on the half titles of
each volume and the removal of printed text from the limitation
page. It is set from the same plates and otherwise identical to
the Autograph Edition. It was published in June 1940 to
supply the texts to institutions unable to afford the price of the
Autograph Edition. Knopf was at first opposed to the idea of a
cheaper edition on the grounds that it would cut into sales of
Knopf's Cather titles. A financial arrangement seems to have
been made between Houghton Mifflin and Knopf for sharing of
revenue from sales of the Library Edition. This arrangement is
hinted at in the Ferris Greenslet-Cather correspondence of 1940
and later.

AA2.   WILLA CATHER ON WRITING

a.i.)   First edition, first printing, 1949

WILLA CATHER | [bright red] On Writing | [black] *Critical
Studies on Writing as an Art* | WITH A FOREWORD BY
STEPHEN TENNANT | [bright red rule] | [within a black
double rule panel] 1 9 [bright red borzoi device] 4 9 | NEW
YORK | ALFRED A KNOPF

Collation: [1-10]^8; pp.[π1-2, i-iv] v-xxvi, [1-2] 3-126 [127-
132] = 80 leaves.

Contents: P.π1: blank; p.π2: 'THE WORKS OF | WILLA
CATHER | [20 titles listed]'; p.i: half title, 'WILLA
CATHER | ON WRITING'; p.ii: blank; p.iii: title page; p.iv:
'*Copyright 1920, 1924, 1925, 1926 by Alfred A. Knopf,* | *Inc.*

Copyright 1936 by Willa Cather. Copyright 1927, | *1931, 1938, 1949 by the Executors of the Estate of Willa* | *Cather.* | [5-line 'rights reserved' statement in caps] | FIRST EDITION | [within a panel consisting of thick-thin rules at top, thin-thick rules at bottom and ornamental uprights] THIS IS A BORZOI BOOK, | PUBLISHED BY ALFRED A. KNOPF, INC. | [beneath the panel] PUBLISHED SIMULTANEOUSLY IN CANADA BY | McCLELLAND & STEWART LIMITED | MANUFACTURED IN THE UNITED STATES OF AMERICA'; pp.v-xxiv: 'The Room Beyond', a foreword on Willa Cather by Stephen Tennant; pp.xxv-xxvi: contents; p.1: part title, 'FOUR LETTERS'; p.2: blank; pp.3-32: text of 'Four Letters'; p.33: part title, 'THE NOVEL DÉMEUBLÉ'; p.34: blank; pp.35-43: text of 'The Novel Démeublé'; p.44: blank; p.45: part title, 'FOUR PREFACES'; p.46: blank; pp.47-88: text of 'Four Prefaces'; p.89: part title, MY FIRST NOVELS | [*There Were Two*]'; p.90: blank; pp.91-97: text of 'My First Novels'; p.98: blank; p.99: part title, 'ON | THE ART OF FICTION'; p.100: blank; pp.101-104: text of 'On the Art of Fiction'; p.105: part title, 'KATHERINE MANSFIELD'; p.106: blank; pp.107-120: text of 'Katherine Mansfield'; p.121: part title, 'LIGHT ON ADOBE WALLS'; p.122: blank; pp.123-126: text of 'Light on Adobe Walls'; p.127: blank; p.128: '[borzoi device in oval] | PRINTER'S NOTE | [11-line note in italic: typography and binding based on designs by W. A. Dwiggins, set in Electra Linotype face, composed, printed, and bound by the Plimpton Press, Norwood, Mass.]'; pp.129-132: blank.

Text Contents (first publication as noted):
The Room Beyond. Foreword by Stephen Tennant.
On *Death Comes for the Archbishop. Commonweal* 7 (27 November 1927). D587
On *Shadows on the Rock. Saturday Review of Literature* 8 (17 October 1931). Title: 'A Letter to Gov. Wilbur Cross'. D590
Escapism. *Commonweal* 23 (17 April 1936). D592
On *The Professor's House. The News Letter of the College English Association* 2, no.6 (October 1940). D595
The Novel Démeublé. *The New Republic*, 12 April 1922, supp. First collected in *NUF*. D583

[Preface to *The Best Stories of Sarah Orne Jewett* (Boston: Houghton Mifflin, 1925)]; selected and arranged by WC].
Incorporated in part in the essay 'Miss Jewett' in *NUF*. DD7
[Preface to Gertrude Hall's *The Wagnerian Romances* (New York: Knopf, 1925)]. DD8
[Introduction to *The Work of Stephen Crane*, vol.9, *Wounds in the Rain and Other Impressions of War* (New York: Knopf, 1926)]. DD9
[Preface to Defoe's *The Fortunate Mistress*, Borzoi Classics edition (New York: Knopf, 1925)]. DD5
My First Novels [There Were Two]. *Colophon* Part 6 (1931), 4 unnumbered pp. D589
On the Art of Fiction. In *The Borzoi 1920* (New York: Knopf, 1920). DD4
Katherine Mansfield. In *The Borzoi 1925* (New York: Knopf, 1925). This version was expanded and developed for inclusion in *NUF* (1936) and *OW* (1949). DD6
Light on Adobe Walls. In *OW* for the first time.

Paper: Cream laid paper, vertical chain lines 32mm. apart. No watermark. 205 x 138mm.; top edge trimmed and stained red brown, other edges rough-cut. End papers of heavy wove cream stock.

Binding: Bright blue-green (159) cloth, stamped in copper brown. Front cover has the stylized Dwiggins orn. with 'W S C' above. Spine: '[orn. rule] | Willa | Cather | ON | WRIT- | ING | [orn. rule] | KNOPF'. Back cover has the borzoi device at lower right.

Dust Jacket: Coated cream wove paper. Front cover: '[within a thick olive green (106) rule panel, lettered in light green (136)] *Willa Cather* | On Writing | [thick black rule] | [black] *With a Foreword by Stephen Tennant* | [large Dwiggins floral orn. in olive green (106) and black on a light green (136) panel] | [thick olive green (106) rule] | [black] CRITICAL STUDIES | ON WRITING AS AN ART | [thick light green (136) rule]'. Spine: '[thick black rule] | [reading from top to bottom:] WILLA CATHER [olive green (106)] On Writing | [light green (136) rule] | [Borzoi Books device on a black panel] | [olive (106)

rule] | [perpendicular:] KNOPF'. Back cover: '[light green orn.]
Willa Cather [Steichen photograph] | [34-line biographical
sketch of Willa Cather | [light green rule]'. Front inner flap:
'$2.25 | net | *Willa Cather* | ON WRITING | [double light
green rule] | [35-line blurb | [light green] *Typography, binding,
and jacket based on designs by* | W. A. Dwiggins.' Back inner flap:
'THE WORKS OF | *Willa Cather* | [20 titles listed]'.

Publication: 20 September 1949 at $2.50 in a first printing of
7,500 copies. Presswork by the Plimpton Press, first through
third printings. Two textual alterations were made on pp.xvii
and xxiii of Tennant's foreword between the first and second
printings. The resetting of three lines was required on p.xxiii:

xvii.19   warm] strong
xxiii.15   an intensification of some] some incandescent

WCOW was not published in England. A note in the Knopf
production records dated 21 March 1951: "Before reprinting,
quotation on sheets to be given Cassell." A follow-up note,
dated February 1953 (just before the second printing), indicates
that Cassell had declined an offer of sheets for an English
edition.

a.ii.)   Second printing. 940 copies, March 1953.

a.iii.)   Third printing. 1,650 copies, February 1962.

a.iv.)   Fourth printing. 1,000 copies, August 1968. Presswork:
          Haddon Craftsmen.

AA3.   **WRITINGS FROM WILLA CATHER'S CAMPUS YEARS**

a.)   First edition (collected) 1950

WRITINGS FROM | [within a heavy single-rule oval] Willa |
Cather's | CAMPUS | YEARS | [at left: a drawing of one of the
early University of Nebraska campus buildings] | EDITED BY
JAMES R SHIVELY | UNIVERSITY OF NEBRASKA PRESS

Collation: [1]⁸ [2-5]¹⁶; pp.[i-viii, 9-10] 11-142 [143-144] = 72 leaves.

Illustration: Photographic portrait of Willa Cather as a student, captioned '*WILLA CATHER IN 1893*'. On smooth wove cream stock, tipped in facing the introduction half title (p.9).

Contents: Pp.i-ii: blank; p.iii: title page; p.iv: '*Copyright by* | UNIVERSITY OF NEBRASKA PRESS | Lincoln, Nebraska | 1950 | *Printed in the United States by* | *The Printing Division, University of Nebraska in Lincoln*'; p.v: contents; p.vi: blank; pp.vii-viii: 2-page preface in italic, subscribed 'James R. Shively | February, 1950'; p.9: introduction half title, '*Introduction*'; p.10: blank; pp.11-27: introduction; p.28: blank; p.29: part title, '*Writings from* | *Willa Cather's Campus Years*'; p.30: 7-line statement in italic; pp.31-112: selections of Cather juvenilia; p.113: part title, '*Letters from* | *Willa Cather's Contemporaries*'; p.114: 8-line statement in italic concerning the letters; pp.115-142: text of letters; pp.143-144: blank.

Text Contents (first publication as noted):
'Dramatic Criticism and Comment' (pp.31-40). Excerpts from theatrical reviews first published in the *Nebraska State Journal*, 11 February 1894, 25 February 1894, 4 March 1894 (3), 11 March 1894 (2), 8 April 1894, 15 April 1894 (3). D22, 30, 33, 34, 49, 50

Peter. *Hesperian*, 24 November 1892. C1

Lou, the Prophet. *Hesperian*, 15 October 1892. C2

A Tale of the White Pyramid. *Hesperian*, 22 December 1892. C3

A Son of the Celestial. *Hesperian*, 15 January 1893. C4

The Clemency of the Court. *Hesperian*, 26 October 1893. C6

A Night at Greenway Court. *Nebraska Literary Magazine* (June 1896). C9

Daily Dialogues. *Hesperian*, 15 February 1893. d2

A Sentimental Thanksgiving Dinner. *Hesperian*, 24 November 1892. d1

Shakespeare. *Hesperian*, 1 June 1892. B1

Anacreon. *Sombrero* (1894). B5

Columbus. *Hesperian*, 1 November 1892. B2

Horace, Book I, Ode XXXVIII, 'Persicos Odi'. *Hesperian*, 24
November 1892. B3

Paper: White laid stock with vertical chain lines 24mm. apart.
Watermark: 'TOWN CRIER TEXT | MADE IN U.S.A.'
213x130mm., edges trimmed. End papers of white wove stock.

Binding: Dark yellow-green (137) cloth with an overall pattern of diamond squares made by crisscrossing light yellow-
green (119) lines. Front cover: '[light yellow-green (119)]
WRITINGS FROM | [gilt-stamped within a thick gilt oval
rule] Willa | Cather's | CAMPUS | YEARS | [campus building
at left in light yellow-green (119)]'. Spine: '[light yellow-green
(119)] SHIVELY | [gilt-stamped vertical lettering] Willa
Cather's CAMPUS YEARS | [light yellow-green (119) hori-
zontal lettering] N | NEBRASKA'. Back cover with crisscross
yellow-green lines; otherwise, blank.

Dust Jacket: Heavy wove paper coated in light yellow-green
(119). Lettering and decoration in dark yellow-green (137)
repeat the title page with crisscross lines in dark yellow-green
(137) overall, reversing the binding colors. Spine: '[dark yellow-
green] SHIVELY | [white vertical lettering] Willa Cather's
CAMPUS YEARS | [white horizontal letter on dark yellow-
green square] N'. Back cover as binding with reversed colors.
Inner flaps contain a continued lengthy blurb.

Publication: February 1950 at $2.75. This volume is the first in
what eventually became the University of Nebraska Press series
of the previously uncollected early writings of WC.

AA4. FIVE STORIES

a.i.) First edition, first printing, 1956

WILLA CATHER | [swelling rule] | *Five Stories* | WITH AN
ARTICLE BY GEORGE N. KATES | ON MISS CATHER'S
LAST, | UNFINISHED AND UNPUBLISHED | AVIGNON

STORY | [swelling rule] | [sun orn.] | VINTAGE BOOKS | A
DIVISION OF RANDOM HOUSE | *New York*

Paperback perfect binding, glued at the spine; pp.[i-viii, 1-2]
3-214 [215-216]. Cheap wove paper, 184x109mm., edges
trimmed flush with the cover. Pictorial stiff coated paper
wrapper. Vintage Book V-28, published 13 February 1956 at
$1.95. First printing of 25,000 copies.

Text Contents (first publication as noted):
The Enchanted Bluff. *Harper's* (April 1909). C43
Tom Outland's Story. *The Professor's House*, pp.177-253.
Neighbour Rosicky. *Woman's Home Companion* (April 1930). C57
The Best Years. *The Old Beauty*, pp.73-138.
Paul's Case. *McClure's* (May 1905). C37
Willa Cather's Unfinished Avignon Story. Article by George N.
    Kates, printed here for the first time.

Reprinted: July 1957 (7,500), February 1958 (10,000), December 1959 (10,000), January 1964 (6,000 and 1,000 copies
hardbound), August 1965 (6,000), September 1966 (7,000 and
1,000 hardbound), February 1969 (3,000), December 1969
(3,000), January 1971 (3,000), July 1972 (3,000), May 1973
(3,000), April 1974 (5,000), June 1977 (5,000), January 1979
(4,750).

AA5.   WILLA CATHER IN EUROPE

a.)   First edition, first printing, 1956

WILLA CATHER | in Europe || *Her Own Story of the First
Journey* || With an Introduction | and Incidental Notes by |
George N. Kates | [borzoi hound] | [short rule] | ALFRED A.
KNOPF : *NEW YORK* : 1956

Collation: [1-5]^{16} [6]^4 [7]^{16}; pp.[π1-2, i-v] vi-xii [xiii-xiv, 1-3]
4-178 [179-184]= 100 leaves.

Contents: P.π1: blank; p.π2: 'THE WORKS OF WILLA
CATHER | [21 titles listed]'; p.i: half title, 'WILLA CATHER
IN EUROPE'; p.ii: blank; p.iii: title page; p.iv: '© THE
EXECUTORS OF THE ESTATE OF WILLA CATHER |
[within a panel rule having 2 fleurs-de-lys as uprights:] THIS IS
A BORZOI BOOK | PUBLISHED BY ALFRED A. KNOPF,
INC. | [beneath: 8-line 'rights reserved' notice and note that
the book is published simultaneously in Canada by McClelland
and Stewart Ltd.] | FIRST EDITION | L. C. CATALOG
CARD NUMBER 56-10906'; pp.v-xii: introduction subscribed
on p.xii, 'George N. Kates | Santa Fé | April 1956'; pp.xiii-
xiv: contents; p.1: second half title, 'WILLA CATHER IN
EUROPE'; p.2: blank; pp.3-178: text; p.179: blank; p.180: 'A
NOTE ON THE TYPE | [11 lines in italic: the book set in
Electra Linotype face designed by W. A. Dwiggins, typography
and binding design by Rudolph Ruzicka; the book composed,
printed, and bound by the Plimpton Press, paper made by
S. D. Warren Company]'; pp.181-184: blank.

Text Contents (first publication as noted):
Liverpool. *NSJ*, 13 July 1902 ('First Glimpse of England').
    D546
Chester and Its Cathedral. *NSJ*, 20 July 1902 ('A Visit to Old
    Chester'). D547
Shropshire and A. E. Housman. *NSJ*, 27 July 1902 ('Out of the
    Beaten Track'). D548
The Canals of England. *NSJ*, 3 August 1902 ('The Canal Folk
    of England'). D549
London: the East End. *NSJ*, 10 August 1902 ('Seeing Things in
    London'). D550
London: Burne-Jones's Studio. *NSJ*, 17 August 1902 ('The
    Kensington Studio'). D552
The Merry Wives of Windsor. *NSJ*, 24 August 1902. D553
Dieppe and Rouen. *NSJ*, 31 August 1902. D555
The Cemeteries of Paris. *NSJ*, 14 September 1902 ('Two
    Cemeteries in Paris'). D557
Barbizon. *NSJ*, 21 September 1902 ('One Sunday at Barbizon').
    D558
Avignon. *NSJ*, 28 September 1902 ('The Old City of the
    Popes'). D559

Marseilles and Hyères. *NSJ*, 5 October 1902 ('Country of the Fabulous'). D560

Le Lavandou. *NSJ*, 12 October 1902 ('In a Principality of Pines'). D561

Arles and Provençe Again. *NSJ* 19 October 1902 ('In the Country of Daudet'). D562

Paper: Cream laid stock with vertical chain lines 25mm. apart, watermarked 'WARREN'S | OLDE STYLE'. 206x139mm.; top edge trimmed and stained brown-orange, other edges rough-cut. End papers of heavier white wove stock.

Binding: Gray cloth, stamped on the front cover in purple with an ornament of a cathedral rose window. Spine stamped in purple: '[cathedral window orn.] || Willa | Cather | in | Europe | [circular orn.] || [triple fleurs-de-lys orn.] || KNOPF'. Back cover has the borzoi device stamped in blind at the lower right corner.

Dust Jacket: Cream coated paper. Front cover: '[author's name over a light blue and purple illus.] Willa Cather | in Europe | [lettering in cream on a light blue panel] *Her Own Story of the First Journey* | [black] With an Introduction and Incidental Notes | by George N. Kates'. Spine: '[on a black, blue and purple panel in cream] Willa | Cather | in | Europe | [light blue vertical lettering] *Her Own Story of the First Journey* | [horizontal Borzoi Books device] | [black] KNOPF'. Back cover: photograph and biographical note on WC. Front inner flap: '[blurb for the book (23 lines)] | [blue] Typography, binding, and jacket design | by Rudolph Ruzicka'. Back inner flap: 'THE WORKS OF | *Willa Cather* . . . .'.

Publication: 22 October 1956 in a first printing of 7,500 copies. $3.00.

A collection of articles first published in the *Nebraska State Journal* which give an account of WC's trip to Europe in 1902 with Isabelle McClung. See D546-50, 552-53, 555, 557-62.

AA6.   EARLY STORIES OF WILLA CATHER

a.i.)   First edition, first printing (collected), 1957

[orn.] | Early Stories of | *Willa Cather* | [orn.] | Selected and
with | commentary by | *Mildred R. Bennett* | *Dodd, Mead &*
Company | NEW YORK   1957

Collation: [1]^8 [2-9]^{16} [10]^8; pp.[i-viii] ix [x-xii] 1-275
[276] = 144 leaves.

Contents: P.i: half title; p.ii: advt. '[orn.] | Also by MILDRED
R. BENNETT | The World of *Willa Cather*'; p.iii: title page;
p.iv: copyright, '© 1957 BY MILDRED R. BENNETT | . . . |
LIBRARY OF CONGRESS CATALOG CARD NUMBER:
57-6787 | . . . .'; p.v: dedication; p.vi: blank; p.vii:
introduction; p.viii: blank; p.ix: contents; p.x: blank; p.xi:
second half title; p.xii: blank; pp. 1-275: text; p.276: blank.

Text Contents (first published as noted):
Peter. *Mahogany Tree*, 21 May 1892. C1
Lou, the Prophet. *Hesperian*, 15 October 1892. C2
A Tale of the White Pyramid. *Hesperian*, 22 December 1892.
   C3
A Son of the Celestial: A Character. *Hesperian*, 15 January 1893.
   C4
The Clemency of the Court. *Hesperian*, 26 October 1893. C6
"The Fear That Walks by Noonday". *Sombrero* 3 (1894). C7
On the Divide. *Overland Monthly* 27 (January 1896). C8
A Night at Greenway Court. *Nebraska Literary Magazine* 1 (June
   1896). C9
Tommy, the Unsentimental. *HM*, August 1896. C10
The Count of Crow's Nest. *HM*, September, October 1896. C12
A Resurrection. *HM*, April 1897. C16
The Prodigies. *HM*, July 1897. C17
Nanette: An Aside. *Lincoln Courier*, 31 July 1897. C18
Eric Hermannson's Soul. *Cosmopolitan* 28 (April 1900). C21
The Dance at Chevalier's. *Library*, 28 April 1900. C22
The Sentimentality of William Tavener. *Library*, 12 May 1900.
   C23

The Affair at Grover Station. *Library*, 16, 23 June 1900. C24
A Singer's Romance. *Library*, 28 July 1900. C25
The Conversion of Sum Loo. *Library*, 11 August 1900. C26

Paper: Cream wove, 202 x 132mm., edges trimmed. End papers
of heavier wove stock.

Binding: Tan paper-covered boards with a design of irregular
pale blue and pink vertical lines. Red-orange (40) cloth shelfback. Covers blank. Spine (vertical lettering, gilt): 'Early Stories
of *Willa Cather* | [horizontal] *Bennett* | [vertical] *Dodd, Mead*'.

Dust Jacket: Wove coated paper with a yellow-toned photograph
of wheat fields and sky extending over front cover and spine.
Lettering in white. Front cover: 'EARLY | STORIES | of |
WILLA | CATHER | SELECTED | AND WITH |
COMMENTARY | by | MILDRED | BENNETT'. Spine:
'EARLY | STORIES | of | WILLA | CATHER | BENNETT |
DODD, MEAD'. Back cover (black lettering on white ground):
photograph and biographical note on Mildred R. Bennett. Front
inner flap: blurb on *Early Stories* with price $4.00. Back inner
flap: advt. for Frances Gray Patton's *A Piece of Luck*.

Publication: Mrs. Bennett's extensive subjective commentary is
interspersed throughout the text in bracketed smaller type font.

The book was issued later in a paperback Dodd, Mead Apollo
edition (A-130) at $1.95.

AA7.   **WILLA CATHER'S COLLECTED SHORT FICTION**
       1892-1912

a.)   First edition (collected), first printing, **1965**

       [extending over 2 facing pp.] [thick-thin rule] | WILLA
       CATHER'S 1892-1912 | Collected Short | Fiction | Volume
       I · THE BOHEMIAN GIRL | Volume II · THE TROLL
       GARDEN | Volume III · ON THE DIVIDE | *Introduction by* |

MILDRED R. BENNETT | UNIVERSITY OF NEBRASKA
PRESS · LINCOLN | [thin-thick rule]

Collation: [1-20]¹⁶; pp.[i-vi] vii-xli [xlii, 1-2] 3-594
[595-598] = 320 leaves.

Contents: P.i: half title; pp.ii-iii: title pages; p.iv: copyright; p.v:
dedication to the memory of Elsie M. Cather; p.vi: blank;
pp.vii-ix: publisher's preface; p.x: italic note on the arrangement
of the text; pp.xi-xii: contents; pp.xiii-xli: introduction; p.xlii:
blank; p.1: part title, '*Volume I* | THE | BOHEMIAN | GIRL |
[3 orn.]'; p.2: italic note on vol.1; pp.3-146: text of vol.1;
p.147: part title, '*Volume II* | THE | TROLL | GARDEN | [3
orn.]'; p.148: italic note on vol.2; pp.149-261: text of vol.2;
p.262: blank; p.263: part title, '*Volume III* | ON | THE |
DIVIDE | [3 orn.]'; p.264: italic note on vol.3; pp.265-543:
text of vol.3; p.544: blank; p.545: part title, '*Appendix* |
PSEUDONYMOUS | STORIES | [3 orn.]'; p.546: italic note;
pp.547-572: text of 3 pseudonymous stories; pp.573-575: 'A
Note on the Editing'; p.576: blank; pp.577-581: WC chronology; p.582: blank; pp.583-590: bibliography of Willa
Cather's short fiction, 1892-1912; pp.591-592: checklist of
WC's short fiction, 1915-1948; pp.593-594: bibliography of
biographical and critical writings; p.595: acknowledgments;
pp.596-598: blank.

Text Contents:
Vol.I:
    The Bohemian Girl
    Behind the Singer Tower
    The Joy of Nelly Deane
    The Enchanted Bluff
    On the Gulls' Road
    Eleanor's House
    The Willing Muse
    The Profile
    The Namesake
Vol.II:
    Flavia and Her Artists
    The Sculptor's Funeral

The Garden Lodge
"A Death in the Desert"
The Marriage of Phaedra
A Wagner Matinee
Paul's Case

Vol. III:

The Treasure of Far Island
The Professor's Commencement
El Dorado: A Kansas Recessional
Jack-a-Boy
The Conversion of Sum Loo
A Singer's Romance
The Affair at Grover Station
The Sentimentality of William Tavener
Eric Hermannson's Soul
The Westbound Train
The Way of the World
Nanette: An Aside
The Prodigies
A Resurrection
The Strategy of the Were-Wolf Dog
The Count of Crow's Nest
Tommy, the Unsentimental
A Night at Greenway Court
On the Divide
"The Fear That Walks by Noonday"
The Clemency of the Court
A Son of the Celestial
A Tale of the White Pyramid
Lou, the Prophet
Peter

An appendix contains 3 pseudonymous stories: 'The Dance at Chevalier's', 'The Burglar's Christmas', 'The Princess Baladina—Her Adventure'.

Paper: White wove, watermarked 'WARREN'S | OLDE STYLE'. 240 x 160mm., edges trimmed. End papers of heavy tan wove stock.

Binding and Dust Jacket: Beige and tan horizontal paneled cloth, spine lettered in gilt and black; facsimile WC signature in gilt and black on front cover. Dust jacket with a Cather portrait drawing adapted from the Steichen photograph.

Publication: First printing, September 1965 at $8.50. Edited by Virginia Faulkner. Fourth in the multi-volume series of the University of Nebraska Press to make available the early writings. The stories in 'Volume II' (*The Troll Garden*) are not copy-edited, but follow the 1905 edition text save for 40 obvious emendations supplied by the editor in 'A Note on the Editing' (pp.574-575). The other stories are 'lightly copy-edited'. That is, conspicuously variant or old-fashioned forms are regularized to modern style. A second printing in November 1965; third printing in June 1967.

The fourth printing (November 1970 at $9.50) was revised, corrected, and expanded by Virginia Faulkner, and a newly proved, unsigned story, 'The Elopement of Allen Poole', (*Hesperian*, 15 April 1893) (C5) added to the contents. The dust jacket, with new text, has a portrait photograph of WC on the front cover.

This collected edition is also the third edition of *The Troll Garden* (see A4.c.).

AA8.   THE KINGDOM OF ART

a.)   First edition (collected), 1966

[extending over 2 pp.] [thick-thin rule] *Selected and edited* | *with two essays and* | *a commentary by* | BERNICE SLOTE | The Kingdom | of Art: WILLA CATHER'S FIRST | PRINCIPLES AND | CRITICAL STATEMENTS | 1893-1896 | UNIVERSITY OF NEBRASKA PRESS · LINCOLN | [thin-thick rule]

Collation: [1-14]^{16} [15]^{12} [16]^{16}; pp.[i-vi] vii-xiv [1-2] 3-489 [490] = 252 leaves.

Illustrations: Following p.18, 5 illus. on 4 leaves of coated paper printed on rectos, inserted: the University of Nebraska campus in 1892, 2 early portraits of WC with facsimile signature beneath, portrait of WC in June 1895, the Lansing Theatre in November 1891.

Contents: P.i: half title; pp.ii-iii: title pages; p.iv: copyright; p.v: dedication to Mrs. George Seibel and Elizabeth Shepley Sergeant; p.vi: blank; pp.vii-ix: preface and acknowledgments, subscribed 'BERNICE SLOTE | *University of Nebraska*'; p.x: blank; pp.xi-xiv: contents; p.1: part title, '*Part I* | FIRST | PRINCIPLES | [3 orn.]'; p.2: blank; pp.3-112: Bernice Slote's essays, 'Writer in Nebraska' and 'The Kingdom of Art'; p.113: part title, '*Part II* | CRITICAL | STATEMENTS | [3 orn.]'; p.114: blank; pp.115-417: text of part 2: p.418: blank; p.419: part title, 'APPENDICES | A NOTE ON THE EDITING | BIBLIOGRAPHY | INDEX | [3 orn.]'; p.420: blank; pp.421-489: appendixes, editor's note, bibliography, index: p.490: blank.

Text Contents: Reviews and excerpts from the *Nebraska State Journal* and the *Courier*, essays, and early interviews. The review titles are supplied by the editor. The more than 100 items that comprise the contents may be found in Section D and the index. (Both refer to this entry.)

Paper: White wove, watermarked 'WARREN'S| OLDE STYLE'. 240x163mm., edges trimmed. End papers of heavy gray wove stock.

Binding and dust jacket: Gray and cream-yellow horizontal pan-eled cloth, spine lettered in gilt and black; facsimile WC signature in gilt and black on the front cover. Pictorial and lettered dust jacket.

Publication: The third publication in the University of Nebraska series. Professor Bernice Slote's selection of reviews by WC between 1891 and 1896. The back matter includes a note on editing, a bibliographical note, and a checklist of Willa Cather's critical and personal writing from 1891 to 1896.

AA9.   THE WORLD AND THE PARISH

a.)   First edition (collected; 2 volumes), 1970

[extending over 2 pp.] [thick-thin rule] *Selected and edited* | *with
a commentary by* | WILLIAM M. CURTIN | The World | and the
Parish WILLA CATHER'S | ARTICLES AND REVIEWS, |
Volume One [Two] 1893-1902 | [4-line italic quote, subscribed
'WILLA CATHER'] | UNIVERSITY OF NEBRASKA
PRESS · LINCOLN | [thin-thick rule]

Collation: (Vol. 1) [1-15]^{16} [16]^{8} [17]^{16}; pp.[i-vi] vii-xxi [xxii,
1-2] 3-502 [503-506] = 264 leaves. (Vol. 2) [1-16]^{16} [17]^{4}
[18]^{16}; pp.[i-iv] v-x [xi-xii] 503-1039 [1040-1042] = 276
leaves.

Contents: (Vol. 1) p.i: half title; pp.ii-iii: title pages; p.iv:
copyright; p.v: dedication 'For Mary'; p.vi: blank; pp.vii-xii:
contents; pp.xiii-xvii: Publisher's foreword, subscribed
'VIRGINIA FAULKNER | *Editor* | University of Nebraska Press';
p.xviii: blank; pp.xix-xxi: Editor's preface, subscribed 'WILLIAM
M. CURTIN | *University of Connecticut*'; p.xxii: blank; p.1: part
title '*Part I* | THE | PROVINCES | [3 orn.]'; p.2: chronology
for part 1; pp.3-502: text of part 1; pp.503-506: blank. (Vol. 2)
pp.i-iv: as in vol. 1; pp.v-x: contents; p.xi: part title '*Part II* |
THE | CITY | [3 orn.] | *Continued from Volume I*'; p.xii:
chronology for part 2; pp.503-952: text of part 2; p.953:
'APPENDICES | A NOTE ON THE EDITING |
BIBLIOGRAPHY | ACKNOWLEDGMENTS | INDEX |
[3 orn.]'; p.954: blank; pp.955-1039: end matter; pp.1040-
1042: blank.

Text Content: The more than 200 items that comprise the
contents may be found in Section D and the index. (Both refer
to this entry.)

Paper: White wove, watermarked 'WARREN'S | OLD STYLE'. ·
235 x 152mm., edges trimmed. End papers of heavy dark gray
wove stock.

Binding and Dust Jacket: Orange and tan horizontal paneled cloth, spine lettered in black and gilt; facsimile WC signature in gilt and black on front cover. Pictorial and lettered dust jacket.

Publication: The fourth in the University of Nebraska Press series of WC's uncollected works.

AA10.   UNCLE VALENTINE AND OTHER STORIES

a.)   First edition (collected), 1973

UNCLE VALENTINE | AND OTHER STORIES | *Willa Cather's* | *Uncollected Short Fiction* | *1915-1929* | Edited with an introduction by | BERNICE SLOTE | UNIVERSITY OF NEBRASKA PRESS · LINCOLN

Collation: [1-5]^{16} [6]^8 [7]^4 [8]^{16}; pp.[i-iv] v-xxx [1-2] 3-183 [184-186] = 108 leaves.

Contents: P.i: half title; p.ii: advt. for WC collections published by UNP; p.iii: title page; p.iv: copyright; p.v: contents; p.vi: blank; p.vii: acknowledgment; p.viii: blank; pp.ix-xxx: introduction, subscribed 'BERNICE SLOTE | *University of Nebraska—Lincoln*'; p.1: part title '*Pittsburgh Stories* | Uncle Valentine | *(Adagio non troppo)* | [3 orn.]'; p.2: blank; pp.3-176: text; pp.177-183: appendix and note on editing; pp.184-186: blank.

Text Contents (first publication as noted):
Uncle Valentine (Adagio non troppo). *Woman's Home Companion*
    52 (February, March 1925). C55
Double Birthday. *Forum* 81 (February 1929). C56
Consequences. *McClure's* 46 (November 1915). C47
The Bookkeeper's Wife. *Century* 92 (May 1916). C48
Ardessa. *Century* 96 (May 1918). C51
Her Boss. *Smart Set* 90 (October 1919). C53
Coming, Eden Bower! *Smart Set* 92 (August 1920). C54

The appendix (pp. 177-181) contains variant readings in "Coming, Eden Bower!' and 'Coming, Aphrodite!', the title used in *Youth and the Bright Medusa* (1920).

Paper: White wove, 233 x 153 mm., edges trimmed. End papers of bright orange (48) heavy stock.

Binding and Dust Jacket: Dark brown and cream horizontal paneled cloth, spine lettered in gilt and iridescent green; facsimile WC signature in iridescent green and gilt on front cover. Pictorial and lettered dust jacket.

Publication: The fifth publication in the University of Nebraska Press series of WC's previously uncollected works.

Works Edited by Willa Cather

AAA1. THE LIFE OF MARY BAKER G. EDDY
–GEORGINE MILMINE

a.i.) First edition, first printing, 1909

THE LIFE OF | MARY BAKER G. EDDY | AND THE | HISTORY OF CHRISTIAN SCIENCE | BY | GEORGINE MILMINE | ILLUSTRATED | [publisher's device] | NEW YORK | DOUBLEDAY, PAGE & COMPANY | 1909

Collation: [1-32]⁸; pp.[1-2, i-vi] vii-xiv [1-2] 3-495 [496] = 256 leaves.

Illustrations: 25 photographic illus. on 19 tipped-in leaves of coated paper. Frontispiece portrait of Mary Baker Eddy, 'Photograph by S. A. Bowers | MARY BAKER G. EDDY | From a photograph taken in Concord, N. H., in 1892'. The others follow pp. 10, 34, 48, 62, 66, 114, 128, 152, 168, 252, 270, 294, 308, 328, 348, 384, 414, and 450.

Contents: Pp. 1-2: blank; p.i: half title; p.ii: blank; p.iii: title page; p.iv: copyright, 'ALL RIGHTS RESERVED, INCLUDING THAT OF TRANSLATION | INTO FOREIGN LANGUAGES, INCLUDING THE SCANDINAVIAN | COPYRIGHT, 1907, 1908, BY THE S. S. McCLURE COMPANY | COPYRIGHT, 1909, BY DOUBLEDAY, PAGE & COMPANY | PUBLISHED, NOVEMBER, 1909'; p.v: 'NOTE | The following history was first published in serial form | in *McClure's Magazine*, 1907-1908. It has since been revised | and new material has been added. | G. M.'; p.vi:

blank; pp.vii-xi: contents; p.xii: blank; pp.xiii-xiv: illustrations; p.1: second half title; p.2: blank; pp.3-495: text; p.496: blank.

Paper: Cheap white wove stock, 210x138mm., edges trimmed. End papers of white laid stock with vertical chain lines.

Binding: Deep blue (197) vertical rib cloth, thick-thin double border rule in blind on the front cover. Gilt-stamped lettering overall. Front cover: 'THE LIFE OF | MARY BAKER G·EDDY | AND | THE HISTORY OF | CHRISTIAN SCIENCE | BY | GEORGINE MILMINE'. Spine: 'THE LIFE OF | MARY BAKER | G·EDDY | AND THE | HISTORY OF | CHRISTIAN | SCIENCE | BY | GEORGINE | MILMINE | DOUBLEDAY | PAGE & CO.' Back cover blank.

Dust Jacket: White coated paper, printed in black. Front cover: '[within a single border rule] [cut-out photographic bust portrait of Mrs. Eddy with a baby, flanked at top by: 'MRS. MARY | BAKER G. EDDY | in 1867' and 'Absolute Mental | Ruler To-day of | Over 60,000 | Christian Scientists.' Beneath, 7-line blurb] Mary Baker G. Eddy | and the History of Christian Science | BY | GEORGINE MILMINE | Illustrated from Photographs [space] Net, $2.00'. Spine: 'THE LIFE OF | MARY BAKER | G·EDDY | AND THE | HISTORY OF | CHRISTIAN SCIENCE | BY | GEORGINE | MILMINE | [publisher's device] | Illustrated | Net, $2.00 | DOUBLEDAY, | PAGE & CO.' Back cover: list of 24 titles by Rudyard Kipling. Front inner flap: advt. for Agnes C. Murphy's *Melba*. Back inner flap: advt. for Lorenzo Sears's *Wendell Phillips*.

Publication: November 1909. Published first in 14 installments of *McClure's Magazine*, January 1907 through June 1908:
Part I, *McClure's* 28 (January 1907): 227-242.
Part II, *McClure's* 28 (February 1907): 339-354.
Part III, *McClure's* 28 (March 1907): 506-524.
Part IV, *McClure's* 28 (April 1907): 608-627.
Part V, *McClure's* 29 (May 1907): 97-116.
Part VI, *McClure's* 29 (July 1907): 333-348.
Part VII, *McClure's* 29 (August 1907): 447-462.
Part VIII, *McClure's* 29 (September 1907): 567-581.

Part IX, *McClure's* 29 (October 1907): 688-699.
Part X, *McClure's* 30 (February 1908): 387-401.
Part XI, *McClure's* 30 (March 1908): 577-590.
Part XII, *McClure's* 30 (April 1908): 699-712.
Part XIII, *McClure's* 31 (May 1908): 16-31.
Part XIV, *McClure's* 31 (June 1908): 179-189.

An "Editorial Announcement" of the series is printed in *Mc-Clure's* 28 (December 1906): 211. This was not written by Willa Cather. On the verso of the announcement page is a portrait subscribed in holograph facsimile "Mary Baker Eddy." The portrait is not of Mrs. Eddy, and it aroused much protest before the series began.

Georgine Milmine's *The Life of Mary Baker G. Eddy* in book form is a major entry here by reason of scholarly controversy over the extent of Willa Cather's involvement with its publication. Milmine's manuscript was badly written, disorganized, and factually unreliable when she brought it to *McClure's*. Willa Cather was a new employee of the magazine in 1906, and her first major assignment was to work on the manuscript after *McClure's* editors Will Irwin and Burton J. Hendrick had tried their hands at it without success. In order to verify Milmine's facts and interview all of the people still living who were mentioned in the biography, Cather was sent to Boston, where she worked on the research assignment until the conclusion of the series in 1908. She reorganized the material for each monthly installment after the January issue and rewrote much of it, impressing her journalistic style on the text to its undoubted improvement.

A strong piece of evidence exists to verify the extent of WC's work on the magazine serial: a letter written to her father on 17 December 1906 explaining why she would be unable to come home for Christmas. Though she wishes to be with her family over the holidays, she cannot desert Mr. McClure in "this crisis," which would mean a loss to him in money and influence if the March article failed to appear on schedule. She refers to the glare of publicity and criticism that surrounds the series and says that she had nothing to do with the January article. Her work "begins to appear" in February. Mr. McClure, worried and anxious,

has begged her to stay at work on the series until after Christmas, which she has agreed to do. (This necessarily paraphrased letter was made available through the generosity of the owner Mrs. Helen Southwick, Willa Cather's niece.)

In later years, Willa Cather preferred to minimize her part in the actual composition. She claimed only an editorial association with the work: arranging the mass of notes and documents in a form that would be clear and effective for publication. In a letter to Mrs. Genevive Richmond, dated 8 December 1933 (Archive of the First Church of Christ, Boston), she says that she never saw Milmine's biography after it was published in book form. Her part consisted only of coordinating the material and "in some instances" rewriting a few paragraphs for the McClure's publication.

In one form or another, this was Willa Cather's unvarying response to inquiries on the subject of the Eddy biography after she was established as a major literary figure, and there is no reason to doubt the truth of her few private statements, though it was clearly a conservative truth. As a mature artist she was understandably resentful of efforts to attribute to her a piece of work that had been a professional assignment not of her own choosing. She was justified in wishing to disassociate her name from anything more than a partial responsibility for the published serial text. Neither did she wish, as a public figure, to involve herself in conflict with the Christian Scientists or stir up again the old controversy over the *McClure's* serialization.

The first installment of the series in the January 1907 issue of *McClure's* (pp. 227-242) is a text entirely different from chapter 1 of the book (pp. 2-41) which it incorporates. This is the work of Burton J. Hendrick, one of the other *McClure's* editors first assigned the job. It aroused such a storm of protest that McClure regretted having undertaken to publish the series. Having begun, however, he decided that the facts must be more thoroughly researched and placed it in Willa Cather's hands.

The February and March installments (the first revised and edited by WC) conform to pp. 42-104 of the book with some structural variation. With the April and May issues, some addi-

tional factual matter begins to appear in the series that is not included in the book, but the text substantially conforms to pp. 105-175 of the book. Chapter 11 (book pp. 176-210) is omitted in sequence from the series, but information contained in it is adapted, extended, and completely revised in the concluding series installment. The June 1907 issue contains an editorial announcement on p. 134 that the second part of the biography will begin with the July issue. From the July through the May 1908 issues, periodical and book texts are essentially the same with occasional passages present in or absent from one text or the other, and variant structures are apparent in some passages. To this extent, Willa Cather's statement is substantiated.

The later installments of the series are heavily documented with letters, affidavits, and authorized statements, of which many were the fruit of Cather's investigation. A greater facility of expression and a more professional style reflect Miss Cather's influence in the later installments (and, therefore, the book chapters). The text of the final June 1908 installment incorporates the content of chapter 11, but bears no relationship to the conclusion of the book, which was undoubtedly the unaided work of Georgine Milmine. If any part of the serialization can be conjectured as the sole work of Willa Cather, it is this concluding installment of the series.

The sections in the series that were later excised from the book text can logically be presumed to be Cather's work. These are as follows, with series passages identified by *McClure's* date, page, column (in roman), and line followed by book location (page and line) from which the passage is excised. Only significant passages are given here, and none of the structural variants in the book that do not occur in the periodical text:

April 1907, 611.i.9-613.i.22	*Troubles*. . . . room. Mr. Russell (108.5-6)
April 1907, 616.i.14-ii.11	She arrived. . . . Webster. (114.34-35)
April 1907, 619.i.54-ii.17	There was. . . . his infancy. (119.8)
May 1907, 97.i.1-17	The first. . . . achievement. (134.1)

May 1907, 97.ii.13-18 — Mrs. Glover accordingly . . . influence. (135.9)

May 1907, 108.i.16-44 — During this. . . . of Jesus Christ.* (153.21-22)

May 1907, 110.ii.48-56 — These men, . . . and morals." (159.7-8)

May 1907, 114.i.9-28 — By 1875 Quimby's. . . . do with it. (165.31-166.1)

May 1907, 115.i.26-ii.25 — As Mrs. Glover. . . . worked at all. (168.7-172.16)

August 1907, 447.i.21-ii.14. — In April, 1878. . . . plaintiff in court. (245.14-15)

August 1907, 453.ii.22-29. — In the absence . . . against himself. (258.11-12)

August 1907, 445.ii.53-ii.8. — and even the. . . . shoulders. But (261.16)

February 1908, 390.i.19-43. — It was on. . . . much for her. (347.13)

February 1908, 393.ii.31-37. — There was certainly. . . . been taught. (356.19-357.4)

February 1908, 396.i.15-17. — (To-day the . . . healers.) (364.10-11)

March 1908, 580.ii.45-581.(I)5. — The reader will. . . . $200 tuition." (386.2-3)

March 1908, 585.i.21-46. — But, however. . . . its columns." (396.33-34)

March 1908, 585.ii.21-31. — "I require. . . . under her." (397.18-19)

April 1908, 702.ii.38-703.i.43. — In her chapter. . . . not greatly changed. (419.8-9)

April 1908, 703.ii.56-704.i.7. — Mrs. Eddy herself. . . .interfered with. (420.25-26)

April 1908, 709.i.22-30. — The withdrawal of. . . . were made him. (432.16-17)

April 1908, 712.i.14-ii.3. — "The doom of. . . . "Babylonish woman." (439.17-25)

May 1908, 19.i.21-46. — Lord Dunmore. . . . EDDY." (448.15-16)

May 1908, 21.i.51-ii.6.	According to. . . . and anxiety. (453.1)
May 1908, 21.ii.29-52.	Mrs. Eddy has stated. . . . excellent record. (453.14-15)
May 1908, 26.ii.2-4; 7-8.	Lest . . . saving. . . . Mrs. Eddy herself seems— arrangement. (463.15)
May 1908, 27.ii.26-30; 38-45.	indeed, it was . . . vice-regents. . . . Rumors are ever. . . . her loyalty. (465.13; 19)
May 1908, 28.i.36-43.	Again, the by-laws. . . . especial legislation. (470.21-22)
May 1908, 28.ii.-29.ii.18.	What, one might ask. . . . of the Mother Church. (472-473.6: this text is present, but in entirely different form)
May 1908, 29.i.46-50.	Since the branch . . . self-government. (473.25-26)

Extensive revision begins in the final pages (pp. 30-31) of the May 1908 issue, and lengthy passages do not appear which are later added to the book version. These passages in addition to 3 appendices (pp. 486-495) are Milmine's work. With the exception of the editorial revision retained by Milmine—there is no objective means of determining its extent—the text of the published work in book form is here concluded to be her own, strongly influenced by Willa Cather's journalistic style. Willa Cather's direct contribution was limited to the text of the *McClure's* serial publication.

a.ii.)   Second printing, 1971

THE LIFE OF | MARY BAKER G. EDDY | AND THE | HISTORY OF CHRISTIAN SCIENCE | BY | GEORGINE MILMINE | ILLUSTRATED | BAKER BOOK HOUSE | Grand Rapids, Michigan

Photographic facsimile of the first edition. [1-10]^{16} [11]^{8}
[12-18]^{16}; pp.[i-vi] vii-xxxiv [1-2] 3-10 [2], 11-34 [2], 35-48
[2], 49-66 [2], 67-114 [2], 115-128 [2], 129-152 [2],
153-168 [2], 169-252 [2], 253-294 [2], 295-328 [2], 329-384
[2], 385-414 [2], 415-542 [2], 453-498 = 280 leaves.

Twenty of the original illustrations (including the frontispiece
portrait) are included in the text on 15 unpaged integral leaves,
which account for the breaks in pagination. 209 x 136mm. Red-
orange (36) fabric binding with simulated morocco pattern, gilt-
stamped on spine, covers blank. Copyright (p.iv) refers to this
as the 'Second Edition': 'Reprinted 1971 by Baker Book House |
by exclusive arrangement with | Doubleday & Company, New
York | Copyright © 1909 by Doubleday, Page, & Co. | Copy-
right © renewed 1937 by Georgine Milmine Adams | Introduc-
tion to Second Edition Copyright © 1971 | by Baker Book
House Company'. The introduction (pp.xv-xxxiv) by Stewart
Hudson makes an argument for Willa Cather's authorship of the
greater part of the text.

English Editions

AAA1.a.i.(e)   First English edition (American sheets of the first printing).
London: Hodder, 1909. Not seen. American sheets with English
imprint. Suppressed in England by the Christian Scientists.

AAA Historical Note

Between 1906 and 1912, during the years of her employment
by *McClure's*, Willa Cather undoubtedly edited many manuscripts that came over her desk. One other should perhaps be
particularly mentioned: the theater reminiscences of Ellen Terry
printed in *McClure's* in 15 installments between June 1907 and
October 1908 (*McClure's* 29, nos.2-3, 6; 30, nos.1-6; 31,
nos.1-6). Since Willa Cather spent most of 1907 and part of
1908 in Boston working on the Milmine biography of Mary
Baker Eddy, it seems unlikely that she had much to do with
Ellen Terry's manuscript, but A. L. Rowse states ("On the Track
of Willa Cather in Nebraska" in *Blackwood's Magazine* 328
(1978), "Elsie [Cather] told me. . . . that Willa had ghost-

written some of the *Autobiography* [*sic*] of Ellen Terry, whom she adored." This interview with the youngest of Willa Cather's sisters occurred in 1957, when she was in her seventies. Involvement with the Terry memoirs may have been wishful thinking on the part of the new *McClure's* employee. She would surely have preferred it to the Milmine work. It is quite possible that she was given editorial control over later Terry installments as a reward for her diligence on the Eddy biography. Ellen Terry's autobiography, *The Story of My Life*, was published in book form in 1909 by Doubleday, Page & Co.

Part Two

B

Poems, 1892-1931

1892

B1. SHAKESPEARE | A FRESHMAN THEME. (1) *Hesperian*, 1
June 1892, p.3. (2) *Prairie Schooner* 22 (Spring 1948): 98-99.
(3) *WCCY*, pp.109-110. (4) In "Willa Cather,
Undergraduate–Two Poems," by John P. Hinz, *American
Literature* 21 (March 1949): 112-113. (5) *AT* (1968), p.61.

B2. COLUMBUS. (1) *Hesperian*, 1 November 1892, p.9. (2) *Prairie
Schooner* 22 (Spring 1948): 99-100. (3) In "Willa Cather,
Undergraduate–Two Poems," by John P. Hinz, *American
Literature* 21 (March 1949): 114-115. (4) *WCCY*, p.111.
(5) *AT* (1968), p.63.

B3. HORACE | BOOK I, ODE XXXVIII | "PERSICOS ODI."
(1) *Hesperian*, 24 November 1892, p.12. (2) *WCCY*, p.112.

1893

B4. ['AH LIE ME DEAD IN THE SUNRISE LAND'] [with the
story, 'A Son of the Celestial']. (1) *Hesperian*, 15 January 1893,
p.7. (2) *Early Stories*, pp.25-26. (3) *WCCSF*, p.523.

1894

B5. ANACREON. (1) *Sombrero* 3 (1894), p.222. (2) *WCCY*, p.110.

1896

B6. MY LITTLE BOY [signed 'John Esten']. (1) *HM*, August
1896, p.21. (2) *AT* (1968), pp.64-65.

B7. 'THINE EYES SO BLUE AND TENDER' [signed 'Emily
Vantell']. (1) *HM*, October 1896, p.15. (2) *AT* (1968), p.66.

B8. JINGLE | BOBBY SHAFTO [signed 'John Esten']. (1) *HM*, October 1896, p.18. (2) *AT* (1968), p.67.

B9. MY HORSEMAN. (1) *HM*, November 1896, p.15. (2) *AT* (1968), p.68.

B10. THE THREE HOLY KINGS [translation from Heine]. (1) *HM*, December 1896, cover and p.1; hand-lettered in a page illustration.

1897

B11. THE ERRAND [translation from Heine]. (1) *Courier*, 6 November 1897, p.2.

B12. ['HAD YOU BUT SMOTHERED THAT DEVOURING FLAME'] [translation of 3 stanzas from Musset's "Malibran"]. (1) *Courier*, 11 December 1897, p.2.

B13. ['THE SEINE DIVIDES OLD PARIS STILL'] [stanzas used in 1899 revision, 'Then Back to Ancient France Again' (B15)]. (1) *HM*, September 1897, p.14.

1898

B14. ['O! THE WORLD WAS FULL OF THE SUMMER TIME'] [with the story 'The Way of the World']. (1) *HM*, April 1898, p.10. (2) *Courier*, 19 August 1899, p.8. (3) *WCCSF*, p.395.

1899

B15. ['THEN BACK TO ANCIENT FRANCE AGAIN'] [see B13]. (1) *Courier*, 22 April 1899, p.2. (2) *AT* (1968), p.69.

1900

B16. ['IN THAT VOICE WHAT DARKER MAGIC'] [translation from Heine]. (1) *Courier*, 6 January 1900, p.2.

B17. IN THE NIGHT. (1) *Library*, 17 March 1900, p.16. (2) *Courier*, 7 April 1900, p.3.

B18. THOU ART THE PEARL [signed 'John Charles Esten']. (1) *Library*, 24 March 1900, p.16. (2) *AT* (1903 et seq.). (3) *Commonweal* 13 (25 February 1931), 465.

B19. "GRANDMITHER, THINK NOT I FORGET". (1) *Critic*
36 (April 1900): 308. (2) *PL*, 29 March 1900, p.2. (3) *Courier*,
28 April 1900, p.2. (4) *Current Literature* 28 (May 1900): 161.
(5) *AT* (1903 et seq.). (6) *Chicago Tribune*, 23 May 1903, p.9.
(7) *Poet Lore* 14 (Winter 1903): 114. (8) *McClure's* 32 (April
1909): 649. (9) *Current Literature* 47 (July 1909): 106. (10) In
The Home Book of Verse, ed. B.E. Stevenson (New York: Holt,
1912), pp.1015-1016. (11) *The Little Book of Modern Verse*
(Boston: HM Co., 1913), pp.75-77. (12) In *The Answering Voice:
One Hundred Love Lyrics by Women* (Boston: HM Co., 1917),
pp.108-110. (13) *Verse by Willa Cather* (New York: Knopf
1922). Single folded sheet containing the first 2 stanzas (A12).
(14) *The Women Poets in English*, ed. Ann Stanford (New York:
McGraw-Hill 1972), pp.175-176.

B20. AFTERMATH [version 1 (see B53 for version 2)]. (1) *Library*,
7 April 1900, p.22.

B21. IN THE GARDEN. (1) *Library*, 14 April 1900, p.20.

B22. FLEUR DE LIS [signed 'Clara Wood Shipman']. (1) *Library*,
26 May 1900, 13.

B23. A LOVE FRAY [signed 'Clara Wood Shipman']. (1) *Library*,
23 June 1900, p.13. *Note:* The Shipman attribution is doubted
by some Cather scholars.

B24. BRONCHO BILL'S VALEDICTORY. (1) *Library*, 30 June
1900, p.6. (2) *Courier*, 14 July 1900, p.3. (3) *AT* (1968),
pp.70-72.

B25. THE LONELY SLEEP. (1) *Library*, 14 July 1900, p.18.

B26. ARE YOU SLEEPING, LITTLE BROTHER | TO J. E.
(1) *Library*, 4 August 1900, p.14. (2) *Courier* 11 August 1900,
p.9. (3) *AT* (1968), pp.73-74. (4) *WCPM Newsletter*, Fall 1967,
p.1.

B27. THE POET TO HIS PUBLIC [in *AT* as 'The Encore']. (1)
Lippincott's 66 (December 1900): 74 (in a separately paged

insert, 'Walnuts and Wine'). (2) *NSJ*, 16 December 1900, p.19. (3) *AT* (1903 et seq., as 'The Encore').

B28.   ASPHODEL. (1) *Critic* 37 (December 1900): 565. (2) *NSJ*, 17 December 1900, p.4. (3) *AT* (1903, 1962, 1968). (4) In *The Humbler Poets (Second Series): A Collection of Newspaper and Periodical Verse, 1885-1910*, comp. W. and F. Rice (Chicago: McClurg & Co., 1911), p.126.

1901

B29.   IN MEDIA VITA. (1) *Lippincott's* 67 (May 1901): 623. (2) *AT* (1903, 1923, 1933, 1962, 1968).

B30.   WINTER AT DELPHI. (1) *Critic* 39 (September 1901): 269. (2) *AT* (1903 et seq.). (3) *New York Times Saturday Review*, 20 June 1903, p.434.

1902

B31.   ARCADIAN WINTER. (1) *Harper's Weekly*, 4 January 1902, p.24. (2) *High School Journal* (Pittsburgh Central High School), January 1902, p.1. (3) *Courier*, 18 January 1902, p.8. (4) *AT* (1903 et seq.).

B32.   THE NAMESAKE | TO W. L. B. OF THE THIRTY-FIFTH VIRGINIA [or 'To W. S. B. of the Thirty-Third Virginia']. (1) *Lippincott's* 69 (April 1902): 482. (2) *Courier*, 12 April 1902, p.3. (3) *AT* (1903, 1962, 1968; subtitle is 'To W. S. B. of the Thirty-Third Virginia').

B33.   THE NIGHT EXPRESS. (1) *Youth's Companion* 76 (26 June 1902): 328. (2) *NSJ*, 20 July 1902, p.12. (3) *PG*, 3 August 1902, p.12. (4) *AT* (1903, 1962, 1968).

B34.   IN ROSE TIME. (1) *Lippincott's* 70 (July 1902): 97. (2) *PG*, 13 July 1902, p.2. (3) *AT* (1903 et seq.). (4) *Lincoln Star*, 30 October 1921, p.7. (5) *Poetry Review* (London) 16 (1925): 408. (6) *Golden Book* 5 (June 1927): 723 (last 7 lines only).

1903

B35. DEDICATORY. (1) *AT* (1903, 1962, 1968). (2) *The Women Poets in English*, ed. Ann Stanford (New York: McGraw Hill, 1972), pp.174-175.

B36. MILLS OF MONTMARTRE. (1) *AT* (1903, 1962, 1968). (2) *Academy and Literature* (London) 65 (18 July 1903), 57-58. (3) *Poet Lore* 14 (Winter 1903): 114-115.

B37. THE HAWTHORN TREE. (1) *AT* (1903 et seq.). (2) *Poet Lore* 14 (Winter 1903): 115. (3) In *The Answering Voice: One Hundred Love Lyrics by Women* (Boston: HM Co., 1917), p.34. (4) Song, set to music by Jessie L. Pease (New York: Boosey, 1923). (5) In *Willa Cather*, by René Rapin (New York: McBride & Co., 1930), p.15.

B38. SLEEP, MINSTREL, SLEEP. (1) *AT* (1903 et seq.).

B39. FIDES, SPES. (1) *AT* (1903 et seq.). (2) *McClure's* 32 (February 1909): 362.

B40. THE TAVERN. (1) *AT* (1903 et seq.). (2) *New York Times Saturday Review*, 20 June 1903, p.434. (3) *McClure's* 31 (August 1908): 419.

B41. ANTINOUS. (1) *AT* (1903 et seq.).

B42. PARADOX. (1) *AT* (1903 et seq.).

B43. PROVENÇAL LEGEND. (1) *AT* (1903 et seq.). (2) *McClure's* 33 (September 1909): 519.

B44. ON CYDNUS. (1) *AT* (1903 [title misspelled: 'On Cyndus'], 1923 et seq.). (2) *PG*, 26 April 1903, sec. 2, p.4. (3) *Commonweal* 13 (25 February 1931): 466.

B45. LAMENT FOR MARSYAS. (1) *AT* (1903 [last stanza omitted], 1923 et seq.). (2) *McClure's* 30 (February 1908): 453.

B46. WHITE BIRCH IN WYOMING. (1) *AT* (1903, 1962, 1968).

B47.   I SOUGHT THE WOOD IN WINTER. (1) *AT* (1903 et seq.).
(2) *Golden Book* 13 (January 1931): 70 (third stanza only). (3) In
Under the Bridge, by Ferris Greenslet (Boston: HM Co., 1943),
p.116 (8 lines of the last stanza only).

B48.   EVENING SONG. (1) *AT* (1903 et seq.). (2) *McClure's*
29 (August 1907): 365 ('From "April Twilights."').

B49.   EURYDICE. (1) *AT* (1903, 1962, 1968). (2) *Commonweal*
13 (25 February 1931): 465.

B50.   THE ENCORE. [See 'The Poet to His Public' (B27).]

B51.   LONDON ROSES. (1) *AT* (1903 et seq.). (2) *McClure's*
34 (November 1909): 61.

B52.   PRAIRIE DAWN. (1) *AT* (1903 et seq.). (2) *Dial* 35 (16 July
1903): 40-41. (3) *McClure's* 31 (June 1908): 229. (4) *NSJ*,
10 June 1917, p.3-c. (5) In *Willa Cather*, by René Rapin (New
York: McBride & Co., 1930), p.16. (6) *Commonweal* 13 (25
February 1931): 466. (7) In *Willa Cather*, by David Daiches
(Ithaca, N.Y.: Cornell University Press, 1951) p.177.

B53.   AFTERMATH [version 2 (see B20 for version 1)]. (1) *AT* (1903
et seq.). (2) *PG*, 26 April 1903, sec.2, p.4.

B54.   THINE ADVOCATE. (1) *AT* (1903, 1962, 1968).

B55.   POPPIES ON LUDLOW CASTLE. (1) *AT* (1903 et seq.).

B56.   SONNET. (1) *AT* (1903, 1962, 1968). (2) *Commonweal* 13
(25 February 1931): 464.

B57.   FROM THE VALLEY. (1) *AT* (1903, 1962, 1968).

B58.   I HAVE NO HOUSE FOR LOVE TO SHELTER HIM. (1) *AT*
(1903, 1962, 1968). (2) *Poet Lore* 16 (Summer 1905): 50.

B59.   THE POOR MINSTREL. (1) *AT* (1903 et seq.). (2) *McClure's*
36 (February 1911): 376. (3) In *The Days and the Nights: Prayers*

for *Today's Woman*, ed. Candida Lund (Chicago: Thomas More Press, 1978), pp.77-78.

B60. PARIS. (1) *AT* (1903, 1962, 1968). (2) In *The Garden of the Heart*. . . . (Boston: Badger, 1903), p.13. Signed 'Willa Sibert Cather'; beneath: 'From "April Twilights"'. This printing may have preceded *AT*.

B61. SONG. (1) *AT* (1903, 1923, 1933, 1962, 1968).

B62. L'ENVOI. (1) *AT* (1903 et seq.). (2) In *The Humbler Poets (Second Series): A Collection of Newspaper and Periodical Verse*, comp. W. and F. Rice (Chicago: McClurg, 1911), p.248. (3) In *The Home Book of Verse*, ed. B. E. Stevenson (New York: Holt, 1912), pp.3217-3218. (4) *Poetry Review* (London) 16 (1925): 411. (5) *Commonweal* 13 (25 February 1931): 465.

1907

B63. AUTUMN MELODY. (1) *McClure's* 30 (November 1907): 106. (2) *AT* (1923, 1933, 1937).

B64. THE STAR DIAL. (1) *McClure's* 30 (December 1907): 202.

1909

B65. THE PALATINE/(IN THE "DARK AGES"). (1) *McClure's* 33 (June 1909): 158-159. (2) *New York Times Saturday Review* 14 (22 May 1909): 317. (3) In *Mark Twain: A Biography*, by Albert Bigelow Paine, 3 (New York: Harper, 1912): 1501-1502 (first 3 stanzas only). (4) In *New Poetry*, ed. Harriet Monroe and A. Corbin Henderson (New York: Macmillan, 1917), pp.43-44. (5) *AT* (1923, 1933, 1937).

1911

B66. THE SWEDISH MOTHER/(*Nebraska*). (1) *McClure's* 37 (September 1911): 541. (2) *AT* (1923, 1933, 1937).

1912

B67. SPANISH JOHNNY. (1) *McClure's* 39 (June 1912): 204. (2) In *New Poetry*, ed. Harriet Monroe and A. Corbin Henderson (New York: Macmillan, 1917), pp.44-45. (3) *AT* (1923, 1933, 1937). (4) *Literary Digest* 78 (21 July 1923): 34. (5) *Poetry*

Review (London) 16 (1925): 410. (6) In *American Ballads and Folk Songs*, comp. John A. and Alan Lomax (New York: Macmillan, 1934), pp.123-124 (music by Charles Elbert Scoggins). (7) Song sheet, music by Elmo Russ (New York: U.S. Music, Inc., 1940). (8) Song sheet, music by John Charles Sacco (New York: G. Schirmer, Inc., 1941). (9) In *Willa Cather: A Memoir*, by Elizabeth S. Sergeant, rev. ed. (Lincoln: University of Nebraska Press, 1963), pp.183-184.

B68.   PRAIRIE SPRING. (1) *McClure's* 40 (December 1912): 226. (2) *O Pioneers!* (Boston: HM Co., 1913), epigraph, p.ix. (3) *NSJ*, 10 June 1917, 3-c ('From *O Pioneers!*'). (4) *AT* (1923, 1933, 1937). (5) In *Willa Cather: A Memoir*, by Elizabeth S. Sergeant (Lincoln: University of Nebraska Press, 1953, 1963), pp.84-85.

1913

B69.   A LIKENESS/(PORTRAIT BUST OF AN UNKNOWN, CAPITOL, ROME). (1) *Scribner's Magazine* 54 (December 1913): 711-712. (2) *Literary Digest* 48 (31 January 1914): 219. (3) *NSJ*, 6 February 1914, p.12. (4) In *Anthology of Magazine Verse for 1913*, ed. W. S. Braithwaite (Cambridge, Mass.: W. S. Braithwaite, 1913), pp.46-47. (5) *AT* (1923, 1933, 1937). (6) *Poetry Review* (London) 16 (1925): 408.

B70.   THE DEAD FORERUNNER. (1) *Scribner's Magazine* 54 (December 1913): 743.

1915

B71.   ['ON UPLANDS']. (1) *The Song of the Lark* (Boston: HM Co., 1915), dedication to Isabelle McClung, p.v. (2) In *Willa Cather: A Memoir*, by Elizabeth S. Sergeant (Lincoln: University of Nebraska Press, 1953, 1963) p.26. (3) In *Willa Cather*, by E. K. Brown (New York: Knopf, 1953), p.97.

B72.   STREET IN PACKINGTOWN. (1) *Century Magazine* 90 (May 1915): 23. (2) *AT* (1923, 1933, 1937).

1923

B73.   RECOGNITION. (1) *AT* (1923, 1933, 1937).

B74. MACON PRAIRIE. (1) *AT* (1923, 1933, 1937).

B75. GOING HOME. (1) *AT* (1923, 1933, 1937). (2) *Poetry Review*
(London) 16 (1925): 409. Last stanza only. (3) In *Willa Cather:
A Memoir*, by Elizabeth S. Sergeant (Lincoln: University of
Nebraska Press, 1953, 1963) p.24. Third stanza only.

B76. THE GAUL IN THE CAPITOL. (1) *AT* (1923, 1933, 1937).

B77. A SILVER CUP. (1) *AT* (1923, 1933, 1937).

1931
B78. POOR MARTY. (1) *Atlantic Monthly* 147 (May 1931):
585-587. (2) *Literary Digest* 109 (9 May 1931): 24. (3) *AT*
(1933, 1937).

1968
B79. THE EASTER RABBIT [*subtitle*: 'Respectfully Dedicated to
Miss Elsie Cather on the Ides of March 1896']. (1) *WCPM
Newsletter* Spring 1968, p.1. In holograph facsimile.

B80. THE HILLS OF SLEEP. (1) *WCPM Newsletter*, Winter
1975-1976, p.1.

1978
B81. THE OLD CLIFF-DWELLER | (WALNUT CANYON,
ARIZONA) | A.D. 1400. (1) Privately printed by the Pedigrus
Press, San Francisco, Calif., 1978. Subject content relates to
SOL, suggesting that the poem was written in about 1915.

B Appendix

Four poems of Willa Cather were set to music in April 1973 by
the composer Robert Beadell for the occasion of a Willa Cather
Centennial Concert in Red Cloud, Nebraska, under the auspices
of the University of Nebraska School of Music and the Nebraska
Arts Council. The theme of the program was music from Willa
Cather's writings. The narration was by Bernice Slote. Leta
Powell Drake, Bernice Slote, and Sandy Dennis were featured as
narrators with the University of Nebraska Symphony Orchestra

and the University Singers. Beadell's musical settings were for
the poems:
Spanish Johnny (B67)
Prairie Dawn (B52)
Prairie Spring (B68)
Prairie Roads (adapted from the text of the story, 'Two Friends'
    [C58])

The 3 "prairie" works were arranged together with the title
"Prairie Trilogy."

Part Three

C

Short Fiction

1892

C1. PETER. (1) *Mahogany Tree*, 21 May 1892, pp.323-324.
(2) *Hesperian*, 24 November 1892, pp.10-12; 16 textual
alterations. (3) *Library*, 21 July 1900, p.5. Title: 'Peter
Sadelack, Father of Anton.' Additional revision. (4) *WCCY*,
pp.41-45. *Hesperian* version. AA3. (5) *Early Stories*, pp.1-8.
Hesperian and *Library* versions alternating by sections separated with bracketed subjective notes by the editor. AA6.
(6) *WCCSF*, pp.541-543. *Mahogany Tree* version. AA7.

C2. LOU, THE PROPHET. (1) *Hesperian*, 15 October 1892,
pp.7-10. (2) *Prairie Schooner* 22 (Spring 1948): 100-104.
(3) *WCCY*, pp.46-53. AA3. (4) *Early Stories*, pp.9-17. AA6.
(5) *WCCSF*, pp.535-540. AA7.

C3. A TALE OF THE WHITE PYRAMID. (1) *Hesperian*,
22 December 1892, pp.8-11. (2) *WCCY*, pp.54-60. AA3.
(3) *Early Stories*, pp.19-24. AA6. (4) *WCCSF*, pp.529-533.
AA7.

1893

C4. A SON OF THE CELESTIAL. (1) *Hesperian*, 15 January 1893,
pp.7-10. (2) *WCCY*, pp.61-68. AA3. (3) *Early Stories*,
pp.25-32. AA6. (4) *WCCSF*, pp.523-528. AA7.

C5. THE ELOPEMENT OF ALLEN POOLE. (1) *Hesperian*,
15 April 1893, pp.4-7. (2) *KA*, (1966), pp.437-441. AA8.
(3) *WCCSF* (1970), pp.573-578. AA7.

C6. THE CLEMENCY OF THE COURT. (1) *Hesperian*, 26 October
1893, pp.3-7. (2) *Prairie Schooner* 22 (Spring 1948): 104-111.

(3) *WCCY*, pp.69-79. AA3. (4) *Early Stories*, pp.33-43. AA6.
(5) *WCCSF*, pp.515-522. AA7.

1894

C7. "THE FEAR THAT WALKS BY NOONDAY" [with Dorothy Canfield]. (1) *Sombrero* 3 (1894), pp.224-231. (2) Separate publication (New York: Phoenix Book Shop, 1931). A17. (3) *Early Stories*, pp.45-57. Publication date erroneously given as 1895. AA6. (4) *WCCSF*, pp.505-514. AA7.

1896

C8. ON THE DIVIDE. (1) *Overland Monthly* 27 (January 1896): 65-74. (2) *Early Stories*, pp.59-75. AA6. (3) In *Pulitzer Prize Reader*, ed. Leo Hamalian and Edmond L. Volpe (New York: Popular Library, 1961). (4) *WCCSF*, pp.493-504. AA7.

C9. A NIGHT AT GREENWAY COURT. (1) *Nebraska Literary Magazine* 1 (June 1896): 215-224. (2) *Library*, 21 April 1900, pp.5-7. Revised. (3) *WCCY*, pp.80-92. Original version. AA3. (4) *Early Stories*, pp.77-91. Alternating version sections separated with bracketed subjective notes by the editor. AA6. (5) *WCCSF*, pp.483-492. Original version AA7.

C10. TOMMY, THE UNSENTIMENTAL. (1) *HM*, August 1896, pp.6-7. (2) *Early Stories*, pp.103-113. AA6. (3) *WCCSF*, pp.473-480 AA7.

C11. THE PRINCESS BALADINA—HER ADVENTURE [signed 'Charles Douglass']. (1) *HM*, August 1896, pp.20-21. (2) *WCCSF*, pp.567-572. AA7.

C12. THE COUNT OF CROW'S NEST. (1) *HM*, September, October 1896, pp.9-11; 12-13; 22-23. (2) *Early Stories*, pp.115-145. AA6. (3) *WCCSF*, pp.449-471. AA7.

C13. WEE WINKIE'S WANDERINGS. (1) *National Stockman and Farmer*, 26 November 1896, p.18. (2) *Vogue*, June 1973, p.113. (3) *WCPM Newsletter*, Literary Issue, Summer 1973, pp.2-3.

C14. THE BURGLAR'S CHRISTMAS [signed 'Elizabeth L. Seymour']. (1) *HM*, December 1896, pp.8-10. (2) *WCCSF*, pp.557-566. AA7.

C15. THE STRATEGY OF THE WERE-WOLF DOG. (1) *HM*, December 1896, pp.13-14, 24. (2) *WCCSF*, pp.441-448. AA7. (3) *Wildlife's Christmas Treasury* (National Wildlife Federation, 1976), pp.82-89. Title: 'The Year Santa Claus Came Late'.

1897

C16. A RESURRECTION. (1) *HM*, April 1897, p.4-8. (2) *Early Stories*, pp.147-167. AA6. (3) *WCCSF*, pp.425-439. AA7.

C17. THE PRODIGIES. (1) *HM*, July 1897, pp.9-11. (2) *Courier*, 10 July 1897, pp.4-5; 17 July, pp.8-9. (3) *Early Stories*, pp.169-185. AA6. (4) *WCCSF*, pp.411-423. AA7.

C18. NANETTE: AN ASIDE. (1) *Courier*, 31 July 1897, pp.11-12. (2) *HM*, August 1897, pp. 5-6. (3) *Early Stories*, pp.93-102; publication date erroneously given as August 1896. AA6. (4) *WCCSF*, pp.405-410. AA7.

1898

C19. THE WAY OF THE WORLD. (1) *HM*, April 1898, pp.10-11. (2) *Courier*, 19 August 1899, 9-10. (3) *WCCSF*, pp.395-404. AA7.

1899

C20. THE WESTBOUND TRAIN. (1) *Courier*, 30 September 1899, pp.3-5. (2) *WCCSF*, pp.381-393. AA7.

1900

C21. ERIC HERMANNSON'S SOUL. (1) *Cosmopolitan* 28 (April 1900): 633-644. (2) *Early Stories*, pp.187-215. AA6. (3) *WCCSF*, pp.359-379. AA7. (4) Separate publication. Perfection Micro-Classic (Logan, Iowa: The Perfection Form Co., n.d. [1975?]). MC 200. (5) See J1.

C22.   THE DANCE AT CHEVALIER'S [signed 'Henry Nickle-mann']. (1) *Library*, 28 April 1900, pp.12-13. (2) *Early Stories*, pp.217-229. AA6. (3) *WCCSF*, pp.547-555. AA7.

C23.   THE SENTIMENTALITY OF WILLIAM TAVENER.
(1) *Library*, 12 May 1900, pp.13-14. (2) *Early Stories*, pp.231-237. AA6. (3) *WCCSF*, pp.353-357. AA7. (4) In *The Dimension of Literature*, by James E. Miller, Jr., and Bernice Slote (New York: Dodd, Mead, 1967). (5) *By Women* (Boston: HM Co., 1976). (6) McFarland, Feagin, Hay, Liu, McLaughlin, Willson, eds., *Focus on Literature: America* (Boston: HM Co., 1978), pp.608-613. (7) *Types of Literature* (Ginn & Co., 1979). (8) *America in Literature: The Midwest* (NY: Scribner's, 1979). (9) *Woman: An Affirmation* (D. C. Heath, 1979). (10) *United States in Literature* (Scott, Foresman, 1980). (11) *Adventures in Appreciation* (Harcourt, Brace, Jovanovich, 1980).

C24.   THE AFFAIR AT GROVER STATION. (1) *Library*, 16 June 1900, pp.3-4; 23 June, pp.14-15. (2) *Courier*, 7 July 1900, pp.3-5, 8-9. (3) *Early Stories*, pp.239-256. AA6. (4) *WCCSF*, pp.339-352. AA7. (5) Separate publication. Perfection Micro-Classic (Logan, Iowa: The Perfection Form Co., n.d. [1975?]). MC 201.

C25.   A SINGER'S ROMANCE. (1) *Library*, 28 July 1900, pp.15-16. (2) *Early Stories*, pp.257-263. AA6. (3) *WCCSF*, pp.333-338. AA7.

C26.   THE CONVERSION OF SUM LOO. (1) *Library*, 11 August 1900, pp.4-6. (2) *Early Stories*, pp.265-275. AA6. (3) *WCCSF*, pp.323-331. AA7.

1901

C27.   JACK-A-BOY. (1) *Saturday Evening Post*, 30 March 1901, pp.4-5, 25. (2) *Prairie Schooner* 33 (June 1959): 77-86. (3) *WCCSF*, pp.311-322. AA7. (4) Separate publication. Title: *Friend of My Springtime*, illus. Arlene Noel (Kansas City, Mo.: Hallmark Crown Editions, 1974). 400HED11-5.

C28.   EL DORADO: A KANSAS RECESSIONAL. (1) *New England Magazine* 24 (June 1901): 357-369. (2) *WCCSF*, pp.293-310. AA7.

1902

C29.   THE PROFESSOR'S COMMENCEMENT. (1) *New England Magazine* 26 (June 1902): pp.481-488. (2) *WCCSF*, pp.283-291. AA7.

C30.   THE TREASURE OF FAR ISLAND. (1) *New England Magazine* 27 (October 1902): 234-249. (2) *Prairie Schooner* 38 (Winter 1964/65): 323-343. (3) *WCCSF*, pp.265-282. AA7.

1903

C31.   "A DEATH IN THE DESERT". (1) *Scribner's* 33 (January 1903): 109-121. (2) *TG* (1905), pp.111-154. 25 substantive textual alterations; 14 minor alterations. Numerous changes in spelling, capitalization, punctuation. The character 'Windermere Hilgarde' becomes 'Everett Hilgarde'. A4.a. (3) *YBM* (1920), pp.273-303. Additional revision by the author. A10.a. (4) In *Love throughout the Ages*, ed. R.Lynd (New York: Coward McCann, 1932). (5) *TG* (New York: Signet Classics, 1961), pp.65-86. The 1905 text with silent corrections and alterations by the publisher. A4.b.i. (6) *WCCSF*, pp. 199-217. *TG* (1905) text. AA7.

1904

C32.   A WAGNER MATINÉE. (1) *Everybody's Magazine* 10 (February 1904): 325-328. (2) *TG* (1905), pp.193-210. Substantially revised by the author. Significant additions and 3 major cuts. A4.a. (3) *YBM* (1920), pp.235-247. Additional revision by the author. A10.a. (4) In *Great Short Stories of the World*, comp. B.H.Clark and M.Lieber (McBride, 1925), pp.1050-1056. (5) In *Book of Modern Short Stories* ed. D.Brewster (Macmillan, 1928; 1940 [13th ptg.]), pp.228-235. (6) In *Three Centuries of American Poetry and Prose*, ed. A.G.Newcomer, A.E.Andrews, H.J.Hall (Scott, 1929). (7) *AE*, 6 (1937): 247-61. *YBM* (1920) text. A10.b. (8) In *Study and Appreciation of the Short Story*, ed. R.I.Johnson, E.M.Cowan, M.S.Peacock (Silver, 1938). (9) *Scholastic*, 30 April 1938, pp.17E-19E. (10) *TG*

(New York: Signet Classics, 1961, pp.107-115. The 1905 text with silent corrections and alterations by the publisher. A4.b.i. (11) In *Modern Talent*, ed. J.E. Hardy (Holt, Rinehart, & Winston, 1964), pp.91-104. (12) *WCCSF*, pp.235-242. *TG* (1905) text AA7. (13) In *Women and Fiction: Short Stories by and about Women*, ed. Susan Cahill (New York: New American Library, Mentor Books, 1975), pp.29-35. A biographical sketch of WC at pp.27-28. ME1858. (14) In *Focus on Literature: Forms*, ed. McFarland, Feagin, Hay, Liu, McLaughlin, Willson (Boston: HM Co., 1978), pp.84-93. *YBM* (1920) text.

1905

C33. THE SCULPTOR'S FUNERAL. (1) *McClure's* 24 (January 1905): 329-336. (2) *TG* (1905), pp.55-84. One minor sentence alteration; numerous changes in wording, spelling, capitalization, punctuation by the author. A4.a. (3) *YBM* (1920), pp.248-272. Additional author revision. A10.a. (4) In *Prose Preference*, ed. S. Cox, E. Freeman (Harper, 1926). (5) In *Century Readings in the American Short Story*, ed. F.L. Pattee (Century, 1927), pp.463-470. (6) In *Representative Short Stories*, ed. A.M. Ellis (Nelson, 1928). (7) In *Book of Modern Short Stories*, ed. D. Brewster (Macmillan, 1928), pp.76-90. (8) In *Short Stories*, ed. W.T. Hastings, B.C. Clough, K.O. Mason (HM Co., 1924; 1929). (9) In *Literature of America*, ed. A.H. Quinn, A.C. Baugh, W.D. Howe, vol.2 (Scribner's, 1929). (10) In *College Omnibus*, ed. J.D. McCallum (Harcourt, 1933), pp.590-600. (11) *Golden Book* 19 (February 1934): 162-172. (12) *AE* 6 (1937): 263-289. *YBM* (1920) text. A10.b. (13) In *American Harvest*, ed. A. Tate, J.P. Bishop (L.B. Fischer, 1942). (14) In *Modern American Short Stories*, ed. B. Cerf (World Pub., 1945). (15) In *The Family Reader of American Masterpieces*, ed. R.L. Wood (Crowell, 1959). (16) *TG* (New York: Signet Classics, 1961), pp.35-49. The 1905 text with silent corrections and alterations by the publisher. A4.b.i. (17) *WCCSF*, pp.173-185. *TG* (1905) text. AA7. (18) Separate publication. Perfection Micro-Classic (Logan, Iowa: The Perfection Form Co., n. d. [1975?]). MC 61.

C34. FLAVIA AND HER ARTISTS. (1) *TG* (1905), pp.1-54. A4.a. (2) *TG* (New York: Signet Classics, 1961), pp. 7-34. Spelling

and punctuation silently modernized by the publisher. A4.b.i.
(3) *WCCSF*, pp.149-172. *TG* (1905) text with 4 corrections of
spelling and punctuation. AA7.

C35. THE GARDEN LODGE. (1) *TG* (1905), pp.85-110. A4.a. (2)
TG (New York: Signet Classics, 1961), pp.51-63. Spelling and
punctuation silently modernized by the publisher. A4.b.i.
(3) *WCCSF*, pp.187-197. AA7.

C36. THE MARRIAGE OF PHAEDRA. (1) *TG* (1905), pp.155-
192. A4.a. (2) *TG* (New York: Signet Classics, 1961), pp.87-
105. Spelling and punctuation modernized by the publisher.
A4.b.i. (3) *WCCSF*, pp.219-234. AA7.

C37. PAUL'S CASE [subtitled 'A Study in Temperament']. (1) *TG*
(1905), pp.213-253. A4.a. (2) *McClure's* 25 (May 1905):
74-83. 2 passages, totaling about 400 words, cut by the author
for periodical publication. The passages are restored in subsequent reprintings. (3) *YBM* (1920), pp.181-212. Subtitle
omitted. A10.a. Revision of the *TG* (1905) version. (4) In
Contemporary Short Stories, ed. K. A. Robinson (HM Co., 1924),
pp.44-69. (5) *Golden Book* 5 (May 1927): 681-690. (6) In *Recent
Short Stories*, ed. M. Pendleton and D. S. Wilkins (Appleton,
1928), pp.20-41. (7) In *Modern American and British Short
Stories*, ed. L. Brown (Harcourt, 1929), pp.97-123. (8) In *Great
Modern Short Stories*, ed. G. M. Overton (Modern Library, 1930).
(9) In *Century Readings in American Literature*, ed. F. L. Pattee
(Century, 1932). (10) In *The Bedside Book of Famous American
Stories*, ed. J. A. Burrell and B. Cerf (Random House, 1936),
pp.681-697. (11) *AE*, 6: 207-245. *YBM* (1920) version.
A10.b. (12) In *Modern Short Stories*, ed. L. Brown (Harcourt,
1937). (13) In *Modern English Readings*, ed. R. S. Loomis and
D. L. Clark (Farrar, Rinehart, 1939; 1946 [5th ed.]), pp.491-
506. (14) In *Patterns for Living*, ed. O. J. Campbell, J. Van
Gundy, and C. Shrodes (Macmillan, 1940). (15) In *A Pocket-book
of Short Stories*, ed. M. E. Speare (New York: Washington Square
Press, 1941; 1968 [75th ptg.]), pp.49-70. (16) In *Great Modern
Short Stories*, ed. B. Cerf (Modern Library, 1942). (17) In *Golden
Argosy*, ed. C. Grayson and Van H. Cartmell (Dial, 1947).
(18) In *Literature of Crime*, ed. E. Queen [pseud.] (Little, Brown,

1950). (19) In *Reading Modern Fiction*, ed. W. C. Lynskey (Scribner's, 1952). (20) In *Greatest American Short Stories*, ed. A. G. Day (McGraw, Hill, 1953). (21) In *Anthology of Famous American Stories*, ed. J. A. Burrell and B. Cerf (Modern Library, 1953). (22) In *Contemporary Short Stories*, ed. M. Baudin, American Heritage series, vol. 1 (Liberal Arts, 1953-1954). (23) *Five Stories*, 149-174. AA4. (24) In *Stories*, ed. F. G. Jennings and C. J. Calitri; (Harcourt, 1957). (25) In *The Britannica Library of Great American Writing*, ed. L. Untermeyer, vol. 2 (Lippincott, 1960). (26) *TG* (New York: Signet Classics, 1961), pp. 117-138. A4.b.i. (27) In *Two and Twenty*, ed. R. H. Singleton (St. Martin's, 1962). (28) In *When Women Look at Men*, ed. J. A. Kouwenhoven and J. F. Thaddeus, (Harper, 1963). (29) *WCCSF*, pp. 243-261. AA7. (30) Separate publication. Perfection Micro-Classic (Logan, Iowa: The Perfection Form Co., n. d. [1975?]. MC 60.

1907

C38. THE NAMESAKE. (1) *McClure's* 28 (March 1907): 492-497. (2) *WCCSF*, pp. 137-146. AA7.

C39. THE PROFILE. (1) *McClure's* 29 (June 1907): 135-140. (2) *WCCSF*, pp. 125-135. AA7.

C40. THE WILLING MUSE. (1) *Century* 74 (August 1907): 550-551, 553-557. (2) *WCCSF*, pp. 113-123. AA7.

C41. ELEANOR'S HOUSE. (1) *McClure's* 29 (October 1907): 623-630. (2) *WCCSF*, pp. 95-111. AA7.

1908

C42. ON THE GULLS' ROAD. (1) *McClure's* 32 (December 1908): 145-152. (2) *WCCSF*, pp. 79-94. AA7.

1909

C43. THE ENCHANTED BLUFF. (1) *Harper's* 118 (April 1909): 774-778, 780-781. (2) *Five Stories*, pp. 3-15. AA4. (3) *WCCSF*,

1911

C44. THE JOY OF NELLY DEANE. (1) *Century* 82 (October 1911): 859-867. (2) *WCCSF*, pp. 55-68. AA7.

1912

C45. BEHIND THE SINGER TOWER. (1) *Collier's*, May 1912, pp.16-17, 41. (2) *WCCSF*, pp.43-54. AA7.

C46. THE BOHEMIAN GIRL. (1) *McClure's* 39 (August 1912): 420-424, 426-427, 430, 432-443. (2) *WCCSF*, pp.3-41. AA7.

1915

C47. CONSEQUENCES. (1) *McClure's* 46 (November 1915): 30-32, 63-64. (2) *UV*, pp.67-84. AA10.

1916

C48. THE BOOKKEEPER'S WIFE. (1) *Century* 92 (May 1916): 51-52, 54-56, 58-59. (2) *Golden Book* 10 (November 1929): 74-78. (3) *UV*, pp.87-97. AA10.

C49. THE DIAMOND MINE. (1) *McClure's* October 1916, pp.7-11. (2) *YBM* (1920), pp.79-139. A10.a. (3) *AE*, 6 (1937): 75-140. A10.b.

1917

C50. A GOLD SLIPPER. (1) *Harper's* 134 (January 1917): 166-174. (2) *YBM* (1920), pp.140-168. A10.a. (3) *Trumps* (New York: Putnam, Community Workers of the New York Guild for the Jewish Blind, 1926). (4) *AE*, 6:141-172. A10.b.

1918

C51. ARDESSA. (1) *Century* 96 (May 1918): 105-116. (2) *UV*, pp.101-115. AA10.

1919

C52. SCANDAL. (1) *Century* 98 (August 1919): 433-445. 'Connie' for 'Kitty'. (2) *YBM* (1920), pp.169-198. A10.a. Name changed to 'Kitty'. (3) In *More Acres* (New York: Putnam, Community Workers of the New York Guild for the Jewish Blind, 1925). (4) In *Tales from Far and Near*, ed. S. Rhys and C. A. D. Scott (Appleton, 1930), pp.302-323. (5) *AE*, 6: 173-205. A10.b.

C53. HER BOSS. (1) *Smart Set* 90 (October 1919): 95-108. (2) *UV*, pp.119-139. AA10.

1920

C54. COMING, APHRODITE! ['Coming, Eden Bower!']. (1) *Smart Set* 92 (August 1920): 3-25. Title: 'Coming, Eden Bower!' See *UV*, appendix, pp.177-181, for Bernice Slote's textual comparison of this and subsequent texts. (2) *YBM* (1920), pp.11-78. Significantly revised for book publication by the author. A10.a. (3) *Golden Book* 4 (November 1926): 591-609. *YBM* (1920) text. (4) *Samples* (New York: Boni & Liveright, Community Workers of the New York Guild for the Jewish Blind, 1927). *YBM* (1920) text. (5) *AE* 6:1-74. A10.b. (6) *Coming, Aphrodite! and Other Stories* (New York: Avon, 1955). (7) *UV*, pp.143-176. The *Smart Set* text.

1925

C55. UNCLE VALENTINE. (Adagio non troppo). (1) *Woman's Home Companion*, February 1925, pp.7-9, 86, 89-90; March 1925, pp.15-16, 75-76, 79-80. (2) *UV*, pp.3-38. AA10.

1929

C56. DOUBLE BIRTHDAY. (1) *Forum* 81 (February 1929): 78-92, 124-128. (2) In *Best Short Stories of 1929*, ed. E.J.O'Brien (Dodd, Mead, 1929), pp.60-85. (3) In *A Modern Galaxy* (HM Co., 1930), pp.115-155. (4) In *Modern American Short Stories*, ed. E.J.O'Brien (Dodd, Mead, 1932). (5) In *Fifty Best American Short Stories 1915-1965*, ed. M.Foley (HM Co., 1965). (6) *UV*, pp.41-63. AA10. (7) In *From These Hills, from These Valleys*, ed. David P. Demarest (Pittsburgh, Pa.: University of Pittsburgh Press, 1976), pp.143-162.

1930

C57. NEIGHBOUR ROSICKY. (1) *Woman's Home Companion*, April 1930, pp.7-9, 52, 54, 57; May 1930, pp.13-14, 92, 95-96. Title: 'Neighbor Rosicky'. (2) *OD*, pp.3-71. A19.a. (3) *AE*, 12:5-62. A19.b. (4) In *This Is My Best*, ed. W.Burnett (Dial, 1942). (5) In *Americans One and All*, ed. H.Shaw and R.Davis (Harcourt, 1947). (6) In *Great Short Stories*, ed. W.L.Schramm (Harcourt, 1950). (7) In *Adventures in Modern Literature*, ed. R.M.Stauffer, W.H.Cunningham, and C.J.Sullivan (Harcourt, 1951). (8) In *American Poetry and Prose*, ed. Norman Foerster (HM Co., 1952). (9) In *America's Literature*, ed. J.D.Hart and

C. L. Gohdes (Dryden, 1955). (10) *Five Stories*, pp.72-111. AA4. (11) In *More Stories to Remember*, ed. T. B. Costain and J. Beecroft (Doubleday, 1958). (12) In *A Quarto of Modern Literature*, ed. L. Brown (Scribner's, 1964 [5th ed.]). (13) In *Stories from the Quarto*, ed. L. Brown (Scribner's, 1968). (14) In *Call Us Americans*, ed. D. Chernoff (Doubleday, 1968).

1932

C58. TWO FRIENDS. (1) *Woman's Home Companion*, July 1932, pp.7-9, 54, 56. (2) *OD*, pp.193-230. A19.a. (3) In *Woollcott's Second Reader*, ed. A. Woollcott (Viking, 1937). (4) *AE*, 12: 63-158. A19.b. (5) In *Fifty Years*, ed. C. Fadiman (Knopf, 1965).

C59. OLD MRS. HARRIS. (1) *OD*, pp.75-190. A19.a. (2) *Ladies' Home Journal*, September 1932, pp.3, 70, 72, 74, 76-77; October 1932, pp.18, 85-87; November 1932, pp.16, 84-85, 89. Title: 'Three Women'. (3) *AE*, 12: 63-158. A19.b.

1948

C60. THE OLD BEAUTY. (1) *OB*, pp.3-72. A23.a.

C61. BEFORE BREAKFAST. (1) *OB*, pp.142-166. A23.a.

C62. THE BEST YEARS. (1) *OB*, pp.75-138. A23.a. (2) *Five Stories*, pp.112-148. AA4.

CC

Excerpted Fiction in Anthologies

CC1. THE MIRACLE. In *Literary Studies for Rhetoric Classes*, ed. B. L. Jefferson, P. Landis, A. Secord, and J. Ernst (Thomas Nelson, 1928). Excerpt from *DCA*.

CC2. WHITE MULES. In *The Southwest in Literature*, ed. M. Major and R. W. Smith (Macmillan, 1929). Excerpt from *DCA*.

CC3. PAVEL AND PETER. *Golden Book* 17 (May 1933). Excerpt from *MA*.

CC4. ANCIENT PEOPLE. In *Modern American Prose*, ed. C. C. Van Doren (Harcourt, 1934). Excerpt from *SOL*.

CC5. MY MORTAL ENEMY. In *Borzoi Reader*, ed. C. C. Van Doren (Knopf, 1936). Complete text of *MME*.

CC6. MRS. HARLING. In *American Sketchbook*, ed. T. McDowell, W. H. Rogers, J. T. Flanagan, and H. A. Blaine (Macmillan, 1938). Excerpt from *MA*.

CC7. MISSIONARY JOURNEYS. In *The Oxford Anthology of American Literature*, ed. W. R. Benét and N. H. Pearson, vol. 2 (Oxford University Press, 1938; 1947 [7th ptg.]). Excerpt from *DCA*.

CC8. THE STONE LIPS. In *Literature and Life in America*, ed. D. Miles and R. Pooley [Life Reading Service] (Chicago and New York: Scott, Foresman, 1943). Excerpt from *DCA*. *Note:* a revision of

Literature and Life, Book 3 (Philippine Islands: SF Co., 1929, 1936) [not seen].

CC9. MISSIONARY JOURNEYS. In *As You Were*, ed. A. Woollcott (Viking, 1943). Excerpt from *DCA*.

CC10. MY ÁNTONIA. In *A Complete College Reader*, ed. J. Holmes and C. S. Towle, vol.2 (HM Co., 1950). Complete text of *MA*.

CC11. O PIONEERS!; A LOST LADY [brief quotes]. In *Literary America: A Chronicle of American Writers from 1607–1952* . . . , ed. David E. Scherman and Rosemarie Redlich (New York: Dodd, Mead & Co., 1952).

CC12. MY MORTAL ENEMY. In *Bennett Cerf's Take-Along Treasury*, ed. L. Hornblow and B. Cerf (Doubleday, 1963). Complete text of *MME*.

CC13. MY MORTAL ENEMY. In *Fifty Years*, ed. C. Fadiman (Knopf, 1965). Complete text of *MME*.

CC14. THE SHIMERDAS. In *The Outnumbered* [stories, essays, and poems about minority groups], ed. C. Brooks (Dell, Laurel Leaf Library, 1967). Excerpt from *MA*.

CCC

Novels First Published in

Periodicals

CCC1. ALEXANDER'S BRIDGE [title: *Alexander's Masquerade*].
McClure's 38, nos.4, 5, 6 (February, March, April 1912):
384-395, 523-536, 658-668.

CCC2. A LOST LADY. *Century* 105 (April 1923): 803-822; 106 (May,
June 1923): 73-94, 289-309.

CCC3. THE PROFESSOR'S HOUSE. *Collier's*, 6 June, pp.5-7; 13
June, pp.24-32; 20 June, pp.22-23; 27 June, pp.28-35; 4
July, pp.30-35; 11 July, pp.24-25; 18 July, pp.22-23; 25 July,
pp.22-23; 1 August, 1925, pp.22-23.

CCC4. DEATH COMES FOR THE ARCHBISHOP. *Forum* 77, nos.1-6
(January, February, March, April, May, June 1927): 22-29,
130-137, 286-297, 450-461, 612-625, 770-784, 930-942.

CCC5. LUCY GAYHEART. *Woman's Home Companion*, March, pp.7-10;
April, pp.14-17; May, pp.23-26; June, pp.16-18; July 1935,
pp.15-17.

Part Four

D

Articles, Reviews, and Essays in Newspapers and Periodicals

A Preliminary Note to Section D

Completion (in so far as it is complete) of this section would not have been possible without reference to the early research of Bernice Slote—partially reflected in her *The Kingdom of Art* and substantially augmented since—and the work of William M. Curtin. Most of the entries are taken directly from Professor Slote's published work and notes and from Professor Curtin's *The World and the Parish*. Title entries here are adapted from these 2 publications.

Authentication of unsigned material from the beginning to 1903 or 1906 is variable and depends upon the authority of editors Slote, Virginia Faulkner, and Curtin, whose judgment can neither be surpassed nor gainsaid. Some pieces are un-decided, and attribution of authorship is still in flux—for ex-ample, Bernice Slote doubts the authenticity of many articles signed 'Clara Wood Shipman'—and discovery of new material goes on. Many recently located articles are represented here through the generosity of Professor Slote.

In this listing, established pseudonyms are given where present; otherwise, it may be assumed that the articles are either un-signed, with authorship determined from internal evidence, or signed with one of the variations of WC's name: 'Willa Sibert Cather', 'Willa Cather', 'W. S. Cather', or 'W. Cather'.

Historical Note on Willa Cather's journalistic Juvenilia and Contributions to the University of Nebraska Hesperian

In files of the *Red Cloud Chief* for 1888 and 1889, a column called "High School Items" lists WC as editor for 3 numbers. The first (19 October 1888, p.5) has her name—incorrectly spelled 'Wella'—as joint editor. For the second (8 February 1889, p.5), she is sole editor. The third (22 February 1889) spells her name 'Cathers'. Her high school commencement address, 'Superstition vs. Investigation', was printed in the *Chief* (13 June 1890, p.5).

During her years as a student at the University of Nebraska in Lincoln, WC was a major contributor to the *Hesperian*. As editor in 1893, she wrote nearly the entire issue for that year. The selective listing given below makes no claim to completeness (work on authentication of her contributions is still in process), but provides a sampling of pieces known to be from her hand between 1892 and 1894:

d1. A SENTIMENTAL THANKSGIVING DINNER IN FIVE COURSES [play]. (1) *Hesperian*, 24 November 1892, pp.4-7. (2) *WCCY*, pp.100-108.

d2. DAILY DIALOGUES OR, CLOAK ROOM CONVERSATION AS OVERHEARD BY A TIRED LISTENER [play]. (1) *Hesperian*, 15 February 1893, pp.3-5. (2) *WCCY*, pp.93-99.

d3. [Editorial comment on the Lansing curtain]. (1) *Hesperian*, 15 March 1893, pp.3-5. (2) *KA*, pp.173-174.

d4. [Editorial comment on football]. (1) *Hesperian*, 15 November 1893, p.9. (2) *KA*, p.212.

d5. [Sketch of Roscoe Pound in 'Pastels in Prose']. (1) *Hesperian*, 10 March 1894, pp.4-5. (2) *W&P*, p.122.

1891

D1. CONCERNING THOS. CARLYLE. (1) *Hesperian*, 1 March 1891, pp.4-5. (2) *NSJ*, 1 March 1891, p.14. (3) *KA*, pp.421-425.

D2. SHAKESPEARE AND HAMLET [part 1]. (1) *NSJ*, 1 November 1891, p.16. (2) *KA*, pp.426-432.

D3. SHAKESPEARE AND HAMLET [part 2]. (1) *NSJ*, 8 November 1891, p.11. (2) *KA*, pp.432-436.

1893

D4. ONE WAY OF PUTTING IT [*series title;* sketch of a Salvation Army service]. (1) *NSJ*, 5 November 1893, p.13. (2) *W&P*, pp.5-7, 10, 25-26.

D5. ONE WAY OF PUTTING IT [description of a Roman Catholic church; the Lincoln cemetery, Wyuka; sketches of Lincoln street personalities]. (1) *NSJ*, 12 November 1893, p.13. (2) *W&P*, pp.9-10, 14-15, 16, 21-22.

D6. ONE WAY OF PUTTING IT [sketches of Lincoln, Nebraska, and townspeople]. (1) *NSJ*, 19 November 1893, p.9. (2) *W&P*, pp.17-19, 23, 26-27.

D7. AMUSEMENTS [*series title;* review of Walker Whiteside in *Richelieu*]. (1) *NSJ*, 22 November 1893, p.6

D8. AMUSEMENTS [review of Clara Morris in *Camille*]. (1) *NSJ*, 23 November 1893, p.5. (2) *KA*, pp.262-263. (3) *W&P*, pp.43-44.

D9. ONE WAY OF PUTTING IT. (1) *NSJ*, 26 November 1893, p.10. (2) *W&P*, pp.10-11, 13-14, 44-45.

D10. AMUSEMENTS [review of Robert Downing in *Virginius*]. (1) *NSJ*, 30 November 1893, p.6.

D11. ONE WAY OF PUTTING IT [vignettes, Robert Downing]. (1) *NSJ*, 3 December 1893, p.13. (2) *W&P*, pp.11-13, 15-16, 24-25, 26, 27-28.

D12. AMUSEMENTS [review of *Friends* with title '"Friends" is Purely Ideal', signed 'W. C.']. (1) *NSJ*, 14 December 1893, p.6. (2) *KA*, pp.263-264. (3) *W&P*, pp.28-29.

D13. ONE WAY OF PUTTING IT. (1) *NSJ*, 17 December 1893, p.13. (2) *W&P*, pp.7-9, 16-17, 19-20, 20-21, 29.

1894

D14.   AMUSEMENTS [review of Emily Bancker in *Gloriana* with the title 'Even the Servants were Ideal', signed 'W.C.']. (1) *NSJ*, 10 January 1894, p.6. (2) *KA*, pp.264-265.

D15.   AMUSEMENTS [review of Lewis Morrison's *Faust*]. (1) *NSJ*, 18 January 1894, p.5. (2) *W&P*, pp.76-77.

D16.   AMUSEMENTS [review of Hoyt's *A Trip to Chinatown*]. (1) *NSJ*, 20 January 1894, p.3.

D17.   ONE WAY OF PUTTING IT [comments on theatre]. (1) *NSJ*, 21 January 1894, p.16. (2) *KA*, pp.140, 174-175, 205-206, 207, 256-257.

D18.   AMUSEMENTS [review of James O'Neill in *Monte Cristo*]. (1) *NSJ*, 26 January 1894, p.6. (2) *KA*, p.256.

D19.   ONE WAY OF PUTTING IT [Mme. Doenhoff; remuneration to artists]. (1) *NSJ*, 28 January 1894, p.13. (2) *KA*, pp.175-176, 182-183.

D20.   AMUSEMENTS [the Kendals in *The Ironmaster*]. (1) *NSJ*, 7 February 1894, p.3. (2) *W&P*, pp.33-35.

D21.   AMUSEMENTS [review of *The Spider and the Fly*]. (1) *NSJ*, 9 February 1894, p.6. (2) *KA*, pp.252-253.

D22.   THE CRITIC'S PROVINCE [editorial]. (1) *NSJ*, 11 February 1894, p.12. (2) *W&P*, pp.68-69.

D23.   PLAYS AND PLAYERS [*series title*; Lincoln theatregoers, the Kendals, the Gerry Society; signed 'Deus Gallery']. (1) *NSJ*, 11 February 1894, p.13. (2) *W&P*, pp.50-51, 84.

D24.   AMUSEMENTS [review of *Fantasma*]. (1) *NSJ*, 13 February 1894, p.5.

D25.   THE CURTAIN FALLS [Greek and Latin plays at the Lansing Theatre]. (1) *NSJ*, 17 February 1894, p.5. (2) *W&P*, pp.72-74.

D26.   AMUSEMENTS [review of *A Duel of Hearts* with Craigen and Paulding]. (1) *NSJ*, 20 February 1894, p.2. (2) *KA*, pp.265-267.

D27.   AMUSEMENTS [reviews of *The Setting of the Sun* and *The Dowager Countess*, with Craigen and Paulding]. (1) *NSJ*, 21 February 1894, p.3. (2) *KA*, p.267.

D28.   AMUSEMENTS [review of *In Old Kentucky*]. (1) *NSJ*, 22 February 1894, p.5.

D29.   AMUSEMENTS [review of Greek and Latin plays]. (1) *NSJ*, 24 February 1894, p.6. (2) *KA*, p.216.

D30.   WITH PLAYS AND PLAYERS [Greek tragedy, Lillian Lewis, Ostrovsky, Modjeska]. (1) *NSJ*, 25 February 1894, p.9. (2) *KA*, pp.134-135, 220-221. (3) *W&P*, pp.37-38, 61-62, 74-75, 96.

D31.   AMUSEMENTS [review of Julia Marlowe in *The Love Chase*]. (1) *NSJ*, 1 March 1894, p.3. (2) *WCPM Newsletter*, Summer 1976, pp.1-2.

D32.   AMUSEMENTS [review of *The Ensign*]. (1) *NSJ*, 2 March 1894, p.3. (2) *WCPM Newsletter*, Summer 1976, pp.2-3.

D33.   WITH PLAYS AND PLAYERS [Julia Marlowe, Steele Mac-Kaye, Sarah Bernhardt, Olive May; signed 'Deus Gallery']. (1) *NSJ*, 4 March 1894, p.13. (2) *WCCY*, pp.33-34, 35-36. (2) *W&P*, pp.36-37, 39-40, 41-42.

D34.   WITH PLAYS AND PLAYERS [Modjeska, Maggie Mitchell, Warde, James, English taste]. (1) *NSJ*, 11 March 1894, p.13. (2) *WCCY*, pp.36, 37. (3) *KA*, pp.199, 221-222, 223, 224. (4) *W&P*, pp.38, 51, 62-63.

D35.   AMUSEMENTS [review of *Romeo and Juliet* with Craigen and Paulding]. (1) *NSJ*, 13 March 1894, p.2. (2) *W&P*, pp.84-86.

D36.   AMUSEMENTS [review of *A Duel of Hearts* with Craigen and Paulding]. (1) *NSJ*, 14 March 1894, p.2.

D37.   AMUSEMENTS [review of *The White Squadron*]. (1) *NSJ*, 16 March 1894, p.3. (2) *KA*, p.253.

D38.   AMUSEMENTS [review of *The Idea*]. (1) *NSJ*, 17 March 1894, p.3.

D39.   AMUSEMENTS [review of *The Voodoo*]. (1) *NSJ*, 22 March 1894, p.6. (2) *KA*, pp.251-252.

D40.   AMUSEMENTS [review of Lewis Morrison in *Richelieu*]. (1) *NSJ*, 23 March 1894, p.3.

D41.   BETWEEN THE ACTS [*series title;* on criticism, Clara Morris, Lewis Morrison]. (1) *NSJ*, 25 March 1894, p.13. (2) *KA*, pp.186-187. (3) *W&P*, pp.46-49, 77.

D42.   AMUSEMENTS [review of Herrmann the Magician]. (1) *NSJ*, 30 March 1894, p.8. (2) *WCPM Newsletter*, Summer 1976, p.3.

D43.   BETWEEN THE ACTS [Lincoln theatres, Marie Tempest]. (1) *NSJ*, 1 April 1894, p.13. Authenticity conjectured by Slote and Curtin.

D44.   AMUSEMENTS [review of *The Black Crook*]. (1) *NSJ*, 3 April 1894, p.5.

D45.   AMUSEMENTS [review of Marie Tempest in *The Fencing Master*]. (1) *NSJ*, 4 April 1894, p.5. (2) *W&P*, pp.169-170.

D46.   AMUSEMENTS [review of William Crane in *Brother John*]. (1) *NSJ*, 5 April 1894, p.6. (2) *W&P*, pp.78-79.

D47.   AMUSEMENTS [review of *Police Patrol*]. (1) *NSJ*, 6 April 1894, p.6.

D48.   AMUSEMENTS [Della Fox and DeWolf Hopper in *Panjandrum*]. (1) *NSJ*, 7 April 1894, p.2. (2) *W&P*, pp.170-171.

D49.   BETWEEN THE ACTS [Cora Tanner, Mounet-Sully, Marie Tempest]. (1) *NSJ*, 8 April 1894, p.13. (2) *WCCY*, pp.37-38. (3) *KA*, pp.127-128, 215-216. (4) *W&P*, pp.51, 80-82.

D50.   BETWEEN THE ACTS [Mrs. Kendal, Gilbert and Sullivan, Rider Haggard's *She*]. (1) *NSJ*, 15 April 1894, p.13. (2) *WCCY*, pp.38-40.

D51.   AMUSEMENTS [review of a minstrel show]. (1) *NSJ*, 18 April 1894, p.3.

D52.   AMUSEMENTS [review of *She*]. (1) *NSJ*, 20 April 1894, p.6. (2) *KA*, pp.267-268.

D53.   BETWEEN THE ACTS [on dramatizing novels; Sousa, Richard Mansfield]. (1) *NSJ*, 22 April 1894, p.13. (2) *KA*, pp.209, 253.

D54.   AMUSEMENTS [review of Mansfield in *Beau Brummell*]. (1) *NSJ*, 24 April 1894, p.5. (2) *KA*, pp.122-123.

D55.   AMUSEMENTS [review of *The District Fair*]. (1) *NSJ*, 26 April 1894, p.5.

D56.   AMUSEMENTS [vaudeville]. (1) *NSJ*, 27 April 1894, p.6.

D57.   BETWEEN THE ACTS [Richard Mansfield, Shakespeare's birthday]. (1) *NSJ*, 29 April 1894, p.13. (2) *Prairie Schooner* 38 (1964): 67-68. Title: 'Willa Cather on Shakespeare'. (3) *KA*, p.123. (4) *W&P*, pp.54-56, 83-84.

D58.   AMUSEMENTS [review of Salvini in *The Three Guardsmen*]. (1) *NSJ*, 4 May 1894, p.6. (2) *KA*, pp.121-122, 247.

D59.   AMUSEMENTS [review of Sousa band concert]. (1) *NSJ*, 5 May 1894, p.2. (2) *KA*, pp.199-201.

D60.   AMUSEMENTS [review of recital by Fred Emerson Brooks]. (1) *NSJ*, 5 May 1894, p.2.

D61.   AMUSEMENTS [review of Blind Tom, Negro pianist]. (1) *NSJ*, 18 May 1894, p.6. (2) *Prairie Schooner* 38 (1964): 343-344. Title: 'Willa Cather: A Portfolio'. (3) *W&P*, pp.166-167.

D62. UNDER THE WHITE TENTS [feature story on circus].
(1) *NSJ*, 27 May 1894, p.13. (2) *W&P*, pp.100-102.

D63. THE COMPETITIVE DRILL [feature story]. (1) *NSJ*, 28 May 1894, p.13.

D64. AMUSEMENTS [review of *Lady Windermere's Fan*, signed 'W.C.']. (1) *NSJ*, 5 June 1894, p.1. (2) *KA*, pp.388-389. (3) *W&P*, pp.90-92.

D65. AMUSEMENTS [review of *The Chimes of Normandy*, signed 'W.C.']. (1) *NSJ*, 7 June 1894, p.2. (2) *WCPM Newsletter*, Summer 1976, pp.3-4.

D66. THE FOURTH AT CRETE. (1) *Lincoln Evening News*, 5 July 1894, p.8. (2) *Prairie Schooner* 43 (1969): 119, 121, 123. Title: 'Willa Cather Reports Chautauqua 1894' (selections). (3) *WCPM Newsletter*, Summer 1975, pp.1-2.

D67. AT THE CHAUTAUQUA. (1) *Lincoln Evening News*, 6 July 1894, p.1. (2) *Prairie Schooner* 43 (1969): 120, 122. Title as in D66(2). (3) *WCPM Newsletter*, Summer 1975, p.2.

D68. NOTABLE CONCERT. (1) *Lincoln Evening News*, 7 July 1894, p.5. (2) *Prairie Schooner* 43 (1969): 119, 123-124. Title as in D66(2).

D69. SUNDAY AT CRETE. (1) *Lincoln Evening News*, 9 July 1894, p.5. (2) *Prairie Schooner* 43 (1969): 120-121, 122. Title as in D66(2). (3) *WCPM Newsletter*, Summer 1975, pp.2-3.

D70. LIFE AT CRETE. (1) *Lincoln Evening News*, 10 July 1894, p.5. (2) *Prairie Schooner* 43 (1969): 120, 124-125. Title as in D66(2).

D71. IN DUNNING HALL. (1) *Lincoln Evening News*, 11 July 1894, p.5. (2) *Prairie Schooner* 43 (1969): 126. Title as in D66(2).

D72. CRETE CHAUTAUQUA. (1) *Lincoln Evening News*, 12 July 1894, p.4. (2) *Prairie Schooner* 43 (1969): 125. Title as in D66(2).

D73. MRS. FISK'S CONCERT. (1) *Lincoln Evening News*, 13 July 1894, p.5.

D74. EMPTY COTTAGES. (1) *Lincoln Evening News*, 14 July 1894, p.1. (2) *Prairie Schooner* 43 (1969): 126-127. Title as in D66(2).

D75. AN OLD RIVER METROPOLIS [feature story on Brownville, Nebraska]. (1) *NSJ*, 12 August 1894, p.13. (2) *American Heritage*, October 1970, pp.68-72. Omits last 2 paragraphs. Title: 'Ghost Town on the River'. (3) *W&P*, pp.103-112.

D76. AMUSEMENTS [review of Cora Potter and Kyrle Bellew in *In Society*]. (1) *NSJ*, 29 August 1894, p.6. Slote questions authenticity in *KA*.

D77. AMUSEMENTS [review of Roland Reed in *The Woman Hater*]. (1) *NSJ*, 13 September 1894, p.5.

D78. AMUSEMENTS [review of Royal Entertainers in vaudeville]. (1) *NSJ*, 14 September 1894, p.6.

D79. AMUSEMENTS [review of *Underground*]. (1) *NSJ*, 16 September 1894, p.3.

D80. UTTERLY IRRELEVANT [*series title;* art exhibits at the State Fair, du Maurier's *Trilby*]. (1) *NSJ*, 16 September 1894, p.13. (2) *KA*, pp.183, 362.

D81. UTTERLY IRRELEVANT [use of libraries, Annie Kenwick, Marion Manola, Sarah Grand's *The Heavenly Twins*, the duty of an author]. (1) *NSJ*, 23 September 1894, p.13. (2) *KA*, pp.180-181, 406-407.

D82. AMUSEMENTS [review of *The Devil's Auction*]. (1) *NSJ*, 28 September 1894, p.3.

D83. AMUSEMENTS [review of *Uncle Tom's Cabin*]. (1) *NSJ*, 30 September 1894, p.2. (2) *KA*, pp.269-270. (3) *Horizon* 9 (Spring 1967): 118. Title: 'Willa Cather, "The Meatax Girl"'.

D84.   UTTERLY IRRELEVANT [music and theatre]. (1) *NSJ*, 30
September 1894, p.13. (2) *KA*, pp.216-217.

D85.   AMUSEMENTS [review of Robert Downing in *The Gladiator*].
(1) *NSJ*, 2 October 1894, p.3. (2) *KA*, pp.270-272.

D86.   AMUSEMENTS [review of *The Derby Winner*]. (1) *NSJ*, 5
October 1894, p.6.

D87.   UTTERLY IRRELEVANT [William McKinley, Robert
Downing, church music, theatre notes]. (1) *NSJ*, 7 October
1894, p.13. (2) *KA*, pp.177-178. (3) *W&P*, pp.117-118.

D88.   AMUSEMENTS [review of *Gloriana*]. (1) *NSJ*, 9 October
1894, p.2.

D89.   AMUSEMENTS [review of *Charley's Aunt*]. (1) *NSJ*, 12 October
1894, p.5.

D90.   AMUSEMENTS [review of *Rush City*]. (1) *NSJ*, 14 October
1894, p.6.

D91.   UTTERLY IRRELEVANT [Duse, Bernhardt, town and gown,
Oliver Wendell Holmes, war in China, practical education].
(1) *NSJ*, 14 October 1894, p.13. (2) *KA*, pp.117-118.
(3) *W&P*, pp.112-115, 129-130.

D92.   UNDER THE GOLD LEAVES OF AUTUMN [account of the
Woods wedding]. (1) *NSJ*, 20 October 1894, p.6.

D93.   UTTERLY IRRELEVANT [Lincoln concert season, Queen
Victoria, the artist's role, standards of criticism]. (1) *NSJ*,
21 October 1894, p.13. (2) *KA*, pp.141-142, 176-177, 253,
257-258. (3) *W&P*, pp.52, 70-71.

D94.   AMUSEMENTS [review of *The Hustler*]. (1) *NSJ*, 25 October
1894, p.2.

D95.   UTTERLY IRRELEVANT [*Trilby*, theatre audiences, Sordello
Clubs, interview with an actor in the penitentiary]. (1) *NSJ*, 28

October 1894, p.13. (2) *KA*, pp.142-143, 179-180, 184-185. (3) *W&P*, pp.115-116, 131-132.

D96. AMUSEMENTS [review of *A Wife's Honor*]. (1) *NSJ*, 30 October 1894, p.2.

D97. AMUSEMENTS [review of *Married for Money*]. (1) *NSJ*, 31 October 1894, p.6.

D98. MUSIC AND DRAMA [*series title;* review of Hoyt's *A Trip to Chinatown*]. (1) *NSJ*, 1 November 1894, p.2. (2) *KA*, pp.241-242.

D99. MORE OR LESS PERSONAL [Hoyt, *The Green Carnation*, Bacon and Shakespeare, Duse]. (1) *NSJ*, 4 November 1894, p.12. (2) *Prairie Schooner* 38 (1964): 68-71. Title: 'Willa Cather on Shakespeare'. (3) *KA*, pp.135-136, 152-153, 242. (4) *W&P*, pp.56-57, 86-89.

D100. AMUSEMENTS [review of Royle's *Friends*]. (1) *NSJ*, 6 November 1894, p.8. (2) *KA*, pp.272-273.

D101. AMUSEMENTS [review of *Hot Tamales*]. (1) *NSJ*, 7 November 1894, p.5.

D102. AMUSEMENTS [review of *Oh, What a Night*]. (1) *NSJ*, 9 November 1894, p.6.

D103. AMUSEMENTS [review of *H.M.S. Pinafore*]. (1) *NSJ*, 10 November 1894, p.6.

D104. AS YOU LIKE IT [*series title;* Olga Nethersole, private libraries, Bliss Carman, Pauline Hall, the French]. (1) *NSJ*, 11 November 1894, p.13. (2) *KA*, pp.137, 181, 224. (3) *W&P*, pp.58-59, 116, 119-120, 134-135.

D105. MUSIC AND DRAMA [review of *Jane* and *The Great Mogul;* Gustave Frohman's Company No.13]. (1) *NSJ*, 14 November 1894, p.2.

D106.   AS YOU LIKE IT [on criticism, Mrs. Kendal, Lillie Langtry, Bernhardt]. (1) *NSJ*, 18 November 1894, p.13. (2) *KA*, pp.172, 258-259. (3) *W&P*, pp.40-41, 63-65, 93-95.

D107.   AMUSEMENTS [review of Pauline Hall in *Dorcas*]. (1) *NSJ*, 21 November 1894, p.2.

D108.   AMUSEMENTS [review of the Wilber Entertainment Company]. (1) *NSJ*, 22 November 1894, p.6.

D109.   AS YOU LIKE IT [Pauline Hall, operetta stars, death of Anton Rubinstein]. (1) *NSJ*, 25 November 1894, p.13. (2) *KA*, pp.134, 228-229. (3) *W&P*, pp.65-66, 121, 167-169, 172-174.

D110.   AS YOU LIKE IT [football, stage marriages, Robert B. Mantell, Maurice Barrymore]. (1) *NSJ*, 2 December 1894, p.13. (2) *KA*, pp.151-152, 212-213.

D111.   AMUSEMENTS [review of Nat Goodwin in *A Gilded Fool*]. (1) *NSJ*, 4 December 1894, p.8. (2) *KA*, pp.128-129.

D112.   MUSIC AND DRAMA [review of *A Summer Blizzard*]. (1) *NSJ*, 5 December 1894, p.3. (2) *KA*, p.252.

D113.   AMUSEMENTS [review of *Killarney*]. (1) *NSJ*, 8 December 1894, p.2.

D114.   AMUSEMENTS [review of the Tavary Grand Opera Company]. (1) *NSJ*, 9 December 1894, p.4. (2) *KA*, pp.131-132.

D115.   AS YOU LIKE IT [Nat Goodwin, William Crane in *Brother John*, Lillian Russell, living pictures]. (1) *NSJ*, 9 December 1894, p.13. (2) *KA*, pp.129-130, 229. (3) *W&P*, pp.59-60, 79-80, 121.

D116.   AMUSEMENTS [review of Helena von Doenhoff in *Il trovatore*]. (1) *NSJ*, 10 December 1894, p.8. (2) *KA*, p.132.

D117.   AMUSEMENTS [review of Thomas Q. Seabrooke in *Isle of Champagne*]. (1) *NSJ*, 14 December 1894, p.6.

D118.   AMUSEMENTS [review of *O'Neil, Washington, D.C.*]. (1) *NSJ*, 15 December 1894, p.2. (2) *KA*, pp.250-251.

D119.   AS YOU LIKE IT [Shakespearean comedy, stage realism, the artist's social role, von Doenhoff]. (1) *NSJ*, 16 December 1894, p.13. (2) *KA*, p.132. (3) *W&P*, pp.52-54, 96-97, 122-123.

D120.   AMUSEMENTS [review of *Lady Windermere's Fan*]. (1) *NSJ*, 18 December 1894, p.2. (2) *W&P*, p.92.

D121.   AMUSEMENTS [review of *In Old Kentucky*]. (1) *NSJ*, 20 December 1894, p.3.

D122.   AS YOU LIKE IT [Stevenson, Kipling, *Trilby*]. (1) *NSJ*, 23 December 1894, p.13. (2) *KA*, pp.311-313, 316-318, 363-365.(3) *W&P*, pp.132-134, 135-139.

D123.   AS YOU LIKE IT [Zola and Bernhardt]. (1) *NSJ*, 30 December 1894, p.13. (2) *KA*, pp.116-117. (3) *W&P*, pp.139-142.

1895

D124.   AMUSEMENTS [review of Sol Smith Russell in *The Heir at Law*]. (1) *NSJ*, 4 January 1895, p.6.

D125.   AMUSEMENTS [review of Belasco's *The Charity Ball*]. (1) *NSJ*, 6 January 1895, p.6. (2) *KA*, p.237. (3) *W&P*, p.220.

D126.   AS YOU LIKE IT [Haydon Art Club, Belasco, criticism]. (1) *NSJ*, 6 January 1895, p.13. (2) *KA*, pp.217-219. (3) *W&P*, pp.124-127, 233-234.

D127.   AMUSEMENTS [Review of *Thro' the War*]. (1) *NSJ*, 8 January 1895, p.2.

D128.   AMUSEMENTS [review of *A Jolly Good Fellow*]. (1) *NSJ*, 11 January 1895, p.8. (2) *KA*, p.252.

D129.   AMUSEMENTS [review of *Yon Yonson*]. (1) *NSJ*, 12 January 1895, p.6. (2) *KA*, p.273.

D130.   AS YOU LIKE IT [Sappho, Elizabeth Barrett Browning,
Christina Rossetti]. (1) *NSJ*, 13 January 1895, p.13. (2) *KA*,
pp.346-349. (3) *W&P*, pp.143-147.

D131.   AMUSEMENTS [review of Warde and James in *Henry IV*].
(1) *NSJ*, 18 January 1895, p.8. (2) *KA*, pp.288-290.

D132.   AS YOU LIKE IT [Shakespeare's histories, Julia Marlowe].
(1) *NSJ*, 20 January 1895, p.13. (2) *Prairie Schooner* 38 (1964):
71-73. Title: 'Willa Cather on Shakespeare' (selection). (3) *KA*,
pp.290-291. (4) *W&P*, pp.230-231.

D133.   AMUSEMENTS [review of Belasco's *Men and Women*]. (1) *NSJ*,
22 January 1895, p.8. (2) *KA*, pp.237-238.

D134.   AMUSEMENTS [review of elocutionist and violin recital].
(1) *NSJ*, 23 January 1895, p.6.

D135.   AMUSEMENTS [review of J. K. Emmett in *Fritz in a
Madhouse*]. (1) *NSJ*, 26 January 1895, p.6. (2) *KA*,
pp.139-140.

D136.   AMUSEMENTS [review of Belasco's *The Girl I Left behind Me*].
(1) *NSJ*, 27 January 1895, p.6.

D137.   AS YOU LIKE IT [Belasco, Bernice Wheeler, von Doenhoff,
Dumas fils, Nat Goodwin]. (1) *NSJ*, 27 January 1895, p.13.
(2) *KA*, pp.238-240, 247-248. (3) *W&P*, pp.175-176,
220-223.

D138.   AMUSEMENTS [review of *Hendrick Hudson*]. (1) *NSJ*,
1 February 1895, p.5.

D139.   AMUSEMENTS [review of *Charley's Aunt*]. (1) *NSJ*, 2 February
1895, p.6.

D140.   AS YOU LIKE IT [interview with Gustave Frohman]. (1) *NSJ*,
3 February 1895, p.13. (2) *W&P*, pp.224-228.

D141.   AMUSEMENTS [review of Hoyt's *A Temperance Town*]. (1) *NSJ*,
7 February 1895, p.6.

D142.   AS YOU LIKE IT [Mendelssohn concert, Charles Hoyt, Russian ballerina Ksheninka]. (1) *NSJ*, 10 February 1895, p.13. (2) *KA*, pp.242-243. (3) *W&P*, pp.177-178, 234.

D143.   AMUSEMENTS [review of *The Passport*]. (1) *NSJ*, 14 February 1895, p.2.

D144.   AS YOU LIKE IT [François Coppée]. (1) *NSJ*, 17 February 1895, p.9. (2) *KA*, pp.326-327. (3) *W&P*, pp.147-149.

D145.   AMUSEMENTS [review of Eddie Foy in *Off the Earth*]. (1) *NSJ*, 22 February 1895, p.8.

D146.   AS YOU LIKE IT [Browning, Max O'Rell lecture, Katherine Kidder as Madame San Gêne]. (1) *NSJ*, 24 February 1895, p.13. (2) *KA*, pp.137-138, 150-151. (3) *W&P*, pp.188-190, 204-205.

D147.   AMUSEMENTS [review of Steele MacKaye's *The New 'Paul Kauvar'*]. (1) *NSJ*, 26 February 1895, p.6.

D148.   AMUSEMENTS [review of Clay Clement in *The New Dominion*]. (1) *NSJ*, 2 March 1895, p.6. (2) *KA*, pp.124-125.

D149.   AMUSEMENTS [review of Marie Tempest in *The Fencing Master*]. (1) *NSJ*, 3 March 1895, p.8. (2) *KA*, p.137.

D150.   AS YOU LIKE IT [Dorothy Morton, Clay Clement]. (1) *NSJ*, 3 March 1895, p.13. (2) *KA*, p.124.

D151.   AS YOU LIKE IT [Clay Clement, Modjeska, *Hamlet*, Mrs. James Potter]. (1) *NSJ*, 10 March 1895, p.13. (2) *KA*, pp.144-145. (3) *W&P*, pp.190-193, 194-195, 231-232.

D152.   AS YOU LIKE IT [*Falstaff*, Emma Eames in *Otello*]. (1) *NSJ*, 31 March 1895, p.13. (2) *KA*, pp.214-215. (3) *W&P*, pp.178-182.

D153.   AMUSEMENTS [review of Griffith's *Faust*]. (1) *NSJ*, 2 April 1895, p.8.

D154. AS YOU LIKE IT [dramatization of *Trilby*, actors' private lives]. (1) *NSJ*, 7 April 1895, p.13. (2) *KA*, p.133. (3) *W&P*, pp.193-194, 240-241.

D155. AS YOU LIKE IT [*Nebraska* (play), Beerbohm Tree, Hamlin Garland]. (1) *NSJ*, 14 April 1895, p.13. (2) *KA*, pp.223-224. (3) *W&P*, p.198.

D156. AMUSEMENTS [review of Bronson Howard's *Shenandoah*]. (1) *NSJ*, 17 April 1895, p.5. (2) *KA*, pp.253-254. (3) *W&P*, pp.228-229.

D157. AMUSEMENTS [review of *The Black Crook*]. (1) *NSJ*, 18 April 1895, p.3. (2) *KA*, pp.274-275.

D158. AS YOU LIKE IT [Shakespeare, Sardou, Madame Réjane]. (1) *NSJ*, 21 April 1895, p.13. (2) *Prairie Schooner* 38 (1964): 73-74. Title: 'Willa Cather on Shakespeare' (selections). (3) *KA*, pp.286-288. (4) *Horizon* 9 (Spring 1967): 117-118. 'Willa Cather, "The Meatax Girl"'. (5) *W&P*, pp.199-200, 232-233, 234-235.

D159. AMUSEMENTS [review of the Spooners in *Inez*]. (1) *NSJ*, 23 April 1895, p.5. (2) *KA*, pp.275-277.

D160. AMUSEMENTS [review of Effie Ellsler in *Doris*]. (1) *NSJ*, 25 April 1895, p.8. (2) *KA*, p.139.

D161. AMUSEMENTS [review of the Spooners in *The Buckeye*]. (1) *NSJ*, 26 April 1895, p.8.

D162. AS YOU LIKE IT [Marie Wainwright in *The Daughters of Eve*, John L. Sullivan, Lillian Russell]. (1) *NSJ*, 28 April 1895, p.14. (2) *KA*, pp.230-231.

D163. AS YOU LIKE IT [Bernhardt, Salvini, Max O'Rell, Mark Twain]. (1) *NSJ*, 5 May 1895, p.14. (2) *W&P*, pp.150-151.

D164. AS YOU LIKE IT [Clara Morris and others, Julia Magruder's *Princess Sonia*]. (1) *NSJ*, 12 May 1895, p.12. (2) *W&P*, pp.152-153, 196, 216-217.

D165. AMUSEMENTS [review of Emily Bancker in *Our Flat*]. (1) *NSJ*, 14 May 1895, p.6.

D166. AS YOU LIKE IT [Lillian Russell, Ada Rehan, Nethersole, *Lady Windermere's Fan*]. (1) *NSJ*, 19 May 1895, p.12. (2) *KA*, pp.208, 389-390. (3) *W&P*, pp.153-154.

D167. AS YOU LIKE IT [Marie Tempest, Chicago *Chap-Book*, Hobart Chatfield-Taylor]. (1) *NSJ*, 26 May 1895, p.12. (2) *KA*, pp.224-225. (3) *W&P*, pp.155-157.

D168. AS YOU LIKE IT [Trilby fad, Warde and James, *Henry IV*, Sardou]. (1) *NSJ*, 2 June 1895, p.9. (2) *W&P*, pp.118, 205.

D169. AMUSEMENTS [review of Oriole Opera Company]. (1) *NSJ*, 7 June 1895, p.6.

D170. AS YOU LIKE IT [*Princess Sonia*, Melba]. (1) *NSJ*, 9 June 1895, p.12. (2) *KA*, p.132.

D171. AS YOU LIKE IT [Marie Burroughs, Duse, French taste]. (1) *NSJ*, 16 June 1895, p.12. (2) *KA*, pp.118-119, 153-154, 260-261. (3) *W&P*, pp.195, 207-209, 235.

D172. AS YOU LIKE IT [Henry Irving, Beerbohm Tree, Rubinstein, Max O'Rell, French and American women]. (1) *NSJ*, 30 June 1895, p.12. (2) *KA*, pp.160-161, 189-191.

D173. AS YOU LIKE IT [William Winter as critic, Lillian Russell, Otis Skinner, Katherine Fisk]. (1) *NSJ*, 7 July 1895, p.9. (2) *W&P*, p.198.

D174. AS YOU LIKE IT [*When Dreams Come True* (Edgar Saltus), William Dean Howells, Bernhardt's book] (1) *NSJ*, 14 July 1895, p.9. (2) *W&P*, 198-199, 259-260, 260-261.

D175. THE PASSING SHOW [*series title*; Dumas fils, Bernhardt, Zola, Mary Anderson, Augustin Daly, Clara Morris]. (1) *NSJ*, 21 July 1895, p.9. (2) *KA*, pp.155, 181. (3) *W&P*, pp.196-197, 200-202, 224.

D176. THE PASSING SHOW [Henry Guy Carleton, Belasco, Olive May interview, Howells, Henry James, Browning]. (1) *NSJ*, 4 August 1895, p.9. (2) *KA*, pp.243-246. (3) *W&P*, pp.203-204, 237-239.

D177. THE PASSING SHOW [death of Madame Carvalho, Melba, America and Rome, Marlowe in *Henry IV*, Stanley Weyman]. (1) *NSJ*, 11 August 1895, p.9. (2) *KA*, pp.161-162, 195, 216, 323. (3) *W&P*, pp.182-185, 205-206.

D178. THE PASSING SHOW [Patti, de Reszke, Calvé, Mansfield, Shaw, *Hamlet*, DeWolf Hopper, *Trilby*, opening of the Creighton Theatre in Omaha]. (1) *Courier*, 24 August 1895, pp.6-8. (2) *KA*, pp.254-255.

D179. THE PASSING SHOW [Felix Morris, Eddie Foy, Rubinstein's son, Royle's *Mexico*, the Bowery]. (1) *Courier*, 31 August 1895, p.6-8. (2) *KA*, pp.195-197. (3) *W&P*, pp.235-236.

D180. AMUSEMENTS [review of exhibition of hypnotism]. (1) *NSJ*, 3 September 1895, p.6.

D181. AMUSEMENTS [review of Roland Reed in *The Politician*]. (1) *NSJ*, 5 September 1895, p.2.

D182. THE PASSING SHOW [Julia Arthur, dramatizing *Romola*, Ella Wheeler Wilcox, Calvé, Mascagni]. (1) *Courier*, 7 September 1895, pp.6-7. (2) *KA*, pp.162-163, 201, 209-210. (3) *W&P*, pp.210-211, 241.

D183. THE THEATRES [*series title*; review of Roland Reed in *The Politician*, the Flints' hypnotism act]. (1) *Courier*, 7 September 1895, p.8. (2) *KA*, pp.277-278.

D184. AMUSEMENTS [review of the Spooners in *The Buckeye*]. (1) *NSJ*, 10 September 1895, p.8.

D185. AMUSEMENTS [review of Griffith's *Faust*]. (1) *NSJ*, 11 September 1895, p.8. (2) *KA*, pp.279-280.

D186. THE PASSING SHOW [George Sand's *Consuelo*, Kipling, Anthony Hope Hawkins, the Dovey sisters]. (1) *Courier*, 14 September 1895, pp.6-7. (2) *KA*, pp.146-147, 210, 318-321.

D187. THE THEATRES [review of Griffith's *Faust*, the Spooners]. (1) *Courier* 14 September 1895, p.8. (2) *KA*, pp.280-281.

D188. THE PASSING SHOW [Hall Caine, Duse, Sir Henry Irving, Marion Crawford]. (1) *Courier*, 21 September 1895, pp.6-7. (2) *KA*, pp.119, 329. (3) *W&P*, pp.209-210, 211-212, 261-262.

D189. AMUSEMENTS [review of *The Hustler*]. (1) *NSJ*, 24 September 1895, p.8.

D190. AMUSEMENTS [review of Belasco's *The Wife*]. (1) *NSJ*, 25 September 1895, p.3.

D191. AMUSEMENTS [review of *Rush City*]. (1) *NSJ*, 27 September 1895, p.8.

D192. THE PASSING SHOW [Oscar Wilde, Judith Gautier, Zélie de Lussan, Clara Morris]. (1) *Courier*, 28 September 1895, pp.6-7. (2) *KA*, pp.133, 138-139, 390-393. (3) *W&P*, pp.263-266.

D193. THE THEATRES [review of Belasco's *The Wife*]. (1) *Courier*, 28 September 1895, p.8. (2) *KA*, pp.281-282.

D194. MAN AND WOMAN | A SYMPOSIUM [1 part only signed by WC]. (1) *Courier*, 28 September 1895, p.10. (2) *W&P*, p.127.

D195. AMUSEMENTS [review of William Gillette in *Too Much Johnson*]. (1) *NSJ*, 2 October 1895, p.3.

D196. THE PASSING SHOW [Nell Gwyn, Maude Adams, Richard Harding Davis, Howells, *Harper's*, Paganini]. (1) *Courier*, 5 October 1895, pp.6-7. (2) *KA*, pp.164-165, 358-359. (3) *W&P*, pp.266-267.

D197. THE THEATRES [review of William Gillette in *Too Much Johnson*]. (1) *Courier*, 5 October 1895, p.8.

D198. AMUSEMENTS [review of Hoyt's *A Contented Woman*]. (1) *NSJ*, 10 October 1895, p.5. (2) *KA*, p.243.

D199. THE PASSING SHOW [Edgar Allan Poe]. (1) *Courier*, 12 October 1895, pp.6-7. (2) *KA*, pp.380-387. (3) *W&P*, pp.157-163.

D200. AMUSEMENTS [review of *Human Hearts*]. (1) *NSJ*, 15 October 1895, p.6.

D201. AMUSEMENTS [review of the Dovey sisters]. (1) *NSJ*, 17 October 1895, p.2. (2) *KA*, p.148.

D202. THE PASSING SHOW [Richard Harding Davis, Anne Reeve Aldrich, Amélie Rives Chandler, Margaret Mather, Cora Potter]. (1) *Courier*, 19 October 1895, pp.6-7. (2) *W&P*, pp.213-214.

D203. AMUSEMENTS [review of Lillian Lewis in *Cleopatra*]. (1) *NSJ*, 23 October 1895, p.6. (2) *KA*, pp.292-293. (3) *Horizon* 9 (Spring 1967): 116-117. Title: 'Willa Cather, "The Meatax Girl"'.

D204. AMUSEMENTS [DeWolf Hopper in *Wang*]. (1) *NSJ*, 25 October 1895, p.6. (2) *KA*, p.140.

D205. THE PASSING SHOW [Lillian Lewis as Cleopatra, Josef Hofmann]. (1) *Courier*, 26 October 1895, pp.6-7. (2) *KA*, pp.148-149, 293-297. (3) *Horizon* 9 (Spring 1967): 117. Title: 'Willa Cather, "The Meatax Girl"'. (4) *W&P*, pp.185-186, 242-246.

D206. AMUSEMENTS [review of *The Globe Trotter*]. (1) *NSJ*, 30 October 1895, p.6.

D207. AMUSEMENTS [review of *The Black Crook*]. (1) *NSJ*, 31 October 1895, p.2. (2) *KA*, p.275.

D208. THE PASSING SHOW [DeWolf Hopper, Romance, Stevenson's letters, Nat Goodwin]. (1) *Courier*, 2 November 1895, pp.6-7. (2) *KA*, pp.130-131, 231-233, 313-314. (3) *W&P*, pp.214-216, 268-270, 271.

D209. THE THEATRES [reviews of Mrs. Dion Boucicault in *The Globe Trotter; The Black Crook*]. (1) *Courier*, 2 November 1895, p.8.

D210. AMUSEMENTS [review of *The Colonel's Wives*]. (1) *NSJ*, 7 November 1895, p.3.

D211. THE PASSING SHOW [Hope's Zenda stories, Pierre Loti's *The Romance of a Spahi*, Dumas's *La route de Thèbes*, Death of Eugene Field, *The Colonel's Wives*]. (1) *Courier*, 9 November 1895, pp.6-7. (2) *KA*, pp.215, 321, 322, 365-367. (3) *W&P*, p.272.

D212. THE PASSING SHOW [overproductive writers, James]. (1) *Courier*, 16 November 1895, pp.6-7. (2) *KA*, pp.222-223, 360-361. (3) *W&P*, pp.273-275.

D213. AMUSEMENTS [review of Walker Whiteside in *Hamlet*]. (1) *NSJ*, 21 November 1895, p.6. (2) *KA*, pp.304-305. (3) *W&P*, pp.247-248.

D214. THE PASSING SHOW [Ouida and women novelists, Whiteside's *Hamlet*]. (1) *Courier*, 23 November 1895, pp.7-8. (2) *KA*, pp.305-308, 408-409. (3) *W&P*, pp.248-251, 275-277.

D215. AMUSEMENTS [review of Robert Downing in Sardou's *Helena*]. (1) *NSJ*, 24 November 1895, p.3.

D216. AMUSEMENTS [Emily Bancker in *Our Flat*]. (1) *NSJ*, 26 November 1895, p.6.

D217. THE PASSING SHOW [Swinburne, Scottish writers, Ian Maclaren, Samuel Crockett, James M. Barrie]. (1) *Courier*, 30 November 1895, pp.6-7. (2) *KA*, pp.338-341, 349-350. (3) *W&P*, pp.277-279.

D218. AMUSEMENTS [Effie Ellsler in *As You Like It*]. (1) *NSJ*,
6 December 1895, p.6. (2) *KA*, p.298. (3) *Horizon* 9 (Spring
1967): 118-119. Title: 'Willa Cather, "The Meatax Girl"'.

D219. AMUSEMENTS [*Newest Devil's Auction*]. (1) *NSJ*, 13 December
1895, p.3.

D220. AMUSEMENTS [Louis James in *Othello*]. (1) *NSJ*,
14 December 1895, p.6. (2) *KA*, pp.299-300. (3) *W&P*,
pp.252-253.

D221. THE PASSING SHOW [Dumas fils, Paderewski, Heine,
Cavalleria Rusticana Intermezzo]. (1) *NSJ*, 15 December 1895,
p.9. (2) *KA*, pp.183-184, 204, 248-249.

D222. THE PASSING SHOW [Louis James as Othello, Mansfield, a
charity concert]. (1) *NSJ*, 22 December 1895, p.9. (2) *KA*,
pp.202, 300-302. (3) *W&P*, pp.253-254.

1896
D223. THE PASSING SHOW [Stevenson's letters, Victor Maurel,
Calvé, Clay Clement]. (1) *NSJ*, 5 January 1896, p.9. (2) *KA*,
pp.214, 314-316.

D224. THE PASSING SHOW [Hall Caine's *The Bondman*, Campanini,
divorce of Sadie Martinot, *Ladies' Home Journal*]. (1) *NSJ*,
12 January 1896, p.9. (2) *KA*, pp.165-166, 187-189,
329-330.

D225. THE PASSING SHOW [Yvette Guilbert, Poet Laureate Alfred
Austin, monument to Stevenson, Lillie Langtry, Walt
Whitman]. (1) *NSJ*, 19 January 1896, p.9. (2) *KA*, p.166-167,
192, 225-228, 351-353. (3) *Horizon* 9 (Spring 1967): 119.
Title: 'Willa Cather, "The Meatax Girl"'. (4) *W&P*,
pp.280-282.

D226. THE PASSING SHOW [James Lane Allen, Bernhardt, death of
Pearl Etynge]. (1) *NSJ*, 26 January 1896, p.9. (2) *KA*,
pp.120-121, 330-331.

D227.   AMUSEMENTS [Albert Hart in *Wang*]. (1) *NSJ*, 31 January
1896, p.6.

D228.   THE PASSING SHOW [death of Verlaine, Hardy's *Jude the
Obscure*]. (1) *NSJ*, 2 February 1896, p.9. (2) *KA*, pp.359-360,
393-397. (3) *W&P*, pp.282-286.

D229.   AMUSEMENTS [the Holdens in *Roxy, The Waif*]. (1) *NSJ*,
4 February 1896, p.6.

D230.   THE PASSING SHOW [the English poet laureate, Dumas fils,
Robert G. Ingersoll]. (1) *NSJ*, 9 February 1896, p.9. (2) *KA*,
pp.192-193, 210-211, 225, 249.

D231.   THE PASSING SHOW [Zola's *The Fat and the Thin*, Bernhardt,
Margaret Mather]. (1) *NSJ*, 16 February 1896, p.9. (2) *KA*,
pp.368-371.

D232.   THE PASSING SHOW [Eugene Field's *The Love Affairs of a
Bibliomaniac*, Oscar Hammerstein, Marie Corelli]. (1) *NSJ*,
23 February 1896, p.9. (2) *KA*, pp.193-194, 202-203,
208-209, 254, 332-333.

D233.   THE PASSING SHOW [Saltus's *Mary Magdalen*, Richard
Hovey, Ambroise Thomas, and Père-Lachaise, Duse-Bernhardt
duel]. (1) *NSJ*, 1 March 1896, p.9. (2) *KA*, pp.167-168,
354-356, 415-417.

D234.   THE PASSING SHOW [Byron, Herbert Bates, Amélie Rives,
summary of theatre season]. (1) *NSJ*, 8 March 1896, p.13.
(2) *KA*, pp.203-204, 334-335, 398-399. (3) *W&P*,
pp.254-255.

D235.   THE PASSING SHOW [Conan Doyle, Dumas père, prodigies,
Max Nordau, Anatole France]. (1) *NSJ*, 15 March 1896, p.9.
(2) *KA*, pp.324-325, 327-328.

D236.   THE PASSING SHOW [Herbert Bates, *Anna Karenina*,
mystery stories, Stevenson's *The Wrecker*, Duse]. (1) *NSJ*,

22 March 1896, p.9. (2) *KA*, pp.154, 193, 335-336, 378-379.
(3) *W&P*, pp.287-288.

D237.   AMUSEMENTS [review of *Fleur de Lis*]. (1) *NSJ*, 26 March
1896, p.2. (2) *KA*, pp.283-284.

D238.   AMUSEMENTS [Richard Mansfield in *A Parisian Romance*].
(1) *NSJ*, 29 March 1896, p.5. (2) *KA*, pp.284-285. (3) *W&P*,
pp.217-218.

D239.   THE PASSING SHOW [dramatization of James's *The Tragic
Muse*, Sol Smith Russell in *Mr. Valentine's Christmas* and *An
Everyday Man*]. (1) *NSJ*, 29 March 1896, p.9. (2) *KA*,
pp.361-362. (3) *W&P*, pp.288-289.

D240.   THE PASSING SHOW [Murger's *Scènes de la vie de Bohème*,
death of Jennie Kimball. (1) *NSJ*, 5 April 1896, p.16. (2) *KA*,
pp.410-414. (3) *W&P*, pp.292-296.

D241.   THE PASSING SHOW [*The Crime of Sylvestre Bonnard*, *Tom
Brown's Schooldays*, Mansfield, Minnie Maddern Fiske]. (1) *NSJ*,
12 April 1896, p.13. (2) *KA*, pp.328-329, 336-338.

D242.   THE PASSING SHOW [Anthony Hope's *Phroso*, Beatrice
Harraden, Chicago *Chap-Book*, Sir Richard and Lady Burton,
'Kathleen Mavourneen']. (1) *NSJ*, 19 April 1896, p.13.
(2) *KA*, pp.168-169, 185-186, 322. (3) *W&P*, pp.289-290.

D243.   THE PASSING SHOW [Hovey and Carman, Bernhardt, Lillian
Russell]. (1) *NSJ*, 26 April 1896, p.13. (2) *KA*, pp.353-354.
(3) *W&P*, pp.290-292.

D244.   THE PASSING SHOW [Mary Anderson, Paderewski's prize for
American composers]. (1) *NSJ*, 3 May 1896, p.13. (2) *KA*,
pp.155-159. (3) *W&P*, p.202.

D245.   THE PASSING SHOW [*The Rivals*, prolific authors, notes on
stars]. (1) *NSJ*, 10 May 1896, p.13. (2) *W&P*, pp.262-263.

D246. THE PASSING SHOW [Ruskin, Tolstoi's new art]. (1) *NSJ*, 17 May 1896, p.13. (2) *KA*, pp.378, 400-404. (3) *W&P*, pp.291-292, 297-301.

D247. THE PASSING SHOW [Burns, Scottish writers, Kipling, the Balestiers]. (1) *NSJ*, 24 May 1896, p.13. (2) *KA*, pp.341-344.

D248. THE PASSING SHOW [Mrs. Humphry Ward and George Eliot, Nethersole and Daly, Henry Irving]. (1) *NSJ*, 31 May 1896, p.13. (2) *KA*, pp.216, 375-377.

D249. THE PASSING SHOW [letter from Clay Clement, Daudet and the roman à clef]. (1) *NSJ*, 7 June 1896, p.13.

D250. AMUSEMENTS [Boston Comic Opera Company in *Olivette*]. (1) *NSJ*, 12 June 1896, p.6.

D251. THE PASSING SHOW [F. H. Burnett's *A Lady of Quality*, Abbey and Grau, death of Clara Wieck Schumann]. (1) *NSJ*, 14 June 1896, p.13. (2) *KA*, pp.169-170, 197-198, 372-374.

D252. LA PUCELLE AGAIN [editorial]. (1) *HM*, August 1896, p.12.

D253. STEVENSON'S MONUMENT. (1) *HM*, September 1896, p.3.

D254. TWO WOMEN THE WORLD IS WATCHING [Mrs. William McKinley and Mrs. William Jennings Bryan; signed 'Mary K. Hawley']. (1) *HM*, September 1896, pp.4-5. (2) *Library*, 14 July 1900, pp.13-15. Title: 'The Personal Side of William Jennings Bryan' (parts of the original article included). (3) *W&P*, pp.309-313.

D255. THE BURNS CENTENARY. (1) *HM*, September 1896, p.12. (2) *W&P*, p.314.

D256. [Review of Roland Reed in *The Wrong Mr. Wright*]. (1) *PL*, 22 September 1896, p.9.

D257. NORDICA HAS RETURNED [editorial]. (1) *HM*, October 1896, p.14.

D258. PRODIGAL SALARIES TO SINGERS [editorial]. (1) *HM*, October 1896, p.14. (2) *W&P*, pp.315-316.

D259. [Review of Sol Smith Russell in *A Bachelor's Romance*]. (1) *PL*, 13 October 1896, p.10.

D260. THE ORIGIN OF THANKSGIVING [signed 'Helen Delay']. (1) *HM*, November 1896, p.8.

D261. DEATH OF GEORGE DuMAURIER. (1) *HM*, November 1896, p.11. (2) *W&P*, pp.316-318.

D262. THE RETURN OF THE ROMANTIC DRAMA [editorial]. (1) *HM*, November 1896, p.12. (2) *W&P*, p.318.

D263. [Review of Joseph Jefferson in *Rip Van Winkle*]. (1) *PL*, 10 November 1896, p.6. (2) *W&P*, pp.422-423.

D264. [Review of the Hollands in *A Superfluous Husband* and *Colonel Carter of Cartersville*; signed 'Willa']. (1) *PL*, 24 November 1896, p.5. (2) *WCPM Newsletter*, Fall 1977, p.2. Title: 'The Hollands at the Grand'.

D265. THE THREE HOLY KINGS [WC, trans.]. (1) *HM*, December 1896, cover and p.1.

D266. "IAN MACLAREN" AS A MINISTER [editorial] (1) *HM*, December 1896, p.12.

D267. [Review of Hoyt's *A Milk White Flag*; signed 'Sibert']. (1) *PL*, 1 December 1896, p.4. (2) *W&P*, pp.467-468.

D268. THE PASSING SHOW [Massenet's *Eve*, E. M. Holland in *A Social Highwayman*, Campanini. (1) *NSJ*, 6 December 1896, p.13. (2) *W&P*, pp.377-381.

D269. [Review of *Thoroughbred*; signed 'Sibert']. (1) *PL*, 8 December 1896, p.2. (2) *WCPM Newsletter*, Fall 1977, pp.2-3. Title: 'It Lacks Continuity'.

D270. THE PASSING SHOW [Nordica and Jean de Reszke, Howells, *Princess Osra* dramatized]. (1) *NSJ*, 13 December 1896, p.13. (2) *W&P*, pp.381-384.

D271. [Review of Frank Daniels in *Wizard of the Nile* (Victor Herbert); signed 'Sibert']. (1) *PL*, 15 December 1896, p.6. (2) *W&P*, pp.385-386.

D272. THE PASSING SHOW [Henry James's *The Other House*, Frank Daniels in *Wizard of the Nile*]. (1) *NSJ*, 20 December 1896, p.13. (2) *W&P*, pp.551-553.

D273. BEAUTIFUL ANNA HELD [signed 'Sibert']. (1) *PL*, 22 December 1896, p.6. (2) *WCPM Newsletter*, Fall 1977, p.3.

D274. THE EDITOR'S TALK [feature; signed 'The Editor']. (1) *National Stockman and Farmer*, 24 December 1896, p.18. (2) *WCPM Newsletter*, Literary issue, Summer 1973, pp.3-4. Title: 'About Jim and Elsie'.

D275. [Review of James Herne's *Shore Acres*; signed 'Sibert']. (1) *PL*, 29 December 1896, p.6. (2) *W&P*, pp.469-471.

1897
D276. ITALO CAMPANINI. (1) *HM*, January 1897, p.11.

D277. BOOKS OLD AND NEW [romances, Edna Lyall, children's classics; signed 'Helen Delay']. (1) *HM*, January 1897, p.23. (2) *W&P*, pp.333-337.

D278. THE PASSING SHOW [Anna Held]. (1) *NSJ*, 3 January 1897, p.13. (2) *W&P*, pp.389-393.

D279. [Review of Jessie Bartlett Davis and the Bostonians in *Robin Hood*; signed 'Sibert']. (1) *PL*, 5 January 1897, p.4. (2) *W&P*, p.386.

D280. THE PASSING SHOW [Handel's *Messiah*, Anna Held and Henry C. Frick, Henry E. Abbey's career]. (1) *NSJ*, 10 January 1897, p.13. (2) *W&P*, pp.471-473, 505-506.

D281.   [Review of Otis Skinner in *A Soldier of Fortune;* signed 'Sibert'].
(1) *PL*, 12 January 1897, p.10. (2) *WCPM Newsletter*, Fall
1977, p.3.

D282.   THE PASSING SHOW [Jessie Bartlett Davis, Sunday music,
Elia W. Peattie]. (1) *NSJ*, 17 January 1897, p.13. (2) *W&P*,
pp.506-507.

D283.   [Review of Fanny Davenport in Sardou's *Gismonda;* signed
'Sibert']. (1) *PL*, 19 January 1897, p.10.

D284.   [Review of *My Friend from India;* signed 'Sibert']. (1) *PL*,
26 January 1897, p.8. (2) *W&P*, pp.468-469.

D285.   THE PASSING SHOW [Fanny Davenport in Sardou's *Gismonda*
and *La Tosca*]. (1) *NSJ*, 31 January 1896, p.13. (2) *W&P*,
pp.424-426.

D286.   A MODERN MAN [editorial on Prince Michael Hilkoff].
(1) *HM*, February 1897, p.12.

D287.   OLD BOOKS AND NEW [romances, *The Prisoner of Zenda*,
Treasure Island; signed 'Helen Delay']. (1) *HM*, February 1897,
p.19. (2) *W&P*, pp.338-339.

D288.   [Review of Julia Marlowe in *Romeo and Juliet*]. (1) *PL*,
2 February 1897, p.5.

D289.   THE PASSING SHOW [Carreño in concert]. (1) *NSJ*,
7 February 1897, p.13. (2) *W&P*, pp.397-400.

D290.   [Review of *Pudd'nhead Wilson;* signed 'Sibert']. (1) *PL*,
9 February 1897, p.4. (2) *W&P*, pp.477-478.

D291.   THE PASSING SHOW [Julia Marlowe as Juliet, E. S. Willard].
(1) *NSJ*, 14 February 1897, p.13. (2) *W&P*, pp.427-429.

D292.   [Review of Margaret Mather in *Cymbeline;* signed 'Sibert'].
(1) *PL*, 23 February 1897, p.4.

D293. THE PASSING SHOW [Nordica in concert, Sothern in *An Enemy to the King*]. (1) *NSJ*, 28 February 1897, p.13.

D294. THE CARNEGIE MUSEUM. (1) *HM*, March 1897, pp.1-4.

D295. THE PASSING OF "THE DUCHESS". (1) *HM*, March 1897, p.7.

D296. "MARK TWAIN'S" POVERTY [editorial]. (1) *HM*, March 1897, p.12.

D297. THE SULTAN'S MUSICAL TASTE [editorial]. (1) *HM*, March 1897, p.12.

D298. OLD BOOKS AND NEW [*Kings in Exile, The Crime of Sylvestre Bonnard, Phroso;* signed 'Helen Delay']. (1) *HM*, March 1897, p.16. (2) *W&P*, pp.340-343.

D299. [Review of *The Sporting Duchess;* signed 'Sibert']. (1) *PL*, 2 March 1897, p.6.

D300. [Review of *Lohengrin;* signed 'A Woman Lover of Music']. (1) *PL*, 4 March 1897, p.2. (2) *W&P*, pp.400-402.

D301. [Review of *Tannhäuser;* in a prefatory note the author is described as 'a lady who wields a trenchant pen']. (1) *PL*, 6 March 1897, p.6. (2) *W&P*, pp.402-404.

D302. THE PASSING SHOW [Margaret Mather in *Cymbeline, The Heart of Maryland*]. (1) *NSJ*, 7 March 1897, p.13. (2) *W&P*, pp.429-432.

D303. [Review of Nat Goodwin in *An American Citizen;* signed 'Sibert']. (1) *PL*, 9 March 1897, p.4. (2) *WCPM Newsletter*, Literary Issue, Summer 1972, pp.1-2.

D304. THE PASSING SHOW [*Lohengrin* and *Tannhäuser*]. (1) *NSJ*, 14 March 1897, p.13. (2) *W&P*, pp.404-408.

D305. [Review of Nethersole in *Carmen;* signed 'Sibert']. (1) *PL*, 16 March 1897, p.4. (2) *WCPM Newsletter*, Literary Issue, Summer 1972, p.2.

D306. [Review of DeWolf Hopper in *El Capitan* by John Philip Sousa; signed 'Sibert']. (1) *PL*, 23 March 1897, p.4. (2) *W&P*, p.387.

D307. THE PASSING SHOW [Nethersole in *Carmen, Camille,* and *The Wife of Scarli*]. (1) *NSJ*, 28 March 1897, p.13. (2) *W&P*, pp.432-436.

D308. THE BYRONIC RENAISSANCE [editorial]. (1) *HM*, April 1897, p.12.

D309. GERMAN OPERA IN PITTSBURGH [editorial]. (1) *HM*, April 1897, p.12.

D310. LITTLE GREECE [editorial]. (1) *HM*, April 1897, p.12.

D311. OLD BOOKS AND NEW [*Les misérables*, *A Kentucky Cardinal;* signed 'Helen Delay']. (1) *HM*, April 1897, p.16. (2) *W&P*, pp.343-345.

D312. THE PASSING SHOW [Nat Goodwin in *An American Citizen,* DeWolf Hopper in *El Capitan,* Julia Marlowe]. (1) *NSJ*, 4 April 1897, p.13.

D313. [Review of Maude Adams and John Drew in *Rosemary;* signed 'Sibert']. (1) *PL*, 6 April 1897, p.4. (2) *WCPM Newsletter*, Literary Issue, Summer 1972, pp.2-3.

D314. [Review of Richard Mansfield in *The Merchant of Venice;* signed 'Sibert']. (1) *PL*, 20 April 1897, p.9. (2) *WCPM Newsletter*, Literary Issue, Summer 1972, p.3.

D315. NURSING AS A PROFESSION FOR WOMEN [signed 'Elizabeth L. Seymour']. (1) *HM*, May 1897, pp.3-5. (2) *W&P*, pp.219-324.

D316. KING GEORGE OF GREECE [editorial]. (1) *HM*, May 1897, p.12.

D317. OLD BOOKS AND NEW [*David Copperfield*, Mark Twain, Mrs. Humphry Ward, George Eliot; signed 'Helen Delay']. (1) *HM*, May 1897, p.18. (2) *W&P*, pp.346-349.

D318. THE PASSING SHOW [Maude Adams and John Drew in *Rosemary*, Mansfield in *The Merchant of Venice*]. (1) *NSJ*, 2 May 1897, p.13. (2) *W&P*, pp.437-438, 439-441.

D319. THE PASSING SHOW [Yvette Guilbert, Kipling]. (1) *NSJ*, 16 May 1897, p.13. (2) *W&P*, pp.555-556.

D320. THE PASSING SHOW [Calvé in concert]. (1) *NSJ*, 23 May 1897, p.13. (2) *W&P*, pp.409-411.

D321. [Review of Lizzie Hudson Collier in *Rosedale;* signed 'Sibert']. (1) *PL*, 25 May 1897, p.9.

D322. THE PASSING SHOW [Lizzie Hudson Collier in *Rosedale*, Mrs. Fiske in *Tess of the D'Urbervilles*]. (1) *NSJ*, 30 May 1897, p.13. (2) *W&P*, pp.443-447.

D323. VICTORIA'S ANCESTORS. (1) *HM*, June 1897, pp.1-4. (2) *W&P*, pp.325-332.

D324. THE PAPER AGE [editorial]. (1) *HM*, June 1897, p.12.

D325. EMMA CALVÉ. (1) *HM*, June 1897, pp.13-14.

D326. OLD BOOKS AND NEW [Moore, Byron, Ouida; signed 'Helen Delay']. (1) *HM*, June 1897, p.14. (2) *W&P*, pp.350-353.

D327. [Review of *The People's King;* signed 'Sibert']. (1) *PL*, 1 June 1897, p.4.

D328. THE GREAT WOMAN EDITOR OF PARIS [Juliette Adam, editor of *Nouvelle revue*]. (1) *HM*, July 1897, p.8.

D329. NOT TO THE QUEEN'S TASTE. (1) *HM*, July 1897, p.12.

D330. OLD BOOKS AND NEW [Emerson, Hall Caine's *The Bondman;* signed 'Helen Delay']. (1) *HM*, July 1897, p.14. (2) *W&P*, p.353-354.

D331. OLD BOOKS AND NEW [Gilbert Parker's *The Seats of the Mighty*, Dickens' *A Tale of Two Cities;* signed 'Helen Delay']. (1) *HM*, September 1897), p.14. (2) *W&P*, pp. 355-357.

D332. [Review of *Never Again;* signed 'Sibert']. (1) *PL*, 28 September 1897, p.4.

D333. OLD BOOKS AND NEW [Housman, F. H. Burnett's *A Lady of Quality*, Thackeray, *Alice in Wonderland;* signed 'Helen Delay']. (1) *HM*, October 1897, p.14. (2) *W&P*, pp.358-361.

D334. [Review of Augustin Daly's *Divorce;* signed 'Sibert']. (1) *PL*, 5 October 1897, p.4.

D335. SOUSA'S OPENING [signed 'Sibert']. (1) *PL*, 12 October 1897, p.4.

D336. BOOKS AND MAGAZINES [*Tales from McClure's: Tales of Humor, Edgar Allan Poe, Old Ebenezer* by Opie Read, *Hugh Wynne: Free Quaker* by S. Weir Mitchell]. (1) *PL*, 15 October 1897, p.2.

D337. [Review of *The Prisoner of Zenda;* signed 'Sibert']. (1) *PL*, 19 October 1897, p.4.

D338. BOOKS AND MAGAZINES [Kipling's *Captains Courageous*, M. H. Catherwood's *The Days of Jeanne d'Arc*]. (1) *PL*, 22 October 1897, p.2.

D339. THE PASSING SHOW [horse show, Charles Stanley Reinhart]. (1) *Courier*, 23 October 1897, pp.8-9. (2) *W&P*, pp.508-512.

D340. [Review of *The Wedding Day;* signed 'Sibert']. (1) *PL*, 26 October 1897, p.4.

D341. THE PASSING SHOW [Sousa and Kipling, Carnegie Prize Committee]. (1) *Courier*, 30 October 1897, p.3. (2) *W&P*, pp.387-389, 513-514, 562.

D342. ANTHONY HOPE'S LECTURE [review, signed 'Sibert']. (1) *PL*, 30 October 1897, p.6.

D343. OLD BOOKS AND NEW [Eliot's *The Mill on the Floss;* signed 'Helen Delay']. (1) *HM*, November 1897, p.14. (2) *W&P*, pp.361-365.

D344. BOOKS AND MAGAZINES [S. Weyman's *For the Cause* and F. Palmer's *How the Greeks Were Defeated*, in *Forum* (November 1897)]. (1) *PL*, 5 November 1897, p.12.

D345. THE PASSING SHOW [Heine and Hugo, Evangelina Cisneros, Lillian Russell in *The Wedding Day*]. (1) *Courier*, 6 November 1897, p.2. (2) *W&P*, pp.393-395, 515-517.

D346. THE PASSING SHOW [Writers' Club dinner for Anthony Hope Hawkins and interview]. (1) *Courier*, 13 November 1897, pp.2-3. (2) *W&P*, pp.564-570.

D347. [Review of Mrs. Fiske in *Tess of the D'Urbervilles;* signed 'Sibert']. (1) *PL*, 16 November 1897, p.11. (2) *W&P*, pp.447-448.

D348. BOOKS AND MAGAZINES [*The Charm and Other Drawing Room Farces* (W. Besant and W. Pollock), *The Love Affairs of Some Famous Men*]. (1) *PL*, 19 November 1897, p.4.

D349. THE PASSING SHOW [President McKinley in Pittsburgh, Campanari concert]. (1) *Courier*, 20 November 1897, pp.2-3. (2) *W&P*, pp.517-521.

D350. [Review of Belasco's *The Wife;* signed 'Sibert']. (1) *PL*, 23 November 1897, p.8. (2) *W&P*, pp.479-480.

D351. BOOKS AND MAGAZINES [*The Latimers* (H. McCook), *A Fountain Sealed* (W. Besant), *Blown Away* (Richard Mansfield),

Thro' Lattice Windows (W. J. Davidson)]. (1) *PL*, 26 November 1897, p.4. (2) *WCPM Newsletter*, Literary Issue, Spring 1972, pp.1-2. 'The Latimers' only.

D352.   [Review of *The Sporting Duchess;* signed 'Sibert']. (1) *PL*, 30 November 1897, p.10.

D353.   OLD BOOKS AND NEW [William Allen White, *Captains Courageous* (Kipling); signed 'Helen Delay']. (1) *HM*, December 1897, p.12. (2) *W&P*, pp.365-367.

D354.   THE WANDERING JEW [review of the Eugène Sue novel; signed 'Helen Delay']. (1) *HM*, December 1897, p.19. (2) *W&P*, pp.367-368.

D355.   WITH NANSEN TO THE POLE [article signed 'Sibert']. (1) *PL*, 1 December 1897, p.2.

D356.   THE PASSING SHOW [Victor Herbert's *Serenade*, Anton Seidl and the United Singers]. (1) *Courier*, 4 December 1897, p.2. (2) *W&P*, pp.412, 525-526.

D357.   PITTSBURGH ORCHESTRA [review signed 'Sibert']. (1) *PL*, 10 December 1897, p.13. (2) *WCPM Newsletter*, Literary Issue, December 1979, pp.1-2.

D358.   THE PASSING SHOW [Mrs. Fiske in *Tess of the D'Urbervilles*]. (1) *Courier*, 11 December 1897, pp.2-3. (2) *W&P*, p.448-452.

D359.   [Review of *Salt of the Earth;* signed 'Sibert']. (1) *PL*, 14 December 1897, p.4.

D360.   THE PASSING SHOW [Writers' Club dinner for Fridtjof Nansen and interview]. (1) *Courier*, 18 December 1897, pp.4-5. (2) *W&P*, pp.521-525.

D361.   THE PASSING SHOW [Nansen's views on literature, Dvořák's *New World* Symphony, musicians' stories]. (1) *Courier*, 25 December 1897, pp.2-3. (2) *Prairie Schooner* 38 (Winter 1964-1965): 344-345. (3) *W&P*, pp.413-414.

D362. PHASES OF ALPHONSE DAUDET [signed 'Sibert']. (1) *PL*, 26 December 1897, p.16.

D363. [Review of *The Lost Paradise;* signed 'Sibert']. (1) *PL*, 28 December 1897, p.4.

1898

D364. OLD BOOKS AND NEW [*Hugh Wynne: Free Quaker* (S. Weir Mitchell), *Rupert of Hentzau* (Anthony Hope), *Jane Eyre* (C. Brontë); signed 'Helen Delay']. (1) *HM*, January 1898, p.12. (2) *W&P*, pp.369-372.

D365. THE PASSING SHOW [Olive May in *White Heather, Secret Service* (William Gillette)]. (1) *Courier*, 1 January 1898, pp.2-3. (2) *W&P*, pp.480-481.

D366. [Review of Melba in *The Barber of Seville;* signed 'Sibert']. (1) *PL*, 4 January 1898, p.4.

D367. BOOKS AND MAGAZINES [*The School for Saints* (J. O. Hobbes), *The Habitant* (W. H. Drummond)]. (1) *PL*, 7 January 1898, p.13. (2) *W&P*, pp.570-571.

D368. [Review of William H. Crane in *A Virginia Courtship;* signed 'Sibert']. (1) *PL*, 11 January 1898, p.6.

D369. [Review of E. S. Willard in *Garrick* (A. Daly); signed 'Sibert']. (1) *PL*, 18 January 1898, p.4.

D370. THE PASSING SHOW [the death of Daudet]. (1) *Courier*, 22 January 1898, pp.2-3. (2) *W&P*, pp.572-576.

D371. BOOKS AND MAGAZINES [*Reminiscences of William Wetmore Story* (Mary E. Phillips), *There is No Devil* (Marius Jokai)]. (1) *PL*, 28 January 1898, p.5. (2) *W&P*, pp.577-579.

D372. THE PASSING SHOW [Melba in *The Barber of Seville*, Yone Noguchi]. (1) *Courier*, 29 January 1898, p.2. (2) *W&P*, pp.414-417, 579-580.

D373. OLD BOOKS AND NEW [death of Daudet, *Quo Vadis?*; signed 'Helen Delay']. (1) *HM*, February 1898, p.12. (2) *W&P*, pp.372-374.

D374. THE PASSING SHOW [Ethelbert Nevin's Carnegie Hall recital]. (1) *Courier*, 5 February 1898, pp.3-4. (2) *W&P*, pp.533-538.

D375. MISS MOULD TALKS [interview]. (1) *PL*, 6 February 1898, p.5.

D376. [Review of *Ash Wednesday*]. (1) *New York Sun*, 9 February 1898, p.7. Probable attribution.

D377. [Reviews of Modjeska in *Mary Stuart; Way Down East*]. (1) *New York Sun*, 11 February 1898, p.7. Probable attribution.

D378. THE PASSING SHOW [on interviewing Adelaide Mould, daughter of Marion Manola]. (1) *Courier*, 19 February 1898, pp.2-3. (2) *W&P*, pp.527-532.

D379. THE PASSING SHOW [on E. S. Willard]. (1) *Courier*, 26 February 1898, pp.2-3. (2) *W&P*, pp.485-488.

D380. [Review of Vesta Tilley in vaudeville; signed 'Sibert']. (1) *PL*, 1 March 1898, p.10.

D381. BOOKS AND MAGAZINES [*Going to War in Greece* (F. Palmer), 'English as Against French Literature' by Henry D. Sedgwick (*Atlantic*, March 1898); signed 'Sibert']. (1) *PL*, 4 March 1898, p.8. (2) *W&P*, pp.582-584.

D382. THE PASSING SHOW [New York productions of *The Lady of Lyons*, Ada Rehan in *The Country Girl*, Modjeska in *Mary Stuart*]. (1) *Courier*, 5 March 1898, pp.2-3. (2) *W&P*, pp.452-457, 459-460.

D383. BOOKS AND MAGAZINES [*The Tales of John Oliver Hobbes* (Pearl Craigie), *The Story of Evangelina Cisneros* (Cisneros and Decker); signed 'Sibert']. (1) *PL*, 11 March 1898, p.4. (2) *W&P*, pp.585-586.

D384.   THE PASSING SHOW [New York productions of *The Tree of Knowledge, The Conquerors*]. (1) *Courier*, 12 March 1898, pp.2-3. (2) *W&P*, pp.482-485.

D385.   BOOKS AND MAGAZINES [*The Barnstormers* (Mrs. Harcourt Williamson); signed 'Sibert']. (1) *PL*, 18 March 1898, p.3.

D386.   THE PASSING SHOW [Melba, Nat Goodwin, Vesta Tilley]. (1) *Courier*, 19 March 1898, pp.2-3. (2) *W&P*, pp.395-397, 417-419.

D387.   BOOKS AND MAGAZINES [*Across the Salt Sea* (J. Bloundell-Burton), *In the Midst of Life* (Bierce); signed 'Sibert']. (1) *PL*, 25 March 1898, p.9. (2) *W&P*, pp.586-587.

D388.   [Review of Mansfield in *The Devil's Disciple;* signed 'Sibert']. (1) *PL*, 29 March 1898, p.4. (2) *W&P*, pp.489-490.

D389.   BOOKS AND MAGAZINES [*The Romance of Zion Chapel* (R. Le Gallienne), *Woman's Bible*, vol.2 (E. C. Stanton); signed 'Sibert']. (1) *PL*, 8 April 1898, p.9. (2) *W&P*, pp.538-541, 587-589.

D390.   THE PASSING SHOW [letter to Nat Goodwin]. (1) *Courier*, 9 April 1898, p.3. (2) *W&P*, pp.461-464.

D391.   BOOKS AND MAGAZINES [*Fantasia* (G. Egerton); signed 'Sibert']. (1) *PL*, 15 April 1898, p.14.

D392.   THE PASSING SHOW [*The Barnstormers* (Mrs. H. Williamson)]. (1) *Courier*, 16 April 1898, p.3.

D393.   [Review of Charles Coghlan in *The Royal Box;* signed 'Sibert']. (1) *PL*, 19 April 1898, p.10.

D394.   THE PASSING SHOW [the sinking of the *Maine*, Mansfield in *The Devil's Disciple*]. (1) *Courier*, 23 April 1898, pp.3-4. (2) *W&P*, pp.544-546.

D395.   THE PASSING SHOW [Charles Coghlan's *The Royal Box*]. (1) *Courier*, 30 April 1898, pp.3-4. (2) *W&P*, pp.481-482.

D396.   BOOKS AND MAGAZINES [*A Bride of Japan* (C. Dawe), *Here and There and Everywhere* (Mrs. M. E. W. Sherwood); signed 'Sibert']. (1) *PL*, 6 May 1898, p.9. (2) *W&P*, pp.541-543.

D397.   BOOKS AND MAGAZINES [*The French Market Girl* (Zola); signed 'Sibert']. (1) *PL*, 27 May 1898, p.5. (2) *W&P*, pp.592-594.

D398.   BOOKS AND MAGAZINES [*The Brown-Laurel Marriage* (Landis Ayr); signed 'Sibert']. (1) *PL*, 24 June 1898, p.5.

D399.   THE WAR AND THE MAGAZINES [signed 'Sibert']. (1) *PL*, 8 July 1898, p.2.

D400.   BOOKS AND MAGAZINES [*The Aurelian Wall and Other Poems* (Bliss Carman); signed 'Sibert']. (1) *PL*, 22 July 1898, p.6. (2) *W&P*, pp.580-581.

D401.   [Review of *The Bride Elect* by John Philip Sousa; signed 'Sibert']. (1) *PL*, 25 October 1898, p.2. (2) *W&P*, pp.610-611.

D402.   [Review of *The Tree of Knowledge;* signed 'Sibert']. (1) *PL*, 1 November 1898, p.11.

D403.   BOOKS AND MAGAZINES [*The Romance of the House of Savoy* (Althea Wiel); signed 'Sibert']. (1) *PL*, 4 November 1898, p.13.

D404.   [Review of Modjeska in *Mary Stuart;* signed 'Sibert']. (1) *PL*, 15 November 1898, p.6. (2) *W&P*, pp.460-461.

D405.   BOOKS AND MAGAZINES [*A Yankee Boy's Success* (H. S. Morrison), *The Changeling* (W. Besant); signed 'Sibert']. (1) *PL*, 19 November 1898, p.5.

D406.   [Review of Nat Goodwin in *Nathan Hale* (Clyde Fitch); signed 'Sibert']. (1) *PL*, 29 November 1898, p.5.

D407.   BOOKS AND MAGAZINES [*In the Cage* (H. James), *Plays, Pleasant and Unpleasant* (G. B. Shaw); signed 'Sibert']. (1) *PL*, 2 December 1898, p.13. (2) *W&P*, pp.553-554, 595-597.

D408.   BOOKS AND MAGAZINES [*Dream Days* (K. Grahame), *The Money Captain* (W. H. Payne), *Ashes of Empire* (R. W. Chambers); signed 'Sibert']. (1) *PL*, 10 December 1898, p.9. (2) *WCPM Newsletter*, Literary Issue, Winter 1973, pp.3-4.

D409.   [Review of E. H. Sothern in *The King's Musketeers;* signed 'Sibert']. (1) *PL*, 20 December 1898, p.8.

D410.   THE PASSING SHOW [Mrs. Fiske in *A Bit of Old Chelsea* and *Love Will Find a Way*]. (1) *Courier*, 24 December 1898, p.3.

1899
D411.   THE PASSING SHOW [Israel Zangwill's lecture "The Drama as a Fine Art"]. (1) *Courier*, 7 January 1899, p.11. (2) *W&P*, pp.491-494.

D412.   [Review of Julia Marlowe in *The Countess Valeska;* signed 'Sibert']. (1) *PL*, 10 January 1899, p.10.

D413.   THE PASSING SHOW [on interviewing Mrs. Fiske]. (1) *Courier*, 14 January 1899, p.3. (2) *W&P*, pp.660-664.

D414.   BOOKS AND MAGAZINES [*Omar the Tentmaker* (N. H. Doyle), *The Borderland of Society* (C. B. Davis); signed 'Sibert']. (1) *PL*, 20 January 1899, p.13.

D415.   THE PASSING SHOW [Nat Goodwin in C. Fitch's *Nathan Hale*]. (1) *Courier*, 21 January 1899, p.4. (2) *W&P*, pp.667-668.

D416.   [Review of *Mr. Barnes of New York;* signed 'Sibert']. (1) *PL*, 24 January 1899, p.10.

D417.   THE PASSING SHOW [Julia Marlowe in *As You Like It* and *The Countess Valeska*]. (1) *Courier*, 28 January 1899, pp.2-3. (2) *W&P*, pp.669-673.

D418.   THE PASSING SHOW [Johnstone Bennett, Rosenthal concert, Sothern in *The King's Musketeers*]. (1) *Courier*, 4 February 1899, p.3. (3) *W&P*, pp.495-497, 543-544, 611-613.

D419. GENIUS IN MIRE [article on Richard Realf, signed 'Sibert'].
(1) *PL*, 12 February 1899, p.20.

D420. BOOKS AND MAGAZINES [*The Day's Work* (Kipling)]; signed
'Sibert']. (1) *PL*, 18 February 1899, p.5.

D421. THE PASSING SHOW [Richard Realf]. (1) *Courier*, 25 February 1899, pp.3-4. (2) *W&P*, pp.598-603.

D422. THE PASSING SHOW [*The Day's Work* (Kipling)]. (1) *Courier*,
4 March 1899, pp.2-3. (2) *W&P*, pp.555-561.

D423. BOOKS AND MAGAZINES [*The Two Standards* (W. Barry),
The Maine (C. D. Sigbee); signed 'Sibert']. (1) *PL*, 10 March
1899, p.12. (2) *W&P*, pp.590-591.

D424. THE PASSING SHOW [Lizzie Hudson Collier in *Jane*, Maude
Adams in *The Little Minister*]. (1) *Courier*, 18 March 1899, p.5.
(2) *W&P*, pp.547-548, 673-675.

D425. [Review of Mansfield in *Cyrano de Bergerac* (Rostand); signed
'Sibert']. (1) *PL*, 21 March 1899, p.4.

D426. BOOKS AND MAGAZINES [Frank Norris's *McTeague;* signed
'Sibert']. (1) *PL*, 31 March 1899, p.8.

D427. THE PASSING SHOW [Richard Realf, Norris's *McTeague*].
(1) *Courier*, 8 April 1899, pp.2-3. (2) *W&P*, pp.603-608.

D428. THE PASSING SHOW [Rostand's *Cyrano de Bergerac*]. (1) *Courier*, 15 April 1899, pp.2-3. (2) *W&P*, pp.497-502.

D429. THE PASSING SHOW [Mansfield as Cyrano]. (1) *Courier*,
22 April 1899, pp.2-3. (2) *W&P*, pp.675-677.

D430. BOOKS AND MAGAZINES [*A Daughter of the Vine* (Gertrude
Atherton), *'Ickery Ann and Other Girls and Boys* (Elia W. Peattie); signed 'Sibert']. (1) *PL*, 22 April 1899, p.5. (2) *W&P*,
pp.694-696. (3) *WCPM Newsletter*, Literary Issue, Winter
1973, p.4.

D431.   RICHARD REALF, POET AND SOLDIER [article signed 'Helen Delay']. (1) *HM*, May 1899, pp.10-11.

D432.   [Review of Francis Wilson in *The Little Corporal;* signed 'Sibert']. (1) *PL*, 2 May 1899, p.2.

D433.   BOOKS AND MAGAZINES [*The Perfect Wagnerite* (G. B. Shaw), *Holland As Seen by an American* (J. H. Gore); signed 'Sibert']. (1) *PL*, 27 May 1899, p.5. (2) *W&P*, pp.617-618.

D434.   BOOKS AND MAGAZINES [*The Professor's Daughter* (Anna Farquhar), *The Wind among the Reeds* (W. B. Yeats), *War Is Kind* (S. Crane); signed 'Sibert']. (1) *PL*, 3 June 1899, p.6. (2) *W&P*, pp.700-702, 705-706.

D435.   THE PASSING SHOW [Metropolitan Opera Company in Pittsburgh, *Lohengrin*]. (1) *Courier*, 10 June 1899, p.3. (2) *W&P*, pp.619-623.

D436.   BOOKS AND MAGAZINES [*The Market Place* (H. Frederic), *Oliver Cromwell* (S. H. Church); signed 'Sibert']. (1) *PL*, 10 June 1899, p.5. (2) *W&P*, pp.709-711.

D437.   THE PASSING SHOW [the Metropolitan Opera Company in Pittsburgh, *Die Walküre*]. (1) *Courier*, 17 June 1899, p.5. (2) *W&P*, pp.623-626.

D438.   BOOKS AND MAGAZINES [*No. 5 John Street* (R. Whiteing), *More* (M. Beerbohm); signed 'Sibert']. (1) *PL*, 17 June 1899, p.5. (2) *W&P*, pp.696-697, 712-714.

D439.   THE PASSING SHOW [death of Augustin Daly]. (1) *Courier*, 1 July 1899, p.3. (2) *W&P*, pp.473-476.

D440.   BOOKS AND MAGAZINES [*The Vengeance of the Female* (M. Wilcox); signed 'Sibert']. (1) *PL*, 1 July 1899, p.6.

D441.   BOOKS AND MAGAZINES [*The Awakening* (K. Chopin), *What Women Can Earn, Outsiders: An Outline* (R. W. Chambers); signed 'Sibert']. (1) *PL*, 8 July 1899, p.6. (2) *W&P*, pp.697-699.

D442.   THE PASSING SHOW [title: 'An Evening at Vineacre'. On
Ethelbert Nevin]. (1) *Courier*, 15 July 1899, pp.4-5. (2) *W&P*,
pp.626-634. *Note:* Parts of this article are used in WC's *Ladies'
Home Journal* (November 1900) article on Nevin, 'The Man Who
Wrote "Narcissus"'. See D503.

D443.   BOOKS AND MAGAZINES [*George Borrow: Life and Correspondence* (W. Knapp), *A Silent Singer* (C. Morris); signed 'Sibert'].
(1) *PL*, 15 July 1899, p.5. (2) *W&P*, pp.699-700, 714-717.

D444.   THE PASSING SHOW [Nethersole in *The Second Mrs. Tan-
queray*]. (1) *Courier*, 22 July 1899, pp.5, 9. (2) *W&P*,
pp.677-678.

D445.   BOOKS AND MAGAZINES [*A Lost Lady of Old Years*
(J. Buchan); signed 'Sibert']. (1) *PL*, 22 July 1899, p.6.

D446.   THE PASSING SHOW [Buchan's *A Lost Lady of Old Years*,
Arnold Bennett's *A Man from the North*]. (1) *Courier*, 28 July
1899, pp.3-4. (2) *W&P*, pp.718-720, 721-722.

D447.   THE PASSING SHOW [*The Awakening* (K. Chopin), *The Forest
Lovers* (Hewlett)]. (1) *Courier*, 26 August 1899, pp.3-4.
(2) *W&P*, pp.720-721.

D448.   THE PASSING SHOW [Whiteing's *No. 5 John Street*]. (1) *Courier*, 2 September 1899, pp.3-4.

D449.   THE PASSING SHOW [Zola's *Germinal*, Phillpotts's *Children of
the Mist*]. (1) *Courier*, 16 September 1899, pp.3-4. (2) *W&P*,
pp.722-727.

D450.   THE PASSING SHOW [Isobel Strong's Stevenson lecture].
(1) *Courier*, 21 October 1899, p.3. (2) *W&P*, pp.562-564.

D451.   BOOKS AND MAGAZINES [*Strong as Death* (Maupassant),
The Vizier of the Two-Horned Alexander (F. Stockton), *The Mormon
Problem* (G. Seibel); signed 'Sibert']. (1) *PL*, 21 October 1899,
p.9.

D452.   THE PASSING SHOW [Elia W. Peattie, Maupassant's *Strong as Death*]. (1) *Courier*, 4 November 1899, pp.3-4. (2) *W&P*, pp.728-732.

D453.   BOOKS AND MAGAZINES [*Blix* (F. Norris), *La princesse lointaine* (E. Rostand), *Where Angels Fear to Tread* (M. Robertson); signed 'Sibert']. (1) *PL*, 4 November 1899, p.5.

D454.   [Review of *The Christian* by Hall Caine; signed 'Sibert']. (1) *PL*, 7 November 1899, p.10.

D455.   BOOKS AND MAGAZINES [*Active Service* (S. Crane); signed 'Sibert']. (1) *PL*, 11 November 1899, p.9. (2) *W&P*, pp.703-705.

D456.   BOOKS AND MAGAZINES [*Germinal* (Zola); signed 'Sibert']. (1) *PL*, 18 November 1899, p.9. (2) *W&P*, pp.732-733.

D457.   THE PASSING SHOW [Hall Caine's *The Christian* dramatized]. (1) *Courier*, 25 November 1899, pp.2-3.

D458.   BOOKS AND MAGAZINES [*Cashel Byron's Profession* (G. B. Shaw), *Don Cosme* (T. H. Tyndale), *The Rubáiyát of Omar Kháyyám* (trans. Mrs. H. M. Cadell), *The Future of the American Negro* (Booker T. Washington); signed 'Sibert']. (1) *PL*, 25 November 1899, p.6. (2) *W&P*, pp.733-736.

D459.   SOME PITTSBURGH COMPOSERS [article signed 'Helen Delay']. (1) *HM*, December 1899, pp.6-7.

D460.   THE PASSING SHOW [letter to Joseph Jefferson]. (1) *Courier*, 2 December 1899, pp.3-4. (2) *W&P*, pp.680-687.

D461.   BOOKS AND MAGAZINES [*The Helpers* (F. Lynde); signed 'Sibert']. (1) *PL*, 2 December 1899, p.6.

D462.   BOOKS AND MAGAZINES [*The Gentleman from Indiana* (B. Tarkington); signed 'Sibert']. (1) *PL*, 9 December 1899, p.9.

D463.   THE PASSING SHOW [letter to Lillian Nordica]. (1) *Courier*,
16 December 1899, p.3. (2) *W&P*, pp.642-646.

D464.   BOOKS AND MAGAZINES [*The Love Affairs of a Bibliomaniac*
(E. Field); signed 'Sibert']. (1) *PL*, 16 December 1899, p.3.
(2) *W&P*, pp.736-737.

D465.   THE PASSING SHOW [Pinero's *Trelawney of the Wells*, Olive
May]. (1) *Courier*, 23 December 1899, p.2. (2) *W&P*,
pp.678-680.

D466.   THE PASSING SHOW [title: 'Two Pianists' (Joseffy and
Pachmann)]. (1) *Courier*, 30 December 1899, p.2. (2) *W&P*,
pp.613-616.

1900

D467.   THE PASSING SHOW [Clara Butt]. (1) *Courier*, 6 January
1900, p.2. (2) *W&P*, p.646.

D468.   A TALK WITH HAMBOURG [signed 'Sibert']. (1) *PL*,
7 January 1900, p.8.

D469.   [Review of Nethersole in *Sapho;* signed 'Sibert']. (1) *PL*, 9 January 1900, p.4. (2) *W&P*, pp.688-689.

D470.   THE PASSING SHOW [Frank Norris's *Blix*]. (1) *Courier*,
13 January 1900, pp.2-3. (2) *W&P*, pp.702-703.

D471.   THE PASSING SHOW [title: 'A Popular Western Novel'. On
Booth Tarkington's *The Gentleman from Indiana*]. (1) *Courier*,
20 January 1900, pp.2-3. (2) *W&P*, pp.737-740.

D472.   THE PASSING SHOW [title: 'The Pianist of Pure Reason'. On
Mark Hambourg]. (1) *Courier*, 27 January 1900, p.3. (2) *W&P*,
pp.650-655.

D473.   THE PASSING SHOW [Irving and Terry in *The Merchant of
Venice*]. (1) *Courier*, 17 February 1900, pp.2-3. (2) *W&P*,
pp.689-692.

D474. THE PASSING SHOW [titles: 'A Great Denver Novel' (Francis Lynde's *The Helpers*) and 'England's New Dramatic Poet' (Stephen Phillips's *Paolo and Francesca*)]. (1) *Courier*, 3 March 1900, pp.2-3.

D475. THE PASSING SHOW [title: 'A Lyric Poet' (A. E. Housman)]. (1) *Courier*, 10 March 1900, pp.2-3. (2) *W&P*, pp.706-709.

D476. Review of the Kendals in *The Elder Miss Blossom;* signed 'Sibert']. (1) *PL*, 13 March 1900, p.10.

D477. THE PASSING SHOW [Jane Addams's lecture on Tolstoi]. (1) *Courier*, 17 March 1900, pp.3-4. (2) *W&P*, pp.743-745.

D478. THE PASSING SHOW [Kendals in *The Elder Miss Blossom*, Mary Johnston's *To Have and to Hold*]. (1) *Courier*, 24 March 1900, p.3. (2) *W&P*, pp.740-743.

D479. SOME PERSONAGES OF THE OPERA. (1) *Library*, 24 March 1900, pp.18-20. (2) *W&P*, pp.755-760.

D480. NEVIN'S NEW SONG CYCLE [signed 'Sibert']. (1) *PL*, 28 March 1900, p.6.

D481. THE PASSING SHOW [title: 'An Heir Apparent' (on Frank Norris)]. (1) *Courier*, 7 April 1900, p.3. (2) *W&P*, pp.746-749.

D482. OUT OF THEIR PULPITS [article on Pittsburgh clergy, signed 'Helen Delay'.]. (1) *Library*, 14 April 1900, pp.7-8.

D483. CALVE AND SEMBRICH [signed 'Sibert']. (1) *PL*, 17 April 1900, p.1.

D484. SUSAN STRONG AND TERNINA [on *Tannhäuser*, signed 'Sibert']. (1) *PL*, 18 April 1900, p.8.

D485. MOZART AT NIGHT [on *Don Giovanni*, signed 'Sibert']. (1) *PL*, 19 April 1900, p.2.

D486.   THE PASSING SHOW [Mrs. Fiske in *Becky Sharp*]. (1) *Courier*, 21 April 1900, p.3. (2) *W&P*, pp.664-666.

D487.   A PHILISTINE IN THE GALLERY [signed 'Goliath']. (1) *Library*, 21 April 1900, pp.8-9. (2) *W&P*, pp.760-764.

D488.   THE PASSING SHOW [*The Barber of Seville, Cavalleria Rusticana, Don Giovanni*]. (1) *Courier*, 12 May 1900, p.11. (2) *W&P*, pp.655-658.

D489.   ONE OF OUR CONQUERORS [signed 'Henry Nicklemann']. (1) *Library*, 2 June 1900, pp.3-4. (2) *W&P*, pp.765-769.

D490.   LETTERS TO A PLAYWRIGHT. (1) *Library*, 9 June 1900, p.7. (2) *W&P*, pp.769-771.

D491.   PITTSBURGH MATINEE DRIVING CLUB [horse racing; signed 'Henry Nicklemann']. (1) *Library*, 16 June 1900, pp.12-13.

D492.   THE HOME OF MINISTER WU (Washington, D.C., Dec. 20). (1) *Lincoln Semi-Weekly State Journal*, 28 December 1900.

D493.   WHEN I KNEW STEPHEN CRANE [signed 'Henry Nicklemann']. (1) *Library*, 23 June 1900, pp.17-18. (2) *Courier*, 14 July 1900, pp.4-5. (3) *Prairie Schooner* 23 (1949): 231-236. (4) *WCCY*, pp.22-24 [brief excerpts]. (5) *W&P*, pp.772-778.

D494.   PITTSBURGH SUMMER AMUSEMENTS [signed 'Clara Wood Shipman']. (1) *Library*, 30 June 1900, pp.12-13.

D495.   THE HOTTEST DAY I EVER SPENT [signed 'George Overing']. (1) *Library*, 7 July 1900, pp.3-4. (2) *W&P*, pp.778-782.

D496.   THE CHILDREN'S PART IN A GREAT LIBRARY [Carnegie Library; signed 'Henry Nicklemann']. (1) *Library*, 7 July 1900, pp.16-17.

D497. PITTSBURGH PEOPLE AND DOINGS. (1) *Library*, 14 July 1900, pp.6-9.

D498. THE PERSONAL SIDE OF WILLIAM JENNINGS BRYAN [signed 'Henry Nicklemann']. (1) *Library*, 14 July 1900, pp.13-15. (2) *Prairie Schooner* 23 (1949): 331-337. (3) *WCCY*, pp.21-22 [brief excerpts]. (4) In *Roundup: A Nebraska Reader*, comp. and ed. Virginia Faulkner, (Lincoln: University of Nebraska Press, 1957), pp.221-226. (5) *W&P*, pp.782-789.

D499. THE PITTSBURGH FIREMEN. (1) *Library*, 21 July 1900, pp.3-4.

D500. A CHINESE VIEW OF THE CHINESE SITUATION [interview, signed 'Henry Nicklemann']. (1) *Library*, 28 July 1900, pp.16-17.

D501. A HOUSEBOAT ON LAND [signed 'Henry Nicklemann']. (1) *Library*, 4 August 1900, pp.17-18. (2) *W&P*, pp.789-791.

D502. THE MEN WHO MAKE THE PITTSBURGH PAPERS. (1) *Library*, 1900, pp.13-14.

D503. THE MAN WHO WROTE 'NARCISSUS' [article on Ethelbert Nevin]. (1) *Ladies' Home Journal*, November 1900), p.11. (2) *W&P*, pp.634-637. Contains some revised sections of 'An Evening at Vineacre' (*The Passing Show*) in the *Courier*, 15 July 1899. See D442.

D504. A STATESMAN AND SCHOLAR [death of Sen. Cushman K. Davis, *Hedda Gabler*]. (1) *NSJ*, 9 December 1900, p.9.

D505. IN WASHINGTON [opening session of the Senate, Carreño's concert]. (1) *NSJ*, 16 December 1900, p.19. (2) *W&P*, pp.794-797.

D506. WINTER SKETCHES IN THE CAPITAL [opening of the Senate, Carreño concert]. (1) *IPL*, 22 December 1900, p.6.

D507. WINTER SKETCHES IN THE CAPITAL [*Hedda Gabler*]. (1) *IPL*, 29 December 1900, p.14. (2) *W&P*, pp.798-801.

D508. WASHINGTON IN OLDEN DAYS [Haddon Chambers, Olga Nethersole, early life in Washington, Christmas in Washington]. (1) *NSJ*, 30 December 1900, p.13. (2) *W&P*, pp.801-802.

1901

D509. WINTER SKETCHES IN THE CAPITAL [Chinese minister to the U.S., Wu T'ing-fang]. (1) *IPL*, 5 January 1901, p.22. (2) *W&P*, pp.803-806.

D510. JEFFERSON, PAINTER ACTOR [exhibition of paintings by Joseph Jefferson]. (1) *NSJ*, 6 January 1901, p.14.

D511. WINTER SKETCHES IN THE CAPITAL [Joseph Jefferson]. (1) *IPL*, 12 January 1901, p.10. (2) *W&P*, pp.807-810.

D512. IN THE CORCORAN GALLERY [racial studies by Hubert Vos, interview with Daniel Frohman]. (1) *NSJ*, 13 January 1901, p.9. (2) *W&P*, p.811-812.

D513. WINTER SKETCHES IN THE CAPITAL [early days in Washington, Hubert Vos's racial studies]. (1) *IPL*, 19 January 1901, pp.10-11.

D514. CLAIMS AGAINST TURKEY. (1) *NSJ*, 20 January 1901, p.9.

D515. WINTER SKETCHES IN THE CAPITAL [the diplomatic corps]. (1) *IPL*, 26 January 1901, pp.10-11.

D516. BERNHARDT IN WASHINGTON [Bernhardt and Maude Adams in *L'aiglon*]. (1) *NSJ*, 27 January 1901, p.9. (2) *W&P*, pp.813-817.

D517. WINTER SKETCHES IN THE CAPITAL [Bernhardt and Maude Adams in *L'aiglon*]. (1) *IPL*, 2 February 1901, pp.10-11.

D518. SECOND VIEW OF BERNHARDT [*La tosca* and *Camille*]. (1) *NSJ*, 4 February 1901, p.8. (2) *W&P*, pp.817-821.

D519. WINTER SKETCHES IN THE CAPITAL [Washington and the White House]. (1) *IPL*, 9 February 1901, pp.8-9.

D520. SETON-THOMPSON AT TEA [Ernest Seton-Thompson, Pittsburgh Symphony Orchestra, death of Queen Victoria]. (1) *NSJ*, 10 February 1901, p.9. (2) *W&P*, pp.822-824.

D521. WINTER SKETCHES IN THE CAPITAL [Ernest Seton-Thompson, Victor Herbert, the Pittsburgh Symphony Orchestra]. (1) *IPL*, 16 February 1901, p.8.

D522. THE CHARM OF WASHINGTON. (1) *NSJ*, 17 February 1901, p.9.

D523. THE GRIDIRON CLUB DINNER. (1) *IPL*, 23 February 1901, p.12.

D524. WASHINGTON GRIDIRON CLUB [annual gridiron dinner, musical debut of Marquis Francesco de Sousa, Clara Clemens]. (1) *NSJ*, 24 February 1901, p.9.

D525. IN WASHINGTON [the poetry of Helen Hay, Mrs. E. D. E. N. Southworth]. (1) *NSJ*, 3 March 1901, p.12.

D526. THE GAY LORD QUEX [review of Pinero's play]. (1) *IPL*, 9 March 1901, pp.8-9. (2) *W&P*, pp.825-828.

D527. IN WASHINGTON [Pinero's *The Gay Lord Quex*]. (1) *NSJ*, 10 March 1901, p.13.

D528. LITERATURE IN THE CAPITAL [Helen Hay's poetry, Edna (Emma) Southworth]. (1) *IPL*, 16 March 1901, pp.8-9. (2) *W&P*, pp.828-832.

D529. HUNTING THE NORTH POLE [the Baldwin-Ziegler expedition, Count Cassini's collections]. (1) *NSJ*, 17 March 1901, p.13. (2) *W&P*, pp.832-835.

D530. MUSIC [Ethelbert Nevin's obituary]. (1) *NSJ*, 24 March 1901, p.13. (2) *W&P*, pp.637-642.

D531.   COMMENT AND COMMENTARY [western railroads, Ernest Seton-Thompson]. (1) *Courier*, 20 July 1901, p.3. (2) *W&P*, pp.837-839.

D532.   OBSERVATIONS ['Real Strike Instigators', 'Lax Denver School', 'A Dramatized Omar', 'Constant's Victoria', 'Edward MacDowell', 'A New Drought Theory', 'Chase', 'Chicago Art Institute', 'The Deterioration of a Composer']. (1) *Courier*, 10 August 1901, pp.1-3. (2) *W&P*, pp.839-855.

D533.   [Review of Eden Phillpotts's *Sons of the Morning*]. (1) *Courier*, 10 August 1901, p.7. (2) *W&P*, pp.846-848.

D534.   OBSERVATIONS ['Schley's Accuser', 'A Tragedy of Environment', 'Small Town Funerals', 'Will White or Funston?', 'A New Library Line']. (1) *Courier*, 17 August 1901, pp.1-3. (2) *W&P*, pp.849-853.

D535.   OBSERVATIONS ['With David Nation', 'Henry of Orleans', 'The Real Homestead', 'Rodin's Victor Hugo', 'Train News Boys', 'Forms of Food Adulteration', 'J. Pierpont Morgan', 'A Fore Runner', 'Warm Praise for Dawes', 'Duse and "Il Fuoco"']. (1) *Courier*, 24 August 1901, pp.1-3. (2) *W&P*, pp.851, 853-854, 855-862.

D536.   THE PHILISTINE IN THE ART GALLERY [signed 'Henry Nicklemann']. (1) *PG*, 17 November 1901, p.6. (2) *W&P*, pp.864-867.

D537.   POPULAR PICTURES [signed 'Henry Nicklemann']. (1) *PG*, 24 November 1901, p.6. (2) *W&P*, pp.867-869.

D538.   PITTSBURGH'S MULBERRY STREET [signed 'Henry Nicklemann']. (1) *PG*, 8 December 1901, sec.5, p.5.

D539.   THE CHRISTMAS SIDE [signed 'Henry Nicklemann']. (1) *PG*, 22 December 1901, sec.4, p.1.

1902

D540.   BOARDING–NOT LIVING [signed 'Henry Nicklemann']. (1) *PG*, 23 February 1902.

D541. STAGE CELEBRITIES WHO CALL PITTSBURGH HOME [signed 'Henry Nicklemann']. (1) *PG*, 2 March 1902, p.8.

D542. A SCHOOL FOR SERVANTS [signed 'Henry Nicklemann']. (1) *PG*, 13 April 1902, sec.4, p.6.

D543. PITTSBURGH'S RICHEST CHINAMAN [signed 'Henry Nicklemann']. (1) *PG*, 15 June 1902, magazine section, p.5.

D544. RICHARD MANSFIELD AS ACTOR [signed 'Willa Sibert Cather']. (1) *PG*, 20 April 1902, pp.3, 183.

D545. A FACTORY FOR MAKING AMERICANS [signed 'Henry Nicklemann']. (1) *PG*, 8 June 1902.

D546. FIRST GLIMPSE OF ENGLAND. (1) *NSJ*, 13 July 1902, p.4. (2) *WCE*, pp.5-11. (3) *W&P*, pp.890-893.

D547. A VISIT TO OLD CHESTER. (1) *NSJ*, 20 July 1902, p.11. (2) *WCE*, pp.15-22. (3) *W&P*, pp.893-897.

D548. OUT OF THE BEATEN TRACK. (1) *NSJ*, 27 July 1902, p.11. (2) *WCE*, pp.27-34. (3) *W&P*, pp.897-901.

D549. THE CANAL FOLK OF ENGLAND. (1) *NSJ*, 3 August 1902, p.11. (2) *WCE*, pp.38-49. (2) *W&P*, pp.901-906.

D550. SEEING THINGS IN LONDON. (1) *NSJ*, 10 August 1902, p.11. (2) *WCE*, pp.54-64. (3) *W&P*, pp.907-911.

D551. THE HOTEL CHILD. (1) *PG*, 10 August 1902, magazine section, p.3. (2) *W&P*, pp.874-879.

D552. THE KENSINGTON STUDIO [Burne-Jones]. (1) *NSJ*, 17 August 1902, p.11. (2) *WCE*, pp.70-79. (3) *W&P*, pp.912-917.

D553. MERRY WIVES OF WINDSOR [Tree revival]. (1) *NSJ*, 24 August 1902, p.16. (2) *WCE*, pp.83-89. (3) *W&P*, pp.917-920.

D554. LIVES IN STREETCAR ALL YEAR ROUND [signed 'Henry Nicklemann']. (1) *PG*, 24 August 1902, sec.4, p.2.

D555. DIEPPE AND ROUEN. (1) *NSJ*, 31 August 1902, p.16. (2) *WCE*, pp.93-100. (3) *W&P*, pp.920-924.

D536. THE STRANGEST TRIBE OF DARKEST ENGLAND. (1) *PG*, 31 August 1902, magazine section, p.4.

D557. TWO CEMETERIES IN PARIS [Montmartre, Père-Lachaise]. (1) *NSJ*, 14 September 1902, p.18. (2) *WCE*, pp.105-114. (3) *W&P*, pp.924-929.

D558. ONE SUNDAY AT BARBIZON. (1) *NSJ*, 21 September 1902, p.18. (2) *WCE*, pp.119-127. (3) *W&P*, pp.929-933.

D559. THE OLD CITY OF THE POPES [Avignon]. (1) *NSJ*, 28 September 1902, p.15. (2) *WCE*, pp.132-141. (3) *W&P*, pp.934-939.

D560. COUNTRY OF THE FABULOUS [Marseilles, Hyères]. (1) *NSJ*, 5 October 1902, p.15. (2) *WCE*, pp.144-151. (3) *W&P*, pp.939-942.

D561. IN A PRINCIPALITY OF PINES [Le Lavandou]. (1) *NSJ*, 12 October 1902, p.15. (2) *WCE*, pp.154-162. (3) *W&P*, pp.942-946.

D562. IN THE COUNTRY OF DAUDET [Monte Carlo, Provençe, Arles]. (1) *NSJ*, 19 October 1902, p.9. (2) *WCE*, pp.168-178. (3) *W&P*, pp.946-952.

D563. PITTSBURGH AUTHORS KNOWN TO FAME [signed 'Henry Nicklemann']. (1) *PG*, 30 November 1902, literary section, pp.20-21.

D564. POETS OF OUR YOUNGER GENERATION. (1) *PG*, 30 November 1902, literary section, p.24.

1903

D565.   THE 100 WORST BOOKS AND THEY THAT READ
THEM. (1) *PG*, 29 November 1903, literary section, pp.11,
14. (2) *W&P*, pp.961-964. Title incorrectly transcribed, 'The
100 Worst Books and They That Wrote Them'.

1904

D566.   THE CASE OF RICHARD STRAUSS. (1) *PG*, 6 March 1904,
pp.8-9. (2) *Prairie Schooner* 55, no.1 (Spring / Summer 1981):
pp.24-33.

1913

D567.   PLAYS OF REAL LIFE. (1) *McClure's*, March 1913, pp.63-72.

D568.   MY AUTOBIOGRAPHY [S.S.McClure], PART 1.
(1) *McClure's*, October 1913, pp.33-45. On p.33: 'I wish to
express my indebtedness to Miss Willa Sibert Cather for her
invaluable assistance in the preparation of these memoirs.'
(2) *Ballymena Observer* (County Antrim, Ireland) 26 December
1913, p.3; 2 January 1913, p.9. Title: 'Story of a County
Antrim Boy Who Made Good in America'.

D569.   TRAINING FOR THE BALLET: MAKING AMERICAN
DANCERS. (1) *McClure's*, October 1913, pp.85-95.

D570.   MY AUTOBIOGRAPHY [S.S.McClure], PART 2.
(1) *McClure's*, November 1913, pp.78-87. (2) *Ballymena
Observer*, 9 January 1914, p.3; 16 January 1914, p.3. Title as
D568(2).

D571.   THREE AMERICAN SINGERS. (1) *McClure's*, December
1913, pp.33-48.

D572.   MY AUTOBIOGRAPHY [S.S.McClure], PART 3.
(1) *McClure's* December 1913, pp.95-106. (2) *Ballymena
Observer*, 30 January 1914, p.4; 6 February 1914, p.4. Title as
D568(2).

1914

D573.   MY AUTOBIOGRAPHY [S.S.McClure], PART 4.
(1) *McClure's*, January 1914, pp.96-108. (2) *Ballymena Observer*,

13 February 1914, p.9; 20 February 1914, p.3. Title as
D568(2).

D574.   NEW TYPES OF ACTING: THE CHARACTER ACTOR
DISPLACES THE STAR. (1) *McClure's*, February 1914,
pp.41-51.

D575.   MY AUTOBIOGRAPHY [S. S. McClure], PART 5.
(1) *McClure's*, February 1914, pp.76-87. (2) *Ballymena Observer*,
27 February 1914, p.4; 6 March 1914, p.5. Title as D568(2).

D576.   MY AUTOBIOGRAPHY [S. S. McClure], PART 6.
(1) *McClure's*, March 1914, pp.95-108. (2) *Ballymena Observer*,
20 March 1914, p.11; 27 March 1914, p.4; 3 April 1914, p.4;
10 April 1914, p.4. Title as D568(2).

D577.   MY AUTOBIOGRAPHY [S. S. McClure], PART 7.
(1) *McClure's*, April 1914, pp.85-95. (2) *Ballymena Observer*,
17 April 1914, p.6; 24 April 1914, p.4; 1 May 1914, p.4;
8 May 1914, p.11. Title as D568(2).

D578.   MY AUTOBIOGRAPHY [S. S. McClure], PART 8.
(1) *McClure's*, May 1914, pp.137-154. (2) *Ballymena Observer*,
15 May 1914, p.8; 22 May 1914, p.11; 29 May 1914, p.5;
5 June 1914, p.4. Title as D568(2).

1915

D579.   THE SWEATED DRAMA. (1) *McClure's*, January 1915,
pp.17-28.

D580.   WIRELESS BOYS WHO WENT DOWN WITH THEIR
SHIP. (1) *Every Week*, 2 August 1915, p.1.

1919

D581.   ROLL CALL ON THE PRAIRIES. (1) *Red Cross Magazine*, July
1919, pp.27-30.

D582.   THE EDUCATION YOU HAVE TO FIGHT FOR. (1) *Red
Cross Magazine*, October 1919, pp.54-55, 68-70. Companion to
the preceding *Red Cross Magazine* article 'Roll Call on the
Prairies' (D581).

1922

D583.   THE NOVEL DÉMEUBLÉ [essay]. (1) *New Republic*, 12 April 1922, supp., pp.5-6. (2) In *Modern Essays*, 2d series, ed. Christopher Morley (New York: Harcourt, Brace, 1924), pp.287-293. (3) In *Book of Modern Essays*, ed. Bruce W. McCullough, E. B. Burgum (New York: Scribner's, 1926), pp.391-395. (4) In *Facts and Ideas for Students of English Composition*, ed. John Owen Beaty et al. (New York: F. S. Crofts, 1931), pp.221-224. (5) *NUF*, pp.43-51. (6) *AE*, 12: 233-241. (7) *OW*, pp.33-43.

D584.   THE HOUSE ON CHARLES STREET. (1) *New York Evening Post*, 4 November 1922, literary review, pp.173-174. (2) *NUF*, pp.52-75. An extended essay incorporating the article, with the title '148 Charles Street'. (3) *AE*, 12: 243-263 (complete essay as in *NUF*).

D585.   [Book review of *Memoirs of a Hostess* (Mark A. DeWolfe Howe, from the diaries of Mrs. James Fields)]. (1) *Atlantic Bookshelf* 130 (December 1922). (2) In *Fact, Fancy and Opinion*, ed. R. M. Gay (Boston: Atlantic Monthly Press, 1923), pp.338-340.

1923

D586.   NEBRASKA: THE END OF THE FIRST CYCLE. (1) *Nation* 117 (5 September 1923): 236-238. In a series, 'These United States'. (2) In *These United States: A Symposium*, ed. Ernest Gruening (New York: Boni & Liveright, 1924), 2: 141-153. (3) In *Further Adventures in Essay Reading*, ed. T. E. Rankin et al. (New York: Harcourt, Brace, 1928), pp.65-76. (4) In *Modern Writing*, ed. W. and M. F. Thorp (New York: American Book Co., 1944), pp.121-129. (5) In *America Is West: An Anthology of Middlewestern Life and Literature*, ed. J. T. Flanagan (Minneapolis: University of Minnesota Press, 1945), pp.618-651. (6) In *Roundup: A Nebraska Reader*, ed. and comp. Virginia Faulkner (Lincoln: University of Nebraska Press, 1957), pp.1-8.

1927

D587.   A LETTER FROM WILLA CATHER [on *Death Comes for the Archbishop*] TO THE EDITOR OF *COMMONWEAL*. (1) *Commonweal* 7 (27 November 1927): 713. (2) *A Letter from Willa*

Cather (London: Heinemann, 1927), 4pp. A promotional booklet published by Heinemann to advertise the first English edition of *DCA*. Back cover: 'BOOKS BY WILLA CATHER | [*DCA, AT, YBM, OO, PH, ALL* listed]'. (3) *Willa Cather: A Biographical Sketch, an English Opinion.* . . . (New York: Knopf, 1933), pp.17-20; (1941), pp.16-19. (4) *OW*, pp.3-13. [See DD Appendix 2.]

D588. WILLA CATHER MOURNS OLD OPERA HOUSE [article]. (1) *Omaha World-Herald*, 27 October 1927, p.9. (2) *Nebraska History* 49 (Winter 1968). Title: 'The Incomparable Opera House' (note by Mildred R. Bennett). (3) *W&P*, pp.955-958.

1931

D589. MY FIRST NOVELS (THERE WERE TWO). (1) *Colophon*, part 6 (June 1931), [4pp.]. (2) *OW*, pp.89-97.

D590. A LETTER TO GOV. WILBUR CROSS. (1) *Saturday Review of Literature* 8 (17 October 1931): 216. In the "Points of View" section, headed ' "Shadows on the Rock" | A Letter by Willa Cather'. (2) *Willa Cather: A Biographical Sketch, an English Opinion.* . . . (New York: Knopf, 1933), pp.22-23; (1941), 21-22. See A16.b.i., c.i. (3) In *Designed for Reading*, ed. H. S. Canby et al. (New York: Macmillan, 1934), pp.596-598. (4) *OW*, pp.14-17.

1933

D591. A CHANCE MEETING [essay]. (1) *Atlantic Monthly* 151 (February 1933): 154-165. (2) *NUF*, pp.3-42. (3) *AE*, 12: 197-231.

1936

D592. ESCAPISM, A LETTER FROM WILLA CATHER. (1) *Commonweal* 23 (27 April 1936): 677-679. (2) *OW*, pp.18-29.

D593. THE BIRTH OF PERSONALITY: AN APPRECIATION OF THOMAS MANN'S TRILOGY. (1) *Saturday Review of Literature* 14 (6 June 1936): 3-4. (2) *NUF*, pp.96-122. Title: 'Joseph and His Brothers'. (3) *AE*, 12: 283-306.

1939

D594. CONTEMPORARY LIT. AGAIN. (1) *The News Letter of the College English Association* (Union College, Schenectady, N.Y.), December 1939, p.2. A letter to the editor containing her views on the teaching of literature.

1940

D595. LETTER ON *THE PROFESSOR'S HOUSE.* (1) *The News Letter of the College English Association* (Union College, Schenectady, N.Y.), October 1940, pp.2, 5. (2) *OW*, pp.30-32 (dated 12 December 1938). (3) In *The Eye of the Story*, by Eudora Welty (New York: Random House, 1977), p.49. Excerpted quote in the essay "The House of Willa Cather".

DD

Introductions, Prefaces, and Contributions to Books

DD1. [Introduction to "Four Years in the Schleusselburg Fortress," by I. P. Youvatshev]. *McClure's* 33 (August 1909): 399-400. Signed 'Editor'. A holograph manuscript is in the Colby College Library collection, signed by WC, with the added note, 'Sign the note either with my name or simply "editor," I dont care which—use whichever Mr. McClure thinks better.' See DDD8.

DD2. [Introduction to "The Secrets of the Schleusselburg: Chapters from the Secret History of Russia's Most Terrible Political Prison," by David Soskice]. *McClure's* 34 (December 1909): 144-145.

DD3. [Biographical sketch in *The Song of the Lark* prospectus]. ([Boston: HM Co., 1915]), pp.1-12. For a full description, see DD Appendix 1.

DD4. ON THE ART OF FICTION [essay]. (1) In *The Borzoi 1920* (New York: Knopf, 1920), pp.7-8. (2) *OW*, pp.99-104.

DD5. [Introduction to *The Fortunate Mistress*, by Daniel Defoe]. (New York: Knopf, 1924), pp.vii-xiii. (2) *OW*, pp.75-88.

DD6. KATHERINE MANSFIELD [essay]. (1) In *The Borzoi, 1925: Being a Sort of Record of Ten Years of Publishing* (New York: Knopf, 1925), pp.47-49. The book exists in 2 states: the first has WC's birth date corrected in ink by hand from 1867 to 1876 on p.246, l.7; the second has the line reset with the date

correctly printed 1876. (2) *NUF*, pp.123-147. Expanded and developed. (3) *AE*, 12: 307-328. (4) *OW*, pp.107-120.

DD7.   [Preface to *The Best Stories of Sarah Orne Jewett* (Boston: HM Co., 1925), pp.ix-xix]. (2) *Bookman* 6 (July 1925): 594-595 (review). (3) *NUF*, pp.76-95. Title: 'Miss Jewett'. A longer sketch using part of the Jewett story collection preface. (4) *OW*, pp.47-59. (5) In *The Country of the Pointed Firs and Other Stories*, by Sarah Orne Jewett (Garden City, N.Y.: Doubleday Anchor Books, 1956), pp.6-11.

DD8.   [Introduction to *The Wagnerian Romances*, by Gertrude (Hall) Brownell (New York: Knopf, 1925), pp.vii-x]. (2) *OW*, pp.60-66.

DD9.   [Introduction to *The Work of Stephen Crane*, vol.9, *Wounds in the Rain and Other Impressions of War* (New York: Knopf, 1926), ix-xiv]. (2) *OW*, pp.67-74.

DD10.   [Biographical sketch in *Willa Cather: A Biographical Sketch, an English Opinion, and an Abridged Bibliography* (New York: Knopf [1926]), pp.1-3]. (2) Same, reprinted and expanded (New York: Knopf [1933]), pp.1-3. (3) *Willa Cather: A Biographical Sketch, an English Opinion, an American Opinion, Reviews and Articles and an Abridged Bibliography* (New York: Knopf [1941]), pp.2-4. Also contains the letter on *Death Comes for the Archbishop* (D587) and 'Letter to Governor Wilbur Cross on *Shadows on the Rock*' (D590). For a full description, see DD Appendix 2.

DD11.   PORTRAIT OF THE PUBLISHER AS A YOUNG MAN. In *Alfred A. Knopf Quarter Century* (New York: Plimpton Press, 1940), pp.9-26.

DD Appendix 1

THE SONG OF THE LARK Prospectus, 1915

The Houghton Mifflin prospectus for *The Song of the Lark*, distributed before publication of the novel, is a 12-page booklet consisting of a single 6-leaf gathering stapled at the center fold and bound in heavy paper wrappers cut flush with the leaves.

150×87mm., edges trimmed. Cover lettering and decoration in dark green. The front cover reproduces the stylized silhouette of the Breton painting used on the dust jacket of the book; beneath: 'The story of a singer, her childhood | in the Colorado desert, her early | struggles in Chicago, her romantic | adventures among the ruins of the | Cliff Dwellers in Arizona, her splendid | triumphs on the operatic stage.' Back cover: 'THE SONG OF | THE LARK | *An American Novel by One* | *of the Younger Novelists* | WILLA SIBERT CATHER | [16-line story synopsis] || THE SONG OF THE LARK $1.40 *net.*' Inside front cover: '*English and American Opinions* | *of the Books of* | WILLA SIBERT CATHER | Author of "THE SONG OF THE LARK" || [6 review excerpts for *O Pioneers!*, 3 for *Alexander's Bridge*] || [price list for the 3 novels]'. Back cover: 'within a single-line border rule] OTHER NOVELS BY | WILLA SIBERT CATHER | [story synopses for *OP* and *AB*]'. Attached to the back cover is a postal order card for *SOL* and the other Cather titles. At the foot: 'Tear this card off, mail it now, and secure an early copy of "The Song of the Lark". Text title (p. 1): 'WILLA SIBERT CATHER | The Development of an | American Novelist'. There follows a 6-part biographical sketch with a photographic portrait at p. 3.

Ferris Greenslet, WC's Houghton Mifflin editor, wrote to her on 21 July 1915 outlining a plan to produce this booklet as part of the advertising campaign for *SOL*. He asked her to provide a 200–500-word story of her life. The literary history he proposed to write himself. On 26 July, Greenslet writes that he has received her copy for the biography section of the booklet (FG to WC, Houghton Mifflin archive, the Houghton Library, Harvard University).

DD Appendix 2

WILLA CATHER: A BIOGRAPHICAL SKETCH, AN ENGLISH OPINION, AND AN ABRIDGED BIBLIOGRAPHY, 1926

[cover title] WILLA CATHER | A Biographical Sketch | An English Opinion | and An Abridged | Bibliography | ALFRED A. KNOPF · *Publisher* · NEW YORK | [borzoi hound orn.]

Single gathering of 8 leaves (pp. 1-16), stapled at the center
fold. The Nicholas Muray portrait photograph reproduced on
the inside front cover. *Contents:* pp. 1-3: biographical sketch;
pp. 4-14: 'An | English Opinion | [star orn.] | WILLA
CATHER | *By* ALEXANDER PORTERFIELD*'; pp. 15-16:
bibliography ending with *My Mortal Enemy.* Cream laid paper,
horizontal chain lines 21mm. apart; watermarked 'Louvain
Book | [device]'. Leaves measure 200 x 130mm., edges trimmed.
Bound in heavy cream wove coated paper cut flush with the text
leaves.

Among Cather scholars, it is now fairly commonly known that
Willa Cather herself wrote the biographical sketch (as she did
the biographical sketch in the prospectus for *The Song of the Lark*
[DD Appendix 1]), although it is unsigned. David A. Randall,
in *New Paths in Book Collecting* (London: Constable, 1934), refers
to it "not as a minor piece of Catheriana, but as an authentic
first of considerable importance, as she wrote the *Sketch* herself."
The pamphlet was reprinted and expanded in 1933 with the
new title *Willa Cather: A Biographical Sketch, an English Opinion,
Reviews and Articles Concerning Her Later Books, and an Abridged
Bibliography.* This edition was the first to include her letter on
Death Comes for the Archbishop in *Commonweal* (D587) and 'Letter
to Gov. Wilbur Cross' (D590). A third edition in 1941 also
contains the 2 letters and has the extended title *Willa Cather: A
Biographical Sketch, an English Opinion, an American Opinion,
Reviews and Articles and an Abridged Bibliography.* The biographical sketch is textually the same in all 3 editions. Dating
of the pamphlets derives from the last listed title in the
bibliography of each.

DDD

Personal Letters, Statements, and Quotations, Printed or Reproduced

[This list does not include facsimile illustrations of manuscript material for sale or letters quoted in auction or dealers' catalogues.]

DDD1.   [Letter to Leonard Charles Van Noppen]. In *Vondel's Lucifer* (Greensboro, N.C.: Leonard C. Van Noppen, 1917), pp.441-442. Ten lines from a letter to Van Noppen written from Pittsburgh, 5 January 1899, subscribed in print 'Willa Cather'. Included in this advertising booklet for Van Noppen's translation from the Dutch of Joost van den Vondel's *Lucifer*. The book was published by the Continental Publishing Company, New York, 1898. $5.00, illustrated. This booklet is made up of excerpted letters about Van Noppen's translation. See also DDD6.

DDD2.   [Letter to 'My Dear Miss Olganova']. In *What Does Your Handwriting Reveal?*, by Nadya Olganova (New York: Grosset & Dunlap, 1929), p. 65. Full-page facsimile (reduced) of a letter written in thanks for an appreciation of *My Ántonia*, dated 21 March [1920], signed. On facing p.64 is an analysis of WC's handwriting.

DDD3.   [Letter to the Staff of the New York Public Library]. *New York Public Library Staff News* 18 (18 October 1928): 119. Used

in a campaign by the NYPL Staff Association for salary adjustments.

DDD4.   MISS WILLA CATHER ACCEPTS THE HOWELLS AWARD [Literary Exercises in the American Academy of Arts and Letters Auditorium, 14 November 1930]. *Proceedings of Ceremonies to Mark the Formal Opening of the New Building of the American Academy of Arts and Letters*, American Academy of Arts and Letters Publication no.75 (1931), pp.333-334. Willa Cather's acceptance speech.

DDD5.   [Letter to 'My Dear Miss Olganova' (excerpt)]. In *Handwriting Tells*, by Nadya Olganova (New York: Covici, Friede, 1936), p. 151. Facsimile (full size) in the text. The last 5 lines of the letter, signed. Incorporated in the printed analysis of WC's handwriting. See DDD2.

DDD6.   [Inscription to Howard Pyle; letter to Leonard Charles Van Noppen]. *The Colophon*, New Graphic Series 3 (September 1939):90, 92. Quoted in "The Crow's Nest" section. The inscription to Pyle, dated 26 April 1906, is in a copy of *The Troll Garden* presented to him by the author. The letter to Van Noppen (January 1900) concerns theatrical essays called 'The Player Letters', written by WC in 1899. She writes of sending the manuscript to Arthur Stedman in the hope that he may find a publisher for them. See DDD1.

DDD7.   'WHATEVER IS FELT UPON THE PAGE WITHOUT BEING SPECIFICALLY NAMED THERE—THAT, IT SEEMS TO ME, IS CREATED.' In *Form and Format: Abstract Design and Its Relation to Book Format*, by John Begg (Brooklyn, N.Y.: George McKibbin & Son, 1949), [p. 23]. Quoted from 'The Novel Démeublé' D583).

DDD8.   [Introduction to Youvatshev's "Four Years in the Schleusselburg Fortress"]. *Colby College Quarterly* 8, no.2 (June 1968):92. Facsimile of the final holograph MS page. First published in *McClure's* 33 (August 1909). See DD1.

DDD9.   [Letter to H. L. Mencken]. In *Mencken*, by Carl Bode (Carbondale: Southern Illinois University Press, 1969), p.184. 'I hope it is not too late to tell you how glad I am that you liked my book. I've tried to telephone you several times. . . .' This letter, dated 27 February 1925, is tipped into Mencken's copy of *PH*.

DDD10.   [70 quotes from Willa Cather's poetry, fiction, and essays]. In *Willa Cather: A Pictorial Memoir* (Lincoln: University of Nebraska Press, 1973). Photographs by Lucia Woods and others, text by Bernice Slote.

DDD11.   [3 quotes from Willa Cather's work]. In *Willa Cather: The Willa Cather Centennial Festival, 1873-1973* (Lincoln: The University of Nebraska, 1973). P.1: WC in an interview with Walter Tuttle, *Century*, July 1925; p.8: *SOL* (pp.276-277); inside back cover: "Nebraska: The End of the First Cycle," *Nation*, 5 September 1923.

DDD12.   WILLA CATHER'S TRIBUTE TO MARK TWAIN. *Mark Twain Journal* 17, no.1 (Winter 1973-1974), back cover. Photographic facsimile of a typed letter, signed, with authorial holograph corrections.

DDD13.   [Letters to Yehudi Menuhin]. In *Unfinished Journey*, by Yehudi Menuhin (New York: Knopf, 1977), pp.130, 145. Personal letters written to Menuhin in 1936.

DDD14.   [Letter on Milmine's *Life of Mary Baker G. Eddy*]. In *Mary Baker Eddy: The Years of Authority*, by Robert Peel (New York: Holt, Rinehart & Winston, 1977), p.472 n.29. Letter to Mrs. Genevive Richmond, dated 8 December 1933. See AAA1.

DDD15.   [11 quotes from Willa Cather's novels and stories]. In *Willa Cather's Red Cloud*, ed. and introd. Gabriel North Seymour (Salisbury, Conn.: Lime Rock Press, Inc., 1980). 100 copies, signed by the editor and photographer). With suite of photographs, ed., and introd. by Gabriel North Seymour. Text quotations are located in the first editions of the works: *O Pioneers!*: pp.64-65, 83-84.

My Ántonia: pp.74-75, 181-182, 190-191, 200-201, 250-251, 373-374.

The Professor's House: p.16.

Obscure Destinies: ('Old Mrs. Harris') pp.80-81, 98-99; ('Two Friends') pp.197-198.

Part Five

E

Translations of Novels and Stories into Foreign Languages

[This list of translations is not to be supposed exhaustive, although the standard sources have been searched to make it as extensive as possible where the volume has not been seen or reported. In most instances, names and titles in languages using another alphabet or ideographic symbols have been transliterated into roman. Where transliteration was not convenient, the English title in full is provided in brackets. Original titles of novels are identified by bracketed initials preceding the entry. Arrangement is chronological within language categories. Foreign publications of works in the original language follow in the EE and EEE sections.]

Arabic

E1. ['Paul's Case'] [*A Rainbow of Short Stories*]. Edited and translated by Abbas Mahmoud Akhad. Cairo: Akhbar, 1954.

E2. [*AB*] RAJUL WA IMRA'ATĀN. Translated by Fathī 'Abū-Rafī'ah. al-Qāhirah: al-Dār al-Qawmīyah, 1966.

Chinese

E3. [*DCA*] TSUNG CHU CHIAO CHIH SZŬ. Translated by Wang Ching Hsi. Hong Kong: Kowloon World Today Press, 1965.

E4. [OP] K'AI K'ÊN TI JÊN. Translated by Hsin-Mei Tong.
Taipei: Cheng Wên, 1967.

E5. [MA] WO TI AN TUNG NI YA. Translated by Su Hsüeh Yin.
Taiching: Tung Ha'i Pub. Ser., 1968.

E6. [ALL] SHIH CH'U TI MEI KUEI. Translated by Ch'ên Ts'ang
Tuo. Taipei: Cheng Wên, 1969.

E7. [OP] K'AI K'ÊN TI JÊN. Translated by Hsin-Mei Tong. Hong
Kong: World Today Press, 1975.

Czech

E8. [ALL] ZTRACENA. Translated by O. Vocadlo. Prague:
Aventinum, 1930.

E9. [DCA] SMRT SI JDE PRO ARCIBISKUPA. Translated by
Z. Wattersonová. Prague: Kvasnicka a Hampl, 1930.

E10. [SOR] STÍNY NA ÚSKALÍ. Translated by Alice Schiffová.
Prague: Vorový, 1932.

E11. [OD] FARMÁŘ ROSICKÝ. Translated by L. Weinfurterová.
Prague: F. Topič, 1933.

E12. [LG] LUCY GAYHEARTOVÁ. Translated by Marie Fantová.
Angloamerická knihovna Standard Library no. 34. Prague:
Nakladatelské družstovo Máje, 1936.

E13. [MME] MÔJ ÚHLAVNÝ NEPRIATEL. Translated by Helena
Corvagová. Trnava: Spolok sv. Vojecha, 1948.

E14. [MA] MOJE ANTONIE. Translated by Olga Fialová and
Emanuela Tilschová. Prague: Mladá fronta, 1966.

E15. [DCA] SMRT SI JDE PRO ARCIBISKUPA. Translated by
Z. Wattersonová. Prague: Vyšhrad, 1972.

E16. [PH] PROFESOROV DOM. Translated by Eduard Castiglione.
Bratislava: Tatran, 1972.

E17. [*MA*] MOJE ANTONIE. Translated by Olga Fialová and Emanuela Tilschová. Prague: Práce, 1975.

E18. [*LG*] LUCY GAYHEARTOVÁ. Translated by Elena Dzurillová. Bratislava: Smena, 1975.

E19. [*MA*] NÅSE TONIČKA. Translated by Karel Pelant. Prague: Simáček, n.d.

Danish

E20. [*PH*] PROFESSORENS HUS. Translated by Ingeborg Simesen. Copenhagen: Gyldendal, 1929.

E21. [*MA*] UNDERVEJS. Translated by Ingeborg Simesen. Copenhagen: Gyldendal, 1930.

E22. [*DCA*] DÖDEN HENTER AERKEBISKOPPEN. Translated by Ingeborg Simesen. Copenhagen: Gyldendal, 1934.

E23. [*SOR*] SKYGGER PAA KLIPPEN. Translated by Ingeborg Simesen. Copenhagen: Gyldendal, 1939.

E24. [*SSG*] SAPPHIRA. Translated by Ingeborg Simesen. Copenhagen: Gyldendal, 1941.

E25. [*LG*] LUCY GAYHEART. Translated by Ingeborg Simesen. Copenhagen: Gyldendal, 1945.

Dutch

E26. [*ALL*] EEN VERLOREN VROUWE. Translated by J. van Schaik-Willing. The Hague: H. P. Leopold, 1927.

E27. [*DCA*] DE STRIJD VAN DEN AARTSBISSCHOP. Translated by J. Boekman. Universeele bibliotheek, no. 3. Helmond: Drukkerij Helmond, 1937.

E28. [*PH*] HET HUIS VAN DEN PROFESSOR. Translated by G. Smit. The Hague: Ten Hagen, 1938.

E29.   [*LG*] LUCIE GAYHEART. Translated by M. S. F. Wibaut-
Bastert. Amsterdam: Wereldbibliotheek, 1953.

E30.   [*SOR*] SCHADUWEN OP DE ROTS! Translated by
J. W. Hofstra. Hasselt: Heideland, 1954.

E31.   [*DCA*] DE STRIJD VAN DE AARTSBISSCHOP. Translated by
M. van Loosdrecht. Hasselt: Heideland, 1954.

E32.   [*DCA*] DE STRIJD VAN DEN AARTSBISSCHOP. Translated
by M. van Loosdrecht. Utrecht: Het Spectrum, 1955.

E33.   [*SOR*] SCHADUWEN OP DE ROTS. Translated by
J. W. Hofstra. Heemstede: Hofboekerij, 1955.

E34.   [*MA*] MIJN ANTONIA. Translated by J. Wagener-Schilperoot.
Antwerp: J. van Tuyl, 1958.

E35.   [*AB*] ALEXANDERS BRUG. Translated by M. G. Binnendijk-
Paauw. Amsterdam: Querido, 1963.

Finnish

E36.   [*MA*] ANTONIA YSTÄVÄNI. Translated by Leena Karro.
Helsinki: Werner Söderström, 1940; 1963.

E37.   [*PH*] PROFESSORIN TALO. Translated by Alex Matson.
Helsinki: Tammi, 1950.

E38.   [*DCA*] KUOLEMA NOUTAA ARKKIPIISPAN. Translated by
Sirkka-Liisa Norko-Turja. Helsinki: Werner Söderström, 1955.

French

E39.   [*MA*] MON ANTONIA. Translated by Victor Llona. Paris:
Payot, 1924.

E40.   ['Coming, Aphrodite'] PROCHAINEMENT APHRODITE.
Translated by Victor Llona. Les cahiers nouveaux, no. 12. Paris:
Éditions du Saggittaire, 1925. The frontispiece is a reduced

facsimile of the original holograph MS of 'Coming, Aphrodite!' ('Coming, Eden Bower!').

E41. [*SOR*] LES OMBRES SUR LE ROCHER. Translated by Maurice Rémon. Paris: Hachette, 1933.

E42. [*MME*] MON ENNEMI MORTEL. Translated by J. Balay and J. E. Burton. Paris: Les Oeuvres Libres, 1935.

E43. [*DCA*] LA MORT ET L'ARCHEVÊQUE. Translated by M. C. Carel. Paris: Editions Stock (Delamain et Boutelleau), 1940.

E44. [*ALL*] UNE DAME PERDU. Translated by Hélène Malvan. Paris: La Nouvelle Edition, 1944; 1947. Bibliothèque Américaine.

E45. [*MA*] MON AMI ANTONIA. Translated by Blaise Allan. Vent d'ouest, vol. 22. Paris: Seghers, 1967.

German

E46. [*MA*] ANTONIA. Translated by Walter Schumann. Stuttgart: Engelhorn, 1928.

E47. [*OO*] EINER VON UNS. Translated by Marielis Mauk. Freiburg, 1928.

E48. [*ALL*] FRAU IM ZWEILICHT. Translated by Magda Kahn. Freiburg: Urban, 1929.

E49. [*DCA*] DER TOD KOMMT ZUM ERZBISCHOF. Translated by Sigismund von Radecki. Stuttgart, 1940. *Note*: This edition was burned by the Nazis, and the plates were destroyed. The translator carried carbon sheets of his translation into Switzerland concealed under the lining of 2 suitcases. The edition that follows (E50) was subsequently published in Zurich.

E50. [*DCA*] DER TOD KOMMT ZUM ERZBISCHOF. Translated by Sigismund von Radecki. Zurich: Scientia AG., 1940; 1942.

E51.   [OP] NEUE ERDE. Translated by Augusta V. Bronner. Vienna: Amandus-Editions, 1945; 1946.

E52.   [MA] MEINE ANTONIA. Translated by Walter Schumann. Stuttgart: Engelhornverl Ad. Spemann, 1948.

E53.   [OP] ZWEI FRAUEN. Translated by Wolf and Ursula Hermann. Bremen: Johs. Storm, 1948.

E54.   [DCA] DER TOD KOMMT ZUM ERZBISCHOF. Translated by Sigismund von Radecki. Ullstein Buch, no.91. Frankfort: Das Goldene Vlies, 1955.

E55.   [SSG] SAPHIRA. Translated by Elisabeth Schnack. Zurich and Cologne: Benziger, 1955.

E56.   [SOR] SCHATTEN AUF DEM FELS. Translated by Elisabeth Schnack. Zurich and Cologne: Benziger, 1956.

E57.   [DCA] DER TOD KOMMT ZUM ERZBISCHOF. Translated by Sigismund von Radecki. Zurich and Cologne: Benziger, 1956; 1957.

E58.   [LG] LUCY GAYHEART. Translated by Elisabeth Schnack. Zurich and Cologne: Benziger, 1957.

E59.   [ALL] DIE FRAU, DIE SICH VERLOR. Translated by Magda Kahn. Zurich and Cologne: Benziger, 1958.

E60.   [MA] MEINE ANTONIA. Translated by Walter Schumann. Basel: Herder, 1959.

E61.   [PH] DAS HAUS DES PROFESSORS. Translated by Elisabeth Schnack. Zurich and Cologne: Benziger, 1959; 1961.

E62.   [LG] LUCY GAYHEART. Translated by Elisabeth Schnack. Vienna: Deutsche Buchgemeinschaft, 1960.

E63.   [MA] MEINE ANTONIA. Translated by Walter Schumann. Zurich and Cologne: Benziger, 1960.

E64. [*MA*] MEINE ANTONIA. Translated by Walter Schumann. Freiburg: Herder, 1961.

E65. [*MME*] EINE ALTE GESCHICHTE. Translated by Elisabeth Schnack. Zurich and Cologne: Benziger, 1961.

E66. [*ALL*] DIE FRAU, DIE SICH VERLOR. Translated by Magda Kahn. Frankfort: Fischer-Bücherei, 1962.

E67. [*MA*] MEINE ANTONIA. Translated by Walter Schumann. Zurich: Buchclub Ex Libris, 1963.

E68. [*OD, YBM, OB*] VOR DEM FRÜHSTÜCK. Translated by Elisabeth Schnack. Zurich and Cologne: Benziger, 1963.

E69. [*AB*] TRAUM VERGANGENER ZEIT. Translated by Elisabeth Schnack. Zurich and Cologne: Benziger, 1964.

E70. [*LG*] AUF EINER GOLDENEN WOLKE. Translated by Elisabeth Schnack. Munich: Goldman, 1964.

E71. [*MA*] MEINE ANTONIA. Translated by Walter Schumann. Munich: Goldmann, 1968.

Greek

E72. [*MA*] I ANTONIA MOU. Translated by V. Damianakon. Athens: Icaros, 1954.

E73. [*DCA*] O EPISKOPOS TOU SANTA FE. Translated by D. Oikonomides. Athens: Ekdoseis, 1956.

E74. [*DCA*] O EPISKOPOS TOU SANTA FE. Translated by D. Oikonomides. Athens: Atlantis, 1964.

Hebrew

E75. [*MA*] ANTONIA SHE-LI. Translated by Amihudi Arbel. Tel Aviv: Am-oved, 1948; 1953; 1955.

E76. [MA] ANTONIA SHELI. Translated by Amihudi Arbel. Haifa: Moazat Poalim, 1957; 1959.

Hungarian

E77. [ALL] AZ ARANYSHINÜ DÓM. Translated by Kázmér Pogány. Budapest: Szt. István társ., 1934.

E78. [SOR] ARNYÉKOK A SZIKLÁN. Translated by Iván Boldizsár. Budapest: Franklin, 1936.

E79. [MA] AZ ÉN ANTÓNIÁM. Translated by Arpád Göncz. Budapest: Europa Kíadó, 1968.

Icelandic

E80. [MA] HÚN ANTÓNIÁ MÍN. Translated by Friorik A. Friorikson. Reykjavik: Almenna bókafélagio, 1965.

Indian and Pakistani Languages

E81. [OP] AGRAGAMI [Hindi]. Translator anonymous. New Delhi: Adhunik Sahitya prakasan, 1955.

E82. [OP] RE AGRAGAMI [Gujarati]. Translator anonymous. Bombay: Nutan Sahitya prakashan, 1956.

E83. [DCA] MANJUPEYYUNA RATRIKAL [Malayalam]. Translated by Joseph Mathan. Ernakulam: Book-a-Month Club, 1957.

E84. [DCA] MARAN MADHURI [Bengali]. Translated by Abdul Bashan. Dacca: M.M.Ali, 1957.

E85. [DCA] DEVACHIN MANSEN [Marathi]. Translated by Vijay Dhondopont. Bombay: G.P.Parchure, 1958.

E86. [MA] [My Ántonia] [Bengali]. Translated by Shahid Akhand and Golam Quadir. Dacca: Leman & Co., 1959.

E87. [OP] [O Pioneers!] [Bengali]. Translated by A. Mateen. Dacca: Purbachal Prakashani, 1959.

E88. [MA] [My Ántonia] [Urdu]. Translated by Qaisi Rampuri. Lahore: Lark Publisher, 1960.

E89. [DCA] ARCH BISHOPER MRITYU [Bengali]. Translated by Bhavani Mukherji. Calcutta: M. C. Sankan, 1961.

E90. [OD] BHAVITAVYA [Bengali]. Translated by Bhavani Mukherji. Calcutta: M. C. Sankan, 1961.

E91. [DCA] PARINIRVAN [Gujarati]. Translated by Harindra Dave. Ahmedabad: Ravani Prakašan Griha, 1962.

E92. [OD] SUNDAR JIVANA ITHEN LABHLEN [Marathi]. Translated by D. K. Hasabnis. Amraoti: Nagvidarbha Prakasan, 1962.

E93. [OB] SEI BRIDDHARUPASI [Bengali]. Translated by Ranu Bhavmilc. Calcutta: Asia Pub. Co., 1963.

E94. [OD] BHABITABYA [Oriya]. Translated by Sachidananda Rautaray. Cuttack: Rashtrabhasa pustak bhandan, 1963.

E95. [DCA] ARCCUBISPPINTO ANTYAM [Malayalam]. Translated by K. Narayana Pilla. Kottayam: Manorama, 1963.

E96. [OD] CHARAN RUKE TYAM [Gujarati]. Translated by Harindra Dave. Ahmedabad: Ranvani Prakasan, 1964.

E97. [MA] PREMIKA [Hindi]. Translated by Syamu Sannyasi. Delhi: Rajpal & Sons, 1966.

E98. [MA] PREMAKA [Panjabi]. Translated by Ajit Kaur. Jullundur: Asian Publishers, 1967.

E99. [OD] AJNATAJIVITANGAL [Malayalam]. Translated by E. K. Purushottaman. Kozhikoda: Nava Kerala, 1967.

E100. [*MA*] MAJHI SAKHI [Marathi]. Translated by Vidyadhar Pundalik. Bombay: Majestic, 1969.

Italian

E101. [*DCA* selection] ['Le visite d'un vicario apostolico'] Translated by Igino Giordani. In *Contemporanei nord-americani*, Pagine Christiane, vol. 10. Turin: Società Editrice Internazionale, 1930.

E102. [*SOR*] OMBRE SULLA ROCCA. Translated by Gino de Negri. Il Grappolo: Collana di Romanzi, no. 1. Milan: Instituto de Propaganda libraria, 1935; 1956; 1970.

E103. [*DCA*] LA MORTE VIENE PER L'ARCIVESCOVO. Translated by Alessandro Scalero. Milan: A. Mondadori, 1936; 1956.

E104. [*MME*] IL MIO NEMICO MORTALE: Translated 'a curia di Livia Agnini'. Milan: Jandi Sapi, 1944. Pirated edition.

E105. [*MME*] IL MIO MORTALE NEMICO. Translated by Arnoldo Maria Gallone. Medusa, vol. 177. Milan: A. Mondadori, 1946.

E106. [*MA*] LA MIA ANTONIA. Translated by Gabriele Baldini. La Gaja scienza, nuova series, vol. 24. Milan: Longahesi, 1947.

E107. [*MA*] LA MIA ANTONIA. Translated by Pinna Pintor. Turin: Einaude, 1947.

E108. [*PH*] LA CASA DEL PROFESSORE. Translated by Fluffy Mella Mazzuccato. Milan: A. Mondadori, 1950.

E109. [*OP*] IL GELSO BIANCO. Translated by Arjo. Turin: Soc. Apost. Stampa, 1953.

E110. [*OO*] UNO DEI NOSTRI. Translated by "A. Ph." Milan: A. Mondadori, 1955.

E111. [*OD*] DESTINI OSCURI. Translated by Fluffy Mella Mazzuccato. Milan: A. Mondadori, 1956.

E112.   [*MA*] LA MIA ANTONIA. Translated by Jole Jannelli and Pinna Pintor. Milan: A. Mondadori, 1959.

E113.   [*MME*] IL MIO MORTALE NEMICO. Translated by A. M. Gallone. Milan:A. Mondadori, 1974.

Japanese

E114.   [*LG*] WAKARE NO UTA. Translated by Naotaro Tatsunokuchi. Tokyo: Shincho-sha, 1940.

E115.   [*LG, ALL*] AI NO TASOGORE / MAYOERU ONNA. Translated by Yoshizo Nakamura. Complete Collection of American Fiction, vol.9. Tokyo: Mikasa shobô, 1940. Title for *ALL* is 'Mayoeru Onna.' Pirated edition.

E116.   [*SSG*] SAFAIRA TO DOREI-MUSUME. Translated by Yaichiro Takano. Tokyo: Taikando, 1941. Pirated edition.

E117.   ['Neighbour Rosicky']. RINJIN ROSSICKY. Translated by Samburo Yamaya. Tokyo: Modan Nihon-sha, 1941.

E118.   [*OD*] SACHI USUKU TOMO. Translated by Hoitsu Miyanishi. Tokyo: Shoshin-sha, 1942.

E119.   [*LG*] WAKARE NO UTA. Translated by N. Tatsunokuchi. Tokyo: Mikasa shobô, 1949; 1951; 1953.

E120.   [*OP*] O KAITAKUSHA YO! Translated by Seikei Okamoto. Tokyo: Kaizô-sha, 1950.

E121.   [*MA*] WATASHI NO ANTONIA. Translated by Masajirô Hamada. Tokyo: Kawade shobô, 1951.

E122.   [*LG*] AI NO TASOGARE. Translated by Y. Nakamura. Tokyo: Kawade shobô, 1955.

E123.   [*LG*] WAKARE NO UTA. Translated by N. Tatsunokuchi. Tokyo: Kadokawa shoten, 1955.

E124.   ['Paul's Case', 'Scandal'] PAUL NO BAAI / WARUI UWASA.
        Translated by Yukio Kobayashi, Masajiro Hamada. Tokyo:
        Eihô-sha, 1956.

E125.   [ALL] SAMAYOU ONNA. Translated by Noboyuki Hayashi.
        Tokyo: Dabiddo-sha, 1956.

E126.   [ALL] MAYOERU FUJIN. Translated by Keiko Kuriyagawa.
        Tokyo: Kenkyû-sha, 1957.

E127.   [DCA, ALL, OP] SHI O MUKAERU DAISHIKYÔ.
        Translated by Karita Motoshi et al. Gendai Amerika Bungaku
        Zenshû, no.2. Tokyo: Kôchi Shuppan-sha, 1957; 1967.

E128.   ['The Enchanted Bluff'] MA NO ZEPPEKI. Translated by
        Tetsuo Shinjô. Tokyo Shin'ei-sha, 1957.

E129.   [OD] ROSICKY TÔSAN / TORTILLA-DAIRA. Translated by
        Fumi Takano. Tokyo: Nan'un-dô, 1959. 'Neighbour Rosicky'
        with Steinbeck's Tortilla Flat.

E130.   ['Neighbour Rosicky', 'A Wagner Matinée', 'Old Mrs. Harris']
        ROSICKY TÔSAN. Translated by Isuzu Tanabe and Fumi
        Takano. Tokyo: Nan'un-do, 1960.

E131.   [MME] MY MORTAL ENEMY. Translated by Y. Deguchi and
        S. Tadokoro. Tokyo: Seibido, 1960.

E132.   [PH] THE PROFESSOR'S HOUSE. Translated by M. Kasai and
        Y. Itatsu. Tokyo: Seibido, 1962.

E133.   [LG] WAKARE NO UTA. Translated by Kameyama Tatsuki.
        Tokyo: Kodan-sha, 1966.

E134.   [MA] WATASHI NO ANTONIA. Translated by Kameyama
        Tatsuki. Tokyo: Kodan-sha, 1967.

E135.   [PH] KYÔJU NO EI. Translated by Masahide Ando. Tokyo:
        Eihô-sha, 1974.

E136. ['Paul's Case', 'Neighbour Rosicky'] PAUL NO BAAI / RINJIN
ROSSICKY. Translated by Masami Nishikawa. Tokyo: Kenjyu-
sha, 1977.

Korean

E137. [*DCA*] BULMYEOLEUI SINANG. Translated by Eul'yu'
Mun'hawa'sa. Seoul: Bong Sik Kang & Yo Seob Ju, 1957.

E138. [*MA*] SIGOL CHEONYEO. Translated by Eul'yu'
Mun'hawa'sa. Seoul: Bong Sik Kang & Yo Seob Ju, 1957.

E139. [*MA, DCA*] NA EUI ANTONIA / DAEJUGYOEUJUKEUM.
Translated by Eul'yu' Mun'hawa'sa. Seoul: Bong Sik Kang & Yo
Seob Ju, 1960; 1961.

Norwegian

E140. [*LG*] LUCY GAYHEART. Translated by Signe Undset Thomas.
Oslo: H. Aschehoug & Co., 1936.

E141. [*DCA*] DØDEN HENTER ERKEBISKOPEN. Translated by
Margarethe Kjaer. Oslo: Gyldendal, 1940.

E142. [*MA*] MIN ANTONIA. Oslo: Aschehoug, 1954.

Persian

E143. [*MA*] [*My Ántonia*]. Translated by P. Daryoush. Teheran: Amir
Kabir, 1956.

Polish

E144. [*DCA*] ŚMIERĆ PRZYCHODZI PO ARCYBISKUPA.
Translated by Hanna Malewska. Paris: Wyd. świgtego
Antoniego, 1957.

E145. [*PH*] DOM PANA PROFESORA. Translated by Aleksandra
Frybesowa. Warsaw: Państwowy Instytut Wydawniczy, 1959;
1961; 1965.

E146. [*YBM, OB*, et al.] PORANEK WAGNEROWSKI. Translated by Zofia Siwicka. Warsaw: Czytelnik, 1971.

E147. [*MME*] MÓJ SMIERTELNY WRÓG. Translated by Ariadna Demkowska-Bohdziewicz. Warsaw: Państwowy Instytut Wydawniczy, 1974.

E148. [*ALL*] UTRACONA. Translated by Ariadna Demkowska-Bhodziewicz. Warsaw: Skiaźka i Wiedza, 1976.

E149. [*OP*] DRZEWO BAILEJ MORWY. Translated by Ariadna Demkowska-Bhodziewicz. Warsaw: Skiaźka i Wiedza, 1977.

Portuguese

E150. [*SSG*] SAFIRA E A ESCRAVA. Translated by Miroel Silveira. Pôrto Alegre: Livraria do globo, 1943.

E151. [*OP*] PIONEIROS. Translated by Jorge Cardoso Avres. Rio de Janeiro: Revista Branca, 1953.

E152. [*DCA*] A MORTE DO ARCEBISPO. Translated by Licia de Sonza. Rio de Janeiro: 1955.

E153. [*MA*] MINHA ANTÓNIA. Translated by Bernard Gersen. Rio de Janeiro: Civilização Brasileira, 1956.

E154. ['Paul's Case'] O CASA DE PAULO. Translated by Becker Taliaferro Washington. São Paulo: Cultrix, 1957.

E155. ['Coming, Aphrodite!'] Translator anonymous. AI VEM AFRODITE! Lisbon: Ed. Originazações, 1957.

E156. [*OD*] DESTINOS OBSCUROS. Translated by Olivia de Krâhenbühl. São Paulo: Cultrix, 1965.

E157. [*DCA*] A MORTE VEM BUSCAR O ARCEBISPO. São Paulo: Cultrix, 1968.

Romanian

E158. [*MA*] ANTONIA MEA. Translated by Vera Berceanu and Cezar Radu. Bucharest: Univers., 1971.

E159. ['On the Divide'] Translator anonymous. [Fifteen stories from *Collected Short Fiction, 1892-1912*]. Bucharest, 1979.

Russian

E160. ['A Chance Meeting'] MADAM GRU. Translated by Ye. Tselikov. Leningrad: Dnei, 1935.

E161. [*MA*] MOJA ANTONĪJA. Translated by V. S. Janovskij. New York: Chekhov Pub. House, 1952.

E162. ['The Sculptor's Funeral'] POHORONĬ SKYL'PTORA. Translated by N. Daruzes. Moscow: Goslitizdat, 1958.

Serbo-Croatian / Slovene

E163. [*DCA*] ŠKOF NOVE MEHIKE. Translated by Anton Anžič. Ljubljana: Založila Družba, 1936.

E164. [*LG*] LUCY GAYHEARTOVÁ. Translated by K. Müllera. Belgrade: Nakladatelské Družstovo máje, 1946.

E165. [*MA*] MOJA ANTONIJA. Translated by Tadija Gavrilović. Montenegro: Narodna knjiga, 1956.

E166. [*MA*] MOJA ANTONIJA. Translated by Sonja Cuderman and Nada Dobravec. Ljubljana: Državna založba Slovenije, 1964.

Spanish

E167. [*ALL*] UNA DAMA PERDÎDA. Translated by Léon Felipe [pseud.]. Nuevo Mundo, 1942.

E168. [*MA*] MI ANTONIA. Translated by Julio Fernández Yáñez Gimeno. Barcelona: Caralt, 1955.

E169. [DCA] LA MUERTE VIENE HACIA EL ARZOBISPO. Translated by Horace Laurora. Buenos Aires: Emecé Editores, 1944.

E170. [OP] LOS COLONOS. Translated by Antonio Guardiola. Barcelona: Caralt, 1955.

E171. [PH] LA CASA DEL PROFESSOR. Translated by Guillermo A. Maxwell. Buenos Aires: Alboreal, 1963.

Swedish

E172. [OP] HELL, BANBRYTARE! Translated by Hildegard Wieselgren. Stockholm: C. E. Fritzes, 1919.

E173. [SOL] LÄRKSÅNGEN. Translated by Hildegard Wieselgren. Stockholm: C. E. Fritzes, 1920.

E174. [ALL] ETT FÖRLORAT IDEAL. Translated by Sigrid Gustafson. Stockholm: P. A. Norstedt, 1924.

E175. [PH] PROFESSORNS HEM. Translated by Jenny Jusélius. Stockholm: Hugo Gebers, 1927.

E176. [LG] AV ALLT DITT HJÄRTA. Translated by Siri Thorngren Olin. Stockholm: Hugo Gebers, 1936.

E177. [DCA] LANDET LÅNGT BORTA. Translated by Siri Thorngren Olin. Stockholm: H. Gebers, 1938.

E178. [MA] MIN ANTONIA. Translated by Aslög Davidsson. Stockholm: H. Gebers, 1939.

E179. [SOR] SKUGGOR ÖVER KLIPPEN. Translated by Siri Thorngren Olin. Stockholm: H. Gebers, 1940.

E180. [SSG] SAPPHIRA OCH SLAVINNAN. Translated by Siri Thorngren Olin. Stockholm: H. Gebers, 1941.

E181. [OP] BANBRYTARE. Translated by Hildegard Wieselgren. Stockholm: Saxon & Lindströms, 1943.

E182.   [OP] O PIONJÄRER! Translated by Hildegard Wieselgren. Stockholm: Folket i Bild, Seelig & Co., 1948.

E183.   [OB] DE BÄSTA ÄREN OCH ANDRA NOVELLER. Translated by Nils Jacobssen. Stockholm: H. Gebers, 1950.

E184.   [MA] MIN ANTONIA. Translated by Aslög Davidsson. Stockholm: Folket i Bild, 1959.

Thai

E185.   [MA] NONG NANG BAN RAI. Translated by Pava Watanasup. Bangkok: Thai Library Association, 1972.

Turkish

E186.   [PH] BIR HANIMEFENDI. Translated by Haldun Derin. Istanbul: Nebioglu Yayineva, 1959.

Vietnamese

E187.   [DCA] DUÕC THIÊNG TRONG SA-MAC. Translated by Lê Bá-Kông. Saigon: Ziên-Höng, 1959.

EE

Tauchnitz Editions

[The Tauchnitz Edition Collection of British and American Authors, published by Bernhard Tauchnitz in Leipzig, printed new editions in English in cheap paperback format. These volumes were intended for sale on the European continent only and were not to be introduced into the British Empire or America.]

EE1. THE PROFESSOR'S HOUSE. No.4716. 1926.

EE2. MY MORTAL ENEMY. No.471. 1927.

EE3. A LOST LADY. No.4781. 1927.

EE4. TOM OUTLAND'S STORY. Edited by Albert Eichler. Student Series, n.s. no.30. Leipzig, 1930. *Note:* This is the first separate edition in English of the middle section of *The Professor's House.*

EE5. DEATH COMES FOR THE ARCHBISHOP. No.4809. 1931.

EE6. SHADOWS ON THE ROCK. No.5082. 1933.

EE7. OBSCURE DESTINIES. No.5108. 1933.

EE8. MY ÁNTONIA. No.5194. 1935.

EEE

Foreign Editions in English and Piracies

[These editions, in the language of original publication, are listed chronologically by country. The piracies from Taiwan are crudely produced by photographic process from the original American editions.]

China (Taiwan)

EEE1. [*MA*] MY ANTONIA. Taipei: Shuang Yeh Shu-tian, 1978. A Taiwanese piracy of the Riverside Press edition.

EEE2. [*DCA*] DEATH COMES FOR THE ARCHBISHOP. Taipei: Shuang Yeh Shu-tian, 1979. A Taiwanese piracy of the Knopf trade edition.

Germany

EEE3. ['Neighbour Rosicky'] NEIGHBOUR ROSICKY. Berlin: Velhagen & Klasing [1958].

EEE4. ['Paul's Case'] PAUL'S CASE. Edited by Karl Schlenk. Brunswick: Georg Westermann, 1963.

Japan

EEE5. [*OB*] THE OLD BEAUTY. Edited by Nobuyuki Hayashi. Tokyo: Gakusei-sha, 1948; 1961.

EEE6. ['The Sculptor's Funeral', 'Paul's Case']. Edited by Hikaru Saitô. Tokyo; Nan'undo, 1956.

EEE7. [PH] THE PROFESSOR'S HOUSE. Edited by M. Kasai and Y. Itatsu. Tokyo: Seibido, 1962.

EEE8. ['Old Mrs. Harris'] OLD MRS. HARRIS. Edited by Kiyoshi Okui. Tokyo: Shimizu Shoin, 1967.

EEE9. ['The Best Years'] THE BEST YEARS. Edited by Yayoi Toyama. Tokyo: Kenjyû-sha, 1967.

EEE10. ['The Enchanted Bluff'] JEWETT, CATHER, AND PORTER. Edited by Kenzo Sakai and Naoko Ouchi. Tokyo: Eihô-sha, 1970.

EEE11. ['A Singer's Romance', 'The Affair at Grover Station', 'The Sculptor's Funeral']. Edited by Katsugi Takaura and Haruma Okada. Tokyo: Kinseido Ltd., 1971.

EEE12. [ALL] A LOST LADY. Edited by Tadamasa Shima. Tokyo: Hokuseido, 1974.

EEE13. ['The Sculptor's Funeral', 'Scandal', 'Coming, Aphrodite'] WILLA CATHER'S THREE STORIES. Edited by Tatsuo Yamaguchi and Hiroko Sato. Tokyo: Bunri Co., 1979.

The Netherlands

EEE14. [PH] ['Tom Outland's Story']. Edited by A. G. van Kranendonk. Groningen: New English Library, 1937.

Part Six

F

Large-Type Books

F1. MY ÁNTONIA. 2 vols. National Aid to the Visually Handicapped, 1949. Spiral. NAVH is a nonprofit agency that does not sell its books, but seeks reimbursement, where possible, at $5.00 per volume.

F2. MY ÁNTONIA. New York: Keith Jennison Books, Franklin Watts, Inc., [1966].

F3. O PIONEERS! New York: Keith Jennison Books, Franklin Watts, Inc., [1966].

F4. THE SONG OF THE LARK. New York: Keith Jennison Books, Franklin Watts, Inc., [1966].

G

Books for the Blind (Braille and Moon Type)

[Braille grade 1 1/2 contains 44 contractions; grade 2 contains 185 contractions and is standard English braille. The Moon system of embossed type, developed by an Englishman, Dr. William Moon (1818-1894), is easier to learn than braille, but requires more space. It is less frequently used in the United States.]

G1. APRIL TWILIGHTS AND OTHER POEMS. Grade 1 1/2, hand-copied.

G2. DEATH COMES FOR THE ARCHBISHOP. 3 vols. Grade 2, press braille.

G3. DEATH COMES FOR THE ARCHBISHOP. 5 vols. Moon.

G4. EARLY STORIES. Selected and with commentary by Mildred R. Bennett. 5 vols. Grade 2, hand-copied.

G5. FIVE STORIES. With an article by George N. Kates on Cather's last, unfinished, and unpublished Avignon story. 4 vols. Grade 2, hand-copied.

G6. "FRIENDS OF CHILDHOOD" (*The Song of the Lark*). 2 vols. Grade 1 1/2, press braille.

G7. "KRONBORG" (*The Song of the Lark*). Grade 1 1/2, press braille.

G8.   A LOST LADY. 4 vols. Grade 1 1/2, hand-copied.

G9.   LUCY GAYHEART. 2 vols. Grade 2, press braille.

G10.   MY ÁNTONIA. 3 vols. Grade 2, press braille.

G11.   MY ÁNTONIA. 6 vols. Moon.

G12.   MY MORTAL ENEMY. 2 vols. Grade 1 1/2, hand-copied.

G13.   "NEIGHBOUR ROSICKY" (*Obscure Destinies*). Grade 1 1/2, hand-copied.

G14.   NOT UNDER FORTY. 2 vols. Grade 1 1/2, hand-copied.

G15.   O PIONEERS! 2 vols. Grade 1 1/2, press braille.

G16.   O PIONEERS! 2 vols. Grade 2, press braille.

G17.   OBSCURE DESTINIES. 3 vols. Grade 1 1/2, hand-copied.

G18.   OBSCURE DESTINIES. 3 vols. Grade 2, hand-copied.

G19.   THE OLD BEAUTY AND OTHERS. Grade 2, hand-copied.

G20.   ON WRITING. 2 vols. Grade 2, hand-copied.

G21.   ONE OF OURS. 4 vols. Grade 1 1/2, hand-copied.

G22.   ONE OF OURS. 4 vols. Grade 2, hand-copied.

G23.   THE PROFESSOR'S HOUSE. 5 vols. Grade 1 1/2, hand-copied.

G24.   THE PROFESSOR'S HOUSE. 4 vols. Grade 2, hand-copied.

G25.   SAPPHIRA AND THE SLAVE GIRL. 2 vols. Grade 2, press braille.

G26.   SHADOWS ON THE ROCK. 2 vols. Grade 1 1/2, press braille.

G27.   SHADOWS ON THE ROCK. 4 vols. Grade 2, hand-copied.

G28.   THE SONG OF THE LARK. 5 vols. Grade 1 1/2, press braille.

G29.   THE SONG OF THE LARK. 9 vols. Grade 2, hand-copied.

G30.   THE TROLL GARDEN. 3 vols. Grade 2, hand-copied.

G31.   "TWO FRIENDS" (*Obscure Destinies*). Grade 1 1/2, hand-copied.

G32.   YOUTH AND THE BRIGHT MEDUSA. 2 vols. Grade 1 1/2, hand-copied.

Note: Titles may be requested by readers with qualifying visual handicaps from regional and subregional network libraries of the National Library Service for the Blind and Physically Handicapped. Their complete list of books and pamphlets in braille or recorded form is available in *Reading Materials for the Blind and Physically Handicapped*, a microfiche catalog issued quarterly. Information on these materials was kindly supplied by Frank Kurt Cylke, director, National Library Service for the Blind and Physically Handicapped, Library of Congress, Washington, D.C.

Cather titles are also available in Braille editions produced by the Iowa Commission for the Blind (*Obscure Destinies*, *My Mortal Enemy*, *On Writing*, *The Professor's House*, *Sapphira and the Slave Girl*, and *The Song of the Lark*); the Woodside Terrace Kiwanis Braille Project, Hillsborough, Calif. (*A Lost Lady*); Child Service Center, Portland, Ore. (*My Ántonia*); IHB Braille Library, West Hempstead, New York (*Shadows on the Rock*); and Philadelphia Regional Library (*The Song of the Lark*).

H

Books for the Blind (Recorded)

Abbreviations

CB Cassette book; 2-track 1 7/8 i.p.s. cassettes (commercial speed)

MT Magnetic tape (limited edition); 3 3/4 i.p.s. open-reel tapes. NLS ceased production of MTs in 1970. Network libraries no longer provide playback equipment for these tapes, but readers can play them on machines commercially available.

NLS National Library Service for the Blind and Physically Handicapped, Library of Congress, Washington, D.C.

RC Recorded cassette; 4-track 15/16 i.p.s. cassette tapes requiring special playback equipment available only to readers with qualifying visual or physical handicap through NLS.

TB Talking book; discs recorded at 16 r.p.m.

TB33 1/3 Talking book 33 1/3 r.p.m. disc recordings, limited edition. NLS ceased production in 1963.

["Talking Books," recorded for the blind, are produced by the NLS and are available through the Library of Congress and regional libraries.]

H1. DEATH COMES FOR THE ARCHBISHOP. Read by Alexander Scourby, 1948. 20 records. TB33 1/3. NLS.

H2. DEATH COMES FOR THE ARCHBISHOP. Read by Donald Madden, 1959. 10 sides, 10-inch, 16 r.p.m. TB1247. NLS.

H3. DEATH COMES FOR THE ARCHBISHOP. RC. In process. NLS.

H4. DEATH COMES FOR THE ARCHBISHOP. RC. Recording for the Blind.

H5. DEATH COMES FOR THE ARCHBISHOP. Tape. New Mexico Regional Library.

H6. DEATH COMES FOR THE ARCHBISHOP. CB. West Valley Federated Women's Club, San Jose, Calif.

H7. FIVE STORIES. RC. Recording for the Blind.

H8. A LOST LADY. Read by George Patterson, 1946. 6 records. TB33 1/3. NLS.

H9. A LOST LADY. Read by Mary Jane Higby, 1963. 6 sides, 10-inch, 16 r.p.m. With *O Pioneers!* (H21) below. TB75. NLS.

H10. A LOST LADY. Read by John Stratton. RC1119. NLS.

H11. A LOST LADY. RC. Recording for the Blind.

H12. LUCY GAYHEART. Read by Suzanne Toren. RC11292. NLS.

H13. LUCY GAYHEART. Tape. Philadelphia Regional Library.

H14. LUCY GAYHEART. CB. Illinois Regional Library.

H15. MY ÁNTONIA. Read by Alexander Scourby, 1948. 17 records. TB33 1/3. NLS.

H16. MY ÁNTONIA. Read by Norman Rose, 1958. 10 sides, 10-inch, 16 r.p.m. TB1374. NLS.

H17. MY ÁNTONIA. Read by Bob Watson. CB1. NLS.

H18. MY ÁNTONIA. CB. San Jose, Calif.: Variety Audio, Inc., San Jose Public Library.

H19. MY ÁNTONIA. Read by Bob Askey. RC13491. In process. NLS.

H20.   MY MORTAL ENEMY. Read by Jean Muir, 1966. 6 sides, 10-inch, 16 r.p.m. TB987. NLS.

H21.   O PIONEERS! Read by Ethel Everett, 1963. 8 sides, 10-inch, 16 r.p.m. With *A Lost Lady* (H9 above). TB75 and TB3498. NLS.

H22.   O PIONEERS! Tape. North Carolina Regional Library.

H23.   OBSCURE DESTINIES. Read by Mildred Dunnock, 1962. 8 sides. With *Shadows on the Rock* (H28 below). TB33 1/3. NLS.

H24.   ONE OF OURS. Read by Alexander Scourby, 1951. 20 records. TB33 1/3. NLS.

H25.   ONE OF OURS. Read by Robert Donley, 1968. 18 sides, 10-inch, 16 r.p.m. RB1796. NLS.

H26.   THE PROFESSOR'S HOUSE. Read by Michael Moodie. RC9578. NLS.

H27.   THE PROFESSOR'S HOUSE. CB. Washington Regional Library.

H28.   SAPPHIRA AND THE SLAVE GIRL. Read by Eugenia Rawls. RC11978. NLS.

H29.   SHADOWS ON THE ROCK. Read by Mary Jane Higby, 1962. 18 sides. With *Obscure Destinies* (H23 above). TB33 1/3. NLS.

H30.   SHADOWS ON THE ROCK. Tape. Santa Monica, Calif.: Madison School.

H31.   THE SONG OF THE LARK. Read by Kate McComb, 1949. 30 records. TB33 1/3. NLS.

H32.   THE SONG OF THE LARK. Read by Ann Pitoniak, 1958. 18 sides, 10-inch, 16 r.p.m. TB736. NLS.

H33.   THE TROLL GARDEN. Read by Winifred Taylor Keene.
       MT545. NLS.

H34.   THE TROLL GARDEN. Tape. New York: New York Associa-
       tion for the Blind.

H35.   UNCLE VALENTINE AND OTHER STORIES. Read by
       Barbara Caruso. RC12472. NLS.

I

Adaptations on Film

I1. A LOST LADY. Warner Brothers Pictures, Inc., 1924. Director: Harry Beaumont. Featured players: Irene Rich (Marion Forrester), George Fawcett (Daniel Forrester), John Roche (Ellinger), Matt Moore (Niel Herbert), June Marlowe (Constance).

Note: A cheap reprint of *ALL* (A13.1.vi) with photographic illustrations from this film was published by Grosset and Dunlap in 1925.

I2. A LOST LADY. Warner Brothers Pictures, Inc., 1934. Director: Alfred E. Green. Featured players: Barbara Stanwyck (Marian Ormsby [so called]), Frank Morgan (Daniel Forrester), Ricardo Cortez (Ellinger), Henry Kolker (John Ormsby), Hobart Cavanaugh (Robert).

Note: Willa Cather was dissatisfied with the 1924 film adaptation for which she had given permission. When the 1934 version was filmed without her knowledge or approval, she was infuriated. According to Mildred R. Bennett, who cites as her authority a conversation with Carrie Miner Sherwood, it was after this unauthorized film of *ALL* that Cather took legal measures to forbid future adaptations of her work in any form. This version drastically alters and distorts the story; Ellinger is represented as a World War I pilot.

I3. PAUL'S CASE. Television film series, "The American Short Story," PBS Television, 1980. Produced by *Learning in Focus, Inc.;* Robert Geller, Executive Producer. Teleplay by Ron Cowen. Director: Lamont Johnson. Featured player: Eric Roberts (Paul).

Note: Cather's legal restrictions could be circumvented for this television adaptation because the story was published first in 1905 and is, therefore, in the public domain. (See A4.a, C37.)

14. [Excerpted quotations from *O Pioneers!*, *My Ántonia*, and *Death Comes for the Archbishop*]. In *Willa Cather's America* (Films for the Humanities, Inc.). Written, produced, and directed by Richard Schickel for WNET-13. Narrated by Hal Holbrook and Gena Rowlands. FFH 145. 60 minutes, 16mm. color.

J

Adaptations for Theater

J1. [ERIC HERMANNSON'S SOUL]. *Out to the Wind.* A musical drama in 2 acts, adapted from Willa Cather's short story, 'Eric Hermannson's Soul'. Music by Robert Beadell; book and lyrics by Virginia Faulkner. Produced and presented by the University of Nebraska School of Music Opera Theatre. Premiere performance in Kimball Recital Hall, Lincoln, Nebraska, 1-4 February 1979.

Index

References in the index are to items, not to pages. Numbers in boldface type indicate principal descriptions of entries. Inferred references, such as those to an alternate title or the contents of a book, are enclosed in square brackets.

Abbey, Henry E., D251, 280
"About Bernice Slote,"
A1.b.iii.
"About Jim and Elsie," D274
'Abu-Rafi'ah, Fathī, E2
Academy and Literature
(London), B36
Across the Salt Sea (Bloundell-
Burton), D387
Active Service (Crane), D455
Actors, WC on: character of,
D574; private lives of,
D154; as stars, D245
"Adagio non troppo," C55.
See also "Uncle Valentine"
Adam, Juliette, D328
Adams, Bruce, A9.e.i.
Adams, Frederick B., Jr.,
A4.a., 5.a.i., 8.a.i., 18; on
WC, A1.a.*note* 2, 4.a.
Adams, Maude, D196, 313,
318, 424, 516-17
Adler, Elmer, A12.a.,
16.b.i., 16₁
"Affair at Grover Station,
The," AA6-7, C24;
Japanese edition, EEE11
"Aftermath": version 1, B20;
version 2, A1-3, AA1, B53
"Ah, lie me dead in the
sunrise land," [AA6-7], B4
aiglon, L' (Rostand), D516-17
Akhad, Abbas Mahmoud, E1
Akhand, Shahid, E86
Akins, Zoë, A14.a.i.
Aldrich, Anne Reeve, D202
Alexander's Bridge, A3, 5;
AA1; CCC1; DDD10; and
April Twilights (AE), A3,
5.c.; AA1; biographical
sketch of WC in, A5.d.;

and Coote's illustrations,
A5.a.i.-b.i., [5.b.ii.-
b.iv.], *5.a.i.*(e); [CCC1];
note by WC in, A5.a.i.;
photograph of WC in,
A5.d.; with preface by
WC, A5.b.i., [5.b.ii.-
b.iv.], 5.d.; publication
of, A5.a.i.-b.i., 5.d.,
5.a.i.(e); reviews of,
A5.a.i.-b.i.; serialization
of, A5.a.i., CCC1; and
Bernice Slote's introduc-
tion, A5.e.; textual variant
in, A5.a.i., 5.b.i. Transla-
tions: Arabic, E2; Dutch,
E35; German, E69. See also
*Alexander's Bridges; Alex-
ander's Masquerade*
Alexander's Bridges, A5.a.i.(e).
See also *Alexander's Bridge*
Alexander's Masquerade,
A5.a.i., *5.a.i.*(e); CCC1.
See also *Alexander's Bridge*
*Alfred A. Knopf Quarter Cen-
tury*, DD11
Alice in Wonderland, D333
Allan, Blaise, E45
Allen, Ralph, A18
American Academy of Arts
and Letters, DDD4
Americana Series, A16₂
American Book Company,
D586
American Book Prices Current,
A1.a.*note* 2
American Book-Stratford
Press, A10.c.vi., 11.a.xix.,
11.c.i., 13.a.xv.,
14.a.xvii., 15.c.vii.-c.x.,
17.a.xxxiv.-a.xxxvii.,

"Arcadian Winter," A1-3,
AA1, B31; textual variants
in, A2.a., 3.a.
"Ardessa," AA10, C51
"Are You Sleeping, Little
Brother?," A1.c., B26
Arjo, E109
"Arles and Provence Again,"
AA5, [D562]
Armed Services Editions,
A6.c., 9.d, 16.d.
Arthur, Julia (Ida Lewis),
D182
Artists, WC on: remuneration
of, D19; role of, D119,
294
Ashes of Empire (Chambers),
D408
Ash Wednesday, D376
Askey, Bob, H19
"Asphodel," A1; B28;
withdrawn from *ATOP*,
A2.a.
As You Like It, D218, 417
"As You Like It" (column,
NSJ), D104, 106, 110,
115, 119, 122-23, 126,
130, 132, 137, 140, 142,
144, 146, 150-52, 154-55,
158, 162-64, 166-68,
170-74
Atherton, Gertrude: *A Daugh-
ter of the Vine*, D430
Atlantic Bookshelf, D585
Atlantic Monthly, A2.b.iii.,
17.a.i., 21.a.i.; B78;
D381, 591
Atlantic Monthly Press, D585
"At the Chautauqua," D67
*Aurelian Wall and Other Poems,
The*, (Carman), D400

Austin, Alfred, D225, 230
Autograph Edition, A1.a.,
8.a.i., 16.b.i., 16.b.v.,
16.e.i.; AA1; [B18-19, 27,
30-32, 34, 37-45, 47-48,
51-53, 55, 59, 62-63,
65-69, 72-78]; C32-33,
37, 49-50, 52, 54, 57-59;
D583-84, 591, 593; DD6;
books in, A3, 5.b., 6.b.,
8.b., 9.c.i., 10.b., 11.b.,
13.b., 14.b., 15.b., 16.c.,
17.b., 19.b., 20.b., 21.b.,
22.b.; AA1
Autumn Melody, A2-3, AA1,
B63
"Avignon," AA5, [D559]
Avignon story (unfinished),
AA4, G5
Avon Books, C54
Avres, Jorge Cardoso, E151
Awakening, The (Chopin),
D441, 447
Ayr, Landis: *The Brown-Laurel
Marriage*, D398

Bachelor's Romance, A, D259
Bacon, Sir Francis, D99
Badger, Richard G., A1.a.
Baker Book House,
AAA1.a.ii.
Bà-Kông, Lê, E187
Balay, J., E42
Baldini, Gabriele, E106
Baldwin, Evelyn Briggs,
D529
Baldwin-Ziegler expedition,
D529
Balestier, Caroline (née
Kipling), D247